Emerging Financial Markets
and the Role of
International Financial Organizations

International Economic Development Law

VOLUME 4

Series Editor

J. J. Norton
Centre for Commercial Law Studies,
Queen Mary and Westfield College,
University of London,
London, U.K.

The titles published in this series are listed at the end of this volume.

SMU, School of Law
Dallas Texas

Centre for Commercial Law Studies
Queen Mary and Westfield College
University of London

Emerging Financial Markets and the Role of International Financial Organizations

Editors

Joseph J. Norton, S. J. D., D. Phil.

Mads Andenas

KLUWER LAW INTERNATIONAL

LONDON – THE HAGUE – BOSTON

Published by Kluwer Law International
Sterling House
66 Wilton Road
London SW1V 1DE
United Kingdom

Sold and distributed in the USA and Canada
by Kluwer Law International
675 Massachusetts Avenue
Cambridge MA 02139
USA

Kluwer Law International incorporates
the publishing programmes of
Graham & Trotman Ltd,
Kluwer Law & Taxation Publishers
and Martinus Nijhoff Publishers.

In all other countries, sold and distributed
by Kluwer Law International
P.O. Box 85889
2508 CN The Hague
The Netherlands

© Kluwer Law International 1996
First published in 1996

ISBN 90-411-0909-9

British Library Cataloguing in Publication Data and Library of Congress
Cataloging-in-Publication Data is available

Proceedings of a conference entitled "Emerging Financial Markets and International Financial Institutions (IFIs)" held in London on 25–26 May 1995 at the European Bank for Reconstruction and Development

Typeset in 10/11 pt Palatino by EXPO Holdings, Malaysia
Printed and bound in Great Britain by Hartnolls Limited, Bodmin, Cornwall

Table of Contents

II. BANKING MARKET ISSUES

III. SECURITIES MARKET ISSUES

List of Contributors

Editors (and Contributors)

Joseph J. Norton, Sir John Lubbock Professor of Banking Law, Centre for Commercial Law Studies, Queen Mary and Westfield College, University of London; James L. Walsh Distinguished Faculty Fellow in Financial Institutions and Professor of Law, School of Law, Southern Methodist University, Dallas, Texas and of Counsel, Andrews & Kurth, LLP, Gilchrist, P.C.

Mads Andenas, Director, Centre of European Law, King's College, University of London, Honorary Director of Studies, Institute of Advanced Legal Studies, University of London and former Legal Adviser, European Bank for Reconstruction and Development, London.

Contributors

Ziad A. Baha-Eldin, Postgraduate Researcher in Development Law, London School of Economics, University of London.

Paolo Clarotti, Head of Banking and Financial Institutions Division of the European Commission, Brussels.

John D. Crothers, Legal Counsel, European Bank for Reconstruction and Development, London.

Steven M. Fries, Office of the Chief Economist, European Bank for Reconstruction and Development, London.

Benjamin Geva, Professor of Law, Osgoode Hall Law School, York University, North York, Ontario.

Christos D. Hadjiemmanuil, Fellow in European Banking Law, London Institute of International Banking, Finance and Development Law, Centre for Commercial Law Studies, Queen Mary and Westfield College, University of London.

John H. Jackson, Hessel E. Yntema Professor of Law, University of Michigan, School of Law, Ann Arbor, Michigan.

N. Kofele-Kale, Associate Professor of Law, School of Law, Southern Methodist University, Dallas, Texas.

Eva Lomnicka, Professor of Law, King's College, University of London.

Jonathan R. Magnusen, Attaché, Ghanaian Embassy, London; Research Fellow in Development Law, London Institute of International Banking, Finance and Development Law, Centre for Commercial Law Studies, Queen Mary and Westfield College, University of London.

F. R. Malan, Professor of Banking Law and Director of Banking Institute, Rand Afrikaans University, Johannesburg.

Chizu Nakajima, Senior Lecturer in Law, City University, London.

Stilpon Nestor, Counsel on Legal and Enterprise Reform, Organisation for Economic Co-operation and Development (OECD), Paris.

A. Newburg, Former General Counsel, European Bank for Reconstruction and Development, London and Senior Visiting Fellow, London Institute of International Banking, Finance and Development Law, Centre for Commercial Law Studies, Queen Mary and Westfield College, University of London.

Gerald N. Olson, Associate Director, London Institute of International Banking, Finance and Development Law; Senior University Visiting Fellow, Centre for Commercial Law Studies, Queen Mary and Westfield College, University of London.

J. M. Otto, Professor of Mercantile Law, Rand Afrikaans University, Johannesburg.

Barry A. K. Rider, Director of the Institute of Advanced Legal Studies and Professor of Law, University of London and Fellow, Tutor and Dean, Jesus College, Cambridge.

Jan-Hendrick M. Röver, Consultant, European Bank for Reconstruction and Development, London.

Hani Sarie-Eldin, Research and Teaching Fellow in Development Law, London Institute of International Banking, Finance and Development Law, Centre for Commercial Law Studies, Queen Mary and Westfield College, University of London; Lecturer in Commercial Law, Cairo University.

Vlatko Sekulovic, Attorney at Law, Belgrade and Fellow of the London Institute of International Banking, Finance and Development Law, Centre for Commercial Law Studies, Queen Mary and Westfield College, University of London.

Stanley Siegel, Professor of Law, New York University School of Law, New York.

John L. Simpson, Consultant, European Bank for Reconstruction and Development, London.

Georgi Spasov, Senior Assistant Professor of Commercial Law, Kliment Ohridski University, Sofia, Bulgaria; Partner with Bratoev, Konov, Krastevich & Spasov Lawyers' Partnership.

Marc I. Steinberg, Rupert and Lillian Radford Professor of Law, School of Law, Southern Methodist University, Dallas, Texas. Visiting Professorial

Fellow, Banking and Finance Law Unit, Centre for Commercial Law Studies, University of London. Of Counsel, Winstead, Sechrest & Minick, Dallas, Texas.

Joel P. Trachtman, Associate Professor of International Law, The Fletcher School of Law and Diplomacy, Tufts University, Massachusetts.

Jane Welch, Head of Legal Advice Department, The Securities and Investment Board, London.

Foreword

Andre Newburg[1]

The Office of the General Counsel of the European Bank for Reconstruction and Development was very pleased to have co-sponsored and hosted in London at the EBRD's headquarters a high level, international "research seminar" entitled "Emerging Financial Markets and International Financial Institutions", along with the London Institute of International Banking, Finance and Development Law at the Centre for Commercial Law Studies, Queen Mary and Westfield College, University of London, the Centre of European Law at King's College, University of London and the Law Institute of the Americas at the Law School, Southern Methodist University, Dallas, Texas. The theme of this conference is central to the mission of the EBRD and other international financial institutions (IFIs): this is why it was important to formalise the Proceedings of this seminar into this most impressive volume, for which we are most grateful to Professor Joseph Norton of London and SMU and Mr Mads Andenas of King's College for their significant efforts in organising the seminar and editing these Proceedings. Without detracting from the broad intellectual and international scope of the following 24 chapters produced by leading experts, I wish to make a few remarks concerning my own experiences with the role of law in the transition process occurring in Central and Eastern Europe (CEE).

The transformation of the command economies of the CEE into democratically governed market economies – the "transition" as it has become known – involves not only fundamental changes of an economic nature, but also profound institutional, political and cultural changes. The replacement of command systems by market economies, and of party-controlled state institutions by democratic institutions and processes governed by the rule of law, implies a complete overhaul of the country's legal infrastructure, as well as of the public attitudes toward law. Respect for the rule

---

[1] Former General Counsel, European Bank for Reconstruction and Development, London and Senior Visiting Fellow, London Institute of International Banking, Finance and Development Law, Centre for Commercial Law Studies, Queen Mary and Westfield College, University of London. A version of this Foreword was given as a talk by the author in February 1994 at the Institute of Advanced Legal Studies, University of London. He wishes to thank Mads Andenas for preparing the draft for that talk.

of law must replace the cynicism with which law was widely regarded in communist societies as an instrument for the exercise of state power.

The focus of the transition process has, however, been principally on macroeconomic issues. The main features of the reform have been the introduction of tight fiscal and monetary policies, the phasing out of price controls and privatisation. In most countries, the creation of a legal framework for economic activity in the emerging private sector has not had the same priority. This is not surprising, as recent reform both in communist and non-communist economies has taken place in an institutional environment, in which the focus quite naturally has been on economic policy issues.

Contemporary economic theory has emphasised the negative or unintended effects of regulation, and reform in Western economies during the past two decades has tended to be characterised by deregulation. Economic advisers from the OECD countries have not always been concerned with what appear to be the legal technicalities of executing economic policy: they may even regard legal issues with impatience, if not disdain. In addition, ideological attitudes (the wish to limit the role of the state as much as possible) may impede one's ability to appreciate that only the state, with its power to legislate and enforce, can guarantee the market economy's efficiency and stability.

Law plays a key role in creating the conditions for a sound market economy: it creates the institutional framework, the essential infrastructure, for the peaceful interaction of economic agents and helps to establish the political and social atmosphere, the "climate of confidence congenial to the businessman" (in the words of Keynes), on which economic prosperity depends. Unless the rule of law prevails, investors will shy away and the creative energies of entrepreneurs will not be released. Unless the state creates a legal system defining the rights and duties of the entrepreneur, and is able to engender respect for that system, there is a risk that the self-same interest that bears such rich fruit in a civil society governed by the rule of law will lead to chaos and anarchy. Russia is an example of a country in which entrepreneurial private sector activity has outpaced the building of the new legal and regulatory system and in which the lack of a satisfactory legal framework has deterred investment and slowed the transition process.

There seems to be a growing realisation that without modern commercial laws and regulation of business activities, including effective mechanisms for dispute resolution and enforcement, the realisation of the benefits of economic reforms will be held back. The World Bank has noted that while, over the longer term, foreign direct investment may provide the major impetus for growth in the former Soviet Union, "the single most important factor continuing to hamper foreign direct investment is the instability of the investment climate, created by the succession of often conflicting laws and regulations".

Commercial law reform has met with many obstacles. A major obstacle is the immense pressure on the political and legislative process of a country in transition: in some cases, the legal framework for a new state must be developed. Preparation of new constitutions has been high on the agenda, often immediately followed by amendments. Central banking laws and regulations, currency regulations and tax and customs legislation also have a high priority. Each country is redefining or identifying the legal framework of its external relations, including memberships of international organisations and treaties, as well as its bilateral and multilateral trading relations. The sheer volume of legislation that the political institutions must process, together with the limited expertise and resources available for the task, make it difficult to cope.

Providing assistance in the development of elements of a suitable legal infrastructure in the former communist states surely ranks as a major challenge. Western countries and international organisations have responded with a broad range of initiatives. Many countries have bilateral legal assistance programmes, with the largest commitments from the United States. The World Bank has used trust funds for legal assistance, and has included law reform projects in its sectoral adjustment loans. The IMF provides assistance to new members in setting up economic institutions and drafting of legislation in areas such as taxation and banking supervision. The Europe Agreements between the European Union and Bulgaria, the Czech Republic, Poland, Hungary, Romania and the Slovak Republic include undertakings by these countries to adjust their laws to the *acquis communautaire* of EU legislation relating to the internal market. The European Union's ambitious technical assistance programmes, Phare and Tacis, provide legal assistance focusing on this "approximation" effort, thus providing a route to law reform which was recently followed by Greece and Portugal with a measure of success. The EBRD uses funds made available by its Member States, and by the European Union, for legal assistance projects. The EBRD's efforts have tended to concentrate on law reform relevant to its investment operations and the fostering of foreign investment. In spite of its magnitude, what has been achieved is not significant in relation to the enormity of the task in hand. It has been difficult to coordinate the various programmes, and some degree of duplication has ensued.

The methodology of legal assistance programmes must be devised in the light of the circumstances of each country. The former communist countries have very different legal traditions. They have also reached different stages in the transition process. Several central European countries in which the law reform process took off in the late 1980s have experienced substantial private sector investment, both foreign and domestic, and have had the opportunity to test their early law reform initiatives. When bottlenecks are identified, only remedial action may be required. On the other hand, in countries in early stages of transition, it may be necessary rapidly to enact legislation for a specific purpose. The legislative and regulatory framework for a major new industry may be required. In such cases, it may be expedient to import a "ready-made" law, but any such exercise should be approached with great caution. Although there have been times in history when countries have received an entire body of law, there is a significant risk that the transplant will be rejected, or ignored in practice, by the existing system. Legislation based on models developed in a mature market economy may not be suitable. Such models are likely to reflect the needs of sophisticated and developed markets, and postulate administration by an experienced and relatively efficient bureaucracy, as well as recourse to a knowledgeable and independent judiciary. Foreign models and experience can, of course, provide valuable guidance on a comparative basis, but indigenous lawyers and legislators must take the lead and be involved from the outset of the legislative process.

One of the more important legal assistance projects undertaken by the EBRD is an example of the practical application of a comparative law approach. In the early years of its existence, as the bank made its first investments in eastern Europe, it became evident that the laws of many of the countries of the region did not provide an effective and practical way for the bank and other lenders to obtain security interests or charges over a borrower's assets. Among other things, the inability of lenders to obtain non-possessory liens frustrates the use of modern financing techniques and deters commercial lending. The EBRD therefore initiated an effort to stimulate reform in this field by undertaking a project to develop a model law on secured transactions for its countries of operations. Rather than proposing to transplant a *prêt à porter* set of rules from a single legal system, the effort became an exercise in comparative law, drawing on a number of legal systems and a broad range of practical sources in various parts of the world, with assistance from an international advisory board that includes several eastern European legal experts.

A guiding principle of this project has been to develop a framework that is compatible with the civil law traditions of central and eastern Europe, while drawing on the experience of common law jurisdictions which have developed legal systems appropriate for modern financing techniques. The model also had to balance the interests of borrowers and lenders and provide a relatively simple and economically efficient system from which more sophisticated rules could in time evolve. Although the model's simplicity is intended to encourage the rapid introduction of a modern secured transactions law, it must be emphasised that the model was never intended to be a "turnkey" law for instant adoption: instead, it is a simple system, which can be adapted by national legislatures in the light of a country's laws and legal traditions, as well as its commercial requirements. The model has already achieved its goal of contributing to the legislative process in several countries which are in the process of adjusting their legislation to the requirements of the market economy.

Law reform is not a two- or three-year exercise. Enacting laws is a necessary, but not sufficient, first step: to be effective, laws need to be administered equitably by the executive and enforced by an independent judiciary. Unless that is the perception of the population, law will be abused or disregarded. Moreover, legislation that is constantly amended or changed fails to provide the stable environment so critical to investors. Hastily enacted legislation can, at times, work against the transition process: it can discredit the rule of law and reassert the role of particular parties or special interests. The challenge lies in building a sound legal infrastructure with all appropriate speed.

Editors' Note and Acknowledgements

This volume concerns the development of financial markets (*i.e.*, banking and securities markets) in "emerging economies". One primary emphasis is placed on the role of a range of international financial organizations, as well as certain regional and governmental organizations, on this development. In certain cases the involvement of such organizations takes the form of direct intervention, while in others it is indirect, through the provision of comparative legal models. More generally, this volume addresses the overall dynamics of the law reform processes in emerging economies as these relate to the construction of viable, sustainable and relevant banking and capital market structures.

As the chapter authors come from different jurisdictions, flexibility as to citations and certain spelling has been permitted, although consistency is maintained within each chapter. Each chapter author reserves the right to use his or her respective chapter for other academic or professional purposes subsequent to the publishing of this volume and provided that any such usage recognizes derivation from this volume.

The editors wish to specially acknowledge the support of the following organizations in the preparation of the research seminar of May 1995, of which this volume contains the Proceedings: Office of the General Counsel, European Bank for Reconstruction and Development, London; Centre for Commercial Law Studies, Queen Mary and Westfield College, University of London, in particular the London Institute of International Banking, Finance and Development Law; Centre of European Law, King's College, University of London and the School of Law, Southern Methodist University, Dallas, Texas.

I.   General Policy and Institutional Issues

1. Regulating International Economic Behavior – Reflections on the Broader Settings of International Financial Markets and Institutions

John H. Jackson[1]

1 INTRODUCTION

This chapter addresses the broader context of its subject matter, namely the important developments of the Uruguay Round which have now been ratified, and which have brought into existence a new international organization – described as the most significant new international economic organization since the Bretton Woods Institutions were created in 1944–45. In doing this, I want to reflect broadly on some of the economic principles that world markets generally (not just financial) are facing, particularly in the context of growing international economic interdependence. But I also want to discuss the implications of the Uruguay Round and the new WTO, concluding with some remarks of what those implications might be for financial services.

Just to add some color to my remarks, I would like to point out that two recent events (of May 1995) relate rather poignantly to some of the fundamental policies underpinning the general landscape of international economic relations which I will be addressing.

The first of these events was the celebration of the 50th anniversary of VE Day (Victory in Europe). Indeed, the celebrations here in Britain were extraordinarily interesting, and in many ways profound. Of course, the fact that we have had relative peace for 50 years is a very remarkable achievement. No single cause of that achievement can claim full responsibility, but certainly the leadership and farsightedness of statesmen at the end of World War II, in establishing the Bretton Woods System for guiding international economic relations, deserves some of that credit.

The other event was the eruption of a serious dispute between the U.S. and Japan, focused on automobile trade. This dispute created rather

---

[1] Hessel E. Yntema Professor of Law at the University of Michigan, School of Law, Ann Arbor, Michigan.

acrimonious statements and media presentations. It seems reasonably clear that some of the threats used by the U.S., for example, could involve U.S. actions that would violate the recently ratified Uruguay Round Agreements which the U.S. has accepted.[2] But one of the facets of the dispute that is intriguing is the degree to which some of the diplomacy and general discussion about the controversy made reference to the GATT and WTO rules, as well as dispute settlement procedures. This may indeed be a constructive reflection on the importance and potential of the WTO as the newest addition to the Bretton Woods System.

My remarks below will be divided roughly into three parts, moving from very broad ideas to increasingly specific subjects. In Part 2, I will reflect very broadly on certain economic principles that relate to questions of international economic relations. In Part 3, I want to address more particularly the results of the Uruguay Round and the new WTO. Finally, in Part 4, I am going to suggest a few attributes of this new UR/WTO system which can have a very significant influence on international banking and other questions of international financial markets and institutions.

2 THE PROBLEM OF REGULATING INTERNATIONAL ECONOMIC BEHAVIOR IN AN INCREASINGLY INTERDEPENDENT WORLD

"Economic interdependence" has become a common phrase to describe the developing conditions of international economic relations. Manifestations of the "gallop" towards linking economies are everywhere: enterprises must cope with competition and development from abroad; national governments find it increasingly difficult to regulate their economies; democratic political leaders find it hard to fulfill election promises and to satisfy constituencies because of forces beyond their control; and resentment against foreign competition and influence stirs the electorate and could even endanger democratic governments.

Since the 1940s world economics has been guided but not governed by a set of institutions nobly put in place by visionary leaders during the immediate post-World War II years – the Bretton Woods System (including the IMF, World Bank and GATT), the United Nations complex of organizations and agencies, OECD, etc. Subsequently many thousands of treaty instruments and organizations have been designed for commodity regulation, transport regulation, taxation and many other subjects. Yet the problems today are so dramatically different from those of 1945, that there is developing concern that this elaborate network of international institutions may not be able to cope over the next few decades.

---

[2] Jackson, "U.S. Threat to New World Trade Order", *Financial Times*, May 23, 1995, at 13. Later developments resulted in a "settlement agreement" between the U.S. and Japan regarding this dispute.

Part of this is inevitable in the light of growing international economic interdependence. Such interdependence brings many benefits from increased trade in both products and services across national borders, resulting in efficiencies and economies of scale which can raise world welfare (but not necessarily *everyone's* welfare, since some groups will be required to adjust in the face of such increased competition). These trends require a different sort of attitude towards government regulation. Within a nation, such government regulation as consumer protection, competition policy, prudential measures (of banking and financial institutions), measures protecting health and welfare (*e.g.*, alcohol and abortion control), and human rights (*e.g.*, prohibiting discrimination), are all designed by governments to promote worthy policies which sometimes clash with market-oriented economic policies. When economic interdependence moves a number of these issues to the international scene, they become (at least in today's defective international system) much more difficult to manage. The circumstances and the broader context of the international system create in many contexts (not just those concerning environmental policies) a series of problems and questions including:

– General questions of effectiveness of national "sovereignty" in the face of a need to cooperate with other countries to avoid some aspects of the "prisoner's dilemma" or "free rider" problems. Unless there is cooperation, individual countries can profit from the efforts of other countries without contributing to those efforts, but in the longer run all may suffer.
– Perplexing questions of how new international rules should be made, questions that often involve voting procedures.
– General questions of the appropriateness and degree to which national sovereignty will submit to international dispute settlement procedures to resolve differences on various policy matters.
– Problems of a single national sovereign using the extraterritorial reach of its regulation (sometimes termed "unilateralism") to impose its will on actions of other nations, or citizens of other nations.
– Significant legitimate differences of view between nations as to economic structure, level of economic development, different forms of government, different views of the appropriate role of government in economic activities, etc. Developing countries, for example, will have different views from those of rich countries, on many "trade-off" matters, arguing that environmental regulations can unfairly restrain their economic development.

In economic terms, most reasons for governments to intervene in the economy can be understood in one of three categories: correction of market failures (distortions); redistribution of income; and certain non-economic objectives. In each of these categories, economists are able to describe, in principle, what the optimal intervention to deal with them should look like. These optimal policies, though not always attainable in practice, provide benchmarks relative to which actual policies can be compared. These principles, however, assume that countries act in isolation. Once we allow for international interactions of various sorts, the picture becomes more complex. Costs and benefits are no longer exclusively national, and the policies to correct distortions and achieve other objectives may also have international repercussions. Once these considerations are taken into account, it is not clear that governments following traditional economic principles will succeed in achieving their objectives. Therefore, both the judgments about the need for government intervention, and what such intervention should be, become altered by the international dimension.

One way to address this issue is to ask, first, under what circumstances countries and their governments can be left to their own devices. That is, under what conditions will independent national governments, forming policy in their own interests, achieve a world-wide configuration of policies that will be optimal for the world as a whole. In fact, these conditions are likely to be extremely restrictive and unlikely to be met in practice, so that some form of international coordination is almost certain to be needed. Preliminary analysis suggests that independent national policies will be optimal *only if* at least the following three conditions are met:

(1) The market failures, distortions, or non-economic objectives that are addressed by government policy are themselves local, in the sense that both their costs and benefits and the behavior that causes them are confined to the same national economy.
(2) The countries that set policies to deal with these problems are small in the world markets impacted by them, in the sense that the policies of the individual countries do not have a perceptible effect on world prices.
(3) National policies are set so as to maximize aggregate national welfare, rather than sacrificing aggregate welfare for distributional or political-economy purposes.

A policy analysis of the various questions raised about the appropriateness and difficulty of government market intervention suggests the necessity of establishing some form of international cooperation. It then becomes necessary to explore a series of questions relating to the modalities of such international action or cooperation, including the impossibility of designing institutions for that purpose.

Clearly, there are a number of different ways to approach the cooperation issue. We can inventory them roughly under the sub-topics of "unilateral", "bilateral", "regional", and "multilateral". Running through all of these levels ("vertical analysis") are several general questions, such as:

(i) Should cooperative approaches be basically voluntary, or binding (under international law)? If binding, should there be sanctions?
(ii) Should the emphasis on cooperation be procedural, or relate more substantively to the rules being applied?
(iii) With respect to substantive rules, should the approach be that of national treatment (non-discrimination between domestic and imported goods), most-favored-nation (non-discrimination among

imported goods and exporting countries), or should there be some sort of minimum standards as the basis of a rule to apply?

In addition, one can explore several different "principles of managing interdependence" that would influence the techniques of cooperation:

- Harmonization, a system that gradually induces nations towards uniform approaches to a variety of economic regulations and structures. An example would be standardization of certain product specifications. Another example would be uniformity of procedures for applying countervailing duties or escape clause measures.
- Reciprocity, a system of continuous "trades" or "swaps" of measures to liberalize (or restrict) trade. GATT tariff negotiations are in this mold.
- Interface, which recognizes that different economic systems will always exist in the world and tries to create the institutional means to ameliorate international tensions caused by those differences, perhaps through buffering or escape clause mechanisms.

Obviously, a mixture of all these techniques is the most likely to be acceptable, but that still leaves open the question of what is the appropriate mixture. For example, how much should the "trade constitution" pressure nations to conform to some uniform "harmonized" approaches, or is it better to simply establish buffering mechanisms that allow nations to preserve diversity but try to avoid situations where one nation imposes burdens (economic or political) on other nations?

Closely connected to this previous point is an issue that may be loosely characterized as being similar to "federalism". This is the issue of the appropriate allocation of decision-making authority at different levels of government. Each federal nation faces this question, *i.e.*, what is the appropriate allocation of power between the national government and subordinate state or municipal governments? The international system broadly, and the international trade system in particular, also face this question. As interdependence drives nations to more concerted action, there also arises the question whether a gradual shift of decision-making authority upward to international institutions is always best for the world. How much power do we want to delegate to such international institutions? In what instances do we wish to preserve local or subordinate government control on the grounds that such government is closer to the affected constituents? To what degree does a "harmonization" approach to managing interdependence unduly interfere with these "federalist" principles of maintaining decision-making closer to affected individuals and firms?

Because most questions of regulating international economics today will likely involve more than two countries, there is a very high probability that the international community will turn toward the formation and designing of a treaty-based multilateral institution which could enable it appropriately and efficiently to respond to the problems of such regulation. Thus it is particularly important to begin thinking about some of the key questions that should be considered in designing international institutions, recognizing that inappropriate design could result in international governmental responses that would be harmful to world welfare and in some cases defeat some of the very policies which have motivated this type of response. A series of "lawyer-type questions" then emerge, such as:

- Questions of rule-making at the international level, and whether it adequately considers some of the scientific and moral concerns involved in the subjects that are linked to trade.
- Questions of international dispute settlement procedures and to what extent they adequately consider opposing policy goals, or provide for appropriate advocacy from interested authorities and citizen groups.
- Questions of whether the international procedures incorporate adequate democratic processes, including transparency and the right to be heard.
- The relation of international rules to domestic constitutional and other laws.
- The operation and procedures of national constitutional bodies and how these promote or inhibit international cooperation.
- The activity of interest groups, both those broadly oriented and those more oriented to specific interests or single issues, and how this activity relates to international institutions and procedures.
- Problems of regulatory competition: governments seeking lower standards of regulation in order to attract economic activity to their societies (sometimes called the "race to the bottom", or in the U.S. the "Delaware Corporation" problem).

It is our assumption that these questions, which have perhaps become most apparent in the context of environmental and competition policy, also relate to a long list of other potential policy areas that can cause clashes with international trade and other international economic policy goals. Such policy areas could certainly include:

- labor standards;
- commodity agreements and regulation;
- product standards (food, pharmaceutical, safety of goods, etc.);
- insurance;
- banking and fiduciary institutions;
- investment protection;
- securities regulation and institutions;
- government procurement procedures and preferences;
- shipping and transport (including air transport);
- intellectual property protection and regulation;
- taxation.

Fundamental differences among societies and governmental structures obviously affect some, if not all, of the questions above. For example, in a market economy many of these questions, particularly as to competition policy, will be answered differently from the situation of a non-market economy.

3 THE URUGUAY ROUND RESULTS AND THE WTO AS THE "NEW KID ON THE BLOCK" FOR THE BRETTON WOODS SYSTEM

The Uruguay Round, the eighth broad trade negotiation round under the auspices of the General Agreement on Tariffs and Trade (GATT), is clearly the most extensive undertaken by the GATT system, and exceeds any similar endeavor in history. The goals of the September 1986 Ministerial Meeting at Punta del Este which set forth the agenda for the Uruguay Round were extremely ambitious. If half the objectives were achieved, the Uruguay Round would still be the most extensive and successful trade negotiation ever. In fact, despite the many years of delay and negotiating impasses, the Uruguay Round has achieved considerably more than half of its objectives. As an example of the magnitude of the effort, it is reported that the Final Act signed in Marrakesh, Morocco on April 15 weighed 385 pounds and included over 26,000 pages![3] Even the basic texts reproduced as part of the Final Act totalled 424 pages.[4]

3.1 Achievements of the Uruguay Round

From the beginning, a most important objective of this trade round was to extend a GATT-type treaty of rule-based discipline to three new subject areas: trade in services, agriculture product trade, and intellectual property matters. Of these three, services and intellectual property were truly new for GATT. GATT had always formally applied to agriculture product trade, but for a variety of reasons agriculture had escaped the GATT discipline. Attempts to bring agriculture "into the GATT fold" had failed in the two previous negotiating rounds (the Kennedy Round of 1962–1967, and the Tokyo Round of 1973–1979).

The overall Uruguay Round result fulfills the original intentions remarkably, although with some gaps. An additional important result (the WTO charter) stemmed from a proposal that only later emerged. A list of the important achievements of the Uruguay Round includes:

(1) Services: The Services Agreement (GATS – General Agreement on Trade In Services) is a major new chapter in GATT history. Although in some ways seriously flawed, this text now offers an overall "umbrella" concept for trade in services that, it is hoped, will allow an ongoing negotiating process for additional detail (probably at least a 50-year process) to occur. In this respect the structure of the new WTO (*see* below) is vital.

---

[3] Final Act Embodying the Results of the Uruguay Round of Multilateral Trade Negotiations, signed in Marrakesh, Morocco (April 15, 1994), 33 I.L.M. 1140–1272 (1994). See also H.R. Doc. No. 316, 103d Cong., 2d Sess. (1994).
[4] Jackson, "Managing the Trading System: The World Trade Organization and the Post-Uruguay Round GATT Agenda", in *Managing the World Economy: Fifty Years After Bretton Woods* 131 (Peter B. Kenen, ed., 1994).

(2) Intellectual property: The TRIPS agreement (Trade Related Intellectual Property) is a splendid new achievement.

(3) Agriculture: The result in agriculture may be meager, but nevertheless there is now, for the first time, some realistic expectation for trade rule discipline over agriculture trade.

(4) Subsidies/countervailing duties: The results include a new improved subsidies "code".

(5) Textiles: Textiles have been covered in the UR with a "phase-out" agreement for the special textile regime.

(6) Standards: Trade rules for product standards have been further addressed, after the accomplishment of the Tokyo Round Code.

(7) Safeguards: Here the Uruguay Round succeeded where the Tokyo Round failed, and a very impressive and ambitious Safeguards Code is part of the UR results.

(8) Market access: The Uruguay Round results include impressive advances in so-called "market access", including a reduction in the use of quotas (and a shift of quotas to tariffs), as well as very substantial tariff cutting (some say the most of any round).

(9) Developing country integration: Developing countries are more fully integrated into the GATT/WTO system than before.

(10) Dispute settlement procedures: One of the many achievements of the GATT, despite its "birth defects", has been the four-decade development of a reasonably sophisticated dispute settlement process. However, there have been a certain number of flaws recognized in those procedures. The Uruguay Round, for the first time, establishes an overall unified dispute settlement system for all portions of the UR agreements, and a legal text (rather than just customary practice) to carry out those procedures. These new procedures include measures to avoid "blocking" which occurred under previous consensus decision-making rules, and provides for the first time a new "appellate procedure" which will sub-stitute for some of the procedures that were vulnerable to blocking.

(11) WTO Charter: One of the interesting achievements of the Uruguay Round is the development of a new institutional charter for an organization which will help facilitate international cooperation concerning trade and economic relations and fundamentally change the GATT system to accommodate the vast new terrain of trade competence thrust on the trading system by the Uruguay Round. Some people have even said that this may be the most important element of the Uruguay Round result.

3.2 WTO – The new institution[5]

Several general characteristics of the WTO can be mentioned.

First, the WTO can be described as a "mini-charter." It is devoted to the institutional and procedural structure that will facilitate and in some cases

---

[5] Jackson, "The World Trade Organization: Watershed Innovation or Cautious Small Step Forward?", 18 *The World Econ.*, (manuscript at 5–7, on file with author); Jackson, *supra* note 4, 135–136.

be necessary for effective implementation of the substantive rules that have been negotiated in the Uruguay Round. The WTO is not an ITO (the 1948 ITO draft Charter never came into force.) The WTO Charter itself is entirely institutional and procedural, but it incorporates the substantive agreements resulting from the Uruguay Round into annexes.

Second, the WTO essentially will continue the GATT institutional ideas and many of its practices in a form better understood by the public, media, government officials and lawyers. To some small extent, a number of the GATT "birth defects" are overcome in the WTO. The WTO Charter (XVI:I) expressly states the intention to be guided by GATT "decisions, procedures and customary practices" to the extent feasible. The practice of consensus is better defined and for the first time becomes a legal procedure in some important decisions, rather than just a practice.

Third, the WTO structure offers some important advantages for assisting the effective implementation of the Uruguay Round. For example, a "new GATT 1994" is created to supersede the "old GATT," called "GATT 1947". This procedure avoids the constraints of the amending clause of the old GATT which might make it quite difficult to bring the Uruguay Round into legal force. At the same time, the WTO ties together the various texts developed in the Uruguay Round and reinforces the "single package" idea of the negotiators, namely, that countries accepting the Uruguay Round must accept the entire package (with a few exceptions). No longer will the Tokyo Round approach of side codes, resulting in "GATT *à la carte*," be the norm.

The WTO Charter establishes (for the first time) the basic explicit legal authority for a Secretariat, a Director-General and other institutions such as the General Council. It does this in a way similar to many other international organizations, and it also adds the obligation for nations to avoid interfering with the officials of the organization.

The WTO also facilitates the extension of the institutional structure (GATT-like) to the new subjects negotiated in the Uruguay Round, particularly services and intellectual property.

Fourth, the WTO Charter, hopefully, offers considerably better opportunities for the future evolution and development of the institutional structure for international trade cooperation.

3.3 The dispute settlement procedures

One of the many achievements of the GATT, despite its "birth defects," has been the development of a reasonably sophisticated dispute settlement process. The original GATT treaty contained very little on this, although it did specifically provide (in Articles 22 and 23) for consultation, and then submittal of issues to the GATT Contracting Parties. As time went by, however, the practice began to evolve more towards a "rule-oriented" system. For example, in the late 1950s the practice was introduced of a "panel" of individuals to make determinations and findings and recommend them to the Contracting Parties. Before that, disputes had been considered in much broader working parties comprised of representatives of governments.

During the next several decades, the Contracting Parties utilized the panel process more and more. Increasingly, the reports began to focus on more precise and concrete questions of "violations" of treaty obligations. At the end of the Tokyo Round in 1979, the GATT Contracting Parties adopted an understanding on dispute settlement which embraced some of these concepts, and embodied the practice concerning dispute settlement procedures which had developed during the previous decades.

In the 1980s, the dispute settlement panels were for the first time assisted by a new legal section of the GATT Secretariat. The panels began to write reports that were much more precise and better reasoned (and much longer!). Many countries, including the U.S. (which has been the largest single applicant for dispute settlement procedures in the GATT) found it useful to take issues to panels as part of their broader approach to trade diplomacy.

However, as might be expected given the history of GATT, there were a number of defects and problems in the dispute settlement process. Some of the problems were gradually overcome through practice in the GATT. But in the Uruguay Round there is a major new text concerning dispute settlement procedures, the "Understanding on Rules and Procedures Governing the Settlement of Disputes".

The new text solves many, although not all, of the issues that have plagued the GATT dispute settlement system. It accomplishes the following:

(1) It establishes a unified dispute settlement system for all parts of the GATT/WTO system, including the new subjects of services and intellectual property. Thus, controversies over which procedure to use will not occur.

(2) It confirms that all parts of the Uruguay Round legal text relevant to the matter in issue and argued by the parties can be considered in a particular dispute case.

(3) It reaffirms the right of a complaining government to have a panel process initiated, preventing blocking at that stage.

(4) It establishes a unique new appellate procedure which will substitute for some of the former procedures of Council approval of a panel report. Thus, a panel report will effectively be deemed to be adopted by the new Dispute Settlement Body (DSB), unless it is appealed by one of the parties to the dispute. If appealed, the dispute will go to an appellate panel. After the appellate body has ruled, its report will go to the DSB, but in this case it will be deemed to be adopted unless there is a consensus *against* adoption, and presumably that negative consensus can be defeated by any major objector. Thus the presumption is reversed, compared to the previous procedures, with the ultimate result that the appellate report will come into force as a matter of international law in virtually every case. The opportunity of a losing party to block adoption of a panel report will no longer be available.

4 IMPLICATIONS FOR INTERNATIONAL FINANCIAL MARKETS AND INSTITUTIONS, INCLUDING EMERGING MARKETS[6]

As suggested above, one of the most significant achievements of the Uruguay Round has been the addition of a major treaty agreement concerning international trade and services. The GATT dealt solely with products, and in many ways has been remarkably successful. But in recent decades it has become apparent to world leaders that services also need some type of international treaty framework. Services have become an increasing and in many cases the major part of the gross domestic product of leading advanced economies. More and more there has been a tendency for service industries (whether they be financial, such as banking, insurance, brokerage, etc., or one of another hundred different sectors of services, such as tourism, transportation, professional services, software development, etc.), to try to develop overseas markets. A somewhat more ominous counter-development, has been a tendency for some countries' governments to try to inhibit the foreign service providers from serving their markets, so as to protect their own providers. This has some of the classical detriments to the welfare of their own countries and of the world, which have traditionally occurred in the area of product trade. Thus many people began in the 1980s to focus on the need for an international framework, and when the Uruguay Round was launched at Punta del Este in September 1986, one of the most important new agenda items was the negotiation of an international agreement for trade in services.

This agreement was not easy to negotiate. First there was a general question of whether some of the traditional international trade rules relating to products (particularly most-favored-nation, and national treatment) could be applied to the area of services. The answer to that question is still not

---

[6] *See e.g.,* Broadman, "GATS: The Uruguay Round Accord on International Trade and Investment in Services", 17 *World Econ.* 281 (1994); D. Brown, A. Deardorff, A. Fox and R. Stern, "Computational Analysis of Goods and Services Liberalization in the Uruguay Round", Conference on the Uruguay Round and the Developing Countries at the World Bank, Washington, D.C. (January 26–27, 1995); Fontevecchio, "The General Agreement on Trade in Services: Is It the Answer to Creating a Harmonized Global Securities System?", 20 *N.C. J. Int'l L. & Com. Reg.* 115 (1994); GATT Secretariat, "Commitments on Services", in *The Results of the Uruguay Round of Multilateral Trade Negotiations: Market Access for Goods and Services: Overview of the Results* (1994); Hoekman and Sauve, "Liberalizing Trade in Services", The World Bank Discussion Paper No. 243 (1994); B. Hoekman, "Tentative First Steps: An Assessment of the Uruguay Round Agreement on Services", The World Bank Policy Research Working Paper No. 1455 (1995); *The International Legal Framework for Services* (K. Sauvant and J. Weber, eds., 1994); Key and Scott, "International Trade in Banking Services: A Conceptual Framework", Group of Thirty Occasional Papers 35 (1991); McNevin, "Policy Implications of the NAFTA for the Financial Services Industry", 5 *Colo. J. Int'l Envtl. L. & Pol'y* 369–399 (1994); Spero, "Trade in Services: Achilles Heel of G.A.T.T. Negotiations?", *A.B.A. Sec. Int'l L. & Prac.* (1991); *Trade in Services: Sectoral Issues,* UNCTAD/ITP/26 (1989); UNCTAD & The World Bank, *Liberalizing International Transactions in Services: A Handbook* (1994); U.S. SPAC, *Report of the Services Policy Advisory Committee on Results of the GATT Uruguay Round Negotiation* (January 1994).

apparent.[7] Likewise, when dealing with intangibles such as many types of services, the question of when there was an international trade incident was more difficult. To have effective international trade often required the development of branches or agencies in the importing market, or the travel of individual persons to such markets, or in some cases the "bouncing of signals off a satellite" into the importing market. How could governments respond and "regulate" these activities, even when such regulation was designed for such worthy reasons as protecting consumers or the quality and standards of services.

I cannot go much more into detail here about the services sector, except to note that the Services Agreement does apply to "financial services", and this has very far-reaching implications. Indeed, financial services is probably the most significant and most controversial part of the Uruguay Round services negotiation results. It was so controversial that the negotiations for financial services rules have in fact not been completed, but are continuing.[8] Activities involved in the financial services sector will surely engage many of the issues that I have discussed above. Will there be cross-border activity that national governments will find very difficult to regulate? What should government responses be to such difficulties? What type of international cooperation must be established to prevent competitive policies that effectively reduce world welfare? How will these international cooperative mechanisms work? The institutions of the WTO, and its new dispute settlement procedures, clearly apply to these questions. The issues that remain yet uncertain include the question of whether the new institutions can cope satisfactorily with some of the problems I have raised in this chapter, and also the question to what degree will professionals be able to appreciate this new institutional context which will affect much of what they will do.

---

[7] Jackson, *International Competition in Services: A Constitutional Framework* (1988).

[8] *See* Lewis, "Global Services Pact Concluded: Good News and Bad for the U.S.", *N.Y. Times*, July 29, 1995, at 35; Lewis, "Trade Chief Sees a U.S. Loss of Pact", *N.Y. Times*, July 28, 1995, at D2; Lewis, "Trade Accord Without U.S. Set in Geneva", *N.Y. Times*, July 27, 1995, at D1; Lewis, "Financial Services Plan Advances Without U.S.", *N.Y. Times*, July 1, 1995, at 33; Sanger, "U.S. and Japan Told to Solve Trade Dispute", *N.Y. Times*, June 14, 1995, at D1.

2. The EU as a Model for Financial Market Reform

Paolo Clarotti[1]

1 INTRODUCTION

The title given to this chapter is very challenging: whether the EU is a model for financial reform in the so-called emerging financial markets of the former communist countries (or command countries).

I will try to explain why we, in the European Commission, believe that the answer should be a straightforward "Yes" and to give some information on what we are doing in order to achieve such an objective. Of course, while the general arguments which support the idea that the EU regulation of financial markets is the best model for any emerging financial market, not only in Europe, may apply to all such markets, there are special additional arguments to follow the EU model for those countries which have expressed their intention to join, on a later stage, the European Union.

I must emphasise, from the outset, that the fact that the European Union has a common regulatory framework does not mean that there was the intention of setting up a European financial centre which will replace the existing financial centres already existing in Europe or which might develop there in the near future. The traditions, the expertise, and the peculiarities of the main financial centres in Europe are an asset which has to be maintained, in order to better serve the multivarious requirements of the European industry, and of the financial community at large.

What we are achieving within the framework of the European Union, is to ensure, within the European Union, a level playing field, for all the operators in such a market, in order to avoid significant distortions in competition.

My purpose is to present an outline of what has already been achieved, which is already very important, even if new initiatives are still in progress.

2 ACHIEVEMENTS IN THE BANKING AREA

Let us start with banking. We will see later what has been achieved in the sector of other financial institutions.

---

[1] Head of Banking and Financial Institutions Division, EC Commission, Brussels.

2.1 The First Banking Directive and background to the Second Directive

The European Union banking legislation covers all credit institutions which receive deposits and similar repayable funds and which also grant credits. This fundamental principle, whose importance I cannot over-emphasise, was established in the Council's First Banking Directive of 1977.

All types of credit institution are, thus, in principle, treated in the same way and there is thus equality of competitive conditions in relation to prudential rules: the famous "level playing field" which is often mentioned.

The reason for this is that all Member States have experienced, to varying degrees, a process of "despecialisation" in which some if not all providers of financial services have broadened their scope of activities and have begun to compete in new markets. Traditional areas of specialisation and demarcation of activities between groups of credit institutions have been eroded, largely, as the result of market forces. The Second Banking Directive of December 1989 reflects this development, by incorporating a full range of banking services within the scope of the single banking licence. Such a development needed to be underpinned by common prudential standards for all banks.

The principle is well demonstrated in the case of the directives on solvency ratio and capital adequacy where the same risk weights and overall capital requirements apply without reference to the composition of business of the institution in question. To take concrete examples, there is the same capital requirement for a mortgage credit extended by a specialised mortgage credit institution as there is for a mortgage credit granted by a truly universal bank or a bank which, typically, concentrates on trade finance; and there are the same capital requirements to face market risks for a credit institution and for a non-bank investment services undertaking, when they are involved in the same transactions in securities.

During the course of the discussions leading up to the Second Banking Directive there were several requests for the emergence of final prudential standards: with one set applicable to those institutions operating at Union level, across national boundaries, and another, unharmonised or partially harmonised set, applicable to those confining their attention to purely domestic markets. It was decided that to take such a path would have been inconsistent with the basic freedom to supply services conferred by the Treaty of Rome, a freedom which is available to all, and with the aim of achieving equality of competition between institutions. Clearly, those credit institutions operating across the Union compete in the national markets of those engaging only in domestic business.

The Union's banking legislation seeks to protect depositors and to safeguard the integrity of the European banking system. In other words, it pursues on a Union-wide scale that which national supervisory authorities have been undertaking for decades.

We are, of course, in the process of redefining supervisory rules across the Union at a time of considerable change in financial markets. Indeed, we are redefining those rules in order to be ready for and to enable major changes in the European market. For this reason it seems especially important to draw up strong prudential guidelines. It would be wise to err on the side of caution rather than to set inadequate standards. The European financial system survived the October 1987 stock market crash but it would be wrong to be complacent. It seems equally important, at a time when the fifteen national markets are about to fuse into one and money and capital markets have an international dimension stretching beyond the European time zone, that the European banking legislation should be readily adaptable in the event of further changes in market structure and financial instruments.

The fact that the standards set in the Union legislation are minimum standards is helpful in making such adaptation easier. Member States are always free to apply tougher standards if they judge it necessary to do so. These conditions range from the minimum level of capital required, to the "fitness" and "properness" of directors. These minimum conditions not only comply with, but are among the highest international standards for credit institutions.

In this framework cooperation between the respective supervisors becomes paramount and they have a duty to consult each other regarding the supervision of institutions operating cross-border. More importantly, our legislation has removed all barriers on banking secrecy that might prevent important information being passed from a supervisor in one Member State to their colleague in another.

Equally important, we have been working to ensure that our liberal trade philosophy, allowing financial services to be provided to the customer in a competitive environment with the greatest possible choice, is extended beyond the frontiers of the European Union. This is witnessed, for example, by our commitment to a strong financial services agreement emanating from the Uruguay Round negotiations in Geneva and by the discussions we have had with our EFTA neighbours, which have been concluded with the signature of the Treaty which has created, from 1 January 1994, a single European Economic Area. Three of the EEA Member countries are now members of the EU.

The European Union has succeeded in getting fifteen Member States to agree on a system that is opening up markets, some of which had been relatively closed and underdeveloped, and at the same time gives adequate protection to the savers, investors and other users or consumers of financial products.

I will outline all the current progress made and the different measures which have been taken in the financial services field.

The first banking coordination directive of December 1977 achieved three main goals:

- it cleared away most of the obstacles to freedom of establishment of banks and other credit institutions;
- it laid down common standards for the granting of banking licences;
- it introduced the basic principle of the cooperation between the supervisory authorities of different Member States and set up the Banking Advisory Committee.

2.2 The Second Banking Directive

The Second Banking Coordination Directive of December 1989 took important steps forward:

- it laid down the idea of a single banking licence valid throughout the whole Union which would authorise a bank or credit institution to supply its services throughout Europe either by branches or by provision of cross-border services;
- the licence would be mutually recognised by other EU banking supervisors;
- a minimum level of capital (own funds) of 5 Million Ecus was prescribed for new banks;
- supervisory rules have been spelt out in respect of internal management and audit system.

Beyond this, and this is the feature of the Second Banking Directive which is most far-reaching, the freedoms above are provided for a wide range of banking activities. A list of such activities which benefit from the liberalisation has been annexed to the directive; the list follows more or less the universal banking model and includes not only the traditional banking services, but also trading in securities, derivatives, etc. If a bank is author- ised to engage in these activities under the terms of its home country licence, it may offer them in other Member States.

The White Paper of 1985 established the principle that harmonisation of national legislation would be pursued only where truly necessary, while in other cases differing national standards would be retained and mutually recognised and respected.

In the banking sector, which is already relatively well integrated on a Union basis, but which is also subject in each country to detailed prudential regulation and supervision, the first decision was the extent to which mutual recognition could operate without jeopardising prudential standards. It was decided that, provided certain key areas of prudential control relating to the tests for authorisation of credit institutions and to standards in relation to ongoing business were harmonised and applied by the supervisors granting authorisation, mutual recognition could be accepted.

The essential minimum harmonisation agreed by the Commission in con- sultation with the Union's banking supervisors comprises:

- minimum capital for authorisation and continuing business (in the Second Banking Coordination Directive);
- adequacy of capital in relation to credit risk incurred (in the Own Funds and in the Solvency Ratio Directives of, respectively, April and December 1989);
- the full implementation of the supervision on consolidated basis (Directive of April 1992);
- limits on concentrations of lending (in the Large Exposures Directive of December 1992);

- effective supervisory control of major shareholders; and
- control of banks' substantial shareholdings in the non-bank sector (both in the Second Banking Coordination Directive);
- the existence of deposit guarantee schemes covering all credit institutions in the Union (Directive of May 1994).

The effect of this is the replacement of national banking licences with a Union-wide licence, valid for establishing branches anywhere without the need for separate authorisation. In other words, one authorisation has replaced fifteen. The system does not, of course, embrace subsidiaries, which are incorporated by the appropriate national supervisory authorities.

The enabling mechanism of home country control, together with the details of operation of the single banking licence, is set out in the Second Banking Coordination Directive.

The Second Banking Directive also contains, as mentioned before, some harmonisation of control of major shareholders. There is a basic information requirement and a provision that supervisors should intervene to end shareholders' influence being detrimental to the sound management of the credit institution. As such, both authorisation and ongoing supervision are involved.

The prudential considerations behind this provision are what one might call "traditional" and "modern". The "traditional" consideration is the supervisor's basic and customary concern about the suitability of those connected with banking institutions and particularly with those taking decisions. The "modern" consideration is that the emergence of more complex forms of business structure in which banks may be part of diversified conglomerates raises problems of cross-financing and conflicts of interest.

These considerations also underlie the provision which limits credit institutions' individual stakes in non-financial companies to any amount greater than 15% of own funds, and the aggregate participations of this kind to the equivalent of 60% of own funds. However, it seems most important to note that these ceilings need not be applied if the participations in question are deducted from own funds (of course, if the bank has sufficient own funds in addition to those required to cover the solvency ratio).

2.3 Further Union legislation

Further legislation is also designed to ensure equality of competition between banks and other credit institutions within the Union. This legislation includes:

- a directive approved in December 1986 which contains the rules on the annual and consolidated accounts of banks and which was followed in February 1989 by another directive on the disclosure requirements of foreign branches. They are not, strictly speaking, directives which deal with prudential regulations, but their implementation has certainly improved the transparency of the European banking market;

– a directive approved in June 1991 which has the aim of obliging banks to participate in the prevention of money laundering. It cannot, as those above, be considered as a prudential regulation, but it plays a positive role in the combating of fraud within the national EU banking systems. In addition, this last directive does not apply only to banks, or credit institutions, but to all kinds of so-called "financial undertakings", which include investment firms, insurance companies, bureaux de change, etc. Of course, the EU action has not been limited to banks or credit institutions only.

3 THE CAD AND ISD DIRECTIVES

Two other important directives which have been approved in 1993 do not apply only to banks but also to non-bank investment firms: they are the Capital Adequacy Directive and the Investment Services Directive.

3.1 The CAD

The Capital Adequacy Directive (CAD) was proposed in 1990 and approved on 15 March 1993. It will enable supervisors to lay down capital requirements for banks, as well as non-bank investment firms, in the securities markets, which are prudent, and which provide for a level playing field for both banks and non-banks which are in the same business. That is why the CAD provides for the measurement of the capital requirement against a particular securities position to be practically the same for a bank, as for a non-bank investment firm, which holds it.

This directive makes provision for market risk related to movements of interest rates and equities which have not been taken into account at all by either European Union legislation, or most national supervisors, and provides that supervisors of universal banks could apply the non-bank capital requirements to the trading book part of their operations. This directive entered into force only on 1 January 1996, because of the significant changes it will bring about in the financial markets of most of the EU countries.

The CAD was a necessary follow-up to the proposal for a directive on investment services in the securities field (the ISD) which was first presented by the Commission in January 1989. The ISD was intended to open the way for investment firms authorised in their home Member State to have access to all other Member States' financial markets – either by establishing branches, or by providing services, therein – on the basis of certain conditions that closely follow those for banks in the Second Banking Coordination Directive. These freedoms had to be based on a coordination of key rules as regards the authorisation, and the ongoing supervision, of the relevant institutions.

The coordination had to achieve the main objective of ensuring that both the health of the general financial system, and in particular investors, will be adequately protected in a new integrated European market. It had also to meet two other goals. First, it had to establish a broadly level playing field between investment firms and banks trading in the securities markets. Consistent with this objective, the rules set out in the directive would not provide an incentive for a bank engaged in investment activities to opt for one institution structure, *e.g.* that of an investment firm, rather than another, *e.g.* a bank. Second, the directive had to enhance, or at least not impair, the attractiveness of European financial centres.

3.2 The ISD

The ISD Directive was approved by the EC Council of Ministers on 10 May 1993, but, as the CAD, it entered into force on 1 January 1996.

The Member State in which an investment firm is set up is the firm's "home Member State". The Member State in which the firm carries on the activities in question may either be its home state or another EU Member State, described as the "host Member State". Once authorised in its home state, the investment firm is free to carry on any investment service for which it is authorised in its home state in any other Member State, either by way of establishment of a branch, or by way of cross-border activities. This is usually referred to as the "European passport".

With the above directives one can say that the "shopping list" of the more important directives in the field of financial services is completed. But this list will not really be complete, without mentioning one directive which has been approved by the European Parliament and the EU Council of Ministers very recently (29 June 1995); this is the directive which aims at the reinforcement of prudential supervision in the field of all financial under-takings (the so-called "post-BCCI" directive) and which will apply not only to banks and non-bank investment firms, but also to insurance companies.

4 THE SIGNIFICANCE AND IMPLEMENTATION

This shopping list demonstrates that the regulatory framework is an ad-equate one, and that there is practically one financial market which needs to have the same rules for all those who operate in such a market, and that the segmentation or specialisation of the different actors is something which should be left to the decision of the interested institutions and not imposed artificially by law or by regulation, as is the case in the U.S. and in Japan, notwithstanding the recent reforms.

The number of banking and other financial firms' crises in Europe (if we leave aside the case of Scandinavian banks which was due mainly to macro-economic causes; and the relevant institutions were not yet supervised at that time according to European rules) has been very limited and the Barings case, with its very special connotations, does not contradict this statement. It shows that the European model is not so bad. That is why, in the framework of the White Paper which the European Commission issued in April 1995, and whose purpose is to define the pre-accession strategy for the associated countries of Central and Eastern Europe (so-called CEECs), it identifies the key measures in each sector of the internal market and suggests a sequence in which the approximation of legislation should be tackled. Equal importance is attached to the establishment of adequate structures for implementation and enforcement. This also applies, of course, to the financial sector.

4.1 Key underpinnings

One of the cornerstones in a successful transformation from a centralised economy to a market economy is the creation of a well-developed financial sector. The financial sector is one of the key elements for economic performance because it is via the financial sector that private savings and other available capital is allocated to investment. Another important function for the financial sector is to coordinate economic activities towards the most productive use of available capital. Therefore, a market economy cannot function without a well-developed and competitive financial sector.

A financial sector cannot be established overnight but has to be created in stages. The order in which the different elements have to be implemented depends on the type of financial system which has been chosen. Independent of this, it is of the greatest importance that the users of the financial system (both domestic and internationally) have full confidence in the system. This trust can only be created via prudential legislation and the creation of efficient supervision or control of the companies in the financial sector.

The three elements needed in order to develop a well-functioning financial sector are: (a) trained and reputable personnel; (b) appropriate legislation; and (c) effective supervisory bodies to ensure that the financial institutions respect the laws and regulations under which they work. Financial services in a centralised economy are quite different from financial services in a market economy. Therefore, training is one of the most urgent needs, not only for the employees in the industry but as much for the staff of the supervisory bodies. When the CEECs are drafting laws and regulations for the financial sector it is important that they have the actual "know-how" level of the industry in mind and do not allow the sector to do more than it is qualified to do. Finally, qualified supervisory bodies mean that the supervisory staff must be well trained but also be sufficient in number to make it possible to supervise or control all the authorised firms on a timely basis. Without a well-functioning supervisory body even the most advanced regulations will make no sense. Therefore, every effort must be made to strengthen the quality of the supervisory bodies so that they are able to perform their duties adequately.

4.2 Inputting the EU framework

It should be stressed that the order in which the EC directives within the financial sector have been adopted and the different elements they have coordinated do not always reflect the most logical order for a country which has to build up a financial sector from scratch. The different directives include elements and principles for which coordination was needed at the time of adoption. Before then national discretion was sufficient. This means that the CEECs ought to make themselves acquainted with all the directives within the sector and implement in the first stage those which are considered as essential.

The creation of an efficient banking system in which savings are transformed into loans to industry on market (economy) terms is of the utmost importance. The creation of an efficient payments system is also needed. Furthermore, the capital market can contribute to the allocation of capital to industry via well-functioning stock exchanges, just as the establishment of collective or mutual investment funds together with other institutional investors can provide valuable capital for investment in the industrial and private sectors, especially the housing sector, while at the same time giving a larger section of the population a stake and interest in the financial markets.

At the time when the EC started its coordination of the financial sector all Member States already had well-developed financial sectors. The coordination which took place was, therefore, more a question of fixing minimum standards for the industry in preparation for the internal market rather than an attempt to develop the financial sector. In the CEECs, the main objective will be to facilitate the emergence of a sound financial market.

In this context the most important first step will be the establishment of a supervisory authority to oversee the credit institutions (or banks as they are normally called). The role of the supervisory authority is to make rules for granting authorisation to credit institutions and rules on prudential requirements and then to ensure that the credit institutions fulfil these requirements (especially solvency).

The pre-conditions mentioned above will be sufficient for most of the different banking activities but not for all of them. One very important activity, and especially in economies transforming themselves into market economies, is mortgage credit. A well-functioning mortgage credit sector cannot exist without a legal infrastructure, such as clear rules for ownership of real estate, transparency concerning old claims (*e.g.* taxes) on the property, a well-functioning land-register, where mortgages can be registered, and legal provisions to enforce the mortgages. Development of a valuation profession could also be recommended. It is clear that without the existence of such other pre-conditions, it will not be possible to create in the CEECs an efficient mortgage credit activity.

Before stock exchanges can be established it is necessary that laws concerning issue and ownership of securities be adopted.

A pre-condition for the establishment of collective investment funds is that securities are issued and traded on regulated markets. One could continue with such a list of additional pre-conditions.

All directives or measures which are an integral part of a well-functioning financial sector have been included as key measures, whereas those directives whose main purpose has been to facilitate the functioning of the market have been left out for the time being.

4.3 First stage implementation

As mentioned above, the EC directives dealing with financial institutions have not been tailored to serve as a model for creating from scratch a financial sector. The directives chosen to form the first stage measures have been those which introduce the basic principles for establishment of financial institutions, but there are elements in the second stage measures which the CEECs, from a rational point of view, could benefit by introducing them at an early stage. Having this in mind the CEECs should in the first stage concentrate their efforts on implementing the principles laid down in the following directives from each of the following financial sectors.

4.3.1 *Credit institutions*

(1) First Banking Directive, which lays down the principles of right of establishment and the freedom to provide services and the establishment of a supervisory authority.
(2) Own Funds Directive, which defines which capital elements can be counted as regulatory capital.
(3) Solvency Ratio Directive, the main purpose of which is to harmonise the prudential supervision and to strengthen solvency standards among Community credit institutions, thereby protecting both depositors and investors as well as maintaining banking stability.
(4) Deposit Guarantee Directive, which will guarantee depositors their savings – up to a fixed maximum – in case of insolvency of a credit institution. The principles of this directive will strengthen the trust of the depositors in the banking system.

4.3.2 *Securities*

(1) The Directive on public offer prospectuses, which applies to securities which are offered to the public for subscription or sale for the first time in a Member State. The prospectus must include all information needed to make an informed financial assessment of the securities. A competent authority shall be appointed to agree prior scrutiny of the prospectus.
(2) The Directive on stock exchange listing particulars to securities which are admitted or are the subject of an application for admission to official listing on a stock exchange. Such securities must comply with the conditions and fulfil the obligations set out in the annex to the Directive. Member States may require issuers of securities to publish information regularly on their financial position and on the general course of their business. A competent authority to decide on the admission of securities and the application of the directive shall be designated.
(3) The Directive on notification of major holdings, which is meant to give investors adequate information on persons who acquire or dispose of major holdings in listed companies. When the voting rights of holdings held by one person exceed or fall below certain thresholds the company and the public must be notified.
(4) The Directive on insider trading, the main purpose of which is to protect investors against improper use of inside information. This directive is also helpful in creating confidence in the market-place.

(5) The Directive on undertakings for collective investment in transferable securities (UCITS), which provides principles for authorisation
of "open ended" investment funds; rules for sale and repurchase of
their units; obligations concerning management, investment, depositaries and prospectuses. Some of the basis principles of this Directive
should be implemented in the first stage (but pre-suppose the existence of transferable securities and regulated markets) in order to give
small investors an alternative to bank savings.

The right of establishment has, in the EC (now "Union"), been an important
element due simply to the Treaty obligation. In the European Agreements
between the EC and CEECs which have been made until now, it is agreed
that EC financial companies shall have the right to set up operations in the
territory of the respective CEECs, at the latest by the end of the transitional
period of the Agreement. Nevertheless, the Community strongly recommends the CEECs to make such establishments feasible as soon as possible
because it would be very much to the benefit of the countries in question to
avail themselves of the know-how of such companies.

To the directives above must be added the very important Council
Directive of 10 June 1991 on prevention of the use of the financial system for
the purpose of money laundering, which is a horizontal directive covering
credit institutions, financial institutions and insurance companies. The
Union strongly recommends the CEECs to establish suitable standards
against money laundering as soon as possible in order to avoid their
financial sector being used for laundering of proceeds from criminal activities in general and drug offences in particular. Without such measures
confidence in their financial system might be jeopardised. The existing
European Agreements contain already an article concerning this objective.

4.4 Second stage implementation

As soon as one of the above-mentioned financial sectors has implemented
its first stage programme it should continue without waiting for the others.
The measures in the second stage will aim in particular to strengthen the
prudential regulation for the firms in order to bring them up to a more
international standard.

Some of the key directives which are proposed for the second stage will
include provisions directly related to the creation of the Community internal market, such as the freedom of establishment and the freedom to
provide cross-border services without further authorisation and the
principle of home country supervision.

The directives to be implemented in the second stage would be the
following.

4.4.1 Credit institutions

(1) The Second Banking Directive, which is the main instrument for
completing the single market in banking.
(2) The Directive on annual accounts and consolidated accounts of banks
and other financial institutions, which specifically addresses this

sector but has to be read together with the Fourth and Seventh Company Law Directives.

(3) The Directive on capital adequacy of investment firms and credit institutions, which deals with the risks other than credit risk to which investment firms and banks are exposed.

(4) The Large Exposures Directive, which limits the exposure a bank can have to a single client to a maximum of 25% of its own funds.

(5) The Directive on supervision of credit institutions on a consolidated basis, which applies to all banking groups, including those the parent undertakings of which are not credit institutions. Supervision on a consolidated basis is all the more effective if it can be exercised on a worldwide basis or at any rate on the widest possible geographical basis. It is, therefore, necessary to ensure that there are no impediments in CEEC countries to the transfer of the necessary information and, where such impediments exist, to endeavour to make agreements with the countries in question.

4.4.2 *Securities*

(1) The Investment Services Directive.

(2) Directive on capital adequacy of investment firms and credit institutions, which applies to investment firms as to banks, as mentioned above.

The White Paper is addressed to the ten countries which already have association agreements (Poland, Hungary, the Czech Republic, Slovakia, Bulgaria, Romania, the three Baltic Republics, and Slovenia). The White Paper is a general reference document which does not adapt its recommendations to the requirements of any particular country. Each CEEC will establish its own priorities and determine its own timetable in the light of its economic, social and political realities and of the work it has achieved so far.

5 THE ROLE OF TECHNICAL ASSISTANCE

Another contribution of the White Paper, as indicated above, is to provide guidelines for the content and organisation of technical assistance. Ensuring that the White Paper's analytical contribution is translated into coherent and effective technical assistance covering both legislation and structures, in response to the needs emerging from the CEECs' national strategies, is the second main objective which should be achieved.

It is the responsibility of each associated country to coordinate its requests for assistance and to provide information about progress made in implementing the White Paper, so as to ensure that assistance from the Union, Member States and other bodies is consistent and mutually reinforcing.

On the Union side, the key objective must be to organise technical assistance in this wide and diverse field in a way which makes the best possible use of scarce resources. Finance is not unlimited and the expertise on which the associated countries need to draw is concentrated in a relatively small number of officials and practitioners, mainly in the Member States. The Union is already providing technical assistance, notably through PHARE, and this should now be enhanced and adapted to the White Paper's recommendations. Other Community programmes open to the associated countries, as well assistance from the Member States and private bodies, also have a useful contribution to make. Special attention needs to be given to ensuring that all these efforts are mutually reinforcing and well focused. Improved information exchange and transparency concerning developments in the associated countries and the assistance on offer will help match supply and demand and provide common services where common needs are identified.

Technical assistance form the Union should cover the programming and drafting of legislation and its implementation and enforcement. Assistance could include the following:

- assistance with appraising the costs and benefits of difference sequences of approximation;
- direct and rapid access to complete and up-to-date EU legislative texts and jurisprudence, as well as translation services;
- a "one-stop-shop" on the Union side to which requests for help with specific problems relating to legislation and its application can be addressed;
- advice from legal and technical experts, on the Union's legal system and, about the interpretation of Community texts and the drafting of national laws;
- information concerning implementation and enforcement mechanisms in the Member States and firsthand experience of their functioning through participation in exchange programmes;
- access to administrative, language and specialised technical training;
- information about the functioning of the internal market for financial operators and for the public at large.

For each associated country, national framework programmes for the approximation of internal market legislation could be established which would ensure complementarity among all PHARE programmes relevant to the objectives of the White Paper.

The national programmes in each associated country should be placed under the authority of a body responsible for assistance and coordination in the framework of the pre-accession strategy. Regular reports on the work of the national programmes should made to the Association Council and the competent structures of the European agreements.

PHARE programming for the five-year period starting this year is already well advanced. The Commission will invite each associated country to hold discussions with it as soon as possible after the publication of the White Paper, to help clarify each country's programme and priorities in the light of the White Paper. Existing national framework programmes for the reform and approximation of law can be adjusted accordingly.

Certain assistance needs are common to all associated countries. To respond to these needs, the Commission intends to establish a Technical Assistance Information Exchange Office supported through a multi-country PHARE programme. The Office will be located in Brussels and managed by the Commission. It will provide for the exchange of information and will help ensure the adequate delivery of services to the associated countries. It will facilitate the provision of the highest possible quality of assistance in the most cost-effective way from a variety of public and private sector bodies.

The assistance covered by the Office will include Community legislation, its transposition into national legislation, legal terminology, translation, training and exchanges, including short-term placements in the Commission's services and relevant bodies in the Member States. In addition, the Office will serve as a "one-stop-shop" or clearing house to which requests for assistance with the recruitment of specialist advisers can be addressed.

6 CONCLUDING OBSERVATIONS

Transition in central and eastern Europe to political and economic systems compatible with those in the European Union is a complex process. It involves the strengthening of democracy and civil society; the implementation of sound macro-economic policies; privatisation and industrial restructuring; legal and institutional changes; and trade liberalisation, aiming at free trade with the Union and with neighbouring countries. Although the situation varies from country to country, this process of transformation is now well under way.

The primary responsibility for the success of this process lies with the associated countries themselves. But the strategy suggested in the White Paper provides for additional support from the Union, including a closer working relationship with its own institutions, the adaption of PHARE priorities to changing needs, and a major new effort to prepare the associated countries for their future integration into the internal market in general, and in the European financial market in particular.

3. The Applicability of Law and Economics to Law and Development: The Case of Financial Law

Joel P. Trachtman[1]

"It is ... the costs of transacting that are the key obstacles that prevent economies and societies from realizing well-being."[2]

1 INTRODUCTION

1.1 The problem

Law and development has seen a significant revival in practice, if not in theory.[3] Law and development advice has become an important part of legal reform and economic development efforts in emerging markets and developing countries. However, this advice lacks a sound theoretical basis, and therefore lacks a disciplined and complete methodology.[4] Without theoretical and methodological underpinnings, (i) it is impossible to evaluate whether this advice is useful or not; (ii) it is impossible to evaluate whether the work needed has already been done, or must be reinvented; and (iii) it is impossible to plan a programmatic approach to law and development.

This chapter suggests that at least one version of the economic analysis of law holds promise as a source of a theoretical and methodological basis for law and development activities. This chapter suggests a comparative

---

[1] Associate Professor of International Law, The Fletcher School of Law and Diplomacy, Tufts University, Mass. I would like to thank Jefferey Atik, Jeswald Salacuse and Ann and Robert Seidman, for their helpful comments, and Xavier Diaz and Daniel Grunberg for their diligent and thoughtful research assistance.
[2] North "Institutions, Transaction Costs and Economic Growth", 25 *Econ. Inquiry* 419, 420 (1987).
[3] The term "law and development" refers to legal reform efforts in developing (third world) and emerging (Eastern European) countries aimed at enhancing economic development. The term "economic development" is much more difficult to define, but refers to changes in economic structure that result in increased wealth. This subject may be viewed as included in a wider topic known as "law and social change".
[4] For an elaboration on the importance of theory and methodology, *see* A. Seidman and R. Seidman, *State and Law in the Development Process: Problem-Solving and Institutional Change in the Third World*, 57–141 (1994) (hereinafter, *State and Law*).

institutional analysis[5] as the appropriate theoretical and methodological basis for law and development. This comparative institutional analysis sees transaction costs not as simple material expenses of doing business, but as the fundamental determinant of how, and whether, people relate to one another to achieve their goals.

Comparative institutional analysis engages in comparative transaction cost economizing, seeking the institutional formula that will best facilitate all manner of social exchange. By social exchange, I mean not simply market transactions, but also politics and all of the social relationships that enhance life: all of the things that we must cooperate with others in order to achieve. This transaction cost economizing approach does not consider the values that each of us attach to various goods, but assumes that we all have different values. It assumes that there are gains from trade: that our different values make it possible for us to get more of what we want by cooperating with others. From this assumption, it works to minimize the costs of cooperating with others, in order to facilitate trade. Obviously, if the gains from trade are smaller than the transaction costs, no trade will take place.

The central problem, or symptom, of developing countries is poverty. Poverty can be explained domestically as arising from inadequate production or distribution of production that leaves some people without sufficient resources.[6] Developing countries face two types of limits to their increase in productivity: (i) a technical production frontier; and (ii) a structural production frontier.[7] "Technical production frontier" means the set of technologies available for production. "Structural production frontier" means the set of institutional relationships, including law, available for organizing production. These two frontiers are related, as the structural production frontier acts as a limit on the ability to utilize higher technologies, with greater specialization of production and better resource allocation. While assistance with technology problems can push forward the technical production frontier, law and development addresses the structural production frontier. It is important to recognize that law and development is a dynamic process, relating the technical production frontier to the structural production frontier as each (hopefully) advances over time. This dynamic process must include not only all of the activities necessary to study local needs and institutions and to legitimate legislation,[8] but it must, in addition, be extended in time after the date when legislation is enacted or

---

[5] *See* N. Komesar, *Imperfect Alternatives* (1994); Mercuro, "Toward a Comparative Institutional Approach to the Study of Law and Economics", in N. Mercuro, ed., *Law and Economics* (1989). *See* also Rubin, "Institutional Analysis and the New Legal Process", 1995 *Wic. L. Rev.* 463 (1995) (reviewing Komesar's book).

[6] Poverty may also be sought to be explained in international terms by reference to adverse terms of trade, economic domination by multinational corporations, or other international phenomena. This chapter does not address those issues, but concentrates on domestic issues. Even if it were possible to show that the domestic issues are not the sole cause, or the most important cause, of poverty, one may speculate that they are at least an important cause of poverty.

[7] *See* Calabresi, "The Pointlessness of Pareto: Carrying Coase Further", 100 *Yale L.J.* 1211 (1991).

[8] *State and Law, supra* note 4.

regulation is promulgated. Thus, the structural production frontier includes not only law, but also (i) other social rules,[9] and (ii) the reaction of people over time to law.[10] It also is affected by changes in the technical production frontier, as, for example, telecommunications or information processing capability reduces transaction costs.

Multilateral financial institutions such as the World Bank, the International Monetary Fund, the International Finance Corporation; regional development banks such as the European Bank for Reconstruction and Development, the Inter-American Development Bank, the Asian Development Bank and the African Development Bank; national government development agencies such as the U.S. Agency for International Development; non-governmental organizations such as the Harvard Institute for International Development, the American Bar Association and many private law firms, accounting firms and consulting firms have sought to contribute to the efforts of emerging and developing countries to develop appropriate legal infrastructures for market economies. The hope of those providing funding and intellectual resources for these efforts is that these infrastructures will facilitate more efficient economies, leading to greater welfare in these poor countries: to expansion of the structural production frontier. However, there seems to be little way to know whether the structural production frontier is actually advanced, and whether it is advanced more than it would be by other available legal structures. Finally, we must ask whether these efforts might actually contract the structural production frontier: whether welfare could be diminished by these efforts.

The current law and development activity, which has grown significantly since the late 1980s, brings to mind an earlier heyday of law and development. Supported by government organizations as well as by foundations such as the Ford Foundation, this earlier period seems to have ended, at least in the U.S., in the mid-1970s.[11] At that time, a powerfully symbiotic combination of reduced funding and theoretical disorientation resulted in the reduction of efforts toward law and development. While funding seems to be less of a problem today, as some of the institutions mentioned above reorient their efforts away from intergovernmental lending for big infrastructure and energy projects toward the framework for a market economy, the theoretical concerns that debilitated the earlier law and development movement[12] have not been addressed. Importantly, current law and

---

[9] *See* R. Ellickson, *Order Without Law* (1991) (examining the dominance of informal social rules over legal rules under the circumstances of cattle ranching in Shasta County, California).

[10] *See* North, *supra* note 2.

[11] *See* Tamanaha, "Book Review: The Lessons of Law-and-Development Studies", 89 *Am. J. Int'l. L.* 470, 474 (1995).

[12] For a useful review of the pre-1977 literature on law and development, *see* Burg, "Law and Development: A Review of the Literature & a Critique of 'Scholars in Self-Estrangement' ", 25 *Am. J. Comp. L.* 492 (1977). *See* also Merryman, "Comparative Law and Social Change: On the Origins, Style, Decline & Revival of the Law and Development Movement", 25 *Am. J. Comp. L.* 457 (1977); Trubek and Galanter, "Scholars in Self-Estrangement: Some Reflections on the Crisis in Law and Development Studies in the United States", 1974 *Wisc. L. Rev.* 1062 (1974); International Legal Center, *Law and Development: The Future of Law and Development Research* (1974).

development advice emphasizes the private sector, rather than the techniques of establishment and administration of the public sector.

Given the theoretical and methodological gap mentioned above, and these resulting questions about the effectiveness of law and development activity, lawyers who become involved in law and development activities may today feel some of the discomfort concerning law and development activities that David Trubek and Marc Galanter expressed in 1974.[13] These discomforts are rooted in ethical concerns: am I overselling the solutions of the West to social problems in emerging markets? If I describe and adapt these solutions for use in emerging markets, am I performing a useful service or is this activity comparable to selling infant formula to countries with inadequate water sterilization facilities, when breast feeding is a safer and more nutritious method of feeding infants?[14] Are these solutions empowering antidemocratic and oppressive elements of society? Finally, how can I know whether I am performing a service or a disservice?

Lawyers and scholars trained in the developed world who are engaged in law and development activities thus oscillate between arrogance and modesty. Sometimes we err by thinking arrogantly that our solutions are unquestionably appropriate for an emerging world that we think has no potential solutions of its own. Sometimes we err by excess modesty, denying the utility of our history, experience and prior work. Between arrogance and modesty is the confidence earned by methodologically sound and contextually sensitive analysis that will be used not to dictate solutions, but to inform politics in the emerging market country.

The purpose of this chapter is to suggest the possibility for a methodologically sound and contextually sensitive analysis based on principles of law and economics. It should be re-emphasized that this analytical method will not be a basis for determining policy. Rather, it will be a basis for informing the political determination of policy, because it is only through politics, not through arid analysis, that social goals can be determined and expressed. Thus, in the end, the quality of politics in the developing or emerging country is critical to the success of any law and development program.[15] However, a strong law and development analysis may contribute to the quality of politics through greater transparency and greater information about the possible effects of legislation.

Economic analysis of law uses many diverse tools: it is an eclectic approach. First, it may use price theory, mathematical modelling or econometric methodology typical of neo-classical economics. Second, it may use game theory or public choice analysis of legislation or other legal activity. Third, with the new institutional economics, it may focus on transaction costs, as I do here. This chapter proceeds without attempting to distill and evaluate the many critiques and defenses of different tools, or schools, of law and economics. This would be too long a project to undertake in this context; all that can be hoped for here is a modest and suggestive introduction.

---

[13] *See* Trubek and Galanter, *supra* note 12.

[14] *See, e.g.,* P. Cateora, *International Marketing* 655–60 (1993) (describing the case of Nestlé marketing infant formula in the third world).

[15] The quality of politics is also a transaction costs problem. *See* Komesar, *supra* note 5.

In most social science, and in law in particular, there is no laboratory; no place in which all other factors can be held constant and a particular regulatory device evaluated for efficiency. Rather, the laboratory available to law is the comparative or historical method.[16] This laboratory provides historical or comparative settings for evaluation of law or regulation. Cappelletti, Seccombe and Weiler describe the utility of the comparative method as follows:

> Comparative legal analysis will then be brought to "evaluate" laws, institutions and techniques in relation to that particular problem and need. This approach represents, in a real way, a "Third School" of legal thinking, different both from mere positivism, for which law is a pure *datum* not subject to evaluation, and from evaluation of such *datum* based on abstract, airy, inevitably subjective criteria such as "natural law" principles.[17]

As noted above, we must extend this comparative approach to compare not simply legal mechanisms, but other kinds of social rules or mechanisms. Thus, regulatory solutions must be compared with market solutions, or with private institutional solutions. So, for example, if Bulgaria is seeking to determine what its approach to insider trading in the securities markets should be, it must first determine its goals in this context and second examine what social structures, including perhaps regulation, would achieve these goals most efficiently. Its domestic goals might include, perhaps, systemic stability, consumer protection, protection of allocative efficiency, and lowest cost to the government budget. It might examine, for example, U.S. securities law and German securities law; the U.S. law because of its reputation for completeness, and the German law because of Germany's geographic proximity and membership in the European Union. It might compare these legal regimes, however, with a non-legal approach that lets markets decide whether to allow insider trading,[18] or allows self-regulatory organizations to regulate this conduct.

Furthermore, legislated regulatory structures must be compared with common law structures: how is law best made and best made dynamic in its ability to respond to change? A rule that might be second best might be preferred to the rule that is otherwise first best, perhaps because the second-best rule is easier to change, with less disruption.

1.2 Financial regulation

Significant law and development efforts are being made in the field of financial regulation, and in particular, bank regulation and securities

---

[16] *See, e.g.*, Komesar, *supra* note 5; Frey, "Institutions Matter: The Comparative Analysis of Institutions", 34 *Eur. Econ. Rev.* 443 (1990); M. Cappelletti, Monica Seccombe & Joseph Weiler, *Integration Through Law: Europe and the American Federal Experience* 5–12 (Vol. 1, Bk. 1 1986); E. Stein, "Uses, Misuses – and Nonuses of Comparative Law", 72 *Nw. U.L. Rev.* 198 (1977). *See* also F. Zimring & G. Hawkins, *Deterrence: The Legal Threat in Crime Control*, 263–70 (1973) (discussing "natural experiments").

[17] *Id.* at 5 (citations omitted).

[18] This approach might be associated with the former German approach. *See, e.g.*, Hopt, "The European Insider Dealing Directive", 27 *C. M. L. Rev.* 51 (1990).

regulation. I use these fields as examples by which to assess, anecdotally and speculatively, the possible utility of law and economics methodologies in law and development activities. Thus, this chapter is an attempt to stimulate and indicate a path for further research, and its legal analysis of certain areas of financial regulation is nothing more than some opening conjectures.

1.3 The structure of the chapter

Part 2 of this chapter is devoted to a brief review of selected literature relevant to the theoretical and methodological problem in law and development and to the potential applicability of the economic analysis of law in the law and development context. The literature regarding the use of economic analysis of law in law and development is scanty, and does not address bank regulation or securities regulation specifically. The literature regarding the use of economic analysis of law in developed countries and especially U.S. bank and securities regulation is deeper.

Part 3 examines the problem of goals, and more particularly of defining efficiency,[19] in law and economics. This is a central problem for this chapter because the question of the goals of law must be at the base of any analysis of the utility of law. Are goals homogeneous or heterogeneous across societies? Assuming heterogeneity, what use will the laws of one society be for another society?

Part 4 turns to the law and economics of finance regulation, examining two representative, and central, areas of finance regulation: deposit insurance for banks and mandatory disclosure regulation in securities offerings. This section considers the goals and mechanisms of regulation in these areas in the developed world, and then turns to the applicability of these goals and mechanisms in the circumstances of the developing or emerging world.

This chapter concludes that law and economics generally, and comparative institutional analysis in particular, is a useful methodology for legal reform efforts in emerging and developing countries. One of the problems with adopting this methodology is that it is more difficult to use than many current, seat-of-the-pants methodologies.[20] It will require substantial

---

[19] *See* Mattei, "Efficiency in Legal Transplants: An Essay in Comparative Law and Economics", 14 *Int'l Rev. L. & Econ.* 3 (1994); Margolis, "Two Definitions of Efficiency in Law and Economics", 16 *J. Leg. Studs.* 471 (1987); G. Becker, *The Economic Approach to Human Behavior* (1976); Kitch, "The Intellectual Foundations of 'Law and Economics' ", 33 *J. Leg. Educ.* 184 (1983). *See* also Hirshleifer, "The Expanding Domain of Economics", 75 *Am. Econ. Rev.*, Dec. 1985, at 53.

[20] This problem is reminiscent of the joke about the drunk who has lost his keys. The drunk is searching for his keys in the light of a street lamp. A policeman arrives and asks what the drunk is doing. Hearing the explanation, the policeman asks whether the drunk lost his keys near the street lamp. The drunk replies "no, but the light is much better here". In order to do effective law and development, we must be willing to go to where the light is not so good. The place where the light is good is in simple copying of developed country legislation, performed in short-term missions by private sector experts who do not apply a comparative methodology. It is necessary to seek better organized help, to search more widely, and to bring some additional light to bear in order to find the key to law and development problems.

intellectual and economic resources. However, despite the conclusion that each country must chart its own path, countries may share some of the analytical work. Thus, this chapter suggests that resources be pooled in order to provide enough resources to do the job right, rather than leaving resources dispersed, with many separate inadequate pools of resources. While a law and economics reflex might recommend competition among sources of law and development assistance, the economies of scale here may override this reflex. Rather, transaction costs should be overcome to allow the pooling of resources. Moreover, there need not be competition among sources of law and development assistance, because this product competes with many easily substituted products, such as internal legislative analysis. In addition, this is a product that is difficult to evaluate and purchase accurately – consumers may not have the expertise to choose among sources, and the market is not especially liquid. This difficulty of evaluation may argue for a high level of independent professionalism in law and development practice, or perhaps for the development of qualified intermediaries capable of evaluating these products. Finally, public choice analysis might argue that until a customized product is actually created, along with advice regarding the utility of the particular legal institution recommended, states as consumers may have interests in choosing the wrong sources of advice, to obtain advice that will empower governing classes, rather than enhance welfare for society at large.

Thus, institutions with financial and intellectual resources for law and development should pool them in order to be able to create a library of comparative institutional data and an academy for the analysis, adaptation and transfer of this data, and for the evaluation and revision of its use over time.

2 LAW AND DEVELOPMENT THEORY AND LAW AND ECONOMICS THEORY

Despite the dominance of economists in much economic development activity, the economic analysis of law has not thus far been a strong force in law and development, perhaps because the economic analysis of law is not a strong area of economics. Certainly the academic literature on law and development has, with few exceptions, either ignored or eschewed the economic analysis of law.[21] However, this does not show much, because the academic literature on law and development largely preceded the rise of the law and economics movement.

2.1 Coase and transaction cost economics

Law and economics might begin with a Coasean analysis of the need for regulation. The Coase Theorem, which has been extensively elaborated and

---

[21] But *see*, Black, Kraakman & Hay, "Corporate Law From Scratch", Harvard Law School Program in Law and Economics, Discussion Paper No. 155, (March 1995); Brietzke, "Designing the Legal Frameworks for Markets in Eastern Europe", 7 *Transnat'l Law.* 35 (1994).

critiqued,[22] though never explicitly articulated as such by Coase himself, indicates that, without transaction costs, the initial allocation of property rights, or the initial determination of regulatory responsibilities, would not affect efficiency.[23] The reason that this initial allocation would, assuming zero transaction costs, not affect efficiency, is that market participants would engage in costless reallocative transactions that would result in an efficient outcome,[24] and all externalities would thus be internalized: no decision-maker would fail to take into account all of the costs of his or her decision.[25] Coase argues that, "if market transactions were costless, all that matters (questions of equity apart) is that the rights of the various parties should be well defined and the results of legal actions easy to forecast".[26] This is an argument that the specifics of the rules of law or regulation are irrelevant *in a zero transaction costs world*, so long as the rules are predictable and their application is administrable. Indeed, even this may be too conservative a position in a zero, as opposed to low, transaction costs world. In the absence of any transaction costs at all, even property rights may be

---

[22] For a summary and reference to further literature, *see* Cooter, "The Coase Theorem", in *The New Palgrave: a Dictionary of Economics* 457, 457–60 (1987). *See* also Hoffman & Spitzer, "The Coase Theorem: Some Experimental Tests", 25 *J.L. & Econ.* 73 (1982); Cooter, "The Cost of Coase", 11 *J. Leg. Stud.* 1 (1982).

[23] Ronald Coase, *The Firm, the Market and the Law* 95–185 (1988), incorporating and commenting upon earlier work, including Coase's seminal articles: "The Nature of the Firm", 4 *Economica* 386 (1937) and "The Problem of Social Cost", 3 *J.L. & Econ.* 1 (1960). Coase explains that these articles are related. "In order to explain why firms exist and what activities they undertake, I found it necessary to introduce . . . the concept that has come to be known as 'transaction costs'." *Id.* at 6. Transaction costs may be viewed narrowly or broadly, but it appears appropriate in the current context to view them quite broadly, as Coase does:

> In order to carry out a market transaction, it is necessary to discover who it is that one wishes to deal with, to inform people that one wishes to deal and on what terms, to conduct negotiations leading up to a bargain, to draw up the contract, to undertake the inspection needed to make sure that the terms of the contract are being observed, and so on. These operations are often extremely costly, sufficiently costly at any rate to prevent many transactions that would be carried out in a world in which the pricing system worked without cost.

Id. at 114. However, there seems to be little consensus on the content of the term "transaction costs". *See* Williamson, "Transaction Cost Economics: The Governance of Contractual Relations", 22 *J.L. & Econ.* 233 (1979). *See* also the commentary listed in Schlag, "The Problem of Transaction Costs", 62 *S. Cal. L. Rev.* 1661, at 1662, n. 3 (1989).

[24] Of course, we must define efficiency in this context. By efficiency, I mean the allocation of resources to their highest value uses. The valuation of uses is effected through a price, or shadow price, system. Either Pareto efficiency or Kaldor-Hicks efficiency have been used in pursuing this concept. *See* Markovits, "A Constructive Critique of the Traditional Definition and Use of the Concept of 'The Effect of a Choice on Allocative (Economic) Efficiency': Why the Kaldor-Hicks Test, the Coase Theorem, and Virtually All Law-And-Economics Welfare Arguments Are Wrong", 1993 *U. Ill. L. Rev.* 485 (1993).

[25] Another way of stating the Coase Theorem, which formulation has been cited with approval by Coase, is that under conditions of zero transaction costs, "private and social costs will be equal". Coase, *supra* note 23, at 174, citing G. Stigler, *Theory of Price*, at 113 (1966).

[26] *Id.* at 119.

unnecessary to be specified.[27] Thus, in a world without transaction costs, not only is the firm unnecessary, but law is also unnecessary: the state would wither away. As Coase says, "[i]t would not seem worthwhile to spend much time investigating the properties of such a world".[28]

As Coase notes, transaction costs exist. Coase suggests that legal decisions should be made with a view to "reduce the need for market transactions and thus reduce the employment of resources in carrying them out".[29] "The same approach which, with zero transaction costs, demonstrates that the allocation of resources remains the same whatever the legal position, also shows that, with positive transaction costs, the law plays a crucial role in determining how resources are used."[30]

Thus, a Coasean approach to bank and securities regulation, as adopted by this chapter, would seek regulation, or deregulation, that minimizes the sum of (i) deadweight losses due to the failure to maximize the achievement of social goals (including those achieved through the market); and (ii) the transaction costs incurred in making such allocation. This approach is ignorant of distributive concerns, but is not necessarily hostile to distributive action by government. Rather, it would simply evaluate the cost in allocative efficiency of redistributive allocations, perhaps pointing out that a direct subsidy or a tax, rather than regulation, is the more efficient means to achieve a particular redistributive goal.[31] Douglass North[32] and Oliver Williamson[33] have built significantly on this Coasean perspective.

2.2 Stigler

In the 1970s, law and economics began to address problems of regulation as a specialized area, and in a way that, from one perspective, competes with the Coasean perspective.[34] George J. Stigler's article, "The Theory of Economic Regulation",[35] began a debate that continues today as to whether regulation can best be explained by public choice,[36] which examines the supply and demand factors that influence legislators and regulators (the "economic" theory or "public choice" theory), or by concern for the public interest (the "public interest" theory). Of course, the answer to this

---

[27] Cheung, "Will China Go 'Capitalist'?" 37, Hobart Paper No. 94 (1968).

[28] Coase, *supra* note 23, at 15.

[29] *Id*. at 119.

[30] *Id*. at 178. Coase argues that with positive transaction costs, the "market transactions" by which private action would reallocate resources may become too costly to effect.

[31] *See* Kaplow and Shavell, "The Efficiency of the Legal System versus the Income Tax in Redistributing Income" Harvard Working Paper on Law and Economics No. 130 (1993).

[32] North, *supra* note 2; North, "Institutions", 5 *J. Econ. Persp.* 97 (1991).

[33] O. Williamson, *The Economic Institutions of Capitalism* (1985).

[34] Stigler, "The Theory of Economic Regulation", 2 *Bell J. Econ. & Management Sci.* 3 (1971); Posner, "Theories of Economic Regulation", 5 *Bell J. Econ. & Management Sci.* 335 (1974); Peltzman, "Toward a More General Theory of Regulation", 19 *J. Law & Econ.* 211 (1976).

[35] *Id*.

[36] There is a wide literature describing the public choice perspective on law. *See, e.g.*, Farber and Frickey, "The Jurisprudence of Public Choice", 65 *Tex. L. Rev.* 873 (1987); Kahn, "The Politics of Unregulation: Public Choice and Limits on Government", 75 *Cornell L. Rev.* 280 (1990), and sources cited in note 1 thereof.

Hobson's choice is "yes"[37] for any honest politician is interested both in doing good and in being reelected, and while the best politicians are interested only in doing good, they need to be reelected in order to continue to do good. Most of us would find the public interest theory more attractive, and the law and economics version of "public interest" is that regulation is justified when it is able to reduce the sum of transaction costs and deadweight losses from what it otherwise would be. Regulation should be used where the market is a higher social cost alternative.

In fact, comparative institutional analysis can be applied to compare the efficiency of government institutions to that of market structures. In this sense, comparative institutional analysis considers the possibility not just of market failure, but of government failure: the possible relative inefficiency of government as a structure for effecting social goals. In this sense, public choice analysis is useful to assess government as a structure, to compare it with a market structure for allocation, and to recommend modifications to government to reduce government failure, just as we recommend modifications to the market – regulation – to reduce market failure.[38] In addition, public policy analysis must recognize that government and the market are parts of an integrated social system. These parts affect one another, and so a change in one part should not be considered without addressing the potential affects on the other.

2.3 Trubek and Galanter

I begin here to review selected material in the literature of law and development that antedated, but provides some support for, the introduction of law and economics to law and development. In 1974, David Trubek and Marc Galanter provided a seminal criticism of the "liberal legalism" that they argued characterized the law and development literature to date.[39] One of their most trenchant criticisms charged the law and development literature with making the state the primary focus of social control, and using law instrumentally to control the conduct of individuals. This is a criticism that resonates with the law and economics movement, at least one branch of which might argue that law is not about control, but about facilitating and enhancing social/economic interaction in society.[40] Another of their important criticisms regarded the possible misuse of law to "further domination by elite groups".[41] Finally, they criticized the ethnocentric bias of law and development work.[42] A law and economics approach to law and development may respond to each of these three criticisms.

---

[37] *See* Priest, "The Origins of Utility Regulation and the 'Theories of Regulation' Debate", 36 *J. L. & Econ.* 289 (1993).

[38] *See* the discussion of public choice theory in Komesar, *supra* note 5, at 53–97.

[39] Trubek and Galanter, *supra* note 12.

[40] Burg points out that at least some of the law and development literature reflected this perspective. Burg, *supra* note 12, at 502, citing Meagher and Smith, "Law and the Development Practitioner" (1974) (report prepared for AID). Burg notes that this concept can be traced to Fuller, "Human Interaction and the Law", 14 *Am. J. Jurisprudence* 1 (1969).

[41] *Id.* at 1083.

[42] *Id.* at 1080–82.

Trubek and Galanter end their article with the prediction of "competing articulations" of continuing law and development studies, which they call (i) pragmatic problem solving; (ii) positivism; and (iii) eclectic critique. Pragmatic problem solving is atheoretical,[43] and implicitly wholly political: when a need is articulated, a law and development exercise can address the specific need. The second articulation, "positivistic pure science", relies on other social sciences, perhaps economics, to provide a neutral basis for action. Trubek and Galanter implicitly challenge the possibility of neutrality, and turn to their favored articulation, the "eclectic critique". The eclectic critique is close to the liberal legalism that Trubek and Galanter criticize, retaining its assumptions as aspirations. The law and economics approach might be considered a positivistic pure science response that rejects these assumptions but considers law a technique of facilitating and enhancing social interaction, given a particular social context. I argue here that law and economics is not a positivistic pure science, and that to the extent that it is such, it is a failure. Rather, law and economics is a tool of analysis that may be used to facilitate politics by allowing the transparent assessment of the effects of law.

2.4 Robert Seidman

Robert Seidman has authored some of the leading works in law and development.[44] In this section, I will concentrate on an article that strongly rejects the potential applicability of neo-classical law and economics to law and development.[45] This article characterizes the law and economics movement as rooted in neo-classical economics. The law and economics described and attacked in this article is more a political preference than a methodology: it is a demand for market solutions as opposed to public sector solutions. While Seidman and Makgetla are correct that neo-classical economics emphasizes the model of perfect competition, the type of law and economics that Coase describes addresses the world of imperfect competition: the world of positive transaction costs. Indeed, law and economics and the "new institutional economics" reject or severely question important aspects of neo-classical economics, for both methodological and political reasons.[46] The Seidman and Makgetla article predates the rise to prominence of this "new institutional economics" and of the transaction cost approach to law and economics.

---

[43] "Practical men, who believe themselves to be quite exempt from any intellectual influences, are usually the slaves of some defunct economist. Madmen in authority, who hear voices in the air, are distilling their frenzy from some academic scribbler of a few years back . . . soon or late, it is ideas, not vested interests, which are dangerous for good or evil." J. Keynes, *The General Theory of Employment, Interest and Money.*

[44] *See,* most recently, A. Seidman and R. Seidman, *State and Law in the Development Process* (1995).

[45] Makgetla and Seidman, "The Applicability of Law and Economics to Policymaking in the Third World", 23 *J. Econ. Issues* 35 (1989).

[46] But *see,* Posner, "The New Institutional Economics Meets Law and Economics", 149/1 *J. Institutional and Theoretical Econ.* 73 (1993). Posner writes that "Coase's famous articles on transaction costs are better regarded as correcting errors, induced by collectivist leanings, in neoclassical theory than as jettisoning that theory." *Id.* at 75.

Seidman and Makgetla rightly attack the law and economics that finds that "government intervention in economic decisionmaking can only cause inefficiency and impinge on personal freedom". However, Coase's transaction costs methodology calls for government intervention wherever such intervention reduces transaction costs below those that would exist absent government intervention: it is a rationalization of regulation, not a condemnation.[47] While the views Seidman and Makgetla reflect an atheist approach to government regulation, Coase, and the transaction costs methodology that follows him, set an agnostic tenor.[48] This literature invites research into comparisons of transaction costs. While Seidman and Makgetla argue that law and economics makes prescriptions for goals without regard to the actual circumstances of real world contexts, this transaction cost comparison necessarily takes real world situations as they are and assesses particular transaction cost structures. With Seidman and Makgetla, perhaps, transaction costs economics sees the state and the market as two of many possible methods of social organization.

Of course, Seidman and Makgetla are correct that any approach that would seek to remake the developing world in the image of the developed world is doomed to failure. However, as Cooter[49] and a few others[50] have shown, law and economics can be used in diverse circumstances, and can sometimes arrive at results that recognize the efficiency and value of customary law. It does so not by ignoring local differences, but by evaluating local rules against potential substitutes in order to determine which structure is more efficient *to achieve local preferences*. Far from ignoring local differences, this requires painstaking research into local structures, both as they address the problem at hand, and as they would interact with proposed substitutes.

Seidman and Makgetla focus on the state-centered approach to law and development identified by Trubek and Galanter as a component of legal

---

[47] Coase puts it as follows:

> The discussion of the problem of harmful effects ... has made clear that the problem is one of choosing the appropriate social arrangement for dealing with the harmful effects. All solutions have costs and there is no reason to suppose that government regulation is called for simply because the problem is not well handled by the market or the firm. Satisfactory views on policy can only come from a patient study of how, in practice, the market, firms and government handle the problem of harmful effects ... It is my belief that economists, and policy-makers generally, have tended to over-estimate the advantages which come from governmental regulation. But this belief, even if justified, does not do more than suggest that government regulation should be curtailed. It does not tell us where the boundary line should be drawn. This, it seems to me, has to come from a detailed investigation of the actual results of handling the problem in different ways.

Coase, "The Problem of Social Cost", *supra* note 23, at 18–19.

[48] *See* Dahlman, "The Problem of Externality", 22 *J.L. & Econ.* 141, 160–61 (1979). But *see*, Kreuger, "Government Failures in Development", 4 *J. Econ. Persp.* 9 (1990).

[49] *See* text accompanying notes 60 to 61, *infra*.

[50] Black, Kraakman & Hay, "Corporate Law From Scratch", Harvard Law School Program in Law and Economics, Discussion Paper No. 155 (March 1995); Mattei, "Efficiency in Legal Transplants: An Essay in Comparative Law and Economics", 14 *Int'l Rev. L. & Econ.* 3 (1994); Mattei and Pardolesi, "Law and Economics in Civil Law Countries: A Comparative Approach", 11 *Int'l Rev. L. & Econ.* 265 (1991).

liberalism. This state-centered approach, and assumption that law and economics too is state-centered, causes Seidman and Makgetla to deny the possibility that law and economics would examine law in society, and compare varying social structures.

Seidman and Makgetla point out the danger that law and economics can quantify productivity at the firm level, but has trouble quantifying other social goals, and therefore might tend to dismiss such concerns, including distributive concerns. While this is a real danger, it is a danger that can be recognized[51] and avoided. Complexity is not a sufficient reason to reject this methodology, although we must recognize that it requires a great deal of work. In addition, the issue of quantification and commensurability is a real one, that raises difficult philosophical problems.[52] However, because from a practical standpoint, commensuration is inescapable, we do not dwell on these issues here.

Seidman and Makgetla are concerned about the prejudice of the neo-classical perspective toward markets: "By accepting the neoclassical identification of utopia with the idealized market of perfect competition, liberal law and economics scholars relinquish the task of investigating alternative perceptions of freedom, which look more to collective decision-making about the economy as well as to political questions."[53] Although I am unsure Seidman and Makgetla would accept this interpretation, their argument is consistent with the kind of comparative transaction cost economizing that is supported by Coasean[54] or Williamsonian[55] analysis: the state or other social structures may have transaction cost advantages over the market for particular functions, and no *a priori* allocation of the burden of proof exists.

In conclusion, Seidman and Makgetla seem to attack a version of law and economics that accepts uncritically all market allocations. As Seidman and Makgetla state, this vision is untenable in the developing world,[56] and one would add that it is also untenable in the developed world. But it is not necessarily the only vision of law and economics, or the strongest. The law and economics that may be useful for law and development would recognize, with Seidman and Makgetla, that markets in the developing world may be weak and inefficient. Thus, in a comparative transaction cost economizing mode, developing world markets[57] may be less successful competitors than state or other non-market means of economic organization. The complexity of social interaction that Seidman and Makgetla see constraining the efficiency of markets may be viewed instead as efficient

---

[51] R. Posner, *Economic Analysis of Law* 27 (4th ed. 1992).
[52] *See* Sunstein, "Incommensurability and Valuation in Law", 92 *Mich. L. Rev.* 779, 780 (1994) ("[E]fforts to insist on a single kind of valuation and to make goods commensurable, while designed to aid in human reasoning, actually make such reasoning inferior to what it is when it is working well.")
[53] Seidman and Makgetla, *supra* note 45, at 48.
[54] Coase, "The Nature of the Firm", *supra* note 23.
[55] *See, e.g.*, O. Williamson, *The Economic Institutions of Capitalism* (1985).
[56] *Id.* at 56.
[57] *Id.* at 57.

systems to achieve efficiencies other than simple market allocative efficiency. Alternatively, we can begin to see markets everywhere, and in every kind of value.[58] Economics can encompass values beyond simple material goals.[59] And once we see all institutions as markets, and all markets as institutions, the question left to us is which market or which institution is more efficient in a particular context to get people more of what they want.

2.5 Cooter

Robert Cooter's work takes up the challenge of Seidman and Makgetla and applies law and economics analysis to legal structures in developing countries, not necessarily to advocate the modernization of law, but at least in one case to show the efficiency of customary rules and law.[60] For example, in an article on land tenure in Papua New Guinea, he finds that the freehold solution, giving absolute, unitary ownership over land to individuals, ending the kin group's customary role in resource allocation, would be disruptive and inefficient. The alternative of reconstituting kin groups as co-operatives with ownership rights would also disrupt the incentive system of the customary economy. He finds that the better solution would be to allow custom to evolve and modernize itself through a common law process.[61] At least implicit in Cooter's approach is a dynamic understanding of the dislocation and potential loss that accompanies any change. Thus, while a complete freehold regime in a complete market system such as the U.S. might (or might not) be more efficient in the aggregate than the customary system in Papua New Guinea, an abrupt shift to a complete freehold system would bring with it greater costs than a gradual shift that is able to retain customary order to the extent it is not replaced by legislated systems.

This type of economic analysis is culturally sensitive, and adopts a modest and respectful approach to local (non-legal) custom, as well as local law. While this perspective does not depend on arguments of the efficiency of the common law, it recognizes that custom or local law may have developed for reasons of efficiency, and may indeed be more efficient than the alternatives. Certainly in former colonies and other authoritarian societies, and even in independent parliamentary democracies, there may be inefficient laws. Cooter is simply looking for an efficient method for exchange of land. But he recognizes the embedded social nature of land tenure in Papua New Guinea.

---

[58] *See* Jensen and Meckling, "The Nature of Man", 7 *J. Applied Corp. Fin.* 4 (1994) (developing a vision of man as a rational, evaluative maximizer, maximizing a basket of values according to individual priorities).

[59] *See* Ellickson, "Bringing Culture and Human Frailty to Rational Actors: A Critique of Classical Law-and-Economics", 65 *Chicago-Kent L. Rev.* 23 (1989); G. Becker, *Human Capital* (3rd ed. 1993).

[60] *See* Cooter, "Structural Adjudication and the New Law Merchant: A Model of Decentralized Law", 14 *Int'l Rev. L. & Econ.* 215 (1994); Cooter, "Inventing Market Property: The Land Courts of Papua New Guinea", 25 *L. & Soc'y Rev.* 759 (1991).

[61] *Id.*

2.6 Application of law and economics to public law

While law and economics had its early successes in antitrust law and regulated industries, and has been used in other public law areas like environmental law and securities law, the deepest recent law and economics literatures are in private law of property, tort and contract, and quasi-private corporation law. Moreover, the arguments regarding law and economics in the U.S. have been addressed more towards judges than towards legislators and regulators, although this is changing rapidly. In fact, public law and private law are not truly separate and there are many more revealing parameters by which to distinguish types of law. However, certain aspects of what we think of as "public law" make it more amenable to the application of law and economics in law and development, at least in areas of economic regulation like banking and securities regulation.

First, public law is often historically new.[62] Banking law only becomes appropriate when a banking system exists, and the kind of prudential regulation that this chapter is concerned with only becomes appropriate when government becomes concerned with the overall stability of the economy or with consumer protection. Of course, the advent of deposit insurance or other governmental safety nets increases the need for governmental regulation. Similarly, while securities law has antecedents in common law fraud, it can barely trace its roots past the beginning of the 20th century. In addition, of course, securities law is not needed without a securities business.

Thus, these areas are quite distinct from the land tenure system addressed by Cooter or other areas of law that have subsisted for ages and have become embedded in a specific local culture. This type of law provides a more fertile area for law and development assistance, due to the fact that emerging markets often have little pre-existing law in this area, and what law they have in this area is more (although certainly not completely) severable from society at large: it exists in a more isolated social space.[63] This isolation results in reduced complexity.

3 THE PROBLEM OF GOALS: EFFICIENCY IN LAW AND ECONOMICS

In order to be able to indicate how law and economics methodology may be applied to banking and securities regulation in emerging markets, it is useful to consider the broad themes of the law and economics literatures of (i) deposit insurance; and (ii) mandatory disclosure. In turn, in order to examine the law and economics methodology, it is necessary to examine its goals of efficiency, and to compare these goals with traditional goals of banking and securities law.

---

[62] Public law, especially in the finance area, seems to involve higher levels of organization of economic relations. *See* North, *supra* note 2.

[63] S. Sassen, *Cities in a World Economy* (1994).

This part first examines the goals of bank and securities regulation. It appears that a broad social view of efficiency is the appropriate goal for bank regulation and securities regulation to seek. This broad view of efficiency would include not simply allocative efficiency in the market, but also efficiency in achieving public policy goals, including economic stability and consumer protection as potential separate goals.[64] Of course, these goals may conflict with one another, and must be traded off against one another in order to maximize the efficiency of the regulatory system as a whole. Thus, these goals may be weighted and integrated to comprise an appropriately broadened efficiency goal.

Of course, each society will weigh and integrate relevant goals differently. Thus, the best that law and development advisers can do is to relate different legal and regulatory structures to different goals, leaving it to the domestic goal-setting process to determine the goals, and thereby, the appropriate legal and regulatory structures. To sum up, while broad efficiency/maximization in achieving social goals is a uniform social aspiration, each society's vision of this aspiration is different, just as each individual's vision of this goal is at least somewhat different.

A broad efficiency goal must also be broad enough to encompass international-type values,[65] including competitiveness, reciprocity in international trade, regulatory effectiveness and free movement of capital. These international factors must be integrated with domestic factors in order to engage in effective policy analysis. Internationalization provides incentives to scrutinize heterogeneity and ensure that domestic society is not paying too high a price for its local goals in terms of trade and regulatory cooperation. Given these variable ends and means, can the experience of one society ever be relevant to that of another?

3.1 Goals of bank regulation and securities regulation

3.1.1 Traditional goals

The ends of bank regulation and securities regulation remain, in large measure, disputed, in the developed world as in the world of emerging markets.[66] Is the goal consumer protection, market integrity, economic stability or economic efficiency, or are these all different guises of the same goal? Even if a particular society could reach agreement on goals, there may

---

[64] Thus, we express our social preferences in two alternative ways. First, we act through the medium of the market, expressing our preferences as inputs into the price system. Second, we act through the medium of politics, expressing our preferences through votes and other political activity. *See* A. Hirschman, *Exit, Voice and Loyalty* (1974). The choice between the market and the political system is one of institutional design.

[65] *See*, Trachtman, "Unilateralism, Bilateralism, Regionalism, Multilateralism and Functionalism: A Comparison with Reference to Securities Regulation", 4 *Transnat'l L. & Contemp. Probs.* 69 (1994).

[66] *See, e.g.*, Flannery, "Government Risk-Bearing in the Financial Sector of a Capitalist Economy", Chapter 4 in M. Sniderman, ed., *Government Risk Bearing* at 72 (1991) ("A broad public debate has sought to evaluate the best means of implementing and enforcing financial regulations, but the debate is handicapped by its reluctance to specify the fundamental economic goals of financial regulation and government risk-bearing").

be widely varying views regarding appropriate means to reach those goals, and it is clear that both ends and means may differ depending on the particular social context in which they are introduced. Thus, means as well as ends are variable, and efficiency of means, or other values with respect to means, including, for example, due process, may be viewed as ends.[67]

While the goals of bank regulation and securities regulation are unsettled and socially contingent, there are a number of purported goals that are frequently cited as forming the basis for regulation.[68] Often cited are consumer protection, market integrity, market stability, protection of the payments system, protection of the banking safety net or economic efficiency.[69] The problem with these goals is that they tell us little about the degree, or even the type, of regulation that is called for. In fact, these goals might be rationales for high levels of government intervention. Of course, some kind of cost-benefit analysis is necessary to determine the kinds and degrees of regulation that are warranted.

3.1.2 Efficiency

At least some practitioners of economic analysis of law posit allocative efficiency as the overarching social goal.[70] Of course, efficiency is not a complete goal; it must be defined in terms of the goods that are to be produced efficiently – in terms of some function of individuals' preferences. A contractarian social goal might be maximization of each individual's preferences through cost-benefit analysis, as opposed to simple wealth maximization.[71] Discussion of efficiency might start, but should not end, with allocative efficiency: allowing markets in perfect competition to freely allocate through the price system. As markets are imperfect – there exist market failures – it is necessary to consider, but not always to accept, measures to address these market failures. If the measure is less costly than the market failure it corrects, it may be efficient. The analysis of the existence and implications of market failure, and of whether regulation should address market failure, is a comparative transaction costs exercise.

---

[67] H. Garten, *Why Bank Regulation Failed: Designing a Bank Regulatory Strategy for the 1990s* (1991). On the question of the special purpose of bank regulation, *see* Corrigan, "Are Banks Special?", Federal Reserve Bank of Minneapolis, *1982 Annual Report*. But *see* Aspinwall, "On the Specialness of Banking", 7 *Issues Bank Reg.* 16 (1983). *See* also E. Corrigan, *Financial Market Structure: A Longer View* (1987).

[68] Clark, "The Soundness of Financial Intermediaries", 86 *Yale L.J.* 1 (1976) (regarding banks, insurance companies and investment companies).

[69] *See* the sources cited in note 67, *supra*.

[70] For a general work on law and economics, *see* R. Posner, *Economic Analysis of Law* (4th ed. 1992). Posner discusses the role of efficiency at 12–18. *See* also Cooter, "The Best Right Laws: Value Foundations of the Economic Analysis of Law", 64 *Notre Dame L. Rev.* 817 (1989); Coleman, "Efficiency, Utility and Wealth Maximization", 8 *Hofstra L. Rev.* 509 (1980).

[71] *See* Cooter, *supra* note 70, at 829. We will not address here issues of distribution. Suffice it to say that the distribution of incomes may be the subject of the preferences of individuals, and so may be included within the more general approach to efficiency. Distribution might further be considered as a function of individuals' preferences, with a Rawlsian veil of ignorance as a place where we each might (or might not) agree, and express a preference, that the justification for income disparities is benefit to the poorest.

Furthermore, this comparative transaction costs exercise forces us to discard the language of "market failure" as too categorical. A more nuanced approach would recognize that markets never "fail", but simply may be more costly than government or other institutions as tools by which to achieve certain social goals.

Thus, efficiency must be construed as the maximization of social goals, broadly defined. These goals include all of the goals that individuals find it useful to express through society.[72] This is no simple wealth maximization technique; rather it must include in its analysis all things that people value, recognizing that valuation is fundamentally subjective and intersubjective. These goals include not only the wealth-type goals normally addressed through the market in a market economy, but also goals that might be considered altruistic, public spirited or just. These goals would thus include constitutional-type principles regarding the way that goals are expressed in government processes. These are all things that people value, *ex post* or *ex ante*.[73]

Carried over to bank regulation and securities regulation, the law and economics perspective would seek efficiency. As described above, the search for efficiency is a transaction cost economizing exercise, evaluating various institutions, including the market, the state, and all institutions in between,[74] on a comparative basis to determine the most efficient structure. It is critical to note that the transaction cost economizing exercise does not stop at simple Weberian predictability or stability;[75] nor does it necessarily seek only clarity of rights. Rather, this complex exercise seeks regulation that will either anticipate or facilitate private reallocative transactions: that will allow people more easily to enter society to achieve their goals.[76] It need not, as Seidman and Makgetla fear, transform society completely to a conforming capitalist utopia. Rather, as Cooter shows, it is able to take circumstances as they are, and to take social preferences as they are. Given these circumstances and preferences, the law and economics methodology evaluates the efficient technique to maximize social preferences, given the circumstances extant. Of course, once this technique is generalized and used in a variety of areas of law, circumstances may change. For example, a relatively rudimentary securities law, with little delegation to an administrative agency, may be efficient in a context where administrative law is relatively incomplete or unclear. However, a more complex securities law

---

[72] *See* Jensen & Meckling, "The Nature of Man", *supra* note 58.

[73] In fact, Rawls' veil of ignorance might be interpreted as a structure that allows for bargaining about constitutional principles *ex ante*, before any individual knows what stratum or position she will occupy in society. J. Rawls, *A Theory of Justice* (1971).

[74] Not to mention institutions that transcend the state.

[75] Many economists, and even sophisticated law and development experts, focus on simple predictability. *See* D. Trubek, *Law, Planning and the Development of the Brazilian Capital Market: A Study of Law in Economic Change* at 10 (1971).

[76] In this sense, each piece of regulation is a new entry into society, or perhaps an incremental entry into society, just as each market transaction is a social act. The enhancement of the achievement of peoples' goals through society – through the various available social institutions (including the market) – is the goal of transaction cost economizing.

may become possible once a more complete administrative law is legislated, and may yield greater efficiency at that time.

Thus, efficiency is a relative and context-determined concept; moreover, efficiency is a dynamic process in which complex changes over time may interact, with the result that a law that is efficient today may be inefficient tomorrow. This relative and contextual approach to efficiency cannot posit an overarching ideal system, a capitalist utopia of zero transaction costs. It must engage in comparative transaction cost economizing. This imperative fits well into the law and development process: it provides a motivation for the comparative law approach to law and development. Thus, a country that identifies some social preferences that would be served by a new or revised banking law should not simply say, "let the market operate freely". While under some preferences and circumstances, this may be the best policy prescription, it could only be formulated and recognized as such after an evaluative process.

3.2 Goals of efficiency in banking and securities regulation

As in any area of regulation, there are certain social goals that are especially associated with banking and securities regulation – particular sub-goals that these types of regulation seek to achieve. These are sub-goals of the general efficiency goal described above. These are the goals that those charged with regulation in these areas, in the U.S., the various federal bank regulatory authorities and the Securities and Exchange Commission, are mandated to achieve. These goals are not more valuable than other social goals, and eventually they must be integrated with a full program designed to achieve a full range of social goals. Moreover, these goals are not more valuable than the goal of avoiding undue regulatory costs, and unintended adverse regulatory consequences.

In commercial banking regulation, we have a number of possible rationales for regulation, including the ostensible "special" nature of banks,[77] financial system stability and consumer protection. There are also rationales that one might call secondary, or compound, rationales. Two of these are obvious. First, assuming that the government provides safety net-type protection, such as deposit insurance or lender-of-last-resort functions, the government must protect its own interests as contingent creditor of the protected banks. Thus the primary regulatory instrument gives rise to the need for secondary regulation. Second, and similarly, regulation may have the effect of distorting allocative efficiency, giving rise to a possible need to make adjustments to restore allocative efficiency, depending on a comparison between the cost of the distortion and the cost of the adjustment. For example, if deposit insurance premia or bank capital requirements are set in ways that are not based on market-based pricing, banks will have incentives to engage in lending in ways that may not be consistent with allocative efficiency. Thus, regulators may be faced with a need to restore, or re-create, market disciplines.

---

[77] *See* sources cited in note 67, *supra*.

Economic theory indicates two overriding goals: capital mobilization and accuracy of capital allocation.[78] While providing incentives for capital mobilization is probably included, to the extent it is appropriate, in establishing accuracy of capital allocation, both these goals may be viewed as intermediate goals that themselves are subordinated to the broader efficiency goals described above.

Transaction cost economizing requires that each regulatory measure be compared to the full universe of alternative regulatory, non-governmental and market structures; as stated above, the goal is to minimize the sum of (i) deadweight losses due to the failure to maximize the achievement of social goals; and (ii) the transaction costs incurred in making such allocation. And of course, regulation operates in systems, so that it is appropriate to evaluate a system of regulation, rather than a single regulatory measure. Thus, once this evaluation is complete, the various regulatory measures may be integrated into a complete system of regulation that is optimal for the given society, insofar as it achieves the society's goals in accordance with the society's priorities. This model is both dynamic and interconnected: all regulation must be constantly re-evaluated in light of other social changes. This model declines to consider regulation in the way that regulation is often formulated: in terms of simple references – to fairness, consumer protection, systemic stability, competitiveness, etc. Rather, it demands to know the value of these concerns, and to compare these values to the prices at which they are achieved.[79] This is obviously an invitation to great complexity, but if we decline to enter the world of complexity, we are destined to remain in a world of waste.

3.3 Application to emerging markets

In assessing the relevance of this model to emerging markets, it is necessary to recognize the variability of both conditions and preferences in these societies. For example, private institutional infrastructure for investment analysis or consumer protection might not be as well developed as it is in developed markets, leading to the possibility that regulation may be easier to justify in some cases in emerging markets. On the other hand, equal regulatory costs may comprise a greater burden on smaller businesses in emerging markets than on larger businesses in more developed markets, thus arguing against regulatory intervention in emerging markets.

Furthermore, as noted above, efficiency is a relative concept that varies by reference to the goals sought efficiently to be achieved. Thus, even if a regulatory system achieves efficiently the goals of a particular society, there is no reason to believe that it would achieve efficiently the goals of another society. Rather, it is necessary to engage in this process for each society, and to engage in the process dynamically, as social preferences and the available set of regulatory tools change. Thus, contrary to Seidman and Makgetla's concern, efficiency is heterogeneous, as it seeks to maximize a

---

[78] Trubek, *supra* note 75, at 11.
[79] But *see*, Sunstein, *supra* note 52.

basket of goals. In addition, the goals of regulation are determined by the process that forms the regulation. Thus, regulation is essentially a political process. However, we can compare the institutions of public regulation with the institutions created by the market. The market is able to express goals and to achieve goals in society, and represents a competing method of human relation to that formed by public regulation.

Finally, the method of implementation of regulatory goals will differ according to the legal, political and social context – different methods of regulation will work better in different contexts. We may begin to consider issues like moral persuasion[80] and self-regulation as tools that may fit varying circumstances in varying ways. The economic approach would apply an incentive theory of the law, considering that people respond to penalties much as they respond to prices.[81]

Thus, to summarize the discussion above, the heterogeneity of efficiency provides good reasons for the heterogeneity of regulation. However, regulation need not be completely heterogeneous; rather, the homogeneity of the broad contours of at least some major goals, combined with the fact that the same mechanism may work well in multiple contexts, militate toward a degree of homogeneity of regulation. Policy is derived from a complex social cost-benefit analysis seeking maximal efficiency in achieving social goals. This limited case for homogeneity exists even before we consider the international context.

3.4 Intranational versus international goals

In the modern setting, policy analysis cannot stop at the relevant society's geographic borders. Rather, it must continue its analysis beyond this artificial border, considering international issues in determining public policy.[82] These international concerns include issues of regulatory effectiveness, of trade, of regulatory overlap and of regulatory underlap. Due to the transnational nature of the market for large amounts of capital, regulation that is formulated with a closed domestic economy in mind is simply based on an inaccurate assumption. For emerging markets, internationalization presents special problems and opportunities.

Special problems include the possibility of importation of techniques of financial abuse; this possibility deprives emerging markets of the luxury of experiencing their own history. While in the U.S., regulation has grown more complex and comprehensive as abuse has grown more devious, it will not necessarily be efficient for emerging market countries simply to accept

---

[80] *See* Norton, "The Bank of England's Lament: The Struggle to Maintain the Traditional Supervisory Practices of 'Moral Suasion'," in J. Norton, ed. *Bank Regulation and Supervision in the 1990's* (1991).

[81] *See* Cooter, *supra* note 70, at 829, citing Kornhauser, "The New Economic Analysis of Law: Legal Rules as Incentives", in *The New Economic Analysis of Law* (Mercuro ed. 1984).

[82] *See* Trachtman, "Unilateralism, Bilateralism, Regionalism, Multilateralism and Functionalism: A Comparison with Reference to Securities Regulation", 4 *Transnat'l L. & Contemp. Probs.* 69 (1994); Trachtman, "Recent Initiatives in International Financial Regulation and Goals of Competitiveness, Effectiveness, Consistency and Cooperation", 12 *Northwestern J. Int'l L. & Bus.* 241 (1991).

this kind of dynamic time-sequenced augmentation. Rather, given the ease of adaptation of abuse from developed markets to emerging markets, there may be good reasons to adapt regulatory protections from developed markets to emerging markets in more of a "big bang".

Another special problem involves the relatively small size of emerging market financial markets. These markets may not be large enough to justify sufficient regulatory apparatuses – to generate regulatory economies of scale. In addition, in the securities field, the small size of the market, and low liquidity, may in and of itself make abuse easier. For example, a relatively illiquid market will be more susceptible to manipulation.

These kinds of problems may be viewed as paired with some opportunities. The problem of importation of abuse is paired with importation of regulatory devices. The problem of low liquidity is paired with the possibility of sharing resources through international integration and co-operation.

4 THE LAW AND ECONOMICS OF FINANCE REGULATION: DEPOSIT INSURANCE AND MANDATORY DISLOSURE

In this section, I briefly summarize some of the ways law and economics analysis might address two central problems of financial regulation: deposit insurance for banks and mandatory disclosure in securities markets. My goal is neither to be exhaustive nor to be conclusive, but rather to be indicative of the kind of general path a law and economics analysis might take, and how it might differ in an emerging market.

4.1 The law and economics of deposit insurance

Deposit insurance, while it appears to be unshakable politically in the U.S., and, for example, in Argentina[83] is on shaky economic foundations: it implies state responsibility for private decisions. Under some circumstances, this type of state responsibility could be justified. In order to do so, state responsibility must be compared with the alternatives. As described above, economic analysis of regulation seeks to minimize the sum of (i) deadweight losses due to the failure to maximize the achievement of social goals; and (ii) the transaction costs incurred in making such allocation.

Under circumstances of no government regulation of banks, the contention over control of economic decisions by banks is market-based and contractual between banks, their depositors, their shareholders, their debtholders and their borrowers. If banks fail, their stakeholders all suffer particular losses by virtue of their individual relationships. Depositors would be treated as unsecured creditors, and would normally experience loss. Due to a collective action problem, there would be incentives for precipitous action, for runs on banks. Due to the so-called asset-liability

---

[83] Miller, "The Politics of Deposit Insurance Reform: The Case of Argentina", forthcoming.

mismatch – the fact that banks borrow on a demand deposit basis and lend on a term basis – banks are vulnerable to runs. Deposit insurance protects depositors from any loss, and thereby reduces the possibility of runs on a bank.

Public insurance, created in part to discourage runs, also reduces the risk of placing money with a bank or S&L. It leaves depositors no reason to monitor the riskiness of their investments. If all investments in banks are equally risky, why not go to the one offering the highest interest – and coincidentally the highest risk to the fund? When risky banks can attract money as easily as sound ones, too much capital flows to the hands of inferior managers. Failure is the wedge to separate good from bad; capitalist economies rely on failure to improve efficiency. When we use public funds to create a no-risk, no-failure sector of the economy, we purchase extra (but disguised) risk and failure. Deposit insurance subsidizes failure, obtaining the cash by taxing success in and out of the financial services industry. Subsidy creates more of the thing subsidized and less of the thing taxed; we produce more failure and less success.[84]

As is now well understood, government-provided deposit insurance is not without unwanted consequences.[85] In effect, it makes government the contingent creditor of the covered bank. The first consequence of this fact, as noted above, is that it severely diminishes the incentive for depositors to discriminate among banks, and thereby to impose the discipline of the market on banks. The second consequence, and the one on which we will focus, is that it gives rise to a need for government to impose substitute disciplines on banks in the form of capital requirements, powers limitations and other prudential regulation. It appears that this regulation can never be as dynamic or precise as the market is able to be: in this dimension, the market has an advantage of precision over government control.[86] Socialism, on the other end of the spectrum, involves complete government control over allocation of capital, but the quality of this control has been severely criticized.

The market's advantage of precision comes at a cost, and may not be as effective in limiting the possibility of runs as government-provided deposit insurance, so we may not on the basis of this fact alone condemn deposit insurance and the concomitant regulation. However, it is necessary to compare costs and benefits to determine which system is appropriate for use.

In this vein, we may consider the whole system of prudential regulation as a transaction cost of providing deposit insurance. There are other

---

[84] Easterbrook, "Regulation and Responsibility: A Note on Banking", 77 *Cornell L. Rev.* 1079, 1082 (1992).

[85] *See, e.g.,* E. Kane, *The S&L Insurance Mess: How Did it Happen?* (1989); L. White, *The S&L Debacle: Public Policy Lessons for Bank and Thrift Regulation* (1991); Fischel, Rosenfield & Stillman, "The Regulation of Banks and Bank Holding Companies", 73 *Va. L. Rev.* 301 (1987); Macey & Miller, "America's Banking System: The Origins and Future of the Current Crisis", 69 *Wash. U.L.Q.* 769 (1991); Scott, "Never Again: The S&L Bailout Bill", 45 *Bus. Law.* 1883 (1990).

[86] *See* Trachtman, "Perestroika in Bank Regulation: Advantages of Securities Regulation for a Market Economy", in J. Norton, ed., *Bank Regulation and Supervision in the 1990's* (1991).

ostensible rationales for prudential regulation, but they are not compelling bases for the kinds of broad programs in existence. Thus, on the cost side would have to be considered the cost of providing the deposit insurance, the cost of imposing the prudential regulation and the cost of compliance with the prudential regulation. The cost of compliance with the prudential regulation may be considerable, including misallocation of resources due, *inter alia*, to the failure of capital requirements and deposit insurance premia to distinguish bad credits from good ones. If deposit insurance were not provided, the banking business would look a good deal more like the investment company or mutual fund business, including the money market fund business. Investors could select these investments on the basis of their portfolios, or could decide to invest in those that pay premiums to private insurers to insure the portfolio. A full range of risk to return ratios could be made available, with market-based pricing.

Thus, in a developed capital market such as the U.S., there would be a plausible, and perhaps convincing, argument to do away with government-provided deposit insurance, subject to the political difficulty of implementing such a strategy. This argument might not be so strong in a less-developed capital market which might not provide the institutions or financial innovation necessary to satisfy investor demand for safety. Internationalization can provide greater liquidity and access to foreign financial institutions and innovation. This type of strategy would put greater pressure on securities-law type regulation, on disclosure of information regarding management and investments of investment vehicles. Obviously, the ability to provide, absorb and regulate this information may be limited in emerging markets.

In addition, emerging markets investors may lack the sophistication, and the sources of reliable advice, necessary to evaluate and choose alternative investment vehicles. Thus, some governmentally protected savings scheme may be necessary. Of course, this does not mean that the deposit insurance model must be used. Where government takes the responsibility, in order to reduce agency costs and moral hazard, which are simply types of transaction costs, government should have control over the investment of the savings. Thus a scheme like Japan's postal savings system might be more appropriate.[87]

4.2 The law and economics of mandatory disclosure

At first, disclosure regulation[88] seems the perfect complement to the information-driven nature of a capital market, which in turn is congruent with the decentralized decision-making process that characterizes a private market for goods and services. In fact, the discussion above of deposit insurance might lead to consideration of a system that allows and relies more on disclosure as a basis for market discipline on "banks". However,

---

[87] *See* Calder, "Introducing . . . The World's Largest Financial Institution", *The International Economy* 53–55 (May/June 1993).

[88] For a current perspective on mandatory disclosure in the U.S., *see* Seligman, "The SEC's Unfinished Soft Information Revolution", 63 *Fordham L. Rev.* 1953 (1995).

there are significant questions regarding the efficiency of the mandatory disclosure system in the U.S. and elsewhere, and this issue has not been conclusively settled in academia.[89]

Here, the question that law and economics asks is why is regulation necessary in the context of a market comprised of willing buyers – why would the market under-provide disclosure if left unregulated? Is it not possible for these buyers to contract directly, or through intermediaries, for the amount of information they feel is necessary, with the market equilibrium equal to the efficient level of information? Will not private insurers, gatekeepers and certifiers spring up in response to market demand to provide the efficient level of support to investors? Or do transaction costs prevent these efficient contracts from being made? Is disclosure a public good,[90] meaning that it will be underproduced because those who produce it cannot enjoy alone all of its benefits? If it is, how can legislators and bureaucrats determine the "correct" level of information to require?

We need to keep in sight our goal of efficiency. In connection with disclosure regulation in the securities market, perhaps there is no broader concept of efficiency, but only the narrower vision of allocative efficiency. While a society will have many goals that are left unaddressed by the allocative efficiency of the securities market, these goals are probably better addressed by mechanisms other than disclosure regulation.[91] Allocative efficiency in the securities market depends on the distribution of information, and is thus "ultimately a function of the cost of information to traders".[92] Traders will always act as much as they can to reduce the cost to them of information, and therefore, to enhance efficiency. Of course,

---

[89] *See, e.g.*, Cunningham, "Capital Market Theory, Mandatory Disclosure, and Price Discovery", 51 *Wash. & Lee L. Rev.* 843 (1994); Langevoort, "Theories, Assumptions and Securities Regulation: Market Efficiency Revisited", 140 *U. Pa. L. Rev.* 851 (1992); Stout, "The Unimportance of Being Efficient: An Economic Analysis of Stock Market Pricing and Securities Regulation", 87 *Mich. L. Rev.* 613 (1988); Thel, "The Original Conception of Section 10(b) of the Securities Exchange Act", 42 *Stan. L. Rev.* 385 (1990); Easterbrook & Fischel, "Mandatory Disclosure and the Protection of Investors", 70 *Va. L. Rev.* 669 (1984); Coffee, "Market Failure and the Economic Case for a Mandatory Disclosure System", 70 *Va. L. Rev.* 717 (1984); Jarrell, "The Economic Effects of Federal Regulation of the Market for New Security Issues", 24 *J.L. & Econ.* 613 (1981); Manne, "Economic Aspects of Required Disclosure under Federal Securities Laws", in *Wall Street in Transition: The Emerging System and Its Impact on the Economy* 21 (College of Business and Public Administration, New York University ed. 1974); Benston, "Required Disclosure and the Stock Market: An Evaluation of the Securities Exchange Act of 1934", 63 *Am. Econ. Rev.* 132 (1973); Stigler, "Public Regulation of the Securities Markets", 37 *J. Bus.* 117 (1964).

[90] *See* R. Musgrave, *The Theory of Public Finance* 61–89, 116–35 (1959); M. Olson, *The Logic of Collective Action: Public Goods and the Theory of Groups* (1965). The conventional definition of a public good is a good that is non-excludable – free-riders cannot be prevented – and indivisible – its use by free-riders does not diminish its utility to others. Information has different degrees of excludability, but is generally indivisible in this sense.

[91] *See* Kaplow & Shavell, "The Efficiency of the Legal System versus the Income Tax in Redistributing Income", Harvard Working Paper on Law and Economics No. 130 (1993). On the other hand, disclosure regulation is sometimes seen as a deterrent to environmental degradation, corruption and abuse of shareholders.

[92] Gilson and Kraakman, "The Mechanisms of Market Efficiency", 70 *Va. L. Rev.* 549, 593 (1984).

information comes from both public (non-issuer) sources and from the issuer.

With respect to information that is appropriable, there may be a public goods problem, in which the producer of information cannot exclude other users from using the information, and therefore cannot realize the full social value of the production of information.[93] Public goods problems are transaction costs problems insofar as a good becomes a pubic good because the costs of excluding others from using it are too high to be worthwhile. The consequence of this problem is the under-production of information, with resulting allocative inefficiency. By requiring a single person – the issuer – to produce the information, the securities laws can overcome this problem, although this analysis does not determine how much information they should require.

With respect to the issuer, additional difficulties might, without the intercession of regulation, prevent the supply of sufficient information.[94] First of all, the issuer has a monopoly over certain kinds of information – access is limited to internal accounting and management information.[95] We might begin to consider the securities market as a complex, multi-player game, where there are honest issuers and dishonest issuers, all seeking financing at the lowest prices possible. Under these circumstances, it is necessary to recognize the costs of obtaining and verifying information, and consider the role of securities disclosure requirements and antifraud rules in shifting those costs from large groups of individual securities purchasers to smaller groups of underwriters and ultimately, to issuers that prepare inadequate or misleading disclosure.[96] Game theory would indicate the need for a mechanism to verify information, in order to avoid the suboptimal outcome of a prisoner's dilemma, in which each issuer provides more and more misleadingly positive information in order to obtain financing. Securities law provides a remedial mechanism: mandatory disclosure regulation, including underwriters' liability and issuer liability for material misstatements and omissions.

Thus, a law and economics analysis of mandatory disclosure could initially take at least two perspectives that would support mandatory disclosure. One perspective would find that the public goods character of disclosure – of information – arises from the high transaction costs of requiring each user of information to pay for it. In other words, it is too costly to exclude free-riders. Another perspective would consider the problem of cooperation and trust between investors and issuers, on the one hand, and among issuers, on the other hand. This problem may be resolved by mechanisms to verify disclosure. Mandatory disclosure minimizes

---

[93] *See* F. Easterbrook & D. Fischel, *The Economic Structure of Corporate Law* 290–91 (1991); Coffee, "Market Failure and the Economic Case for a Mandatory Disclosure System", 70 *Va. L. Rev.* 717 (1984).

[94] *See* Coffee, "Market Failure and the Economic Case for a Mandatory Disclosure System", 70 *Va. L. Rev.* 717 (1984).

[95] For an argument that issuers will have incentives to make optimal disclosure, *see* Easterbrook & Fischel, *supra* note 89, at 683–85.

[96] *See* Gilson & Kraakman, *supra* note 92, at 600–608.

verification costs by providing a uniform set of requirements for disclosure and a uniform type of recourse, and thus eliminating the need to contract separately for disclosure, with varying standards and recourse. Both of these types of problems could be resolved by market mechanisms, but the presumption on which regulation is based is that the transaction costs of a market response would be too high: that the regulatory solution is the cheaper one.

Assuming that the costs of complying with mandatory disclosure requirements are not an inappropriate barrier to use of the capital markets, and subject to the efficient capital markets hypothesis argument described below, mandatory disclosure would seem an appropriate response to these problems. Of course, at some monetary level of financing, the work necessary for compliance with mandatory disclosure will become too expensive, and this may be the case more often in developing countries than in developed countries.

On the other hand, much of the criticism of disclosure regulation argues simply that it is unnecessary, based on the efficient capital markets hypothesis (ECMH). The ECMH holds that market forces incorporate all available information into stock prices so quickly that arbitrage opportunities cannot be exploited systematically.[97] The ECMH relies on highly liquid markets with highly sophisticated market institutions to operate to incorporate information into stock prices. There is significant reason to doubt the applicability of the ECMH in emerging markets. Thus, while emerging market reformers might seek to be more *laissez-faire* than Milton Friedman, the argument for *laissez-faire* in disclosure regulation has less of a basis in emerging markets.

Of course, emerging markets pose other problems for disclosure regulation. Often they lack the infrastructure in terms of accounting, legal and investment banking skills, as well as investment analysis skills, that make it possible to make and use disclosure efficiently. It is possible that internationalization and the development process may, to some extent, supply these skills. Other more general problems include a weak administrative law system and a weak judicial system.[98]

5 IMPLICATIONS FOR METHODOLOGY AND POLITICAL PROCESS

Only the least sensitive operator in law and development, or law and economics, would take a law from one society and introduce it to another

---

[97] The ECMH is not impervious to criticism. *See* Gilson & Kraakman, *supra* note 92; Langevoort, *supra* note 89; Cunningham, "From Random Walks to Chaotic Crashes: The Linear Genealogy of the Efficient Capital Market Hypothesis", 62 *Geo. Wash. L. Rev.* 546 (1994); Cunningham, "Capital Market Theory, Mandatory Disclosure, and Price Discovery", 51 *Wash. & Lee L. Rev.* (1994); R. Romano, *The Genius of American Corporate Law* 91–96 (1993).

[98] *See* Black, Kraakman & Hay, "Corporate Law From Scratch", Harvard Law School Program in Law and Economics, Discussion Paper No. 155, at 13–15 (March 1995) (discussing weaknesses in Russian judicial system).

society without a full analysis of the ramifications in the transferee society. This analysis would in effect be a dynamic and speculative comparative law analysis that would require significant expertise and resources. Thus, both appropriate goals and appropriate means of implementation will be heterogeneous. The law and development operator must maintain a modest perspective.[99]

On the other hand, where goals may be similar, and where legal rules are less deeply embedded in a longstanding social system, a degree of homogeneity may be appropriate. Homogeneity offers two kinds of benefits. One is the benefit of using international "best practices" where a number of cultures have engaged in a comparative analysis and found that a particular shared goal may best be achieved by a particular regulatory technology. Science and real technology are also socially embedded, but many societies can share particular sciences and technologies. In addition, trade disciplines provide incentives toward homogeneity, where a degree of homogeneity can reduce barriers to trade, either unilaterally or reciprocally. This perspective argues for linking law and development efforts to multinational searches for regulatory "best practices" and to trade liberalization negotiations.

Law and development requires sophisticated, disciplined and sustained work. There is little reason to have a competition among providers of law and development assistance, especially because it would be exceedingly costly and difficult for the customers to separate the good from the bad. Rather, given the limited resources available for these efforts, economies of scale may indicate that it is most efficient for providers of assistance in this area to pool their resources, and for countries that are engaged in the law reform process to pool their resources. This would allow for advancement and for the pooling not only of resources, but of experience with various approaches to implementation and transition.

---

[99] In addition, the law and development operator needs ultimately to be immersed in local law and culture. This argues that a large part of the work of law and development is involved with instructing local people regarding foreign practices so that they can design adaptations as appropriate. *See* Frankel, "Knowledge Transfer: Suggestions for the Developing Countries on the Receiving End", 13 *Boston Univ. Int'l. L.J.* 141 (1995).

4. Financial Reform and Development in Transition Economies and the Role of IFIs

Steven M. Fries[1]

1 INTRODUCTION

The importance of financial reform and development to the transition toward a market economy is clear. A well-functioning domestic financial system is the linchpin of high domestic savings, private investment and growth in a market economy, channelling domestic savings into fixed investment and imposing financial discipline on enterprises. In contrast, the command economy delivered only low growth despite high investment because the investment was of low quality, with savings allocated through a government's budget and largely passive banking system. Inappropriate incentives in enterprises further undermined the quality of investment.

The comparatively marginal and tranquil existence of bankers in the region changed abruptly with the introduction of market reforms. Two-tier banking systems were created, separating central and commercial banking functions; and the newly created state-owned commercial banks gained more autonomy in credit allocation decisions, as the government withdrew from budgetary financing of enterprise investment. At the same time, however, the enterprise sector experienced considerable upheavals, with the liberalisation of trade and prices, collapse of intra-regional trade and economic contraction. Many outstanding loans soured and the quality of new lending became difficult to judge. Moreover, the financial reforms necessary to impart clear incentives for the prudent management of state banks and new private banks took time to implement, allowing the initial spate of bad loans to proliferate in many countries.

Despite the initial setbacks, headway has since been made in overhauling the financial sectors in the region. Many countries have enacted legal and

[1] Office of the Chief Economist, European Bank for Reconstruction and Development, London. This chapter draws in part from Chapter 10 of the EBRD's 1995 *Transition Report*, which was prepared by the author with assistance of Mayamiko Kachingwe and Carlo Sdralevich. The views expressed in the chapter are those of the author and do not necessarily represent those of the EBRD.

regulatory frameworks for banks that draw upon international standards. Procedures for resolving bad loans have been implemented in a number of countries in eastern Europe, while others in the Baltics and CIS have relied on high inflation and negative real interest rates to shrink the asset quality problem. In some eastern European countries, governments have re-capitalised state-owned commercial banks, raising their capital to minimum international standards, while committing to their privatisation. Other countries, particularly those in the Baltics and CIS, have allowed the extensive creation of new private banks.

Securities activities in the region are typically less developed than banking. The authorities in a number of countries have moved to create the basic legal and regulatory framework for securities activities. Development of the securities markets themselves, though, has been largely shaped by broader developments, in particular the nature of privatisation pro-grammes. Mass privatisation programmes have led to rapid increases in stock market capitalisations, but markets swelled in this way have little liquidity. In contrast, a selective approach to privatisation and to listing companies on the stock exchange has fostered relatively liquid markets, but their capitalisations remain limited.

Regardless of the chosen reform path, however, the scale of bank lending, particularly to the private sector, and of securities activities throughout the region remains small relative to the size of the economies in which they are provided. This observation provides a simple illustration of the limited pro-vision of financial services in transition economies. An important challenge for the International Financial Institutions (IFIs) is thus to help strengthen financial sectors in transition economies and fill the void in provision of these services which are vital to a market economy.

This chapter examines the transformation of banking and emergence of securities activities in eastern Europe, the Baltics and CIS. The focus is on both the changing role of government in finance and the development of financial institutions themselves. Examples of how the IFIs have helped to promote financial reform and development in the region are also pro-vided, emphasising operations with both government and financial institutions.

2 TRANSFORMATION OF BANKING

The transformation of banking in transition economies is taking place at two levels. The role of government in banking is changing dramatically; and, at the same time, the banks themselves must adapt to and develop in their new market environment.

2.1 Changing role of government

The changing role of governments in banking involves a number of dimensions, apart from the basic creation of a two-tier banking system and credit market liberalisation. These include the introduction and strengthen-ing of prudential regulation and supervision, recapitalisation and privatisation of state banks, and policies toward entry and exit of private banks. Some countries in eastern Europe have attempted to move along these various dimensions in a deliberative manner, while others in the Baltics and CIS have engineered a more abrupt break with the past by allowing a period of liberal entry of new private banks as very high inflation reduced the significance of state banks and former state banks.

2.1.1 Prudential regulation and supervision

Many countries in the region have enacted a basic framework for prudential regulation. Given the bad loan problems in most countries, capital adequacy standards and rules on classification of asset by quality and on provisions against identified loan losses have assumed particular importance. Limits on concentrated or connected lending have also taken on added significance in transition economies.

Capital adequacy regulations have been introduced throughout most of the region, and in many countries these draw upon the Basle Committee or EU standards for capital adequacy. In some countries, such as Bulgaria, the Czech Republic, the Slovak Republic and Ukraine, these standards are being phased in over a transition period to allow time for the banks to adjust. Procedures for classifying assets and for making specific provisions against doubtful and unrecoverable loans have also been introduced in most countries. However, there remains in some countries significant departures from Basle Committee or EU standards in the definition of regulatory capital, as well as scope for discretion in application of loan classification and provisioning rules owing to weakness in prudential supervision.

Restrictions on large exposures to a single borrower range widely in the region, although a number of countries have enacted rules that are in line with international standards. Some countries in the region also impose a tighter ceiling if the large exposure is to a person or entity connected with the bank, such as director, manager, employee or shareholder. The strict enforcement of prudent exposure limits is particularly important in transition economies because of the close ties between enterprises and state banks and the widespread ownership of banks by enterprises in some countries.

While well-conceived regulations are important, they do not ensure that the prudential regulations achieve their objective of a safe and sound banking system. Realisation of that objective requires adequate supervision of banks to ensure compliance and to enforce the applicable laws and regulations. Effective supervision, in turn, hinges upon development of staff and the provision of accurate information to the regulatory authorities.

A significant challenge for implementing effective supervision is to attract and to train bank examiners. In some of the more advanced countries in the region, such as the Czech Republic, Hungary and Poland, supervisory staff levels have been built up to levels comparable to those in western European countries with similar banking structures. However, such simple comparisons do not take into account the considerable variation in staff skills and financial accounting and reporting systems among these countries and those in western Europe. Throughout the region, much remains to be done in terms of both recruiting and training supervisory staff.

Apart from adequate staff resources, the other basic input into banking supervision is the financial accounts of banks. However, the accounting practices in much of the region still reflect more the information requirements of central planning and tax administration than those of prudential supervision and financial analysis.

Overall, while prudential regulations in banking have developed towards international standards, and continue to do so, the capacity to enforce these regulations has expanded at a slower pace. More effective enforcement will require the sustained development of supervisory staff skills, recruitment of additional staff in many countries and improvements in accounting standards.

2.1.2 *Recapitalisation and privatisation of state banks*

While effective prudential regulation and supervision aim to prevent banking troubles from emerging, an important aspect of the incentive framework for banks is the regulatory authorities' approach toward bank recapitalisation or closure if difficulties do arise. Instilling discipline while recapitalising state banks in eastern Europe, however, has proven particularly challenging. Governments were essentially unlimited liability shareholders in the dominant state banks, and the behaviour of bank managers was not, at least in the first instance, the primary cause of the bad loan problem.

There have been two broad approaches to direct bank recapitalisation in the region, both of which aim to create in somewhat different ways conditions under which discipline can be imposed should future difficulties arise.

One approach focuses on creating strong incentives for the commercial operation of banks through full recapitalisations, efficient frameworks for resolving bad loans, and commitments to bank privatisation. In this approach, the extent of a bank's loan losses is broadly ascertained through an independent audit or other means of verification, with the recapitalisation of the bank designed to restore its capital adequacy after writing down these loans. To resolve the debt overhang in the enterprise sector and to enhance the recovery on problem loans, the approach strongly encourages the work out of bad loans within a fixed time frame through direct negotiations between creditors and debtors or legal bankruptcy proceedings. To strengthen incentives, the approach also includes a commitment on the part of government to bank privatisation, in which their managers may be invited to participate as owners. While these schemes can be relatively complicated, examples of this approach are found in Poland and Slovenia, as well as in the 1993–94 recapitalisation programme in Hungary.

The second approach to bank recapitalisation aims to create a quick break with the past by limiting compensation for losses on loans to those that were in some way clearly linked with the past. This approach typically restricts the types of loan on which compensation for losses would be available. This restriction has taken the form of either a cut-off date, so that losses made after a particular point in time would not be eligible, or a restriction on loans made for a particular purpose. Losses on any loans not covered by the scheme remain in principle the responsibility of the bank and thus are to be met out of either its earnings or capital. In some cases this clear break with the past has been reinforced by rapid privatisation of banks. The virtues of this approach are simplicity and speed in implementation, but it does require that banks have sufficient capital or earnings to absorb any uncompensated loan losses. Examples of this approach can be found in Bulgaria and the former Czechoslovakia.

There exists a serious risk of distorting incentives for prudent and commercial operation of banks if the recapitalisations are inadequate. In this case, even if there is a commitment to bank privatisation, the inadequate recapitalisation could limit the credibility of the commitment and raise expectations of future assistance. For those recapitalisations that attempt to achieve a clear break with the past, the potential for an inadequate recapitalisation is present. Loan losses are unlikely to be confined to particular types of loans or those made before a cut-off date.

In those countries that have pursued a comprehensive approach to bank recapitalisation, with a clear framework for the work-out of bad loans and commitment to bank privatisation, implementation of these complicated schemes has been relatively slow, particularly the pace of bank privatisation.

2.1.3 Liberal entry and exit of private banks

While one approach to the overhaul of banking has focused primarily on the recapitalisation and privatisation of state banks, a number of countries in the region have relied extensively on the liberal entry of new private banks to help transform the industry. This strategy aims to reduce the prominence of state banks through not only their privatisation but also the emergence of viable new private banks. These new banks have gained significant shares of domestic markets in a number of Baltic and CIS countries. However, the liberal entry of banks almost inevitably raises the issue of how to manage exit from the industry.

Estonia and Latvia, for example, have relied extensively on the entry of new private banks. Between 1989 and 1992, 42 commercial banks were established in Estonia and 55 in Latvia. Entry was much facilitated by the erosion of minimum capital requirements through the high inflation of 1991–92, when most of these new banks were established. However, following this expansion of banks there has been a period of consolidation in each country. In the early stages of this consolidation most new private banks were closed, creating strong financial discipline within banking, but in the advanced stages, the failure of some of the larger new private banks has elicited some government support.

Some countries in the CIS have also relied extensively on the liberal entry of new private banks to help transform their banking systems. In Russia, for example, the number of commercial banks has proliferated since the start of reforms, reaching almost 2,600 by the middle of 1995. However, most of these banks are quite small, with over 40 per cent of them having capital of less than ECU 100,000. Nevertheless, some of the new private banks have gained a significant market position. The total assets of each of the seven largest new private banks now amount to about one-third to one-half of the total assets of each to the former state banks, apart from the Sperbank.

As has happened in Estonia and Latvia, a consolidation of new private banks in some CIS countries will almost inevitably be required. The management of any financial difficulties, however, will require a careful balancing of concerns about financial stability against possible adverse impact of support for banks on public finances. This trade-off can become more severe as the private banks gain a more prominent role in the domestic financial systems.

2.2 Market structure and profitability in banking

Three distinguishing features tend to characterise the market structure and profitability of banking in transition economies: the high concentration of banking markets, which is often a direct legacy from the structure of pre-reform banking; the relatively small scale of banking in most countries, which has been largely caused by high inflation and banks' limited capacity to expand their balance sheets in real terms; and the adverse impact of asset equality problems on bank profitability. Nevertheless, there are indications that the industry has the potential to become profitable and to attract the resources necessary for its real expansion.

2.2.1 Market structure

The high level of market concentration in many countries stems from the way in which the two-tier banking systems were created. Typically, this reform has involved splitting the monolithic state bank under central planning into several large banks, which are specialised by activity, economic sector or geographical region. The extent of entry by new private banks has also had an impact on market concentration in some countries.

The banking markets in much of the region are highly concentrated. Market shares for the top five banks in Belarus, Bulgaria, the Czech Republic, Hungary, Poland, Romania, the Slovak Republic, Slovenia and Ukraine ranged from about 60 to 80 per cent in 1994. The high market shares in these countries reflects largely the continued dominance of state banks and former state banks. In contrast, the market shares of the top five banks in Russia was around 30 per cent in 1994. The low concentration of these banking markets reflects the impact of high inflation on state banks and former state banks and of liberal policies toward the entry of new private banks and their aggressive expansion.

Another distinguishing feature of the banking systems in much of the region is their small relative size. In some countries in eastern Europe, (Poland, Romania and Slovenia), the Baltics and CIS, high inflation and negative real interest rates have limited the relative size of bank credits. The ratio of domestic credit to GDP in these countries was roughly between 20 and 40 per cent of GDP in 1994, and even less in previous years. With the easing of inflation and transformation of banking, there has been some recovery in bank lending, but the relative size of the systems remains small. In the Czech and Slovak Republics, where periods of high inflation have been avoided, the ratio of total domestic credit to GDP ranges between 70 per cent and 100 per cent of GDP in 1994, approaching the ratios in advanced industrial countries.

Not only is the scale of bank credits relatively small, in most countries in the region the dominant share of the outstanding credits is to government and state enterprises. The ratio of outstanding private sector credits to GDP in Estonia, Poland and the Slovak Republic ranges from about 10 per cent to 30 per cent. Only in the Czech Republic, does the share of private sector credit in GDP, at about 65 per cent, approach the levels found in industrial countries, reflecting the impact of the mass privatisation programme.

The analysis of concentration and scale of banking in the region thus points to markets that are dominated by a handful of banks and that are small relative to the sizes of the economies in which they operate. Basic consideration of supply and demand thus suggests that the return to the provision of banking services should be relatively high, although conditions exist under which the exercise of market power can become possible.

2.2.2 *Bank profitability*

To gauge the recent financial performance of banks in eastern Europe, the Baltics and CIS, measures of banks' financial performance have been calculated based upon 1990–93 annual reports of selected institutions. The country coverage includes Bulgaria, the Czech Republic, Hungary, Poland, Romania, Russia, the Slovak Republic and Slovenia. While coverage does not include all institutions within these countries, it does cover the major commercial and savings banks in most countries.

According to these data, the financial performance of banks in the region has been dominated by the asset quality problems. In most countries, the annual provisions have ranged between 2 per cent and 6 per cent of total assets. Where provisions remain small relative to total assets, the countries have yet to tackle the asset quality problem in a comprehensive way or have relied on high inflation to reduce the significance of the problem. As a comparison, annual loan loss provisions of banks in advanced industrial countries is typically no more than 1 per cent of total assets.

While loan loss provisions have been high, the net interest and other income of banks has also been quite high, with banks in most countries earning between 4 and 8 per cent on total assets. To some extent, however, these wide margins in banking reflect the impact of high inflation when interest margins widen partly to preserve the real value of banks' capital. The income of banks in industrial countries is typically in the range of 2 to 5 per cent of total assets.

The operating expenses of banks in the region tend to be in line with that of banks in industrial countries, that is in the range of 2 to 3 per cent of total assets. Banks in some countries fall below this range, possibly reflecting shortages in staff levels and skills, while the operating costs of banks in one country lie well above it.

Once the asset quality problem of banks has been resolved, two considerations thus point to their potential ability to attract the resources required to expand the scale of their operations and to meet the financing needs for private investment in the region. The net interest and other income of banks is relatively high, although this may reflect in part the impact of past high inflation. The operating costs of banks relative to their total assets appear to be in line with those of banks in industrial countries. However, the concentrated market structures and small scale in banking point to the need for disciplined new entry, including foreign banks which can bring much needed technical expertise.

2.3 The role of IFIs

IFI support for financial sector reform and development in transition economies has been aimed at supporting both the changing role of government and the strengthening of banks themselves. This support has also been tailored to the stage of transition in banking.

In the early stages of transition, IFI support has tended to concentrate on technical assistance operations to build up basic infrastructure in banking. The World Bank and other multilateral and bilateral agencies have funded a number of such technical assistance operations in eastern Europe to strengthen banking supervision and to build commercial banking skills through twinning arrangements with international banks. The IMF co-ordinated an extensive technical assistance programme for the Baltics and CIS, in which experts from central banks in a number of industrial countries participated.

Perhaps the most comprehensive example of this approach is the Financial Institutions Development Project in Russia, which the EBRD has co-financed with the World Bank. This project consists of three basic components: the strengthening of a core of 30 to 40 commercial banks by financing twinning contracts with international banks and technology development programmes; the building up of bank supervision, in particular through an on-site inspection programme and legal assistance for the central bank of Russia; and the improving of bank accounting, focusing on the modernisation of accounting and auditing practices.

Once some of the basics in banking are in place, and skills have been strengthened, deeper reforms can be considered. This involves, in particular, the recapitalisation of insolvent banks and financial restructuring of heavily indebted enterprises. The restoration of positive net worth in banks, along with a strong commitment to bank privatisation, are the keys to developing market-oriented and competitive banking system. The sustained health of the banking system, of course, also requires a solvent enterprise sector. For this reason, bank restructuring programmes must be linked with the financial restructuring of enterprises.

Perhaps the most successful IFI-supported financial restructuring programme in eastern Europe and the CIS to date has been in Poland through the World Bank's Enterprise and Financial Sector Adjustment Loan. Following extensive audits of the nine major state banks in Poland, which identified non-performing loans in their portfolio, the banks were provided with a financial injection in the form of government bonds to restore their capital adequacy on the condition that the banks restructure their non-performing enterprise loans by a fixed deadline. The incentive for undertaking these workouts came from the up-front capitalisation and commitment to bank privatisation, as well as from losses to the bank and enterprise if an agreement is not reached.

Strengthening of banks themselves through IFI projects requires an approach that builds incrementally upon existing operational capabilities. This is very much the approach taken in the EBRD's financial sector operations. Since institutional strengthening is largely a learning process, it should start at the earliest possible stage to help ensure that the institutions develop in step with their operating environment.

For relatively undeveloped and/or weakly regulated banks, IFI credit lines supported with technical assistance for credit evaluation and monitoring, trade finance, and other basic banking functions can serve both to build basic banking skills and to expand the availability of credit. This credit can be targeted to certain enterprises or activities that can have special economic benefits, such as small enterprise and trade. These credit lines may rely on sovereign guarantee or strong risk mitigation measures (short-term revolving credit lines). As the operational capabilities financial institutions develop and their solvency and risks can be more accurately assessed, IFI projects can involve more extensive risk exposures. Long-term investment by IFIs, particularly equity investments alongside those of other investors in banks that are being privatised or newly created, are instrumental to the transition, improving the ownership and governance of banks. Such investment can help to expand the capital base of domestic financial systems and thereby multiply the amount of financing available for private investment. But these investments must be in line with the operational capabilities of the institutions.

3 THE EMERGENCE OF SECURITIES ACTIVITIES

The securities exchanges and non-bank financial institutions in transition economies can be an important complement to the banking sector in mobilising and channelling domestic savings into investment and in imposing financial discipline over companies. Moreover, the lack of market liquidity in those countries that pursued mass privatisation programmes can pose a serious impediment to the post-privatisation restructuring of enterprises.

A wide range of institutions actually make up a securities market, including the physical or electronic exchanges and their market makers, clearance and settlement organisations, agents for the issuers of securities (share registrars and transfer and payment agents) and agents for investors (depositories, custodians, proxy services and brokers). Effective regulations are also required to ensure an organised and stable environment for securities activities. These regulations include rules governing the eligibility to issue and to list securities, such as those on financial disclosure, and prohibitions on fraud and insider trading. Moreover, investors in securities often rely on vehicles such as investment companies, pension funds and insurance companies, which are, typically, subject to prudential regulation. A number of countries in the region have enacted basic law and regulations for the creation of securities and the exchanges upon which they trade, as well as for the trading of these instruments.

3.1 Development and performance of securities markets

The development of securities markets in the region has so far been largely shaped by the nature of privatisation programmes. The formation of securities markets began in 1990–91 with the re-establishment of exchanges in Bulgaria, Croatia, Hungary, Poland and Slovenia. The implementation of mass privatisation programmes in the Czech and Slovak Republics propelled the reopening of the Prague and Bratislava Stock Exchanges in 1993. Similarly, in Lithuania, the National Stock Exchange was established in 1993 to support the mass privatisation programme. In Russia, the completion of the first phase of mass privatisation fuelled the development of securities activities on a number of exchanges which had been established in the early 1990s, primarily for the trading of commodities. Latvia and Romania opened exchanges in the course of 1995.

In Hungary, Poland and Slovenia, the institutions that make up a securities market have been able to develop in step with the expansion of securities. This reflects the selective approach to privatisation and demanding disclosure requirements, which have limited the rate of increase in securities. These markets provide adequate liquidity, but their total capitalisation remains small relative to the size of the economies they support. In the Czech and Slovak Republics and Russia, however, the mass privatisation programmes have contributed to a surge in equities that has outstripped the capabilities of the market to handle them. These markets have achieved high capitalisations, but suffer from a shortage of liquidity. In the Czech Republic, the market lacks liquidity in part because of problems in trade settlement and non-transparent trades on the organised exchanges. Moreover, an estimated 80–90 per cent of all share transactions take place outside of the organised exchanges in the Securities Centre, which was originally established to register securities holders. In Russia, the mismatch between the volume of securities and the capacity of the market to handle them is even greater, and there are fundamental weaknesses in the systems for the registration of shares and for the clearance and settlement of trades. The weak legal protection of shareholders' interests and securities fraud are also significant problems.

In transition economies, there thus appears to be a trade-off between the scale and speed of privatisation and the liquidity of shares in privatised companies. Moreover, the nature of the trade-off is such that no stock exchange in the region performs satisfactorily when performance is measured in terms of liquidity provided to the overall economy. The levels of stock market liquidity relative to the size of the economy throughout the region are well below the levels achieved in industrial and fast-growing developing countries. This lack of liquidity can significantly restrict the ability of companies to raise capital through securities issues and impede the emergence of an active market for enterprise control.

3.2 Role of government and self-regulation

Those counties that have achieved at least modest levels of cash-based securities activities, either in the form of new issues or trading in outstanding shares, have, typically, enacted a range of securities regulations. These include financial disclosure requirements for publicly offered securities and investor protection codes related to fraud and insider trading. Such regulations are complemented by the listing requirements imposed by the exchanges themselves.

The quality of financial disclosure is determined not only by regulatory requirements, but also by accounting practices. As with banking supervision, a critical input into investment decisions of investors is the accounts of the listed companies. The accounting practices of many countries continue to reflect more the needs of central planners and tax administrators than of outside investors. However, the overhaul of accounting practices is under way throughout the region.

In addition to disclosure and accounting requirements, a number of countries have implemented investor protection codes, by making illegal securities fraud and insider trading. However, the extent of enforcement is often limited.

3.3 Role of IFIs

In transition economies, the institutions that make up a securities market must be created from scratch. An important role for IFIs in development of securities markets is thus to help alleviate bottlenecks in the institutional infrastructure and enable these markets to function more effectively. This role is performed through the IFIs' financial capacity to share in the risks of starting up new institutions, along with the ability to access technical co-operation funds to address project design and regulatory issues.

Examples of IFI support for the development of securities market institutions include the National Share Registry project in Russia, which was launched in 1995 by the Bank of New York, two Russian companies, the IFC and EBRD. The main business of the Registry is to provide share registration and transfer services in Russia that meet the highest operational standards and meet the requirements of large Russian enterprises. A significant obstacle to development of the Russian securities market has been the lack of reliable share registrars. In Russia, the only proof of share ownership is an extract from a share register which has been, typically, managed by the enterprise itself. This situation created fundamental uncertainties regarding the security of ownership claims and increased transactions costs for trading shares. The EBRD has also made investments in a number of non-bank financial institutions in the region, in particular insurance companies and investment funds, that serve as vehicles for domestic investors to participate indirectly in securities markets.

More generally, IFI projects with the local private sector contribute to raising the standard of financial accounting and disclosure by individual enterprises. This improvement in information can represent an important first step toward access to domestic and international securities markets for local enterprises.

4 CONCLUSION

This chapter has highlighted the fact that the relative scale of banking and securities activities in transition economies is well below the levels in advanced industrial countries and fast-growing developing countries. Much remains to be done in the region to transform the role of government in the financial sector, with a focus on the effective enforcement of laws and regulations, and to strengthen the financial institutions and markets themselves.

Governments in a number of eastern European countries have pursued a measured strategy to transform their role in banking, strengthening prudential regulation and supervision while recapitalising and privatising state banks. Further progress along these lines will require more stringent prudential regulation, along with more rapid progress in privatisation to strengthen incentives and to attract the resources necessary for the expansion of services. Support of the EBRD and other IFIs for bank privatisation can be instrumental in this process.

The transformation of banking in some countries in the Baltics and CIS has occasioned the liberal entry and aggressive expansion of new private banks, as very high inflation eroded the significance of state banks and former state banks. However, the liberal entry of banks will almost inevitably raise the issue of how to manage exit from the industry. If recapitalisations of new private banks does prove necessary, it is vitally important that the conditions imposed by the authorities on the troubled banks' managers and shareholders impose financial discipline. At the same time, the EBRD and other IFIs can help to strengthen a core of private banks that can serve as a nucleus of a viable private banking system.

For securities activities, the challenge is to achieve both high stock market capitalisation and liquidity. This will require development of effective regulations and institutions, more accurate and fuller financial disclosure, and greater transparency in trades. The EBRD and other IFIs have an important role to play in fostering development of the necessary institutional infrastructure for securities activities and in supporting the issuance of securities by local enterprises.

5. A Submerged Challenge for IFIs' Efforts: Proscription of Economic Spoliation

N. Kofele-Kale[1]

1 INTRODUCTION

Any discussion on emerging financial markets, particularly in developing countries, and the role international financial institutions can play in sustaining them, cannot be complete if it ignores issues of governance. It has been observed that the transition from command to market-driven economies currently taking place in Central and Eastern Europe (CEE) is both a process of economic reform as well as political reform. This is an implicit acknowledgement that one cannot be accomplished without the other: the two go hand in hand. If the emerging economies of CEE are to avoid repeating the mistakes that "older" developing countries in Africa made, then one of the issues that must be raised and confronted *now* – not later when it would be too late – is the leadership question. More to the point, the vexing problem, usually discussed *sotto voce*, of internal forms of wealth exploitation by indigenous élites must be confronted head-on. As Professor Reisman pointed out some years ago, the "ritual of condemnation of foreign corporations' spoliations of the resources of developing countries and their elevation to the level of international concern have obscured the problem of spoliations by national officials of the wealth of the states of which they are temporary custodians".[2] These unspeakable depredations occurring daily in the Third World must now command the attention of the international community.

The leadership question which is so central to the problem of capital accumulation – this after all is what capital-starved countries are trying to generate through the help of international financial institutions – raises Juvenal's enduring question: "But who is to guard the guardians?" (*"sed quis custodiet ipsos custodes"*) (*Satires*, 6.347). Juvenal's satire was addressed

---

[1] Ph.D., J. D., Associate Professor of Law, School of Law, Southern Methodist University, Dallas and serves as an Associate Editor of *The International Lawyer*.
[2] *See* M. Reisman, "Harnessing International Law to Restrain and Recapture Indigenous Spoliations", 83 Am. J. Int'l. L. 56 (1989).

to Postumus, trying to dissuade him from his plan to marry, worried as he was about the profound spiritual sickness of Roman society brought about by the collapse of family life and sexual morality and the depravity of Roman women. The satirist could not see how anyone could be contemplating marriage at a time when a woman's honor could not be vouched for. Apparently it had become standard practice for the *praetorian* guards, the designated guardians of the honor of the women of Rome, to take advantage of their charges. Hence the celebrated lament. In the same vein, this author does not see why aid and bank loans continue to be poured into developing Third World economies by international financial institutions and friendly donor governments when all indications are that these funds, targeted for development projects, will end up in the personal accounts of national leaders. For these custodians of Third World wealth, like the Roman bodyguards of Juvenal's time, have demonstrated repeatedly a particular fondness for the "treasures" entrusted to their care! Who then is going to protect these valuable but scarce resources from the pilfering hands of heads of states and other high ranking officials?

In the past three decades or so, the developing countries of the Third World have become the victims of a coordinated plan, whose effect, if not objective, is the destruction of the essential foundations of the economic life of most of their economies. This period has witnessed the systematic and organized plunder of the resources of Third World countries by their leaders, elected and appointed. This wholesale assault on the economic rights of citizens occurs almost daily in military regimes as well as civilian governments across the Third World political landscape. Yet nothing is being done. Following Reisman, I have referred elsewhere to this activity as *indigenous spoliation*[3] and have argued that it is so reprehensible it not only deserves a new name[4] but belongs to that genre of crimes that the venerable International Law Commission refers to as "crimes under international law". For this reason its proscription should be of some concern to the managers of international financial institutions in their role as formulators of global economic policy. This task should not be left to the victim states and peoples to resolve by themselves.

---

[3] *See* Ndiva Kofele-Kale, "Patrimonicide: The International Economic Crime of Indigenous Spoliation", 27 Vand. J. Transnat'l L. 45–108 (1995) (hereinafter "Patrimonicide"); Ndiva Kofele-Kale, *International Law of Responsibility for Economic Crimes: Holding Heads of States and Other High Ranking State Officials Individually Liable for Acts of Fradulent Enrichment* (1995).

[4] A new crime deserves a new name and for this new crime of economic spoliation what better name than *"patrimonicide"*; a word coined from combining the Latin words *"patrimonium"* meaning "[t]he estate or property belonging by ancient right to an institution, corporation, or class; especially the ancient estate or endowment of a church or religious body" and, of course, *"cide"* meaning killing. The new word clearly conveys what economic spoliation really is: the deliberate and systematic destruction of the sum total of a nation's endowment; the laying waste of the wealth and resources belonging by right to her citizens; the denial of present and future generations of what is theirs by right.

2 THE PROBLEM OF ECONOMIC SPOLIATION

Economic spoliation is an illegal act of depredation committed for private ends by constitutionally responsible rulers, public officials and their close associates in the private sector. As a matter of fact, other terms such as embezzlement, misappropriation, corruption, graft, kleptocracy have been employed to describe this widespread practice of office holders confusing the public fisc with their private accounts. However, they fail to convey the full force of this relatively new phenomenon of indigenous spoliation since all these terms signify is the raw act of forcible taking but not its effect, *i.e.*, the systematic destruction of the social, economic and moral foundation of the victim state. The practice I write about occurs on a scale so vast as never before seen in the history of the modern state system. This is not to suggest that misappropriation of a nation's wealth by its political leadership is a novel phenomenon. However, the new generation of pillage differs from the old in at least four respects. First, the modern version is characterized by great *mobility of wealth* and the capacity to hide and disguise this wealth. Purloined national wealth is almost always exported to "safe havens" abroad and hidden in banks in Western Europe and North America.

Second, the amount of wealth involved is so stupendous that it goes beyond shame and almost beyond imagination. We are talking of individual fortunes that are munificent by anyone's standards. For instance, Mexico's fugitive former Deputy Attorney-General Ruiz Massieu is reported to have deposited almost $32 million in personal funds in U.S. banks and an unspecified amount in Mexican banks. Ferdinand Marcos while in office for two decades drew an annual salary of $5,700 yet court records filed by the successor Aquino government placed his net worth in the billions of dollars. Nigeria's Umaru Dikko, an *eminence grise* in the civilian government of Shehu Shagari, escaped to England with close to two billion pounds sterling when that government was overthrown in a military coup on New Year's Eve 1984.

Thirdly, the spoliated funds that are cached abroad usually exceed the total external debts of many of the victim states. For instance, President Mobutu of Zaire's estimated net worth is enough to wipe off a substantial part of his country's $11 billion external debt. Between 1986–1990 $2.1 billion were embezzled by public officials in Cameroon (as against $1.9 billion in export receipts for a comparable period (1985–90), an amount equal to 50 per cent of the country's external debt based on 1990 estimates! Unfortunately, the bulk of this purloined wealth is hardly ever reinvested in productive enterprises at home.

Finally, there is a strong linkage between contemporary capital flight and domestic economic growth and development. The kind of massive capital flight resulting from spoliation tends to be directed at all the wealth-generating sectors of the economy, leaving in its wake profound social and economic devastation. In effect, the relationship between capital flight and domestic economic growth and development is a *zero-sum game*. Resources that might otherwise be used for domestic development are diverted into the private pockets of a few individuals. As this scarce capital flees, the victim-States are left with little alternative than to borrow funds from foreign lenders to prosecute their development programs. However, these external borrowings create new liabilities that must be paid off by governments that are already overburdened by prior unpaid debts. Consider this: all of Africa spends four times more on debt servicing than on health care; Burundi (which is currently experiencing its own internal convulsions) uses up 30 per cent of its budget each year to service its external debt; sub-Saharan Africa as a whole uses up one-fifth of its export earnings on debt service.

Two points bear noting. First, while only a small highly visible oligarchy engages in, and profits from, economic spoliation, the consequences almost always are borne by the rest of society – particularly the *hoi polloi*. Ayi Kwei Armah's biting satire of Ghanaian society *The Beautyful Ones Are Not Yet Born* (1969) graphically captures this contradiction. In short, the price of outflows of scarce resources to the West is billions of dollars-worth of un-surfaced roads, unpurified water and untreated illnesses. The Haitians have a saying: "We live, we die and in between we suffer". The second point worthy of note is that persistent and unrestrained spoliation invariably leads to serious social and political instability. The continued plunder of a nation's wealth by its leadership will gradually erode the base of legitimacy of any government. This point was underscored in the Plan of Action drawn up at the 1994 Miami Summit of the Americas which was attended by President Clinton and leaders of 33 other nations from this hemisphere. These heads of state and government acknowledged with uncharacteristic candor that corruption has now become a serious problem not only in their hemisphere but in all regions of the world. They called attention to the fact that high level corruption "weakens democracy and undermines the legitimacy of governments and institutions".[5] With time even the most anesthetized masses will say "enough is enough" and rise up in revolt against their corrupt rulers. Such was the case in the Philippines in 1986 and in Romania in 1989. Alternatively, self-appointed agents of the masses may take it upon themselves to restore accountability in government using extra-constitutional methods. This partially explains the frequency of military coups in the Third World. In coup after coup the justification usually given is that of putting an end to high level corruption.

While it is true that economic spoliation is the work of indigenous élites, their success depends on the assistance, tacit or express, provided by the rest of the international community. This assistance has come in various forms: the conspiracy of silence in the face of brazen acts of plunder and pillage; a predisposition to turn the other way and pretend not to see what is occurring; an eagerness to provide safe havens for spoliated national wealth and asylum for fugitive dictators. The case of Lt. Gen. Raoul Cedras, head of the military junta that toppled President Aristide in 1991 – a man whom President Clinton once described as a dictator and thug – is illustrative. In exchange for his voluntary departure from Haiti for asylum in Panama, the U.S. State Department agreed to lease three of his villas for an

---

[5] *See* Summit of Americas, Plan of Action, item 5: Combating Corruption. Done at Miami, Florida, on December 10, 1994 (hereinafter "Plan of Action").

estimated $3000 a month with a total of $60,000 paid to him for the first year's rent![6]

To be sure, the ravaging effects of economic spoliation are more directly felt in the developing countries who are the least capable of absorbing the consequences on their economies. But the industrialized countries of Western Europe and North America will not be spared the fall-out. It is therefore in their own self-interest to ensure that this conduct is proscribed. Internal instability, civil strife and social conflict have already been cited as likely consequences flowing from the destruction wrought on an economy by rapacious national leaders. Any one of these can trigger a mass exodus of people across territorial boundaries thus globalizing a conflict that began as a local, internal affair. The specter of hordes of "economic" refugees from the Third World flooding the shores of Western Europe and North America is very real indeed. Consider the social and financial costs of absorbing and resettling hundreds of thousands of unwanted, unskilled and semi-literate people who are, in the main, culturally and racially different from their hosts. How long before the generosity of struggling taxpayers in the host countries is replaced by compassion fatigue and even violent backlash?

Even if the refugee problem can be contained there still remains unresolved the underlying cause. It has been shown time and time again that prolonged conflicts provoked by economic deprivation may require military assistance or direct intervention from the industrialized countries which tend to be costly and politically difficult to justify to domestic taxpayers. Furthermore, developing economies shattered by years of relentless plunder and pillage will have to be rebuilt and it is the West that invariably shoulders this tremendous financial burden (it cost U.S. taxpayers an estimated $500 million in the initial phase of restoring Jean-Bertrand Aristide back to the Haitian presidency). Finally, internal instability leads to the disruption of the global financial markets as the recent skirmishes between the Mexican government and the Chiapas Indians so recently demonstrated.

3 INDIVIDUAL ACCOUNTABILITY FOR ECONOMIC SPOLIATION

The peculations of national resources I have described deserve to be treated as an international economic crime (a) responsibility for which should be attributed to the individual perpetrator; and (b) whose capture and punishment becomes an obligation of the community of nations. This would extend the Nuremberg principle of individual responsibility to a broader reach than traditional international law has heretofore permitted. Resulting from this effort would be a regime that treats the Head of State or any

---

[6] *See New York Times*, October 15, 1994, 1, 6:5.

high-ranking State official who spoliates his nation's resources like the pirate and slave trader before him – as an enemy of mankind.[7]

3.1 The doctrine of individual responsibility

It is worth recalling that the Nuremberg War Crimes Tribunal remarked that "crimes against international law are committed by men, not by abstract entities, and only by punishing individuals who commit such crimes can the provisions of international law be enforced".[8] The Nuremberg Tribunal went on to single out three crimes that entail personal responsibility: crimes against peace, war crimes, and crimes against humanity.[9] When in 1946 the United Nations General Assembly adopted the Nuremberg principles, it also directed the International Law Commission (ILC) to prepare a draft code of offenses against the peace and security of mankind. The first draft was submitted in 1950 and in 1991 the ILC adopted a Draft Code of Crimes Against the Peace and Security of Mankind. Article 3 of the Draft Code codifies the principle of individual responsibility; Article 13 specifically targets Heads of States as persons who can be charged for Draft Code violations while Article 2 reaffirms the doctrine of the supremacy of international law over municipal or national law.

The ILC Draft Code of Crimes has opened the door for the inclusion of economic spoliation among its enumerated "crimes under international law", *i.e.*, "crimes *by* individuals" as opposed to crimes of state or international crimes proper (in the language of Article 19 of the ILC's Draft Articles on State Responsibility). Under the Draft Code of Crimes the following crimes when committed by individuals subject the authors to *personal* responsibility: genocide, torture, aggression, apartheid, terrorism, intervention, colonial domination, drug trafficking, environmental damage, and mercenarism. The ILC has enunciated a two-pronged test for conduct that qualifies as a "crime under international law". First, the degree to which the conduct is found to be reprehensible to the universal conscience. Second, its seriousness. The prohibited conduct, whether directed against persons or property, must be so serious that it undermines the very foundations of human society such that its proscription becomes the obligation of the community of nations. The seriousness of the conduct is to be "gauged according to the public conscience ... the disapproval it gives to, the shock it provokes, the degree of horror it arouses within the national or international community".

3.2 An international problem giving rise to a universal obligation to resolve

Economic spoliation undermines two fundamental interests of mankind: the right to self-determination and the right of permanent sovereignty over

---

[7] *See* Ndiva Kofele-Kale, *International Law of Responsibility for Economic Crimes: Holding Heads of States and Other High Ranking State Officials Individually Liable for Acts of Fraudulent Enrichment* (1995).

[8] *See* the judgment of the International Military Tribunal at Nuremberg, 6 F.R.D. 69, 119, 129 (1946).

[9] 6 F.R.D. 69, 110 (1946).

natural resources and national wealth. Because all States have a *legal* interest in protecting these obligations, they also have a legal duty to capture and punish those guilty of violating them.

3.3 The right to self-determination and permanent sovereignty

Self-determination is now accepted as an inalienable right of all human beings. It speaks to the right of all peoples freely to determine, without external interference, their political status and to pursue their economic, social, and cultural development.[10] While self-determination represents the essence of political independence, the doctrine of permanent sovereignty is the very embodiment of economic independence. This right was enunciated in the celebrated United Nations General Assembly Resolution 1803 of 1962 as the right of all peoples freely to use, exploit and dispose of their natural wealth and resources as they see fit.[11] Article 21, paragraph 1 of the African Charter on Human and Peoples' Rights goes one step further by providing that this right shall be exercised in the exclusive interest of the people; and in no case shall a people be deprived of it. The African Charter acknowledges that citizens of a sovereign State have a fundamental and "inalienable" right to utilize the benefits from the disposition of natural resources and that national leaders have an obligation to ensure that these resources are used for the "well-being of the people".

It is something of an irony that the drafters of this Charter which purports to celebrate "peoples' rights" have turned out to be the most dedicated practitioners of economic spoliation. The massive looting of a nation's wealth for the personal benefit of its political leaders deserves to be recognized as part of the list of international crimes that have risen to the status of *jus cogens*. Because the effects of indigenous spoliation are so severe and profound – the impoverishment of the nation concerned, retardation of its economic, social and cultural development, and, ultimately, the compromising of the dignified survival of its people – the case for making this kind of depredation a peremptory norm of customary law is all the more compelling.

---

[10] *See* 1970 United Nations Declaration of Principles of International Law Concerning Friendly Relations Among States in Accordance with the Charter of the United Nations; Article 1 of the International Covenant on Civil and Political Rights, and Article 1 of the International Covenant on Economic, Social and Cultural Rights; *see* also *Western Sahara Case* 1975 I.C.J. Reports 12 (where the International Court of Justice characterized this right as a peremptory or *jus cogens* norm of international law, *i.e.*, a non-waivable obligation from which States cannot contract out); and the Commentary to Article 19 of the Draft Articles on State Responsibility. For a definition of *jus cogens*, *see* Article 53 of the Vienna Convention on the Law of Treaties, May 22, 1969, U.N. Doc. A/CONF. 39/27, reprinted at 8 I.L.M. 679 (1969) (opened for signature May 23, 1969; entered into force January 27, 1980).

[11] *See* Resolution on Permanent Sovereignty over Natural Resources, GA Res. 1803, 17 UN GAOR Supp. (No. 17) at 15, UN Doc. A/5217 (1962); *see* also Article 13 of the 1978 Vienna Convention on Succession of States in Respect of Treaties; Article 1(2) of both the International Covenant on Civil and Political Rights, and Economic, Social and Cultural Rights; and Article 2(1) of the Charter on Economic Rights and Duties of States.

4 SOME SOLUTIONS

The industrialized world has a major part to play in reducing the incidence of economic spoliation. If legal and moral reasons are not persuasive enough for wanting to join the fight against this scourge then these States need to be reminded that it is in their self-interest to help make such acts so unattractive that few national leaders would be tempted to engage in them.

4.1 A multilateral treaty

One way the international legal community can begin to tackle this problem is through a multilateral convention or treaty. In this vein, Professor Reisman has proposed the drafting of an international declaration that would (1) characterize acts of spoliations by national officials as a breach of national trust and international law; (2) impose on other governments an obligation of supplying information and cooperation; and (3) treating the failure of other governments to prevent such funds from being cached in their jurisdiction and to aid in their recapture as complicity, after the fact, and as itself, an international delict.[12] The idea of drafting an international agreement that would provide the legal framework for restraining and recapturing spoliated wealth and punishing its authors is perhaps the ideal remedy. Treaties representing, as it were, the express consent of state parties to be bound by their undertakings[13] occupies the highest rung in the hierarchy of international legal authorities.[14] A promising first step in this direction is the anti-corruption accord[15] that was signed by President Clinton and leaders of 33 other nations at the Summit of the Americas in Miami in December 1994 wherein the leaders issued a call on the governments of the world to "adopt and enforce measures against bribery in all financial or commercial transactions within the Hemisphere; toward this end, invite the OAS to establish liaison with the OECD Working Group on Bribery in International Business Transactions".[16] For their part, the Hemisphere's leaders pledged to "[d]evelop within the OAS, with due regard to applicable treaties and national legislation, a hemispheric approach to acts of corruption in both the public and private sectors that would include extradition and prosecution of individuals so charged, through negotiation of a new hemispheric agreement or new arrangements within existing frameworks for international cooperation".[17] This might take a while to work out but in the short term international financial

---

[12] *See* M. Reisman, "Harnessing International Law to Restrain and Recapture Indigenous Spoliations", 83 Am. J. Inl'l L. 56 (1989).

[13] *See* Article 2(1)(a), Vienna Convention on the Law of Treaties, *supra* note 10.

[14] *See* Article 38(1) of the Statute of the International Court of Justice which is usually treated as the most convenient and concise statement regarding the sources of international law. International conventions appear first in the list of the rules to be applied by the Court in deciding cases before it. And most publicists assign legal rules drawn from international agreements the highest rank among all sources of international law.

[15] *See* Plan of Action, *supra* note 5.

[16] *Id.*

[17] *Id.*

institutions with their enormous financial leverage can take the lead in bringing about desirable changes in international lending practices.

4.2 Spoliation as a conditionality for receipt of aid and IFIs' credits

Major aid donors, including key international financial institutions such as the International Bank for Reconstruction and Development (World Bank) and the International Monetary Fund (IMF), have increasingly been including democratic reforms and observance of human rights as conditionalities for extending aid and credits to authoritarian and totalitarian governments.[18] The World Bank, for example, has expanded its traditional role as a financial institution to include a new governance role that allows it to dictate legal and institutional change through its lending policies.[19] It has frequently exercised its enormous governance power:

through its financial leverage to legislate entire legal regimes and even alter the constitutional structure of borrowing nations. Bank-approved consultants often rewrite a country's trade policy, fiscal policies, civil service requirements, labor laws, health care arrangements, environmental regulations, procurement rules, and budgetary policy.[20]

The Bank's principal tool in nudging borrowing members towards prescribed social objectives is "conditionality".[21] Bank loans impose conditions requiring legislative and policy changes by borrowing governments.[22] As one critic of the World Bank's new and expanded lending policy observed "[t]hese non-financial conditions frequently derive from assumptions about the normative and economic task of development"[23] and are justified on grounds that so long as governance (a euphemism for Western liberal democratic system of government) issues are related to economic development, the Bank may impose conditions on governance.[24] For its part, the

---

[18] *See e.g.* Section 11B of the Foreign Assistance Act of 1961, as amended, 22 U.S.C. s. 2151n (1988) (Prohibition of Foreign Assistance to Gross Violators of Human Rights) and Section 502B of the Foreign Assistance Act of 1961, as amended, 22 U.S.C. s. 2304 (1988) (Prohibition of Security Assistance to Gross Violators of Human Rights.

[19] *See* Jonathan Cahn, "Challenging the New Imperial Authority: The World Bank and the Democratization of Development", 6 Harv.- Hum. Rts. J. 159, 160 (1993).

[20] *Id.*

[21] For the origins of the concept of conditionality, *see* Joseph Gold, *Conditionality* (I.M.F. Pamphlet Series No. 31, 1979); Manuel Guitan, *Fund Conditionality: Evolution of Principles and Practice* (I.M.F. Pamphlet Series No. 39, 1981); John Williamson, "IMF Conditionality" in *IMF Conditionality* (John Williamson ed. 1983).

[22] The purpose of conditionality has shifted from that of maximizing "the probability of repayment a World Bank loan, but rather. . . to enable the borrower to remove what the lender sees as fundamental policy induced obstacles to economic growth." *See* Paul Mosley, Jane Harrigan & John Toye, *Aid and Power: The World Bank and Policy-Based Lending: Analysis and Policy Proposals* (1979), pp. 66–77.

[23] *Id.*

[24] *World Bank, Governance and Development* 46 (1992); *see* also World Bank, *Sub-Saharan Africa: From Crisis to Sustainable Growth* 60–61 (1989) (the issue of borrowing members' governance raised for the first time whereupon the Bank publicly called upon African governments to become accountable to their citizens).

Bank has taken the position that its governance concerns extend from broad macroeconomic policy to the proper structure and role of government institutions that administer the economy, to environmental impacts, and even military spending.[25]

Given this role shift it should not be too difficult to include in loan agreements specific requirements for the repatriation of spoliated wealth in foreign accounts held by high-ranking officials of the borrowing governments. This along with the requirement of leadership incorruptibility and progress toward democratization should be made conditions that must be fulfilled before donor governments and international financial institutions can extend financial assistance to the countries concerned. This can be accomplished in one of four ways:

(1) By requiring that when extradition treaties between victim-States and States where spoliated wealth is banked or invested are negotiated or renegotiated, as the case may be, economic spoliation should be included as an extraditable crime. The willingness of victim-States to renegotiate extradition treaties for this purpose can be used as a test of their good faith commitment to democratic reforms. Should a victim-State balk at the idea then it leaves itself open to charges that it has no serious intention of pursuing democratic reforms and as such should not be eligible for foreign aid and credits.

(2) Given the importance developing countries attach to private foreign investment, treaties of friendship, commerce and navigation as well as bilateral investment treaties between investment-starved developing countries and capital-rich industrial countries can be drafted to include a provision to assist a government, *e.g.*, the successor government of Corazon Aquino, that has been the victim of economic spoliation by former high-ranking officials in recovering and repatriating any funds found stashed in the industrial country.

(3) Including in bilateral and multilateral Mutual Legal Assistance on Criminal Matters Treaties a provision for mutual assistance in the recovery and return of spoliated wealth.[26]

(4) By insisting that victim-States be actively involved in the prevention and punishment of economic spoliation. Donor countries and IFIs should encourage victim-States to pass and enforce national legislation for the prevention and punishment of persons guilty of such acts. The international community can start by assisting fragile democratic successor governments to restore "the legitimacy and effectiveness of their own judicial and political systems";[27] encourage them

---

[25] *Id.* at 164; *see* also Ibrahim Shihata, "The World Bank and 'Governance' Issues in its Borrowing Members", in *The World Bank in a Changing World* 53, 67–72 (Franziska Tschofen & Antonio R. Parra eds. 1991).

[26] The Summit of the Americas' Plan of Action suggests multilateral "mechanisms of cooperation in the judicial and banking areas to make possible rapid and effective response in the international investigation of corruption cases".

[27] *See* Ann-Marie Burley, Remarks during the panel presentation "Pursuing the Assets of Former Dictators" at the *Proceedings of the 81st Annual Meeting of the American Society of International Law* 394, 402 (M. Malloy ed. 1990).

to incorporate in their national laws "stiff penalties for those who utilize their public position to benefit private interests";[28] and help them to establish national legal guarantees that (a) judgments against high-ranking officials, including former heads of state, will be enforced; and (b) the courts will not permit a deposed dictator to successfully invoke sovereign immunity or act of state defenses when the new government requests such immunity to be revoked. Many African states have taken the position that economic rights for individuals and peoples take precedence over civil and political (so-called Western liberal) rights. For these countries, there can be no better barometer for measuring their professed commitment to this principle than their willingness to pass and enforce strict laws on leadership conduct.[29]

5 REFERENCES

C. Braeckman, *Le Dinosaure* (1990).

Ann-Marie Burley, Comments during the panel presentation *Pursuing the Assets of Former Dictators* at the Proceedings of the 81st Annual Meeting of the American Society of International Law 394, 401 (1987) (M. Malloy ed. 1990).

Charter of Economic Rights and Duties of States, Dec. 12, 1974, U.N.G.A. Res. 3281 (XXIX), 29 U.N. GAOR, Supp. (No. 31) 50, U.N. Doc.A/9631 (1975), reprinted in 14 I.L.M. 251 (1975).

B. Chayes, Comments during the panel presentation *Pursuing the Assets of Former Dictators* at the Proceedings of the 81st Annual Meeting of the American Society of International Law 394, 395 (1987) (M. Malloy ed. 1990).

D. Delamaide, *Debt Shock: The Full Story of the World Credit Crisis* (1984).

E. Denters, "IMF Conditionality: Economic, Social and Cultural Rights, and the Evolving Principle of Solidarity", in *International Law and Development* 235, 237–46 (P. De Waart, P. Peters & E. Denters eds. 1988).

---

[28] *See* Plan of Action, *supra* note 5.

[29] *See* "Limburg Principles on the Implementation of the International Covenant on Economic, Social and Cultural Rights (1986)", 9 Human Rts. Q. 128, 143 (1987); World Commission on Enviroment & Development, *Our Common Future* (1987). In 1979, the Assembly of Heads of States and Governments of the Organization of African Unity meeting in Monrovia, Liberia passed a resolution calling for a meeting of experts to draft a human rights charter. The resolution stressed the "importance that the African peoples have always attached to the respect for human dignity and the fundamental human rights, *bearing in mind that human and people's rights are not confined to civil and political rights, but cover economic, social and cultural problems, and that the distinction between these two categories of rights does not have any hierarchical implications but that it is nevertheless essential to give special attention to economic, social and cultural rights in the future. . ."* *See On Human and People's Rights in Africa*, OAU Document AHG/Dec. 115 (XVI) (emphasis added).

S. George, *A Fate Worse Than Debt* (1990).

R. Higgins, *The Development of International Law Through the Political Organs of the United Nations* (1963).

M. Janis, *An Introduction to International Law* (1988).

N. Kofele-Kale, "Patrimonicide: The International Economic Crime of Indigenous Spoliation", 27 Vand. J. Transnat'l L. 45–108 (1995).

————, *International Law of Responsibility for Economic Crimes: Holding Heads of States and Other High Ranking State Officials Individually Liable for Acts of Fraudulent Enrichment* (1995).

J. Marks, "Emerging Human Rights: A New Generation for the 1980s?", in *International Law: A Contemporary Perspective* 501 (1985).

Meagher, "Act of State and Sovereign Immunity: The Marcos Cases", 29 Harv. Int'l L.J. 129 (1988).

M. Reisman, "Harnessing International Law to Restrain and Recapture Indigenous Spoliations", 83 Am. J. Int'l L. 56 (1989).

M. Shaw, *International Law* (2nd ed. 1986).

L. Sohn, "The New International Law: Protection of the Rights of Individuals Rather than States", 32 Am. U. L. Rev. 1 (1982).

J. Starke, *An Introduction to International Law* (9th ed. 1984).

Trubek, "Economic, Social and Cultural Rights in the Third World: Human Rights Law and Human Needs Programs", in *Human Rights in International Law: Legal and Policy Issues* 215 (T. Meron ed. 1984).

Turk, "The Human Right to Development", in *Restructuring the International Economic Order: The Role of Law and Lawyers* 85 (P. Van Dijk, F. Van Hoof, A. Koers & K. Mortelmans eds. 1987).

United Nations General Assembly, *Declaration on the Right to Development*, U.N. Gaor, 41st Sess., Resolutions and Decisions, Agenda Item 101, at 3–6, 9th plenary meeting, 4 Dec. 1986 U.N. Doc. A/Res/41/128.

6. Structural Adjustment Policies and the Evolution of a New Legal Framework for Economic Activity in Ghana

Jonathan R. Magnusen[1]

1 INTRODUCTION

The period of the 1980s witnessed profound changes in international finance and economic relations as the World Community grappled to come to terms with the Debt Crisis[2] and the need to address the threat posed by economic crises of the Third World. In discussing these issues, the developing countries called for more favourable prices for their exports, access to international markets and a general realignment of international economic relations. The International Financial Institutions[3] and the developed world, however, saw the solution in terms of developing countries undertaking structural adjustment designed to enhance their competitive advantages and better integrate them into a world economic system based on principles of free trade, open markets and liberalisation.

In Africa, Ghana was one of the first countries to embark on a Structural Adjustment Programme (SAP).[4] Ghana's SAP was generally consistent with the neo-classical economic policies advocated by the Bretton Woods Institutions in other developing countries, and inspired by the liberal economic analysis which believed in the market as the mechanism for the

---

[1] LL.M. (London), attaché, Ghanaian Embassy, London and Research Fellow in Development Law, London Institute of International Banking, Finance and Development Law, Centre for Commercial Law Studies, Queen Mary and Westfield College, University of London.

[2] The Debt Crisis emerged in 1982 when the developing world, led by Mexico, served notice that it was unable to continue servicing its external debt. For a discussion of the issue, *see* S. Dell, "Crisis Management and the International Debt Burden", *International Journal* (Autumn 1985); *see* also J. Clark, "The Sovereign Debt Crisis: A Lawyer's Perspective", in Hazel Fox (ed), *International Economic Law and Developing States* (British Institute of International and Comparative Law, London, 1992).

[3] These institutions include multilateral aid agencies such as the World Bank, the International Monetary Fund and the European Bank for Reconstruction and Development.

[4] For a full discussion of the SAP, *see* the World Bank, *Ghana: Policies and Program for Adjustment* (Washington D.C., 1983).

regulation of economic activity. Its basic tenets included fiscal discipline, financial liberalisation, establishment of market determined exchange rates, trade liberalisation, privatisation, deregulation of internal prices, attraction of foreign direct investment and rationalisation of public expenditure through, *inter alia*, removal of subsidies, retrenchment of public sector employees and cost recovery in social programmes like health and education.

Structural adjustment as promoted by the Bretton Woods Institutions[5] in developing countries can be criticised for their ideological bias, concentration on a narrow set of macro-economic objectives of demand management to promote sustainable balance of payment and reduce budget deficits, and excessive political, economic and social consequences.[6] Despite the single country approach to design, the adjustment programmes supported by the two institutions tend to be uniform across countries with minor differences in detail. The underpinning liberal economic philosophy leads to such automatic responses as privatisation, reliance on market mechanisms and promotion of free trade and free access. Indeed, in many developing countries, the Bretton Woods Institutions are widely viewed as powerful international bodies which use their political leverage to promote the interests of Western capital.

Some of the assumptions on which SAPs have been founded could also be questioned in a number of ways. The theoretical and empirical foundations of adjustment programmes are uncertain, especially as they assume that markets, especially capital and commodity markets, are free and uncontrolled. Secondly, the concepts of comparative advantage and free trade which constitute the bedrock of structural adjustment are relevant to economies which are static or growing, but of dubious applicability to African economies that have been in many years of decline. Given the bias towards export-led growth and the dependence of the export sector of many of these economies on a few agricultural and mineral products, the tendency has been for structural adjustment to integrate these economies further into the international economic system in a more or less servient-dominant relationship *vis-à-vis* the developed western world. The classical dependency arguments used by the opponents of the IMF in Ghana have sometimes assumed greater relevance in the light of these considerations.

Apart from these, much attention has been drawn to the negative social consequences of structural adjustment on the most vulnerable groups in society – the urban poor, rural crop farmers, women, children and the elderly.[7] Other problems include the impact of SAP on the environment and human development, especially education, health, nutrition and employment, the aggravation of income inequality between the rich and the poor,

---

[5] These institutions are the World Bank and the International Monetary Fund.
[6] *See* "Embracing the Future ... Response to the World Bank's Vision for the Bretton Woods System" by OXFAM (U.K. and Ireland) London, July 1994.
[7] *See* Mosley, Harrigan and Toye, *Aid and Power: The World Bank and Policy Based Lending*, Volume 2 (Routledge, 1991), p. 169.

and the perpetuation of external dependence with consequences for national sovereignty.[8]

Despite the criticisms, alternatives to neo-classical structural adjustment programmes have not been many. The major ones view adjustment as a means to address long-term development issues. This alternative approach sees as the ultimate goal a human-centred development aimed at alleviating poverty and raising the welfare of the people through sustained improvement in living standards. It also proposes integration of African economies though national and regional collective self-reliance.[9] However, because these alternative approaches have not been adopted on an international scale, the efficacy of the policy measures they recommend are yet to be seen.

It is, however, not the intention of this chapter to launch into a discussion of the successes and failures of the SAP in Ghana. Much has already been written on the subject. Also, for reasons of brevity, it would not be possible to examine all the salient areas of Ghana's SAP. Emphasis will therefore be placed on the reforms within the monetary and financial sectors, although reference will be made to reforms in other areas when necessary.

Within these narrow confines, this chapter seeks to explore the legal significance of reform measures and the consequences, if any, that the adjustment programme has had on the development of the legal order in the country. The intention would be to show that the reform process has led to the emergence of a new legislative framework for economic activity in Ghana, and that the effect of these new legislations has been to advance the objectives of the SAP itself. Whether these objectives are desirable or not, is a value judgement that would depend on the individual's socio-economic and political persuasions.

The chapter has been structured to give a chronological account of the interplay between the political economy and the development of law in the period since independence in Ghana and at the same time to explore the legal issues which form its core. Part 2 provides a general background to structural adjustment in Ghana. It also examines the role of the IMF and the World Bank in the adjustment process, the use of conditionalities as an instrument for directing the process and the linkages between all these and international law.

The next two Parts discuss, in turn, legislative reforms in the monetary and financial sectors. In each section, a survey of the economic and legal conditions prior to adjustment precede a discussion of the reform measures that were implemented. These measures are discussed from a legal standpoint, with a view to emphasising their implications for the law (or absence of law) regulating activities in these areas, and how the legal framework

---

[8] *See* D. Hogg, "The SAP in the Forest: The Environmental and Social Impact of Structural Adjustment Programmes in the Philippines, Ghana and Guyana" (Friends of the Earth, London, 1993).

[9] For a discussion of this approach, *see* Adebayo Adedeji, "African Alternative Framework to Structural Adjustment Programmes for Socio-Economic Recovery and Transformation" (United Nations Economic Commission for Africa, Addis Ababa, E/ECA/CM.15/6/Rev 3).

they provide supports the attainment of the objectives of the adjustment programme.

In the concluding Part, an attempt is made to draw together the various strands of argument in the preceding sections to support the proposition that the reform process has resulted in the emergence of a new legal order in Ghanaian economic life. This new regulatory regime is shown to consist of both framework laws to bring specified sectors within the realm of legislative control, and substantive rules made to regulate new economic activities that had emerged as a result of the SAP. At the same time, the evolution of the new legislative framework is shown to have involved a substantial revision of the pre-adjustment regulatory regime. And, in terms of the consequences of this development, it is argued that the new legal order promotes and facilitates the objectives of the SAP, *i.e.* deregulation, liberalisation and the eventual creation of a market economy in Ghana.

2 ECONOMIC, LEGAL AND INSTITUTIONAL BACKGROUND TO STRUCTURAL ADJUSTMENT

2.1 Ghana's political economy – 1957–1983

On 6 March 1957, Ghana became the first African country south of the Sahara to achieve political independence, under Dr. Kwame Nkrumah, its first President. The Conventional Peoples' Party (CPP) regime, which he led, devoted itself to the creation of a welfare state within a largely centrally planned economy.

Nkrumah's regime can be credited with policies which ensured a significant improvement in the indicators of social welfare. Substantial public resources were expended on health and education. Life expectancy and school enrolment went up, and infant mortality fell. The establishment of hundreds of state-run, import substitution industries under the Industrial Investment Programme ensured ready jobs for the urban organised workers who had helped to bring Nkrumah to power.

Paradoxically, the industrialisation and social welfare programmes of the Nkrumah government also sowed the seeds for the subsequent economic instability and decline. Much of the wealth generated by the country was used to service the government's social welfare services and largely inefficient, domestic import substitution industries, leading to severe pressure on public finances. Without additional revenue from other sources, the budget deficit began to increase, whilst the regime became increasingly marginalised.

It was against this background that the Nkrumah government was ousted by a military coup on 24 February 1966. The National Liberation Council, which was ushered into power, made feeble attempts at stabilisation with the support of the IMF and World Bank, including a devaluation of the currency. The attempt was, however, doomed to failure, and devaluation as an economic measure became extremely unpopular.

Despite its inclination towards liberal economic policies, the popularly elected Busia government, which succeeded the NLC late in 1969, also failed to reverse Ghana's economic decline. Informal dealings with the IMF and World Bank eventually led the government to privatise some state enterprises and announce another devaluation in December 1971 in a tentative step towards economic adjustment. This measure, together with the effects of dwindling foreign exchange earnings due to the decline in cocoa prices, largely precipitated the overthrow of the government the next month by a military junta led by Col. I.K. Acheampong. What followed was the gradual paralysis of economic policy making and plunder of the economy in what has been called a rule of Kleptocracy.[10]

During this period, the growth dynamic of the economy fell as domestic savings, investment and cocoa output fell. The tendency of the regime to resort to deficit financing resulted in strong inflationary pressure, worsened by the over-valuation of the Cedi, whose exchange rate had been pegged at a parity rate of $1.15 to a Cedi since 1973. As the situation worsened, the government imposed price controls which only succeeded in driving goods into the parallel markets in a phenomenon which became known in Ghana as "Kalabule". Corruption became endemic, whilst the government's penchant for printing more money spiralled inflation out of control. Negative real rates of interest ensured huge profits for officials and their cronies who could secure bank loans through corruption and rent-seeking activities.[11]

General Akuffo, who ousted General Acheampong in a palace coup in 1978, put together an economic technocratic team to consult with the IMF. As a result, some stabilisation measures including a devaluation of the exchange rate of the Cedi to ¢2.75 to a dollar were introduced. The economic crisis was, however, so deep that the measures only had superficial effects.

In the midst of the discontent that followed, the regime was overthrown in 1979 in a coup led by Flt. Lt. J.J. Rawlings. The new regime allowed the ongoing transitional process to civilian rule to proceed, and permitted the economic technocratic team to continue its consultations with the IMF. However, it purged the country of many of its corrupt senior officials in what became known as the revolutionary clean-up campaign. After four months in office, Rawlings handed over power to Dr. Hilla Limann who had been elected the new President.

Despite the continuation of negotiations with the IMF, the Limann government tried to avoid a formal IMF programme, demonstrating in the process a remarkable degree of indecisiveness and ineptitude. This inaction by the Limann regime was so stark in the face of the severe economic crisis that some writers have concluded that the IMF's stabilisation programme was all but abandoned.[12]

---

[10] *See* Mosley, Harrigan and Toye, 1991 , *op. cit.*, Volume 2, p. 152.

[11] Rent-seeking activity refers to the excess profits made by the favoured few who could secure bank loans and rationed foreign exchange to import controlled goods at World Market prices and sell at inflated prices in the domestic economy.

[12] *See* generally E. Hutchful, "IMF Adjustment policies in Ghana since 1966", *Africa Development*, Vol. X No.1/2 1985; D. Rothchild and E. Gyimah-Boadi, "Ghana's Economic Decline and Development Strategies", in J. Ravenhill (ed), *Africa in Economic Crisis* (London, Macmillan, 1980).

At the time when Rawlings returned to power on 31 December 1981 as Chairman of the military-led Provisional National Defence Council (PNDC), Ghana's economic devastation was almost complete. By 1983, the prospect of economic collapse looked real. Real Per Capita had declined by 30% of its 1970 levels, Real Export Earnings by 52% and GDP by 20% of its 1974 level. Real Minimum Wage fell to 10% of its 1975 level, inflation shot up to 123% and the Cedi sold on the black market for more than 3000% of the official rate of 2.75 to the dollar.

1983, therefore, appears to have been a watershed year for Ghana. A series of radical mass mobilisation techniques employed by the PNDC provided some temporary relief but failed to make any significant impact. Behind the scenes, discussions were carried on with the IMF, but the regime became embroiled in a bitter power struggle over whether or not to call in the IMF. The ensuing political turbulence resulted in the departure from the government of the anti-IMF faction, composed mainly of activists of leftist political persuasions.

2.2 Pre-adjustment legal framework for economic activity

A survey of the pre-adjustment legal framework for economic activity reveals that, with the exception of investment regulation, which changed in line with the perceptions and political persuasions of successive governments, the most important legislations governing economic activity were enacted in the immediate post-independence era. Most changes which occurred did so in the 1980s and were motivated by the stabilisation, economic rehabilitation and liberalisation programmes that came with the SAP.

Another factor which emerges from an overview of the pre-adjustment regulatory regimes is that, despite being prohibitory and restrictive in character, many of the laws also provided a framework for future economic policy measures. In the view of one senior legal officer of the Central Bank of Ghana, "the nature of the Ghanaian economy did not allow for full advantage to be taken of the envisaged legal framework".[13] The prohibitions contained in those laws were qualified, not absolute. In many cases, licences and permits could be issued by designated authorities to permit economic activities which would otherwise be prohibited by law. However, the issue or otherwise of such licences and exemptions became a part of economic policy based on the political choices of successive governments.

An example of the above can be found in the area of monetary policy. One of the early laws enacted by the first post-independence government was the Exchange Control Act of 1961, Act 71. The object of the Act was to introduce an exchange control regime in Ghana. The Act laid down a long list of prohibited activities relating to, *inter alia*, foreign exchange transactions, but all the prohibition clauses were preceded by the following phrase: "Except in circumstances as may be prescribed, no person shall ..." The Act also stated that the Minister responsible for Finance shall prescribe

---

[13] Interview with Mr Andrew Boye-Doe, Senior Legal Executive, Bank of Ghana, 22 November 1994.

such banks or other bodies as he thinks fit to be authorised dealers in gold and external currency.[14]

Within a month of Act 71 coming into effect, the Minister of Finance, in pursuance of powers granted him under Section 38 of the Act, issued the Exchange Control Regulations 1961 (Legislative Instrument No. 133) which specified the authorised dealers in gold and foreign currency. Almost all the prohibitions stipulated by Act 71 were made inapplicable where the Bank of Ghana had consented to the transaction concerned. Thus, for example, the Bank of Ghana had power to consent to private companies and individuals buying and selling foreign currency, although this was prohibited by the Act. The fact that this was not done until five years after the introduction of structural adjustment reforms underscores the dependency of the legislative framework on the deliberate economic choices made by successive governments. Because of its anticipatory nature and the framework it provided, Ghana did not need to repeal the Exchange Control Act or enact new laws to, for example, give statutory backing to the operation of private forex bureaux in the country. All that was needed was a Notice from the Bank of Ghana in exercise of its powers under LI 133.

Within the banking sector, Part IV of the Bank of Ghana Act 1963, Act 182 gave the Central Bank a general supervisory jurisdiction over the banks operating in Ghana. Additionally, in order to deal in gold and foreign currency, the banks needed to be designated as authorised dealers by the Minister of Finance. The supervising role of the Central Bank was generally limited to monitoring the operations of and demanding information from the banks. The banks, therefore, had a considerable latitude of activity and generally operated free of stringent controls.

The Banking Act of 1970, Act 339 made inroads into the regulatory framework for banking in Ghana by requiring that banks be licensed by the Bank of Ghana.[15] Several statutory, financial and prudential obligations were imposed on the banks, and the special powers and supervisory role of the Bank of Ghana was strengthened. New accounting and auditing regulations were also introduced and, for the first time, banks were required by law to make annual reports to the Bank of Ghana.[16]

Despite the apparently strong regime of supervision and control instituted by Act 339, the economic abyss into which the country sunk from the mid-1970s mirrored itself in the dismal performance of the banking sector in Ghana. Corruption in domestic banking was facilitated by laxity in the accounting and auditing procedures of the banks. The Central Bank failed to fulfil its supervisory role as it increasingly came under the influence and control of rent-seeking officials and politicians. The consequent failure to utilise the legislative framework to control and regulate banking activity was further compounded by the absence of an adequate regulatory framework to govern informal and non-banking financial institutions.

---

[14] Section 1(1).
[15] Section 2.
[16] Section 24.

Thus, although the legal framework for economic activity was neither evolutionary nor dynamic, it generally tended to contain within it provisions which could be the basis of future economic activity directed at arresting the economic decline. That this did not happen was a result of economic inaction and inappropriate policy choices rather than a failure of the legal order to regulate and direct economic activity.

2.3 Structural adjustment, the IMF and the World Bank

Given the economic abyss into which Ghana had sunk when the PNDC came into power on 31 December 1981, urgent action was needed to prevent chaos. It was agreed that recovery would depend to a large extent on a significant infusion of external capital. The issue of sources of financial support turned out to be a contentious one and resulted in a rift within the PNDC between the radical left using classic dependency argument to oppose an agreement with the IMF, and the moderate faction, whose leaders, including the key economic players of the regime, favoured negotiations and were already having discussions with the IMF.

The decision in August 1982 to call in the IMF was the result of a number of factors some of which pre-dated the PNDC. Toye[17] has noted that serious discussions with the IMF had been going on under previous regimes. It has also been argued that the PNDC was left with no alternative but to go the IMF. Callaghy is of the view that the government had no choice, and refers to the failure of the Soviets to assist when asked by the revolutionary government in Ghana.[18]

Finally, there is the view that the decision to embark on IMF stabilisation was reached largely from necessity.[19] Confronted with the reality of a bankrupt economy on the brink of collapse and chaos, and with very little help coming from elsewhere, the regime had to act quickly or risk eroding its legitimacy. But whatever the reason was, the decision to negotiate with the IMF was a profound one which precipitated violent political consequences and the departure from the PNDC of the radical left.

The programme that was eventually agreed upon between the government and the IMF and World Bank was designed to span three overlapping phases – stabilisation, economic rehabilitation and liberalisation.[20] It was presented to Ghanaians under the label "Economic Recovery Programme" (ERP). The complexity of the ERP lay in the fact that, although these phases were conceptually distinct, they overlapped in implementation, and were carried out under two banners, the ERP I from 1983–86 and ERP II from 1987–1989. Table 1 (opposite) provides an illuminating view of the phasing and sequencing of the SAP.

---

[17] Toye, "1991, Ghana", in Mosley, Harrigan and Toye, *op. cit.*, Volume 2, p. 157.
[18] T. M. Callaghy, 1990, "Lost Between State and Market: The Policies of Economic Adjustment in Ghana, Zambia and Nigeria", in J. Nelson (ed), *Economic Crisis and Policy Choice* (Princeton University Press, 1991), p. 271.
[19] I. Hussain and R. Faruqee (eds), *Adjustment in Africa; Lessons from Country Case Studies* (World Bank, Washington D.C., 1994), p. 160.
[20] *See* World Bank, *Ghana: Policies and Program for Adjustment* (Washington D.C., 1983), p. 73.

Table 1: Ghana: Phasing and Sequencing of Adjustment Process

Policy Reforms	Stabilisation Phase	Rehabilitation Phase	Liberalisation and Growth Phase
(a) *Pricing Reform Package*			
1. Exchange Rate	x	o	+
2. Interest Rate		x	o
3. Wage Rate	x	o	+
4. Energy Prices	x	o	+
5. Infrastructure Prices	x	o	+
(b) *Trade & Industrial Policy Package*			
6. Industrial Incentives		x	o
7. Non-Traditional Export Promotion			x
8. Price Controls		x	o
9. Trade Restrictions			x
(c) *Investment Package*			
10. Public Investment Programme			x
11. Private Sector Initiatives			x
(d) *Taxation & Subsidy Package*			
12. Tax Reforms	x	o	+
13. Consumer Subsidies	x	o	+
14. Producer Subsidies	x	o	+
(e) *Human Resource Development*		x	o
(f) *Institutional Reforms*			
15. Planning Process		x	o
16. Investment, Appraisal, Monitoring & Evaluation		x	o
17. State Enterprises		x	o
18. Export Marketing Boards	x	o	+
19. Mining Companies	x	o	+
20. Statistical & Information System	x	o	+
21. External Debt Management	x	o	+
22. Financial Intermediation		x	o
23. Agriculture Support Services		x	o
24. Civil Service Reform		x	o

Legend: x – initiate action
  o – continue action, evaluate and adjust
  + – sustain action

Source: World Bank, 1983, *Ghana: Policies and Program for Adjustment*, Washington D.C., page 73.

The evolution and progress of Ghana's SAP provides an interesting illustration of IMF/World Bank collaboration and the respective roles they played in the reform policies implemented by many developing countries in the 1980s. Contemporary writers have pointed out that the recent lending policies of the two institutions tend to blur the traditional distinction between the IMF as being concerned with macro-economic programmes intended to ensure stabilisation and correction of balance of payment difficulties, and the World Bank as an international development organisation concerned mainly with micro-economic issues related to project lending.[21]

While this may be so to a large extent, the fact remains that of the one billion dollars of financial assistance received by Ghana between 1983–86, the IMF provided about 60% whilst the World Bank provided only 14%.[22] The financial role of the Fund was to provide foreign exchange needed to support stabilisation measures and to facilitate imports for rehabilitation. This task was executed through three successive Stand-By Arrangements[23] during the first phase of the ERP.

With the advent of the ERP II, however, the respective roles of the IMF and the World Bank appeared to have reversed,[24] with the World Bank emerging from its junior partner role into the dominant position in the design and implementation of micro-economic measures of development policy and financial assistance. The IMF's role was generally limited to providing funds under its Extended Fund Facility,[25] Structural Adjustment Facility[26] and the Enhanced Structural Adjustment Facility[27] mainly to reschedule Ghana's debt servicing problem that had arisen as a result of the short-term Stand-By Arrangements of the ERP I.

The reform measures were continued through the early 1990s resulting in an inflation rate of 11.5% by September 1992. However, a significant increase in money supply in the last quarter of 1992 due to a minimum wage increase resulted in the resurgence of inflationary pressures in the economy.[28] An increase in the price of petroleum products early in 1993

---

[21] Toye, *op. cit.*, p. 162.

[22] J. Loxley, *Ghana: Economic Crisis and the Long Road to Recovery* (Ottawa, The North South Institute, 1988), p. 24.

[23] The Stand-By Arrangement is the traditional mode for the use of the IMF's resources in the upper credit tranches. Usually of one year's duration, their conditionalities focus on demand reduction to reduce payment imbalances.

[24] D. Hogg, *op. cit.*, pp. 28–29.

[25] The Extended Fund Facility was introduced in 1974 by the IMF in a shift towards medium-term financing. Usually of 3 years' duration, they are of a more structural nature and are accompanied by tough conditionalities similar to ESAFs.

[26] The Structural Adjustment Facility was the IMF's response to demands to integrate growth into the adjustment process. Introduced in 1986, it was limited to 70% of a member's Fund quota, was of 3 years' duration and had relatively looser conditionalities attached.

[27] The Enhanced Structural Adjustment Facility was designed to make more funds available to credit-seeking members of the IMF. Members could draw up to 300% of their quota, but had to agree to more stringent conditionalities. Additionally, slippage on an increased number of performance criteria could result in suspension of disbursements.

[28] Bank of Ghana, *Quarterly Economic Bulletin* (Accra, Ghana, October–December 1992), p. 1.

fuelled a rise in the National Consumer Price Index and generated further inflationary pressure. Combined with adverse conditions on the commodity markets and a continuing depreciation of the exchange rate of the Cedi, which had fallen from ¢434 to one U.S. dollar in March 1992 to ¢935 by March 1994;[29] the situation posed a threat to the economic stability of the country.

Although various measures including upward interest rate adjustments, increased open market operations by the Central Bank to mop up excess liquidity and restrictive monetary policies have been employed since then to readjust the economy and reduce inflationary pressure, it might perhaps be over optimistic to assert that Ghana's economy is firmly on the road to recovery. The "fragile strength" tag with which the economic situation in Ghana at the end of 1988 was summed up[30] might still be more appropriate.

2.4 The ERP, conditionality and international law

The implementation of a structural adjustment programme in Ghana generated debates regarding the legal basis of IMF and World Bank activity in the country and other developing countries, the obligations of members in relation to these Bretton Woods Institutions, the legal framework within which conditionalities[31] were used to influence policy choices and the implications of slippage[32] in the implementation of these conditionalities. Discussion of the legal consequences flowing from a breach of the conditionalities has also focused on the fact that, despite significant slippage in some areas of the adjustment process in Ghana, suspension of future drawings was hardly a viable sanction. One reason advanced for this state of affairs is that there was, especially during the latter part of the ERP, the will within the IMF and World Bank to support the adjustment reforms in Ghana.[33]

One of the purposes of the IMF is to make the general resources of the Fund temporarily available to members under adequate safeguards to correct maladjustments in their balance of payments.[34] The preambular clause of the new Article IV stresses that the principal objective of the international monetary system was the development of the orderly underlying conditions necessary for financial and economic stability. Thus, each member undertakes to collaborate with the Fund to, *inter alia*, promote stability by fostering orderly economic and financial conditions and a stable monetary system.

---

[29] Bank of Ghana, *Quarterly Economic Bulletin* (Accra, Ghana, January–March 1994), p. 22.
[30] Callaghy, *op. cit.*, p. 286.
[31] The term "conditionality" is used to describe policy prescriptions which credit-seeking members were compelled to commit themselves to as a prerequisite for IMF and World Bank programme facilities.
[32] "Slippage" refers to non-implementation of specific policy reform that governments commit themselves to in their loan agreements with the World Bank and the IMF.
[33] Interview with Mr Boye-Doe, *op. cit.*
[34] Article 1(v) of IMF Articles of Agreement.

This obligation, within the context of the formulation of structural adjustment programmes for which Fund assistance is being sought, exposes members to the increasing use of the Fund's conditionalities to secure desired policy changes. The employment of conditionalities could be traced to its apparent endorsement in Article V 3(a) of the Articles of Agreement. This article empowers the Fund to adopt policies on the use of its resources that will, *inter alia*, establish adequate safeguards for the temporary use of its resources.

The practice has been for the Fund to use its conditionalities as a tool for ensuring adequate safeguards for the use of its resources. And because members do not have any legal rights to these stand-by arrangements, they are obliged to accept the conditionalities agreed with the Fund in order to gain access to the facilities. Thus, in practice, the use of conditionality has expanded the effective powers and influence of the Fund. In Ghana, IMF conditionality provided a framework for strong Fund influence on domestic policy formulation and implementation, especially during the earlier phases of the ERP.

In contrast to the IMF, the World Bank has traditionally been ascribed with the developmental functions set out in its purposes.[35] The Bank's traditional role has been that of project financing, although under Article III 4 (vii) of its Articles of Association, it was empowered to grant non-project, *i.e.*, programme loans to members for "special circumstances". The thrust of the World Bank lending shifted in 1979 with the decision to embark on programme aid linked to policy changes, and the introduction the next year of the Structural Adjustment Loans (SAL)[36] and Sectorial Adjustment Loans (SECAL).[37] Hogg has remarked that the SALs were closely connected with the IMF's stabilisation programme, since the Bank's Articles of Agreement precluded lending with policy conditions attached unless the member was faced with exceptional circumtances – a situation that could apply to countries implementing IMF stabilisation programmes.[38]

Between 1983 and 1986, World Bank loans to Ghana consisted of programme aid to support balance of payments and project lending for rehabilitation. In 1986, the first World Bank SECAL was extended to Ghana. By 1987, the Bank had ceased to employ the word "condition" in its agreements with Ghana, opting instead for a scheme in which "agreed actions" by the Ghanaian government were listed. The legal significance of this development would lie in the distinction between liabilities arising from a

---

[35] *See* Article 1 of IBRD Articles of Association.

[36] "SALs" are World Bank Programme loans directed at balance of payment support and premised on the existence of an IMF supported stabilisation programme. They are an important element in the World Bank's move from project lending to structural adjustment lending. For a full discussion, *see* Mosley, Harrigan and Toye, *op. cit.*, Volume 1.

[37] "SECALs", which are also programme loans, place greater emphasis on supply-related factors and focus on restructuring a particular sector deemed important in increasing the supply response of the economy. Like SALs, they are medium-term loans, but unlike SALs, they could be granted without the recipient country necessarily having an IMF stabilisation programme already in place.

[38] D. Hogg, "The SAP in the Forest" (Friends of the Earth, 1993), p. 24.

breach of the conditions of a credit agreement, and slippage in the execution of agreed actions.

It may also be pertinent to note the link between conditionality and the concessional character of several of the programme credits. Helleiner is of the view that, in Africa, the need for conditionality is no longer argued primarily on the need to ensure repayment. He suggests that the high degree of concessionality in IMF and World Bank loans implies that, in economic terms, most of these loans would never be repaid.[39] While this may be so, it must be acknowledged that the conditionalities themselves have facilitated the concessions, especially within the context of the structural adjustment programme of Ghana.

2.5 Observations

The preceding sections provided an outline of the economic, legal and institutional background of Ghana's ERP, the general content and thrust of the ERP itself, and the legal basis on which the involvement of the Bretton Woods Institutions in the design and implementation of the ERP could be founded. Ghana's economic problems at the beginning of the 1980s have been shown to be the results of deliberate policy choices and economic inaction. Although adverse external factors contributed to the decline, the effects of these developments could have been minimised by appropriate remedial action, had the political will been present.

This does not in any way imply an uncritical acceptance of IMF and World Bank prescriptions. Given the adverse terms of trade that had affected the country since the late 1970s, the process of economic recovery would have been more difficult without an infusion of capital from external sources. What was required was a process of negotiation which would place the developmental needs of the people at its core, and which would take adequate account of local understanding of the measures and pace of reforms required within the general framework of structural adjustment. Probably, given the economic conditions at the time, Ghana's bargaining position could not have been stronger than it turned out to be. Nevertheless, the country's experience has shown that the leverage exercised by governments in negotiations with the international financial institutions is bound to increase as the reform measures begin to show signs of reversing the decline.

Neither could it be seriously argued that the legal framework which existed at the time was inhibitory to a reform programme. Successive governments possessed the power but lacked the will to take advantage of the legislative framework to promote a real developmental effort. Secondly, although such laws as existed were prohibitory in nature, they also provided a framework for other instruments and notices to be published to accommodate and give a legal basis for policy measures in pursuance of a reform programme. The failure of the legal framework to develop during

---

[39] G. K. Helleiner, "The IMF, the World Bank and Africa's Adjustment and External Debt Problems: An Unofficial View", *World Development*, Volume 20, No. 6 (1992).

those years was therefore the result of the stagnation and decline which characterised the economy between 1972–83. The vigorous legislative activity witnessed in the late 1980s and early 1990s must, therefore, be seen in the light of the resurgence of economic activity that came with the drive towards the market economy promoted by the SAP.

3 MONETARY POLICY REFORMS

This section examines in greater detail the monetary policies pursued by Ghana prior to the ERP and the legal framework underpinning the system as it existed at that time. The term "monetary policy" is employed somewhat loosely to embody policies pursued in the areas of exchange rate, interest rate, money supply and fiscal/revenue activities. This discussion is followed by a general outline of the trajectory of the reform measures in the areas outlined above. More particularly, the role of law in the implementation of the monetary sector reforms is highlighted, and some emphasis is also placed on the legal implications of the reform measures and the impetus given by the reform process to the development of law in this area. New laws which have come into force as a result of the reforms are discussed in some detail. Finally, the argument is put forward that, although the pre-existing legal framework did not necessarily inhibit reforms, the reform process has resulted in an enhanced legal order to regulate fiscal and monetary activities.

3.1 Law and monetary policy before 1983

One of the important factors which contributed to the severe balance of payment difficulties in the 1970s and early 1980s was the disincentive for exports as a result of the over-valuation of the domestic currency, the Cedi. Since the early 1960s, Ghana had followed a fixed exchange rate system. Although this form of exchange arrangement was permitted under the Articles of Agreement of the IMF,[40] it was anticipated that the value of a country's currency would be adjusted periodically to reflect changes in selected economic indices in relation to its major trading partners.

Ghana's Cedi was pegged to the U.S. dollar originally at ¢1.15 to a dollar in 1973. Despite adverse terms of trade, falling purchasing power parity, rapidly rising consumer price index and high inflation rates relative to its major trading partners, the exchange rate of the Cedi remained pegged at ¢1.15, thereby becoming grossly over-valued. In August 1978, the Cedi's value was adjusted to ¢2.75 to the dollar and this rate remained until 1983. By this time, the differential between the official and the parallel market rates was in excess of 2000%. In the circumstances, export volumes declined considerably.

Fiscal policy before adjustment was characterised by falling government revenues, increasing expenditures and severe budget deficits. By 1983,

---

[40] *See* Article IV(2)(B).

government revenue had fallen to 5% of GDP, as against 20% in 1970. Meanwhile, capital expenditure, grants to inefficient public enterprises and a host of other factors resulted in increasing government expenditure, rising from ¢587m in 1972 to ¢11,374m in 1982. The net result of these trends was a large government deficit, which, for the decade before 1983, averaged 7% of GDP.

To compensate for this lopsided fiscal policy, the government increasingly resorted to domestic deficit financing. It has been calculated that between 1972–83, the monetary base expanded by an average annual rate of 40%.[41] The use of direct lending from the Central Bank as the major source of monetary growth had dire consequences on inflation, especially as net foreign assets played a minor role in monetary policy. This thwarted any efforts at arresting the economic decline.

The classical economic view has been that higher interest rates discourage credits and encourage savings, thereby mopping up excess liquidity and helping to control inflation. In Ghana, it would appear that successive governments did not have any coherent policies with regard to interest rates, even when inflation was running out of control. Interest rates remained low during the pre-adjustment period, and over the years, large negative real rates of interest were allowed to develop. In addition, there was hardly any regulation of credits granted by the banks, and large windfall gains therefore accrued to those who could gain access to bank credits. The low interest rates also encouraged consumptive activity and served as a positive disincentive to savings.

Unsurprisingly, the economic inaction and vicious cycle of policy mistakes manifested themselves in a general regulatory inactivity and the gradual emergence of an outdated, inadequate and a largely ignored legal order. Within this dated legal framework, however, possibilities existed for use of relevant provisions to advance policy reforms. The provision in the Exchange Control Regulations of 1961 giving the Bank of Ghana power to consent to dealings in gold and foreign exchange could have been used in an attempt to absorb the parallel foreign exchange market at a much earlier stage than 1989. That it was not done was a classic example of policy inaction which resulted in the non-utilisation of relevant legal provisions.

Another example can be found in the sphere of exchange rate reform. Section 25 of the Bank of Ghana Act 1963, Act 182 gave the Minister for Finance power to take decisions to regulate the exchange rate regime. It therefore provided a mechanism for review of the exchange rate of the Cedi through Executive Instruments and Bank of Ghana notices. But the issue of exchange rate adjustment became highly politicised as governments grappled with public opposition to devaluations. Thus, the Cedi was allowed to become over-valued in the face of dwindling export earnings.

---

[41] *See* C. Leechor, "Ghana: Frontrunner in Adjustment", in I. Hussain and R. Faruqee (eds), *Adjustment in Africa: Lessons from Country Case Studies* (World Bank, Washington D.C., 1994), p. 158.

Regarding interest rate regulation, Section 23 of the Banking Act of 1970 provided that the Bank of Ghana may, by Executive Instrument, make rules with respect to, *inter alia,* the borrowing and lending rates, commissions and other charges of banks, and each bank was obliged to comply with the rules. But even when inflation began to spiral out of control, interest rates were not used as a response measure. Instead, large negative real rates of interest were allowed to develop.

The contention that aspects of the legal order regulating monetary policy were largely ignored is borne out by the obscurity into which provisions relating to money supply fell. Section 22 of the Bank of Ghana Act of 1963, Act 182 required the Bank to report to the Minister any increase in currency circulation exceeding 15% of the figure for the preceding year, indicating the causes and recommending remedial measures. However, in a situation where direct lending from the Central Bank constituted the primary source of deficit financing, it is hardly surprising that the framework for action provided by Act 182 was ignored. It is doubtful if, given the policy choices made by the government at that time, the Bank of Ghana felt obliged to comply with the requirements of the law.

3.2 Monetary reforms under the ERP

As early as 1983, the World Bank identified exchange rate reform as the major source of distortion in the Ghanaian economy and therefore the main plank of the ERP.[42] What happened under the ERP was essentially a deregulation of the foreign exchange regime in Ghana. Dr. Kwesi Botchway, Ghana's Finance Minister since 1982 and a principal architect of the ERP has described reform in exchange rate policy as "one critical dimension in the Ghanaian experience where deregulation was most challenging and, incidentally, also most rewarding".[43] For want of a more eloquent and authoritative statement, his account of the process of exchange control and exchange rate reform is summarised here.

The reform process was accomplished through four phases. The first phase saw a series of discrete exchange rate adjustments, implemented through a multiple exchange rate system leading to a depreciation of the Cedi by about 90% in U.S. dollar terms. The system was, however, abandoned towards the end of 1983 and the official rates were unified with a further devaluation of about 90%. The exchange rate was thereafter adjusted quarterly and by mid-1986, the differential between the official and parallel market rates had been reduced to about 100%.

In order to further depreciate the Cedi, a floating system was introduced in the second phase in September 1986. A dual arrangement was introduced under which foreign exchange was auctioned at two windows – one at a fixed rate for debt service repayments and essential imports, and a second at a higher rate for all other imports. The auction system

---

[42] The World Bank, *Ghana: Policies and Programme for Adjustment* (Washington D.C., 1983).
[43] Botchway, "Deregulating the Foreign Exchange Market in Ghana", in Douglas Rimmer (ed), *Action in Africa* (Royal Africa Society, Heinemann, London, 1993).

was later modified through unification of the two windows. This made possible the abolition of the Import Licensing System in January 1989. By this time, the Cedi had depreciated to about ¢300 to a dollar. However, a large parallel market in foreign exchange persisted, with the differential standing at 25%.

The third phase involved policies to strengthen the role of market forces in the determination of the exchange rate, and to absorb the parallel market. Early in 1988, a major policy decision was taken to permit any corporate or natural person licensed by the Bank of Ghana to operate a foreign exchange bureau to buy and sell foreign exchange at freely negotiated rates. The bureaux operated alongside the official weekly retail auction, but the two were segmented to the extent that the bureaux were not permitted to purchase foreign exchange at the weekly auction. Thus, there remained a wide difference between the bureaux and the official exchange rates.

In 1990, the parallel exchange systems were unified by abolishing the retail auction system. Instead, a weekly wholesale auction in which all authorised dealers, including the bureaux, could participate was instituted to operate alongside an inter-bank and retail foreign exchange market. The adoption of a flexible exchange rate system through the floatation of the Cedi was completed in April 1992 when the Wholesale Auctions were abolished. Since then, the Central Bank's management of the exchange rate has taken place directly in the inter-bank markets. This has entailed a depreciation of the exchange rate of the Cedi to ¢1,100 to one U.S. dollar by early 1995.

The reforms in the exchange rate regime were accompanied by appropriate fiscal and monetary policies. The key element of fiscal policy was resource mobilisation. Tax compliance was improved while collection efforts strengthened. The absorption into official channels of goods and services previously passing through the parallel markets helped to boost government revenue. Meanwhile, the elimination of subsidies to public sector enterprises, restraint on public expenditure and retrenchment within the civil and public service resulted in a rationalisation of government expenditure. The result was a net reduction of the budget deficit.

The improved fiscal discipline made monetary policy more manageable and stabilised the monetary base. The policy goal was to reduce the rate of increase of money supply, through cutbacks in domestic borrowing by Central government, and the use of intensive open market operations as a means of regulating the level of money supply.

During the same period, interest rate reforms became a dynamic aspect of monetary policy in Ghana. The Central Bank rate was periodically adjusted upwards until late 1987 when interest rates were liberalised. The commercial banks were given the power to determine their own savings and lending rates. By 1990, the lending rates had increased from 10% in 1983 to between 24–30%.[44] Table 2 (over) provides an overview of changes in selected economic indices including interest rates between 1982–1994.

---

[44] Bank of Ghana, *Annual Reports 1984–90*.

Table 2:   Ghana: Selected Economic Indices

Year	GDP Growth Rate (%)	Exchange Rate of Cedi to One U.S.$	Average Rates of Inflation (%)	Central Bank Interest Rate (%)
1982	–	2.75	–	8
1983	–	30	–	11
1984	–	52	–	–
1985	5.1	90	10.4	–
1986	5.2	135	24.6	18.5
1987	4.8	180	39.8	21
1988	5.6	230	31.4	–
1989	5.1	300	25.2	–
1990	3.3	360	37.2	21.5
1991	5.3	420	18.0	–
1992	3.9	534	10.0	30
1993	5.0	820	25.0	35
1994	3.3	1050	24.9	33
1995 (*Projected*)	5.0	1135	18	39

Sources: Bank of Ghana Data, *Republic of Ghana Budget Statements, 1985–95*.

Towards the end of 1992, a wage increase granted by the government led to a rise in the rate of increase in money supply from 7.4% to 41.8%.[45] As a result, there was a resurgence of inflationary pressure in the economy. To mop up the excess liquidity in the system, a tight monetary policy was pursued and interest rates increased to about 35%. These measures were, however, not enough to prevent a budget deficit re-emerging in 1992 and 1993, as well as high rates of increase in money supply. Although the high rates of increase in money in circulation continued, an exceptional performance of tax revenues helped the budget to record a surplus in 1994.

Monetary policy in 1995 is projected to be tightened to support a more stable exchange rate and to stem the considerable pressure on prices that the 40% increase in money supply in 1994 is bound to exert. As a first step, the Bank Rate was increased in January 1995 from 33% to 39%. A reduction in the growth in money supply to an ambitious 8% and a budget surplus of 1.2% of GDP have also been programmed. It is also intended to stabilise the exchange rate of the Cedi to the US dollar at around ¢1.135.[46]

3.3 Legal implications of the reforms

One significant factor in the evaluation of the legal implications of monetary reforms under the ERP is the timing of the legislative changes that took place. As noted, before the reforms started in 1983, the monetary sector was regulated largely through the relevant provisions of the Exchange Control Act of 1961, the Bank of Ghana Act of 1963 and the Banking Act of 1970.[47]

---

[45] Bank of Ghana, *Quarterly Economic Bulletin* (October–December 1992), p. 1.
[46] Ghana, *Budget Statement and Economic Policy of the Government* (Accra, 1 February 1995).
[47] *See* Section 2.2.

Despite the fact that monetary reforms were a significant component of the early stabilisation measures, new laws were not enacted until six years after the reforms had started. The new Banking Law was passed in 1989, and it was not until 1992 that the new Bank of Ghana Law was passed to repeal the 1963 Act. Thus, one observation which could be made was that rather than being enacted earlier to give a legal basis for reform measures, the new legal framework was created at a late stage to accommodate reforms already being implemented, and to enable further reform measures to proceed. In a sense, then, the new legal order was a result rather than the catalyst of monetary policy reforms.

Thus, the reform measures described previously were carried out within the framework of the existing law at the time. It has already been noted that, though generally prohibitory in nature, those old laws also contained a framework for future action consistent with the reform measures implemented under the ERP. These provisions were employed to formulate and direct the monetary reforms until a new monetary order had been established, whereupon a legal framework was created to accommodate the changes and give impetus to further reforms.

In this regard, it is significant to recall the relatively small extent to which the IMF and World Bank conditionalities were employed as an instrument for directing the monetary reforms.[48] For example, until 1987, the reform of the foreign exchange rate was handled outside the area of formal bank conditionality. The minor loan conditions later employed dealt more with timetables for further reforms than with the content of the reform measures themselves. The issue of whether Ghana had been in breach of its obligations to the international financial institutions did not, therefore, become pertinent.

It may be useful at this point to examine some of the changes introduced by the new laws, and the legal implications of these changes. The most significant of these changes came via the Bank of Ghana Law of 1992. In order to buttress the role that the Bank had played in shaping fiscal and monetary policy reforms, the institutional structure of the Bank was strengthened, its functions enhanced and its supervisory powers over the banking system placed within a legal framework for the first time.[49] The Bank's principal objects were expanded to include an obligation to act as Banker and Financial Adviser to the Government.[50] Section 29, another new provision, defined the Bank's advisory role by requiring it to proffer advice to government on the monetary operations of the government and its agencies.

Part IV of the Law improved upon the legal framework within which the Bank was to employ mechanisms to fulfil its other object of administering, regulating and directing the currency system. Section 22 of the 1963 Act merely required the Bank to make a report to the Minister when a growth in money supply of more than 15% occurred. In contrast, the new law provided for such a report whenever there was an unusual movement in

---

[48] *See* Toye, *op. cit.*, p. 177.
[49] Bank of Ghana Law 1992, Part II.
[50] Bank of Ghana Law 1992, Section 3(d).

money supply and prices detrimental to balanced growth of the economy.[51] It also granted the Bank for the first time power, after due consultations, to use any instruments of control conferred on it by law to counteract the unusual movements. And in contrast with Act 182, Section 31 of the 1992 Law set out ten mechanisms of monetary policy which the Bank had power to use for the purpose of monetary management.

The provision on interest rate provides an interesting illumination of the manner in which the 1992 law reflects the liberalisation policy pursued within the framework of the financial sector reforms. Section 53 of the 1963 Act gave the Minister power to prescribe maximum interest rates. This power was transferred to the Bank in 1970.[52] However, as already noted, the interest rate regime was liberalised under the ERP. In amending the law to reflect the change in economic policy, the 1992 Law provided only for the alteration of the discount and interest rates of the Central Bank as a means of influencing developments in commercial bank interest rates.

It may also be observed from a reading of Sections 29 to 31 of the 1992 Act that it grants the Bank power to control the level and rate of growth of money supply. The Bank had limited powers to engage in open market operations under the 1963 Act.[53] However, the 1994 Act expanded the range of instruments of monetary control to accommodate the varieties of open market mechanisms employed during the reforms. The 1992 Law also introduced an innovation by extending the requirement that counteracting measures be taken to combat unusual movement in money supply, to include also such movements in prices.

Although exchange rate reforms were one of the critical areas of Ghana's structural adjustment process, it was also one of the areas where legislative reform witnessed the least activity. Article 49 of the 1994 Law was the only provision dealing with exchange rate. Even then, it was a virtual repetition of the earlier provision in the 1963 law giving the Minister power to take decisions relating to the exchange rate.[54] The only change made was a minor amendment requiring that the decision must not merely relate to, but be for the determination of the exchange rate. However, it would appear that this absence of a clearly defined regulatory framework for the exchange rate regime is consistent with the objectives of monetary reforms, which included liberalisation of the exchange rate regime and promoting reliance on market mechanisms.

3.4 Observations

It may be observed from the foregoing analysis that monetary policy reforms in Ghana during the SAP have entailed a revision of the law in this area. The reform process has resulted in an enhanced order for the regulation of fiscal and monetary activities. In so doing, the law has been

---

[51] Bank of Ghana Law 1992, Section 30.
[52] Banking Act 1970, Act 339, Section 23.
[53] *See* Section 28 of the 1963 Act.
[54] *See* Bank of Ghana Act 1963, Section 25 (as amended).

reformed to accommodate the policy reform measures that were pursued and the mechanisms they employed to achieve the objectives, and also to reflect the changing role of the central players in the process of policy formulation. But the changes in the regulatory regime did not imply that the pre-existing legal framework for monetary activities was inhibitory of SAP-type policy measures. As noted, the regime it provided contained flexible mechanisms which could have been used by governments, if so minded, to provide a legal basis for reform oriented policy actions.

This observation is reinforced by the fact that monetary reforms under the SAP were pursued largely within the framework of the legal order that had existed since the early 1960s. In doing so, greater advantage was taken of the general powers of the Minister and the Central Bank under the old legal regime. The various notices issued by the Bank and legislative instruments made by the Minister during the reforms helped to widen the parameters of the emerging legal framework and define its scope. But it was not until a decade after the reform began that laws were passed to give shape to the new legal order.

Ultimately, the reforms in the legislative framework for monetary activity have added a dimension of adequacy and sophistication to the law in that area of economic activity. This development also emphasises the dialectical relationship between law and economic activity in the adjustment process. The cumulative effect of this trend has been to facilitate economic and legal reforms in other sectors of the economy.

4 FINANCIAL SECTOR REFORMS

This section describes initially the legal framework which governed financial activities before structural adjustment, and the actual operations of the institutional arrangements within the financial sector. This is followed by a discussion of the reforms carried out under the Financial Sector Adjustment Programme (FINSAP) and the objectives that they sought to achieve. The relatively high conditionality character of the FINSAP is also underlined. And, because an improvement of the legal framework to ensure effective supervision and enforcement constituted an important part of the World Bank conditionalities, those new legal provisions are discussed in some detail. The implications of these changes for banking operations, the securities markets and other non-banking institutions are also discussed. In concluding, the financial sector is identified as one of the areas where the legal implications of reforms have been most significant. Another argument put forth is that the reforms have resulted in an enhancement of the legal framework for financial activities in Ghana, and the creation of new institutional arrangements with requisite legal underpinnings to promote the intermediation role of the banking sector.

4.1 The background to the reforms

Before the commencement of the FINSAP reforms in 1986, the banking sector was dominated by institutions either owned wholly by the state or in which the state had substantial equity holdings. Of the 11 banks operating in Ghana, seven were state-owned. The over 100 rural banks which existed also operated as public concerns. The operations of the four private foreign-owned banks were limited by provisions in the investment laws of the country which stipulated that at least 40% of their capital must be owned by Ghanaians.[55] The largest existing non-bank financial institutions were also public concerns. The financial sector was therefore largely para-statal in character and operated under direct governmental influence or control.

To this effect, the banking sector in Ghana was regulated by the relevant provisions of the Bank of Ghana Act of 1963 and the Banking Act of 1970. Section 3 of the 1963 Act provided that one of the principal objects of the Central Bank of Ghana was to regulate and direct the banking system in accordance with the economic policy of the government and the provisions of the Act. Part IV of the Act provided a mechanism for fulfilling this obligation by granting the Bank certain powers of control. These included powers to prescribe liquid assets of a specific amount or composition, request from any banking institution any information it requires to ensure compliance with other legal requirements, direct the banks to impose restrictions on expansion of credits and investments and fix minimum paid-up capital.[56]

The Banking Act of 1970 gave further scope and content to the framework provided by the 1963 Act. Section 18 gave the Bank of Ghana (BOG) overall supervisory authority over the business of banking in Ghana. Under the Act, banks had to be licensed by the BOG before they could operate, open, close or relocate any branch. Several other statutory restrictions were imposed on the banks. And, unless otherwise exempted, a bank could not engage in commercial, agricultural, industrial or real estate undertakings.

Other requirements of the banks related to accounting and auditing procedures. Every bank was to maintain proper books of accounts and records of all transactions, appoint an auditor to audit its books annually and furnish copies of the same to the BOG. The auditor's report was to contain full information on the accounts, assets and liabilities and affairs generally of the bank. The auditor was also required to state, *inter alia*, whether or not the bank's transactions were within its powers. The banks were further required to submit to the BOG a monthly statement of assets and liabilities and a half-yearly analysis of loans, advances and overdrafts granted during the period.[57]

However, the BOG was not merely a passive recipient of information. It could lay down policies on granting of advances and make rules in respect of the liquid assets of the banks, borrowing and lending rates, and commissions and other charges.[58] The Chief Examiner of Banks appointed by the BOG was required to examine the affairs of every bank annually to

---

[55] *See* the Investment Policy Decree 1975, Section 7, and the Investment Code of 1981, Second Schedule, Part B, Section 2.
[56] Sections 29–34 of the Act.
[57] *See* Part V of the Banking Act 1970.
[58] Banking Act 1970, Sections 22–23.

ascertain compliance with the law.[59] And to give effect to these powers, the Act gave special enforcement powers to the BOG in cases where a bank's business activities were not in the best interest of its depositors and creditors, where its assets were insufficient to cover its liabilities to the public or where BOG had been notified of inability to meet obligations to creditors and depositors.[60]

It may thus be observed that the legal framework for banking was fairly strict, combining prudential, accounting and auditing requirements with obligations to submit reports to the BOG, which itself had strong powers of supervision and oversight. Thus, within the financial sector, provisions existed for adequate regulation of banking institutions.

However, the same cannot be said in relation to non-banking financial institutions. Apart from the Stock Exchange Act of 1971, which provided a framework for regulating the activities of companies dealing in shares, stocks, bonds, debentures and other marketable securities, there were no comprehensive legal regimes for other non-banking financial activities, like the taking of deposits, making of loans and advances, leasing and hire-purchase activity. Paradoxically, the Stock Exchange, which was anticipated by the 1971 Stock Exchange Act, did not materialise until after the commencement of FINSAP. As a result of the factors above, the non-banking financial sector remained largely unregulated.

Despite this, the failure of the financial sector to fulfil its intermediation role during the years before adjustment was due mainly to the political and economic climate of the period, which promoted corruption and rent-seeking activity and encouraged non-compliance with the statutory obligations imposed on the banks. Further, in view of the prevailing socio-economic climate, there was no will or incentive for BOG to exercise its powers of control, supervision and oversight. Prudential, accounting and auditing requirements were largely ignored and loans and credits were made in contravention of the rules. Most of these loans were neither repaid nor written off. This led to dwindling liquid assets and declining capital bases and adequacy ratios, thereby weakening the financial soundness of the banks. By the early 1980s, the banking system was hovering on the edge of collapse, with the banks generally failing to provide adequate financial intermediation.

4.2 The Financial Sector Adjustment Programme (FINSAP)

FINSAP was divided into two phases. FINSAP I, which ran from 1988–90 had, among its objectives, the creation of a sound prudential and regulatory framework for banking in Ghana; a more effective Banking Supervision Department to enforce prudential rules and regulations and the development of fully liberalised money and capital markets in Ghana.[61] These goals

---

[59] Banking Act 1970, Section 25.
[60] Banking Act 1970, Section 20.
[61] Bank of Ghana, *Annual Report 1989–90*, p. 3.

of FINSAP were in consonance with the World Bank policy objectives of financial sector reforms during the liberalisation and growth phase of Ghana's SAP, *i.e.*, strengthening the financial bases, removing restrictions on financial intermediation and eliminating interest rate and sectoral credit ceilings.[62] Indeed, FINSAP was formulated, designed and implemented under the supervision of the World Bank, which laid down the conditionalities for the process and provided the finance to sustain it.

The reforms were preceded by diagnostic studies of individual para-statal banks, to look at their managerial structure, accounting policies and procedures, loan portfolios, non-performing assets, etc. The banks were then restructured. And in order to strengthen the financial soundness of the banks, the Non-Performing Assets Recovery Trust (NPART) was set up by the Non-Performing Assets (Loans, Investments) Recovery Law of 1990, PNDCL 242 to take over the non-performing portfolios of the banks. This was done through the issue of long-term bonds to the banks in exchange for government guaranteed loans and other obligations of state enterprises and some non-performing obligations of the private sector. The non-performing assets thus taken over were then put up for sale or liquidated. The PNDCL 242 also established an adjudicating Tribunal and gave NPART enforcement powers.

In addition to these, reforms were carried out in other areas of financial activities. Institutional development efforts and prudential regulations were upgraded in 1988 and 1989. The Central Bank ceased to regulate commercial interest rates and rather sought to use the bank rate to influence interest rate movement. Sectoral lending requirements were abolished and in 1992, global and institution-specific credit ceilings were removed in a switch to fully fledged open market operations. Around the same time, a variety of new financial institutions started operating in Ghana, including two discount houses and a leasing company. A Stock Exchange also started operations in Ghana for the first time late in 1990.

The main thrust of FINSAP II, which is still being implemented, is the divestiture of state interest in banking. In 1991, the government broadened the use of government securities as an indirect instrument of monetary control and announced its intention to divest the ownership of the commercial banks. The FINSAP Secretariat was set up to manage the continuation of the adjustment process leading up to privatisation of state interests in banking institutions.

One of the consequences of FINSAP II has been the merger of two state-owned banks and a programme to revitalise the financial sector through the divestiture of 60% of public sector shareholding in selected banking institutions. It is expected that the privatisation exercise would attract individual and corporate as well as strategic foreign investor participation. In addition to these measures, three new private banks were licensed by the BOG to commence operations in 1995 to promote and enhance the benefits of competition.[63]

---

[62] *See* World Bank, *Ghana: Policies and Program for Adjustment* (Washington D.C., 1983), p. 68.
[63] Ghana, *Budget Statement and Economic Policy of the Government of Ghana* (Accra, 1 February 1995), pp. 44–45.

Reforms in the financial sector also encompassed measures to take into account the role of the non-banking financial institutions in promoting intermediation. Initial measures taken included the enactment of new legislations to regulate areas like home mortgage finance, finance lease, the securities industry, discount, finance and acceptance houses, leasing and hire-purchase companies, credit unions, etc.[64]

In addition to these legislative measures, the government is in the process of preparing, in collaboration with the World Bank's IDA, the Non-Bank Financial Institutions Programme. The objective of this project is to implement changes, especially legislative reforms, to promote greater private sector participation in the financial sector. Key areas of support are expected to include the reform of contractual savings institutions and securities markets, diversification of financial instruments and restructuring of incentives attached to financial instruments as well as privatisation of state-owned non-bank financial institutions.[65]

It may be useful to consider at this point, the influence, if any, which World Bank conditionalities had on the FINSAP. In Ghana, FINSAP was one area where the use of conditionalities was most evident. The conditions attached to the World Bank's Financial Sector Adjustment Credit (FINSAC) of mid-1988 were concerned mainly with the promulgation of new banking regulations relating especially to accounting and audit, and their enforcement.[66] These conditions were almost certainly related to the passage, in December of that year, of the Banking (Capital, Audit and Prudential Requirements) Regulations, LI 1389 to prescribe new rules for minimum capital for licences, capital adequacy of banks, payment of dividends, credit control and auditing. Release of later tranches of FINSAC were also conditional on progress in the restructuring of the assets and liabilities of banks, as well as a study for the setting up of a Stock Exchange. The strigent conditionalities attached to FINSAC, which was a World Bank Sectorial Adjustment Loan, were characteristic of the stricter conditionality nature of SECALs, as noted above.

These conditionalities have all been implemented without slippage through the enactment of new laws to facilitate the issue of long-term bonds in exchange for the non-performing assets of the banks, the promulgation of a new Banking Law in 1989 and the establishment of the Stock Exchange in 1990. The conditionalities could, therefore, be regarded as having played an important role in giving impetus and direction to the financial sector reforms.

4.3 The legal effects of financial sector adjustments

The Financial Sector Reforms have resulted in a revision of the legal framework to improve supervision and financial discipline, and the enactment of new laws and regulations to govern areas previously outside the

---

[64] *See* Financial Institutions (Non-Banking) Law 1993 (PNDCL 328).
[65] Ghana, *Budget Statement, op. cit.*, p. 45.
[66] Toye, *op. cit.*, p. 182.

regulatory framework. Between 1988 and 1993, vigorous legislative activity took place as FINSAP unfolded. Nearly a dozen new laws and regulations were promulgated, mostly to regulate specific areas of financial activity and sometimes as apparent responses to World Bank conditionalities. It is proposed to review briefly some of these laws and regulations and assess the changes they introduced.

The earliest of these laws was the Banking (Capital, Audit and Prudential Requirements) Regulations, LI 1389 which was made at the end of 1988. This regulation, passed in response to World Bank demands for the promulgation of such a regulation and for its enforcement, imposed new and higher levels of minimum paid-up capital, capital adequacy ratios and credit controls for banks. The scope of audit reports of the banks was extended beyond the statutory report to include a new and more detailed long report. Reporting requirements to the Central Bank were also strengthened. LI 1389, despite the changes it made, was more of an interim measure, pending a more fundamental review of the banking laws of the country.

That review was achieved in the form of the Banking Law of 1989, PNDCL 225, which was promulgated almost exactly a year later. What this law did was to codify and, in many cases, modify the regime introduced by the Banking Act of 1970 and LI 1389 to reflect the objectives of FINSAP. In some cases, new provisions were enacted to regulate specific and previously unregulated areas of financial activity. For example, the scope of the rules governing minimum paid-up capital was expanded to include new provisions for development banks and rural banks.[67] In addition, some of the new provisions reflected the liberalisation of banking activities that FINSAP was intended to achieve. For example, the 1970 Banking Act prohibited banks from engaging in commercial, agricultural or industrial and real estate activity. The 1989 Act revised this restriction, permitting those activities where the banks established a subsidiary company for that purpose.[68]

In addition, the overall supervisory authority of the BOG over the business of banking in Ghana contained in the 1970 Act was retained and reporting procedures to the BOG were further improved. The banks were now required to submit reports monthly instead of twice a year to show their assets and liabilities, as well as outstanding loans, advances and credits.[69] A new offence was also created for providing the BOG with false or misleading information.[70] Further, in a bid to institutionalise the policy of recapitalisation of the banks started by the NPART, a new provision was made in Section 19 giving the BOG power to fix minimum liquid assets that a bank shall hold. In the area of auditing, the long-form report introduced by LI 1389 was retained, and the auditor's right of access to records and right to demand information expanded.

---

[67] Banking Law 1989, Section 3(2).
[68] Banking Law 1989, Section 14.
[69] Banking Law 1989, Section 17.
[70] Banking Law 1989, Section 20.

The 1989 law made a significant revision of the law relating to disclosure of information by the banks. One important omission of the 1970 Banking Law, which codified the law on banking in Ghana for the first time, was the failure to provide for information disclosure, although arguably, that area of banking activity could be said to have been regulated by the general banking rules relating to confidentiality.

Interestingly, the first domestic regulation on confidentiality, the Banking and Financial Institutions (Request for Information) Decree of 1979, made inroads into the general principles of banking law by imposing on the bank and its employees a duty to disclose any information on the affairs of any customer requested by the government, and making it an offence for failing to do so. This Decree, which, more than any other, eroded public confidence in the banks, was repealed by the 1989 Law. Section 44 of the new Law forbids any official of any bank from disclosing such information except where such disclosure is required by a Court or authorised by the customer or is in the interest of the bank.

An important legal consequence of developments within the area of non-bank financial institutions was the promulgation, in 1993, of the Financial Institutions (Non-Banking) Law, PNDCL 328. Law 328, which was the first of its kind in the history of the country, sought to provide a legal framework for the operation of the emerging non-bank financial institutions. It defined these institutions in its schedule to cover the following:

(a) discount houses;
(b) finance houses;
(c) acceptance houses;
(d) building societies;
(e) leasing & hire purchase companies;
(f) venture capital funding companies;
(g) mortgage financing companies;
(h) savings & loans companies; and
(i) credit unions.

The law, which was based on the model of the banking law, required all such institutions to be licensed by the BOG and prescribed levels of minimum paid-up capital, capital adequacy and liquidity ratios and liquid assets. It also gave the BOG supervisory authority over the business of these institutions. The Central Bank was given special powers to revoke licences, direct remedial steps to be taken, be notified of changes in the operations of the institutions and to make rules for the proper functioning of all non-bank financial institutions. Specific obligations relating to accounting, auditing, submission of returns and reports to the BOG and other prudential requirements were imposed on the non-bank financial institutions.

Another area of financial activity which received legislative attention as a consequence of FINSAP was the securities industry. It may be recalled that Ghana had no Stock Exchange despite the creation of a legislative framework to that effect by the Stock Exchange Act of 1971. In an apparent response to the World Bank conditionalities, the first Council of a Stock

Exchange was constituted in 1990. One of the first Acts of the Council done in exercise of its powers under the 1971 Act was to issue two regulations to lay the foundations for the operation of the Stock Exchange pending the enactment of a new law to regulate the securities industry in general. The Stock Exchange Listing Regulations of 1990, LI 1509 outlined the requirements for admission as a member of the Stock Exchange, and the procedure, criteria and methods for listing on the exchange. The Stock Exchange Membership Regulations, LI 1510 which were issued alongside LI 1509, set out in greater detail the rules governing eligibility and conditions for membership of the Stock Exchange, the relationship between both members and the investing public, and members and the Stock Exchange authorities.

The Securities Industry Law of 1993, PNDCL 333 was passed to both accommodate the developments in the regulation of the securities market and also to lay down a broad framework for the industry in general. Its most important contribution in this regard was to institutionalise the reforms in the industry by establishing a Securities Regulatory Commission with advisory, supervisory, regulatory and oversight powers.[71] The 1971 Law was modified to empower the Commission to receive and approve applications for the establishment of a Stock Exchange. In addition, rules were made on the issue and regulation of dealer's licences, registers of interest in securities, conduct of securities business, accounts and audits and trading in securities. The Law, therefore, sought both to regulate existing institutional arrangements and provide a framework for other anticipated activities within the securities industry, such as Unit Trusts, Mutual Funds and Fidelity Funds.

Several other of the laws enacted in the financial sector were promulgated to give legal backing to specific securities institutions that had already been set up or were in the process of being set up, whilst others facilitated the implementation of certain policy measures that were part of FINSAP. For example, the Home Mortgage Finance Law of 1993, PNDCL 329 was promulgated to give legal backing to the establishment of the Home Mortgage Finance Scheme and the creation of the Home Mortgage Finance Company to administer the scheme. In doing so, the Law gave scope and substance to the framework for the regulation of mortgage finance business provided by the Financial Institutions (Non-Banking) Law of 1993, PNDCL 328.

Yet another example of legislation made to provide substantive rules within the framework provisions of PNDCL 328 was the Finance Lease Law of 1993, PNDCL 331. Under the Law, the BOG was given power to prescribe eligibility requirements, issue licences for the business of financial leasing and receive reports from the leasing companies. The substantive rules imposed by the Law covered such diverse areas as the requirements for and contents of a lease agreement, rights and obligations of both the lessee and the lessor, registration and assignment of lease agreement,

---

[71] *See* Parts I and II of the Law.

repossession by lessor, third party claims and variations of the rights, duties and liabilities of the parties.

It can thus be observed that, whilst in economic terms, FINSAP has resulted in the liberalisation of banking business and the emergence of new non-bank financial sector institutions, its legal effects have been both profound and far reaching. The general legislative framework has been enhanced by the revisions made in the existing law and the enactment of new laws to accommodate and give further impetus and direction to the reform process. The enforcement of these new rules and regulations may be expected to improve financial discipline and promote the ability of the banking and other non-bank financial institutions to play their role of financial intermediation effectively.

4.4 Observations

The financial sector has been one area of economic activity in Ghana where structural adjustment has had the most significant legal implications. It is arguable whether this trend was the result of the profound nature of the changes brought about by FINSAP or was due to the need to comply with the conditionalities laid down by the World Bank, or indeed, whether it was the conditionalities that generated the steadfast pursuance of far-reaching reforms. Whichever be the case, there is little doubt that the implementation of FINSAP has entailed very little slippage on the World Bank conditions.

The new laws and regulations called for in the conditions have mostly been put in place. Liberalisation of banking business has been achieved to a large extent, whilst measures to privatise the state-owned banks are being implemented. Of these, the privatisation measures have been the most controversial. Irrespective of the value judgments placed on these developments, there can be little controversy over the fact that FINSAP has helped develop the regulation of financial activities in Ghana through reform of the existing law relating to banking and the provision of a new framework for non-banking financial business in Ghana.

In addition to the development of the legal framework for financial activities, the new legislations have also been geared towards the promotion of a market-based approach to banking and non-bank financial activities. In pursuance of the twin objectives of deregulation and liberalisation, less reliance has been placed on direct state intervention in preference for market instruments as a means of indirect control of the financial markets. The stricter accounting, auditing and prudential requirements imposed on the financial institutions do not necessarily conflict with the goals of the reform process. This is because it may be necessary to impose such higher standards if the institutions are to be allowed to exercise greater freedom of activity without undermining financial discipline and the need to prevent a relapse into the corruption and decay of the 1970s. It is for the same reason that the strengthening of the overall supervisory role of the BOG can be viewed as consistent with liberalisation as a policy objective of the reform programme.

Finally, it is submitted that the new legal framework has also improved the compliance mechanism to ensure that the widespread disregard of the rules characteristic of the decade before the ERP does not repeat itself. The new rules on requirements and procedures for the submission of periodic returns and reports to the BOG, and for the Bank to direct remedial measures, are an important part of this process. Given the political will to encourage respect for, and enforcement of these new rules, the new legal order created by the financial sector reform process has the potential of emerging as one of the more significant achievements of the ERP.

5 CONCLUSIONS

In this chapter, an attempt was made to trace the effects of the structural adjustment reforms on the domestic law affecting monetary and financial activities in Ghana. As a prerequisite to this, attention was drawn to the state of economic and legal conditions prior to adjustment. The respective roles of the IMF and the World Bank during ERP I and II were also addressed within the context of how their conditionalities impinged on the reform process. The link between the new regulatory regime that evolved and the reform process has also been highlighted to show how the development of law influences, and is in turn influenced, by economic policy.

One point that emerges from the previous discussion is the fact that the regulatory regime governing financial and monetary activity prior to adjustment was restrictive in character and limited in scope and substance. But it also provided a framework within which new instruments, rules and regulations could be made to accommodate the effects of the reforms, and also to regulate new and emerging areas of economic activity resulting from the reforms. Again, the character of the regulatory framework was such that these rules could be made even where the reform measures were inconsistent with the neo-classical economic philosophy which lies behind policy measures advocated by the IMF and the World Bank.

The fact that some aspects of the reform process were carried out within the framework of the legal order established in the 1960s and 1970s, is an indication of the potential of the pre-adjustment legal regime. The supervising and licensing powers of various authorities were utilised to carry the reform process forward. As a result, most of the rules and regulations which accompanied the reform measures came by way of legislative and executive instruments, Bank of Ghana notices and regulations, and the granting of permits and licences. The enactments which were made later fell into two categories: those that created a new regulatory framework by amending or repealing previous laws and those that provided substantive rules to regulate specific areas of activity that had emerged with the move towards a market economy.

Ghana's SAP has had significant legal consequences. The role of law in the reform process has depended, to an extent, on the specific sector in question. In some areas like monetary policy, the role played by legal considerations during the implementation of the ERP was minimal. But in others like the financial and investment sectors, laws played a much more significant role. Secondly, whilst in some areas, the new order provided the legal framework for economic reform measures, in others, the new regulatory framework came to accommodate reform measures already in place.

The SAP has also exposed Ghana to the influence of the IMF and World Bank through the conditionalities imposed upon the process. The legal basis of conditionality has been traced to relevant provisions in the Articles of Agreement of the Bretton Woods Institutions. In Ghana, conditionalities were employed more in financial sector reforms that in monetary policy reform. This does not, however, mean that the SAP in general was a low conditionality process. Nevertheless, slippage in the areas discussed above were minimal. And, given the Ghanaian circumstances, it is questionable if serious consideration would have been given to the employment of sanctions had there been significant slippage.

The character of the new laws and regulations has differed from the old legal order in that they have provided for a wider scope of economic activity. The framework has broadened beyond that established by the old order. The new laws have also added greater clarity, content and substance to the regulation of domestic economic activity. In this regard, these new laws have enhanced the legal underpinning of the current economic environment in Ghana which seeks to promote deregulation and privatisation and diminish the intervention of the state in the economy.

Finally, the legal effect of SAP has been to change the character of domestic economic law. The old framework regime has been replaced with a legal order that combines a general framework with substantive laws that underpin the adjustment process, strengthen its institutional structure and arrangements and regulate the new economic activities that have emerged in the wake of the ERP. In this sense, then, the SAP can be said to have revised the regulatory regime as it affects monetary and financial activities, and initiated the evolution of a new legal order for economic activity in Ghana. Ultimately, because of its underlying economic philosophy, this new legal order could be expected to facilitate and promote the creation of a market economy in Ghana.

II.   Banking Market Issues

7. The Domestic Payment System: Policies, Structure, Operation and Risk

Benjamin Geva[1]

1 INTRODUCTION

Being the lifeline of any financial activity and in fact of the exchange economy in general, the payment system is more than paper money and coin ("currency"). The payment system was thus broadly defined to consist of the set of rules, institutions and technical mechanisms for the transfer of money.[2] It was similarly stated that "[t]he modern payment system is a complex set of arrangements involving such diverse institutions as currency, the banking system, clearinghouses, the central bank, and government deposit insurance".[3] In turn, it was said that "it is useful to think of payment clearing and settlement as analogous to a motor – a crucial component necessary for every car and truck but only part of the total from the viewpoint of the final purchaser".[4]

This chapter will focus on the interbank delivery and settlement mechanism of the payment system, namely, only the "motor" of the entire payment apparatus. The chapter will thus address the structure, underlying basic policies, requirements and design of the payment system. It will further discuss the components and risks of the domestic large-value payment system ("LVTS"), whose operation lies at the heart of the payment system. Ultimately, the chapter will set out the fundamentals of the legal regime governing large-value transfers.

---

[1] LLD., Professor of Law, Osgoode Hall Law School, York University, North York, Ontario.

[2] B. J. Summers, "The Payment System in a Market Economy", in B. J. Summers (ed.), *The Payment System* (Washington, D.C., IMF, 1994), 1 at 1.

[3] M. S. Goodfriend, "Money, Credit, Banking and Payment System Policy", in D. B. Humphrey (ed.), *The U.S. Payment System: Efficiency, Risk and the Role of the Federal Reserve* (Boston/Dordrecht/London, Kluwer Academic Publishers, 1990), 247 at 247.

[4] B. K. Stone, "The Electronic Payment Industry: Changes, Barriers and Success Requirements from a Market Segments Perspective", in Humphrey (ed.), *supra* note 3, 13 at 21.

2 POLICIES AND STRUCTURE

Bruce Summers[5] enumerates seven principles that can serve as building blocks in the development of modern payment systems. The first general principle is that a payment system that relies on fiat money as a store of value and medium of exchange must enjoy price stability if an effective and efficient payment system based on the national currency is to develop. Stated otherwise, high inflation is the principal enemy. A second general principle is that a nation's monetary regime, which defines the terms and conditions under which deposit money held in commercial banks and the central bank can be used, plays a major part in determining the choice of design for the payment system. Factors such as the level of commercial banks' required reserves at the central bank, eligibility of assets to meet reserve requirements, and whether reserve balances earn interest, may influence the relative attractiveness of clearing through correspondent banking networks versus clearinghouses and of relying on net versus gross settlement.

The third general principle is that the technical efficiency of the payment system influences the efficiency with which the stock of deposit money balances in banks is used and the degree of credit and liquidity risk and fraud risk carried by a particular payment system. The fourth principle is that the payment process in a modern economy centers around economic actors' management of their stocks of currency and bank deposits and their access to sources of credit that can be used to obtain money balances. Identifying and managing credit and liquidity risks is thus an inherent part of the payment process. The fifth principle concerns the legal framework contributing substantially to the certainty of payment and to the overall risk inherent in the payment process.

The sixth principle recognizes that the payment system has public good characteristics that require a certain amount of official oversight and supervision. Finally, under the seventh principle, it is universally accepted that final interbank settlement is best accomplished by the transfer of balances held in accounts with the central bank. However, in this context, the nature of such settlement (whether gross or net), the choice of technology, and the precise division of labour between the commercial and central banks, remain open questions.

According to Hans Blommenstein and Bruce Summers,[6] the banking system is the instrumentality through which payments are made. It consists of commercial banks and the central bank. Under a two-tier banking structure, commercial banks provide services to the non-bank public, including non-bank financial firms, as well as other commercial banks. On its part, the central bank provides services to commercial banks and issues bank notes and coins (currency). Core services provided by banks are deposits

---

[5] In Summers (ed.), *supra* note 2 at 4–7.
[6] H. J. Blommestein and B. J. Summers, "Banking and the Payment System", in Summers (ed.), *supra* note 2 at 15.

and loans. The former are bank liabilities, the latter are bank assets. Payment services are stated to be related to deposits, loan, and associated account services that banks provide to their customers. Bank payment services must be competitive *vis-à-vis* currency supplied by the central bank. Banks must thus provide interaccount transfer facilities as well as conversion facilities allowing interconvertibility of payment mechanisms. Especially for wholesale customers, credit services are offered as a direct extension of account and payment services. Commercial banks thus provide settlement accounts and liquidity needed to meet their customers' needs in making payments. Interbank settlement occurs through interbank correspondent relationships, and the nostro accounts commercial banks hold with the central bank. It is by means of these nostro accounts that commercial banks achieve final settlement in central bank money. The payment system hierarchy is described as an "inverted pyramid",[7] with the central bank at the very pinnacle, and commercial bank customers at the base.

Together with the conduct of monetary policy and oversight of banking and financial markets, involvement in the payment system is an integral component of the central bank's three-part overall mandate.[8] Until the 1980s, the central bank's interest was limited to operational and automation aspects of the payment system. In contrast, operational and policy linkages between the payment system and other primary central bank responsibilities are overwhelmingly recognized today. Thus, in connection with the payment system, the central bank has supervisory, operational, as well as policy responsibilities. The supervisory role relates primarily to clearing organizations and banks participating in the payment system. Operational tasks are in the areas of interbank settlement and the large-value transfer system. Policy responsibilities address the structure of private clearing and settlement arrangements. A complex and delicate balance characterizes the central bank's multiple responsibilities, as a supervisor, operator, and policy setter, in the payment area.

From the point of view of the banking system, delivery and clearing mechanisms for payment instruments are interbank systems, interbank correspondent arrangements, interbank clearing house arrangements, and central bank arrangements. Credit arrangements and ancillary banking facilities are also important in the construction and operation of a national payment system.[9]

Historically, "the evolution of the payment system has been driven by efficiency gains from substituting credit (claims on particular institutions) for commodity money".[10] Thus, in early history, recognizability and

---

[7] *Ibid* at 25 where the source is acknowledged to be E. G. Corrigan, "Perspectives on Payment System Risk Reduction", in Humphrey (ed.), above note 3 at 129.

[8] *See* J. A. Spindler and B. J. Summers, in Summers (ed.), above note 2 at 164. Some aspects of those functions may be carried out, at least in part, by other public authorities.

[9] *See e.g.*, J. C. Marquardt, "Payment System Policy Issues and Analysis", in Summers (ed.), above note 2 at 116.

[10] Goodfriend, above note 3 at 248, on whom the ensuing discussion (until the paragraph preceding the one containing note 15) draws. The analysis (up to the emergence of paper money) further draws on B. Geva, "From Commodity to Currency in Ancient History – On Commerce, Tyranny and the Modern Law of Money" (1987), 25 *O.H.L.J.* 115.

portability led to particular commodities ("primitive money")[11] to be used as money (namely universal medium of exchange and unit of account). Recognizability was further enhanced with standardization and ultimately the attachment of the state seal to standardized metallic pieces ("coins") attesting to the quality and quantity of each metallic unit.[12] Further efficiency was ultimately achieved with the bank note serving as a warehouse receipt or document of title for deposited ("lent") coins, or more specifically, their sum. Being lighter than the coin, the bank note was also more easily portable. As such, it was put in circulation as paper money.[13]

Warehousing developed into banking relatively quickly. Depositaries ("banks") realized that not all deposited coins must be permanently stored and that only a quantity designed to meet anticipated demand for coins by depositors ("fractional reserve") must be kept idle. The rest could be invested (or lent) thereby reducing storage charges and enhancing efficiency. This, however, meant that each bank note was not fully collateralized and its value had become dependent on the creditworthiness of its issuer. Ultimately, it was thus only the bank note of the central bank, being backed by the state, which survived as paper money.

Nonetheless, banks remained instrumental in the development of the payment system. Indeed, further saving in portability (and hence reduction in the risks of loss and theft) could be accomplished by carrying out payments not in *specie* but rather by means of interdeposit transfers. Through the establishment of interbank correspondent relationships, non-cash payments could be carried out among customers of different banks primarily by means of the cheque (drawing on deposited coins).[14] An efficient interbank system purporting to reduce interbank cash deliveries required banks to keep interbank balances, thereby forcing them to monitor each other. Thus, to support efficient payment services for their customers, banks specialized in information-intensive credit extension, first with respect to their fellow bankers. They promptly carried over this specialization to non-financial firms as well, namely outside the payment system. Non-traded information-intensive loans have thus become the principal assets of banks. In turn, specialization in non-traded loans is an explanation to the par valuation of bank deposits, that is, to the fact that depositors' return is independent of the fortune of the bank's investment. This is so in the absence of

---

[11] "Primitive money" was defined to be "a unit or an object conforming to a reasonable degree to some standard of uniformity, which is employed for reckoning or for making a large proportion of the payments customary in the community concerned, and which is accepted in payment largely with the intention of employing it for making payment". In fact, it was a chattel with intrinsic utility and economic value, which is served as a unit of account and medium of exchange. *See e.g.*, P. Einzig, *Primitive Money*, 2nd ed. (Oxford, Pergamon Press, 1966), 317.

[12] The process took place in ancient history, during the Greek and Roman eras.

[13] This occurred during the 17th and 18th centuries in England.

[14] That is, in a typical setting, a customer of a bank delivered a cheque to his or her creditor. The cheque instructed the customer's bank to pay the creditor. The creditor deposited the cheque in his or her bank that collected payment, ultimately through an adjustment in an interbank account.

an objective cost-effective mechanism facilitating the ongoing evaluation of non-traded information-intensive loans. A linkage between the value of demand deposits and the value of the bank's investment would have required such a mechanism. Furthermore, par-value deposits, like bonds, are an optimal part of a financial package to most efficiently monitor management and ensure an efficient choice of assets.

Subsequently, efficiency generated the establishment of multilateral clearing arrangements to substitute numerous bilateral interbank correspondent clearing facilities. The private clearing house introduced central collection, collective settlement, centralized holding of reserves, more extensive interbank lending, and payment finality. Ultimately, however, it was only settlement on the books of the central bank that could provide finality equivalent to that of the physical delivery of gold or central bank paper money. Also, the central bank's monetary policy has become instrumental in maintaining the stability of the payment system. Finally, deposit insurance and prudential supervision of banks have contributed to the public confidence and hence the stability and safety of the payment system.

The principal operational and financial goal of payment system policy is the safe and efficient transfer of money. In this context, efficiency includes the reliable, timely, and low-cost transfer of money. Auxiliary goals are to promote liquid money markets, to facilitate the conduct of monetary policy, and to promote open and competitive financial markets.[15]

Payment system policy is designed to promote efficiency and reduce risk. Efficiency for users implies that benefits of using a particular payment instrument must outweigh its costs. Efficiency for suppliers implies that benefits, including revenues, of providing particular payment, clearing and settlement services, must outweigh their costs, including a market-based return on investment. Overall efficiency in the payment services market requires that both users and suppliers of such services behave efficiently. Policies stimulating payment system efficiency are in the area of standards, competition, law, monetary regulation, and central bank services.

Payment system float undermines efficiency.[16] Float is constituted by the accounting effects of the asynchronous posting of payment entries to the accounts of the payor and the payee. Stated otherwise, payment system float is the balance sheet effect of crediting (in a debit transaction like a cheque) or debiting (in a credit transfer) the originator's account before the offsetting entry is made to the receiver's account.

Float can cause significant distortions to the payment system and decrease its efficiency. Because of the float, some parties may have the use of funds at the expense of others who are legally owed those funds. Float thus means that somebody grants or receives free or subsidized credit. Float poses credit and liquidity as well as fraud risks and has an impact on the implementation of monetary policy.

---

[15] *See* Marquardt, *supra* note 9.
[16] *See* J. M. Veale and R. W. Price, "Payment System Float Management", in Summers (ed.), *supra* note 2 at 145.

Float is caused by posting procedures, transportation, holdovers, back-logs, and processing errors. Accordingly, improvement in delivery and processing efficiency that reduces delays is one approach to dealing with float. A second means of controlling float is to use availability schedules that synchronize accounting entries for the payor and the payee regardless of the time it takes to process the payment item itself. Cash management services offered by banks help customers to handle float. Such services are cash concentration, disbursement, and investment.

Electronic delivery and processing of payment orders ("electronic banking" or EFT) reduces and ultimately eliminates payment system float. Electronic banking may further enhance efficiency by substituting automation equipment costs for labor costs. Obviously, the latter is an efficiency again only where, taking into account also payment volumes, labour is more expensive than advanced technology.[17]

3 MULTILATERAL NETTING: BASIC PRINCIPLES[18]

Broadly speaking, a machinery facilitating the multilateral exchange ("clearing") of obligations and their payment ("settlement") is a clearing house. In any given country, so far as cashless payments are concerned, the national payment system consists of nationwide clearing house arrangements for the multilateral interbank clearing and settlement of payment orders. The payment orders exchanged could be embodied in pieces of paper or in electronic messages. Settlement could be for each payment order individually ("gross" settlement), or for resulting balances ("net" or "net net" settlement). Ultimately, the nationwide interbank settlement is usually completed on the books of the central bank. Indeed, for each currency, "central bank money", in the form of credit in an account held at the central bank, is as good as cash, *i.e.* bank notes and coins.

Gross settlement requires individual payment for each obligation. Netting reduces the number of actual payments; payment is made solely for netted amounts of obligations rather than for each one individually. In bilateral netting, one payment is made between each pair of counterparties for a series of bilateral obligations, whereas in multilateral netting ("net nettings"), one payment is made by or to each of the counterparties, to or from a central counterparty, for a series of multilateral obligations.

According to Jeffrey Marquardt,[19]

Since multilateral net settlement systems settle payments on a multilateral net basis at the end of a banking day instead of sequentially in real time, these systems can

---

[17] *See* Marquardt, *supra* note 9 at 123.
[18] This and the ensuing section(s) draw heavily on my previous 3 works: *The Law of Electronic Funds Transfer* (New York, Matthew Bender, 1992 updated to 1994), particularly Chapters 3 and 4; "The Clearing House Arrangement" (1991), 19 *Can. Bus. L. Rev.* 138, and "International Funds Transfers: Mechanisms and Laws", in J. J. Norton, C. Reed and I. Walden (eds.), *Cross-Border Electronic Banking* 1 (Lloyd's of London Press, 1995).
[19] J. C. Marquardt, "Monetary Issues in Payment System Design", in Summers (ed.) *supra* note 2, 41 at 44.

generally be expected to require less central bank money to settle a given value of payments than a real-time gross settlement system. Thus, the higher the relevant measure of the cost of using central bank money to settle payments, the greater the monetary incentives for commercial banks, holders of central bank money to install and use multilateral net settlement systems rather than real-time gross settlement systems.

Stated otherwise, "[m]ultilateral net settlement systems tend to economize on the use of central bank money relative to gross settlement systems, essentially by substituting explicit or implicit interbank intraday credit, extended through netting for central bank money".[20] As a rule, the lower are reserve requirements in the form of accounts at the central bank, as well as the interest (if any) payable on such reserve accounts, the greater is the monetary incentive to install a multilateral net settlement system.

According to the Lamfalussy Report,[21] the following are minimum standards for the design and operation of cross-border and multi-currency netting and settlement schemes:

(1) Netting schemes should have a well-founded legal basis under all relevant jurisdictions.

(2) Netting scheme participants should have a clear understanding of the impact of the particular scheme on each of the financial risks affected by the netting process.

(3) Multilateral netting systems should have clearly defined procedures for the management of credit risks and liquidity risks which specify the respective responsibilities of the netting provider and the participants. These procedures should also ensure that all parties have both the incentives and the capabilities to manage and contain each of the risks they bear and that limits are placed on the maximum level of credit exposure that can be produced by each participant.

(4) Multilateral netting systems should, at a minimum, be capable of ensuring the timely completion of daily settlements in the event of an inability to settle by the participant with the largest single net-debit position.

(5) Multilateral netting systems should have objective and publicly disclosed criteria for admission which permit fair and open access.

(6) All netting schemes should ensure the operational reliability of technical systems and the availability of back-up facilities capable of completing daily processing requirements.

"Netting" is the process of establishing the amount owed by one counterparty to another by adjusting the mutual claims of each one on the other. In that process, the net amount owed by one counterparty to another is established by subtracting the gross amount owed by the latter to the former, from that owed by the former to the latter.

---

[20] *Id*. at 52.

[21] *Report of the Committee on Interbank Netting Schemes of the Central Banks of the Group of Ten Countries* (Bank for International Settlement, Basle, November 1990).

Netting arrangements are in the form of either "position netting" or "netting by novation".[22] "Position netting" is an arrangement which facilitates the discharge of two bilateral gross obligations between two counterparties by one payment of the net amount. This is also known as "payments netting" or "bulking of payment". It can be carried out either on the basis of a pre-existing agreement ("binding payments netting") or by the actual acceptance of the net amount in discharge of the two debts. Either way, until payment is made, each party remains legally obligated for the gross amounts.

"Netting by novation" is a species of "novation". In general, "novation amounts to the extinction of [an] old obligation, and the creation of a new one".[23] Stated otherwise:[24]

Novation is a transaction by which, with the consent of all the parties concerned, a new contract is substituted for the one that has already been made. The new contract may be between the original parties ... or between different parties, e.g. where a new person is substituted for the original debtor or creditor ...

Where substitution is involved, novation is thus "a contract between debtor, creditor and a third party that the debt owed by the debtor shall henceforth be owed to [or by] the third party".[25]

"Netting by novation" is the replacement of two mutual gross obligations by one single net obligation for the net amount. In effect, the original gross obligations are discharged.

Netting, whether position or by novation, can be either bilateral or multilateral. As discussed, bilateral netting involves solely two counterparties and establishes the net amount owed from one to another. Multilateral netting involves more than two counterparties and establishes the net amount owed between each one and all others. This amount is referred to as a "net net" and is reached by transforming all bilateral debts between a pair of counterparties to multilateral net nets between each counterparty and all others. The mutuality between two of the counterparties in a bilateral netting is thus replaced by the mutuality between each counterparty and all others often represented by a central counterparty.[26] Multilateral netting underlies the operation of the clearing house arrangement.

---

[22] *See*, in general, *Report on Netting Schemes* (Bank for International Settlement, Basle, February 1989) known as the Angell Report, as well as P. R. Wood, *English and International Set-Off* (London, Sweet & Maxwell, 1989), particularly at 185–92.

[23] P. S. Atiyah, *An Introduction to the Law of Contract*, 4th ed. (Oxford, Clarendon Press, 1989), 402.

[24] *Cheshire and Fifoot's Law of Contract*, 11th ed., M. P. Furmston (ed) (London, Butterworths, 1986), 505–6.

[25] G. H. Treitel, *The Law of Contract*, 7th ed. (London, Stevens & Sons, 1987), p. 498.

[26] "Mutuality" is premised on the principle that "one man's money shall not be applied to pay another man's debt": *Jones v. Mossop* (1844), 3 Hare 568 at 574, 67 E.R. 506, *per* Wigram V.C. In connection with the set-off required for netting, mutuality means that "the two claims must be between the same parties in the same right". *See* R. M. Goode, *Legal Problems of Credit and Security*, 2nd ed. (London, Sweet & Maxwell, 1988), 154. For an extensive discussion on principles of mutuality see Chap. 14 of Wood, *supra*, note 22.

Netting avoids the multiplicity of reciprocal payments (in position netting) as well as of reciprocal obligations (in netting by novation) through the exercise of the right of set-off. "Set-off" is defined as "the discharge of reciprocal obligations to the extent of the small obligation". Accordingly, "where a creditor claims a debt from his debtor and the debtor has a cross-claim on the creditor, then, if the debtor can reduce or extinguish the amount of the creditor's claim by his cross-claim, the debtor is said to set-off".[27]

At common law,[28] the right of set-off "is generally characterized as being, not a modification of an obligation, but an incident of its enforcement".[29] It is "merely a convenient mode of settling mutual accounts or preventing multiplicity of actions between the same parties".[30] In contrast to the civil law "compensation" which operates automatically by the sole operation of law to extinguish mutual obligations,[31] set-off at common law is "a personal privilege, and not an incident or an accompaniment of the debt".[32] It "is not a defense, but a cross action [which] concedes the validity of the plaintiff's claim, and is founded upon an independent cause of action in favor of the defendant, who may at his election assert it by way of set-off, or enforce it by a separate suit".[33]

By statute, the right of set-off can be asserted by the defendant by way of defence.[34] The right is available only in an action for payment of a debt due from the defendant to the plaintiff and can be used solely in relation to a debt due from the plaintiff to the defendant;[35] that is, both reciprocal claims must be in liquidated amounts due by one to the other.[36] The right exists in England by statute since 1729[37] and is currently provided for in Ontario in s. 111 of the Courts of Justice Act.[38] It is called "statutory set-off", or

---

[27] Wood, *supra* note 22 at 5.

[28] *See*, in general, B. Geva, *Financing Consumer Sales and Product Defences in Canada and the United States* (Toronto, Carswell & Co. Ltd, 1984), 134.

[29] B. Crawford, *Crawford and Falconbridge Banking and Bills of Exchange*, 8th ed. (Toronto, Canada Law Book Inc., 1986), vol. 2, 1730.

[30] *Falconbridge on Banking and Bills of Exchange*, 7th ed., A. W. Rogers (ed.) (Toronto, Canada Law Book Ltd, 1969), 671. This quote does not appear in the current edition (*see* note 29). Instead, the author states, "[t]o prevent circuity, mutual debts taking the form of liquidated demands may be set-off, the one against the other, with judgment being rendered for the net balance". *Id.*, vol. 1, 786.

[31] G. Nicholls, "The Legal Nature of Bank Deposits in the Province of Quebec" (1935), 13 *Can. Bar Rev.* 635 at 647.

[32] *Lincoln v. Grant*, 47 D.C. App. 475 (1917–18) at 483.

[33] *Id.*

[34] *See* Geva, *supra* note 28 at 132.

[35] Against a plaintiff suing as an assignee of a debt, set-off is also available to the defendant in relation to a debt due to him from the plaintiff's assignor and accruing prior to the notification of the assignment: *see, e.g., Cavendish v. Geaves* (1857), 24 Beav. 163, 53 E.R. 319; s. 40(1)(b) of the Personal Property Security Act, R.S.O. 1990 c. P-10 as am., and for a critical discussion, Geva, *supra* note 28 at 134–7.

[36] Goode, *supra* note 26 at 135. This reciprocity is the "mutuality" requirement referred to in note 26 and the text above.

[37] "Act for the Relief of Debtors with Respect to the Imprisonment of their Persons", 1729, 2 Geo. II, c. 22, s. 13.

[38] R.S.O. 1990, C. 43.

alternatively, "independent set-off", "legal set off", "court set-off" or "procedural set-off".[39]

Statutory set-off is effective only from the time judgment is given.[40] That is, until judgment it produces position netting. As of judgment, it generates netting by novation.

Against a bankrupt debtor, set-off was allowed by common law courts and courts of equity as of the 17th century.[41] The codification of the right to set-off in bankruptcy goes back to 1705.[42] The right is currently provided for in insolvency legislation in England[43] as well as in Canada.[44]

Set-off in insolvency is procedural "in the sense that it is part of the process of proof and requires the taking of an account".[45] Nonetheless, unlike statutory set-off between solvent parties, bankruptcy set-off is mandatory and cannot be excluded by contract.[46]

The specific rationale for bankruptcy set-off which distinguishes it from statutory set-off between solvent parties was explained by Park B. in *Forster v. Wilson*.[47] Accordingly, while the latter "is given by ... statutes ... to prevent cross actions",[48] the object of the former "is not to avoid cross actions ... but to do substantial justice".[49]

Bankruptcy set-off is retroactive to the insolvency date.[50] That is, until claim approval, bankruptcy set-off produces position netting. Once a balance is struck and approved, it generates netting by novation as of the bankruptcy date. Conceptually then, bankruptcy set-off occurs auto-matically at the moment of bankruptcy, even if the calculations have to be done afterwards. That is, at the date of bankruptcy, the account is deemed to have been taken so as to immediately produce a novated obligation.[51]

Netting leads to a payment for amounts sent less amounts received. Consequently, compared to a system where payment is made only for amounts sent, netting reduces insolvency losses, provided netting withstands insolvency. In common law jurisdictions, bilateral netting

---

[39] Wood, *supra* note 22 at 7. This "statutory set-off" is thus distinguished from "equitable" or "transaction" set-off, relating to matters arising from one transaction and discussed by Wood in Chap. 4.

[40] Wood, note 22 at 17 and 84–6.

[41] Goode, *supra* note 26 at 134.

[42] "Act to Prevent Frauds frequently committed by Bankrupts", 1705, 4 & 5 Anne, c. 17, s. 11.

[43] Insolvency Act 1986, 1986 (U.K.), c. 45, s. 323 (set-off bankruptcy); Insolvency Rules 1986, S.I. 1986/1925, r. 4.90 (set-off in winding up).

[44] Bankruptcy Act, R.S.C. 1985, c. B-3, s. 97(3); Winding-up Act, R.S.C. 1985, c. W-11, s. 73. For the application of these pieces of legislation to banks, *see* Crawford, *supra* note 29 at 641–2.

[45] Goode, *supra* note 26 at 177–8.

[46] *National Westminster Bank Ltd. v. Halesowen Presswork & Assemblies Ltd.*, [1972] A.C. 785 (HL). See the discussion by Goode, *id.* at 178.

[47] (1843), 12 M. & W. 191, 152 E.R. 1165.

[48] *Id.*, at 203.

[49] *Id.*, at 204. Thus, where A owes B 8 units and B owes A 6, upon B's bankruptcy, in the absence of effective set-off (to allow B's trustee to collect 2 units from A), A must pay 8 units and receive only dividends for the 2 units owed by B.

[50] Wood, *supra* note 22 at 17 and 292–3.

[51] For this automation effect of bankruptcy set-off *see Stein v. Blake, The Times*, 19 May 1995 (HL).

withstands insolvency of a counterparty due to the effectiveness of the right of set-off in insolvency. However, effective set-off requires pre-insolvency mutuality; only debts between the same counterparties can be set off against each other. For multilateral netting to withstand insolvency, therefore, mutuality between each counterparty and the central counterparty, effectively representing all others jointly, must be established prior to insolvency. Stated otherwise, prior to the insolvency, bilateral debts between all pairs of counterparties must be substituted by bilateral debts between each counterparty and all others (or the central counterparty).

The leading case is *British Eagle International Airlines Ltd. v. Compagnie Nationale Air France.*[52] In that case, the liquidator of a defaulting multilateral net debtor purported to repudiate multilateral netting, by forcing another clearing house member, a bilateral debtor of the defaulter, to pay to the liquidator (for the benefit of all creditors of the defaulter) rather than to the clearing house (for the benefit of multilateral net creditor members of the clearing house). This would increase the amount of loss incurred by the clearing house members from the net net debit of the defaulter to its entire gross multilateral debit, with the gross multilateral credit going to the liquidator. The entire court agreed that the liquidator could not do it with respect to amounts established upon substitution and novation. However, the majority thought that amounts for items exchanged after the previous periodic clearance and before the one that followed (that is, during the cycle within which default occurred), remained owing between each pair of counterparties so that the defaulter's liquidator could appropriate all bilateral credit balances in the defaulter's favour.

The effectiveness of netting arrangements to withstand a counterparty's insolvency can further be enhanced contractually by continuously integrating each individual bilateral obligation, as it is created, into the overall multilateral net. At any point in time throughout the clearing cycle there is, accordingly, one constantly updated obligation of each counterparty to or from all others or the central counterparty. Such "netting by novation and substitution" is carried out, for example, by CHIPS Rule 12.

Specific legislation in the USA[53] and England[54] further reinforces the effectiveness of financial netting arrangements.[55] In contrast, doubts about the legal strength to withstand insolvency of netting arrangements in some European countries have persuaded European central bankers to recommend the real-time gross settlement model for adoption in each of the European Economic Community countries.[56] In such a gross settlement

---

[52] [1975] 2 All E.R. 390 (HL).

[53] Federal Deposit Insurance Corporation Improvement Act (FDICIA) 1993, 12 USC § 4400 *et seq.*

[54] Companies Act 1989, Chap. 40, Pt. VII, particularly s. 159.

[55] In Canada, *see* the proposed Payment Clearing and Settlement Act, introduced on 20 June 1995.

[56] *See* Working Group on EC Payment Systems, *Minimum Common Features for Domestic Payment Systems* (Report to the Committee of Governors of the Central Banks of the Member States of the European Economic Community, November 1993), particularly Principle 4 and p. 24. This document is known as the Padoa-Schioppa Report.

system, each payment order is paid as it is processed so that no insolvency risk is borne by the receiving bank.

4 LVTS – COMPONENTS AND RISK

The segment of the national payment system for the exchange and settlement of large-value credit transfers is referred to as Large Value Transfer System ("LVTS"). For some LVTS, the threshold or floor value for payment orders is specifically prescribed; others allow participants to decide for themselves what payments should be subjected to the more individualized, and hence more expensive, treatment of the LVTS.

There is no uniformity in direct accessibility of local banks to LVTS facilities. In some systems (*e.g.* the American Fedwire or the Swiss SIC), access is broadly based. In others (*e.g.* the English CHAPS), only large banks utilize the facility, with each of the small ones benefitting from its service indirectly through a correspondent large bank direct participant. Furthermore, for some LVTS (*e.g.* the American CHIPS) strict geographical limitations apply so that banks outside the geographical area need establish correspondent relationships with banks within the territory. Finally, access to the communication facility may not be identical with access to the settlement facility; one may be broader than the other, in which case agency and/or correspondent relationships must be established for indirect participation. For example, the American CHIPS facilitates broadly based accessibility to the communication facility but gives a quite restrictive access to the direct settlement facility at the Reserve Bank of New York. Conversely, one could envisage a system where there is a limited access to communication but broad participation in the multilateral settlement.

Automated large-value transfer systems are generally regarded as a key component of the infrastructure in modern financial markets.[57] A major function of these systems is to speed up dramatically the communication, processing, and settlement of large-value payments. Accordingly, from a macroeconomic perspective, an automated large-value interbank system may greatly facilitate the establishment of short-term money markets. At a microeconomic level, the installation of automated large-value transfer systems can enhance the liquidity of both interbank money markets and individual banking organizations.

In the past, the operation of the LVTS has invariably been premised on the interbank exchange of paper vouchers and settlement of resulting balances either separately or as part of the overall daily settlement at the national payment system. The recently closed down London Town Clearing in England was an example for such a facility utilizing special same-day settlement. The Canadian predecessor of the current IIPS system was a paper-based system whose settlement merged into the overall daily settlement at the Bank of Canada.

---

[57] *See*, in general, Marquardt, *supra* note 19. Nonetheless, I submit, whether any developing country should have one, is a matter of cost and benefit analysis.

Today, all major currency countries have computerized (or automated) facilities for the exchange of messages. Also, they either have adopted or are moving towards the adoption of special settlement arrangements for large-value credit transfers.

A technologically advanced LVTS (or "wire transfer system") is characterized by a communication system linking participating banks by means of dedicated lines capable of providing on-line communication in real-time. According to Bernell Stone, "[t]he virtually instantaneous transfer of payment data by a two-way telephone-line communication network shapes the prominent economic operations characteristics" of a LVTS. These characteristics are "speed, single transaction focus and ... security", facilitating a relatively expensive individualized handling, confirmation and notification for each payment.[58]

Typically, large-volume transfer systems accommodate credit transfers, namely payment transfers initiated by the payor, and carried out by "pushing" funds from the payor's account to that of the payee. Small-value transfer systems accommodate also debit transfers, initiated by the payee (under the payor's authority), carried out by "pulling" funds into the payee's account from that of the payor. Namely, the operation of a credit transfer commences with a debit to the payor's account and is completed by means of a credit to the payee's account. In contrast, the operation of a debit transfer commences with a credit to the payee's account and is completed by means of a debit to the payor's account.

A centralized automated transfer facility for the clearing and settlement of small-value electronic payment items is called an "automated clearing house" or "ACH". Such facility exists, for example, in the U.S. as well as in England. Conversely, in Canada, automated systems for small-value transfers are proprietary for each large bank and no central interbank ACH facility is utilized. Interbank communication is by means of physical deliveries of tapes or disks. In any event, the generic name for small-value transfers handled in bulk is "ACH transfers". Accordingly, and irrespective of whether a central ACH facility is utilized, ACH transfers denote debit or credit transfers handled in bulk. Table 1 (over) outlines the principal differences among the wire, ACH and (paper-based) cheque systems.

The ensuing discussion on the operational facilities component – or the "plumbing" – of the payment system draws from Sendrovic.[59] The discussion deals with electronic technologies used to support large-value payment systems. Automated systems that use modern technologies depend on data-processing facilities, data-communication facilities, and highly skilled operations and support personnel.

---

[58] B. K. Stone, "Electronic Payment Basics", 71 *Ec. Rev. Fed. Res. Bank of Atlanta* 3:9 and 3:10 (1986). The wire transfer is relatively expensive compared to other payment mechanisms but not necessarily in relation to the size of the payment.

[59] *See* I. Sendrovic, "Technology and the Payment System", in Summers (ed.), *supra* note 2 at 178.

Table 1

	Wire	*ACH*	*Cheque*
1. Payment applications	Credit transfers	Credit and debit transfers	Debit transfers
2. Processing	Single-transaction (or small group)	Batch	Batch
3. Communication System	Two-way telephone-like communication network	One-way store and forward electronic mail	Physically transported
4. Settlement	Either gross (instantaneous for every transaction) or net-net	Net-net	Net-net
5. Normal transfer execution time	Within day	Next day	Next day or later
6. Instantaneous advise features	Confirmation to sender; advice to receiver	None	None
7. Additional data (beyond payment information)	Limited	Depending on payment application	Limited on cheque but extensive on attached remittance advice
8. Overall Cost	Very high	Low; could be very low if volume increases	Low
9. Fixed Cost	Very high	High	Moderate
10. Variable Cost	High	Low	Relatively high
11. Peak-load problem	Expensive solution (adding telephone lines)	Inexpensive solution ("load smoothing" feature)	Inapplicable
12. Security	Crucial	Important	Important

Data-processing facilities consist of computer equipment, the environmental software needed to operate and control that equipment, the application software designed for processing of payments, and skilled staff. Large computers require special support infrastructure, consisting of primary and backup facilities. Data communication facilities, allowing for the transmission of payment information, are composed of communications equipment and software.

At the most basic level, the telephone network can be used to provide the physical connection between a user's terminal and the computer used to process electronic payments. In this setting, modems are used to convert the digital information used by digital computers to analog signals that can be transmitted over a voice telephone network. Connection requiring the user to dial a telephone number to access the computer system is called a switched circuit.

Alternatively, the connection may be over a dedicated circuit, leased from the telephone company. This option offers better control over the network but is more expensive. It requires individual ports, or connecting points, to the communication equipment that is part of the payment processing system. In contrast, a single port may be shared by switched circuits. Regardless of the type of connection, to ensure confidentiality, encryption devices are frequently used to encode the data transmitted.

Circuit costs, but not the use of computer ports, can be reduced by the use of multiplexer equipment. The latter eliminates the need for an individual communications line for each user. A multiplexer combines the transmission signals from several users into a single, high-speed circuit, to which modems may also need to be connected. At the site of the electronic payment processor, a second multiplexer is required to separate the transmission signals for each user before connection to the computer ports. High-speed circuits using multiplexer equipment are often called backbone or trunk circuits. They may be terrestrial, microwave, or satellite circuits.

Multiple users within a geographical area may further be connected through local access circuits and equipment to communication nodes. Adjacent nodes are linked to one or more high-speed trunk circuits and ultimately to the electronic payments computer. These nodes and trunk circuits form a backbone network. A sophisticated backbone network allows multiple users to share trunk circuits and provides multiple paths over which data can be routed to provide alternatives should a particular circuit fail. Networks that rely on nodes and incorporate multiple paths dividing a stream of data into small units – packets – for transmission over the backbone network, are called packet networks. Typically, the computer system requires one port connection to each communication node. Packet networks thus reduce circuit as well as computer port costs and provide improved network reliability because of their ability to route data over alternative paths.

A packet network can be either private or public. In the former, the payment system provider owns and operates the network. In the latter, the payment network provider leases capacity from a public network vendor over facilities that may be shared with other users.

Four key factors must be carefully considered in the design and the implementation of a communication network supporting an electronic payment system. First, the quantity of data traffic must be determined and the network properly sized to support peak transmission volumes. Second, fallback plans and procedures must be in place to provide backup for circuit and equipment failures. Third, the communication network must be flexible enough to accommodate changes due to volume growth, an expanded user community, or the introduction of new payment services.

Fourth, a communication network must be carefully and continuously managed to ensure proper operations, prevent problems, and diagnose and resolve problems quickly should they occur.

Interbank overseas communication is primarily over the SWIFT network. Furthermore, some LVTS, such as in Canada and France, utilize the SWIFT network for the exchange of domestic bank-to-bank payment orders.

The Society for Worldwide Interbank Financial Telecommunication ("SWIFT") is a non-profit cooperative society organized under Belgian law, and owned by numerous banks throughout the world. The SWIFT system operated by it is a computerized telecommunications network that operates a global data-processing system for transmitting financial messages over dedicated lines among its members and other connected users.

In its current SWIFT II configuration, SWIFT is a central switch system linking numerous and diverse bank terminals all over the world. The central switch currently consists of two slice processors, one situated in the Netherlands and the other in the U.S., each functioning as an independent and *ad hoc* network, linking SWIFT access points. Each country is assigned to a SWIFT access point. Interbank communication is via the SWIFT access points mediated by a slice processor. A system control processor monitors and controls functions of the system but is not involved in routing messages.

More specifically, each SWIFT message travels first on a domestic circuit from the sending bank's terminal to the SWIFT access point for that country. From there, it continues on an international circuit to the slice processor and onward to the SWIFT access point for the receiving bank's country. At that point it is routed on the domestic circuit of that country to the ultimate destination of the receiving bank's terminal. Each message is validated and processed under heavy security.

SWIFT transmittal of domestic messages does not bypass the international circuit; that is, each message travels between two domestic banks via the SWIFT access point for the country, onward to the slice processed in the Netherlands or the U.S., and back to the country SWIFT access point.

Many countries have developed domestic dedicated networks for their LVTS. This is true, for example, for the U.S., England, Germany, Switzerland and Japan, as well as Australia, Hong Kong and Singapore.

Computerized LVTS are either central switch or gateway networks. In the former, interbank communication is intermediated through a central switch. In the latter, interbank communication is facilitated by means of a direct computer-to-computer communication. The American CHIPS is an example of a central switch network while the English CHAPS is a gateway system.

In general, a central switch system facilitates participation by a large number of banks of diverse size and computer capabilities, since only communication to the central switch, and not to each participating bank, is required. A central switch system is thus consistent with an open access policy imposing minimum bilateral compatibility requirements between each participant and the central computer, so as to accommodate a fragmented banking system. A central switch system further requires a centralized organization structure to accommodate the broad range of diverse bank systems.

A gateway architecture, on the other hand, requires a higher degree of multilateral compatibility among all participants, facilitating direct communication between each participant and any other,[60] and is more decentralized in its organization. For each bank it facilitates a better interface between its gateway and payment system. A gateway system is more responsive to technological enhancements and is likely to accommodate a banking system dominated by a small number of large banks.

In an LVTS communication architecture, a central facility may be involved in the itinerary of each payment order. The central facility could be a central switch or a monitoring facility, typically in conjunction with the implementation of risk reduction measures, discussed below. Basically, three models exist. The payment order could thus be routed from the sending bank to the receiving bank via the central facility (a "V" shaped circuit); directly from the sending bank to the receiving bank with a copy generated from the LVTS to the central facility (a "T" shaped circuit); or from the sending bank to the central facility, back to the sending bank, and ultimately, to the receiving bank (an "L" shaped circuit).

As indicated, LVTS settlement could be either on gross or multilateral net basis. For example, in the U.S., CHIPS is a multilateral net settlement system while Fedwire operates on a gross settlement basis. In the U.K., CHAPS is still a multilateral net settlement system. However, following the Padoa-Schioppa Report,[61] it is being transformed into a gross settlement system.

The importance of monetary incentives experienced by commercial banks in deciding what type of an interbank funds transfer system is to be installed was noted earlier.[62] However, the importance of such incentives ought not to be overstated. Issues relating to the stability of the payment system, particularly during times of financial stress, as well as payment system risk, technology, and access to the payment system, must also be addressed. In the final analysis, money and credit issues have an important influence on the choice of the model, and often influence the discussion and analysis of the merits of different types of large-value payment systems. They are nonetheless, not the only considerations.[63]

Payment system risk relates to several areas. Risks may stem from human interference and error, operational error and failure, uncertainty about laws and regulations, and from credit, liquidity, and systemic financial factors.[64] In the final analysis, major risks are credit (or insolvency), liquidity and systemic. They manifest themselves in a participant's (or participants') inability to complete settlement obligations. The ensuring discussion focuses on payment system risk in the context of LVTS.

---

[60] Or at least between each participant and some others, so that ultimately, each participant could communicate to any other either directly, or via another participant.
[61] *See* note 54 and accompanying text, *supra.*
[62] *See* text around notes 19–20, *supra.*
[63] *See* Marquardt, *supra* note 19.
[64] *See* Marquardt, *supra* note 9.

Obviously, in a net net settlement system, while legal means can bolster the effectiveness of netting arrangements to withstand insolvency, they do not eliminate the loss created by settlement failure, namely the default of a net net debtor that fails to meet its multilateral settlement obligation (whether due to insolvency or temporary liquidity problems). The risk of settlement failure may turn into a "systemic risk" where one or more net creditors of the failing participant default as a result of their inability to absorb the loss generated by the original settlement failure.

The risk of settlement failure can be reduced, if not eliminated altogether, by prudential measures restricting access to LVTS, as well as by means of a series of risk reduction measures. Overall, under what came to be known as the "Lamfalussy standard", "[m]ultilateral netting systems should, at a minimum, be capable of ensuring the timely completion of daily settlements in the event of an inability to settle by the participant with the largest single net-debit position".[65]

Specific risk control measures are bilateral credit limits, multilateral debit caps, collateralization of anticipated amounts in default, and loss sharing arrangements.

For each counterparty *vis-à-vis* another, a bilateral credit limit sets the maximum bilateral credit, in the amount of total received less sent that the *other* counterparty may extend to it at any point throughout the exchange. At the same time, for each counterparty *vis-à-vis* all others, the multilateral debit cap represents the maximum net net debit balance that it may be allowed; it is the maximum credit, in the amount of total received less sent, that *all* counterparties are prepared to extend to it at any point throughout the exchange. While the bilateral credit limit measures bilateral debit positions, the debit cap measures the multilateral or overall debit position of a counterparty. A counterparty may have absolute discretion in establishing bilateral credit limits or must act under guidelines. Debit caps are established either on the basis of the total bilateral credit limits or under guidelines, usually referring to capital adequacy standards.

Collateralization is usually in the form of liquid securities. Loss sharing is likely to be based on credit extended (or extendable) by counterparties to the failed one. The size of collateral required may be determined in relation to the total exposure of a counterparty, taking into account its debit cap and anticipated share under the loss sharing scheme.

In the U.S., CHIPS employs all four risk reducing measures. At the same time, in the U.K., CHAPS currently employs bilateral credit limits and multilateral debit caps but not collateralization and loss sharing.

Inasmuch as it requires the instantaneous (*i.e.* real-time) settlement of each payment order as it is processed, a gross settlement system does not involve the risk of settlement failure. Nevertheless, liquidity difficulties of counterparty/ies may cause a gridlock and bring operations to a halt. An intraday funds market, facilitating same-day borrowing and repayment, such as exists in Japan, is one means towards the resolution of the issue.

---

[65] *See* Standard IV, text that follows note 21 *supra*.

From all major currency countries, only Switzerland appears to have an LVTS consisting exclusively of a pure gross-settlement facility, relying on effective liquidity management by each participant. Elsewhere, to bypass liquidity problems, the national payment system does not have a gross settlement facility (*e.g.* Canada), does not limit itself to a gross settlement LVTS (*e.g.* Japan, Germany and the U.S.), permits bilateral netting operations (resulting in one payment which is instantaneously settled) to occur in designated hours (*e.g.* Japan and France once the TBF is in place), or allows a counterparty to overdraw on its account with the central bank (*e.g.* the U.S.).

The latter practice, namely allowing a counterparty to overdraw on its account with the central bank in order to allow real-time gross settlement even in the absence of funds in the account, gives rise to daylight overdrafts. A daylight overdraft is an overdraft in a settlement account with the central bank, generated in the course of the daily payment activity and settled by the end of the day. The practice facilitates the smooth operation of the gross settlement system, but not without generating a risk of its own, that of end of the day settlement failure (namely the failure to provide cover) by the bank that incurred a daylight overdraft. Unlike in a net net settlement system, the settlement risk in a gross settlement system that allows daylight overdrafts is borne by the central bank and not by the other counterparties. This is so since, in a gross settlement system, payment is made to the receiving bank by the central bank as each payment order is processed and settled.

Settlement risks in a gross settlement system providing for a daylight overdraft facility can be reduced if not eliminated altogether by the employment of a series of risk reduction measures. Measures available are a multilateral debit cap (but not bilateral credit limits), collateralization, and intraday overdraft pricing. Such devices are currently employed by Fedwire in the U.S. and will be utilized by the TBF in France.

In sum, there is a trade-off between efficiency and risk in the design and operation of large-value transfer systems.[66] At one extreme, a gross settlement system that does not provide for intraday credit to participants minimizes the concentration of credit risk in the large-value system itself, but at the same time may severely constrain the flexibility with which payments can be made. At the other extreme, a gross payment mechanism that provides liberal quantities of credit, either through the central bank or implicitly through a multilateral netting arrangement, brings significant risks both for participants and for the financial system. No single model is necessarily best for a particular situation. More than one large-value transfer system can serve the same economy, meeting the needs of different types of markets and customer requirements.[67] A mix of public and private

---

[66] *See* A. Horii and B. J. Summers, "Large-Value Transfer System", in Summers (ed.), *supra* note 2 at 73.

[67] In fact, having determined the desirability of real-time gross-settlement systems, the Padoa-Schioppa Report, *supra* note 54, specifically endorsed the continued parallel operation of same-day net-settlement systems, "[p]rovided they settle at the central bank" (Principles 4 and 5 respectively).

arrangements may represent the optimal solution to the needs of participants in markets that give rise to demands for large-value services.

5 THE FUNDAMENTALS OF THE LEGAL REGIME

There are several facets to the legal regime that governs the payment system. First, there is the regulatory and organizational aspect which is closely linked to the regulation and organization of financial institutions in general. Second, there is the legal regime governing netting, clearing and settlement.[68] In part, this is covered by interbank rules and agreements. Finally, there is the private law governing the payment instructions and their execution. So far as large-value ("wire") transfers are concerned, this is the law of credit or funds transfers.

As indicated, one of the principles serving as building blocks in the development of modern payment systems concerns the legal framework governing payment transactions.[69] The legal regime can contribute substantially to the certainty of payment, thus reducing the overall risk inherent in the payment process. Indeed, a sound legal regime outlining rights and obligations of parties and allocating risks is an essential ingredient in the overall scheme securing the safe operation of the payment system.

The ensuing discussion will outline the basic requirements for a law governing credit or funds transfers. Thus, in each jurisdiction, this branch of law must:

(1) identify the participants in the payment transaction and define their legal relationships. This aspect includes the definition of the juridic nature of the payment instructions and the identification of the point of their irrevocabiltity;

(2) identify the point of completion of the funds transfer as well as of that of the resulting discharge of the obligation paid by it; and

(3) allocate risks occurring in the absence of timely and satisfactory completion. This covers three separate general situations: delayed completion, non-completion (*i.e.*, risk of loss) and "miscompletion" (*i.e.*, the misdirection of funds, overpayment and underpayment). Questions that arise in such contexts relate to (i) the identification of the party responsible; (ii) elements of liability (*i.e.*, particularly the choice between fault or "money-back guarantee" schemes); (iii) privity requirements and the existence of vicarious liability; and finally (iv) the scope of damages (namely, in particular, whether consequential loss is recoverable).

In the U.S., almost all jurisdictions have adopted Article 4A of the Uniform Commerical Code as law governing credit transfers. Article 4A was drafted primarily in order to provide a legal regime for large-value

---

[68] *See*, in general, Part 3 of this chapter, *supra*.
[69] *See* text following note 5, *supra* (Principle 5).

wire transfers. In turn, Article 4A strongly influenced the content of the Model Law on International Credit Transfers, prepared by UNCITRAL.

So far, no jurisdiction has adopted the Model Law. Outside the U.S., large-value wire transfers are currently governed by general principles of law. This is true for common as well as civil law jurisdictions. As a rule, compared to laws in such jurisdictions, Article 4A and the Model Law are more pragmatic and less doctrinal in the resolution of pertinent issues. Also, they are more detailed in addressing specific technical issues.

Raj Bhala outlines five rules as underlying Article 4A so as to form the substance of the U.S. legal regime governing large-value credit transfer systems.[70] They are:

(1) A scope rule differentiating the parties and payment instructions that are included in the law governing funds transfers from those that are not. Briefly stated, "payment orders" issued to banks, instructing credit transfers, and given orally, in writing or electronically, fall within the scope of Article 4A.

(2) A trigger event indicating the moment where rights and obligations of a party arise. In principle, "acceptance" of a payment order by a "receiving bank" is such a trigger event.

(3) A receiver finality rule to establish when credit to an account is irrevocable. In general, payment to the beneficiary, or posting credit to the beneficiary's account, marks such finality.

(4) A money-back guarantee rule to cover situations where a funds transfer is not completed, coupled with a discharge rule for cases where the transfer is completed. In principle, such discharge occurs upon "acceptance" by the benificiary's bank.

(5) An antifraud rule allocating liability for fraudulent payment instructions. In general, a purported sender is responsible only for an authorized or properly verified payment order.

I believe that at least another rule ought to be added, namely, a scope of liability rule. This rule provides for strict privity requirements (namely, no vicarious liability, as well as for the insulation of a bank from liability for consequential, even foreseeable, losses).

The combined effect of the "money-back guarantee" rule and the "scope of liability" rule is that, normally, a paying party (the "originator" of the funds transfer) will be able to shift to that party's bank (the "originator's bank") the loss incurred by the non-completion of the funds transfer (risk of loss) occurring due to the default of any participating bank other than the beneficiary's bank. This is, however, true only to the extent of the principal amount, interest, and incidental expenses, but not so far as consequential losses (such as the loss of a profitable contract) arise. The originator's bank may shift the loss it bears initially onward, ultimately up to the defaulting bank.

---

[70] R. Bhala, "Legal Foundations of Large-Value Transfer Systems", in Summers (ed.) *supra* note 2 at 53.

Obviously, Article 4A is much more detailed and fine-tuned. A detailed analysis of Article 4A, and in fact, of any law governing large-value credit transfers, is outside the scope of the present dicussion.

6 CONCLUSION

A study of the payment system increasingly becomes interdisciplinary. As this chapter demonstrated, the current structure of the payment system reflects its historical development and the search for payment system efficiency. It is within the context of efficiency that multilateral netting of payment orders is best understood. It was argued that, in common law jurisdictions, multilateral netting stands on firm ground. Subsequently, LVTS components and risk were explored. It was concluded that no single model can meet all requirements under all circumstances. Finally, the fundamentals of the legal regime governing large-value transfers were highlighted.

7 REFERENCES

Books

B. Geva, *The Law of Electronic Funds Transfers* (updated to 1995).

B. J. Summers (ed.), *The Payment System* (1994).

D. B. Humphry (ed.), *The U.S. Payment System: Efficiency, Risk, and the Role of the Federal Reserve* (1990).

Article

B. K. Stone, "Electronic Payment Basics", 71 *Ec. Rec. Fed. Res. Bank of Atlanta* 3:9 (1986).

Reports

Report on Netting Schemes (BIS, Basle, Feb. 1989) [the Angell Report].

Report of the Committee on Interbank Netting Schemes of the Central Banks of the Group of the Ten Countries (BIS, Basle, Nov. 1990) [the Lamfalussy Report].

Working group on EC Payment Systems, *Minimum Common Features for Domestic Payment Systems* (Nov. 1993) [the Padoa-Schioppa Report].

8. Bank Capitalization Issues in Emerging and Transitional Economies

Gerald N. Olson[1]

1 INTRODUCTION

The term "bankrupt" comes from the Italian "banca rotta", meaning "bank broken" or "broken bench". An old Italian custom, supposedly, called for breaking the tablets or benches of bankers and money lenders whose businesses had failed.[2] It is interesting to note that the term "bankrupt" initially referred to a bank as the failing or defaulting debtor rather than the borrowers from the money lenders.

Banks are no longer considered safe. The banking industry, some might say, has returned to the era of the "broken bench". Bank customers are no longer confident in the safety or purchasing power of their money or the value of their property. Banks are failing or threatened in record numbers, worldwide.[3] The 1980s brought the Latin American debt crisis.[4] The 1980s and 1990s brought the banking industry of the largest economy in the world, the United States, literally to its knees.[5] The Japanese banking system is *in extremis*.[6] Mexico is experiencing a massive banking crisis.[7]

---

[1] Senior University Visiting Fellow, Centre for Commercial Law Studies, Queen Mary and Westfield College, University of London; Associate Director, London Institute of International Banking, Finance and Development Law. The author is currently writing an extended monograph regarding bank insolvency, bank capital and public policy.

[2] *Oxford English Dictionary* (2nd ed. 1989).

[3] *See* "Please, Governor, Can You Spare a Billion?", *The Economist*, p. 115 (March 25, 1995).

[4] *See* F. Morris with M. Dorfman, J. P. Ortiz and M. C. Francoy, "Latin America's Banking System in the 1980's, A Cross Country Comparison", *World Bank Discussion Paper*, No. 81 (1990).

[5] *See* J. R. Macey and G. P. Miller, "Bank Failure: The Politization of a Social Problem", 45 *Stan. L. Rev.* 289 (1992).

[6] *See, e.g.*, J. Sapsford, "Tokyo Concedes Broader Banking Crisis, Tallying $474 Billion of Problem Loans", *Wall St. J.*, Sect. A, p. 10 (June 7, 1995); B. Bremner, "When Will Japan Set the Banks Free?", *Bus. W.*, p. 56 (June 12, 1995); and J. Pitman, "Will Tokyo's River of Bad Debts Burst Its Banks?", *The Times* (London), p. 29 (October 19, 1994).

[7] *See, e.g.*, R. Alm, "Peso Crisis Shakes the Foundation of Mexican Banks", *The Dallas Morning News*, Sect. H, p. 1 (April 30, 1995); and G. Smith and N. Reed, "Pulling the Banks From the Rubble", *Bus. Wk.*, p. 52 (June 12, 1995).

Central and Eastern European countries transitioning to market economies are poised to discover their own banking crises. Government intervention to rescue or bail out their banking systems has been the order of the day.[8] In the midst of banking crises affecting entire economies are well-publicized individual bank failures such as the BCCI collapse,[9] Barings,[10] Credit Lyonnais,[11] Daiwa,[12] and the list goes on.

These failures are driven by two broad categories of threats to bank capital adequacy and solvency. First, and most importantly, bank capital is threatened by a global systemic cycle of inflation, deflation and devaluation. Second, the banking environment created by this cycle provides a fertile opportunity for mismanagement as well as banking crime and fraud, on an unprecedented scale.

2 DESTABILIZATION OF THE BANKING INDUSTRY

Bank insolvency has historically been a relatively rare occurrence. Widespread bank insolvencies have occurred generally only as a result of widespread economic collapse or depression during periods such as the great depression in the United States during 1929 and the 1930s,[13] and the secondary banking crisis in England during the 1970s.[14] The Latin American debt crisis of the late 1970s and early 1980s,[15] and 1990s,[16] the United States banking crisis and the current ongoing global banking crisis[17] present a somewhat different picture. These recent periods of crisis have resulted in waves of blame and recrimination as well as changes in banking laws; specifically those laws designed to ensure the safety and soundness of banking systems generally by insuring bank deposits, by setting standards to assure minimum levels of bank capital, and by establishing complex systems of bank regulation, supervision and enforcement.[18]

Banks historically have provided the primary mechanism for a society to safeguard its funds, establish a means for payment in exchange transactions, and ensure a source of loans and credit to finance trade and investment. In

---

[8] *See The Economist, supra,* note 3.

[9] *See* R. K. Bhala, *Foreign Bank Regulation After BCCI* (1994).

[10] *See* G. T. Milliman, "Barings Collapses: Financial System Bears Up Well", *Wall St. J.* (February 28, 1995).

[11] *See* T. Allen-Mills, "French Elite Blamed For Bank Fiasco", *The Sunday Times* (London) (March 19, 1995); and T. Allen-Mills and K. Hamilton, "Credit Lyonnais Rescue Sparks Political Furor", *The Sunday Times* (London) (March 19, 1995).

[12] *See* J. R. Wilke, T. L. O'Brien and N. Shirouzu, "In A Signal To Japan, U.S. Bars Daiwa Bank and Indicts Institution", *Wall St. J.,* p. 1 (November 3, 1995).

[13] *See* P. P. Swire, "Bank Insolvency Law Now That It Matters Again", 42 *Duke L. J.* 469 (1992), at note 4.

[14] *See* M. Reed, *The Secondary Banking Crisis 1973–75* (1982).

[15] *See* Morris, Dorfman, Ortiz and Francoy, *supra,* note 4.

[16] *See* "Banks In Latin America, An Urgent Case of Disrepair", *The Economist,* p. 69 (July 1, 1995).

[17] *See The Economist, supra,* note 3.

[18] *See* J. Norton, *Devising International Bank Supervisory Standards* (1995).

order for banks to perform these functions, all of which are necessary to broad-based business activity, the legal framework for the banking system and the relationship of bank capital (based on underlying asset and loan collateral values) to cash and cash equivalents or other liquid investments must be transparent and relatively stable and predictable.

Banks no longer dominate the financial industry. The global financial economy has, to a large degree, eroded and displaced banks' and central banks' stabilizing functions.[19] Asset values and liquidity have been de-stabilized by the prevailing system of floating currency exchange rates and by the resulting speculative trading focus of the global financial economy.[20] This destabilization of asset values and liquidity lies at the heart of the global crisis of bank capital adequacy and the resulting destabilization of the banking industry.[21]

While the systemic problem of bank capital adequacy is worldwide, the problem is manifested domestically in each economy, whether a so-called "developed economy" or an "emerging or transitional economy". Government reactions to the problem and government programs of intervention have been varied and unique to each economy. Despite a wide range of government acts of intervention designed to mitigate the problem of destabilization or to assess blame for its effects and impose retribution, the problem has not been eliminated and no satisfactory long-term resolution is likely.

The genesis of the current destabilizing systemic problem of capital adequacy lies in the collapse of the Bretton-Woods Accord caused by the United States' withdrawal in 1973[22] and in its subsequent public policy and legal response to the consequences of its actions. It is ironic that the International Financial Institutions established to oversee global financial stability following World War II as a part of the Bretton-Woods Accord now face a new role in combating the effects of the global sys-temic capital adequacy crisis in emerging and transitional economies.[23] World Bank and IMF studies, reports and discussion papers chronicle the

---

[19] J. Kurtzman, *The Death of Money* (1993), at p. 29.

[20] *Id.*, at pp. 37–40.

[21] *See* M. Hinds, "Economic Effects of Financial Crisis", *World Bank Working Paper*, WPS 104 (October 1988).

[22] *Id.; see* also, Kurtzman, *supra*, note 19, at pp. 50 *et seq.*; J. Shelton, *Money Meltdown: Restoring Order To the Global Currency System* (1994); J. Shelton, "How To Save The Dollar", *Wall St. J.*, Sect. A, p. 10 (July 15, 1994); and W. Angell, "As Good As Gold", *Wall St. J.* (July 22, 1994).

[23] *See* K. Reisman, "The World Bank and the IMF: At The Forefront Of World Transformation", 60 *Ford. L. Rev.* 349 (1992); *see* also, "International Capital Markets: Development Prospects And Policy Issues", *IMF Annual Report* (1994); B. Davis, "U.S. Backs Preventative Role For IMF To Deter Mexico-Style Financial Crises", *Wall St. J.*, Sect. A, p. 10 (June 7, 1995); M. Camdessus, "The IMF Way To Open Capital Accounts", *Wall St. J.*, Sect. A, p. 16 (September 27, 1995); "Fit At Fifty", *The Economist* (July 23, 1994); "Thoroughly Modern Sisters", *The Economist* (July 23, 1994); L. Clark, Jr., "IMF: Another Conference Failure", *Wall St. J.*, Sect. A, p. 12 (July 19, 1994): J. D. Sachs, "IMF, Reform Thyself", *Wall St. J.* (July 21, 1994).

consequences of the systemic capital adequacy crisis in the emerging and transitional economies.[24] The same fundamental issues, however, underly the ongoing banking problems in the so-called "developed economies", including the United States, Japan, France, Germany and Britain. The difference lies in the ability of these countries to diffuse and politicize the issues internally.

The problems in the emerging economies are seemingly intractable. Waves of currency fluctuations followed by dramatic asset value distortions, beginning with the price of oil in the 1970s immediately after the collapse of Bretton-Woods and followed by the global collapse of real estate values and cycles of inflation and recession, have made money management, lending and investment, the traditional purvue of the banking industry, a speculator's game.[25]

3 BANK CAPITAL ADEQUACY STANDARDS

Banking, even in the developed economies, is an inherently risky business. Notwithstanding the recent interest of bank regulators in levels of bank capital and minimum ratios of bank capital adequacy represented by the Basle Capital Adequacy Accord,[26] spawned by ongoing problems of bank capital adequacy and bank insolvency, bank capital levels remain the lowest of any capital intensive industry. In addition, the bulk of bank assets (loans) are themselves highly leveraged. Because bank profits are limited, as a general rule, to interest rates which represent a relatively narrow margin over their cost of funds and operations, augmented by service and transaction fees, significantly higher levels of required bank capital would quickly render most banks' business unprofitable.[27] The relatively low levels of required bank capital are uniquely exposed to risks which are not easily protected against by loan underwriting, documentation and administration. Further, because of banks' relatively high leverage, a relatively low level of absolute losses can impair or eliminate a bank's capital,[28] even under the imposition of the most rigorous capital adequacy standards.

The questions then become:

(a) On what day, with what information, do you determine a bank's capital?
(b) What is the purpose of the determination?
(c) What are the consequences of the determination?
(d) When are losses recognized?
(e) How are losses allocated?

---

[24] *See supra*, notes 4 and 21.
[25] *See* Kurtzman, *supra*, at note 19; *see* also Hinds, *supra*, at note 21, regarding specific implications of global banking destabilization in developing economies.
[26] *See* Norton, *supra*, note 18, Chapter Four.
[27] *Id.*, at pp. 18 and 19 and notes 47 through 51.
[28] *Id.*

(f) Who will bear the loss?

(g) Who, if anyone, is to blame for the loss and who, if anyone should suffer retribution for it?

Despite the comprehensive, and purportedly transparent, bank regulatory environment in the United States, during the current banking crises, the answers to the foregoing questions have not been clear. The answers to these same questions in other developed economies such as England and Japan are less clear. In fact, the public policy in those two jurisdictions appears to be to address the issues through the discretion of the central banking authorities, thus avoiding public inquiry and debate of the policy issues inherent in the rules governing the answers to the questions so posed.[29] The most clearly articulated analysis of these questions and the range of appropriate answers can be found in the various actions taken by the Latin American Countries during the 1980s.[30]

Countries emerging from formerly socialist central-planned economies are striving to implement new market-based economic systems. The establishment by these countries of viable banking systems is an indispensable component of their shift to market economies. Without clearly articulated transparent domestic public policy and laws backed by some degree of international consensus recognizing the different causes of bank capital impairment and the appropriate governmental responsibility to intervene in the resolution process, the increasing manifestations of bank instability and bank capital impairment will have significant ongoing economic and political ramifications in the emerging and transitioning economies. Bank capital adequacy standards, alone, cannot stem this tide.[31]

4 BANK CAPITAL IN EMERGING AND TRANSITIONAL ECONOMIES

Emerging economies come equipped with central banking systems designed to implement centrally planned allocation of capital and operating subsidies to target industries, with little or no reference to underlying economic fundamentals, much less any definitive programs for and identified sources of repayment or collateral for repayment.[32] In fact, the prevalent attitude with respect to bank loans in emerging and transitional

---

[29] *See* J. Norton, "The Bank of England's Lament: The Struggle To Maintain The Traditional Supervisory Practice of 'Moral Suasion'", in J. Norton (ed.), *Bank Regulation And Supervision In The 1990's* (1991); *see also*, T. F. Cargill and G. F. W. Todd, "Japan's Financial System Reform Law: Progress Towards Financial Liberation?", 19 *Brooklyn J. Int. Law* 47 (1993).

[30] *See* Morris, Dorfman, Ortiz and Francoy, *supra*, note 9 and Hinds, *supra*, note 21.

[31] *See* Norton, *supra*, note 18, citing at note 50, on p. 19, remarks by Young, "Bank Capital in the United States", *Issues in Bank Regulation* 3, at p. 4 (Spring 1986): "In a sense 'capital adequacy' is misleading. No amount is adequate if its bank's credit culture goes wrong, No amount is sufficient to weather a liquidity crisis".

[32] *See, e.g.*, R. Lamdany, *Russia, The Banking System In Transition*, World Bank Country Study (1993).

economies is that the loans (formerly, directed credits to pay capital expenses and operating subsidies to debtor businesses) are not really contemplated to be repaid in any event.[33] Many banks in emerging economies are small, with no deposit insurance for depositors, controlled by insiders.[34] Loans are predominately short term, without what experienced bankers would consider adequate documentation, collateral or identified sources of repayment.[35] These loans are repaid through "roll-overs", so that risks of repayment are not recognized.[36] Loans to insiders proliferate, often for speculative or political purposes.[37] Based on the standards of the world banking community, a very high percentage of the loans would be classified as uncollectable and the banks holding them would be considered capital impaired and insolvent.

5 THE RELEVANCE OF BANK REFORM IN EMERGING AND TRANSITIONAL ECONOMIES TO BANK CAPITAL ADEQUACY

Banks in emerging and transitional economies face a range of threats to capital adequacy and, therefore, solvency. Earlier, this chapter described the primary threats to bank capital adequacy and solvency as:

(a) mismanagement, fraud and crime; and
(b) systemic asset devaluation as a consequence of global currency and capital instability.

Banks in emerging economies also face additional threats to capital adequacy including:

(a) political risk; and
(b) a legacy of assets which were originally booked as directed credits in formerly centrally planned socialist systems and which are essentially uncollectable and therefore of no real value.

Further, both developed economies and emerging economies suffer from legislative, regulatory and management denial of the presence or effect of these threats to bank capital adequacy and from chronic avoidance of any open proactive anticipation of, or response to, such threats.

New banks are proliferating rapidly in emerging economies.[38] Banking law reform is widespread, driven largely by the requirements of international financial institutions, including the World Bank, The International

---

[33] *Id.*
[34] *The Economist*, (August 8, 1992).
[35] *Id.*
[36] *Id.*
[37] *Id.*
[38] *See The American Banker, Washington Monday*, p. 8 (November 23, 1992).

Monetary Fund, and the European Bank for Reconstruction and Development.[39] Consultants and advisers abound.[40] Reforms are being implemented, in most cases, without an understanding by these institutions, their consultants and advisers, legislators, regulators, or the bankers, of the global economic context, the unique local culture or of the cumulative interactive effect of their acts of intervention.

Current efforts at banking reform in emerging economies tend to focus on the immediate concerns of the international institutions and the domestic central banking authorities. These reforms tend to be in the areas of structure and control of the central banking system, payment and clearing systems, foreign exchange, operating systems and systems of financial regulation, supervision and enforcement.[41] Current banking law reform in emerging economies does not address satisfactorily the special issues attendant to the highly volatile composition of bank capital, or bank insolvency detection, prevention or resolution.

The current range of law reform does, however, include bankruptcy law reform. This reform has been spawned, in large part, to provide a mechanism to liquidate defunct or obsolete and unproductive formerly state-owned enterprises and to strip them of liabilities, to facilitate subsequent privatization and sale.[42] In addition to the privatization and bankruptcy law reform, the rhetoric of bankruptcy law reform remains to "effect market discipline".[43] The new bankruptcy laws do not address specifically the necessarily unique treatment of bank capitalization and solvency issues.

In most cases, capital impaired or insolvent banks in emerging economies have little prospect of legal or financial resolution. Attempts are made to reorganize or liquidate them under bankruptcy laws characterized by the rhetoric of free market discipline (often for political purposes), accompanied by public outcry and protest from depositors and calls for government intervention and protection.[44] Smaller banks may be liquidated as examples or to facilitate special political or financial objectives.

6 ASSET VALUES AND BANK CAPITAL

Recent political changes in Latin America, Central and Eastern Europe as well as in other formerly centrally planned socialist economies have re-

[39] *See, e.g.,* "Russian Federation Financial Institutions Development Project", *The World Bank Report* (1995); *The World Development Report, 1994,* The World Bank (1994); and *Transition Report,* The European Bank for Reconstruction and Development (1994).

[40] *See The American Banker,* p. 2a. (August 11, 1991).

[41] *See Moscow Times,* Section 382 (January 20, 1994).

[42] *See* S. Nestor, "Insolvency Procedures in Transition Economies", Chapter Nine of this publication; *see* also, S. van Wijnbergen, "Enterprise Reform in Eastern Europe", *World Bank Working Paper,* WPS 1068 (January 1993).

[43] *Id.; see* also, C. Gray, "Evolving Legal Framework For Private Sector Development In Central And Eastern Europe", *World Bank Discussion Paper,* No. 209 (1993).

[44] *See* V. Sekulovic, "Money: Where It Went; State Owned and Privately Owned Banks' Insolvency In Serbia", private LL.M. research paper on file with the author; *see* also, "Venezuelan Banks, From Bad to Worse", *The Economist,* p. 116 (March 25, 1995); and "Debit Lyonnais's Encore", *The Economist,* p. 22 (March 25, 1995).

sulted in massive transfers of state-owned enterprises, including banks, to private ownership in what amounts to a legal vacuum. The global economy is already establishing a hegemony over these assets, before they have found their place in their domestic economies and before underlying issues such as domestic currency valuations and exchange rates, job security programs, government operating and capital subsidies, environmental costs, taxation considerations, accounting rules and other governmental rules and regulations have been addressed. This massive shift of assets into the global financial economy will likely result in dislocations in the emerging and transitional economies and will likely spur the further growth and volatility of the global financial economy.[45]

This growth velocity and volatility will force lawmakers to focus more clearly on what should happen to the participants under these circumstances, when things go wrong; when companies and their assets unexpectedly hit the bottom of the unexpected cycle; and when the global ripples of devaluation and financial failure spread to other economies, debtor companies, their assets and creditors.

For the economies now emerging from previously socialist systems, private asset values have no foundation in private property and collateral security laws or in a viable marketplace.[46] Therefore, asset values in these economies are highly uncertain and volatile. Consequently, credit transactions based on such uncertain and volatile asset values present a relatively high risk of loss, at the very time when political objectives and economic policies dictate that substantial credit transactions are required to attract hard currency investment transactions and investment capital, fuel economic growth and provide a mechanism to privatize state-owned enterprises and to engage entrepreneurial vigor in these systems.

7 SUGGESTIONS REGARDING ISSUES OF BANK CAPITAL ADEQUACY IN EMERGING AND TRANSITIONAL ECONOMIES

Most developed economies have provided for the regulation and supervision of banks, including provisions for minimum capitalization and for the resolution of banks whose capital base is impaired or eliminated. Because of the quasi-public nature of banks as the foundation of an economy's financial and economic structure as well as agents of government monetary policy, issues relating to bank capitalization and bank solvency are best resolved in the context of banking laws rather than commercial bankruptcy laws.[47] The public's interest in bank solvency and in the stability of a

---

[45] Kurtzman, *supra*, note 19, at pp. 65, 66 and 75.

[46] *See* S. Handelman, "The Russian 'Mafia'", 73 *Foreign Affairs* No. 2, p. 83 (March/April 1994).

[47] *See, e.g.*, Corrigan, "Are Banks Special?", Fed. Res. of Minn., *Annual Report* (1982); *see also*, R. Clark, "The Soundness of Financial Intermediaries", 86 *Yale L.J.* 1, at p. 99 (1976), to the effect that the theory supporting a special regime of bank insolvency appears not to have received "careful and sustained attention".

market economy's banking system is self-evident. The maintenance of depositor confidence avoids runs on the banks and resulting systemic threats to the banking system and permits banks to make prudent loans and investments which have less liquidity than their deposit base. Stable banks in a stable banking system are integral to an effective system of deposit, lending and investment and payment in exchange transactions. These conditions are vital to the conversion of formerly socialist centrally planned economies to functional market-based economies.

The global phenomenon of deteriorating bank capital adequacy can be explicated and understood by policymakers and legislators. First, it will be necessary to examine, analyze and articulate the public policies and laws of the leading developed economies and to assess the effectiveness of these systems of laws and policies in healing the wounded global financial system. Based upon an understanding of (i) the nature and identity of the threats to bank capitalization; (ii) the effectiveness of existing and possible new laws and policies in mitigating these threats, or alternatively, recognizing and fairly allocating losses in a transparent manner consistent with the threats realized and the consequences which can be attributed to them, the public interest in a stable, predictable and safe banking system in an emerging economy can be preserved and protected.

Banking systems in the developed economies seek to create the same conditions, *e.g.* stability, predictability and safety, although the extent to which they have been successful and the particulars of their respective systems are highly varied. Notwithstanding common public perception regarding the homogeneity and uniformity of the "global banking system", in fact the systems are highly individualized and efforts to achieve homogeneity and uniformity are really quite recent in time.[48] Public policy and legal responses to the basic threats to bank capital and bank solvency; regulatory and management processes to mitigate the risks of capital inadequacy; the methods of systemic and depositor protection; and the legal alternatives available for the resolution of bank insolvencies: all these are vastly dissimilar among the countries constituting the so-called "developed economies".

The literature regarding the issues germain to bank insolvency is scant, excepting only the recent literature examining capital adequacy standards.[49] The major issues to be faced by the emerging economies relating to bank capitalization, however, are not related to technical bank capital adequacy standards, but rather centre on the nature of the capital, its valuation, revaluation reflecting global and domestic economic changes and the realization of identified threats to capital and the consequences which flow from that realization. Notwithstanding the adoption of bank capital adequacy standards, in the absence of a methodology for measurement of the value of components of bank capital, the political will to address adverse changes in value or an accurate recognition of the causes of adverse value changes, in a manner which reflects the cultural necessity for blame and recrimination, if

---

[48] *See* generally, "Symposium: Global Trends Toward Universal Banking" 19 *Brooklyn J. Int'l L.* No. 1 (1993).

[49] *See* P. Swire, *supra*, note 12, at p. 473, note 3.

appropriate, neither the developed economies nor the emerging and transitioning economies can avoid systemic financial crisis.

The emerging economies will benefit from an examination of the methods by which banks in developed economic systems identify and mitigate threats to capital adequacy and solvency as well as the methods by which these systems protect the public interest in banking system stability and depositor safety. An examination of the comparative and contrasting public policies and legal systems in the major developed economies will also provide a framework for analysis of the public policy issues and the legal implications of those policies in emerging economies.

The issue of bank insolvency and capital inadequacy in newly emerging economies is largely nascent. Explication of the threats to bank insolvency, depositor safety and banking system stability in the context of the public policy and legal alternatives for their implementation will benefit these emerging economies as the problems associated with capital deterioration and insolvency inevitably rise to levels of national and international concern.

8 CONCLUDING OBSERVATIONS

Based upon a study of existing systems of banking law among the developed economies, recent international experience (primarily in Latin America) and recognition of the effects of the global capital adequacy crisis, the emerging economies should, in principle, be able to successfully confront the threats to bank capital adequacy. These emerging economies are struggling to initiate new political systems and develop and integrate public policies with unfamiliar financial and legal systems in a manner which will reflect disparate cultural and national identies.[50] This struggle will develop and define the balance for allocation of the financial benefits of new banking systems as well as the allocation and absorption of the losses to be expected.

---

[50] *See* Kurtzman, *supra*, note 19, at pp. 194 and 224–227.

9. Insolvency Procedures in Transition Economies

Stilpon Nestor[1]

1 INTRODUCTION

Insolvency legislation is a fundamental component of the institutional/ legislative framework in every market economy:

- It is the main tool for imposing financial discipline on enterprises. It sets out the main criteria that separate "the dead from the living" in commercial firms. These criteria bear directly on the strategic behaviour of commercial agents and determine the financial soundness of their risk/return policies.
- It provides a mechanism for an orderly enforcement of property rights. One of the fundamental issues in the context of insolvency is the "common pool" problem, *i.e.* the fact that several creditors have to be satisfied by an insufficient pool of assets. The consequence might be a run on the debtor's assets which, in turn, can result in both an inequitable distribution of these assets among creditors and the unwarranted (and thus socially wasteful) demise of the debtor firm.[2] In order to preclude such behaviour, the state creates, in the context of insolvency legislation, a set of rules that introduce order in the enforcement of creditor rights. These rules are based on some hard and often criticised choices regarding the outcome of the zero-sum game that is insolvency.
- It is the "bottom" segment of the market for corporate control (or assets), through which sick firms (or their assets) are allocated to the most efficient owners through their reorganisation or liquidation. In contrast to the first insolvency objective of prescribing the moment of death and its consequences, the corporate control function of

---

[1] Counsel on Legal and Enterprise Reform, Organisation for Economic Co-operation and Development (OECD), Paris. The opinions expressed here are the author's own and do not necessarily reflect the views of the OECD.
[2] For a more elaborate analysis of the common pool problem *see* T. Jackson, *The Logic and Limits of Bankruptcy Law* (1985).

insolvency proceedings signals the new life of the firms, or parts of them.[3] The efficient functioning of this market results in higher welfare for the debtor's stakeholders and for society as a whole; it depends largely on the prescriptions and structure of the insolvency law in force.

The purpose of this chapter is to identify the role and functioning of insolvency legislation in the context of the transition from a centrally planned to a market economy and to offer certain suggestions on the design of the insolvency framework. Part 2 sets out the main issues and problems in this debate. Part 3 contains a brief overview of the current status and problems of insolvency law implementation in transition economies. Part 4 views the structure of insolvency legislation; it contains an analysis of the main subject-matter areas and offers some alternative legislative approaches to outstanding problems in the transition context. In Part 5, the purpose, implementation and effectiveness of certain "quasi-insolvency proceedings" that have been employed in transition economies as a tool for the privatisation of state-owned enterprises (SOEs) are discussed. Finally, Part 6 offers some concluding remarks.

2 MAIN ISSUES

Rapid change in the economic environment has rendered many normative approaches to the insolvency question in OECD countries inadequate.[4] In some jurisdictions (Germany,[5] Switzerland and Australian), the enforcement of secured creditor rights takes place outside the insolvency framework; the debtor is not discharged of pre-insolvency debts, once the insolvency process comes to an end. The result might be a net transfer of wealth from junior to senior creditors and a net increase in social costs, resulting from the liquidation of a going concern with a positive present value. In contrast, some countries have adopted rules that over-emphasise the goal of debtor protection (like the U.S. and, to some extent and for different reasons, France); this might increase credit risk and shield inefficient management from a much needed change.

Recently, novel approaches are being adopted (as in the case of the new German law) or proposed by academics.[6] Instead of focusing the law on the

---

[3] For a description of the tensions and conflicts between these two objectives, *see* P. Legros and J. Mitchell "Bankruptcy as a Control Device in Economies in Transition", 20 *Journal of Comparative Economics* (1995), pp. 265–301.

[4] For a comparison between different OECD jurisdictions and their classification according to the protection they extend to debtors/creditors, *see* P. Wood "Effectiveness of Corporate Re-organisations and Liquidation Proceedings in OECD Economies" in *Trends and Policies in Privatisation*, Vol II No. 2, OECD (1995).

[5] Germany has passed a new insolvency law in 1994 which will not, however, be implemented for another five years. We refer to the 1994 legislation as the "new German law" and to the currently enforced one as the "German law".

[6] *See* P. Aghion, O. Hart, J. Moore "The Economics of Bankruptcy Reform", *LSE Discussion Paper*, No. 148 (1992).

protection of the debtor, certain classes of creditors or the employees, these new approaches underline the idea of market-conformity, *i.e.* the function of the law as a tool for the facilitation of negotiation between different stakeholders with a view to maximising the present value of the debtor's assets.[7] This presupposes an unusual flexibility of proceedings that allow corporate control decisions to be taken by creditors or their representatives on the basis of the highest of alternative bids for the assets of the debtor (either on an individual or going-concern basis).

The design and implementation of insolvency legislation in economies in transition is faced with additional problems:

- Insolvency procedures did not exist in centrally planned economies. Procedures for closing down enterprises did not resemble at all insolvency procedures as we know them in the West.[8]
- Externalities, such as the collapse of CMEA, have exacerbated liquidity problems of business firms.
- Dysfunctional financial markets, where state-owned banks were, at least in the first transition phase, forced to lend to SOEs, where banking supervision is deficient and where property rights (including rights related to secured lending) are unclear, contributed to a growing stock of bad debt, *i.e.* non-performing loans, in the banks' portfolios.[9] These problems are compounded by enormous information asymmetries that make external monitoring of a firm's performance and financial health very difficult. The above, combined with the high cost of capital due to the implementation of macroeconomic stabilisation policies,[10] have resulted in banks becoming extremely reticent to lend. In the absence of external financing, enterprises have resorted to non-payment of commercial debt.
- Monopolistic upstream and downstream product markets are also a fertile ground for inter-enterprise arrears, since alternative suppliers or distributors are scarce and therefore expensive to find.
- There is widespread creditor passivity, caused both by endemic arrears (of which it is also partly the cause) as well as by cultural reasons (bankruptcy being perceived as "death" rather than "a new life"). Moreover, passivity is encouraged by expectations of state bail-outs to avoid systemic collapse.[11]
- Institutional problems are a major stumbling block to the efficient implementation of insolvency procedures. In most transition

---

[7] *See* M. Balz, "Market Conformity of Insolvency Proceedings: the 1994 German Insolvency Law Reform", mimeo (1994).

[8] *See* C. Gray, "Evolving Legal Frameworks for Private Sector Development in Central and Eastern Europe," *World Bank Discussion Papers* No. 209 (1993), p. 10.

[9] *See* Z. Thuma, "Economic Restructuring and Corporate Insolvency Procedures in the Czech Economy" in OECD (1995), *supra* note 4.

[10] *See* D. Begg and R. Portes, "Enterprise Debt and Economic Transformation: Financial Restructuring in Central and Eastern Europe," mimeo, Centre for Economic Policy Research (1992).

[11] *See* G. Calvo and F. Coricelli "Stabilizing a Previously Centrally Planned Economy: Poland 1990", 14 *Economic Policy* (1992), pp. 176–226.

economies courts are ill-equipped, poorly funded and little-trained to deal with complex decisions affecting the economic future of enterprises. The private infrastructure supporting insolvency procedures in OECD countries (*i.e.* trustees/administrators, lawyers, investment bankers, accountants, etc.) is also missing.[12]

Given all the above transition problems and the urgent need to reverse the arrears trend, it is important to adopt laws that prescribe simple procedures and an institutional framework that is decentralised and flexible,[13] allowing creditors to take most of the major decisions and limiting the courts' role to that of oversight and dispute resolution.

3 THE IMPLEMENTATION OF INSOLVENCY LEGISLATION IN TRANSITION ECONOMIES

Among transition economies, Hungary has been the pioneer in adopting and implementing a strict insolvency framework. Between April 1992 (when the law was adopted) and April 1993, enterprises representing close to 14% of the GDP have entered insolvency proceedings.[14] On the other hand, the bankruptcy law has been effective in lowering inter-enterprise arrears. Within less than a year from the date of its implementation, these dropped by approximately two-thirds. The law applies with the same vigor to SOEs and private sector companies and, due to this fact, has been a major privatisation method.

The Hungarian bankruptcy law was, in its first version, one of the strictest among both market and transition economies. It made insolvency proceedings mandatory for the debtor, on the basis of a very narrow cash flow test, *i.e.* the non-payment of debts within 90 days from the day they became due. While it did provide for a period to negotiate a settlement with creditors, it required creditor unanimity for the acceptance of any reorganisation plan and was, therefore, strongly biased against going-concern reorganisation. Amendments to abolish the quasi-automatic triggering of bankruptcy procedures and the unanimity requirement for reorganisation were adopted in late 1993. By abolishing mandatory debtor filings, Hungarian legislators did manage to lower dramatically the number of bankruptcy cases. However, available data since the amendments suggest that reorganisation cases (as opposed to liquidations) have practically vanished.[15] This might be due to the absence of effective monitoring

---

[12] *See* S. Nestor (ed.), *Corporate Bankruptcy and Reorganisation Procedures in OECD and Central and Eastern European Countries,* OECD (1994), p. 13.

[13] *See* P. Sak and H. Schiffman, "Bankruptcy Law Reform in Eastern Europe", 28 *The International Lawyer* (1994), pp. 927–950.

[14] *See* E. Hegedus, "The Hungarian Framework for Bankruptcy and Reorganisation and its Effects on the National Economy" in OECD (1994), *supra* note 12, p. 104.

[15] *See* M. Szanyi, " Bankruptcy Procedures and Enterprise Restructuring in Hungary" in OECD (1995), *supra* note 4.

procedures by creditors on the one hand and on the reticence of debtors to file at an early stage, on the other: the new law requires the appointment of a trustee even in cases of debtor filings.[16]

The Czech approach towards the implementation of insolvency procedures has been very different. The Czech law is quite nebulous when it comes to defining insolvency and prescribes a fairly complicated, court-centred procedure. It also imposes a mandatory grace period for debtors during which they are supposed to work out a reorganisation plan with creditors. The Czech aversion towards rigorous bankruptcy procedures is partly explained by their approach towards privatisation. In contrast to the Hungarians, the Czechs opted for voucher privatisation of a large number of enterprises. This approach aims at decentralising enterprise restructuring decisions, which are taken at a post-privatisation stage by the new owners.[17] Consistent with its mass privatisation logic, the Czech government decided to transfer the politically harmful responsibility of dealing with insolvent enterprises to the new private owners. It delayed implementation of the law until the first wave of privatisation was completed and, even after the law took effect, it exempted from its scope companies undergoing privatisation within the second wave.

However, even after the law had become applicable to privatised enterprises, in September 1993, very few bankruptcy procedures were initiated. Beyond the above-mentioned legal deficiencies of the insolvency framework, the economic causes of this phenomenon appear to be three-fold.[18]

First, the Consolidation Bank (*i.e.* the bank which was created to assume non-performing loans from commercial banks, which received in exchange government bonds) controls a large chunk of the bad-debt while the National Property Fund (*i.e.* the state agency that controls the government's stakes in commercial enterprises) is still a minority – but often controlling – shareholder in a large number of troubled companies. Thus the state, reluctant to be perceived as the enforcer of bankruptcy procedures, becomes the captive of insolvent enterprises and, instead, tries to keep them alive.

Secondly, there seems to be a general reluctance of dominant creditors (*i.e.* semi-private commercial banks) to initiate bankruptcy proceedings. This behaviour may be related to the fact that these banks are still controlled by the NPF. Furthermore, they are at the same time major shareholders in many companies, via the investment funds that they control.

Thirdly, a reason might be the introduction very early on of private incentives through mass privatisation (and the firm expectations on its

---

[16] *Id.*

[17] For a different, more positive assessment of these changes *see* Sak and Schiffman, *supra* note 13, p. 935.

[18] *See* I. Lieberman, "Mass Privatisation in Central and Eastern Europe and the Former Soviet Union: A Comparative Analysis", in *Mass Privatisation: an Initial Assessment*, OECD (1995), p. 13.

implementation) and the consequent acceleration of enterprise restructuring by insiders, hoping to retain their jobs after privatisation. This latter conclusion seems to be supported by the fact that the level of inter-enterprise arrears has remained fairly stable during the last two years, *i.e.*, from a "flow" perspective, payment discipline seems to be improving.[19] However, the fact that this level is quite high indicates a "stock" problem in dealing with the initially accumulated non-performing debt and, consequently, a deficiency in the way the insolvency framework has been functioning.[20]

Poland adopted early on a bankruptcy law (the 1934 Commercial Law provisions) which is applicable to both private entities and SOEs. The application of the law is triggered by a broad insolvency test and there are no mandatory filing requirements for the debtor. It leaves outside the scope of reorganisation arrangements a number of important state claims, such as tax and social security payments, thus making creditor led restructuring unattractive.[21] Another Law on Arrangement (*i.e.*, reorganisation) Proceedings (also a 1934 law) has proven useful when it comes to enterprises with a few large creditors. However, its complicated voting rules and procedural formalities and the considerable benefits it allows the state as creditor have rendered it unworkable when it comes to more complicated cases.[22] While a number of bankruptcy and reorganisation proceedings were initiated during the three years of their implementation, the two Polish laws have not affected seriously SOEs. However, as we shall see below, a number of supplementary quasi-insolvency procedures aimed at SOEs have flourished in the context of Polish privatisation.

Russia adopted a complicated bankruptcy law in 1992, which has only rarely been enforced (a little more than 200 cases in three years). A vague insolvency criterion, excessive reliance on economic decision-making by the courts and a skewed order of claim satisfaction have contributed to these poor results.[23] The continuing rise of inter-enterprise arrears levels testifies to the need for further payment discipline for commercial enterprises. In contrast, Estonia has adopted a strict bankruptcy law which has been applied vigorously; more than 250 companies (a large number for Estonia) have entered bankcruptcy proceedings.[24]

---

[19] The first two reasons are examined in detail by K. Brom and M. Orenstein, "The Privatised Sector in the Czech Republic: Government and Bank Control in a Transition Economy", *Institute of East–West Studies Working Paper* (1994).

[20] *See* Thuma (1995), *supra* note 9.

[21] On the flow and stock problem in general *see* S. Fries and T. Lane, "Financial and Enterprise Restructuring in Emerging Market Economies" in G. Caprio et al. (eds.), *Building Sound Finance in Emerging Market Economies*, IMF/the World Bank (1994).

[22] *See* K. Miszei, "Bankruptcy and the Post-communist Economies of East Central Europe", *Institute for East-West Studies Working Paper* (1993).

[23] *See* P. Rymazewski, "Polish Insolvency Procedures as a Tool for Privatisation" in OECD (1995), *supra* note 4.

[24] *See* L. Bergstrom, "Insolvency Proceedings Regarding State-Owned Enterprises in Russia" in OECD (1995), *supra* note 4.

From a comparative point of view, there seems to be a trade-off between the effective implementation of bankruptcy provisions and the adoption of a rapid/mass privatisation programme.[25] Countries which have followed a more traditional "sales" approach to privatisation, such as Hungary or Estonia, have been forced to introduce at an earlier stage insolvency procedures as an alternative way of enforcing market discipline on companies which had not yet acquired a private incentive structure. On the other hand, where mass privatisation was the norm, as in the Czech Republic or Russia, imposing similar constraints on SOEs could cause considerable delays and generate additional transaction costs to their privatisation.

4 THE STRUCTURE OF GENERAL INSOLVENCY LEGISLATION

4.1 The criterion of insolvency

In many transition economies (Russia, Poland, Czech Republic), insolvency laws use a mixed test of balance sheet and payment default/cash flow criteria. This has created a lot of ambiguities and has been a major disincentive in the implementation of these laws. Judges are often reticent to pronounce a company insolvent just because it has failed to pay some debts. They feel that they have to look at the balance sheet – itself rarely revealing any substantial information – and make an "economically sound" judgment on the long-term solvency of the firm. But this should not be the job of the judge, especially where the latter is ill-equipped to take such a decision. Some OECD countries have employed similarly vague definitions: payment default criteria can, in certain cases, be combined with balance sheet elements such as the existence of excessive debt or available assets.[26] It has taken the courts, which are in these countries in a much better position to interpret such provisions than in post-communist countries, considerable time and effort to develop case law criteria. Some OECD countries provide for clear definitions,[27] much like the Hungarian law, setting precise conditions under which payment default constitutes insolvency.

A clear-cut payment default criterion should be used to indicate insolvency. This avoids bottlenecks and confusion in the courts and allows both the debtor and its creditors to seek timely protection of their interests. There should be a presumption that if an enterprise which does not pay (a) mature debt(s) amounting to a certain sum to one or more creditors, so that payment is overdue for a certain period of time, this is insolvent; the

---

[25] *See* E. Mirsky and A. Weismann, "Central and Eastern European Bankruptcy and Restructuring: Estonia, Latvia, Lithuania", mimeo, USAID/Deloitte Touche (1995).

[26] *See* S. Nestor and S. Thomas, "Privatisation through Liquidation", 192 *OECD Observer* (1995), p. 38.

[27] *See, e.g.,* both the French and the German laws. *See,* respectively, H. Lafont, "The French Bankruptcy System" in OECD (1994), *supra* note 12, p. 17, and H. Fialski, "Insolvency Law in the Federal Republic of Germany", *id.* at p. 22.

threshold of both the amount and time should be reasonably low. The burden of proof to the contrary should be assumed by the debtor and should be quite onerous (for example, proof that payment – including interest – will be effected, beyond reasonable doubt, within the next 30 days). In case of debtor filings the criterion could be somehow broader so that it can include situations where cessation of payments is reasonably expected in the immediate future; the debtor's burden of positive proof in this case would, consequently, be lighter.

Any creditor, acting alone or jointly with other creditors, should be able to initiate bankruptcy proceedings. Debtors could also file under the conditions outlined above. Compulsory debtor filings could also be envisaged, but in this case the amount and time thresholds (*i.e.*, time elapsed since the debt became overdue) of the trigger should be higher. This approach would retain the beneficial effects of the first Hungarian law as regards the lowering of inter-enterprise arrears and the tightening of payment discipline but would avoid some of its negative aspects, *i.e.*, the premature drawing into insolvency procedures of enterprises in a temporary illiquid position, as a consequence of very low thresholds.[28]

4.2 The management of the debtor

In most transition economies, current legislative arrangements postulate outside administration during the insolvency period. Only Poland (in the context of "arrangement", *i.e.*, reorganisation procedures) and Russia (in the context of "sanacyia" or rehabilitation proceedings) include possibilities for debtor-in-possession arrangements. Both of these procedures have been rarely used.

As with the trigger discussion, the main issue here is to make proceedings simple, effective and market-oriented. These objectives are best served with the introduction of a creditor-driven procedure.[29]

In principle, debtor-in-possession arrangements should neither be encouraged nor excluded. While the fact that most incumbent managers in transition economies are of poor quality and unable to promote restructuring is an argument against such arrangements,[30] in some cases it might be prohibitively expensive to hire external administrators. The creditors should decide on the appointment of an external administrator or the maintenance of debtor-in-possession arrangements. However, given the fact that in many transition economies the biggest creditors (such as banks or big suppliers) are often held hostage by the debtor and its managers, it might be advisable to provide for a qualified majority of claims for the approval of the debtor-in-possession arrangements. The court should accept the creditors' choice unless there is strong evidence of a wilful attempt to abuse

---

[28] *E.g.*, Australia. *See* J. Lehane, T. L'Estrange and A. Powles, "Australia Country Review" in "Solving the Insoluble", *International Financial Law Review* (special issue) (1990), p. 9.

[29] *See, contra*, Sak and Schiffman, *supra* note 13, p. 934. It should be noted that the French law also requires the debtor to file for bankruptcy, albeit in quite uncertain terms.

[30] *See* Balz, *supra* note 7, pp. 3–4.

the process. Moreover, where debtor-in-possession arrangements are chosen, it might be advisable to provide for the nomination by the court of an external supervisor.[31] The creditors committee should also be allowed at any point to change existing debtor-in-possession arrangements.

The law should provide for a very flexible regime regarding the trustees remuneration. Performance-linked schemes should be specifically allowed and encouraged. They might be essential to attract capable administrators to insolvent enterprises without excessively raising the costs of the procedure.

The trustee (or debtor-in-possession) should have wide-ranging powers, which should include the disposal of assets not essential to the business.

4.3 The bankruptcy decision and its effects

The creation of an estate which encompasses all property rights of the debtor, including collateral and mortgaged property, is the first and foremost result of a bankruptcy decision.

A thorny issue in some transition economies, mainly the Newly Independent States of the former U.S.S.R. (NIS), is the ownership of a vast array of "social assets", *i.e.*, workers' housing, stadiums, kindergartens, vacation facilities, etc. by the enterprises involved. It seems preferable not to include these assets in the estate for obvious social reasons; the long disturbance in their functioning and their piecemeal liquidation might result in an unbearable cost to the community (sometimes a very large one) that is supposed to benefit from them. However, they should be separated quasi-automatically (*i.e.*, as a direct consequence of the bankruptcy decision) from the enterprise and transferred to the local authorities. This would avoid the debtor holding hostage the community (and perhaps the state) in order to be bailed-out.

A comprehensive, automatic moratorium on creditor action should be a direct consequence of the creation of the estate if real collective proceedings are to function effectively. All pre-insolvency creditors – including secured ones – should be included in this moratorium; the latter should be strictly mandatory for the administrator. Excluding secured creditors from the bankruptcy process, as it is now the case under current Russian, Polish and – to a degree – Estonian and the amended Hungarian law,[32] cancels most of the benefits of collective proceedings. It creates a powerful liquidation bias by allowing secured creditors to "plunder" the estate before its administrator has a chance to explore any reorganisation alternatives (or even assess the net present value of the firm).[33] On the other hand, inclusion of

---

[31] *See* K. Miszei, "Financial Distress and Bankruptcy: The Main Issues and Hypotheses" in OECD (1995), *supra* note 4, p. 5.

[32] That is also the case in Denmark. *See* A. Gammeljord, "Denmark Country Report" in *International Financial Law Review* (1990), *supra* note 28, p. 17.

[33] The latter two make a moratorium conditional on creditor approval: *see* Szanyi, *supra* note 15, p. 4. In Poland, action by secured creditors that was initiated before the bankruptcy decision is not subject to the stay: *see* Szlezak, "Polish Bankruptcy and Re-organisation Law" in OECD (1994), *supra* note 12, p. 113.

secured creditors may constitute an infringement of their priority rights and thus weaken the nascent property rights system. Ensuring that their priority rights are not eroded in the distribution of liquidation proceeds and that interest and the eventual depreciation of collateral are treated as part of their original claim, might remedy to a great extent this infringement.

There should be vast powers of avoidance vested in the administrator of the estate; he/she should be in a position to restore the estate to its true value and rescind all transactions that, objectively, have harmed the creditors as a group, as well as gratuitous acts, irrespective of their cause. Avoidance powers are specifically enumerated in Polish law but are rather vague in the Czech and Hungarian laws and are practically absent in the Russian statutes.[34] Executory contracts (*i.e.*, contracts not fully executed by both parties, such as leases, labour contracts, etc.) should be subject to rejections for their future component, irrespective of the time they were concluded.

A related issue is the capacity of the system to prevent insider deals and the plundering of the estate by insiders. This is especially important in transition economies where the weakening of corporate control by state authorities combined with a lack of clear property rights for a prolonged period of time have become fertile ground for such behaviour by managers.[35] In addition to banning such transactions in the insolvency period, the law might provide for specific civil and criminal sanctions for company directors, if the insolvency is found to be a result of their own illegal behaviour.

4.4 The insolvency procedure

Most transition economies – like the majority of OECD countries – have adopted different, distinct procedures that correspond to different expected outcomes of insolvency proceedings. Reorganisation rules are usually quite different from liquidation rules; a switch from one to the other entails high costs. The Russian law, for example, provides for five different insolvency procedures, each one with different incentives to debtors and creditors and different roles for the courts.[36] Moreover, in a large number of these countries (for example, Czech Republic, Poland, Russia, Slovakia), the courts are expected to play a paramount role in economic decision-making in the context of insolvency.

---

[34] The creation of a comprehensive moratorium on creditor action was one of the main goals in the recent overhaul of the German insolvency framework; *see* M. Balz and H-G. Landfermann, *Die Neuen Insolvenzgesetze* (1995).

[35] Thus, the administrator may reverse "suspicious" pre-insolvency transactions only on the basis of the general (and much harder to administer) civil law remedy of *Actio Pauliana*, which presupposes an intent to defraud or otherwise harm creditors.

[36] *See* S. Nestor and S. Thomas, "Systemic Privatisation and Restructuring in East-Central Europe", *Papers Presented to the Joint Economic Committee of the U.S. Congress* (1994), p. 73.

Given the institutional/implementation problems mentioned above, such reliance on the judiciary is unrealistic. It is more important to put special emphasis on the "user-friendliness" of the law,[37] on the facility and effectiveness with which it can be implemented. The most important item in such an agenda would be the empowerment of creditors to make the major decisions. On the drafting side, three methods to enhance this aspect of the law are: (a) the adoption of "bright lines", *i.e.*, hard and fast rules when it comes to thresholds, amounts, voting rules, etc. as well as clear-cut definitions of the rights and obligations of different agents in the insolvency process; (b) a system of presumptions in areas where court decisions have to be made, entailing shifts of the burden of proof; (c) time limits for all actions in the insolvency procedure and clear default solutions in the case of non-action.

A unitary procedure – like the one adopted in the context of the new 1994 German Insolvency Law – seems to be the most effective way to organise insolvency proceedings.[38] It considerably lowers the costs incurred when switching, say from a reorganisation to a liquidation process, and avoids inefficient solutions that are the result of "path dependency", *i.e.*, of the process (instead of the stakeholders) determining the outcome. The creditors should be able to choose between different plans of selling the business as a whole, selling parts of it as going concerns or separate assets, or reorganising the firm and its capital structure by reshuffling property rights among existing shareholders and creditors. Obviously, the final solution can in any particular case be a combination of the above.

In order to get as many alternatives as possible, the submission of bids should be open to anyone (*i.e.*, including current shareholders, managements, employees, creditors and third parties).[39] Another important prerequisite for the facilitation of bids is the availability of information on the debtor company. There should be specific provisions on the powers and obligations of the administrator of the estate to extract information from management and make it available to potential bidders.

Both cash and non-cash bids should be allowed in the process of reorganisation/liquidation.[40] This is very important in countries where liquidity is very low. Debt-equity conversions in particular should be encouraged (with an exception where the state or enterprises majority-owned by the state are the creditors).

Creditors should be free to accept any amount of debt write-offs they see fit.[41] There is no economic rationale behind the imposition on creditors of a level of claim satisfaction – the state has no role in telling a creditor not to

---

[37] Such an approach has been adopted in the context of French insolvency proceedings: *see* G. Endreo, "France Country Report" in *International Financial Law Review* (1990), *supra* note 28, p. 25.

[38] *See* V. Yakovlev, "The Legislation of the Russian Federation Concerning Bankruptcy" in OECD (1994), *supra* note 12, p. 131.

[39] *See* Sak and Schiffman, *supra* note 13, p. 931.

[40] *See* Balz and Landfermann, *supra* note 34.

[41] In contrast, under U.S. Chapter 11 proceedings, the debtor-in-possession is, in practice, the only party that can submit a reorganisation plan: *see* H. Swaim, "United States Bankruptcy/Reorganisation Laws" in OECD (1994), *supra* note 12, p. 65.

accept 10 cents on a dollar if it thinks that's the best it can manage. On the other hand, the state as creditor should be statutorily obliged to accept to write-off or reschedule debt on conditions that are as favourable as those of the immediately lower class of creditors. This would greatly encourage reorganisation efforts and boost the creditors' incentive to keep the firm as a going concern; it would also serve the transition state's strategic interests in terms of employment and rapid restructuring of the economy better than receiving a few more pennies for the state budget.[42]

A creditor-driven procedure requires an effective decision-making mechanism that allows creditors to examine and vote upon different reorganisation/liquidation options. This mechanism should be based on two precepts: flexibility, *i.e.*, the possibility to approve a plan, even though a minority of creditors disagree; and respect of the absolute priority rule, *i.e.*, the protection of senior creditors from decisions that infringe on their secured property rights.[43] Most transition economies have adopted traditional continental rules requiring a qualified – and usually very large – majority of claims for the adoption of any reorganisation plans. This approach has proven to be quite ineffective in terms of providing incentives for reorganisations. Moreover, it might also infringe the absolute priority rule, in cases where secured creditors are a minority in terms of claims – a likely situation in transition economies where secured lending is a new and not quite established financing technique.

The solution that has been given in the U.S. Bankruptcy Code to address this problem has been the establishment of creditor classes. Voting takes place inside each class of creditors. While the U.S. Code requires a two-thirds majority of claims in each class, the proportion can be a lower figure in a transition economy, eager to promote flexibility and restructuring. In principle, the choice of a lower class cannot be imposed on a higher class. However, the court can, exceptionally, impose such a choice, through a procedure known as "cram-down". The implementation of the cram-down rule by the court should be limited and guided by a number of considerations: the amount of claims dissenting to the proposed solution (in both the upper and the lower classes), the availability of other feasible alternatives or whether the plan is likely to guarantee to secured claimants (or another dissenting class) a fair and equitable treatment.[44]

4.5 The order of claims

The order of claim satisfaction is in most transition economies significantly distorted. State claims rank higher than unsecured claims in almost every

---

[42] *See* Aghion et al, *supra* note 6.

[43] Only Hungary has no thresholds for claim satisfaction in the case of debt restructuring. Czech, Russian and Polish legislation provide for mandatory percentages for claim satisfaction: *see* Sak and Schiffman, *supra* note 13, p. 941 and Yakovlev, *supra* note 38, p. 136.

[44] This was an important reason for the relative success of the Polish bank conciliation scheme: *see* infra and S. van Wijnbergen, "The Role of the Banks in Enterprise Restructuring: the Polish Example", *i.e.* Centre for Economic Policy and Research, *Discussion Paper*, No. 898 (1994).

country in the area. In Latvia they are higher than everything else.[45] Polish law ranks (unsecured) claims to banks higher than other unsecured claims. Finally, provisions on administrative claims (*i.e.*, claims that arise in the post-insolvency context) are either extremely vague (Russia, Lithuania) or non-existent (Latvia).

Administrative/post-insolvency claims should, in principle, have priority over other, pre-insolvency claims. This is especially true for the administrator's fees (not, however, their performance-related bonuses), expenses related to the procedure and post-insolvency wages. Other post-insolvency creditors should not have absolute priority over secured creditors, since this could significantly distort market-based incentives. Nevertheless, it might be advisable to "split the pie" between post-insolvency and secured creditors, so that reorganisation attempts become more likely, with the provision of fresh working capital.

Claims by secured creditors should be on the top of the order. This is a fundamental prerequisite for the market-conformity of the proceedings and for the development of an effective system of corporate finance by the banking sector. Downgrading secured claims might result in a higher cost of capital for the whole economy.[46]

Although in many OECD countries tax arrears and other state budget claims have priority ranking, most experts and policy makers agree that such a ranking is not justified and may actually be an obstacle to successful reallocation of resources within the insolvency framework.[47] It is more rational to treat state authorities as general creditors.

Claims for unpaid wages should also be, in principle, covered by social security in the case of bankruptcy. However, given the current transition difficulties, such claims, limited to a brief period before insolvency, could be ranked above general creditor claims.

5 INSOLVENCY PROCEDURES AND PRIVATISATION[48]

Insolvency procedures and privatisation pursue different policy goals. Bankruptcy is a creditor-driven debt-collection mechanism which imposes financial discipline on enterprises and enforces property rights. Privatisation in transition economies is a major tool for the creation of a private sector; it is, in principle, owner-driven. Yet, there seems to be a broad interface between the two policy areas: both are seen as tools to promote restructuring of enterprises, either on a going-concern basis or through liquidation and subsequent reallocation of their assets to new, more efficient owners.

---

[45] For a thorough analysis of the absolute priority rule, *see* E. Warren, "A Theory of Absolute Priority", 9 *Annual Survey of American Law* (1991), p. 16.

[46] Section 1129(b) of the U.S. Bankruptcy Code defines in detail what is "fair and equitable" for each class of claimants.

[47] *See* Mirsky *et al.*, *supra* note 25.

[48] *See* Miszei (1993), *supra* note 22.

In certain transition economies, general insolvency procedures have been a major tool in the privatisation process. In Hungary almost one-third of the enterprises in the State Property Agency's portfolio have entered into insolvency proceedings. In Poland, a little less than half of the enterprises privatised were actually liquidated.[49] In addition to the perceived trade-off between rigorous implementation of bankruptcy provisions and the adoption of voucher privatisation programmes,[50] one can observe a relationship between speed of privatisation and the amount of SOEs undergoing bankruptcy proceedings. In countries that have emphasised speed in privatisation (Czech Republic, Russia, Lithuania and Estonia) relatively few SOEs have gone through bankruptcy procedures. Where privatisation proper has been slow (Poland, Hungary) a large number of SOEs have been effectively privatised through bankruptcy/liquidation procedures.

The advantage of using general insolvency proceedings for the purposes of ownership transformation and systemic restructuring lies in the decentralisation effect on these two processes. Decisions on ownership changes are taken from the hands of bureaucrats and placed in a market-driven context, at least in theory. Putting in place an effective insolvency mechanism that encompasses both private firms and SOEs constitutes a powerful incentive for SOEs to strive for their privatisation. But this mechanism will hardly be in a position to deal, at least in the short term, with the amount and complexity of privatisation cases in a transition economy.[51] Moreover, its social and political costs might be very high. Therefore, rapid privatisation should still be considered the main tool for ownership transformation: the corporate governance change might reverse the fortunes of some troubled but privatised SOEs; in the worst of cases privatisation might spread insolvency procedures more evenly over time.

It might be necessary to supplement both general insolvency procedures and mass privatisation programmes with transitional arrangements that focus on systemic transformation problems at the enterprise level. These problems include creditor passivity and information asymmetries. Transitional arrangements for insolvent enterprises, typically, consist of out-of-court procedures, usually prescribed in a separate legal instrument, affecting insolvent SOEs and aiming at their privatisation and restructuring (either on an asset or going-concern basis). They are temporary in nature. They aim to create a "half-way house" stage for insolvent/illiquid debtors; courts and the general insolvency framework remain the default solution.

Two main approaches have emerged: the first one consists of the so-called "conciliation" proceedings, *i.e.*, creditor(bank)-led arrangements, usually a forming part of a package aiming at bank restructuring. Poland and, more recently, Hungary, have adopted such procedures. The second one entails the assignment of restructuring/liquidation responsibilities to a state institution, either existing or established for this purpose. This has

---

[49] *See* OECD (1994), *supra* note 12, pp. 7–13.
[50] This section draws substantially on Nestor and Thomas (1994), *supra* note 36, pp. 74–78.
[51] *See* OECD (1995), *supra* note 4.

been the approach in the former East Germany and in Russia. Poland has also provided for such procedures as regards smaller SOEs.

The choice between these two approaches should, to a great extent, be determined by the nature of the debt overhang. Where, as is generally the case in Central European countries, outstanding bad debt is mainly owed to the banking sector, creditor-led proceedings might be the better solution. Where, as is the case in most NIS, inter-enterprise arrears and overdue debts to the state budget are the main culprits, a state institution might be the best agent for SOE clean-up.

5.1 Creditor-led arrangements

The purpose of creditor-led arrangements is to combine two important policy objectives in the transformation process: bank rehabilitation and enterprise restructuring. In the case of Poland, more than 200 generally large SOEs went through the arrangement/conciliation proceedings led by banks. In the Polish scheme, banks are *ex-ante* recapitalised and thus given a powerful incentive to work out their non-performing loans in direct negotiations with debtors, without a pressing liquidity bias. The main creditor bank becomes responsible for initiating and directing proceedings against a particular debtor. These aim at reorganising the debtor on the basis of a restructuring plan, whose central feature is ownership transformation. The decision of whether to pursue liquidation or reorganisation is based on the assessment of the present going-concern value of the debtor. Apart from debt write-offs and rescheduling (in which state claims are mandatorily included) debt-to-equity swaps play an important role in this approach.

In contrast to the relative success of the Polish conciliation scheme, a similar programme in Hungary failed to yield important results on either bank rehabilitation or enterprise restructuring.[52] In the first place, it seems that banking supervision rules and their implementation were ineffective. This, combined with successive bank recapitalisations, intensified moral hazard and weakened the incentives for banks to pursue aggressive debt-collection-cum-enterprise rehabilitation policies. A second reason might be the fact that the state, contrary to the Polish scheme, did not offer to match any debt reduction adopted by other creditors. Thirdly, the evaluation of debtor plans was not carried out by creditors/banks but by a state committee; this denied the scheme much of its flexibility and creditor-driven character.

The advantages of conciliation procedures are their flexible, decentralised nature and relatively low transaction costs. In transition countries that have developed towards a universal banking system with relatively few big players, banks are more likely to possess the necessary information and resources (including expertise) to assess the present value of debtors. There is, however, an important downside. Given the large number of insolvent enterprises and the generally poor state of bank balance sheets and governance, credit institutions may not be able to cope with an extensive

---

[52] *See* Gray, *supra* note 8.

work-out exercise which might considerably divert time and energy from other important banking activities.[53] In this aspect it should be noted that while the Polish government initially envisaged that more than 130 enterprises to go through bank-led conciliation arrangements, the banks did not manage to come to terms with more that 80 SOEs. Moreover, debt work-outs result in large debt-to-equity swaps. Bank balance sheets might, thus, become considerably riskier on the asset side. That is why such schemes will only work if coupled with effective banking supervision.

5.2 State institutions as insolvency agents

Using state institutions as restructuring agents for insolvent SOEs is a method widely employed in the region. In the German case, almost a third of the 13,000 companies privatised went through quasi-insolvency proceedings administered by the Treuhandanstalt.[54] In Russia, the Federal Bankruptcy Agency has started proceedings against more than 500 wholly or partly state-owned enterprises, while another 2000 are on its list. Debtor reorganisation (or liquidation) is usually combined with rapid privatisation. "Normal" privatisation methods may be avoided or circumvented for the sake of expediency. In some cases (as in the Polish liquidation process for small and medium-sized SOEs), the inclusion of enterprises in this insolvency process results in a change of corporate control. Controlling ministries, traditionally serving sectoral or simply bureaucratic goals, which might be less keen on privatising, are replaced by institutions that are either exclusively or primarily focused on privatisation.[55] Furthermore, it is argued that a state institution, being at the same time the owner and a powerful creditor, is better placed than any other agent to assess the present value of a going concern and eventually force its transformation into "privatisable" entities.

In Russia, an important function of the Bankruptcy Agency is actually to file the bankruptcy with the courts. One of its main tasks is, therefore, to forcefully overcome creditor passivity. Not only does it initiate general insolvency proceedings but it also provides the administrators of the insolvent's estate.[56]

This approach has presented certain important drawbacks. There is considerable risk of changing the focus of the process. This might be inherent in the assignment to the same agent of two largely conflicting functions, *i.e.*, creditor and owner – in spite of the "power" argument mentioned above.[57] Unless a clear mandate and scope is provided, the state institution might become more "restructuring" than privatisation-oriented and thus prolong the agony of inefficient SOEs and the waste of public money for a consider-

[53] *See* P. Rymazewski, *supra* note 13; van Wijnbergen, *supra* note 44. *See also* papers in S. Kawalec and M. Simoneti (eds), *Bank Rehabilitation and Enterprise Restructuring* (1995).

[54] For a critique of the Hungarian scheme, *see* M. Szanyi, *supra* note 15, K. Miszei, *supra* note 31, and Szekeres in Kawalec and Simoneti, *supra* note 54.

[55] On this point, *see* H. Blommestein and M. Spencer, "The Role of Financial Institutions in the Transition to a Market Economy" in G. Caprio, et al. (1994), *supra* note 21.

[56] *See* E. Wandel, "The Treuhandanstalt and the Winding up of Companies Incapable of Effective Restructuring" in OECD (1995), *supra* note 4.

[57] *See* J. Bukowski, "Performance of Polish Small and Medium-sized Enterprises Privatised Through Leveraged Buy-outs", mimeo (1995), pp. 1–3.

able period of time. In this respect, separating (at least in certain categories of "severe" insolvency cases) the ownership and creditor functions and assigning them to different institutions should be envisaged. This might also mitigate the risk of an insolvency agency becoming an obvious political target and lower the scope for corruption in the process.[58]

Finally, there is a danger of institutional conflict between the judiciary which is, in principle, the central institution in general insolvency procedures, and specialised state agencies. It is, therefore, important for the legal framework to provide for complementary rather than conflicting mandates and ensure that both substantive tasks and temporal jurisdiction do not overlap.[59]

6 FINAL REMARKS

This chapter has argued for a creditor-driven, "user-friendly" bankruptcy procedure, that would allow firms in transition economies, hit by systemic illiquidity, to reorganise without compromising seriously creditor rights and the absolute priority rule. It has also argued for parallel out-of-court proceedings, of a strictly transitional nature, that would link the survival of troubled SOEs to their privatisation.

Insolvency procedures are the necessary linchpin of a country's financial system. Without a clear-cut normative structure for determining the fate of insolvent firms and their assets, risk management by financial market agents becomes infinitely more complicated, whether this involves banks assessing loan risk or shareholders calculating portfolio risk. But even if such a structure is in place, the absence or illiquidity of markets for assets may make it very difficult for the system to function. In this respect, it might be worth considering the creation of state-backed asset pools, similar to the ones created in Eastern Germany. These pools can provide liquidity to enterprises that need to sell assets (real estate, machinery, etc.) rapidly and, at the same time may help create a market for these assets. Their role as buyers should of course be of a strictly temporary nature, *i.e.*, more of an underwriting than an ownership function.

Another important debate is centred on the social function of the insolvency framework. Certain OECD countries, like France, have included social objectives within the scope of their legislation. This, however, risks undermining the primary goals of bankruptcy laws, which are to enforce property rights and to facilitate the efficient allocation of resources in the economy. Introducing social considerations in the bankruptcy framework might be even more harmful in a transition economy, where both market factors and property rights are in the nascent stage of their development. That is not to say that social stability is not important. It should, however, be the object of other policies that directly focus on unemployment, social welfare and worker retraining rather than becoming the justification for raising obstacles to resource reallocation. The latter is the only long-term way towards sustainable development and, thus, increased prosperity for the transition economies.

---

[58] *See* Bergstrom, *supra*, note 24.
[59] *See* Miszei (1995), *supra*, note 31.

10.   An Introduction to the European Bank's Model Law on Secured Transactions[1]

John L. Simpson[2]
Jan-Hendrik M. Röver[3]

Secured transactions play a vital role in financing in emerging and transitional market economies. Every commercial investor is interested in making a profit from his investment but in many cases the first fundamental concern is to obtain protection against loss of the investment. A legal framework for secured transactions is a key requirement in creating an investor-friendly climate. An investor who knows that he has legally recognised rights to turn to his debtor's assets in case of non-payment may assess the investment risk quite differently. It may influence his decision whether to invest or not; it may also change the terms on which he is prepared to invest (typically by lowering the interest rate or extending the term of a loan). There is a direct relationship between the legal framework and the attitude of the investor. If there is a law on secured transactions which is seen to give practical protection and remedies in the case of non-payment of a debt, then security can become a major part of the investment decision, both for local and international investors. If the investor is not persuaded that the law gives real protection and remedies then it becomes irrelevant.

Shortly after the European Bank was established in 1991 it became evident that central and eastern European countries needed particular support in the area of secured transactions. A Round Table discussion at the First Annual Meeting of 1992 in Budapest indicated clearly that most countries either did not have any rules on secured transactions at all or had to rely on outdated rules from pre-communist regimes. After that meeting the Bank set up its Secured Transactions Project and produced a first

---

[1] Adapted from the introduction published with European Bank for Reconstruction and Development, *Model Law on Secured Transactions* (London, 1994).
[2] Consultant, European Bank for Reconstruction and Development, London.
[3] Consultant, European Bank for Reconstruction and Development, London.

"working draft" for a Model Law on Secured Transactions for the Bank's Second Annual Meeting in April 1993 in London. At that meeting a Round Table discussion on the Model Law was led by the Project's Advisory Board. The next year was spent in wide consultations, both within the region and outside, and in developing the working draft into the final text of the Model Law on Secured Transactions presented at the Third Annual Meeting of the Bank in St. Petersburg in April 1994.

Why a Model Law? If the European Bank's contribution in the area of secured transactions was to be effective it had to be rapid and practical. It also had to recognise that the precise needs and the legal traditions of each country are different. It would have been possible just to give general advice; but the advice would have to be applied and it is often only in the course of the practical drafting of a law that the nature and extent of the legal issues are properly understood. The Bank therefore decided that it would be more efficient, and of more help to those seeking to develop their own laws, if it drew up a guide in the form of a model law. The Model Law is *not* intended as detailed legislation for direct incorporation into local legal systems. It is, however, intended to form the basis for national legislation. It seeks to combine carefully worded and detailed legal text with a high degree of flexibility, to enable adaptation to local circumstances. The principal objectives are both to harmonise the approach to security rights legislation and to provide guidance as to expectations of international investors and lenders.

The Model Law is based on comparative work and has been influenced by a number of legal systems. This was made possible through the support of an international Advisory Board consisting of twenty academic and practising lawyers from fifteen jurisdictions and through the views, suggestions and critique contributed by many others. The draftsmen of the Model Law have combined a civil law and a common law approach and have sought to draw on a broad range of legal and practical sources, both in central, eastern and western European countries and elsewhere in the world.

One principle which has guided the drafting of the Model Law has been to produce a text which is compatible with the *civil law* concepts which underlie many central and eastern European legal systems and, at the same time, draw on common law systems which have developed many useful solutions to accommodate modern financing techniques. This aim underscores the economic function of a law on secured transactions. If the Model Law has in places departed from some of the traditional legal concepts of secured transactions found in laws which date from times when financing had a less important role, it is with a view to achieving a result which is economically efficient for both lender and borrower. The lender must obtain real benefit from holding security but not at the expense of depriving the borrower of the use of the assets given as security or the flexibility needed to operate an efficient business. Although the Model Law should form the basis for modern legislation covering a wide range of sometimes complex matters it had to be kept *simple* in order to be of practical use for market economies in transition. The Model Law is, therefore, a basic system on which more sophisticated rules can be grafted.

1 THE BASIC PRINCIPLES OF THE MODEL LAW

Several features may summarise the content of the Model Law.

1.1 Single security right

The Model Law is based on the idea of a *single security right for all types of things and rights* which is called a "charge". The distinction of various traditional types of security rights, such as pledge of movables, pledge of rights and mortgages is merged in this one right.

1.2 Right in property

A charge under the Model Law is by nature a *property right* and not a mere obligation. The right entitles the person receiving security to a sale of the things and rights taken as security in enforcement proceedings and gives preference over unsecured creditors in enforcement and insolvency proceedings.

1.3 Securing business credits

For charges granted by natural persons the Model Law is limited to securing *business credits* since this is the area of most pressing need. It could be extended to cover personal and consumer transactions in countries where adequate rules on consumer protection exist.

1.4 Minimum restrictions

The parties to the charge are given maximum *flexibility* to arrange their relationship as best suits their particular needs. The mandatory requirements and the restrictions on what the parties can agree have been kept to a minimum.

1.5 Flexible definition of secured debt and charged property

There is also great flexibility in the way in which the parties can define the debt or debts which are secured and the things and rights which are given as security. In both cases they can be described specifically or generally, they can be present or future and they can change during the life of the charge; it suffices that they are identified at the outset.

1.6 Public registration

The Model Law works on the principle that charges are a matter for *public knowledge*. Since Roman law, the idea that a person may create secret rights in his assets has always been received with scepticism. A person who gives assets as security but does not indicate this to his potential creditors creates an impression of "false wealth". The Model Law achieves publicity mainly by relying on registration of charges at a separate charges' registry.

1.7 Broad rights of enforcement

Enforcement relies in the first instance on *self-help*, the person holding the charge being given broad but clearly defined rights to sell the charged property in whichever way he considers most appropriate. This is supported by the right of any interested party to apply to the court for protection and to claim damages from the person enforcing the charge for any loss suffered as a result of wrongful or abusive enforcement. The interests of persons claiming entitlement to the proceeds of sale are further protected by distribution being made through a proceeds depositary.

1.8 Sale of enterprise

Where the charge covers all the assets of an enterprise there is the additional remedy of *selling the enterprise as a going concern*, which may enable an enterprise in financial difficulties to be saved while increasing the recovery of the secured creditor. This is a complex area which will require development in each jurisdiction, in particular by taking account of local insolvency laws, but the Model Law seeks to give at least a preliminary indication of how such a system might be achieved.

1.9 Practical application

A number of provisions have been included in the Model Law to cover practical matters which often give difficulties in secured transactions, such as a continuing *licence* to the chargor to deal in the charged property and the inclusion of a *"charge manager"* to "manage" the charge where there are a number of chargeholders, for example in the case of a syndicated loan.

The law itself is divided in five large parts. Part 1 contains *general provisions* which set out who can give a charge, who can receive a charge, and general rules concerning the secured debt and the charged property.

2 THE STRUCTURE OF THE MODEL LAW

Part 2 deals with rules on the *creation* of charges and introduces the general distinction between *registered charges* which have to be registered at a charges' registry; *possessory charges* where registration is not required but the chargeholder takes possession of the charged property, and *unpaid vendor's charges* which protect suppliers of goods who seek retention of title. Part 2 also contains rules about the defences of a chargor against a charge and the rights and obligations of chargor and chargeholder and introduces the idea of a charge manager, who is designed to stand in the place of the chargeholders for most dealings concerning the charge.

Part 3 provides for the case where *third parties are involved*, in particular the priorities between different chargeholders, the transfer of a secured debt (and a charge), the licence of the chargor to deal in the charged property and the acquisition by third parties of things or rights which are subject to a charge.

Part 4 sets out a system of *enforcement* proceedings. The Model Law allows the person taking security to enforce the charge immediately after a failure to pay the secured debt. There is no requirement of a separate court order to enable the chargeholder to enforce his charge and the Model Law allows considerable flexibility to the person enforcing a charge while including necessary protections against abuse.

The rules on enforcement have to interface with local insolvency laws and will have to be adapted to fit with local procedural rules. It is vital that appropriate provisions on enforcement are included. Without the assurance of a clear right to enforce the chargeholder is deprived of his remedy and a charge becomes valueless.

Part 4 of the Model Law is completed by a definition of the different events which cause a charge to terminate.

Finally, Part 5 sets out rules for *registration* at a separate charges' registry. Again these will need to be supplemented according to the needs of each country. It is of particular importance that registration does not involve cumbersome procedures but remains a simple, low-cost administrative act.

The Model Law is designed to provide a fair balance between the competing but legitimate interests of debtor, secured creditor and other parties. Such a system is necessarily comprehensive, with different parts being dependent on each other. It is not sufficient for central and eastern European countries to have a law on secured transactions: it has to be a law which works and the Model Law will have to be adapted to interface with local law, for example in the areas of contract law, land law, company law, court procedures and insolvency rules. In places the Model Law may give an indication of how that interface may occur but the draftsmen have limited the Model Law intentionally to the field of secured transactions.

A practical commentary was published with the Model Law and gives a short explanation of the concepts developed in the Model Law and the way that it may work in practice. Time was of the essence for this project; the Model Law had to be produced quickly and although eighteen months may seem a long time, it felt very short for those working on the project. The "final" version of the Model Law is intended to be a living text which can be developed further as experience is gained in using it to develop national laws.

The Model Law aims to assist central and eastern European countries in multiple ways. Once the drafting had been completed the task ahead was and remains to use the Model Law as a basis from which national laws can be developed; the way that is being done varies from country to country. In several jurisdictions the drafts of the Model Law contributed to the process of producing new legislation even before the Model Law was completed. In the twenty months since the Model Law has been published an accelerating momentum has been generated for moves from a theoretical model law to the practical changes that are needed to national laws as part of the transition towards open market-oriented economies. The European Bank currently has six technical assistance projects where it is working with the governments of individual jurisdictions to assist in the drafting and implementation of secured transactions laws. More broadly, the Bank is drawing on the Model Law its continuing work to improve the laws and infrastructure for secured transactions in transition economies.

11. Project Finance in Central and Eastern Europe from a Lender's Perspective: Lessons Learned in Poland and Romania

John D. Crothers[1]

1 INTRODUCTION

The European Bank for Reconstruction and Development (the "EBRD" or the "Bank") approved 91 investment projects in 1993.[2] The author as a lawyer in the Office of General Counsel for the Bank was involved in eight of these projects including three projects each in Poland and Romania. The general lessons learned in two of these investments: an ECU35,000,000 chemical plant in Romania[3] and an ECU51,000,000 paper mill in Poland,[4] provide an interesting comparison between the law and practice of project finance from a lender's perspective in two distinct emerging markets within the general emerging market of Central and Eastern Europe. This chapter does not aim to provide an in-depth analysis of the two projects (and confidentiality requirements would not allow it in any event) but rather to make some general observations on the economic and legal background of the countries in which these projects are situated and how this affects the structure and implementation of projects.

2 ROMANIA AND POLAND: THE BACKGROUND FOR FOREIGN INVESTMENT

Romania and Poland are at different stages of transition to a market economy. Poland (along with Hungary and the Czech Republic) is well on

---

[1] Legal Counsel, European Bank for Reconstruction and Development, London; Member of the Bars of New York and Paris; B.C.L. (McGill) 1985; LL.B. (McGill) 1984. The opinions expressed in this chapter are those of the author and not of the European Bank for Reconstruction and Development.

[2] *1993 Annual Report of the EBRD*, London, 7 March 1994, p. 7 (copies available from the Bank upon request).

[3] "Virolite Functional Polymers", *Annual Report*, p. 65 ("Virolite").

[4] "Trebruk/Kostrzyn", *Annual Report*, p. 65 ("Trebruk").

its way to capitalism and receives large amounts of foreign direct investment, while in Romania, like Bulgaria and Slovakia, the pace of reform is slower.

Romania has a diversified industrial and agricultural base, a skilled work force and important natural resources. The total level of foreign investment in Romania remains modest, relative to the size and potential of the economy. Following three years of decline, the Romanian economy grew modestly in 1993 (a 1% increase in GDP), with tighter monetary policy and the resulting progress towards positive interest rates, a reduction in inflation and elimination of price subsidies. Privatisation continues to move forward slowly, however. Romania must still meet the challenges of reducing its heavy public enterprise sector, stimulating foreign investment and developing a more flexible legal framework for private sector development.

Poland ranks first as a target of EBRD investments. GDP growth is strongly positive, with the private sector growing significantly to just under half of GDP. The legal framework for a market economy is substantially in place, privatisation has been moving forward quickly and foreign direct investment strengthened significantly, reaching U.S.$350 million in 1993.

3 STRUCTURING THE INVESTMENT BASED ON RELATIVE COUNTRY RISK

The view of foreign investors and project lenders on relative country risk affects the basic structure of the project investment and its financing. The Virolite Romanian project and the Trebruk Polish investment were structured differently due in large part to the perceived levels of risk.

3.1 Structure of the foreign investment

The Romanian market is less developed and perceived as more risky by foreign investors and, as a result, the foreign sponsor in the Virolite transaction sought a joint venture with an established Romanian industrial partner operating in a similar field. The advantages were numerous: a local partner could help to smooth relations with regional and national authorities, could act as an additional source of cash and equipment and, since the local partner was also a chemical company and industrial entity in its own right, could provide access to a supply of raw materials and energy. There were, of course, also downsides to a joint venture as joint operation required sharing of initial capital contributions, management and profit.

Thus, the borrower under the EBRD financing was initially designed as a special purpose joint stock company organised under Romanian law to which the Romanian partner would contribute land and equipment on the site of its existing operation and the foreign investor would provide know-how, an off-take agreement for the product and management skills. Both parties would also contribute cash. The EBRD would, in turn, provide limited-recourse long-term debt financing.

Because of the difficult economic situation in Romania, it soon became apparent that the Romanian partner would not be in a position to provide the full cash contribution to the project that the parties had initially negotiated. Ultimately, the EBRD was asked to purchase shares in the joint venture in order to make up the Romanian cash shortfall. The Bank thus became an equity investor and lender and the initial investors gained not only a senior creditor but a significant minority shareholder.

The Bank's equity stake was structured as a "bridge" financing under which the industrial investors (with priority to the Romanian partner) were given a call on the Bank shares during the first seven years of the investment. It was hoped that the Romanian partner, given time, would be in a position to buy out the Bank's shares. From the seventh year, the Bank negotiated a "put" of its shares to the joint venture itself (to avoid dilution of the other investors), since the Bank is required by its founding charter to recycle its investments.

The Trebruk project in Poland, on the other hand, did not involve a Polish partner. A Swedish paper manufacturer, with co-investment by Nordic institutional investors, purchased 100% of a financially troubled and environmentally unsound Polish pulp and paper mill through a privatisation auction. The privatised entity was then restructured with the closure of the polluting pulp mill, the introduction of Western technology for the expansion of fine paper production and the renegotiation (including write-offs) of existing enterprise debt.

3.2 Structure of the financing

The relative risks of project finance lending in the Polish and Romanian markets respectively were also reflected in the Bank's ability to attract other lenders to the projects. In Virolite, the EBRD was able to interest only the Overseas Private Investment Corporation ("OPIC"), an agency of the U.S. government, to co-finance the loan to the Romanian joint venture. This represented OPIC's first investment in Romania and OPIC was able to invest because the Western investor was an American entity.

In the Trebruk project, the Bank structured its financing to include participations from two international commercial banks in the Bank's loan and a parallel loan from a syndicate of Polish commercial banks. The co-lending by local Polish banks provides further confirmation of both the advanced economic climate of the country and the soundness of its financial sector. This is not to say that foreign investors and banks see Poland as an investment which is without risk, however.

In both the Polish and the Romanian projects the presence of an international financial institution (or "IFI") such as EBRD acted as the catalyst for the foreign investor and for the participating financial institutions. As an international organisation linked by multilateral international convention[5]

---

[5] The Agreement Establishing the European Bank for Reconstruction and Development is a treaty binding on its shareholders, which are member States and international organisations.

and practice[6] to its countries of operation, the Bank will take the so-called "political risk" of investing in the emerging market. The foreign investor and other participating lenders derive comfort from the Bank's special status *vis-à-vis* the country of the investment. It is felt that the risk of expropriation or nationalisation of the local entity or its assets is reduced by Bank involvement. Furthermore, undue interference by the State in the lawful generation of profit both for repayment of the Bank's loan and the overall profitability of the project is apt to trigger possible sanctions, such as suspension or termination of that country's access to Bank resources and cross-default under Bank and other IFI financing.

With political risk reduced by Bank involvement in the project, or in the case of the Virolite transaction further reduced by the purchase by the American sponsor of political risk insurance which is offered by government agencies such as OPIC to cover specified events such as total expropriation and civil war, investors and co-lenders are free to make investment decisions based on "project risk" – the ability of the project to produce revenues to repay debt and increase shareholder return on investment.

4 STRUCTURING THE INVESTMENT TO REDUCE PROJECT RISK

Both foreign investors and lenders use various means to reduce their project risk.

4.1 The foreign investor

For the investor, reduction of project risk involves taking full advantage of various incentives offered by States to attract foreign investment. Both Romania and Poland offer similar advantages such as tax holidays, exemptions from import duties for "in kind" contributions such as plant and equipment to the capital of the local company and guarantees on access to foreign exchange and the ability to repatriate profits.

Foreign investors may also wish to mitigate the risks of devaluation and expropriation by holding hard currency onshore or in offshore accounts. It is interesting to note that in the more developed economy of Poland, all companies, including those with foreign participation, can open and hold *only* local currency accounts with local banks. Foreign currency accounts in Poland or abroad require National Bank approval, which is rarely granted.

In Romania, on the other hand, where the local currency is in constant devaluation, foreign investors may retain their hard currency capital contributions in hard currency denominated bank accounts, while companies

---

[6] As an IFI, like the World Bank, the International Finance Corporation and other regional development banks, the EBRD also enjoys the so-called "preferred creditor status" under which its investments are by international financial practice free from rescheduling, moratorium and foreign exchange restrictions.

that export for hard currency can retain such earnings to purchase imports. Since foreign investment is still limited in Romania, a major foreign investor is probably better able to seek and receive from the government "one-off" benefits such as increased tax and duty exemptions and approval for offshore bank accounts.

4.2 The lenders

Project finance is limited-recourse lending; in other words, after physical completion and putting into operation of the project, the lenders must look to the project itself and not to the financial backing of the Western sponsors.

4.2.1 Pre-project completion recourse

In both the Trebruk and Virolite projects, the EBRD entered into a form of Project Completion Agreement with the respective foreign sponsors. Under such agreement the foreign sponsor is required to provide additional funds by way of subordinated debt or equity to achieve physical and operational completion of the project, where in the opinion of the Bank such further funds are required. The sponsor is thus responsible to meet cost overruns in the financing plan of the project as well as other contingencies. Furthermore, until completion, the sponsor is liable for the financial obligations of the local borrower under the Bank's loan.

Many sponsors consider these obligations to be harsh, but the Bank, and the other project finance lenders, take the project risk based on a financing plan prepared by the sponsor. When the project facilities are completed and operating, the sponsor's obligations are terminated and the lenders look only to project revenues and ultimately to security.

4.2.2 Post-completion recourse: security

As a prudent lender operating in accordance with sound banking principles, the Bank seeks a full security package to protect its investments. Such a package would, ideally, include a mortgage over real property (land and buildings), a pledge of equipment, inventory, receivables, intangibles (patents and trademarks), insurance proceeds and bank accounts, as well as a pledge over the shares of the project company held by the sponsors. This presents a challenge, however, given the legal environments of the countries in which the Bank operates. Secured lending in the EBRD's countries of operations thus takes place on a "best efforts" basis, where the security package is structured so as to provide maximum protection except where limited by public policy in the country in question or by possible interference with operations of the borrower (*e.g.*, a possessory lien over equipment would provide excellent security but would prevent the company from operating).

In both the Trebruk and Virolite transactions the Bank and its co-lenders were able to take, with varying degrees of comfort, a relatively complete security package.

Not surprisingly, given the higher level of foreign investment and of project lending in Poland, the Trebruk package is a result of established market practice, albeit of limited judicial confirmation. A mortgage over real property may be obtained by a relatively simple notarial act and entry on a local registry. Under the Polish Civil Code, only local Polish banks may take a non-possessory pledge over moveable property. Non-Polish bank lenders use "transfer of moveables" agreements with the borrower, under which title is transferred to the lenders while the borrower remains in possession. This is combined with labelling of the moveable property to provide notice to third parties. The Civil Code also allows the pledge by written contract and notice of other rights such as receivables, shares, insurance proceeds and intangibles. With the exception of shares, which can easily be perfected by delivery of the certificates, the Bank relies not on pledge but rather on assignment agreements, under which the rights are assigned to the Bank up to the amount of the secured debt with the contractual right upon default to apply proceeds received to the satisfaction of the unpaid debt.

The final obstacle to secured lending by the EBRD and foreign banks in Poland is the Code of Civil Procedure under which, in enforcement proceedings, unsecured debt to local banks ranks ahead of debt secured by mortgage or pledge. In the Trebruk transaction, this could be remedied by a contract for security sharing among the local and foreign banks forming the lenders' syndicate. Where local banks do not form part of the financing syndicate (for example, banks providing short-term working capital credit), then foreign bank lenders must either require subordination agreements with such local banks or accept the priority.

Romanian security law and practice is extremely limited and even the question of private ownership of land is not free from doubt. The Romanian Civil Code, which is based on the Napoleonic Code, does contain provisions on mortgages and pledges.

The Virolite project highlighted a major concern for foreign investors and lenders in Romania – while land may now be held privately by Romanian natural and legal persons it is very difficult for them to obtain proof of title. Furthermore, non-Romanian natural or legal persons are not permitted to own land. Apparently, there is, however, no prohibition on a Romanian entity, including a joint venture company such as the Virolite project company, from owning land. A Romanian partner may also contribute land ownership rights to the capital of a Romanian entity as a contribution in-kind.

In the Virolite project, the Romanian partner is, at the date of writing, still going through the process of obtaining title to the land which forms part of its existing plant and which it intends to contribute to the joint venture. Assuming this takes place, the joint venture (with majority foreign participation) must then attempt to register its title to the land. Finally, the Bank can only then seek to obtain a mortgage on the property. Should the Bank wish to enforce its mortgage through judicial sale, it is likely that it would have to form a Romanian company in order to hold the property.

The Bank has obtained a pledge on the shares in the borrower. Apparently, however, Romanian law does not allow a pledge on bank accounts and thus the Bank will have to rely on access to foreign bank accounts, if any, which would be secured under foreign law. Finally, in an effort to anticipate the development of Romanian security practice, the

Bank has relied on current French practice which has developed to deal with a Civil Code substantially similar to that of Romania, and which has evolved to keep pace with modern secured lending. Thus, where security provisions are lacking in the Civil Code, as in pledge of moveables/accounts receivable or insurance proceeds, the Bank may seek to arrive at similar results using non-security devices such as call options on the assets and *délégation de paiements* for insurance.

As in the case of Poland, the security package available to the Bank in Romania is innovative and untested in court. Some comfort can be derived, however, from the shared Civil Code and closer links between France and Romania under which Romanian judges might be convinced by French developments.

5 CONCLUSION

While the discussion above of project finance problems and solutions in two Central and Eastern European countries at different stages of transition to a market economy provides various points of similarity and divergence, it must be emphasised that this is a snapshot. Both countries continue to develop to meet the challenges of transition. Also, when compared with the difficulties facing investors and lenders in CIS countries, which also make up the EBRD's countries of operations, the similarities and accomplishments outweigh the problems.

The EBRD will continue to encourage this transition through continued investment and law reform initiatives[7] but the true test will be continued and increased foreign investment and project finance.

---

[7] *See* EBRD Model Law on Secured Transactions (London, 1994), with introduction by Simpson and Röver.

12. Central Bankers' "Club" Law and Transitional Economies: Banking Reform and the Reception of the Basle Standards of Prudential Supervision in Eastern Europe and the Former Soviet Union

Christos D. Hadjiemmanuil[1]

1 INTRODUCTION

The establishment of a well-functioning banking system is one of the most important challenges facing the countries of eastern Europe and the former Soviet Union as they move from the centralised economic system of the communist period to a market economy. The issue is critical for the future development of these countries.

In addition to providing payment services, banking institutions in a market economy serve as the main conduit for the mobilisation of private savings and other capital resources and for their employment in productive uses, in the form of loans to commercial and industrial enterprises. The quality of their lending decisions is crucial for the efficient allocation of the economy's supply of credit between competing demands. In addition, their willingness and ability to monitor effectively the performance of their borrowers on a continuous basis and to take appropriate measures as soon as a deterioration in their financial situation is detected are decisive for the effectiveness of the prevailing structures of corporate governance and, more generally, for the enforcement of financial discipline on both households and enterprises.

In the case of the post-communist economies, the benefits of an efficient banking system are unlikely to become available at an early stage of the transition process. The ubiquity of non-performing ("bad") loans and the lack of essential skills, in particular insofar as the assessment and monitoring of credit risks is concerned, set strict limits to the ability of the existing banking sector to allocate credit efficiently. The inefficiencies in the supply of credit as a result of the banking sector's inherent imperfections are

---

[1] Fellow in European Banking Law, London Institute of International Banking, Finance and Development Law, Centre for Commercial Law Studies, Queen Mary and Westfield College, University of London.

exacerbated by government policies aiming at the stabilisation of the domestic currency's value. The unwillingness of the central bank to accommodate new demand for credit through increases in the money supply, the removal of the traditional implicit state guarantees on bank loans to enterprises and the prevalence of particularly high real interest rates, due to the initially limited credibility of the new monetary policies, precipitate a credit crunch and a deep and protracted recession.[2] For these reasons, during the early phases of the transition, the recovery of production will probably be slow and will depend primarily on the availability of private investment by the owners for the financing of new industrial and commercial enterprises or on the reinvestment of the retained profits of existing enterprises.[3]

Nonetheless, the experience of the rest of the world shows that, in the long run, the development of the post-communist economies will depend directly on the emergence of a stable and efficient banking system. From this perspective, the policy choices of the transitional period are of fundamental importance, because they are bound to have irreversible implications for the long-term structure and performance of the area's fledgling banking markets. Accordingly, the criterion for the adoption of legal and administrative regulatory frameworks during the transition should be primarily, if not exclusively, their likely contribution to the emergence of a robust banking system within a reasonable time scale, not their suitability for a mature Western-style financial system.

In reality, the actual public policy choices in eastern Europe and the former Soviet Union are heavily influenced by certain regulatory practices and substantive standards of prudential supervision upon which the central banks and banking regulators of the major industrialised nations have gradually converged over the last two decades in an effort to achieve mutual compatibility of their regulatory systems. The informal Basle Committee on Banking Supervision has provided the most important forum for international regulatory convergence, through the development of a core of common prudential requirements, including, in particular, common capital adequacy standards. In the European context, the Committee's work has been paralleled by extensive harmonisation of the banking laws of the Member States of the EC on the basis of principles which, with limited technical exceptions, are consistent with the Committee's pronouncements.

---

[2] *See* G. A. Calvo, "Financial aspects of socialist economies: from inflation to reform", in V. Corbo, F. Corricelli and J. Bossak (eds.), *Reforming Central and Eastern European Economies: Initial Results and Challenges* (Washington, D.C.: The World Bank, 1991).

[3] Evidence from enterprise surveys in a number of eastern European economies suggests that the funding of enterprises' investment relies heavily on internal finance; *see* W. Carlin, J. van Reenen and T. Wolfe, *Enterprise Restructuring in the Transition: An Analytical Survey of the Case Study Evidence from Central and Eastern Europe* (EBRD Working Paper No. 14, London: EBRD, July 1994), p. 43; and comments of Leila Webster, in European Bank for Reconstruction and Development, "EBRD Conference on Banking Reform and Regulation in Eastern Europe", London, 19 and 20 October 1992, summary of proceedings, mimeograph, p. 28. *See* also European Bank for Reconstruction and Development, *Transition Report: Economic Transition in Eastern Europe and the Former Soviet Union* (London: EBRD, October 1994), pp. 49 and 55–56.

Western governments, international financial institutions and the institutions of the European Union actively encourage the post-communist economies to adopt, at the earliest possible date, Basle-style standards of prudential supervision, in order to ensure conformity with the internationally accepted best regulatory practices. However, regardless of their intrinsic merits or disadvantages, it is not clear whether the Basle standards address the special circumstances of the post-communist economies or whether they can make an appreciable contribution to the success of the transition process.

In the following pages, after a short description of the Basle Committee's role in the international regulatory convergence process and, more specifically, of its work on capital adequacy standards, the channels through which its pronouncements exert an influence on the development of banking policy in the countries of eastern Europe and the former Soviet Union are discussed. The special problems that plague the banking systems of the post-communist countries are then identified. Finally, the question is raised, whether, in view of these problems, simple transposition of Basle-style capital-based prudential standards, which are designed for mature, internationally competitive banking systems, can provide appropriate regulatory solutions for the transition process.

2 ORIGINS AND ROLE OF THE BASLE COMMITTEE

The origins of the international regulatory convergence process can be traced back to a series of banking scandals and crises, which erupted in the major industrialised nations in the mid-1970s (failure of Bankhaus I. D. Herstatt in West Germany and of Franklin National Bank in the U.S., the secondary banking crisis in the U.K.) and again in the early 1980s (collapse of Banco Ambrosiano in Italy, international third-world debt crisis, failure of Continental Illinois in the U.S.). The banking failures proved in many cases to have significant cross-border dimensions, reflecting the dramatic explosion of international banking activities in recent decades.

The globalisation of banking created new profit opportunities, but also exposed banks to strong competition and increased risks.[4] Globalisation was a self-reinforcing process, since, in the face of growing foreign competition, most large banks found it necessary to expand their international presence in order to increase, or simply to protect, their market share. Nonetheless, it was not always easy for them to manage the attending risks. The intense competition for market share, in combination with the initially limited understanding of the new environment, resulted, in many cases, at least in the short term, in overtrading and excessively low pricing, which

---

[4] These developments have been analysed in a series of studies commissioned by the OECD in the 1980s, most notably: R. M. Pecchioli, *The Internationalisation of Banking: The Policy Issues* (Paris: OECD, 1983); G. Bröker, *Competition in Banking* (Paris: OECD, 1989); and OECD, Expert Group on Banking of the Committee on Financial Markets, *Trends in Banking in OECD Countries* (Paris: OECD, 1985).

did not reflect the actual risks taken by banks. The difficulties were exacerbated by the widespread macroeconomic disruptions of the 1970s and much of the 1980s. At the same time, the wholesale and predominantly interbank nature of the booming international markets resulted in a sharp increase in bank interdependence. This has been a potentially serious source of contagion risk, insofar as the costs from the failure of one institution are borne by its counterparties in the interbank market and the payment and settlement systems.

The increase in banks' risk-taking as a result of international operations presents national banking authorities with a policy dilemma. Given that every significant banking jurisdiction has an interest in protecting and promoting the national banking industry's international competitiveness, it would be undesirable for the authorities of any such jurisdiction to impose unilaterally countervailing regulatory restrictions on their domestic banks, because this would increase their costs of doing business and, if the restrictions were more burdensome than those applicable to their foreign competitors, undermine their ability to compete globally. On the other hand, a failure of the authorities to contain risk-taking by banks would lead unavoidably to an explosion in the costs of keeping in place the prevailing regimes of implicit and/or explicit public safety-nets for the banking industry, as the authorities would be forced to bail out a growing number of insolvent banks.[5]

In this climate, international regulatory convergence appears probably as the best way of tackling the problem of increased bank riskiness without dissipating the benefits from banking operations abroad. A multilateral approach to the definition of prudential standards could ensure some sort of competitive "level playing field" for international banks, while permitting national authorities to keep the costs from the public safety-nets under control.

The first concrete evidence of the growing risks from international banking operations was provided in 1974, when two significant institutions, the German Bankhaus I. D. Herstatt and the American Franklin National Bank, failed after suffering very heavy losses through unhedged foreign-exchange trading. Central-bank intervention was necessary in order to prevent the contamination of numerous other banks which had not received payment for currency that they had forwarded to the failed institutions immediately prior to their closure. These failures, which illustrated the vulnerability of internationally active banks to uncompleted interbank currency transactions, raised unprecedented concerns with the prudential

---

[5] The implications of risk-taking by banks for the public safety-nets deter the national regulatory authorities from pursuing a simple policy of "competition in laxity". "In the longer run, there are some forces that will help keep capital ratios across countries from getting too far out of line. Low capital requirements that allow institutions to grow faster and take on more risk in their loan portfolios than their international competitors ultimately become a source of concern to their countries' governments"; D. B. Crane and S. L. Hayes, "The evolution of international banking competition and its implications for regulation" (1983) 14 *J.B.R.* 39, p. 51.

aspects of international banking operations amongst banking regulators and triggered a process of convergence of the supervisory standards of different countries.

In response to the Bankhaus I. D. Herstatt failure, the governors of the central banks of the Group of Ten ("G-10") countries and Switzerland formed at the end of 1974 an *ad hoc* committee, the Committee on Banking Regulations and Supervisory Practices.[6] The initiative for the Committee's formation apparently belonged to the Bank of England.[7] The Committee, which became better known as the "Basle Committee" from its permanent meeting place at the Bank for International Settlements in Basle, Switzerland, met for the first time in February 1975. Meetings have taken place regularly (about three to four times a year) ever since.[8]

The purpose of the Basle Committee is to provide a forum for the study of the international aspects of prudential regulation and the discussion of policy issues between the participating national authorities, leading gradually to the elaboration of common principles concerning the strengthening of banking supervision and the harmonisation of prudential standards.

The Committee operates on a totally informal basis. It does not have legal existence as an international institution, does not function on the basis of a formal mandate and does not follow specific procedures or by-laws. Convergence on particular policies is reached through discussion and gradual achievement of mutual understanding, and is based strictly on the principle of consensus. They are set out in policy papers notable for their not strictly technical and relatively flexible language, which eschews the exact style and precise definitions of legal documentation. As the institutions represented in the Committee lack the legal power to conclude binding treaties on behalf of their countries or to legislate domestically, Committee policy pronouncements are set out merely as "reports", "consultative documents", "statements", "guidelines" or "recommendations" and are not purported to have any specific legal effect. In 1984, Peter Cooke, the chairman of the Basle Committee at the time, described its status and role in the following words:

The Committee does not undertake a formal supranational supervisory role; its conclusions do not have, and were never intended to have, legal force. Rather it formulates and recommends broad supervisory principles and guidelines of best

---

[6] *See* Press Communiqué of the Governors of the central banks of the G-10 countries, 12 February 1975, released by the BIS. The Committee, whose full name has since been changed to the Basle Committee on Banking Supervision, is made up of representatives of the central banks and banking supervisory authorities of Belgium, Canada, France, Germany, Italy, Japan, Luxembourg, the Netherlands, Sweden, Switzerland, the United Kingdom and the United States. For a brief introduction to the Committee's work, *see* A. Cornford, *The Role of the Basle Committee on Banking Supervision in the Regulation of International Banking* (Discussion Paper No. 68, Geneva: United Nations Conference on Trade and Development, September 1993).

[7] *See* J. Revell, *Solvency and Regulation of Banks: Theoretical and Practical Implications* (1975), p. 51. The Bank of England's representatives held the chairmanship of the Committee during its early years.

[8] *See* Basle Committee, "Report on International Developments in Banking Supervision, 1981" (July 1982), p. 1; and "Report on International Developments in Banking Supervision: Report No. 8" (September 1992), p. 1.

practices in the hope and expectation that individual authorities will take steps to implement them through detailed arrangements – statutory or otherwise – which are best suited to their own national systems.[9]

The Committee's policy papers are not signed by its members and do not include express references to its composition, other than in a footnote explaining in general terms that the Committee "consists of senior representatives of bank supervisory authorities and central banks" from the twelve participating countries, without, however, naming its members or the institutions that they represent. In fact, until the early 1980s, the Committee's operations were covered by almost total secrecy and its papers were not even publicly available. Since then, however, there has been a marked shift towards openness. The Committee's discussion and final papers are now circulated widely and comments by the banking industry are invited. Moreover, since 1982, the Committee has produced on a regular basis (annual until 1986 and biennial thereafter) a series of "Reports on International Developments in Banking Supervision", whose purpose is to keep bank supervisors and other interested parties around the world informed about the Committee's recent work.[10]

Largely due to the prestige and institutional power of its membership, the regulatory standards that emanate under the Committee's auspices enjoy a far wider legitimacy than would be justified by their doubtful legal status. Through their *de facto* implementation by the represented institutions within the limits of their discretionary powers, but also through their formal adoption by national legislators, Committee pronouncements, despite their lack of formal force, exert in practice a very powerful influence in the generation of national and regional legal rules and formal institutional structures.[11] The process could be described as the inculcation of formal legal systems by central bankers' "club" law.

Although its principles are directed primarily to the participating countries, the Basle Committee makes every effort to ensure their world-wide acceptance. For this purpose, it has encouraged the setting up of several regional groups of banking supervisors, with which it cooperates closely.[12] In addition, the Basle Committee is the organiser, in cooperation

---

[9] Basle Committee, "Basle Supervisors' Committee" (document for external distribution) (21 June 1984).

[10] *See* Basle Committee, "Report on International Developments in Banking Supervision: Report No. 9" (September 1994), p. 1.

[11] *See* the observations of Peter Cooke, a former head of the Bank's banking supervision and chairman of the Basle Committee, "The Basle 'Concordat' on the supervision of banks' foreign establishments" (1984) 39 *Aussenwirtschaft* 151. *See* also J. J. Norton, "The work of the Basle Supervisors Committee on bank capital adequacy and the July 1988 report on 'International Convergence of Capital Measurement and Capital Standards' " (1989) 23 *Int'l Law.* 245, p. 251; and P. C. Hayward, "Prospects for international co-operation by bank supervisors", in J. J. Norton (ed.), *Bank Regulation and Supervision in the 1990s* (1991), p. 68.

[12] At the Committee's instigation, an Offshore Group of Banking Supervisors was set up in October 1980. *See* "Report on International Developments in Banking Supervision, 1981", *loc. cit.*, n. 8, p. 18. Subsequently, the Committee has assisted or encouraged other regional

with the authorities of the host country, of the biennial International Conferences of Banking Supervisors (ICBS), which are held regularly since 1979.[13] The conferences provide a forum for the discussion of supervisory issues and the promotion of cooperation between regulators, permitting the disemmination of the Committee's policy thinking to regulators from every corner of the world. The number of participants in the conferences has increased over the years; currently around 110 countries attend the ICBS.[14]

The Committee has had considerable success in its efforts to export its standards, even though in numerous jurisdictions their effective implementation is resisted in practice or is impeded by the limited resources of the local regulatory authorities. The Committee maintains particularly strong links with the banking fora of the EC,[15] primarily because the membership of the G-10 and the EC is characterised by substantial overlap. In many cases, work has been conducted in parallel, although in certain matters the EC, motivated by the need to complete the internal market, has achieved harmonisation in areas where the Basle Committee has not, for the time being, made concrete progress.

Footnote 12 *cont'd*

groups of regulators who have established permanent contacts in the following fora: in 1981, the Commission of Latin American and Caribbean Banking Supervisory and Inspection Organisations (now renamed the Association of Banking Supervisory Authorities of Latin America and the Caribbean); in 1983, the Caribbean Banking Supervisors' Group and the GCC (Gulf Co-operation Council) Committee of Banking Supervisors; in 1984, the SEANZA (South East Asia, New Zealand and Australia) Forum of Banking Supervisors; in 1990, the Group of Banking Supervisors from Central and Eastern European Countries; in 1991, the Group of Banking Supervision Officials in Arab Countries; in 1993, the East and Southern Africa Banking Supervisors' Group; and in 1994, the West and Central Africa Group of Bank Supervisors.

[13] The first ICBS, which brought together regulators from over eighty countries, took place in London on 5–6 July 1979. *See* "International conference of banking supervisors" (1979) 19 *B.E.Q.B.* 298; and W. P. Cooke and R. M. G. Brown, "Developments in co-operation among banking supervisory authorities" (1981) 21 *B.E.Q.B.* 238. Since then, conferences have taken place in Washington, DC (1981), Rome (1984), Amsterdam (1986), Tokyo (1988), Frankfurt (1990), Cannes (1992) and Vienna (1994).

[14] "Report on International Developments in Banking Supervision: Report No. 9", *loc. cit.*, n. 10, p. 71.

[15] Including the informal Contact Group of Supervisory Authorities; the Banking Advisory Committee, which was formed in accordance with Article 11 of First Council Directive 77/780/EEC of 12.12.77 on the co-ordination of laws, regulations and administrative provisions relating to the taking up and pursuit of the business of credit institutions (the "First Banking Directive"); and the Banking Supervisory Sub-Committee of the European Monetary Institute, which was originally constituted as a sub-committee of the Committee of Governors of the Community's central banks under Article 3(1) of Council Decision 64/300/EEC of 08.05.64 on cooperation between the central banks of the Member States of the EEC, as amended by Council Decision 90/142/EEC of 12.03.90. The Contact Group, in particular, provides an effective channel of communication between the Basle Committee and the relevant Directorate (DG XV) of the European Commission. On the Basle Committee's links with the EC, *see* J. J. Norton, *Devising International Bank Supervisory Standards* (London and Dordrecht: Graham & Trotman/Martinus Nijhoff, 1995), pp. 163–167.

3 THE BASLE ACCORD ON THE INTERNATIONAL CONVERGENCE OF CAPITAL STANDARDS

Initially, the Basle Committee's work focused primarily on the delineation of supervisory responsibilities for the supervision of banks and banking groups operating in more than one jurisdiction and on the achievement of coordination and cooperation between the home and host-country authorities of such banks and banking groups.[16] This effort has continued over the years, but has met with limited practical success.[17]

Since the early 1980s, however, the Committee's attention has increasingly turned to the substance of prudential regulatory norms.[18] The result has been the publication of a series of recommendations on matters such as the assessment and control of country exposures,[19] the expansion of supervision to the off-balance-sheet activities of banks,[20] the imposition of limits on large credit exposures,[21] and even the promulgation of principles for the prevention of money laundering.[22]

The Committee's most important achievement to date, however, involves the elaboration of common minimum standards of capital adequacy for international banks. A historical agreement on this matter, the so-called

---

[16] *See* the Basle Committee's papers: "Report to the Governors on the Supervision of Banks' Foreign Establishments" (the "Concordat") (September 1975); "Consolidation of Banks' Balance Sheets: Aggregation of Risk-Bearing Assets as a Method of Supervisory Bank Solvency" (Oct. 1978); and "Principles for the Supervision of Banks' Foreign Establishments" (the "revised Concordat") (May 1983).

[17] *See* "The Ensuring of Adequate Information Flows between Banking Supervisory Authorities" (April 1990); and "Minimum Standards for the Supervision of International Banking Groups and their Cross-Border Establishments" (June 1992). The "Minimum Standards . . ." suggest a retreat from the Committee's stated preference for consolidated supervision by a bank's home-country authorities, emphasising instead the need for the host country to ensure that these home-country authorities are indeed capable of exercising effective supervision.

[18] Writing in 1984, Peter Cooke, then Chairman of the Basle Committee, noted that "[t]he process of international supervisory co-operation during the last decade has passed through several phases. The first consisted of simple steps to establish the practice of supervisory co-operation and some basic agreement on its essential framework and principles. The second has seen the spread of supervisory co-operation, its practice and its principles around the world, beyond the areas where it first developed. This is now well under way but much remains to be done. The third phase, which has scarcely built up momentum yet, is directed toward a closer convergence of supervisory standards and techniques in different countries reflecting that single international marketplace in which major banks in so ma[n]y countries are now operating extensively"; *loc. cit.*, n. 11, pp. 155–156.

[19] Basle Committee, "Management of Banks' International Lending: Country Risk Analysis and Country Exposure Measurement and Control" (March 1982).

[20] Basle Committee, "The Management of Banks' Off-Balance-Sheet Exposures: A Supervisory Perspective" (March 1986).

[21] Basle Committee, "Measuring and Controlling Large Credit Exposures" (January 1991).

[22] Basle Committee, "Prevention of Criminal Use of the Banking System for the Purpose of Money Laundering" (December 1988).

"Basle Accord", was reached in July 1988.[23] The Basle Accord was the outcome of several years' work. Its significance consists in ensuring multilateral convergence on a consistent definition of the elements of bank capital,[24] on a framework for assessing the adequacy of a bank's capital base as a function of the credit risk of its assets (*i.e.*, of the risk that its assets will become non-performing as a result of its counterparties' default on their obligations)[25] and on the imposition on all internationally active banks of a common minimum standard of 8% of capital to risk-weighted assets, which should be applied on a consolidated basis.[26]

The issue of bank capital was brought to the forefront of the Basle Committee's concerns at the beginning of the 1980s. Responding to the worries of the Governors of the central banks of the G-10 countries relating to a worldwide trend of erosion of capital-to-asset ratios at a time of very aggressive expansion of banks' international lending, the Committee began, in 1981, to monitor systematically the capital ratios of leading banks with a view to preparing a report to the Governors.[27]

On the basis of its fact-finding work, the Committee was able to confirm that further deterioration of capital ratios should be resolutely resisted by banking regulators on prudential grounds and that, at the very least, the major banks should be forced to maintain their capital positions at the levels prevailing at the time, whatever those levels happened to be. These conclusions were strongly endorsed by the G-10 central bank Governors, to whom the Committee's report was presented in June 1982.[28]

The grave threat to the international banking system from the third-world debt crisis, which was met only through the coordinated rescheduling organised by the central banks of the major creditor countries, exposed the total inadequacy of bank capital in comparison to the gigantic volume of international lending and gave new momentum to the search for a solution.

A connected issue, that also attracted the interest of the Basle Committee, concerned the explosion of off-balance-sheet credit exposures, frequently in the form of innovative, securitised instruments. As the various national regulatory authorities relied for the supervision of capital adequacy on gearing ratios, which simply related capital to the total volume of assets on a bank's balance sheet, the rearrangement of their activities by moving assets off-balance-sheet provided banks with an opportunity of avoiding supervisory pressures for the strengthening of capital positions. However,

---

[23] Basle Committee, "International Convergence of Capital Measurement and Capital Standards" (the "Basle Accord") (July 1988). *See* also the Committee's "Proposals for the Inclusion of General Provisions / General Loan-Loss Reserves in Capital" (February 1991), which were followed by an "Amendment to the Basle Accord" (November 1991).

[24] *Id.*, Part I.

[25] *Id.*, Part II.

[26] *Id.*, Part III.

[27] "Report on International Developments in Banking Supervision, 1981", *loc. cit.*, n. 8, p. 7.

[28] Basle Committee, "Report on International Developments in Banking Supervision, 1982" (March 1982), pp. 3–4.

the new instruments were particularly complex and posed previously unknown risks, which the bankers might perhaps underestimate.[29]

Competitive considerations precluded a unilateral solution to the problem of bank capital adequacy. The imposition of capital requirements constrains the ability of banks to expand and increases their costs of doing business. Capital is not only a scarce, but also an expensive, resource. For a bank, it is much cheaper to raise other bank liabilities, especially deposits, when these are effectively protected by explicit or implicit public safety-nets, because capital instruments carry considerable residual risk for the investors. For this reason, the unilateral imposition of more onerous capital rules on the banks of one country only would jeopardise their competitiveness in the international markets and could also have perverse prudential effects, by encouraging a more risky strategy in an attempt to counteract the impact of the regulator-induced cost disadvantage on their profitability.

In the wake of the third-world debt crisis, the U.S. Congress gave statutory legitimacy to the promulgation of federal standards of capital adequacy by enacting the International Lending Supervision Act of 1983 ("ILSA").[30] The enactment of ILSA also provided the Federal Reserve Board and the U.S. Treasury with a mandate to pursue the international convergence of capital standards and the achievement of a competitive "level playing field" through consultations with bank regulators from other nations.[31] In March 1984, Paul Volcker, then Chairman of the Federal Reserve Board, armed with the recent mandate, raised with the other G-10 central bank Governors the issue of an international framework for the measurement of capital adequacy that could ensure the "functional equivalence" of the disparate national regulatory regimes. At the conclusion of the Governors' meeting, the Chairman of the Basle Committee, Peter Cooke, was charged with the task of reporting within the year on how comparability of the different measures of capital adequacy could be achieved.[32]

Of the three elements on which convergence depended, *i.e.*, a common definition of capital, a common framework for measuring capital adequacy and a common minimum standard, the Basle Committee was able to make progress only on the second. Under the influence of the seven participating countries which were also Member States of the EC, where a common framework risk-based measurement of capital was used for observation purposes since the late 1970s, the Basle Committee had reached agreement, by February 1986, that a risk-weighted approach should be preferred over a gearing measure.[33] The collapse of Continental Illinois in May 1984, despite

---

[29] *See* Basle Committee, "Report on International Developments in Banking Supervision, 1984" (April 1985), p. 15; and "The Management of Banks' Off-Balance-Sheet Exposures: A Supervisory Perspective", *loc. cit.*, n. 20.

[30] Pub.L. No. 98-181, Title IX, 97 Stat. 1278 (30 Nov. 1983).

[31] Congressional declaration of policy, 12 USC § 3901.

[32] "Report on International Developments in Banking Supervision, 1984", *loc. cit.*, n. 29, p. 9.

[33] *See* Basle Committee, "Report on International Developments in Banking Supervision: Report No. 5" (September 1986), pp. 16–19.

its relatively high gearing ratio of 5.8%, helped to convince the Americans of the merit of the risk-weighted approach, by showing that straight gearing ratios could be seriously misleading and even perverse, since they could induce banks to take on riskier business as a means of restoring their profitability. On the other hand, fundamental disagreements continued to divide the countries on the issue of the constituent elements of capital. The only commonly acceptable items were shareholders' equity and retained earnings. Regarding the admission of "impure" forms of capital, however, there were insurmountable difficulties: Germany wanted their total exclusion, the U.S. pressed for the inclusion of loan loss provisions, while Japan alone insisted on the admission of unrealised capital gains on a bank's equity portfolio as capital. None of the authorities represented in the Committee was ready to accept a radical departure from its own national approach.[34]

Faced with this impasse, in a meeting on 2 September 1986 the Chairman of the Federal Reserve Board, Paul Volcker, and the Governor of the Bank of England, Robin Leigh-Pemberton, decided that, as there was little chance of a multilateral breakthrough, action should be undertaken on a bilateral basis by the two leading financial jurisdictions.[35] By adopting simultaneously a common set of risk-based capital standards, the authorities in the U.S. and the U.K. could probably convince their national banking industries to abandon their implacable opposition, for well-founded reasons of competitiveness, to their attempts to strengthen bank capital requirements.[36]

By the end of the year, the technical experts of the two central banks, working outside the Basle framework, had managed to generate a fully articulated risk-based capital adequacy measure for the two countries. This was incorporated in an informal "Agreed Proposal of the United States Federal Banking Supervisory Authorities and the Bank of England on Primary Capital and Capital Adequacy Assessment" (the "U.S./U.K. Accord"), released on 8 January 1987.[37] Although agreement had not been

---

[34] *See* S. Solomon, *The Confidence Game: How Unelected Central Bankers Are Governing the Changed Global Economy* (New York and London: Simon & Schuster, 1995), pp. 420–421.

[35] On the Anglo-American bilateral convergence, *see id.*, pp. 413–423; Norton, *Devising International Bank Supervisory Standards, op. cit.*, n. 13, pp. 186–190; and E. B. Kapstein, *Supervising International Banks: Origins and Implications of the Basle Accord* (Essays in International Finance No. 185, Princeton, N.J.: International Finance Section, Department of Economics, Princeton University, Dec. 1991), pp. 9–24.

[36] In the U.S., by adopting a risk-based standard; and in the U.K., by incorporating off-balance-sheet activities in the Bank of England's existing risk-based model.

[37] The U.S./U.K. Accord's text was reproduced in (1987) 27 *B.E.Q.B.* 87. *See* also the related notice issued by the Bank of England's Banking Supervision Division, "Convergence of capital adequacy in the U.K. and U.S." (1987) 27 *B.E.Q.B.* 85. As none of the participating bodies had the power to conclude international agreements, the U.S./U.K. Accord was not presented as a legally binding document, but as a discussion document which should serve "as a basis for consultation with the banking industry and others in the United States and the United Kingdom". However, it was understood that its provisions would be implemented by the participating bodies under their domestic regulatory powers.

achieved on the common minimum standard, the common understanding was that this should be higher than the U.S.'s existing 6%.

Crucially, one of the express aims of the U.S./U.K. Accord was "to promote the convergence of supervisory policy and capital adequacy assessments among countries with major banking centres". This implied that it was not necessarily the intention of the Anglo-American regulators to implement its provisions as such, but to exert pressure on their counter-parties from the other G-10 countries, and in particular Japan, to reach multilateral agreement at Basle. In other words, the U.S./U.K. Accord was intended to provide the "intervening catalyst" in the Basle process.[38] The implicit threat was that, if this process did not bear fruit, other countries would be left with the choice either to comply with the Anglo-American standards or to face exclusion of their banks from New York and London.

Despite some initial negative reactions from the European Commission and elsewhere to such an "ultimatum", the G-10 central bank Governors were generally understanding.[39] It was agreed that the Basle Committee should explore the feasibility of a multilateral alternative, otherwise the bi-lateral Accord would be implemented by the end of 1987. Capital definitions continued to be the biggest stumbling block. Both Germany and Japan resisted the idea of international convergence on the basis of the bi-lateral agreement, but for opposite reasons, leaving the initiative with the Anglo-American axis.[40] With the possibility of a financial trade war looming larger by the day, a compromise was finally achieved with the Japanese. By September 1987, the Basle Committee had concluded its draft report. Three months later, the G-10 central bank Governors finalised the emerging agreement and circulated it for comment in the form of a con-sultative paper. The final agreement was eventually endorsed by the Governors in July 1988. From this point, its implementation was left to the national supervisors represented in the Basle Committee.

The Basle Accord bases its definition of capital on a distinction between "Tier 1" or core capital (comprising equity, disclosed retained earnings and certain types of perpetual preferred stock) and "Tier 2" or supplementary capital (including a number of other sources of more or less permanent bank funding, such as undisclosed reserves, revaluation reserves, general loan loss reserves, certain hybrid instruments combining equity and debt characteristics and subordinated term debt with a minimum maturity of five years). At least half of a bank's minimum capital requirement should be met out of Tier 1 items. Moreover, for the measurement of a bank's capital adequacy, its goodwill, its investments in unconsolidated sub-sidiaries engaged in banking and financial activities, and its holdings of

---

[38] The formulation belongs to Professor J. J. Norton; *see Devising International Bank Supervisory Standards, op. cit.,* n. 15, p. 186.

[39] *See* Solomon, *op. cit.,* n. 34, pp. 425–426.

[40] Germany pleaded for a formal framework based on a very narrow definition, while Japan pressed for maximum informality and the inclusion in a bank's capital base of so suspect an item as unrealised capital gains from shareholdings – a form of capital that could be dissipated quickly in the event of a sharp decline in equity markets. *See id.,* p. 426.

capital instruments issued by other banks or deposit-taking institutions should be deducted from its capital base.[41]

Under the Basle Accord, a bank's capital base should be related to its risk-weighted assets, *i.e.*, the sum of the value of its assets as adjusted to reflect their different credit risk. Assets should be allocated to five risk-weighting categories (0%, 10%, 20%, 50%, 100%), depending on the nature of the relevant counterparty. A 0% weight was assigned to cash, claims on (or guaranteed by) central governments and central banks of the OECD countries, claims collateralised by cash or OECD central-government securities, and claims on (or guaranteed by) other central governments and central banks insofar as they are denominated in the national currency and funded in that currency – in other words, these assets were totally excluded from the calculation of the bank's credit exposure. A weight of between 0% and 50%, at the discretion of the national authorities, should be applied to claims on entities of the domestic public sector and local government. A 20% weight was assigned to claims on multilateral lending institutions and regional development banks, claims on other banks incorporated in the OECD countries, claims on banks incorporated outside the OECD countries with a remaining maturity of less than one year, and claims on non-domestic entities of the public sector of the OECD countries. Loans secured by mortgages on residential property attracted a 50% weight. Finally, a 100% weight was stipulated for almost all commercial and consumer loans or other exposures to the private sector, claims on, or guaranteed by, non-OECD central governments and central banks which are not denominated and funded in the local currency, or longer-term claims on banks incorporated outside the OECD – that is, these assets are taken into account at their full nominal value for the calculation of the bank's capital adequacy. Off-balance-sheet exposures should be converted into estimated equivalent on-balance-sheet exposures to the same counterparties according to specified procedures and then included in the calculation.[42]

The Basle Accord set the minimum ratio of total capital to risk-weighted assets at 8% on a consolidated basis, although the national supervisors were left free to impose higher requirements. The Accord required that all internationally active banks comply with the minimum ratio no later than the end of 1992.[43]

The Basle Accord was expressly adopted as a means for attaining a high degree of consistency in bank capital standards, with the purpose of diminishing an existing source of competitive inequality.[44] Nonetheless, it has by no means achieved real uniformity. The Basle Committee itself accepted in the introduction to the Accord that differences in the fiscal

---

[41] Basle Accord, *loc. cit.*, n. 23, Part I.

[42] *Id.*, Part II.

[43] *Id.*, Part III. Insofar as the deadline for compliance with the 8% minimum standard was concerned, the U.K. had pressed for a short transition period, because all its banks were already operating on high capital levels. However, the other countries insisted on a longer transitional period, and the final date for compliance was set at the end of 1992.

[44] *Id.*, para. 3.

treatment and accounting presentation of various items for tax purposes could distort the measurement of the capital positions of international banks, but noted that there was little that it could do in this connection.[45] Moreover, to ensure widespread acceptance, the Basle Accord has given national authorities a substantial degree of discretion in the interpretation and implementation of its requirements. This has increased the number of countries willing to adhere to the spirit of the agreement, but only at the cost of minimising the Accord's benefits in terms of ensuring competitive equality.[46]

Insufficient uniformity, however, may not be the most significant defect of the Accord. Numerous other fundamental problems have been identified.[47] The division of assets in risk categories, driven by political considerations, is a mechanical accounting exercise with bears little relationship to the assets' actual credit risk, while the relationship of the risk weights between one another is unrealistic. The measurement ensures very favourable regulatory treatment for the sovereign debt of the OECD countries (and of other countries, provided that the relevant claims are denominated and funded in the domestic currency) and for interbank claims on banks incorporated in the OECD countries, but makes no effort to differentiate between various claims on the private sector, which attract a blanket 100% risk-weight. The correlation of risks within a bank's asset portfolio, or the effects of specialisation on its ability to monitor and manage particular categories of risk, are not taken into account and there is no provision for non-credit risks. Moreover, the capital standards apply only to banks, distorting the competition between banks and non-bank financial intermediaries such as securities firms, and creating incentives for the avoidance, or at least minimisation, of regulatory burdens through market adaptation. The Accord also fails to deal directly with the competitive implications of government support in the form of safety-net policies which protect banks and their depositors in many countries.[48]

---

[45] *Id.*, para. 9.

[46] M. J. B. Hall, *Banking Regulation and Supervision: A Comparative Study of the U.K., U.S.A. and Japan* (Aldershot: Edward Elgar, 1993), Ch. 8, identifies examples of resulting discrepancies in the acceptance of Tier 2 capital items, *e.g.*, in the deductions from the capital base and in the assignment of particular risk weights to bank assets, which can have a significant impact on the marginal pricing of banking services. The specification of different capital adequacy requirements for individual banks by their national regulators, subject to the agreed minimum ratio, is also an important source of inequalities.

[47] *See, e.g.*, M. Gossling, "The capital adequacy framework – an introduction" (1988) 3 *J.I.B.L.* 243; E. J. Kane, "Tension between competition and coordination in international financial regulation", and P. M. Laub, "International regulation: how much cooperation is needed?", in C. England (ed.), *Governing Banking's Future: Markets* vs. *Regulation* (Boston: Kluwer Academic Publishers, 1991); and I. Swary and B. Topf, *Global Financial Deregulation: Commercial Banking at the Crossroads* (Cambridge, Mass., and Oxford: Blackwell, 1992), pp. 411–414.

[48] H. S. Scott and S. Inwahara, *In Search of a Level Playing Field: The Implementation of the Basle Capital Accord in Japan and the United States* (Washington, D.C.: Group of Thirty, 1994), p. 69, (Occasional Paper No. 46) summarise the situation with regards to competitive advantages

Nevertheless, for all its technical crudeness, the Basle Accord has probably been beneficial as a multilateral response to the problem of falling capital standards. It has impeded an escalation of competition in laxity between national banking authorities (which could involve the further subsidation of banks risk-taking by these authorities) and set a basis for co-ordinated regulatory responses for the purpose of moving the costs from the globalisation of banking activities back to the private sector.[49]

With the Accord finally in place, the interest of the Basle Committe has turned in recent years to its refinement,[50] but, more importantly, to its expansion to cover non-credit risks undertaken by banks, in particular risks arising in the context of banks' securities business. The significance of securities activities relative to banks' traditional lending business increases steadily from year to year. At the same time, the progressive integration of banking and securities markets is reflected in the growing presence of financial conglomerates, combining in the same group banks and securities firms.

The involvement of banks in the securities markets, whether directly or through affiliated firms, has momentous regulatory implications, forcing banking supervisors to develop prudential mechanisms for the control of the additional risks incurred by the banks in this manner. In its turn, the introduction of prudential controls creates the need for banking supervisors to establish contacts with the regulators of securities firms, because, without coordination of the regulatory responses, banks may find themselves at a competitive disadvantage against their non-bank competitors in the securities markets. The approaches of different jurisdictions towards the

---

Foonote 48 *cont'd*
as follows: first, factors for impact on competition; second, the effect of the Basle Accord is highly influenced by national accounting rules and other balance-sheet regulations – for example, loan loss reserve policies; third, cross-national differences in legal regimes and capital markets can provide significant advantages in utilising various capital instruments and in holding assets of different risk-weights; fourth, differences in the public enforcement of capital requirements have not been remedied by the Basle Accord.

[49] *See, e.g.*, E. B. Kapstein, "Resolving the regulator's dilemma: international coordination of banking regulations" (1989) 43 *International Organization* 323; and L. J. White, "On the international harmonization of bank regulation" (Winter 1994) 10:4 *Oxford Review of Economic Policy* 94.

[50] Over the years, the Committee has made a number of amendments to the Accord, for the following purposes: to refine the definition of capital through a differentiation between different categories of provisions, which may or may not be counted in a bank's capital base; to change the definition of OECD countries for the purpose of calculating capital requirements for exposures to foreign governments, by refusing the lowest risk-weights to countries which have rescheduled their external sovereign debt within the previous five years; to reduce a bank's capital requirements insofar as valid bilateral netting arrangements between that bank and its counterparties are in place, since such arrangements effectively reduce credit risk; and to modify capital requirements in the direction of capturing more accurately the potential future credit exposure associated with off-balance-sheet items. *See*, respectively, "Amendment to the Basle Accord" (Nov. 1991); "Amendment to the Capital Accord of July 1988" (July 1994); "The Capital Adequacy Treatment of the Credit Risk Associated with Certain Off-Balance-Sheet Items" (July 1994); and "Basle Capital Accord: Treatment of Potential Exposure for Off-Balance-Sheet Items" (Apr. 1995).

monitoring and control of risks from securities business is also necessary to ensure a "level playing field" internationally.[51]

Nonetheless, regulatory convergence in this area meets tremendous practical difficulties, due in part to technical difficulties relating to the measurement of risk exposure, but primarily to the fact that the commitment of the regulators of non-bank securities firms to the project of harmonisation is rather limited. The internationalisation of securities markets is a recent phenomenon, and pressures for equal regulatory treatment for all participants are not yet particularly strong. At the same time, regulatory responsibilities for securities markets at the national level are often fragmented, while international coordination between them is still in its infancy.[52] Moreover, securities regulators have fewer incentives than their banking colleagues to converge on uniform standards. Securities activities are organised in discrete national markets and are subject to conduct-of-business constraints, thus facilitating control. There are valid reasons for employing different methods of regulation for different activities or markets. Finally, securities regulators do not provide safety-nets to their regulatees and, accordingly, do not have an immediate budgetary reason to curtail their risk-taking. In contrast, the value of the public safety-nets for banking institutions increases in pace with their expansion to securities activities, putting pressure on banking regulators to control risk-taking, without, however, undermining the ability of their regulatees to compete internationally or domestically with non-banks.

The Basle Committee has undertaken a great deal of work in cooperation with the Technical Committee of the International Organisation of Securities Commissions ("IOSCO") for the purpose of devising common capital standards for financial intermediaries' market risk, *i.e.* the risk of losses on open positions in securities, derivative instruments and foreign exchange in an institution's trading portfolio as a result of adverse movements in market prices, including interest rates, exchange rates and equity values. However, the discussions between the two groups broke down in late 1992, because of the inability of IOSCO's members to reach agreement amongst themselves.[53] Following this, the Basle Committee decided to proceed on its own. Taking account of the banking industry's responses to its original proposals,[54] in April 1995 the Committee issued a set of revised consultative proposals,[55] aiming to issue a definitive Supplement to the

---

[51] *See* "Convergence of capital standards and the lessons of the market crash" (1988) 28 *B.E.Q.B.* 220, pp. 221–223.

[52] *See* "The co-ordination of regulation" (1988) 28 *B.E.Q.B.* 364.

[53] *See* "Report on International Developments in Banking Supervision: Report No. 10", *loc. cit.*, n. 10, pp. 79–80.

[54] Basle Committee, package of consultative proposals, published simultaneously: "The Prudential Supervision of Netting, Market Risks and Interest Rate Risk: Preface"; "The Supervisory Recognition of Netting for Capital Adequacy Purposes"; "The Supervisory Treatment of Market Risks"; and "Measurement of Banks' Exposure to Interest Rate Risk" (Apr. 1993).

[55] Basle Committee, package of consultative proposals, published simultaneously: "Proposal to Issue a Supplement to the Basle Capital Accord to Cover Market Risks"; "An Internal Model-Based Approach to Market Risk Capital Requirements"; and "Planned Supplement to the Capital Accord to Incorporate Market Risks" (Apr. 1995).

Accord by around the end of 1995, which the member countries should implement by the end of 1997.[56] The proposals propose a modified definition of capital and a framework for the calculation of explicit capital charges for market risks.[57] Where a bank uses sophisticated in-house models for measuring and managing its market risk, these may be used, instead of the Committee's standardised methodology, for the calculation of the capital requirements, subject to a number of carefully defined criteria;[58] in this case, however, the bank will be required to hold capital amounting to a multiple (at least three times) of its measured overall market risk exposure ("total value-at-risk").[59] It is still too early to know whether these proposals will bear fruit and, if so, how they will affect competition between banks and non-bank securities firms, who may not be subject to similar requirements.

For the time being, however, comprehensive harmonisation in this area has been achieved only by the EC, where the application of common capital requirements for the trading activities of all financial intermediaries, regardless of whether they are organised as credit institutions or investment firms, has been necessary as a prerequisite for completing the integration of the internal market in financial services and making possible the mutual recognition of national regulatory standards for investment firms.[60]

4 THE EXPORTATION OF BASLE-STYLE SUPERVISORY STANDARDS TO THE TRANSITIONAL POST-COMMUNIST ECONOMIES

As has been explained above,[61] the Basle Committee promotes actively the world-wide acceptance of its "club" law and is seeking to export its standards

---

[56] "Proposal to Issue a Supplement to the Basle Capital Accord to Cover Market Risks", *id.*, para. 25.

[57] "Planned Supplement to the Capital Accord to Incorporate Market Risks", *loc. cit.*, n. 55. In addition to market risks from the trading of debt and equity securities, derivatives and foreign exchange, the framework also covers risks arising in connection with commodities trading.

[58] "An Internal Model-Based Approach to Market Risk Capital Requirements", *loc. cit.*, n. 55.

[59] *Id.*, paras. IV.19–20. "The *multiplication factor* will be set by individual supervisors on the basis of their assessment of the quality of the bank's risk management system, subject to an absolute minimum of 3 (although this minimum number may be reviewed in light of additional experience). *The Committee has agreed that banks should be required to add to this factor a 'plus' directly related to the ex-post performance of the model, thereby introducing a built-in positive incentive to keep high the predictive quality of the model (e.g.,* it could be derived from the outcome of so-called 'back-testing' and be zero when such results are satisfactory)"; para. IV.20 (emphasis in the original). *See* also Patricia Jackson, "Risk measurement and capital requirements for banks" (1995) 35 *B.E.Q.B.* 177.

[60] Council Directive 93/6/EEC of 15.3.93 on the capital adequacy of investment firms and credit institutions (the "Capital Adequacy Directive"). The Capital Adequacy Directive's scope is wider than the Basle Committee's proposals, but the methodology and much of the detail is similar.

[61] *See supra*, pp. 184–185 and nn. 12–15.

even to those countries which are not represented in its ranks. The various regional groups of banking supervisors that have been set up with its assistance provide the main tool for the achievement of this aim. In addition, the biennial international regulatory conferences provide the Committee and its national members with an opportunity to influence the policy thinking of officials from countries with less developed supervisory systems.

The regional groups of banking supervisors are the Committee's preferred channel of interaction with non-G-10 countries. In contrast, direct contacts with individual supervisors at the national level are avoided, because they involve duplication and waste of effort. The Committee has recently initiated regular annual meetings with the chairmen of all regional groups, for the purpose of discussing each group's work, as well as that of the Committee; the first such meeting took place in Basle on 8 December 1993. Moreover, the Committee has expressed its willingness to participate more actively in the regional groups' own work, *e.g.*, through its representation by one or two Committee members at the regional meetings or through the preparation and circulation by its Secretariat of background papers on specific issues and the arrangement of presentations for sessions in the regional meetings.[62]

The same strategy has been followed in relation to the post-communist countries of eastern Europe and the former Soviet Union. Thus, during the Sixth International Conference of Bank Supervisors, held in Frankfurt on 10–11 October 1990, Huib Muller, then Chairman of the Basle Committee, hosted a meeting for regulators from countries of the area which led to the establishment of a Group of Banking Supervisors from central and eastern European Countries.[63] The State Banking Supervision Authority of Hungary hosted the first meeting of the new group, which took place in Budapest on 26–27 March 1991 with the participation of regulators from Bulgaria, Czechoslovakia, Hungary, Poland, Romania and the USSR. A delegation from Russia took the place of the former USSR at the Group's third meeting in Prague in April 1992.[64] Since then, numerous other countries have joined the Group, including Belarus, the FYR of Macedonia, Moldova, Slovenia, Slovakia, the Ukraine and the three Baltic states.[65]

The Group, which receives technical and secretarial assistance from the Secretariat of the Basle Committee, meets twice a year, with a different country hosting each meeting. The Group has agreed that chairmanship

---

[62] "Report on International Developments in Banking Supervision: Report No. 9", *loc. cit.*, n. 10, pp. 69–70.

[63] "Report on International Developments in Banking Supervision: Report No. 8", *loc. cit.*, n. 8, pp. 134–135.

[64] *Id.*

[65] "Report on International Developments in Banking Supervision: Report No. 9", *loc. cit.*, n. 10, pp. 119–120.

should be rotating, with the country hosting the next meeting acting as group chairman in the meantime.[66]

The Group does not have specific decision-making powers, but simply provides a forum for communication between individual supervisory authorities.[67] Its purpose is "to facilitate the exchange of information on supervisory policies and practices and to promote practical cooperation between members".[68] This is considered to be particularly useful, due to the fact that the supervisory authorities in the countries of the area experience common problems in establishing market-oriented banking markets. Significantly, an express subsidiary function of the Group in this context is to ensure consistency between the policies adopted by the countries of eastern Europe and the supervisory practices of western countries. For this reason, the Group is involved in "the identification of common needs in terms of training and technical assistance".[69]

Indeed, the training of the member countries' supervisory personnel plays a central part in the Group's activities. The Group's special attention to the education of staff serves well the general strategy of the Basle Committee for the dissemination of its thinking to the supervisors of non-G-10 countries. In recent years, the Committee has placed increased emphasis on its own week-long training seminars, which, since 1991, have been run on an annual basis. Each of these seminars is attended by delegates from over thirty countries. According to the Committee, the objective of the seminars is:

to give relatively young supervisors, who have the potential to rise to senior positions in their organisation, the opportunity to broaden their understanding of global banking markets and of current supervisory issues. There is a deliberate mix of participants from industrialised and developing countries. The courses inevitably have a strong international flavour and *focus mainly on the issues under discussion in the Basle Committee itself*... . Experience shows that the personal relationships which inevitably develop can prove to be a valuable source of assistance to participants in the course of their subsequent work and in the fostering of international supervisory co-operation.[70]

Insofar as the Group of Banking Supervisors from Central and Eastern European Countries is concerned, a similar approach is applied at the regional level. Thus, a first training seminar for junior supervisors from all central and eastern European countries was held under the auspices of the

---

[66] *Id.*
[67] "Report on International Developments in Banking Supervision: Report No. 8", *loc. cit.*, n. 8, pp. 134–135.
[68] "Report on International Developments in Banking Supervision: Report No. 9", *loc. cit.*, n. 10, p. 119.
[69] *Id.*
[70] *Id.*, pp. 70–71 (emphasis added).

Basle Committee's Secretariat in Poland in June 1991, at the instigation of the National Bank of Poland. Subsequently, training seminars have been organised with the Secretariat's assistance in most countries of the region, with participation of lecturers from the Basle Committee and the G-10 central banks.[71]

As the demand of the transitional economies for training is extremely high, owing to the lack of experience in regulatory issues and the large number of newly hired junior supervisory staff, the seminars provide a particular strong channel for the transplantation of Basle-oriented policy thinking and the organisation of the regulatory debate in the region around concepts based on the experience and current practices of the leading industrialised countries.

The Basle Committee's direct cultural influence on the regulators of the Group of Banking Supervisors from Central and Eastern European Countries is compounded by the advice given to the governments and central banks of the post-communist countries by the international financial institutions, such the World Bank, the IMF and the EBRD, which assist financially and technically the transition process. These institutions promote consistently the adoption of regulatory policies compatible with those of the Basle Committee, as a means of bringing the regulatory and legal infrastructure of the banking system in the countries in question up to western standards.

5 THE INFLUENCE OF THE EUROPEAN UNION

The most immediate pressures for the adoption of Basle-style regimes of prudential supervision, however, come from the direction of the EU.[72] From the latter's pespective, the transplantation of its model of prudential regulation in its entirety is indispensable, not because it offers the most promising strategy for the sustainable recovery of the post-communist economies, but as a prerequisite for the participation by the countries of wider Europe in the Union's single market. More specifically, the uniform application of Community law is necessary for ensuring equality of competitive conditions for all operators within the single market. In the financial sector, this entails the imposition of the application of the common European capital requirements to the credit institutions and other financial intermediaries of the countries of eastern Europe insofar as

---

[71] *See* "Report on International Developments in Banking Supervision: Report No. 8", *loc. cit.*, n. 8, p. 135; and "Report on International Developments in Banking Supervision: Report No. 9", *loc. cit.*, n. 10, p. 120, where it is noted that "[s]ome of these courses cover basic matters of supervisory technique such as licensing, accounting, on/off site supervision and capital requirements whereas other seminars concentrate on more advanced subjects, such as minimum standards, consolidation, treatment of bad loans/provisioning, new financial instruments and market risk regulations".

[72] *See* Dr. Paolo Clarotti (Head of the Banking and Financial Establishments Division, DG XV, European Commission), "EU as a model for financial market reform", Ch. 2 of this volume.

these countries have access to the single market and aspire to eventual accession to the Union.[73]

It is particularly significant that ten of the region's countries (Poland, Hungary, the Czech Republic, Slovakia, Bulgaria and Romania, the Baltic states, and Slovenia) are already associated, or are in the process of becoming associated, to the EC. These countries are bound under their Europe Agreements of association to pursue the approximation of their banking laws to the Community model. A typical example is Poland's Europe Agreement, which contains the following provision:

> The Contracting Parties recognise that the major precondition for Poland's economic integration into the Community is the approximation of that country's existing and future legislation to that of the Community. Poland shall use its best endeavours to ensure that future legislation is compatible with Community legislation.[74]

It is explicitly provided in the Agreement that the necessary approximation of laws extends to the area of banking law and financial services.[75] To assist Poland to achieve approximation, the Community is required to provide technical assistance, in particular by sending experts to Poland, supplying information, organising seminars and training activities, and providing aid for the translation of relevant Community legislation.[76] In addition to the above, a special provision on banking, insurance and other financial services stipulates that:

1. The Parties shall cooperate on the adoption of a common set of rules and standards *inter alia* for accounting and for supervisory and regulatory systems of banking, insurance and financial sectors.
2. Both sides shall establish precise methods of facilitating the process of reform ...[77]

Finally, the Agreeement requires Poland and the Community to cooperate "in order to prevent the use of their financial systems for the laundering of proceeds from criminal activities".[78]

As part of the pre-accession strategy for the associated countries of central and eastern Europe, the European Commission issued in April 1995 a White Paper for the purpose of assisting these countries to prepare themselves for participation in the Union's internal market.[79] Recognising that alignment with the internal market must be distinguished from accession to

---

[73] *Cf.* the reception of EC banking law by the EFTA countries by 1 January 1994, pursuant to the Treaty establishing the European Economic Area.

[74] Europe Agreement establishing an association between the European Communities and their Member States, of the one part, and the Republic of Poland, of the other part, Art. 68.

[75] *Id.*, Art. 69.

[76] *Id.*, Art. 70.

[77] *Id.*, Art. 83.

[78] *Id.*, Art. 85(1).

[79] Commission of the European Communities, White Paper, "Preparation of the Associated Countries of Central and Eastern Europe for Integration into the Internal Market of the Union", COM(95) 163 final, with "Addendum: Annexe", COM(95) 163 final/2.

the Union (which requires the acceptance of the *acquis communautaire* as a whole),[80] the White Paper identifies the key measures of Community law in each sector of legislative activity which form the foundation of the internal market and proposes to the associated countries a sequence for the approximation of their legislation to these measures.[81] At the same time, the White Paper describes the necessary structures for the implementation and enforcement of the relevant legislation, stressing that the establishment of such structures may be the most difficult task facing the associated countries.[82] The associated countries are not bound by the suggestions of the White Paper and are free to establish their own sectoral priorities for their alignment with the internal market in the light of their individual economic, social and political realities. The Union is already providing technical assistance for this purpose, notably through its PHARE programmes. The White Paper, however, indicates how technical assistance can be enhanced and adapted to support its recommendations and announces the creation by the Commission of a new Technical Assistance Information Exchange Office in Brussels, supported through a multi-country PHARE programme, which will serve as a "one-stop-shop" to which requests for assistance can be addressed. Assistance with advice and expertise will come from the Commission, the Member States and private bodies.[83]

With regard to banking legislation in particular, the White Paper encourages the associated countries to become acquainted with all EC directives affecting the financial sector and to implement in the first stage those measures which are considered essential for the operation of a sound banking sector. The White Paper recognises that a functioning basic framework of company law and accounting and financial reporting is a necessary pre-condition for the operation of the proposed legislation. It also stresses the importance of establishing, as soon as possible, an effective settlement system for dealing with transactions between financial institutions. The establishment of a banking supervisory authority responsible for the authorisation of credit institutions, the setting of prudential requirements for the operation of such institutions and the monitoring of the continuing fulfilment of these requirements – especially capital adequacy (or solvency, in the terminology of EC law) requirements – is identified as the most important first step once these pre-conditions are in place.[84]

According to the White Paper, the approximation of banking legislation should concentrate at an early stage on the transplantation of those measures of EC banking law which set the basic principles for the establishment of credit institutions.[85] At this stage, approximation should include, in particular, the recognition of the right of establishment and of the freedom to

---

[80] *Id.*, para. 1.8.
[81] *Id.*, paras. 1.5 and 1.14.
[82] *Id.*, paras. 1.6, 3.25–3.26 and 4.27–4.34.
[83] *Id.*, paras. 1.7 and 5.1–5.17.
[84] *Id.*, "Addendum: Annexe", pp. 282–284.
[85] *Id.*, pp. 284–285 and 287.

provide services, a legal requirement for the authorisation of banking institutions,[86] the introduction of Basle-style capital adequacy standards,[87] the establishment of a deposit guarantee scheme,[88] and the adoption of suitable standards against money laundering.[89] Noting that their Europe Agreements require the associated countries to permit EU financial institutions to set up operations in their territory by the end of their agreement's transitional period, at the latest, the White Paper includes a strong recommendation to the associated countries to allow the establishment of EU institutions as soon as possible, on the ground that this would involve important benefits in terms of the importation of those institutions' superior "know-how".[90]

At a later stage, the White Paper proposes the implementation of those other measures of EC banking law which aim specifically at the strengthening of prudential requirements, for the purpose of bringing prudential regulation in the associated countries up to international standards.[91] The second stage should focus on the adoption of prudential controls regarding the suitability of bank shareholders, the existence of sound administrative and accounting procedures and internal controls, etc.;[92] on the adoption of high standards for the preparation of the annual and consolidated accounts of credit institutions;[93] on the imposition of capital requirements for banks' and other financial firms' securities activities and for related trading risks;[94] on the imposition of controls on large exposures;[95] and on the introduction of supervision of banking groups on a consolidated basis.[96]

It is clear that the implementation by any post-communist country of a legislative package based on the White Paper's proposal ensures

---

[86] Consistent with the First Council Directive.

[87] Consistent with Council Directive 89/299/EEC of 17.4.89 on the own funds of credit institutions (the "Own Funds Directive") and Council Directive 89/647/EEC of 18.12.89 on a solvency ratio for credit institutions (the "Solvency Ratio Directive").

[88] Consistent with Directive 94/19/EC of 30.5.94 of the European Parliament and of the Council on deposit-guarantee schemes (the "Deposit-Guarantee Directive").

[89] Consistent with Council Directive 91/308/EEC of 10.6.91 on prevention of the use of the financial system for the purpose of money laundering (the "Money Laundering Directive").

[90] White Paper, *loc. cit.*, n. 79, "Addendum: Annexe", p. 287.

[91] *Id.*, pp. 288–290.

[92] Consistent with the Second Council Directive 89/646/EEC of 15.12.89 on the co-ordination of laws, regulations and administrative provisions relating to the taking up and pursuit of the business of credit institutions and amending Directive 77/780/EEC (the "Second Banking Directive"). However, provisions of the Directive which are directly related to the creation of the Community's own internal market, such as those establishing a credit institution's freedom of establishment and freedom to provide cross-border services in every Member State on the basis of its home-country authorisation, could be disregarded.

[93] Consistent with Council Directive 86/635/EEC of 8.12.86 on the annual accounts and consolidated accounts of banks and other financial institutions.

[94] Consistent with the Capital Adequacy Directive.

[95] Consistent with Council Directive 92/121/EEC of 21.12.92 on the monitoring and control of large exposures of credit institutions (the "Large Exposures Directive").

[96] Consistent with Council Directive 92/30/EEC of 6.4.92 on the supervision of credit institutions on a consolidated basis (the "Second Consolidated Supervision Directive").

automatically substantial compatibility of such country's regulatory regime with the substantive prudential recommendations of the Basle Committee – although not necessarily with its pronouncements regarding transnational regulatory cooperation for the supervision of banks operating in more than one jurisdiction.

6 OBSTACLES TO THE ESTABLISHMENT OF A FUNCTIONING BANKING SECTOR IN POST-COMMUNIST ECONOMIES

The primary purpose of the convergence to common prudential standards through the Basle process is to guarantee that all banks, regardless of nationality, are subject to equivalent regulatory burdens and to ensure, in this manner, an international "level playing field" for banking competition. A similar need to eliminate regulatory distortions of competition motivates the harmonisation of banking legislation in the EC, which is a precondition for the integration of national banking markets in a single pan-European financial system. On the other hand, the development of policies aiming at the construction of a functioning financial system from scratch has never been pursued by either the Basle Committee or the EC, since all the participating countries have already firmly in place developed payment, banking and financial structures.[97]

This, however, is not the case in the post-communist economies of eastern Europe and the former Soviet Union. Even the most advanced transitional economies of central Europe are finding the establishment of a well-functioning financial sector particularly difficult. Other countries, including Russia, have made much less advance in the direction of banking reform.[98]

Admittedly, every post-communist economy has made at least some first tentative steps in the direction of establishing a market-oriented banking

---

[97] *See* White Paper, *loc. cit.*, n. 79, "Addendum: Annexe", pp. 281 and 283.

[98] *See Transition Report, loc. cit.*, n. 3, pp. 9 and 15. In Table 2.1, pp. 10–11, the *Transition Report* uses a simplified four-tier classification to provide a snapshot of the progress made by 25 countries in the region in connection with banking reform. A group of nine countries, comprising Armenia, Azerbaijan, Belarus, Georgia, Kazakhstan, Tajikistan, Turkmenistan, the Ukraine and Uzbekistan, are found to belong in Category 1, suggesting that they have made "little progress beyond establishment of a two-tier system". Another eight countries, comprising Albania, Bulgaria, the FYR of Macedonia, Kyrgyzstan, Lithuania, Moldova, Romania and, last but not least, the Russian Federation, are classified in Category 2, which means that they have reached the point where "interest rates significantly influence the allocation of credit". A final group of eight countries, comprising Croatia, the Czech Republic, Estonia, Hungary, Latvia, Poland, the Slovak Republic and Slovenia, are assigned to Category 3, in other words these countries are characterised by "substantial progress on bank recapitalisation, bank auditing, and establishment of a functioning prudential supervisory system; significant presence of private banks; full interest rate liberalisation with little preferential access to cheap refinancing". Significantly, none of the 25 countries examined is thought to have reached Category 4, *i.e.* to have achieved "well functioning banking competition and prudential supervision".

system as part of its transition strategy.[99] Typically, the Soviet-style "monobank" system, in which the main national bank served as both central bank and monopolistic commercial bank with a nationwide branch network, has been dismantled and replaced by a two-tier banking system. This has been achieved by breaking up most of the commercial operations of the national bank into several new commercial banks, owned by the state or by state-owned enterprises and organisations. The remaining core of the old monobank functions as a traditional central bank. The degree of fragmentation of the old monobank varies from country to country; it has reached an extreme in the former Soviet Union where the break up of the main state bank (Gosbank), which commenced in 1987 as part of the perestroika reforms, has led to the creation of thousands of regional and sector-oriented commercial and cooperative banks,[100] but has been much more limited in the rest of the region.

In most parts of the region, the deposit and credit markets are still dominated by the state-owned successors of the monobank and of the specialised sector-oriented institutions of the communist era. Only a few countries have achieved large-scale privatisation of their state-owned banks. This is, notably, the case of the Czech and Slovak Republics, Estonia and Lithuania; a number of other countries, such as Poland, Hungary, Latvia and, to a lesser extent, Croatia, are currently making concrete progress in the same direction. In most countries, entry in the banking sector has been liberalised, permitting the establishment of new private banks, domestic or foreign. While entry by foreign banks has generally been very limited, domestic institutions have been created, often in large numbers. These, however, lack the state-owned banks' branch networks and established deposit base and thus tend to be small, although they have the advantage of clean asset portfolios.[101]

Across the region, further banking reform has encountered fundamental difficulties. In many cases, the new central banks do not have the political autonomy, credibility, and technical ability that they need to bring inflation under control and guarantee monetary stabilisation. At the same time, there are serious questions regarding the ability of the new commercial banks to perform their role by ensuring sound lending and the safety of their deposit liabilities.

Commercial banks' loan portfolios contain large amounts of very low-quality assets ("bad loans"), especially to state-owned enterprises, inherited

---

[99] For a review and assessment of transition developments in the area of money and banking in various countries of the region, *see* D. M. Kemme and A. Rudka (eds.), *Monetary and Banking Reform in Postcommunist Economies* (New York and Prague: Institute for East-West Security Studies, 1992); and J. Rostowski (ed.), *Banking Reform in Central Europe and the Former Soviet Union* (Budapest: Central European University Press, 1995).

[100] On 1 June 1994, 2,214 commercial banks were in operation in the Russian Federation alone; *Transition Report, loc. cit.*, n. 3, p. 35.

[101] The EBRD's *Transition Report, id.*, Appendix 2.1: "Transition indicators", pp. 16–41, provides brief individual descriptions of the current structure of the banking system in 25 countries of the region. *See* also *Transition Report Update* (London: EBRD, April 1995), Appendix II: "Transition indicators – update", pp. 51–68.

from the old monobank. Under the centrally administered economic system, bank credit used to be allocated in response to planners' commands, not on the basis of commercial criteria. In many cases, the communist state did not provide sufficient capital to enterprises, and even withdrew their trading profits in order to prevent them from building up excess inventories. Bank loans were instead given to enterprises for planned capital investment, thus ensuring more effective control by the planners, who could apply pressure on an enterprises by reducing its credit. Significantly, the loans did not have definite repayment terms. The allocation of credit on a non-market basis, in combination with the total absence of incentives for financial discipline in either enterprises or banks, led to the accumulation of bad loans in banks' balance sheets.[102] With the transition to a market-oriented system, these bad loans have come to plague the new commercial banks, which are effectively insolvent.

In some countries, such as the Czech and the Slovak Republics, Poland, Hungary, and Estonia, a solution to the problem has been sought through programmes of bank recapitalisation, while in others rapid inflation has eroded the real value of the inherited bad loans. Almost everywhere, however, the accumulation of bad loans continued as the collapse in industrial output deepened. A significant proportion of new loans are extended to borrowers who experience financial difficulties and are unable to service their debt. Usually, these borrowers are the same large state-owned enterprises which were responsible for the old bad loans. On the other hand, private enterprises with promising prospects are often unable to secure credit.[103]

The perpetuation of bad lending is a result both of the general lack of banking skills and of the perverse incentives of the management of state-owned commercial banks. Banks do not have the criteria for assessing the creditworthiness of clients and for evaluating projects. The quality of bank services and management is low and bank infrastructure is inadequate. Matters are made worse by the fact that accounting practices do not meet

---

[102] See *Transition Report, id.*, p. 6. In the words of J. Rostowski, "The banking system, credit and the real sector in transition economies", in Rostowski (ed.), *op. cit.*, n. 99, p. 16, "[b]efore the beginning of the transition to capitalism, all credit in Central Europe and the Soviet Union was 'systemically bad' in the sense that it was not allocated on the basis of commercial criteria, and therefore there was no reason to suppose that once ordinary market conditions were established, any particular loan could be serviced and ultimately repaid by the borrower. Bad credit of this kind is not really an asset belonging to the lender, but rather a transfer to the borrower, occurring at the expense of either the lender or of those financing the lender (the lender's lenders). To the extent that part of any credit could be serviced and repaid, this was accidental and, to the extent that servicing is enforced, could be thought of as a random tax on particular borrowers."

[103] However, there is some evidence that in the most advanced transitional economies, *e.g.*, Poland, the state-owned banks gradually improve their performance, starting to respond to demands for market-oriented finance. See *Transition Report, id.*, p. 50; and comments of S. van Wijnbergen, in D. Hexter *et al.*, "Round table on banking" (1993) 1 *Economics of Transition* 111, p. 120.

the appropriate standards, while the situation in the area of commercial law, including in particular mortgage and security law, is still unsatisfactory. Accordingly, lending is generally biased in favour of borrowers who can offer large fixed assets as collateral, *i.e.* industrial state-owned enterprises.

At the same time, a number of factors make it rational for bank management to continue throwing good money after bad. Because of their weak capital position and the extent of bad loans in their portfolios, which puts their own solvency in question, banks have a strong incentive to misrepresent their borrowers' true condition and to protect them from bankruptcy by refinancing their arrears, in the hope that the government will eventually bail them out or that their situation will gradually improve.[104] This is possible because there are no established accounting disciplines that would ensure the writing-off of non-performing assets.

Moreover, the banks maintain very close links with their large borrowers of the state-owned industrial sector. Indeed, in many cases, especially in the countries of the CIS, the banks are themselves partially owned by borrower enterprises, which use them as vehicles for their financing. The concentration of bank credit exposures is aggravated by the existence of large-scale inter-enterprise arrears, which have built up as a result of the difficulties facing the state-owned enterprises and the inadequacies of the payment system. In their turn, inter-enterprise arrears are further encouraged by the commercial banks' unwillingness to take action against delinquent borrowers. If debts were rigorously enforced, enterprises might be less accommodating to their debtors, because they would need to secure their own cash flow. Under current conditions, however, banks and their borrowers have a common interest in the non-enforcement of financial claims, due to the interdependent nature of their exposures.[105] The governments of the region may not be totally inimical to these practices, which permit the continuing operation of loss-making large enterprises without need for politically unattractive explicit subsidies, which would violate their professed commitment to stabilisation. However, this amounts effectively to the monetisation of enterprise deficits, with untoward inflationary consequences.[106] In short, the underlying insolvency of the commercial banks encourages even higher risk-taking and the continuing refinancing of bad loans. Things are only made worse by the rapid reduction in bank reserve ratios which accompanies the implementation of a macroeconomic stabilisation programme.[107]

---

[104] *See* comments of D. Begg and R. Portes, in Hexter *et al.*, *id.*, p. 117.

[105] *See id.*; and M. Bruno, "Stabilization and the macroeconomics of transition – how different is Eastern Europe?" (1993) 1 *Economics of Transition* 5, pp. 14–15.

[106] *See* E. C. Perotti, "A taxonomy of post-socialist financial systems: decentralized enforcement and the creation of inside money" (1994) 2 *Economics of Transition* 71, pp. 73–75.

[107] In the pre-stabilisation period of the transition, commercial banks tend to operate with very high reserve-to-deposit ratios. This reflects the traditional practices of the monobank system, but also the extreme inefficiencies of the payments system, which force

Beyond the creation of efficient payment systems, the termination of this vicious cycle through the establishment of incentives for the sound allocation of credit and the enforcement of financial discipline (including bankruptcy) would be the most valuable contribution of banking policy during the transition. The explicit recognition and writing down of bad loans in bank balance sheets is an essential aspect of this process. It necessitates, however, state intervention in order to avoid widespread bankruptcy and the complete collapse of the banking system.

As has been mentioned above, the recapitalisation of state-owned banks, with the aim of solving the bad loan problem and of bringing them closer to international capital standards, has already been attempted in several eastern European countries. Recapitalisation can be achieved either through the swapping of non-performing assets on banks' balance sheets for government bonds or through the infusion of cash, leaving the responsibility for sorting out the bad loans to the banks themselves, often subject to incentives for performing this task.[108]

Nonetheless, simple recapitalisation of ailing banks by the state is not of itself sufficient for the emergence of a functional banking system, and can even prove counterproductive: as it confirms the banks' belief that their perverse lending would sooner or later be validated by the state, recapitalisation can become a source of severe moral hazard problems, inducing a new cycle of unsound banking practices and leading to the quick dissipation of the capital injection. Certain additional conditions are necessary. These include the development of expertise and proper procedures for credit evaluation. Training is a critical issue in this context, but the process needs time. Insofar as the achievement of incentive-compatibility is concerned, the early (even prior to restructuring) privatisation of the state-owned banks is of vital importance. Currently, managers are interested in the appropriation of short-term profits, high salaries and other benefits, but are not concerned with the long-term performance of their banks. Private ownership is, accordingly, an essential condition for efficient management, committed at ensuring profitability on a continuous basis. It also puts an end to government interference in banks' lending decisions. The main problem in this context is that privatisation tends to take much longer than initially envisaged and is particularly vulnerable to political instability.

Even a successful privatisation programme, however, may fail to address the inefficiencies of the banking system, if the most fundamental condition

---

Footnot 107 *cont'd*
commercial banks to maintain particularly large deposits with the central bank, as well as the ample availability of central bank credit to commercial banks. Stabilisation induces a rapid reduction in the backing of deposits by reserves and an increase in the proportion of commercial loans in banks' balance sheets. However, the value of these loans is highly uncertain, because of the low quality of credit allocation. J. Rostowski, "Problems of creating stable monetary systems in post-communist economies" (1993) 45 *Europe-Asia Studies* 445, pp. 446–447.

[108] *See Transition Report, loc. cit.,* n. 3, pp. 52–54.

is not ensured. This is the independence of banks from their borrowers. It has been rightly observed that:

It is a terrible mistake to allow enterprises to own a large part of a commercial bank from which they are borrowing heavily. The outcome is the bankruptcy of the bank rather than of the enterprise. The credit process must be independent; this principle is clear from the experience of many countries.[109]

More generally, as long as the fate of banks in eastern Europe and the former Soviet Union continues to depend on that of their ailing borrowers, either as a result of ownership links or of concentrated exposures, the incentives for sound lending will remain poor.

7 WESTERN-STYLE CAPITAL-BASED PRUDENTIAL REGULATION: AN APPROPRIATE TOOL FOR BANKING REFORM?

Neither the Basle Committee nor the European Commission appears to doubt the relevance of their model of prudential supervision for the banking systems of the post-communist economies and, in particular, its suitability for the transitional phase. In its latest "Report on International Developments in Banking Supervision", the Basle Committee stresses the universal validity of its approach:

As banks move away from traditional activities, supervision becomes more judgmental, requiring an assessment of the appropriateness of an individual bank's business strategy in light of its management capabilities and of overall market conditions. Supervisors need to devote sufficient resources to monitoring and understanding the risks which arise as banks develop new funding and trading strategies, new risk management techniques, and new organisational structures ... Supervisors in the emerging markets are subject to very similar challenges, albeit at a less advanced stage of development... . Attention has to be paid more to management capacity and to qualitative aspects of banks' performance than to the straightforward quantitative criteria. Supervision therefore has to be strengthened and contacts between supervisors and the banks in their jurisdictions intensified.[110]

To what extent, however, should a fledgling regulatory system with very limited resources and no experience adopt the essentially discretionary approach advocated by the Committee? To what extent should the diversification of banks away from their core activities be accepted passively as a fact of life by the banking authorities of the post-communist economies while they try to establish from scratch functioning banking

---

[109] Kemme and Rudka (eds.), *op. cit.*, n. 99, p. 158.
[110] "Report on International Developments in Banking Supervision: Report No. 9", *loc. cit.*, n. 10, pp. 2–3.

systems? And to what extent should the strengthening of prudential requirements be the paramount priority during the transition period?

Dr. Paolo Clarotti, the Head of the Banking and Financial Establishments Division of the European Commission, believes that "[i]t would be wise to err on the side of caution rather than to set inadequate standards".[111] Strict prudential policies, however, may not be the best policy for countries undergoing a major transformation, where skills are scarce and the broader economic conditions particularly unstable. The emergence of sound banks in these circumstances depends on a gradual learning process in an environment where there is no easy way to assess risk. In these circumstances, the desideratum of stability might better be pursued through structural measures, rather than prudential regulations.

Indeed, the European Commission recognises itself in its White Paper that the programmes for the approximation of the associated countries' laws to the Community model cannot in all cases be easily reconciled with the need to consolidate economic reforms during the transition, noting in particular that:

in the field of financial services, internal market legislation strengthens prudential requirements and leads to more deregulated markets. Such a regulatory change made too soon could seriously weaken financial entities in Central and Eastern Europe, since most of them still have to cope with a legacy of bad loans.[112]

This insight, however, is not accompanied by specific qualifications of a structural nature to the proposed approximation sequence. Instead, the rapid introduction of EC-oriented prudential regulation and the establishment of efficient supervisory structures are advocated, on the basis that they are necessary for ensuring that the users of the financial system have full confidence in it. Accordingly, the Commission places the main emphasis on the issue of training, not only for the employees in the financial industry, but equally for the staff of the supervisory bodies.[113] In contrast, medium-term alternatives to a system of prudential regulation (*e.g.*, possible structural responses to the problem of stability, or the encouragement of unregulated competition between the new banking institutions) are not explored.

Having established a supervisory authority, many countries in the region have already moved to enact banking laws reflecting the prudential standards of the Basle Committee and the EU (although in certain cases the effect of the new standards is not immediate, but phased over a period of time to permit the gradual preparation of the local banking system). At the same time, a number of eastern European economies have adopted policies for the identification and working out of bad loans and the recapitalisation of state-owned banks, with a view of raising their capital ratios to the level

---

[111] Clarotti, *loc. cit.*, n. 72.
[112] White Paper, *loc. cit.*, n. 79, para. 4.11.
[113] *Id.*, "Addendum: Annexe", pp. 281–282.

required by the Basle Accord and the European directives, in preparation for their privatisation.[114]

A fundamental pre-condition for the successful implementation of the new prudential standards, especially those concerning capital adequacy, is the existence of valid accounting practices and functioning rules regarding the classification of assets and the making of provisions against identified loan losses. In fact, the modernisation and rationalisation of accounting practices, with a view to replacing the unrealistic policies of the communist era with generally accepted international standards, has been pursued throughout the region. However, the accounting and reporting systems are not yet sophisticated enough to guarantee the accuracy and timeliness of information provided to the management of the commercial banks and the regulatory authorities. Residual discretion in the classification of assets in terms of their quality and in the making of provisions is a particularly important problem, given the size of the bad loan problem. Aggressive supervision would be required to confirm the quality of financial accounts, but throughout the region regulators lack the skills and resources necessary for performing their role effectively. Thus, the adoption of prudential rules consistent with the international standards is not accompanied by effective enforcement.

A particular problem is that the banks of post-communist economies often start from a position where compliance with the international capital standards is simply not feasible. The adoption of unrealistically strict regulatory standards can have significant perverse effects. One possibility is that the banks will ignore the standards and continue to pursue risky policies, in the hope of boosting their profitability, since only this would permit them eventually to restore their capital positions. Alternatively, the effective enforcement of the standards may result in further contraction of the relatively small bank sector and reduced competition, since the high start-up costs will dissuade new entry, while the operation of risk-based capital requirements will force the consolidation of existing banks and set constraints on their ability to expand by taking up new risks. Given the limited effectiveness of the supervisory function, it is probable that a mixture of the two responses will prevail, ensuring the worst possible outcome, as the capital regulations will check the competitiveness and growth of the fledgling banking sector, without, however, guaranteeing its safety.

The clear shift in many countries towards a tightening of entry controls for new banks raises special concerns, since the long-term development of a healthy private banking sector depends on competition and innovation. It is true that the lack of significant entry controls is bound to be mirrored in high exit rates, as many of the newly created banks may eventually fail. However, the introduction of barriers to entry in the form of minimum start-up capital requirements and the adoption of policies directed at the consolidation of

---

[114] *See, e.g.,* on the Polish attempts, comments of S. Sikora, in "EBRD Conference on Banking Reform and Regulation in Eastern Europe", summary of proceedings, *loc. cit.*, n. 3, p. 13; and Kate Mortimer, "Banking privatization policy in Poland and Czechoslovakia", in Rostowski (ed.), *op. cit.*, n. 99.

existing small banks encourages further concentration of the banking sector, where already a few state-owned banks tend to predominate. The entrenchment of an oligopolistic banking structure in the name of increased safety should be strongly resisted. Even less acceptable is the gradual expansion of the public safety-nets to the larger new private banks.

It should be repeated at this point that the international capital standards were designed for the needs of the mature banking systems of the industrialised countries; their aim was to keep the cost of public safety-nets under control, ensuring at the same time competitive equality for all international banks. Neither of these aims is relevant to the banking systems of the transitional phase. International competitive considerations are not an issue for them, while their main concern is the disengagement of the state from the banking sector, rather than the continuing solvency of the public safety-nets.

On the other hand, the legacy of accumulated bad loans requires that the regulatory policies pursued by the post-communist economies should be able to address the underlying problems (including the absence of appropriate structures of corporate governance and the commonality of interest between banks and their debtors) and to facilitate the development of banking skills, especially insofar as the assessment of credit is concerned. Moreover, these policies should be easy to implement, even on the basis of relatively unsophisticated reporting information, and their application should not rely unduly on the discretionary judgment of the local supervisors, since these are poorly prepared for their task and in many cases have an inappropriate incentive structure.[115]

A critical question for the future role of banks in the region concerns the limits to their links with industrial and commercial enterprises. An influential view is that banks should be allowed to play an influential role in corporate governance in the post-communist economies. On this view, the securities markets are unlikely to ensure satisfactory mechanisms of corporate control and accountability. While the fragmentation of ownership, *e.g.* through programmes of mass privatisation of state-owned enterprises, does not leave sufficient incentives for the dispersed group of small shareholders to take part in corporate governance, the low liquidity of securities markets deters take-overs of inefficiently managed firms. This can pose a serious impediment to the restructuring of enterprises following privatisation. In this situation, corporate governance should be based on the concentration of control, through significant equity holdings and

---

[115] E. S. Phelps, R. Frydman, A. Rapaczynski and A. Scleifer, *Needed Mechanisms of Corporate Governance and Finance in Eastern Europe* (EBRD Working Paper No. 1, London: EBRD, Mar. 1993), pp. 36–37, observe that reform proposals should not rely on the quality of the regulatory function. The political environment in transitional countries is unstable and does not provide significant rewards for conscientious bureaucrats. Any reasonably qualified person will find employment in the booming private sector materially more attractive. As a result, the turnover in regulatory personnel is high. Moreover, opportunities for corruption abound. In particular, disclosure should prevail over regulatory discretion and licensing should depend on mandatory rules, under clearly defined criteria, not on the balancing of qualitative factors.

representation in company boards, in the hands of groups of "insiders" who are able to exercise it effectively. The policy implication of this view is that inter-enterprise ownership, as well as the close involvement of banks in the funding and control of industry, should be embraced. This would be consistent with the universal banking system of the countries of continental Europe, especially Germany, with which many central and eastern European countries are traditionally closely associated. Although its proponents recognise that such a system of corporate finance and governance involves significant risks in terms both of the structure of the industrial sector and of the safety of banks exposed to concentrated corporate risk, these could be minimised through strong anti-monopoly and prudential regulation.[116]

A related view finds advantages in the participation of banks in the working out of existing non-performing loans and the restructuring of their corporate debtors, *e.g.* through debt-for-equity swaps. Banks may be suitable for this purpose, because they have prior knowledge of their debtors (even though they did not take genuine credit decisions in the past) and an incentive to see the debtors' situation improving – something that may not be the case with the administrators of the special state agencies to which the restructuring of insolvent enterprises can, alternatively, be entrusted. As a result of the restructuring exercise, banks are likely to improve their skills, ensuring at the same time the continuing financing of the enterprises concerned.[117]

These views, however, may be unduly optimistic. Given the incentive problems identified earlier,[118] further involvement by banks in their debtors' affairs would be particularly dangerous. The addition of equity exposures to the underperforming debt claims, would only strengthen the interest of banks in keeping their debtors afloat, regardless of their true situation. Moreover, recapitalisation by the state would create a reasonable expectation of future bail-outs, exacerbating the moral hazard problems. Essentially, behind the façade of German-style universal banking, banks could become the centres of large state-owned holding companies, inhibiting competition and extracting state subsidies. Moreover, the true value of banks' equity holdings would be extremely difficult to ascertain, since these would consist primarily of their debtors' unquoted stock.[119]

For these reasons, putting an end to (rather than reinforcing) the symbiotic relationships between banks and their large corporate debtors

---

[116] *See* J. Corbett and C. Mayer, "Financial reform in eastern Europe: progress with the wrong model" (1991) 7:4 *Oxford Review of Economic Policy* 57; and comments of Colin Mayer, in "EBRD Conference on Banking Reform and Regulation in Eastern Europe", summary of proceedings, *loc. cit.*, n. 3, pp. 18–20.

[117] *See* comments of S. van Wijnberger, in Hexter *et al.*, *loc. cit.*, n. 103, pp. 118–120; and *Transition Report*, *loc. cit.*, n. 3, p. 53.

[118] *See supra*, pp. 205–206 and nn. 104–107.

[119] E. S. Phelps, R. Frydman, A. Rapaczynski and A. Scleifer, *Needed Mechanisms of Corporate Governance and Finance in Eastern Europe* (EBRD Working Paper No. 1, London: EBRD, Mar. 1993), pp. 23–28; and Rostowski, "The banking system, credit and the real sector . . .", *loc. cit.*, n. 102, pp. 28–35.

appears to be an urgent priority for the development of a healthy banking sector. Various solutions to the problem have been proposed. One suggestion is that viable new banking institutions should be created from scratch with state support, with a parallel scaling down of the activities of old banks. This could be achieved by transferring to the new institutions part of the old banks' deposit liabilities equal to the amount of bad loans that are taken up by the special state agency serving as the vehicle of corporate restructuring.[120] Other proposals involve the introduction of "narrow banking", which would prevent institutions accepting deposits and participating in the payment mechanism from lending directly to the industrial and commercial sector by forcing them to back their deposit liabilities with extremely safe assets, such as balances with the central bank or government debt.[121]

Generally, given the nature of banking relationships in eastern Europe and the former Soviet Union, a stronger element of structural regulation than is normally found in the West is probably required to ensure safety. Although, in principle, the Basle model of prudential supervision does not preclude additional structural measures, in practice it encourages a system of universal banking, concentrating on the control of risk through the assessment and implicit pricing of banks' overall asset-profile, but leaving aside questions regarding the mix of their activities. In the case of post-communist economies, however, setting strict limits on banks' permissible activities seems more appropriate, at least until the banks have developed the credit assessment, liability management and other skills which are necessary for efficient credit allocation. The relevant measures could include, in particular, the imposition of tight credit limits and the separation of commercial from investment banking, in order to prevent the involvement of banks accepting retail deposits in enterprise restructuring. Restrictions on the type of credit that commercial banks can extend could be introduced, *e.g.* by confining them to self-liquidating trading finance, but precluding long-term finance for fixed investment.

In contrast, a Basle-oriented system of capital-based prudential regulation would appear incapable of addressing the incentive problems or ensuring safe and sound banking in the region. As Jacek Rostowski has observed:

high capital ratios make less sense as long as bank capital is state-owned (unless, as in Poland, capital adequacy is a criterion for … privatization, and bank managements are very interested in privatization), and as long as bank auditing and super-

---

[120] *See* Phelps *et al.*, *id.*, pp. 28–29; and comments of F. Coricelli and A. Thorne, in Hexter *et al.*, *loc. cit.*, n. 103, pp. 112–115.

[121] *See* Rostowski, "Problems of creating stable monetary systems …", *loc. cit.*, n. 107, pp. 449–452; and A. W. A. Boot and S. van Wijnbergen, "Financial sector design, regulation and deposit insurance in Eastern Europe", in Rostowski (ed.), *op. cit.*, n. 99. The allocation of credit and equity finance under a system of this type would be left to investment funds, private holding companies and special investment banks with access to wholesale funding. The restrictions on bank functions could be lifted gradually, as the banking system matures.

visory skills are rare (valuation of bank equity requires realistic loan classification). High reserve ratios are easier to apply, and as one approaches 100 per cent reserves on deposits the need for high levels of capital to provide a cushion against bad loans disappears.[122]

Where the Basle approach simply encourages holdings of domestic government liabilities by assigning them a 0% risk-weight and thus excluding them from the calculation of a bank's capital requirements, without, however, imposing a mandatory portfolio constraint to this effect, a regulatory policy based on high mandatory reserve ratios would force banks to keep the proportion of government liabilities in their asset port-folios above a specified level. Compliance with a reserve requirement could be enforced on the basis of relatively simple data. The policy could also simplify the operation of monetary policy, because it would decrease the variability of the money supply. Reserve ratios could be gradually brought down, as the condition of the banking system improves and the confidence of the monetary authorities increases.

The one component of the Basle approach which is particularly relevant for the situation of the post-communist economies and whose application would be indispensable for a regulatory policy aiming at increased safety, is that relating to the control of large exposures.[123]

Nonetheless, it should be asked whether bank safety should indeed be the paramount objective of regulatory policy, at least during the transition. An alternative would be to pursue thoroughly a pro-competition policy, involving the complete withdrawal of public safety-nets (possibly after a final recapitalisation of existing banks) and the removal of barriers to entry (including minimum capital requirements). A policy of this type would provide strong incentives for bank managers to improve efficiency and quality of services, and even to innovate, thus accelerating the maturation of the banking system.

Under this scenario, once the authorities had made clear that their implicit responsibility for the safety of bank liabilities has been removed, depositors would be likely to shift their deposits to banks which are perceived to be safe.

Since the depositors' "flight to quality" would make it imperative for banks to protect their credibility in the market for funds and to compete on the basis of their reputation, its effects would be beneficial in terms of ensuring the fundamental safety of banks. The process of "natural selection" of healthy banks would certainly induce in the short run numerous bank failures. This could have negative implications insofar as it might discourage the population's banking habit. However, the problem may not be particularly grave, because, as Arnoud Boot and Sweder van Wijnbergen observe:

---

[122] Rostowski, "The banking system, credit and the real sector . . .", *loc. cit.*, n. 102, p. 38.
[123] *See* "Measuring and Controlling Large Credit Exposures", *loc. cit.*, n. 21; *see* also the European Large Exposures Directive.

[i]nsolvency of private and/or public banks would mainly put corporate depositors at risk as most countries' household deposits still largely flow through a dedicated savings bank.[124]

At any rate, such an effect cannot probably be pre-empted completely without undermining the basic strategy, which would be incompatible with a policy of deposit insurance, since this would remove the incentives for reputational competition and market discipline.

A promising experiment in this direction is already under way in the Russian Federation, in the form of the Russian Financial Institutions Development Programme (FIDP), which is supported by the World Bank and EBRD, and which aims precisely at assisting the emergence of a core group of sound and efficient medium-size private banks, whose reliability is signalled through self-imposed restrictions on their risk-taking and healthy financial ratios. The success of this programme would suggest that supporting the forces of competition may be a better answer to the problems of the transition than relying on imported models of centralised prudential regulation.

---

[124] Boot and van Wijnbergen, *loc. cit.*, n. 121 , p. 51.

13. Evolution of Banking Law in Serbia and the Role of International Institutions

Vlatko Sekulovic[1]

1 INTRODUCTION

Serbian banking law reflects Serbia's entire legal framework as its banking system reflects the whole of economic relations in Serbia. Therefore, the analysis of the evolution of Serbian banking law not only illustrates specific solutions related to banking practice and institutions, but also reveals complex social and economic tendencies and changes. This chapter will review and analyse the banking area of Serbian law in the context of two events: the collapse of socialism and war in the former Yugoslavia.

The International Monetary Fund (IMF), the International Bank for Reconstruction and Development (IBRD or World Bank) and the Organisation of United Nations (UN) influenced significantly the macroeconomic and macropolitical conditions of Serbia, as well as those of the Socialist Federal Republic of Yugoslavia (SFRY).

In 1988 the last federal government of SFRY implemented a programme of reforms designed to build up an economic and political system which would ensure economic efficiency and political democracy over the course of five years. A fundamental element of this transition process in Serbia and SFRY was the reform of the legal system. During forty-five years of socialism, the law reflected an economy based on social ownership of the means of production. Thus, with the advent of democracy and a market economy, drastic changes in the Yugoslav legal system were inevitable. Hence, enterprise law, property law, the Constitution, etc. had to be amended or completely new legislation had to be adopted. The importance of banking system transformation was evident. In 1989, new banking regulations were enacted creating the necessary legal framework for the reconstruction of the Banking system. International financial institutions (IFI), specifically the IMF and the IBRD, had a significant role in the transition process.

---

[1] Attorney at law, Belgrade; Research Fellow of the London Institute of International Banking, Finance and Development Law, Centre for Commercial Law Studies, Queen Mary and Westfield College, University of London.

After the disintegration of SFRY and the consequent war in Croatia and Bosnia-Herzegovina, the evolution of banking law in Serbia continued under vastly different circumstances. UN sanctions, the disintegration of the Yugoslav market, etc. influenced heavily the macroeconomic conditions of Serbia. The virtual collapse of the national economy had dramatic effects on banking in Serbia, modifying the process of its law reforms.

The aim of this chapter is to describe recent banking law reforms in Serbia, and the interactive relation between law and political and economic conditions, under the influence of the IFI. In order to clarify the social context in which reforms were implemented, some basic facts about SFRY and Serbia will be presented, as well as a historical perspective of the relationship between SFRY and the IFI.

The chapter will follow the dynamics of banking law changes in Serbia, during the period of 1988–1994. The second part of the chapter will analyse banking law reforms enacted under the programme of reforms of the last Federal Government of SFRY. The third part of the chapter will focus on the period after the disintegration of SFRY. The economic consequences of the war in Croatia and Bosnia-Herzegovina on Serbia will be presented and its implications for the evolution of the banking system of Serbia will be analysed. The fourth part of the chapter will contain a summary of the evolution of banking law in Serbia and a proposal for further banking law reforms.

2 REFORMS IN THE SOCIALIST FEDERAL REPUBLIC OF YUGOSLAVIA (SFRY)

2.1 What was the Socialist Federal Republic of Yugoslavia?

2.1.1 A different era

In the past five years, circumstances in Eastern Europe have changed dramatically. The collapse of socialism has had deep although different consequences in the former socialist countries. In the light of the rapid development of market economies in Poland, the Czech Republic and Hungary, and the savage ethnic war in the Yugoslav area, it is somehow difficult to believe that the Socialist Federal Republic of Yugoslavia, or former Yugoslavia, was considered as the most liberal of the socialist countries, as well as a country which solved its national relations successfully. Its specific economic system allowed certain forms of private ownership. SFRY was an open country during the period when citizens of other socialist countries could not travel to the West and when a special permit was required even for internal travel. Millions of foreign tourists came to SFRY for their holidays and 1,300,000 Yugoslavs worked abroad.[2] Although ethnic relations had some period of crisis,[3] in general, the situation was normal.

---

[2] Census 1981 – *Statistical Yearbook of SFRY* 1989.
[3] Major crises occurred in 1968 – Kosovo; 1971 – Croatia; 1981 – Kosovo. On these occasions the state authorities used force to restore public order.

People of different ethnic groups worked and lived together. In the Republic of Bosnia and Herzegovina alone there existed more than 60,000 ethnically mixed marriages.

SFRY followed a less dogmatic socialist ideology.[4] Accordingly, SFRY had always tended to accept Western values. The first attempt to introduce market economy practices occurred in the mid-1960s under the leadership of Tito.[5] The second period of intensive reform was initiated in the 1980s. These reforms were supported by two other factors, in addition to the general openness of SFRY: (1) internal problems in the self-managed[6] economy; and (2) external pressure coming mainly from the IMF and the IBRD. This chapter will focus on reforms enacted in the period 1988–1990, based, however, on the context of the reforms which immediately preceded that period.

2.1.2 Yugoslav society

Yugoslavia as a state was founded in 1918 when the process of unification of Southern Slavs[7] was facilitated by the disintegration of the Austro-Hungarian Empire. Yugoslavia in that period was a unitarist monarchy. Sharp social and ethnic tensions characterised that period; Yugoslavia was one of the poorest areas in Europe at that time. During World War II, Nazi forces occupied Yugoslavia and Hitler divided the country into different

---

[4] The rupture of relations between the USSR and SFRY in 1948 caused the sharpest crisis in the socialist world up to that point. After that SFRY had a more independent development outside of Soviet influence.

[5] Josip Broz Tito (1896–1980), leader of the Communist Party of Yugoslavia and of the resistance movement during World War II; co-founder of the Non-aligned Movement; President of SFRY.

[6] Self-management doctrine is a theoretical derivation of Marxism under which: "The goal of liberation of the human being could be achieved only by elimination of exploitation through liquidation of private ownership on the means of production, free association of workers and gradual extinction of the state." (extract from: *The Encyclopedia of Self-management* – Prosveta, Belgrade, 1975). The Yugoslav interpretation of this thesis resulted in the self-management doctrine. Self-management has as its core idea direct management by the working people of all aspects of social life, *e.g.* economy, politics, culture, social care, etc. In order to satisfy their various needs, the workers associate into respective types of organisations, *e.g.* economic, political, etc. Self-management was introduced in 1950 but only on the microeconomic level, where workers were allowed to establish the business policy of the business enterprises. In the following decades, self-management spread into the macroeconomic and macropolitical spheres of Yugoslav society. Under the Constitution of 1974, the political system of SFRY was conceived as a delegate system where representatives on local levels were elected directly by the voters, and the representatives at the local level elected members of assemblies on higher levels, *i.e.* Autonomous Provinces, Republics, Federation.

[7] Yugoslavia means the Land of the Southern Slavs: Serbs, Croats, Slovenes, Macedonians, Montenegrins and Muslims (Muslim in SFRY was also an ethnic category, not only religious). Yugoslavism was born in the twentieth century, in the period of nationalist movements in Europe. The intellectual élite of the Southern Slavs conceived Yugoslavia as a means of emancipation of the Southern Slavs. However, the area envisaged for Yugoslavia was at that time part of two great empires, the Ottoman and Austro-Hungarian, preventing the realisation of the aspirations of the Southern Slavs.

areas.[8] The National Liberation Front, led by the Communist Party, waged a fierce partisan guerrilla war against the occupiers and their domestic allies. In 1945, the Yugoslav Army, which derived from the partisans, liberated the entire area of Yugoslavia and the Socialist Federal Republic of Yugoslavia was founded.[9] SFRY was organised on a federal principle which reflected the multiethnicity of the country. Of the entire population of 22,434,711, SFRY had a total of 25 different ethnic groups.[10] The Federation was conceived as a mechanism which would help every nation to develop freely in association with other nations. SFRY had eight federal units: six Republics: Serbia, Croatia, Bosnia and Herzegovina, Slovenia, Macedonia, and Montenegro; and two Autonomous Provinces: Kosovo and Vojvodina which are incorporated into Serbia.[11] National equality was one of the fundamental principles of society which was implemented explicitly and extensively by the law.[12] The Yugoslav legal system was an unusual and specific creation, attracting much attention and respect.[13] Not only its specific and developed legal system but also an intensive period of human development gave SFRY a distinguished position among other developing countries (*see* Table 1).[14]

Table 1

	1955	1965	1985
illiterate population*	3,162,941	3,066,705	1,780,902
university graduates**	7,972	27,952	51,477
number of doctors	8,136	15,443	40,329
number of hospital beds	68,165	112,958	141,039
printed book titles	5,105	7,980	11,179

*Data for the years 1948, 1961 and 1981.
**Data includes only BA students.

---

[8] Hitler and Mussolini were the first to claim that Yugoslavia was an artificial state which should be broken up. The fascist and Nazi forces split Yugoslavia in eight zones, including the Independent State of Croatia, and Serbia as a Nazi protectorate, as two puppet creations. The rest were zones directly integrated into Germany, Italy, Bulgaria, Albania, Romania and Hungary.

[9] The 29th of November 1943 was the official date when socialist Yugoslavia was founded. Yugoslavia changed its name three times during socialism: Democratic Federal Yugoslavia, 1943–1945; Federal Peoples Republic of Yugoslavia, 1945–1956; Socialist Federal Republic of Yugoslavia, 1956–1991.

[10] The largest seven ethnic groups were: Serbs, Croats, Muslims, Albanians, Slovenes, Macedonians and Montenegrins.

[11] The most significant difference between Republics and Autonomous Provinces is that the former had the constitutional right to secession and the latter did not.

[12] An illustration thereof is that SFRY did not have a single official language but all languages were official and the individual was guaranteed the right to use his mother tongue in all situations, *e.g.* at work, in education, in court proceedings, etc. The predominant language was Serbo-Croatian spoken by Serbs, Croats, Muslims and Montenegrins.

[13] The University of London course of comparative European law has four options: German, French, Soviet and Yugoslav law – syllabus 1994.

[14] *Yearbook of SFRY* – 1989 issue.

2.1.3 The political system of SFRY

Under the Constitution of SFRY, adopted in 1974, significant powers were transferred from the federal jurisdiction to republics and autonomous provinces, and from republics and autonomous provinces to municipalities. This transition was a further step in the implementation of the self-management doctrine and of decentralisation of the state mechanism, which was seen as further development of equality between different ethnic groups and individuals. The main attributes of power were concentrated on the Republics and Autonomous Provinces, *e.g.* internal affairs, economy, social security, education, etc. The Federation had control over the Federal Army and foreign affairs. Other institutions, such as the Central Bank and the Federal Customs Agency, were federal organisations whose main function was to co-ordinate the activity of their members. The Federal Parliament had two chambers and was the supreme legislative body, with large prerogatives to control in respect of the executive power embodied in the Federal Executive Council. Each federal unit had its own Parliament and Executive Council. The chief of state was the federal presidency consisting of the presidents of Republics and Autonomous Provinces. The main decision-making principle in the institutions on the federal level was consensus. This principle guaranteed equality between federal units but often created problems in the efficiency of the federal institutions. Thus the system functioned on a balance between different federal units, and the Federation was the mechanism to facilitate their activities and interrelations.

SFRY had a monoparty system. The sole party was the ruling League of Communists of Yugoslavia (LCY), which was also organised as a federation of the League of Communists of the respective federal units. Political differences between the Leagues of Communists of different Republics and Autonomous Provinces dominated the last years of the Yugoslav federation. The first multiparty elections were held in 1990, resulting in a net victory for the nationalist forces.[15]

2.1.4 The economy of SFRY

SFRY experienced significant economic development in the post-World War II period (*see* Table 2).[16]

Table 2

	1955	1965	1975	1985
GDP (mill of din)**	81,087	164,658	289,893	393,742
number of workers (thous.)	2,161	3,662	4,758	6,516
index of industrial develop*	100	309	613	971
index of agricultural develop*	100	133	177	198
export (mill of din)**	100	336.1	567.2	788.1

*1955 = 100.
**1 U.S.$ = 1262.03 YUdin.

---

[15] *Republicke elite i raspad Jugoslavije* – V. Goati, Institute of Social Studies, Belgrade, 1993.
[16] *Yearbook of SFRY* – issues of 1956, 1966, 1989.

The economy of SFRY passed through three stages: first, an administrative economy with state ownership and large intervention of the state in the economy (1945–1952); second, self-management on a microeconomic level, (1952–1965); and third, self-management on a macroeconomic level, (1965–1989). The economy was based on social ownership of the means of production. Private ownership existed in a restricted form. Agriculture, tourism, small-scale industry, etc. were permitted to develop and a modest private sector emerged in the economy (*see* Table 3).[17]

Table 3

Gross Domestic Product by Forms of Ownership in 1989 in SFRY in mill. of din.

Social ownership	199,083
Private ownership	22,196
Mixed ownership	151
Total GDP	221,430

However, the business activities of the enterprises in social ownership were also influenced by market rules since they operated in a competitive environment.

Nevertheless, by the end of the 1970s and the beginning of the 1980s the Yugoslav economy fell into crisis. Scarcity of goods and unemployment, etc. were the main features of that period.[18] The Federal Government initiated in 1981–1983 a programme of economic stabilisation. After initially positive results, the situation deteriorated and in 1987 the inflation rate achieved its highest peak up to then: 2,400% per year .

The economic crisis, together with the then ongoing global erosion of socialism,[19] created favourable conditions for fundamental changes in the economic system of SFRY. Consequently, the new Federal Government inaugurated its programme of economic reforms in 1988.

2.2 Relations between SFRY and IFIs

SFRY was one of the founder members of the IMF and of the IBRD. Political factors combined with economic factors determined relations between SFRY and the IFIs. SFRY was a socialist country largely outside of the Soviet zone of influence and was a leading member of the Non-aligned Movement. Thus, the West had a strategic interest in preserving the neutral status of SFRY. This interest resulted in a somewhat benevolent attitude of the IFIs, and especially of the IMF to the SFRY, which was followed by the IBRD and other Western creditors.[20] Nevertheless, the relationship was not a one-sided influence of the IFIs on the Yugoslav economy; the relationship

---

[17] *Yearbook of SFRY* – 1989.
[18] *The Economy of Destruction* – M. Dinkic, 1994, p. 39.
[19] Gorbachov started with reforms in USSR known as Glasnost and Perestroika in 1985.
[20] *The Soviet Bloc in the IMF and the IBRD* – Valerie J. Assetto, 1988, p. 95.

was more interactive. Yugoslavia was often cited as an example of successful economic reforms for other socialist countries and its experience heavily influenced the IMF and IBRD policy towards other developing countries.[21] The first loan to SFRY by the IMF was made in 1948. In the period 1962–1984, eight SBA and 25 IBRD loans were granted to SFRY.[22] Although their relations deteriorated in the 1980s, the IMF substantially supported the Yugoslav programme of economic stabilisation when the Yugoslav economic crisis errupted in the begining of the 1980s. The IMF granted Yugoslavia the largest loan ever made to a developing country up to then, 1.6 bill. U.S.$ in 1981.[23] The rationale for this loan is rather illustrative:[24]

- preservation of the non-aligned status of SFRY;
- Yugoslav debt-servicing difficulties stemmed from adverse credit market conditions which derived from the second round of the oil crisis and recession in the Western economies;
- support for Yugoslavia would help to shore up general confidence in the international financial system.

This IMF loan was part of a rescue package set by Western creditors[25] (which amounted to 6 billion U.S.$ in the period 1981–1984) in order to assist Yugoslavia to overcome its liquidity and economic problems.[26] In spite of this massive financial aid, SFRY did not solve its economic problems. Instead, these problems increased in the following period, forcing the SFRY authorities to adopt a more market-oriented approach when they initiated the reforms in 1989, supported by the IFIs. Therefore it is evident that SFRY enjoyed the full confidence of foreign creditors, specifically the IMF, in the decade which preceded its disintegration.

2.3 The period of reconstruction – introduction of a market economy

2.3.1 *Internal and external pressure*

After the introduction of self-management, enterprises were given large autonomy in their business operations.[27] However, the enterprises were in

---

[21] Valerie J. Assetto, *op. cit.*, p. 136.
[22] *The Debt Rescheduling Process* – Milivojevic Marko, 1985, p. 76.
[23] *World Debt Tables* – World Bank, 1993.
[24] M. Milivojevic, *op. cit.*, p. 69.
[25] On the 17th of January 1983 the Advisory Commitee, chaired by an IMF official, was established in order to control the application and stipulate further agreements between SFRY and its foreign creditors.
[26] In 1979 SFRY registered its highest deficit in its balance of payments, 1.7 billion U.S.$.
[27] The 1970s brought the third phase of implementation of self-management to the SFRY economy. Restriction of state interference was characteristic of this period, which allowed more independence to economic entities, although political influence on the decision-making process was still very present; *Changes in the Yugoslav Financial and Economic System* – K. Ott, in: *Finance in Eastern Europe* – D. H. Gowland, 1992, p. 49.

social ownership, which guaranteed to them the assistance of other enterprises and banks in case they faced insolvency and bankruptcy.[28] A large number of enterprises covered their loses with credits from domestic and foreign creditors, thereby avoiding bankruptcy and liquidation. This fundamental imbalance of the Yugoslav economy was the main source of economic problems in SFRY.[29] The National Bank of Yugoslavia (the Central Bank of Yugoslavia) could not control the borrowing activity of domestic enterprises on international financial markets. Consequently, the foreign liabilities of domestic enterprises increased from 2.0 billion U.S.$ in 1970 to 18.48 billion U.S.$ by 1980.[30] In addition, the National Bank of Yugoslavia was not in the position to charge positive real interest rates on its credits to domestic enterprises while facing mounting payments on foreign liabilities.[31] The other main source of economic difficulties was the fiscal deficit of the State, which was covered by the National Bank of Yugoslavia.[32] Monetary expansion and inflation followed. Essentially, Yugoslav society was spending much more than it produced. The situation became critical in the beginning of the 1980s. The oil crisis caused a global problem of liquidity and solvency to all developing indebted countries, including SFRY. Therefore, the Federal Government enacted a programme of economic stabilisation in 1981 which was supported by the first Structural Adjustment Loan (SAL) loan to SFRY. The main conditions of the IMF loan reflected the internal problems of SFRY and demands from foreign creditors for more centralisation, financial discipline and control, namely:[33]

- adjustment of interest rates and improvement of investment planning and allocation;
- liberalisation of external trade policies and allocation of foreign exchange;
- improved pricing policies and enterprise decision-making, with particular emphasis on agriculture and energy sectors.

However, the stabilisation programme faltered for various reasons. SFRY was not at that time committed to a qualitative change of its economy and the SAL itself was addressing too many issues. As a result, in 1987, the economic situation fell back to the levels of 1982–83, despite initial success.

---

[28] K. Ott, *op. cit.*, p. 55.
[29] *See* pp. 225–226.
[30] *World Debt Tables* – World Bank, 1993.
[31] K. Ott., *op. cit.*, p. 58.
[32] The social expenditures of the state budget, education, social care, etc., were higher than state budget incomes due to a restrictive fiscal policy. This created a disequilibrium covered by credits of the National Bank of Yugoslavia.
[33] *Reforming Central and East European Economies – Initial Results and Changes,* Vittorio Corbo, Fabrizio Coricelli, Jan Bosjak, World Bank Symposium, 1991.

2.3.2 Market economy reforms

In December 1989, the new Federal Government[34] announced its programme of reforms. The essential characteristics of the economic reforms were structural issues such as adjustment of the enterprise and banking sectors. Lack of performance in these sectors was seen as the basic cause of the financial instability and poor economic performance of SFRY. The other structural features of the new programme were:[35]

- further liberalisation of the foreign exchange and trade regimes and concomitant domestic price liberalisation;
- enforcement of financial discipline by enterprises through restructuring and tighter bankruptcy procedures, together with an adequate interest rate policy, although in the short run, the enterprise adjustment would be backed by non-inflatory fiscal support to the enterprises;
- broader-based fiscal financing of the social safety net to protect displaced workers, without placing a further burden on productive enterprises. This measure would be complemented by specific programmes to promote small private sector enterprises.

Moreover, the programme was supported by expanding its coverage to the issues of enterprise reform, regulation of the labour market and creation of conditions for banks' financial reconstruction.

The measures applied based on the structural features of the programme included:[36]

- in the area of monetary policy: internal convertibility of the Yugoslav dinar and a frozen exchange rate to the Deutsche Mark of 1DM to 7YUD, currency reform and devaluation of the dinar of 20%, restrictive domestic bank credits and monetarisation of foreign exchange;
- in the area of income: freeze of nominal wages and prices of some goods, energy and transport;
- fiscal policy expenditures: servicing of foreign liabilities, transfers to the bank restructuring programme, transfers to the social safety net;
- liberalisation of trade: only 12% of total imports remained under the quota regime.

---

[34] The candidate for prime minister was Ante Markovic, general director of Rudi Cajavec, a large electrical appliances enterprise. He was appointed as candidate in March 1987. The process of nomination for prime minister lasted a year. In 1988, amendments to the Constitution of SFRY were adopted and, in 1989, new banking and enterprise laws creating the necessary legal conditions for the implementation of economic measures. Thus, the reconstruction of the legal system preceded the economic reconstruction. From M. Dinkic, *op. cit.*, p. 37.

[35] *See* V. Corbo & others, *op. cit.*, p. 78.

[36] *See The Programme of the Federal Government* – edition of the Institute of Economic Studies – Belgrade, 1990.

All the features of the programme and measures applied were in compliance with the demands of the IMF: increase of the National Bank's authority over the monetary system, enforcement of financial discipline, expansion of the fiscal authority on the federal level, and the increase of competition and efficiency through import liberalisation.[37] The legal framework was modified to support the new orientation of the Federal Government. The key pieces of legislation were the new enterprise law (enacted in 1988) and the new banking law (enacted in 1989). Thus, the reconstruction of the legal system preceded the implementation of other measures incorporated in the programme itself. Of course, it was still an open question whether the programme would succeed.

The first results were positive. In the first half of 1990, the inflation rate dropped, the foreign currency black market was eliminated, federal reserves increased to over 10 billion U.S.$, and the foreign debt was reduced from 21 billion U.S.$ in 1988 to 17 billion U.S.$ in 1990.[38] Unfortunately, in the second half of 1990, the disintegrative process of SFRY entered in its final stage, causing financial indiscipline which provoked deterioration of the economic conditions and collapse of the federal reforms.

2.3.3 Political instability – overture to the disintegration of Yugoslavia

The 1980s were a period of renaissance for the nationalist movements in SFRY, with the sole idea of creating different nation-states in the place of Yugoslavia. The strengthening of nationalism had various aspects but the most significant were its disintegrative and conflicting effects. In the mid-1980s there began the process of disintegration of organisations on the federal level. The first organisation to break was the Association of Writers of Yugoslavia[39] in 1985. Other organisations followed and the last was the League of Communists of Yugoslavia, in January 1990.[40] The institutions of the system reflected this trend. The principle of consensus, once a function of political equality, was diverted into a method of blackmail and blockade of federal institutions, *e.g.* Federal Assembly, Presidency, etc. In 1988, Slovenia refused to accept the amendments to the Constitution proposed by the Federal Government. Only under heavy pressure and compromises did Slovenia withdraw its veto of the constitutional reforms. In 1989, Serbia abolished the autonomy of the two Autonomous Provinces in violation of the Federal Constitution which guaranteed the autonomy of the Provinces. The same year, Serbia introduced economic sanctions against Slovenia. Slovenia responded by taking over the duties on imported goods entering into SFRY through its territory. Following the example of Slovenia, in 1990, the National Bank of Serbia burst upon the monetary system, with the

---

[37] *Yugoslavia and the IMF*, Dejan Jovovic, 1991, p. 193.
[38] *Statistical Yearbook of Yugoslavia*, 1991.
[39] Since political activity through parties was forbidden, various cultural organisations and especially the Writers Associations became the main forums of alternative political life in SFRY. Many of their members became active politicians with the advent of democracy. Thus, the fate of this association is illustrative of further developments in SFRY.
[40] V. Goati, *op. cit.*, p. 389.

emission of 1.8 billion U.S.$ "giral" (credit) money,[41] without the authorisation of the Federal Government or of the National Bank of Yugoslavia, causing irreparable damage to the monetary system of SFRY. However, the growing nationalism was not articulated only through institutions. In compliance with its political reforms, the Federal Government urged the Republics to enforce the introduction of democracy. In 1989, all Republics liberalised political life, allowing the registration of new political parties. The majority of the newborn political organisations used nationalist rhetoric to attract voters. The first multiparty elections were held in 1990 with a clear victory of parties of nationalist orientation. In 1991, SFRY *de facto* disintegrated in a bloody conflict and the newborn states were recognised internationally in the first half of 1992.

2.4 Banking law reform

2.4.1 Socialist legislation – banks as servants of their founders

The legal centrepiece of the period of self-management in the 1980s was the Associated Labour Act[42] (ALA), adopted in 1976. ALA was a further step in the process of implementation of self-management on a macroeconomic level. The fundamental principles of this Act were:

- social ownership of the means of production;
- the right to work with socially owned resources;
- the self-management position of the worker.

These notions appear quite cryptic; however, they articulated economic relations based upon the principle of the power of the working people. Under the provisions of ALA workers associated their labour into organisations of associated labour (OALs) where all business decisions were made directly by workers through various mechanisms, *e.g.* internal referenda, workers' councils, etc. The economic function of the OALs was similar to the functions of enterprises in other economies: to provide goods and services. The elementary forms of OALs were the basic organisations of associated labour which could then associate into wider organisations, *e.g.* work organisations and composite organisations of associated labour, or into services which would help the OALs to perform certain activities, *e.g.* social and medical care, pensions, etc.

One important area of these services was financial services. Article 393, section 4 of ALA provided: "... monetary, banking and other financial transactions for the needs of organisations of associated labour and other forms of the pooling of labour and resources shall be carried out by banks in conformity with federal law". This article established the nature of banks and of their activities in the Yugoslav economy from the 1970s until the

---

[41] K. Ott, *op. cit.*, p. 70.
[42] *Official Gazette* of SFRY– issue 56/76.

reform of 1989. The purpose of banks was to finance the development and projects of their OAL founders and not to make a profit. Thus, banks were compelled to conduct their business operations without regard to market conditions. Although banks were independent from state authority, there was heavy influence from political structures on banks' activities. This led to the situation where the majority of banks' assets were invested in their founders, through loans made to cover losses, creating increasing solvency and liquidity problems for the banks. This unsustainable financial activity was, in turn, covered by foreign loans and by credits from the National Bank of Yugoslavia. Banks were one of the important centres of redistribution of wealth in the Yugoslav socialist society. With their policies dominated politically, banks were perceived as "centres of alienated power".[43] As aforementioned[44] this imbalance was the main source of Yugoslav economic problems.

Under the pressure of foreign creditors, the Federal Government attempted to introduce more stability and control in the banking and financial system of Yugoslavia.[45] However, these efforts were tentative and ineffective, since the fundamental Article 393 of ALA was repealed only in 1989 with the introduction of the new enterprise law. The legal framework of the socialist banking system was based on the conjunction of ALA with the National Bank of Yugoslavia Act, the Law on Foundations of Banking and Crediting System, the Foreign Exchange Law and the Foreign Credit Relations Law.

2.4.2 The Central Bank system under the National Bank of Yugoslavia Act[46]

The banking system of SFRY did not have one single institution which could perform the functions of a central bank. The central bank system of SFRY reflected the federal organisation of the state. Each federal unit had its own central bank. The National Banks of Republics and Autonomous Provinces were institutions of Yugoslavia's integral monetary system. The legal position of the National Bank of Yugoslavia (NBY) was governed by the Law on the National Bank of Yugoslavia and Joint Monetary Operations of National Banks of Republics and of National Banks of Autonomous Provinces (NBY Act). Together with the National Bank of Yugoslavia, the National Banks of Republics and Autonomous Provinces were responsible for joint monetary policy (art. 1). They determined the conditions for and the mode of use of monetary resources in their respective Republics and Autonomous Provinces; providing credits to commercial banks (art. 16), supervising the operations of these banks (art. 57), and authorising them to perform foreign currency and foreign exchange operations (art. 39). In addition, they carried out other banking operations entrusted to them by their

---

[43] K. Ott, *op. cit.*, p. 50.
[44] *See* p. 222.
[45] *See* pp. 221–222.
[46] *Official Gazette* of SFRY – 26/84.

respective Republics and Autonomous Provinces. Thus, as a federal institution, the NBY was limited in its duties and activities by the independent role of the National Banks of the respective federal units. The NBY was responsible for the condition of the Central Bank system to the Federal Assembly and to the Federal Executive Council (Federal Government). The NBY policy was devised by the general plan of development of SFRY adopted by the Federal Assembly (art. 2). The NBY had the duty to submit annual reports to the Federal Assembly (art. 5). The Governor of the NBY was appointed by the Federal Assembly. The Federal Government had the authority to intervene directly in the implementation of financial and monetary policy if the NBY was not in the position to make a decision on certain issues (art. 66). The consent of the Federal Government was necessary for the membership and participation of the NBY in international financial organisations and activities. Thus, the activity of the NBY was under the constant surveillance and guidance of the Federal Boards, its independence further eroded by the interfering powers of the Federal Government, set out in article 66.

The main bodies of the NBY were the Council of Governors (Council), members of which were Governors of NBs of Republics and Autonomous Provinces, and the Governor of the NBY (Governor). The Council was the decision-making board of the NBY, while the position of the Governor was purely formal; the Governor represented the NBY and chaired the meetings of the Council. The Council's decision-making principles were consensus and simple majority vote, with a clear predominance of the unanimous vote (art. 62).

The activities of the NBY included:

- joint issuing of notes and coins, and money supply regulation (arts. 16, 42, 43);
- maintenance of external and internal liquidity (this included regulation of methods of maintenance of minimal bank liquidity, structure and time schedule of banks' assets, use of obligatory reserves of banks, etc.);
- financial activities for the needs of the Federation, Federal Army and National Defence (art. 49);
- supervision over the banking system (art. 57).

The NBY did not have the power to enforce its decisions or to carry out direct measures against a bank or other financial institution which did not respect the regulations of the banking system. The ultimate decision on the fate of a bank or other financial institution was in the authority of the Assembly of its respective Republic or Autonomous Province (art. 58).

2.4.3 The Law on Foundations of Banking and Crediting System[47] – commercial banking

The Yugoslav commercial banking system was different from that of other countries. Under the provisions of the Law on Foundations of Banking and

---

[47] *Official Gazette* of SFRY – 70/85.

Crediting System (Law), the aim of a bank was to increase the accumulation of associated labour and expansion of the material basis of associated labour (art. 6).Thus, banks were conceived in the context of their function in a socialist economy, as a device for the development of the organisations of associated labour. The banks had the duty to accept any request for credit if the applicant satisfied administrative conditions, *e.g.* that it was a registered organisation, etc. (art. 14). Therefore, when granting credits, banks were not guided primarily by the assessment of the profitability or credit worthiness of such credits. Banks were founded by agreements concluded between organisations of associated labour, and managed by their OAL founders (art. 18). The NBY did not have the power to regulate the establishment of banks; the NBY's authority was confined to give its opinion without the right of enforcement. The business plan of the banks had to be in compliance with the aims and policy of the economic development of the country established by the Federal Assembly (art. 12). Supervision over banks and other financial institutions was in the competence of the Assemblies, the NBY and the Social Accountancy Service. The Law provided for the following forms of banks and financial institutions: Internal Banks, Basic Banks, Associated Banks, Saving Banks, Postal Saving Banks and Self-managing Funds (art. 24).

(a) Internal Banks   These institutions developed from the internal financial departments of OALs. Their scope was to facilitate financial transactions between OALs, to monitor the use of resources of all the units of an OAL and to deal with internal financial relations within OALs (art. 26).

Internal Banks could collect deposits only from workers working in the respective OAL. Management was performed directly by the workers of its OAL. The founding Act provided the prudential requirements of the business activities of the Bank. The Law provided only the duty to create an Internal Bank's reserve funds but did not set the mode of use and the required amount of the reserves (art. 57). The activities of Internal Banks were under the supervision of the Social Accountancy Service. Internal Banks were liable to the extent of all their assets.

(b) Basic and Associated Banks   These two types of banks were, essentially, elements of the same organisation. Basic Banks, founded by OALs, associated into Associated Banks. A Basic Bank could not refuse a demand for association from an OAL. A Basic Bank's management was in the power of the workers of its founder organisation (art. 71). For example, article 78 provided that the upper limits of a Bank's, Associated or Basic, borrowing in Yugoslavia and abroad were set by its founders.

The financial rehabilitation and liquidation process of a Basic Bank required the approval of the NBY and of the respective Assembly. In the case of liquidation, private deposits had priority over other debts (art. 109). The Law set up the duty of Basic Banks to create "solidarity funds" as coverage for the fund's members' bad loans. The activities of Basic Banks are not specified, which leads to the conclusion that Basic Banks were conceived as a stage in the establishment of Associated Banks. A single Basic Bank could found or associate into several Associated Banks (art. 126). The function of the NBY was restricted to the authority to issue its judgment of the rationale for the establishment of an Associated Bank without any power to enforce its decision. Article 127 sets up the activities of the Associated Banks:

- to associate funds and means;
- to issue bonds;
- to collect deposits from the public in the country and abroad;
- to judge the possibilities of joint interests and development of Basic Banks;
- to create information systems.

From the range of their activities, it is apparent that Associated Banks were the main institutions of commercial banking in Yugoslavia. In addition, these banks could obtain authorisation from the NBY to open accounts in foreign banks and to perform international financial transactions, and were more likely to obtain authorisation from the NBY to take loans from foreign lenders. Associated Banks were managed by the representatives of their founders, and ultimately by OALs (art. 71). The internal structure of the Associated Banks was so loose that the Associated Bank did not even have the authority to impose measures on its Basic Bank members if the Basic Bank caused liquidity problems to the whole system. Associated Banks could only refer the pertinent information to the respective Assemblies, the NBY or the Social Accountancy Service (art. 136).

2.4.4 The Foreign Exchange Law[48] and the Foreign Credit Relations Law[49]

These two Acts were enacted in 1985 with the aim of:

- establishing stronger interdependence between borrowing abroad and outward payment;
- strengthening the unity of the Yugoslav market;
- affirming the dinar as the only legal tender in the country;
- obliging economic entities to deposit all foreign exchange earnings from foreign partners in accounts in Yugoslav banks within specified time limits.[50]

The influence of the IMF requirements for more stability and security can be noticed in the first aim. The authorisation conditions to apply for foreign loans are in the authority of the NBY. Article 12 of the Foreign Credit Relations Law provides that OALs, authorised banks, the Yugoslav Bank for International Economic Co-operation, and socio-political communities can apply for foreign loans under conditions set by the NBY.

---

[48] *Official Gazette* of SFRY – 68/85.
[49] *Official Gazette* of SFRY – 65/85.
[50] Preface to the English edition of the Foreign Exchange Law, Vuk Ognjanovic – deputy finance minister, 1985.

2.4.5 *Reconstruction of the banking system – banks as market entities*

What differentiates the reforms of 1989–1990 from a dozen other Yugoslav banking reforms in the previous forty-five years is their intention to introduce market logic and rules in the Yugoslav banking system. Thus, it can be described as a reconstruction programme which embraced:[51]

- ownership transformation of Yugoslav banks;
- implementation of market methods in the financial reconstruction of banks;
- consideration and adoption of international banking standards and rules.

The aim of the reconstruction process was to create a Yugoslav banking system on the level of international banking criteria, *e.g.* organisation and business activities, international accountant standards, etc. all based on the concept of Universal Banking.[52] This attempt faced significant obstacles, specifically in the process of financial rehabilitation of the banking sector. Banks' losses amounted approximately to 40% of the banks' assets, or close to 60% of deposits. This was three times more than the banks' capital stock.[53] The process of rehabilitation was conceived in two stages: first, adoption of new banking regulations and, second, general or linear financial rehabilitation of banks through the Central Bank and the Federal Agency for Deposit Insurance and Financial Rehabilitation of Banks.

The legal framework of the reconstruction process included three fundamental Acts: the Enterprise Law, the New National Bank of Yugoslavia Act and the Law of Banks and other Financial Institutions. The Enterprise Law[54] was enacted in 1989 and repealed the famous Associated Labour Act. Enterprises replaced the Organisations of Associated Labour. Article 1 of the Enterprise Law provided that "an Enterprise is a legal entity which performs economic activity for the purpose of earning income, *i.e.* profit". This was totally new logic in the Yugoslav economy and a drastic shift in an environment based on socialist values for forty-five years. The Enterprise Law provided two forms of Enterprises: companies with limited liability and stockholding companies. Enterprises could be socially owned or in private ownership. All OALs had to transform into Enterprises and to reform their activities to conform to the new law within the period of one year. Banks also had to transform into one of the two possible forms. The basic three Acts were complemented with the New Law on Foreign Credit Relations, the Law on Money and Capital Markets, the Securities Act, the Law on Financial Rehabilitation,

---

[51] *Program Savezne vlade* – edition of the Institute of Economic Studies, 1990.
[52] Universal Banking refers to banking systems where banks operate all financial services, in contrast with Specialised Banking. The former system is known also as the German model and the latter as the Anglo-Saxon.
[53] K. Ott, *op. cit.*, p. 68.
[54] *Official Gazette* of SFRY – 40/89.

Bankruptcy and Liquidation of Banks and other Financial Institutions, and the Law on the Agency for Deposit Insurance and Financial Rehabilitation of Banks. Thus, after the reforms of 1988–1989, banks had to continue their activities in an environment substantially different from the one in which they were formed. However, the legal reform established necessary conditions for further steps in the process of financial reconstruction of the Yugoslav banking system. The fate of the reforms depended upon two factors: time and money.[55]

2.4.6 *Reform of the Central Bank system*

Difficulties in the work of the NBY stemmed mainly from its inability to impose financial discipline and efficiency. The limits of reforms of the main financial authority were set by the variety of interests in the Federation. The Central Bank system remained constituted by the NBY and the National Banks of Republics and Autonomous Provinces, echoing ultimately the multiethnic structure of the Yugoslav society (art. 1). Hence, preserving the joint responsibility of the NBY and of the NBY of Republics and Autonomous Provinces for the maintenance of the monetary and financial system of SFRY. However, the federal structure of the Central Bank system cannot be seen as the root problem of the inefficiency of the NBY in the previous period. More important were obstacles created by the subordination and dependency of the NBY to Federal bodies, and the principle of a unanimous vote in the decision-making process of the Council of the NBY. The reforms followed this logic. Major changes in the position and the functions of the NBY occurred in its internal decision-making process; its management and relationships with the Federal bodies gaining more independence. The operations of the NBY were no longer attached to the general plan of development of the country adopted by the Federal Assembly following repeal of the previous article 2. The Federal Assembly preserved its powers to nominate the Governor of the NBY and the duty of the NBY to submit annual reports to the Federal Assembly. The Federal Government lost its prerogatives set by the previous article 66 to interfere directly in the discharge of NBY duties. Also, the NBY could join international forums and activities without the prior consent of Federal bodies. Thus, the position of the Federation in respect of the NBY was rather loose. Legal provisions were complemented by the political decision to eliminate the financing of the fiscal deficit of the Federation by the NBY's credits.[56]

The internal organisation of the NBY was submitted to changes in two directions: strengthening of the position of the Governor of the NBY in respect of the Council and elimination of the unanimous vote principle in the Council's decision-making process. The Governor of the NBY was no longer only the representative of the NBY, but also gained effective powers. Article 18 provided that the Governor had the right to take necessary

---

[55] In 1989 political tension escalated: *see* p. 224. An estimated 2 billion U.S.$ were necessary for the reconstruction of the Yugoslav banking system – K. Ott, *op. cit.*, p. 68.
[56] *See* p. 222.

measures in order to carry out the responsibilities of the NBY if the Council was not able to reach a decision on a specific issue. The Governor also had the right to enact by-laws necessary for the discharge of the duties of the NBY. The main board of the NBY, however, remained the Council, having in its authority all decisions regarding discharge of the duties of the NBY.

The Council was the main managing body, formed of eight members – the Governors of the National Banks of Republics and Autonomous Provinces. Its decisions were made by simple and qualified majority. Thus, the principle of unanimity was eliminated, making the decision-making process more efficient and bypassing unnecessary and protracted negotiations in order to reach unanimity.

The activities of the NBY also underwent modifications, particulary the duty of maintenance of internal and external liquidity and supervision. The NBY was responsible for maintenance of the State's liquidity, but article 5 provided that the NBY should not take up the payment liabilities of other entities on the basis of its general responsibility for maintenance of internal and external liquidity. Hence, banks and Enterprises with liquidity problems could no longer count on the automatic intervention of the NBY. The supervision process remained the same, *i.e.* through Assemblies of respective Republics and Autonomous Provinces, the Social Accountancy Service and the NBY. However, the NBY's powers were expanded. The NBY was entitled to take direct measures if the control of business operations of a specific bank showed violation of banking regulations (art. 61); or withdrew its assets (art. 62). These measures included taking over the management of the bank if subsequent controls would reveal further erosion of the bank's stability, liquidity and solvency (arts. 67a and 67b), or undertaking necessary proceedings at the responsible state institutions if the violation was also a criminal act (art. 68). The NBY had the duty to monitor the supervision of the National Banks of Republics and Autonomous Provinces and could take necessary measures if they neglected their duties (art. 63). Departments responsible for the discharge of supervision were completely independent and responsible directly to their respective Governors. Authorisation was introduced as a completely new power of the NBY. In the previous period, the NBY had no role in the banks' establishment process. Now article 66 provided that the authorisation by the NBY was indispensable for the establishment of commercial banks.

2.4.7 Commercial banks as market entities – the Law on Banks and Other Financial Institutions[57]

This Law replaced the Law on Foundations of Banking and Crediting System. Article 2 of this Law provided the following: a bank is independent in its business activities in order to create income. Its business is based on principles of liquidity, security and profitability. This was a substantial change in respect of article 6 of the previous Law,[58] introducing different

---

[57] *Official Gazette* of SFRY – 87/89.
[58] *See* p. 228.

criteria of commercial banking in SFRY. Banks could be organised as companies with limited liability or joint stock enterprises (art. 1a). Banks could be founded by domestic legal persons or by domestic legal and natural persons together with foreign natural or legal persons, *i.e.* Mixed Banks. The provisions specific to Mixed Banks regulated their internal organisation and management, reflecting the dual source of the initial capital (art. 48). The bodies of the bank were: Founders' Assembly, Managing Board, Director and Supervisory Board. The banks' business was regulated by rules common to banking businesses in market economies. Article 4 imposed direct linkage between a bank's obligatory initial capital and reserves, and a bank's business operations, *i.e.* capital adequacy. Large exposure provisions were enacted by article 16, limiting the exposure of the bank to a single borrower to 30% of own[59] funds, and single credit to 20% of own funds. Banks' activities included (art. 63):

- acceptance of all types of deposits;
- credit operations;
- foreign currency exchange operations;
- discount operations;
- issuing of securities and money cards;
- deposit insurance;
- guarantee operations.

Secrecy of banks' business was guaranteed (art. 23). The bank was responsible for its solvency and liquidity (art. 57). The bank's profit was divided into: dividends of its founders, required reserves and other bank's funds. Banks could form syndicates in order to facilitate large projects (art. 63). Basic Banks and Associated Banks had the obligation to adapt their business to the new rules and to transform their internal structure in the period until 1990, 1991, and 30 June 1992 (art. 83). The process of transformation was regulated by the NBY (art. 83b).

Other financial institutions under this Law were: Savings Banks, Postal Saving Banks and Saving Credit Institutions. Significant distinctions between banks and other financial institutions were the different own funds requirements and business activities; thus there were no differences based on form of ownership or source of capital.

This Law was an essential part of the process of transformation of the banking system, despite certain ambiguous provisions. Domestic natural persons could found a bank only as a joint operation with a foreign investor (art. 1). Thus the distinction between mixed and other banks somehow echoes the need to transform socially owned banks from OALs into Enterprises, *i.e.* joint-stock and limited liability companies. Banks were independent in their business operations; they could fix interest rates and charges for their services. This Law proclaimed the creation of profit as the primary aim of a bank's business and set stiff rules in order to induce

---

[59] Own funds = initial capital + reserves.

prudential conduct. However, the necessary prudent management could not have been established by legal decree.

2.4.8 Other relevant Acts and institutions

The new Law on Foreign Credit Relations[60] introduced rigid rules for the access of domestic legal persons to foreign lenders. The number of author-ised entities which could enter foreign credit relations was reduced (art. 1). The authority of the NBY was expanded. The NBY could not only grant au-thorisations but also could undertake measures against banks and Enterprises which endangered the national liquidity by their activities, or restrict their borrowing activity in general (art. 14).

Securities and stock exchanges have been virtually non-existent in post-war Yugoslavia, with the exception of a negligible issue of state securities. The Law on Money and Capital Markets[61] and the Securities Act[62] pro-vided for the introduction of and set conditions for the development of financial markets. Securities included shares, bonds, treasury notes, certificates of deposit and commercial bills (art. 14 of the Securities Act). Securities could be issued by Enterprises, banks and other financial insti-tutions; insurance companies; or any other legal person. Financial markets were founded by banks and other financial institutions which were secur-ing the necessary conditions for their business. The NBY gave authorisa-tion for the start-up of the money markets, and participated in the activities on the money markets, as part of its regulatory function of money supply and demand. The activity of capital markets was supervised by the Federal Securities and Exchange Commission. The introduction of securities and financial markets was met with great euphoria by the public at large, presented as the miracle cure for the problems of the Yugoslav financial system.

The Agency for Deposit Insurance and Financial Rehabilitation of Banks[63] was based upon the model of the United States Federal Deposit Insurance Corporation. The main scope of the Agency was to conduct the process of reconstruction of the banking system as linear financial rehabili-tation. The Agency would purchase banks' bad loans temporarily to improve their position and to prevent further losses. The Agency would issue bonds for the amount of purchased loans or take credits from the NBY to purchase potential losses, with the duty on commercial banks to buy securities from the NBY for the amount of these credits. Further, the Agency would conclude an agreement with each bank regarding the con-ditions it should satisfy during the time it used those funds earmarked for financial support. The Law on Rehabilitation, Bankruptcy and Liquidation of Banks provided the legal basis for this process. Unfortunately, circum-stances were adverse to the aims of the Agency, which, consequently, did not fulfil its task.

---

[60] *Official Gazette* of SFRY – 84/90.
[61] *Official Gazette* of SFRY – 64/89.
[62] *Official Gazette* of SFRY – 64/89 and 29/90.
[63] K. Ott, *op. cit.*, p. 68.

3 REFORMS OF BANKING LAW IN SERBIA

During 1991, the Socialist Federal Republic of Yugoslavia entered in the final stage of its breakdown. Ethnic tensions increased to an unprecedented extent. Armed incidents erupted into a full-scale war. The consequences of the conflict are tragic for all the Republics of the former Yugoslav Federation. The international community has played an important role in the crisis, with United Nations' activity being very intensive in the negotiation process between the warring factions. United Nations' measures heavily influenced the positions of the key participants in the conflict. This chapter will analyse the effects of UN sanctions against Serbia and the fate of banking law reforms in an economic and social environment totally different from the one in which they were initiated.

3.1 Disintegration of SFRY – punishment for Serbia

3.1.1 Events

This chapter does not elaborate the sources of the conflict in the former Yugoslavia or analyse in detail the ideological background of the crisis. However, some elementary facts are necessary to understand the premises on which the United Nations' policy is based, in the crisis of the former Yugoslavia. Hostilities between ethnic groups in SFRY were created mainly by the nationalist forces of respective nations, whose dominant aim and idea is to create their own independent nation-states[64] and to unite all the members of one nation into its state, *i.e.* Greater Serbia, Greater Albania, Greater Croatia, etc. The problem is that the borders of these imaginary states are in collision with each other since all the Republics of SFRY were ethnically mixed and, therefore, it is impossible to establish frontiers based upon ethnic borders. After the elections of 1990, nationalist parties became the dominant political force in all the Republics of SFRY, with the exception of Macedonia.[65] The first armed incidents occurred in Croatia in April 1991. In June of the same year Slovenia declared its independence which caused a war between the Federal Army and the Slovene forces, in July 1991.[66] The war known as the Four Days' War resulted in withdrawal of the Federal Army from Slovenia. The next month, armed conflicts began between nationalist Serbs and the armed forces of Croatia. The leadership of Serbia backed the nationalist Serbs in Croatia in their demands to unite with Serbia. After the international recognition of Croatia in January 1992, the United Nations imposed a peace plan for Croatia.[67] The outcome of this

---

[64] *See* p. 224.
[65] Macedonia is internationally recognised under the name of the Former Yugoslav Republic of Macedonia.
[66] The conflict started after an abortive attempt by the United States' Secretary of State James Baker to stop the process of disintegration.
[67] The plan was based upon UN Resolution 743, adopted on the 21st of February 1992.

plan, known as the "Vance plan", involved the deployment of peace-keeping forces on the front lines between the two sides and a cease-fire which is still in force. Unfortunately, in April 1992, war broke out in Bosnia and Herzegovina, provoked by essentially the same demand of the Serbian nationalists: to unite with Serbia.[68]

Up to now, the conflict in former Yugoslavia has resulted in over 300,000 deaths, more than 3.5 million refugees, and an estimated material damage of over 300 billion U.S.$. The entire world is shocked by the proportions of the conflict and by brutality unseen in Europe since the end of World War II.

3.1.2 The political situation in Serbia

Serbia and Montenegro formed a new Federation in April 1992, under the name of the Federal Republic of Yugoslavia (FRY).[69] Article 2 of the Constitution of FRY provides that "... other republics can join the Federal Republic of Yugoslavia". Bearing in mind the tendencies of nationalist Serbs in Croatia and Bosnia, it is not difficult to detect the purpose of article 2. Although the new Federation bears the name of Yugoslavia, it is clear that FRY is not connected to the ideals of Yugoslavism as a movement of emancipation of Southern Slavs or to the name of Yugoslavia itself. The size, and the economic, political and military power of Serbia[70] ensures its domination over Montenegro. The Constitution defines FRY as a multiparty democracy; nevertheless, foreign and domestic groups and organisations claim that there are irregularities in the electoral procedure. The economy is conceived on a market basis. However, macroeconomic conditions are adverse to any process of economic development. The disintegration of the SFRY market, increasing numbers of refugees, and the scale of military aid to nationalist Serbs in Croatia and Bosnia have all exacerbated economic problems. The United Nations sanctions, introduced in May 1992, were the most important factor which contributed to the breakdown of the economy and are the major obstacle to the recovery of Serbia.[71]

3.1.3 United Nations activity

The UN has expressed its concern for the problems of one of its founder members since the very beginning. In the first period, spring-autumn 1991,

---

[68] Serbian nationalists proclaimed their independent Republics in the areas under their control; Republika Srpska in Bosnia and Republika Srpska Krajina in Croatia.

[69] The Federation was formed without asserting democratic procedures, *i.e.* national referendum.

[70] Serbia has 9.4 million inhabitants and Montenegro 600,000. The relations between the two Republics have periods of tranquillity and tension. Political disagreements between the leadership of the two Republics over the UN peace plan led to the introduction of informal economic sanctions by Serbia against Montenegro in summer 1993.

[71] Official statements describe the UN sanctions as "unprecedented and genocidical" – Mr. Avramovic, Governor of the NBY, at a press conference on the 4th of April 1994. However, only two years earlier, when the sanctions were introduced, Mr. Milosevic, president of Serbia, declared: "UN sanctions will help our economy to develop and achieve higher standards of efficiency." – Daily newspaper *Politika*, 21st of June 1992.

UN activity was blocked by the perception of the European countries that the war in Yugoslavia is an internal, European problem. Following the failure of the European Community policy to stop the war in Croatia, the UN assumed a more active role, by the end of 1991. Since then, over 100 resolutions and presidential statements have been adopted by the UN Security Council. They embrace various measures: deployment of UN peace-keeping forces (UNPROFOR) in Croatia and Bosnia;[72] embargo on weapons export into the Republics of the former Yugoslavia;[73] no-fly zone over Bosnia,[74] etc.

All the adopted documents clearly condemn the policy of Serbia and Montenegro and of their nationalist Serb allies in Croatia and Bosnia, emphasising their responsibility for the conflict[75] and the accompanying atrocities. The UN warned the Serbian leadership of the consequences of its behaviour. Nevertheless, the leadership of Serbia ignored the demands of the international community. Following its previous decisions, in May 1992 the UN imposed economic sanctions on Serbia and Montenegro. The legislative basis of the political and economic isolation of Serbia are UN Resolutions 757, 787, 820, 821 and 943.

UN Resolution 757[76] imposed economic, financial, technical, sporting and cultural sanctions against Serbia, including a full trade embargo and a flight ban (exemptions: foodstuffs, humanitarian and medical supplies and UNPROFOR-related goods and services). Article 5 provides the following:

. . . all States shall not make available to the authorities in the Federal Republic of Yugoslavia (Serbia and Montenegro) or to any commercial, industrial or political utility undertaking in the Federal Republic of Yugoslavia (Serbia and Montenegro), any funds or any other financial or economic resources and shall prevent their nationals and any persons within their territories from removing from their territories or otherwise making available to those authorities or to any such undertaking any such funds or resources and from remitting any other funds to persons or bodies within the Federal Republic of Yugoslavia (Serbia and Montenegro), except payments exclusively for strictly medical or humanitarian purposes and foodstuffs.

---

[72] The United Nations Protection Force was established by Resolution 743, adopted on the 21st of February 1992, which implemented the plan of the UN known by the name of the UN envoy Mr. Cyrus Vance. The plan embraces various measures in order to achieve normalisation of life in the United Nations Protected Areas, which are the zones in Croatia held by nationalist Serb forces.

[73] UN Resolution 713, adopted on the 25th of September 1991.

[74] UN Resolution 816, adopted on the 31st of March 1993.

[75] The United Nations condemned also the behaviour of other paramilitary forces and armed forces, *i.e.* Croatian and Bosnian. However, their activities never led to such drastic consequences as the operations of the Serbian nationalists. A high-ranking officer of the ruling party in Serbia, Goran Percevic, stated that Serbs had 10 times fewer casualties than other nations in the war in Bosnia, clearly indicating the proportions of forces. This, furthermore, directly influenced the behaviour of the UN in respect of the warring sides.

[76] Resolution 757 was adopted on the 30th of May 1992.

The regime of sanctions imposed by UN Resolution 757 had many imperfections producing unsatisfactory effects. Therefore, UN Resolutions 787[77] and 820[78] were adopted to strengthen the sanctions against Serbia, prohibiting transhipment through the Federal Republic of Yugoslavia (Serbia and Montenegro) of petroleum, coal, steel and other products.

Resolution 821[79] reaffirmed that the Federal Republic of Yugoslavia (Serbia and Montenegro) could not maintain the membership of the Socialist Federal Republic of Yugoslavia in the United Nations, and recommended to the General Assembly that it decide that the Federal Republic of Yugoslavia should not participate in the work of the United Nations boards. This decision resulted in the political isolation of Serbia from all major international forums. This has had a significant effect on the Serbian economy. The International Monetary Fund and the World Bank adopted the position of the UN.[80] In addition, they listed the conditions Serbia must fulfil in order to be accepted as a member. Without IMF and IBRD membership and support, the international financial markets were closed to Serbia, with all the consequences such a position could have on its economy.

The Security Council adopted UN Resolution 943 on the 23rd of September 1994, which suspended certain sanctions on the Federal Republic of Yugoslavia (Serbia and Montenegro) for an initial period of 100 days. This was caused by compliance of the Serbian leadership with UN Resolution 942, which further imposed rigid sanctions against Serbian nationalists in Bosnia. UN Resolution 943 called for the re-establishment of flights and the participation of FRY in sports and cultural exchanges. However, the economic sanctions had already produced devastating effects on the economy and social life in Serbia.

3.1.4 *The economic catastrophe – effects of the United Nations sanctions[81]*

The measures of the United Nations resolutions were strictly implemented by its member states. By the end of 1992, the first effects of the sanctions on the Serbian economy were apparent. The industrial production rate decreased in 1992 to 21% of the production of 1991, reaching the level of the year 1963 by the end of 1993, and agricultural productivity reached the level of 1972. GDP decreased in 1993 to 30% of the GDP in 1990. The average wage rate fell from 800 U.S.$ per month in 1991 to 25 U.S.$ per month in 1993. Only 43% of the employed population was actually working.[82] 72% of the state budget was financed by credits of the NBY in

---

[77] Adopted on the 16th of November 1992.
[78] Adopted on the 17th of April 1993.
[79] Adopted on the 28th of April 1993.
[80] The Board of Executive Directors of the World Bank decided that the membership of SFRY terminated on the 25th of February 1993. The Board also established requirements under which five former Republics of SFRY may succeed to SFRY membership.
[81] All data in this section are from *The Economic Drama of Yugoslavia* – T. Popovic, S. Stamenkovic, edition of the Economic Institute in Belgrade, 1994.
[82] Since bankruptcy procedures have been frozen for an indefinite time period and, consequently, there are no job losses, it is not, therefore, possible to establish the exact level of unemployment.

1993.[83] Consequently, the quantity of money in circulation increased nominally over 20,000 times but the real value of the money in circulation decreased from 1.8 billion U.S.$ in December 1992 to 35 million U.S.$ in December 1993. In combination with other factors, this caused hyper-inflation. The inflation rate between December 1992 and December 1993 was 350,000 billion % or 350,000,000,000,000 % per year. In such conditions, the official currency, the dinar, lost its quality as a store of value, and as a measure of value further, it was losing its function as a medium of exchange. This created a situation of psychosis and despair among the population enhancing pathological behaviour, *e.g.* criminality, alcoholism, etc. There is no research which can calculate the damage to the Serbian society stemming from recent political decisions of its leadership. Nevertheless, some experts have calculated that Serbia will need one year of economic recovery for each month that it has been under sanctions.[84]

3.1.5 Chaos in the banking system

The banks in Serbia already suffered under a heavy burden of bad loans made in the previous period,[85] but in 1991 the situation started to deteriorate sharply. After the appearance of Serbia in the monetary system in 1990, the Federal Government lost its fight for financial discipline, forcing it to adopt very unpopular measures to maintain the integrity of the monetary system. In spring 1991 the Federal Government ordered commercial banks to stop payments on foreign currency deposits to the public. This was followed by a siege of banks by enraged citizens wanting their money.[86] Public confidence was further eroded by the speculative activities of banks and a consequent chain of insolvency cases.[87] Hence, by 1993, saving activity in Serbia literally disappeared. International financial transactions declined gradually and virtually disappeared after the introduction of the UN sanctions. In 1992, international financial transactions decreased by 32% in respect of 1991; financial funds and accounts of Serbia were blocked except for the servicing of the IMF loan for the third quarter of 1992. In 1993, all transactions except services related to UN activities were frozen.[88] Thus, banks are operating under extremely hostile conditions which are forcing them to neglect the rules of prudential business. For example,

---

[83] 70% of the federal budget is used for military purposes; Federal Army expenditures and aid to the self-proclaimed Republika Srpska and Republika Srpska Krajina.

[84] With an average growth rate of 10% per year – Prof. Ljubomir Madzar – Faculty of Economy, Belgrade University.

[85] *See supra*, discussion.

[86] The total debt of commercial banks in SFRY to the public on foreign exchange deposits was estimated to be over 10 billion U.S.$: of this, 6.5 billion U.S.$ was in Serbia. The problem of the old foreign currency deposits is still unsolved: Mr. Avramovic stated that that is one of the heaviest burdens on Serbian banks – *Journal of InvestBanka*, Sept–Oct 1994.

[87] In 1993 two private banks, Dafimentbank and Yugoskandik, operating on a pyramidal scheme basis, collapsed with a total amount of 1.5 billion U.S.$ in foreign currency deposits – M. Dinkic, *op. cit.*, p. 235.

[88] *Journal of InvestBanka*, April 1994 issue.

expansion of investments is not followed by the adequate flow of capital; there is no proper valuation of borrowers' credit potential and of non-payment risks; the professional skills and integrity of managers and directors are not appropriate to the level of their business activities. An NBY survey[89] showed the consequences of this deterioration: in 1992, out of 96 operating banks, 26 did not satisfy the prudential business requirements – five ignored capital adequacy and 21 the large exposure criteria. In 1993, out of 103 operating banks, only 19 conducted their business in compliance with binding banking standards. The NBY encountered various obstacles in the discharge of its duties. Problems stemmed mainly from the effects of the UN sanctions and legal insecurity. Some authors have described the banking system in Serbia as chaotic.[90]

3.2 Avramovic[91] Programme – a rescue for a failed economy

In January 1994, Serbia and Montenegro faced total disintegration of the economy. A rescue programme with the sole aim of preventing the collapse of the monetary system was enacted. Measures embraced by this programme had as their priority the elimination of hyper-inflation. Other economic problems, including rehabilitation of the banking sector, are not issues of this programme. As aforementioned, the main sources of inflation were: budget deficit, lack of monetary discipline and speculative activities of banks and other financial institutions. The target of the programme was to impose discipline and stability in the monetary system. To achieve that, two policies have been adopted: restrictive monetary policy and active fiscal policy. The new dinar was introduced as currency with a fixed exchange rate in proportion of 1:1 to the Deutsche Mark. Internal convertibility of the new dinar was proclaimed. NBY issued only 200 million new dinars which were covered by Federal reserves of 200 million Deutsche Marks. Any new quantity of issued dinars had to be justified by increase of Federal reserves in gold or foreign currency. Credit policy was restricted in respect of the Federation and of commercial banks. The programme was supported by massive media propaganda. As a first result, the inflation rate dropped, official sources claim, to 3.7% in the period January–September 1994. Real wage rates increased to 80 U.S.$ per month. However, it is not possible to judge the results of the programme mainly because of two reasons: the alleged "massaging" of official data, and the unknown dimensions of speculative activities and their influence on the economic indicators, *i.e.* inflation. In addition, there is no evidence that the sources of the problems have been eliminated. The war in the former SFRY still requires massive economic support by Serbia.

---

[89] *National Bank of Yugoslavia Annual Survey*, 1992 and 1993.
[90] T. Popovic, S. Stamenkovic, *op. cit.*, p. 39
[91] Mr. Dragoljub Avramovic was for a long time the representative of SFRY at the UNCTAD and an expert of the IMF and World Bank. In January 1994, he was appointed Governor of the National Bank of Serbia and Montenegro.

Nevertheless, the programme lasted longer than was expected by many. One of the important sources of foreign currency is the remittances of citizens living abroad and business operations of banks and enterprises based abroad and operating for the account and under control of legal and personal entities in Serbia. Without reintegration into international economic relations and significant financial aid from international creditors, Serbia cannot expect significant improvement in its economic conditions. As Mr. Avramovic said himself: "Without substantial foreign financial aid, primarily IMF and World Bank loans, the programme is destined to fail".[92]

3.3 Adjustment of the legal system

The period after disintegration of SFRY is characterised in Serbia by the necessity to adapt the legal system to new circumstances and at the same time to continue with reforms in the direction of a market economy. The Constitution of 1992 articulated new political aims and a federal structure with strong unitary elements; proclaiming determination for the principles of a market economy and political democracy. The new National Bank of Yugoslavia Act[93] echoed the same tendency. Though the process of centralisation of the NBY was initiated in SFRY, the new Central Bank is a completely different institution from the previous National Bank, even though its name is the same. The new Law on Banks and Other Financial Institutions reflected the second tendency. Reforms of the legal system of commercial banking continued and developed. In addition, particular attention is due to various other Acts which reflect the specific historic period. These Acts are mainly temporary measures adopted in order to cope with the problems caused by the UN sanctions.

3.3.1 The position of the new National Bank of Yugoslavia

The concept of federalism was abandoned by the new NBY Act. The NBY is established as the independent and centralised institution of the banking system, assuming the role of the Central Bank. The NBY is now responsible for monetary policy, currency stability and financial discipline (art. 1, para. 1).

The NBY contributes to the internal and external stability of and adherence to the international integration of the economy by discharging its duties. The NBY is the only institution which has in its power note and coin issuing, and creation of monetary policy (art. 8). The previous National Banks of Serbia, Montenegro, Kosovo and Vojvodina have been abolished and reconstructed as regional branches of the NBY (art. 19). The duties of the NBY in respect of the Federation have been reduced to annual reports submitted by the Governor of the NBY to the Federal Assembly (art. 22). Federal institutions cannot enforce any decision in the area of competence

---

[92] Daily newspaper *Politika* – 4th of February 1994.
[93] *Official Gazette* of SFRY – 32/93.

of the NBY, thus leaving the NBY out of the political control of the Federation. The NBY acquired the right to submit legal proposals to the Federal Assembly (art. 5). The main board of the NBY is the Council; constituted by six members proposed by the Federal Government and the Governor of the NBY, and appointed by the Federal Assembly (art. 12). The duty of the Council is to establish the general platform of the NBY's policy (art. 14). The Governor of the NBY is responsible for the discharge of the NBY's duties, organises its activities (art. 15) and adopts Acts necessary for the implementation of the general platform adopted by the Council (art. 17). The competencies of the NBY embrace:

- establishment of the monetary policy and the exchange rate of the dinar (art. 24) in co-operation with the federal government, and its credit policy (art. 32);
- issue of notes and coins;
- regulation of money supply and demand, with special emphasis on the activities of financial markets (arts. 25 and 26);
- administration and control over Federal foreign currency reserves (art. 41);
- maintenance of internal liquidity (art. 38);
- establishment of prudential business requirements (arts. 31 and 33);
- supervision over banking activities: the NBY has the authority to supervise the quality and legality of business activities of banks and other financial institutions (art. 53). If a bank does not respect instructions, the NBY can enforce direct measures against the bank in question (art. 54). The NBY grants and withdraws licences of banks and other financial institutions (art. 58);
- judgment of personal skills and integrity of directors (art. 59);
- in extraordinary circumstances, and during the period of the UN sanctions, limitation of interest rates (art. 97).

The formulations and provisions of this Act blatantly reflect the present problems of Serbia. Under article 1, in connection with article 45, the NBY co-operates with international organisations and international financial institutions in the discharge of its duties. This expresses the need to reintegrate Serbia into international economic relations with a dose of servility. The NBY no longer guarantees deposits at banks and other financial institutions (art. 38) as a consequence of previous experience linked to public deposits.[94] The financial markets have been emphasised as a modality of NBY activities. Restrictions set by article 97 – "Exceptionally, during the period of UN sanctions – against FRY, the NBY can restrain the maximum interest rate of banks and other financial institutions; and direct their investments; when it is not possible to regulate interest rates and structure of the assets by means of monetary policy" – introduced insecurity in the banking business. Speculative activities were condemned and prosecuted

---

[94] *See* p. 232.

by the provisions of article 84, which formulated as criminal acts against stability of the monetary system of FRY, imposing a maximum penalty of three years' imprisonment. However, legalistic proclamations have not been followed by concrete political steps. The period following the enactment of this Law coincides with the period of major deformations in the monetary and financial system.

3.3.2 Commercial banking law

The new Law on Banks and Other Financial Institutions continued the reforms enacted in the previous Law, solving some of its contradictions and inconsistencies. This Law defines banks as profit-earning institutions which can be organised as joint-stock companies (art. 2); hence the distinction between Mixed Banks and banks has been repealed. Domestic natural persons also obtained the right to found a bank. Foreign natural and legal persons can found a bank under a reciprocity condition. The supervision and authorisation powers of the NBY have been expanded. Supervision included, with the existing powers, the right to monitor any transfers of initial capital ownership over 15% of its total amount (art. 12). Authorisation embraced licences to foreign banks for their branches or subsidiaries (art. 16). The business activities of banks have been enlarged to financial services which were not provided by the previous Law (art. 22). Article 26 sets the conditions of prudential conduct, adding to the duties of solvency ratio, capital adequacy, and large exposures the duty of banks to inform the NBY about certain specific activities, *e.g.* increase of initial capital, big credits, etc. Articles 46 and 49 set the required criteria for bank managers and directors. Other financial institutions are Postal Savings Banks, Savings Banks, Savings Credit Banks and Mutual Funds.

3.3.3 Ephemeral Acts

Particular attention is due to the enormous number of Acts and bylaws adopted by the Federal Government or by the Governor of the NBY after the implementation of the Avramovic Programme. The most illustrative Acts are:

- the Decision on Regulation of Investments in New Dinars of Banks and Other Financial Institutions and The Mode of Insurance of Foreign Exchange Cover for These Investments[95] – provides that banks can make new investments in new dinars only if they provide the necessary foreign currency basis (art 1);
- the Decision on Obligatory Investments in New Dinars of Banks and Other Financial Institutions[96] – this Act sets the duty of banks and other financial institutions to direct their new dinar investments into the

---

[95] *Official Gazette* of SFRY, issued 21st of January 1994.
[96] *Official Gazette* of SFRY, issued 17th of February 1994.

purchase of Enterprise securities issued on the basis of sale of goods and services (art. 1).

These decisions articulate the fundamental orientation of the Avramovic Programme.[97] The first Act restricts the credit policy of commercial banks and the second directs their investment policy in order to avoid banks' speculative activities. Administrative regulation of banking business is also a characteristic of the two Acts.

4 SUMMARY AND AGENDA

4.1 Summary

Banking law in Serbia evolved in two different stages. The first phase, in 1989, was part of a reform of the economy from self-management to a market economy. The SFRY programme had the financial rehabilitation of banks as one of its priorities. Therefore, large parts of earnings from fiscal and other measures have been diverted as funds for the banks' reconstruction. Hence, banking law provided the legal framework for the ownership, transformation and rehabilitation of banks. The focus in that period was on commercial banking. The reconstruction of the Central Bank system was secondary to the rehabilitation of commercial banks. The purpose of banks was changed from institutions of social redistribution of wealth to profit-earning companies. New prudential criteria were introduced and new institutions were created, *e.g.* the Agency for Deposit Insurance and Financial Rehabilitation of Banks. The programme's discrepancies, *e.g.* the dualism of Mixed Banks and banks, were the result of a necessity; to cope with inherited ownership structure and management and new economic rules and forms, *e.g.* instead of socialism and OALs, market and Enterprises. However, the strategic and ideological orientation of the law was clear. The International Monetary Fund and the IBRD expressed their influence in the area of central banking reform through demands for centralisation and efficiency, which prevailed over the internal opposition of different Federal units.

The essential contradiction of the second phase, after 1991, is continuous deterioration of general macropolitical and macroeconomic conditions, caused mainly by United Nations sanctions and the will of the Serbian authorities to solve the country's problems in the face of those sanctions. Law is used in that context as a form of expression, and at the same time imposed on the legal system tasks which are beyond its powers, therefore, eroding its integrity. This period is characterised by major changes in central banking. The new National Bank of Yugoslavia (Serbia and Montenegro) separated from other National Banks of the former Yugoslav

---

[97] *See* pp. 240–241.

Republics, attributing to itself all the powers of the previous Federal Central Bank system. This shift can be regarded as an inception of a substantially new legal system, where the National Bank is the Central Bank. The new law reflected the difficulties of Serbia, showing its inability to change macroeconomic conditions. Other Acts showed the same characteristic, proving themselves to be more of an administrative than a market nature. Commercial banking continued on the track set by previous reforms and further developing the already implemented notions. Even if the new law is far more consistent than the preceding Act, this diverges from the actual situation in the banking business.

4.2 Political dimensions of future banking law reforms

Without the reintegration of Serbia into the international community, it is difficult to expect any stable improvement of its economic situation. Normalisation of relations with the United Nations, the International Monetary Fund, and the World Bank are the priority in that sense. The policy of Serbia must change in order to be consistent with the United Nations' position and to initiate the process of release of the sanctions, which will inevitably take some time. The economic policy of Serbia is related to the issue of peace in the area of the former Yugoslavia. Stable and permanent peace is fundamental to foreign investors' confidence. Without massive international support in the form of humanitarian aid and financial assistance, *e.g.* loans and investments, the recovery of Serbia and of the entire area of the former Yugoslavia will be very difficult. It is difficult to imagine a foreign investor placing its capital into a region with an inherent danger of escalation of tensions and conflicts, notwithstanding the recent political settlement.

4.3 Legal issues – stabilisation and development of banking

The reconstruction of the Serbian economy and of its banking system is also a complex and difficult task from the legal point of view. The experience of other Eastern European countries can be helpful in the process of the economic and legal reconstruction of Serbia, but cannot be implemented mechanically due to the specificity of the Serbian crisis. The deformation and inefficiency of the legal system of Serbia is one of the most serious consequences of the war and the imposition of UN sanctions. Legal insecurity and lack of public confidence in the institutions and organisations of the system are reflected in the banking system. Thus, the priority is to:

- re-establish the rule of law, *i.e.* legal security, stability and predictability;
- restore public domestic and international confidence in the Serbian economy, *i.e.* the banking and financial systems.

Both of these interrelated aims require institutional and regulatory changes. Primarily, the division of powers must be strengthened, with clear distinctions of competence between the legislature, the executive and the judiciary. Specifically, the executive power must be subordinated to law. The judicial mechanism must be independent from any political or other influence in order to reinstate its integrity. Institutional changes in that direction can create a favourable climate for the reconstruction of the banking system. Institutional changes must be complemented with the following aims to achieve in the banking sector:

- transparency of the banking system: this will have two effects: strengthening of the prudential conduct of banks in their business and restoration of public confidence;
- compatibility with international banking regulations: in the first instance European Union banking regulations, because it is necessary for a future integration of Serbia into European integrative processes; and secondly, Serbian banks must operate on an international level, creating a familiar and stable environment for potential foreign investors;
- liberalisation of the financial services market: the presence of foreign banks can force domestic banks to be more competitive and reinvigorate confidence in the banking system in general;
- improvement of the skills and integrity of managers and directors.

These aims can be realised through the:

- establishment of the Ombudsman for Banking and Financial Services as a special committee of the Federal Parliament or as a completely independent institution with the duty to monitor the development and operation of the banking business;
- establishment of the Association of Bankers with the right to implement direct measures, *e.g.* prohibition to work in banks or other financial institutions for a specified time period to be imposed on managers and bankers whose conduct is contrary to the principles of banking and morality;
- further legal reforms based on existing regulations in the European Union;
- deregulation of the establishment procedure for foreign banks' subsidiaries or branches;
- co-operation with governmental and non-governmental banking and educational organisations and institutions, *e.g.* know-how programmes, seminars of foreign bankers, training courses, exchange programmes, etc.

These aims imply a defrosting of the process of financial rehabilitation of banks. Particularly important is the reactivation of the Agency for Deposit Insurance and Financial Rehabilitation of Banks. However, it is an illusion to assume that the reconstruction of the Serbian economy and its banks will be painless. Bankruptcies will dominate the Serbian banking business at first, as part of a process to eliminate banks which cannot compete under market rules. Enterprise and bank liquidation can create or increase social tensions with unpredictable consequences. Nevertheless, the process of reintegration and adaptation to the international market is the only way for Serbia to achieve satisfactory economic and human development.

14. Contemporary Influences on the Development of South African Banking Law

F. R. Malan[1]

1 INTRODUCTION

1.1 Comparative aspects

Foreign influences on South African law, including banking law, have been immense. The "reception" of the recommendations of the Basle Committee on Banking Supervision[2] in South Africa has been immediate and explicit. The "soft law"[3] of Basle has indeed become positive law through the adoption of its principles in the Banks Act, 1990 and the regulations made under it.[4] This will in turn lead to the reception of these principles and pronouncements in all countries in Southern and South Eastern Africa.[5] Not so pronounced, on the other hand, are the influences of the Directives of the European Union on the harmonisation of company and securities law but,

---

[1] LL.D., Professor of Banking Law and Director of Banking Institute, Rand Afrikaans University, Johannesburg.

[2] It is not possible to refer to all the pronouncements of the Basic Committee on Banking Supervision. For a discussion of their working, *see* J. J. Norton, *Devising International Bank Supervisory Standards* (1995) 171 ff (hereinafter cited as Norton *Standards*); M. J. B. Hall, *Handbook of Banking Regulation and Supervision* 2ed (1993) 9 ff and the literature cited.

[3] Sir Joseph Gold, "Developments in the International Monetary System, the International Monetary Fund and International Monetary Law since 1971" *Recueil des Cours* 107, 156 ff (1982) (cited by Norton, "How International Bank Supervisory Standards are Developed: The Interconnection of Domestic, Regional and International Supervisory Regimes" (Draft 28 October 1994), *Lecture Presentation for Research Institute for Banking Law, Rand Afrikaans University Johannesburg* 39–40 and Norton *Standards* 255–6.

[4] The regulations were first published in *Government Notice* R2799 of 30.10.1990 and amended several times thereafter. The current set of regulations was published in *Government Notice* R2509 (*Government Gazette* 15382) of 28.12.93. The Act and regulations are available in loose-leaf form edited by F. R. Malan & A. N. Oelofse, *South African Banking Legislation* (1990). Amendments made by the Banks Amendment Act 26 of 1994 as well as amendments to the regulations made by *Government Gazette* 16369 (*Regulation Gazette* 5492) of 11.4.95, all of which became effective on 1.5.95, are referred to.

[5] *See* the report on the East and Southern Africa Banking Supervisors Group (ESAF) in South African Reserve Bank Bank Supervision Department, *Annual Report 1994* 21–2.

no doubt, cognisance will be taken of these developments.[6] Of course, not all the recommendations emanating from Basle and Europe have or will be accepted: South Africa has its own institutions and traditions and will continue to develop them.[7] The increase in trade coupled with the abolition of exchange control on non-residents[8] will be added stimuli leading to an era of continuous domestic as well as regional law reform.

Comparative law is not a strange feature in South African law. The common law of South Africa is Roman-Dutch law, reflecting the concepts, divisions and principles characterising Roman legal science. This is particularly true of private law, notably the law of obligations.[9] The British colonisation at the beginning of the nineteenth century, however, led to the swift and far-reaching reception of English law. The adoption of English law, mostly through legislation covering particularly areas of commercial law, left the essential nature of the South African common law unchanged. Although the legislative and other imports brought with them English terminology and the use of English precedents justifying the classification of the South African system as a hybrid one,[10] the essential Roman character of the common law remained. This has made South African law uniquely suitable for comparison, a jurisdiction bridging the grand systems of jurisprudence.

Commercial law displays the character of South African law very well. The Bills of Exchange Act 1964 is an example. This statute is based entirely on the 1882 Bills of Exchange Act – the "best drafted Act of Parliament which was ever passed",[11] with its imposing structure, logical order and simple language.[12] Despite fundamental differences in the legal framework within which negotiable instruments function, such as consideration and conversion, the legislative structure of the 1882 Act has remained basically unchanged. Its interpretation and application, however, have taken an entirely different route: one of "fitting" into the conceptual structure of the South African or Roman-Dutch law the concepts used in this Act. One

---

[6] Delport, "European Community Directives on the Harmonization of Company Law and United Kingdom Company Law. A Status Report", *S.A. Merc. L.J.* 198 (1992).

[7] The Reserve Bank is currently investigating the introduction of a deposit insurance scheme (South African Reserve Bank Bank Supervision Department, *Annual Report 1994* 18; Bank of Lisbon, "Suitability of Bank Deposit Insurance Facilities in South Africa" *Economic Focus* (February 1995). The matter is still very much debated. On the EU proposals *see* M. Dassesse, S. Isaacs & G. Penn, *EC Banking Law* 2ed (1994) 365 ff.

[8] *See* the Press Statement issued by the Minister of Finance on 10.3.95. The abolition of exchange control on non-residents became effective on 13.3.95. *See* Itzikowitz, "Whither the Financial Rand", *T.S.A.R.* 432 (1994) on some of the then envisaged consequences of the abolition. *Cf.* Martinek, "Der Wirtschaftsrechtliche Orientierungsrahmen für Investoren im neuen Südafrika", *R.I.W.* 116, 122–3 (1991).

[9] Zajtay, "The Permanence of Roman Legal Concepts in the Continental Legal Systems", with an addendum by Hosten, "The Permanence of Roman Concepts in South African Law", *C.I.L.S.A.* 181, 192 ff (1969).

[10] Zajtay & Hosten 194.

[11] *Bank Polski v. KJ Mulder & Co.* [1942] 1 All. E.R. 396, 398.

[12] C. M. Schmitthoff, *Commercial Law in a Changing Economic Climate* 2ed (1981) 7.

example will suffice:[13] conversion with its notion of strict liability is unknown in South African law. The Bills of Exchange Act 1964, however, in various sections concerning cheques, regulates the payment and collection of cheques against a background of liability for conversion. At one stage, indeed, the provincial legislation absolved the collecting bank from liability where it acted in good faith and without negligence.[14] This made no sense since a collecting bank was not liable on conversion and there was, consequently, no need to free it from liability! It was only in the 1990s that the appellate division, after a long and tortuous process spanning some seventy years, held what many thought to have been obvious, *viz.* that a collecting bank owed a duty to take reasonable care in the collection of cheques to the owner of a lost or stolen instrument.[15] The resulting similarity in the laws of England and South Africa was brought about by entirely different techniques: in the one case by excluding liability for conversion where the collection is undertaken without negligence[16] and in the other by holding that a duty to care is owed to the owner of a lost or stolen cheque.

Kahn-Freund,[17] when speaking of comparative law as a tool of law reform, warns that the comparative method requires "a knowledge not only of the foreign law, but also of its social, and above all its political context". It is not sufficient to compare the texts of legislation; one should look for "reality", for the customs and practices, to determine how laws are applied, how the law enforcing or supervising authorities functions in practice. Functions should be compared, not institutions. Reality may be quite different from the appearance created by a superficial comparison of legislation.[18]

---

[13] *See* F. R. Malan with J. T. Pretorius & C. R. de Beer, *Malan on Bills of Exchange, Cheques and Promissory Notes in South African Law* 2ed (1994) 35 ff, 83 ff, 413 ff. The *Proposals for the Reform of the Bills of Exchange Act, 1964* (Working Paper 22 of the South African Law Commission) (1988) by F. R. Malan, A. N. Oelofse & J. T. Pretorius is based to a large extent on the work of the United Nations Commission on International Trade Law (*see Malan on Bills of Exchange* 31–4) and seeks to remove some of these ill-fitting rules from the Bills of Exchange Act 1964. Another example of "fitting" foreign precedents into the structure of South African law concerns the so-called fraud exception available to a bank issuing or confirming a letter of credit (*Sztejn v. J. Henry Schroder Banking Corporation* (1941) 31 N.Y.S. 2d 631). This rule is accepted by the South African courts (*Phillips v. Standard Bank of South Africa Limited* 1985 3 S.A. 301 (W)) but is characterised as an example of the general principle that contracts be performed in good faith (F. R. Malan, A. N. Oelofse *et al*, *Provisional Sentence on Bills of Exchange, Cheques and Promissory Notes* (1986) 139 ff). Similarly, the bank and customer relationship (on which *see* R. Cranston (ed.), *European Banking Law* (1993)) in South African law can be characterised as a contract of mandate entailing the many *naturalia* typical of such a relationship (Stassen, "Banke en hul kliënte: 'n Herwaardering van Engelsregtelike eienaardighede in die lig van die Suid-Afrikaanse gemenereg, Bankwet en Wisselwet", 5 *Modern Business Law* 80 (1983); *Malan on Bills of Exchange* 331–2).

[14] The now repealed s. 80 of the provincial enactments. *See* D. V. Cowen & L. Gering, *Cowen on the Law of Negotiable Instruments in South Africa* (1966) 430–5.

[15] *Indac Electronics (Pty) Ltd v. Volkskas Bank Ltd* 1992 1 S.A. 783 (A). For a review of the literature *see Malan on Bills of Exchange* 413 ff.

[16] s. 4 of the Cheques Act 1964.

[17] Kahn-Freund, "On Uses and Misuses of Comparative Law", 37 *Modern L.R.* 1 at 27 (1974).

[18] *Cf.* Blanpain, "Comparativism in Labour Law and Industrial Relations", in R. Blanpain (ed.), *Comparative Labour Law and Industrial Relations* 3ed (1987) 3, 13–14.

The historic Housing Accord signed by the South African government, the Council of Southern African Bankers and other interested parties provides for a mortgage indemnity scheme whereby the government would guarantee losses where the lending institutions are unable to repossess the properties of defaulters. Of particular significance is the commitment of government to ensure "a stable environment in which communities can grow and thrive". Equally important is the undertaking by all parties to campaign intensively "to change the hostilities between financial institutions, local government and the communities and to bring to an end the tradition of non-payment for services, rent and bond boycotts, including the tradition of non-delivery of services".[19]

Another example showing how dangerous a comparison of legislation only could be is money laundering. The warning of the Basle Committee that "[p]ublic confidence in banks and hence their stability, can be undermined by adverse publicity as a result of inadvertent association by banks with criminals"[20] was heeded by the acceptance of the Drugs and Drug Trafficking Act, 140 of 1992. It contains provisions which apply specifically to financial instrument traders, stockbrokers and directors, managers and executive officers of financial institutions (including banks).[21] Although somewhat limited in scope, since it is concerned with offences relating to drugs only, the Act is, nevertheless, a far-reaching and progressive measure. It requires that a stockbroker, financial instrument trader or a financial institution, notwithstanding any obligation of secrecy or any contractual or common-law restriction on the disclosure of information,[22] if he[23] "has reason to suspect that any property acquired by him from any person in the ordinary course of his business is the proceeds of a drug offence",[24] to "(i) as soon as possible report his suspicion to any designated officer; and (ii) at the request of that designated officer, furnish the said officer with such particulars as he may have available regarding the person from whom that property has been acquired". A further offence is created, *viz.* that of the conversion of the proceeds of a defined crime:[25] "No person shall

---

[19] At page 8 of The Housing Accord, "Housing the Nation", signed at Botshabelo on 27 October 1994.

[20] Basle Committee on Banking Regulations and Supervisory Practices (December 1988), *Statement on Prevention of Criminal Use of the Banking System for the Purpose of Money-Laundering*, Ch V document B at 274. *Cf.* Council Directive 91/308 of 10 June 1991 on Prevention of the Use of the Financial System for the Purpose of Money Laundering.

[21] *See* Itzikowitz, "Financial Institutions; Exchange Control", *Annual Banking Law Update 1994* 4 ff; "Money Laundering" 6 *S.A. Merc. L.J.* 318 (1994).

[22] s. 10(4). On the continuing threat to bank confidentiality in South African law *see* W. Faul, *Grondslae van die beskerming van die bankgeheim* (1991) (LL.D., dissertation, Rand Afrikaans University) 440 ff; Fourie, "Duty of Secrecy by Bankers", *South African Banker* (1990) 20, 48; *Malan on Bills of Exchange* 366 ff; Meiring, "Bankgeheimnis en die bank se eie belang", 3 *S.A. Merc. L.J.* 107 (1991).

[23] 10(2) and (3). Section 6 also makes it an offence to acquire property knowing that it is the proceeds of a defined crime.

[24] This is defined in s. 1(1) read with s. 13.

[25] s. 7.

convert any property, while he knows or has reasonable grounds to suspect that any such property is the proceeds of a defined crime". "Property" or money is "converted" if the conduct of the accused has or is likely to have the effect of "concealing or disguising the nature, source, location, disposition or movement of property or its ownership" or of enabling or assisting any person who has committed a drug or other offence, whether in the Republic or elsewhere, to avoid prosecution or to "launder" the proceeds of the offence.[26] These serious provisions are supported by a presumption arising from the possession of the proceeds of a crime[27] and a special section imposing liability on employers and principals.[28] Moreover, specific measures deal with the forfeiture and confiscation of the proceeds of a crime.[29] Despite the existence of the legislative text and the taking of precautionary measures by banks to comply with the Act, one may doubt the ability of the law-enforcing authorities to effectively police the Act. The same could well be said of the comprehensive insider-trading provisions which have been in force for many years but have not as yet, led to a prosecution.[30]

On an entirely different level, the inadequacy of legislation alone as the basis for comparison is illustrated by the Safe Deposit of Securities Act 1992.[31] This Act provides for the collective deposit of securities with a depository institution and is clearly inspired by European systems of collective deposit, notably the German,[32] by introducing the concept of co-ownership to the collective deposit of securities.

Where securities are deposited with a depository institution for safe custody, the institution will be entitled, unless the customer expressly directs otherwise, to redeposit them with a central securities depository or with another depository institution which is a member of a central securities depository.[33] Only a depository institution which is a member of a

---

[26] s. 1(1).

[27] s. 22.

[28] s. 24.

[29] ss. 25 ff and 35 ff.

[30] s. 440F of the Companies Act, 1973. Subsection 1: "Any person who, whether directly or indirectly, knowingly deals in a security on the basis of unpublished price-sensitive information in respect of that security, shall be guilty of an offence if such person knows that such information has been obtained – (a) by virtue of a relationship of trust or any other contractual relationship, whether or not the person concerned is a party to that relationship; or (b) through espionage, theft, bribery, fraud, misrepresentation, or any other wrongful method, irrespective of the nature thereof." *See* H. S. Cilliers, M. L. Benade *et al*, *Corporate Law* 2ed (1992) 145 ff; Botha, "The Economics of the Crime and Punishment of Insider Trading in South Africa", 4 *S.A. Merc. L.J.* 145 (1992). For a discussion of the relevance of the EU Directive 89/592/EEC of 13.11.1989 in South Africa see Van Zyl & Joubert, "The European Union Directive on Insider Trading: A Model for South Africa?", 6 *S.A. Merc. L.J.* 291 (1994); Luiz, "Prohibition against Trading on Inside Information – The Saga Continues", 2 *S.A. Merc. L.J.* 328 (1990).

[31] s. 2(1). *See* Itzikowitz, "Financial Institutions and Exchanges", *Annual Banking Law Update 1993* 52, 54 ff.

[32] F. R. Malan, *Collective Securities Depositories and the Transfer of Securities* (1985) 137 ff; Itzikowitz, "Safe Deposit of Securities", 58 *T.H.R.H.R.* 111 (1995).

[33] s. 2(2).

central securities depository is entitled to deposit securities with the central depository and to have an account with it.[34] The holdings of a person who deposits securities with a depository institution are reflected in securities accounts with the depository institution and the holdings of the depository institution on its account with the central securities depository. All securities held by the central depository will, unless they are bearer securities, be registered in the name of the central securities depository or its wholly owned subsidiary.[35]

Specific requirements are set for the registration of a central securities depository.[36] In addition, a central securities depository must frame rules to ensure proper management and administration.[37] To ensure that a depository institution or central securities depository will not suffer a loss as a result of any claims instituted against it for stolen or forged securities certificates deposited with it, the Act provides that every depositor will be deemed to warrant to the depository institution or the central securities depository, as the case may be, that he is entitled to deposit the securities and that any document relating to such securities is genuine and correct in all respects. He is furthermore deemed to have indemnified the institution against any loss suffered by it as a result of such deposit.[38]

A depository institution may hold all securities of the same kind deposited with it for safe custody collectively in separate securities repositories.[39] A similar provision applies to a central securities depository.[40] Ownership in the individual securities is thus impossible since they cannot be appropriated to a specific customer. Section 4, consequently, sets out the rights of the depositors to the body of securities and provides that the person who was owner of the securities at the time of deposit becomes entitled to an interest as co-owner of all the securities of the same kind comprised in the same repository or central securities repository proportional to his holdings. The total of the rights of the depositor is his collective deposit share and this he cedes or transfers when deliveries are made and pledges when giving them as security.

An interest in securities held in collective deposit is transferred by agreement completed by entry in the securities accounts of the transferor and the transferee.[41] These provisions apply *mutatis mutandis* to the transfer of securities held by a central securities depository.[42] Similarly, a pledge of the interest of a depositor is created by agreement completed by entry in the accounts of the depositor held by the depository institution. This entry must specify the name of the pledgee, the interest pledged and the date.

---

[34] s. 10(1).
[35] s. 10(3).
[36] s. 9.
[37] s. 12.
[38] s. 2(3). *Cf.* s. 138 of the Companies Act 1973.
[39] s. 3.
[40] s. 3.
[41] s. 5.
[42] s. 11(3).

An interest so pledged may not be transferred save with the consent of the pledgee. By precluding the debtor from transferring, the creditor can attach the holder's interest on his failure to perform the secured debt. The pledgee is given the same rights as the pledgee of movable corporeal property in possession.[43]

A depository institution or central securities depository is obliged to deliver the same number of securities, or securities of the same nominal value and of the same kind, to the owner of the securities.[44] The owner must exercise his rights through the depository institution. Dividends and other benefits accruing to the securities are, in the same manner, acquired indirectly, through the depository institution.[45] The attachment of securities held in safe deposit, or, more correctly, of the interest in securities so held, is complete only when notice of the attachment is given to the depository institution, the sheriff has taken possession of the certificate evidencing the securities attached, if any, and he has made an entry of the attachment in the securities account.[46]

Despite this elaborate system for holding securities, little use has been made of it and securities given in safe deposit are held, if not in specie, primarily by bank or broker nominee companies on behalf of customers.

The dangers inherent in comparison are therefore very real when South African law is compared with other legal systems. Not all the pre-conditions for an open and free society have yet been met: the ideals of Chapter 3 of the Constitution entrenching specific fundamental rights have not all been transformed into reality.

South Africa, nevertheless, has a vibrant economy possessing the institutions necessary for sustained development in the region: the Johannesburg Stock Exchange was formed more than a century ago[47] and the South African Futures Exchange[48] was licensed on 10 August 1990. Legislation excluding the right of a liquidator to disclaim adverse contracts in transactions both on the formal exchanges and in derivatives in the informal market is at present before Parliament.[49] The cheque payment system is

---

[43] s. 6.

[44] s. 8.

[45] s. 10(2).

[46] s. 13(1).

[47] In 1887. *See* E. Rosenthal, *On Change through the Years: A History of Share Dealing in South Africa* (1968) 138 ff. Some 670 companies are listed today; *A Guide to the JSE* (1995) 1. The JSE is today licensed in terms of the Stock Exchanges Control Act 1 of 1985.

[48] In terms of the Financial Markets Control Act 55 of 1989 following the *Report of the Committee of Investigation into the Development of Financial Futures Transactions in South Africa* under the chairmanship of Dr. C. L. Stals, the present Governor of the South African Reserve Bank (1988). *See* Malan, "Gambling on the Future? Legal Aspects of the Futures Market", *T.S.A.R.* 577 (1990).

[49] Bill 14 of 1995.

based on a one-day clearing system.[50] Alternative methods of payment exist.[51] Lacking may still be effective ways of enforcing consumer rights embodied in the infant Code of Banking Practice and elsewhere.

South African law has been and will continue to be influenced by contemporary tendencies elsewhere. In banking supervision, the influence of Basle has been immediate and direct. This is best illustrated by the legal regime governing foreign banks in South Africa.

1.2 Foreign banks under South African law

A foreign bank may enter the South African banking scene in one of three ways. The first and most obvious is to register as a bank in terms of the Banks Act 1990. This means that the bank would have to comply in all respects with the legal provisions, including prudential requirements applicable to banks registered in South Africa.

An international financial institution conducting banking business can also, with the approval of the Registrar, establish a *representative office* in South Africa.[52] A representative office is not a "bank" and may not conduct "the business of a bank" in the Republic.[53] "The business of a bank" has a technical meaning and consists essentially in (a) the acceptance of deposits from the general public; (b) the soliciting and advertising for deposits; (c) the utilisation of the deposits for the granting of loans, the making of investments or the financing of any business.[54] The definition of "deposit" is equally wide and, generally, amounts to the receipt of money subject to an agreement to repay it.[55] It follows that the prohibition on a representative office from conducting "the business of a bank" in the Republic means essentially that it cannot accept deposits from the general public and that all operations must be funded from abroad.

---

[50] *Malan on Bills of Exchange* 289 ff. Truncation seems to have been introduced without changes in legislation requiring physical presentment of cheques at the drawee branch: *Navidas (Pty) Ltd v. Essop; Metha v. Essop* 1994 4 S.A. 141 (A). The Bills of Exchange Act 1964, admittedly drafted in an era before electronic "presentment" was either possible or conceivable, however, does not seem to constitute a serious impediment to the smooth functioning of the clearing house system devised by the banks. As Hefer JA said at 148: "A cheque, it will be recalled, is payable on demand. Due presentment on any particular date is accordingly not recalled and there is nothing to prevent presentment in the prescribed manner at the correct place after a 'dishonoured cheque' has been returned to a collecting bank by the clearing house. In every case it is for the holder to decide whether the cheque should be properly presented in order to enable him to sue on it." On truncation, the clearing system and related aspects *see* Meiring, "Holder in Due Course, Truncated Cheques and Presentment for Payment: Recent Developments", 4 *S.A. Merc. L.J.* 377 (1992) and "Die Status van die ACB", 5 *S.A. Merc. L.J.* 321 (1993); Oelofse, "Enkele regsaspekte van ontwikkelings in die bankwese", 7 *Modern Business Law* 6 (1985) and "Onlangse ontwikkelings in die tjekreg", 3 *S.A. Merc. L.J.* 364 (1991).

[51] Meiring, "Elektroniese bankoordragstelsels", 6 *S.A. Merc. L.J.* 318 (1994) and "Die Status van die ACB", 5 *SA Merc. L.J.* 321 (1993).

[52] s. 34.

[53] s. 34(4).

[54] s. 1(1), Para. 6 thereunder.

[55] s. 1(1).

The third and perhaps most acceptable vehicle of entry into the South African financial market is the establishment of a branch of the foreign bank in South Africa.[56] It is also here that the influence of Basle[57] is most pronounced: approval for the establishment of a branch will only be given if the foreign institution, which must have been lawfully established elsewhere to engage in business similar to the business of a bank, confirms its understanding and acceptance of, and adherence to, the minimum standards in respect of consolidated supervision of banking groups and their cross-border establishments set by the Basle Committee.[58] In addition, the Registrar will have to be satisfied that the home-country supervisory authority of the foreign institution "accepts, is committed to and complies with the proposals, guidelines and pronouncements of the Basle Committee on Banking Supervision".[59] Moreover, the branch and the foreign institution will have to enable the home country and host-country supervisory authorities to adhere at all times to the minimum standards of consolidated supervision of banking groups and their cross-border establishments set by the Basle Committee.[60] In addition, the home-country supervising authority must be satisfied that proper risk management standards are maintained by the foreign institution[61] and must inform the supervisory authorities in the Republic of material information regarding the financial soundness of the foreign institution and its branch.[62]

Strict prudential requirements are set for the establishment of a branch in the Republic. The institution must, among other requirements, have held net assets, as certified by its auditors and reflected in its audited financial statements, for a period of eighteen months prior to the application, amounting to U.S. \$ 1 billion.[63] If this is not enough, it must also have been given an acceptable long-term investment grade debt rating by an internationally recognised rating agency.[64] Then the endowment capital of the branch must be maintained at an amount no less than the greater of R 50 million or 8 per cent of the amount of the assets and other risk

---

[56] *See* s. 18A which came into force on 1 May 1995 as well as the Conditions for the Conducting of the Business of a Bank by a Foreign Institution by means of a Branch in the Republic (*Government Notice* R521 of 3.4.95 (*Government Gazette* 16356 (*Regulation Gazette* 5488)). For a discussion of the treatment of foreign branches (*i.e.* branches of banks incorporated in non-member states) in the EU *see* M. Gruson & R. Reisner, *Regulation of Foreign Banks United States and International* (1991 with 1993 *Supplement*) para. 11.05.

[57] *Supervision of Banks' Foreign Establishments* (1975); the *Revised Concordat Principles for the Supervision of Banks' Foreign Establishments* (1983) and *Minimum Standards for the Supervision of International Banking Groups and their Cross-border Establishments* (6.7.92). *See* Norton *Standards* 178–9, 200 ff and Gruson & Feuring, "A European Union Banking Law: The Second Banking and Related Directives", in R. Cranston (ed.), *The Single Market and the Law of Banking* 2ed. (1995) 25, 41 on the EU Directives.

[58] reg. 1(5)(c)(iii).

[59] reg. 1(6)(b)(ii).

[60] reg. 1(6)(e).

[61] reg. (1)(6)(b)(vi).

[62] reg. 1(6)(b)(vii).

[63] reg. 1(3).

[64] reg. 1(3)(b).

exposures of the branch, calculated in the same way as in the case of banks registered under the Banks Act 1990.[65] The prudential requirements the branch must comply with are, in fact, the same as those pertaining to a fully fledged South African bank.[66] A fit and proper test is set for the management of the branch[67] and an executive officer has to comply with the same requirements as those set for directors and executive officers of locally registered banks.[68] Although there is some restriction on the business activity of a branch in that it may accept unlimited deposits from legal entities but deposits in an initial amount of R 1 million only from natural persons, the intention of the legislature was clearly to treat every branch as if it were a bank and to subject it to the same regulatory and supervisory regime as the one applicable to banks.[69]

Following the Basle guidelines for the supervision of international banking groups,[70] the Registrar is empowered to request information concerning the foreign operations of South African banks, whether through subsidiaries, branches, agencies or other undertakings so as to supervise their world-wide activities.[71] This is in line with the approach of the Banks Act, which makes possible the supervision of a group of banks by means of consolidated returns reflecting the financial information of all the banks in the group as well as their subsidiaries and controlling companies, other undertakings and controlled trusts.[72] The Bank Supervision Department of the Reserve Bank is committed to consolidated cross-border supervision in accordance with the Basle standards.[73]

---

[65] reg. 1(3)(c).

[66] In particular s. 72 of the Act applies, *mutatis mutandis*, to a branch as do the provisions relating to the maintenance of minimum reserve balances in terms of s. 10A of the South African Reserve Bank Act 90 of 1989 (reg. 1(3)(d) and (e)).

[67] reg. 1(4)(a).

[68] reg. 1(4)(b) refers specifically to s. 1(1A).

[69] reg. 1(6)(d) specifically provides: "In addition to sections 1(1A), 18A, 70(2) and 72 of the Act, the other provisions of the Act shall, in so far as they can be applied and except where they are inconsistent with the context or clearly inappropriate, apply, *mutatis mutandis*, to branch as if a branch were a bank."

[70] Basle Committee on Banking Supervision, *Minimum Standards for the Supervision of International Banking Groups and their Cross-border Establishments* (6.7.92). Section 52 of the Banks Act 94 of 1990 requires South African banks to obtain the approval of the Registrar before establishing a branch or representative office outside the Republic and places other limitations on them. For a comparison of the Basle guidelines and EU Directives 83/350/EEC and 92/30/EEC *see* Norton *Standards* 130 ff and Dassesse, Isaacs & Penn 73 ff.

[71] s. 75(4)(a).

[72] s. 75(4)(b) and reg. 5 which requires a bank to furnish the Registrar with consolidated annual financial statements for the bank or controlling company and all subsidiaries as well as certain "associates".

[73] South African Reserve Bank Bank Supervision Department, *Annual Report 1994* 20–1.

2 HISTORICAL ASPECTS

The first bank in South Africa, the Bank van Leening, was established in 1793.[74] Before unification of South Africa in 1910, the law relating to commercial banking was governed in the Cape Province by Acts 6 of 1891 and 19 of 1893; in the Orange Free State by Ordinance 20 of 1902 and in the Transvaal by Law 2 of 1893. The Cape Act was promulgated to consolidate[75] and amend the law relating to banking and to secure and regulate the circulation of bank notes.[76] It also secured a degree of publicity for banking operations.[77] A bank was defined as "every foreign banking company and every joint stock company engaged in the ordinary business of banking by receiving moneys on deposit and by issuing in this Colony or elsewhere bills or notes payable at sight or on demand".[78]

In Natal, the Natal Bank (Limited) Laws 1888 to 1912, Private Act 7 of 1912, consolidated all laws relating to the establishment of the Natal Bank.

The Banking Act 38 of 1942 repealed the banking legislation in the Cape Province, Orange Free State and Transvaal, as well as the previous Banks Acts of the Union 7 of 1916 and 31 of 1920. The purpose of the Banking Act 38 of 1942 was to consolidate and amend the law relating to banks and certain similar institutions. In this Act "banking institution" included a commercial bank,[79] a people's bank,[80] a loan bank[81] which carried on the business of accepting deposits of money and of granting small loans,[82] and a deposit-receiving institution.[83]

The Banking Act 7 of 1917 was enacted to provide for the issue of bank notes of the denomination of ten shillings[84] and for the periodical return by banks of statements of assets and liabilities within and outside the Union.[85] The Currency and Banking Act 31 of 1929 was enacted to conserve the specie supplies of the Union by providing for the issue of gold certificates;[86]

---

[74] On the history of banking in South Africa *see* H. B. Falkena, L. J. Fourie & W. J. Kok, *The Mechanics of the South African Financial System* (1989) 63 ff; N. Willis, *Banking in South African Law* (1981) 11; M. V. Kelly, *Financial Institutions in South Africa* (1993) 251 ff.

[75] s. 1.

[76] ss. 24, 25, 30–51.

[77] *e.g.* publicity of the deed of settlement (ss. 3 and 6) and alteration thereof (s. 4) and penalty of non-compliance (s. 5); publicity of the power of attorney (ss. 7–9); publicity of returns of shareholders (ss. 11–12); quarterly statements of assets and liabilities (ss. 13–15); additional statements (ss. 16–18); appointment of inspectors (ss. 19–23); appointment, etc. of auditors (ss. 26–29); statements of unclaimed trust moneys to be published (s. 52); bank licence (s. 55) and legal acceptance (s. 53).

[78] s. 2.

[79] A person who carries on business of which a substantial part consists of the acceptance of deposits of money withdrawable by cheque (s. 1).

[80] An association established for the purpose of promoting thrift among its members and of making loans to its members (s. 1).

[81] A bank other than a people's bank (s. 1).

[82] s. 1.

[83] A person who carries on the business of accepting deposits of money but who is not a commercial bank or a people's bank or a loan bank (s. 1).

[84] s. 1.

[85] ss. 2–5.

[86] Ch. I ss. 1–8.

to provide for the establishment of a central reserve bank for the Union,[87] including its establishment,[88] capital,[89] reserve fund and allocation of surplus,[90] powers and duties,[91] business,[92] and prohibited business;[93] to regulate the issue of bank notes[94] and the keeping of reserves with a view to securing greater stability in the monetary system of the Union[95]; and generally to make provision for matters incidental thereto.[96] The Act[97] described a bank as every person, firm or company using in its description or title "bank" or "banker" or "banking" and every person, firm or company, receiving or accepting deposits of money subject to withdrawal by cheque, draft or order.

The Savings Bank Societies Borrowing Powers Act 6 of 1932 gave savings bank societies (other than building societies) powers to borrow money for their business. The original Act applied to building societies as well, but Act 62 of 1934 repealed it in so far as it affected them. The Building Societies Act 62 of 1934 was enacted to provide for the registration, incorporation, regulation, management and dissolution of building societies. It was repealed by the Building Societies Act 24 of 1965.

Under the terms of the Banks Act 23 of 1965, a major consolidating piece of legislation, "banking institution" included a commercial bank,[98] a discount house,[99] a general bank,[100] a hire-purchase bank,[101] a merchant bank[102] or a savings bank.[103] In a major change, the Financial Institutions

---

[87] Ch. II.

[88] s. 9.

[89] s. 10.

[90] s. 11.

[91] s. 12.

[92] s. 13.

[93] s. 14.

[94] ss. 15–16, 20–22.

[95] ss. 17–19, 23.

[96] Audit and inspection (s. 24); returns (s. 25); falsification of books, statements, etc. (s. 26); banking secrecy (s. 27); offences to be maintained by other banks (s. 30); monthly returns (s. 31).

[97] s. 34.

[98] *i.e.* a person who carries on a business of which a substantial part consists of the acceptance of deposits of money withdrawable by cheque (s. 1(i)). This definition was deleted by s. 10(1) of Act 106 of 1985.

[99] *i.e.* a person whose business consists of discounting or buying and selling or investing in securities ... and also of accepting, predominantly against the pledge of such securities, loans repayable on demand or at short notice from the institutions (s. 1(iv)). Discount houses are no longer recognised in the Banks Act of 1990.

[100] *i.e.* a person who carries on the business of accepting deposits, but not a commercial bank or a hire-purchase bank or a merchant bank or a savings bank (s. 1(v)). This definition was deleted by s. 10(1) of Act 106 of 1985.

[101] *i.e.* a person who carries on the business of accepting deposits, but not a commercial bank or a hire-purchase bank or a merchant bank or a savings bank (s. 1(v)). This definition was deleted by s. 27(c) of Act 103 of 1979.

[102] *i.e.* a person carrying on a business of which the acceptance of bills which are eligible for discount by the Reserve Bank forms a substantial part, and who also accepts deposits (s. 1(xi)). This definition was deleted by s. 10(2) of Act 106 of 1985.

[103] *i.e.* a person who carries on the business of accepting deposits and of whose either business the granting of loans against the security of fixed property or surety bonds forms a substantial part (s. 1(xxi)). This definition was deleted by s. 27(c) of Act 103 of 1979.

Amendment Act 106 of 1985 abolished the distinction between the different classes of banks and differentiated between "banking institutions" and "discount houses" only.[104] However, not all banks were, under this regime, entitled to offer cheque facilities and special permission to that end was necessary.[105] The Banks Act 1990 (originally known as the Deposit-taking Institutions Act 94 of 1990) goes much further and effectively does away with discount houses. Moreover, and this is its novelty, it treats banks and building societies and, for that matter, all deposit-taking institutions alike.

2.1 The South African Reserve Bank

The South African Reserve Bank was established under the Currency and Banking Act 31 of 1920 which gave the South African Reserve Bank the right to transact certain business and the sole right to issue bank notes. Act 29 of 1944 consolidated the laws relating to the Reserve Bank, repealing all previous legislation, and made provision for matters incidental to the regulation of the monetary system of the Union. This Act removed the provisions relating to note issues from the Banks Act but was itself repealed by the South African Reserve Bank Act 90 of 1989 which consolidated all legislation concerning the Reserve Bank.[106]

The interim Constitution of the Republic of South Africa,[107] which came into effect on 27 April 1994, deals in three sections with the constitutional role of the South African Reserve Bank. It provides that the Reserve Bank is the central bank of the Republic[108] with its primary objectives the protection of the internal and external value of the currency in the interest of balanced and sustainable economic growth.[109] The Reserve Bank is entitled, in the pursuit of its primary objectives, "to exercise its powers and perform its functions *independently*, subject only to an Act of Parliament ..."[110] There must, however, be consultation between the Reserve Bank and the Minister of Finance.[111] The powers and functions of the Reserve Bank are those customarily exercised and performed by central banks and are determined by Act of Parliament.[112] The independence of the Reserve Bank will have to be recognised in the final Constitution to be drawn up by the Constitutional Assembly.[113]

---

[104] The activities of discount houses were limited by this Act to the discounting, buying or investing in certain security; s. 22(1) Banks Act.

[105] s. 29(2) Banks Act.

[106] On the history and functions of the Reserve Bank *see* M. H. De Kock, *Central Banking* 4ed (1974) 8ff; Du Plessis, "The Structure and Operation of the Reserve Bank and its Relationship to the Government", 2 *Modern Business Law* 86 (1980); Falkena, Fourie & Kok 41–2; Malan, "Banks, the Reserve Bank and the Bills of Exchange Act, 1964", T.S.A.R. 755 (1993).

[107] Act No. 200 of 1992.

[108] s. 195.

[109] s. 196(1).

[110] s. 196(2).

[111] s. 196(2).

[112] s. 197.

[113] s. 71(1) and Schedule 4 XXIX which provides that "[t]he independence and impartiality of ... a Reserve Bank ... shall be provided for and safeguarded by the Constitution ..."

The Constitution guarantees the independence of the Reserve Bank from government intervention and interference: only consultation between bank and government is called for. However, the independence relates to the exercise of the *powers* and performance of the *functions* of the Reserve Bank in the *pursuit of its primary objectives* only. Arguably, the supervision of banks is not a primary objective, nor is the decision to institute or abolish exchange control.[114]

South African financial institutions are regulated not by a single central authority but by several agencies of which the two most important are the Registrar of Banks and the Financial Services Board.[115] Closely linked to these institutions is the Policy Board for Financial Services and Regulation,[116] whose aim is to advise the Minister with regard to any matter of law dealing with the regulation of financial institutions and services, policy considerations and matters referred by the Minister to the Board.[117] The Board has contributed and will contribute to the elimination of gaps in the existing regulatory structure. No doubt the Policy Board will eventually recommend the creation of a single financial regulatory body.[118]

The Registrar of Banks is an official of the Reserve Bank and he heads the Office of Banks.[119] Extensive powers of supervision and inspection vest in the Registrar,[120] and he may call upon the auditors of the bank whose appointment he has to approve[121] to furnish him with notices and other information.[122] Moreover, the auditors must inform the Registrar of any matter relating to the affairs of a bank which, in their opinion, may "endanger the bank's ability to continue as a going concern or may impair the protection of the funds of the bank's depositors or may be contrary to the

---

[114] Control of foreign exchange vests in the Treasury by virtue of the Currency and Exchanges Act 9 of 1933 and was delegated to the Reserve Bank.

[115] Van Zyl, "The FSB's Role in the Regulation of the Financial Services Industry", *Financial Services Board Bulletin* 2 (1994); Krull, "Preparing for International Financial Markets Discipline: Adapting SA's Regulatory Legal Framework", *Financial Services Board Bulletin* 7 (1994); I. Goodspeed, H. B. Falkena, P. Morgenrood & R. K. Store (eds.), *The Regulation of Financial Markets* (1991) and Malan, "Legal Aspects of the Regulation of Financial Institutions", *T.S.A.R.* 553 (1989).

[116] Established by the Policy Board for Financial Services and Regulation Act 141 of 1993.

[117] s. 5.

[118] *See, e.g.* the *Commission of Inquiry into the Supervision of Financial Institutions, Financial Services and Deposit-taking Institutions* (1993).

[119] s. 3.

[120] Itzikowitz, "The Deposit-taking Institutions Act 94 of 1990: Its History and an Overview of its Main Provisions", 4 *S.A. Merc. L.J.* 170 (1992); Oelofse, "The South African Deposit-taking Institutions Act 94 of 1990", *J.I.B.L.* 98 (1991).

[121] s. 61. The liability of auditors is regulated mainly by the Public Accountants' and Auditors' Act 1981. *See* Van Zyl, "The Role of the Auditor in the Regulation of Financial Institutions", *Financial Services Board Bulletin* 8 (1994); J. T. Pretorius, *Aanspreeklikheid van maatskappy-ouditeure teenoor derdes op grond van wanvoorstelling in die finansiële state* (LL.D. dissertation, Rand Afrikaans University, 1985) 222 ff and Fourie, "Auditors and Corporate Illegality and Fraud", 6 *S.A. Merc. L.J.* 178 (1994).

[122] s. 63.

principles of sound management ... or amounts to inadequate maintenance of internal controls".[123]

Section 88 of the Banks Act absolves from liability the South African Reserve Bank, any director of that Bank, the Registrar or any other officer or employee of the Bank for any loss sustained by or damage caused to any person as a result of anything done or omitted by them in the *bona fide* performance of any function or duty under this Act. No comparable section exists in previous legislation and it is submitted that this provision merely reflects what has been decided in *Yuen Kun-yeu v. Attorney General of Hong Kong*,[124] where the Privy Council declined to hold that a common law duty of care could be imposed on the commissioner of deposit-taking companies appointed under the Hong Kong Deposit-taking Companies Ordinance 1976.

2.2 The emergence of building societies

In South Africa, the building society movement started in the Eastern Province and Natal.[125] The population in these areas was predominantly English, being descendants of the British settlers who emigrated from the United Kingdom, where building societies were well known.[126] The first permanent society was established in Grahamstown in 1877,[127] but the first legislation, applicable to terminating societies only, was passed in Natal. The building society movement spread to the Cape in 1859 but after the dramatic change in the South African economy, with the discovery of diamonds near Kimberley in 1867 and the discovery of gold on the Witwatersrand in 1886, building societies were established countrywide.[128]

By the turn of the century, there were ten permanent societies in the country. After the Union in 1910 and the First World War, the economy received an impetus and societies were enabled to widen their scope and to operate on a nation-wide basis. By 1918, the total assets in the building society movement exceeded three million pounds. During the next decades building societies became substantially bigger, often through amalgamations.[129]

---

123 s. 63(1)(b)(ii) as amended by s. 42 of Act 26 of 1994. *See* reg. 6(5) which requires the auditors to report on "any significant weaknesses in the system of internal controls relating to financial and regulatory reporting, and compliance with the Act and the Regulations . . ."

124 [1987] 2 All. E.R. 705 (PC). *See also Davis v. Radcliffe* 1990 B.C.L.C. 647, 653–6 and *cf. Minorities Finance Ltd v. Arthur Young (a firm) (Bank of England, third party); Johnson Matthey plc (a firm) v. Arthur Young (a firm) (Bank of England, third party)* [1989] All. E.R. 105 (QB).

125 D. G. Alston, "Building Societies", in A. Hamersma & N. Czypionka, *Essays on the South African Financial Structure* (1976) 61; Falkena, Fourie & Kok 97.

126 M. Boleat, *National Housing Finance Systems – A Comparative Study* (1985) 133; D. G. Alston, *Building Societies in South Africa. Their Origin and Development* (1973) 3; J. De Klerk, *Die ontwikkeling van handelsbanke en bouverenigings in Suid-Afrika 1652–1967* (1970, dissertation).

127 Alston 2–3; Boleat 134; De Klerk 48; L. Alcock, *Die belangrikheid van permanente bouverenigings as instrument vir die finansiering van privaatbehuising in Suid-Afrika* (1986, dissertation) 99.

128 Alston 3–4; De Klerk 46; Alcock 100.

129 Alston 5–6; Boleat 134; Alcock 100.

In 1909, the Building (Permanent) Society Act and the County Permanent Building Society Act were adopted in Natal. The next major development took place when, on 23 May 1935, Act 62 of 1934 was brought into force.[130] The Building Societies Act 24 of 1965 repealed the 1934 Act and applied to mutual building societies only.

Changes in the regulation of building societies was brought about as a result of recommendations by the De Kock Commission of Inquiry into the Monetary System and Monetary Policy in South Africa in 1985.[131] The view of the Commission on the role of building societies was as follows:

At the present stage of their evolutionary development, building societies should continue to be accorded special treatment under their own Building Societies Act. This implies the retention of tighter restrictions on their fund-raising and lending activities than those of banking institutions registered under the Banks Act, balanced by certain privileges and advantages not enjoyed by the latter institutions. At the same time, it should be recognised that the societies are dynamic and progressive institutions which have moved away from the traditional concept of mutual thrift institutions and closer to modern deposit banking. And it should be accepted that further evolutionary changes in this direction are probably both inevitable and desirable.[132]

The recommendations of the De Kock Commission demanded amendments to the Building Societies Act, although the Commission was of the opinion that new legislation was necessary to bring the Building Societies Act into line with the Banks Act.

At very much the same time as the report of the De Kock Commission was released, the *Report of the Commission of Inquiry into Certain Matters Relating to Building Societies in South Africa*[133] was published. This Commission saw building societies rather in isolation than as part of the overall financial system. It opined that the major object of societies was the financing of housing from personal savings and the encouragement of home-ownership, although it recognised that building societies had gradually extended their functions and that the favourable treatment afforded them had enhanced their competitiveness against other institutions. The Commission frowned on the extension of their activities and proposed that societies should rearrange them in accordance with the precepts and principles with which they functioned in the past.[134]

The government accepted the recommendations of the De Kock Commission. This resulted in the building societies regime undergoing a fundamental change in 1986. Two Acts were promulgated, *viz.* the Building

---

[130] Alston 6; Boleat 134; Alcock 107–108.
[131] Falkena, Fourie & Kok 103 ff.
[132] *Second Interim Report of the Commission of Inquiry into the Monetary System and Monetary Policy in South Africa* (1982) para. 14; *Final Report by the Commission of Inquiry into the Monetary System and Monetary Policy in South Africa* (1985) Ch. 7.
[133] RP 37/1982.
[134] Paras. 527, 545 and 581.

Societies Act 28 of 1986 and the Building Societies Amendment Act of 1986, resulting in the transformation of building societies into companies and their consequent take-over by the major banks.

3 THE BANKS ACT 94 OF 1990: GENERAL ASPECTS

The purpose of the Banks Act 94 of 1990 (originally named the Deposit-taking Institutions Act) is to provide for the regulation and supervision of the business of public companies taking deposits from the public.[135] Its main object is to create the legal framework for the regulation and supervision of the business of accepting deposits from the public.[136] To this end, the Act governs the establishment and financial soundness of banks, the security of the investments of depositors and the protection of the integrity of banks in the interest of the financial system.[137]

The approach of the Banks Act, it is said, is functional and not institutional. It addresses the function of deposit-taking rather than the institutions accepting deposits. The advantages of this approach are that various groups of banks are regulated by a single Act and that a more level "playing field" is created for the concerned institutions, thereby eliminating past inequalities and discrepancies in the regulation of these groups.[138]

Banks and the former building societies were the major deposit-taking institutions in South Africa in 1990 and were regulated on an institutional basis by the Banks Act 23 of 1965, the Mutual Building Societies Act 24 of 1965 and the Building Societies Act 82 of 1986. The Banks Act 1990 consolidated and revised the then existing legislation. Furthermore, it applies to all deposit-taking institutions which are registered as companies in terms of the Companies Act 61 of 1973. Mutual building societies, as they were then known, were excluded from the operation of the Act since they were not companies.[139]

The consolidation of the Banks Act and the Building Societies Act was a realistic step.[140] The business of banks and building societies were merged in recent years and the new Act established a basis for more equitable competition between them. The convergence of the business of banks and building societies was assisted by two factors, namely the conversion of large

---

[135] *See* the preamble to the Banks Act. For a review of the Act *see* Itzikowitz, "The Deposit-taking Institutions Act 94 of 1990: Its History and a Review of its Main Provisions", 4 *S.A. Merc. L.J.* 170 (1992); Oelofse, "The South African Deposit-taking Institutions Act 94 of 1990", *J.I.B.L.* 98 (1991); Malan & Faul, "Introduction to the Deposit-taking Institutions Act 94 of 1990", *T.S.A.R.* 379 (1991); Malan, "The Business of a Deposit-taking Institution", *T.S.A.R.* 561 (1991); Pienaar, "The Prudential Requirements of the Deposit-taking Institutions Act 94 of 1990", *T.S.A.R.* 475 (1992).

[136] *Memorandum on the Objects of the Banks Bill 1990* 111 (B116B–90(GA)).

[137] *Memorandum* 111.

[138] *Memorandum* 111.

[139] *Memorandum* 111.

[140] Malan, "Legal Aspects of the Regulation of Financial Institutions", *T.S.A.R.* 553 (1989).

mutual building societies into companies in terms of the Building Societies Act[141] and the establishment by building society control companies of banking subsidiaries to supplement their traditional services with banking services.[142] The merging of the activities of banks and building societies is a universal phenomenon and, elsewhere, the call for uniform regulation has also been made.[143] The changes described, however, brought about the virtual disappearance of the building society movement in South Africa.

"Building societies" today exist only in the form of mutual banks registered in terms of the Mutual Banks Act 1993. The two remaining permanent building societies were registered as "mutual banks" under this Act at the beginning of January 1994, and one of them is in the process of being reregistered as a bank under the Banks Act 1990.[144] The Mutual Banks Act 1993 introduces a supervisory regime for mutual banks similar to the system created by the Banks Act 1990. Mutual banks are not incorporated companies, but rather juristic persons established on the basis of mutual membership of investors to whom (non-equity) shares are issued.

An important newcomer is the Community Bank, provisionally registered as a mutual bank on 8 July 1994, which, like all mutual banks, focuses on the mobilisation of the savings and participation of lower-income communities.[145]

3.1 The prohibition of deposit-taking

What a bank is and what banking business entail are questions that have persistently troubled lawyers.[146] The United Kingdom Banking Act of 1979[147] did not define "bank" but instead focused on deposit-taking and the central role of the Bank of England in supervising banking institutions: "One of its [the Act's] functions is to give legal sanction to the *de facto* control that has been exercised in the past by tacit consent."[148] The passing of the Act was prompted by the First Banking Directive[149] and its object was

---

[141] Ch. 6 of the Building Societies Act.

[142] *Memorandum* 111.

[143] Llewellyn, "The Regulation of Building Societies: the Need for Overhaul", *Butterworths Journal of International Banking and Financial Law* 391, 393 (1990). For a discussion of the competition between banks, building societies and life insurers *see* Bank of Lisbon, "Competition for Savings between Banks, Building Societies and Life Insurers", *Economic Focus* (July 1990).

[144] South African Reserve Bank Bank Supervision Department, *Annual Report 1994* Appendix 12 at 84.

[145] *Debates of Parliament* col 12067-8 of 22 June 1993. For a discussion of the Community Bank *see* Itzikowitz, "Financial Institutions; Exchange Control", *Annual Banking Law Update 1994* 27.

[146] E. P. Ellinger & E. Lomnicka, *Modern Banking Law* 2ed (1994) 73 ff; G. A. Penn, A. M. Shea and A. AroraI, *The Law relating to Domestic Banking* (1987) 8 ff; *Paget's Law of Banking* 10ed (1989) by M. Hapgood 6 ff. For a review of recent evolutionary changes in U.K. banking *see* Blair, "Liberalisation and the Universal Banking Model: Regulation and Deregulation in the United Kingdom", in J. J. Norton, C. Cheng & I. Fletcher, *International Banking Regulation and Supervision: Change and Transformation in the 1990s* (1994) 81.

[147] R. R. Pennington, *Banking Supervision* (1989) 18 ff.

[148] F. R. Ryder, *The Banking Act 1979* (1979) 1.

[149] First Council Directive 77/780/EEC of 12.12.1977 on the Co-ordination of Laws, Regulations, and Administrative Provisions to the Taking Up and Pursuit of the Business of Credit Institutions. *See* Ellinger & Lomnicka 33.

the control of deposit-taking and the integrity of the banking system. This was achieved without defining "bank", but instead by regulating deposit-taking. Central to the Act is section 1(1), which prohibited a person, with certain exceptions, from accepting a deposit in the course of carrying on a business which is a deposit-taking business for the purposes of the Act. A business is a deposit-taking business if, in the course of the business, money received by way of deposit[150] is lent to others, or any other activity of the business is financed, wholly or to any material extent, out of the capital or interest of money received by way of deposit.[151]

The subsequent Banking Act of 1987 enacted substantially the same prohibition against conducting a deposit-taking business.[152] The Act does not define "bank" or "banking business" but provides for a system of authorisation and exemption.[153] "Deposit" and "deposit-taking business" are extensively defined[154] and, in addition, the Treasury is given far-reaching powers to amend the definitions.[155]

The South African Banks Act 1990 came into operation on 1 February 1991. The influence of United Kingdom legislation on the Act is at once apparent.[156]

Chapter I deals with the interpretation and application of the Act and contains definitions of the principal concepts. Two new definitions are of overriding importance, namely "deposit" and "the business of a bank".[157]

---

[150] s. 1.

[151] s. 1(2). *See* Ryder 37–38.

[152] s. 3(1).

[153] ss. 3 and 4.

[154] s. 5.

[155] s. 7.

[156] The Banks Act 1990 embodies some of the recommendations made in the main report of the commission of investigation into banking irregularities and contraventions of the Banks Act, 1965; *see* "Kommissie van Ondersoek na Sekere Moontlike Onreëlmatighede", *Hoofverslag* (RP 64/1989).

[157] Section 1(2) gives far-reaching powers to the Minister to amend the definitions of "deposit" and "the business of a bank". The subsection provides as follows: "(a) The Minister may, on the recommendation of the Registrar and after consultation with the Governor of the Reserve Bank, by regulation amend the definitions of 'deposit', and 'the business of a bank' for the purposes of the application of any of or all the provisions of this Act. (b) Every regulation made under paragraph (a) shall be of force and effect unless and until, during the session in which the relevant list has been laid upon the Tables in Parliament in accordance with the provisions of section 17 of the Interpretation Act, 1957 (Act 33 of 1957), every House of Parliament has by resolution disapproved of the regulation, in which event the regulation shall lapse as from a date to be specified in the resolution, but such lapsing of the regulation shall not affect the validity of anything done under such regulation before the date specified in the resolution, and nothing contained in this paragraph shall affect the power of the Minister to make a new regulation as to the subject matter of the regulation which has so lapsed." This subsection is based on s. 7 of the U.K. Banking Act of 1987 but the wording is not the same. R. R. Pennington, *Banking Supervision* (1989) 37–8 justifies this provision by stating that "[t]he rapid diversification of banking activities, particularly in the international financial markets, may well necessitate further reappraisal of these important definitions by the Treasury in the not too distant future". Whatever might have been the considerations leading to the adoption of these provisions, they are unacceptable and contrary to principles of parliamentary democracy. They should be repealed.

Registration as a bank is a prerequisite for conducting the business of a bank. A contravention of this provision is an offence.[158] These definitions are instrumental in bringing about more equitable competition by bringing deposit-taking institutions other than banks[159] into the ambit of the Act and provides a basis for identifying and controlling the conduct of unregistered persons. The definition of "the business of a bank" sets out the features of the business that is to be regulated. The two cardinal concepts, *viz.* "deposit"[160]

---

[158] ss. 11 and 91(4).

[159] Section 1 of the Banks Act 1965 defined "bank" and "banking institution". A "bank" was a person other than a discount house who carried on the business of a banking institution. "Banking institution" referred to a bank or a discount house. Under the present Banks Act discount houses are no longer distinguished from banks.

[160] A "deposit" in terms of s. 1(1) made under s. 1(2)(a) is "an amount of money paid by one person to another subject to an agreement in terms of which – (a) an equal amount or any part thereof will be conditionally or unconditionally repaid, with or without a premium, on demand or at specified or unspecified dates or in circumstances agreed to on or on behalf of the person making the payment and the person receiving it; and (b) no interest will be payable on the amount so paid or interest will be payable thereon at specified intervals or otherwise, notwithstanding that such payment is limited to a fixed amount or that a transferable or non-transferable certificate or other instrument providing for the repayment of such amount *mutatis mutandis* as contemplated in paragraph (a) or for the payment of interest on such amount *mutatis mutandis* as contemplated in paragraph (b) is issued in respect of such amount; but does not include a amount of money – (i) paid as an advance, or as part payment, in terms of a contract of the sale, letting and hiring or other provision of movable or immovable property or of services, and which is repayable only in the event of – (aa) that property or those services not in fact being sold, let and hired or otherwise provided; (bb) the fulfilment of a resolutive condition forming part of that contract; or (cc) the non-fulfilment of a suspensive condition forming part of that contract; (ii) paid as security for the performance of a contract or as security in respect of any loss which may result from the non-performance of a contract; (iii) without derogating from the provisions of paragraph (ii), paid as security of the delivery up or return of any movable or immovable property, whether in a particular state of repair or otherwise; (iv) paid by a holding company to its subsidiary, or by a subsidiary to its holding company, or by one subsidiary to another subsidiary of the same holding company; (v) paid by a person who, at the time of such payment – (aa) is a close relative of the person to whom such money is paid; (bb) is a director or executive officer of the person to whom such money is paid; or (cc) is a close relative of a director or executive officer of the person to whom such money is paid; (vi) paid by any person to a registered insurer as defined in section 1(1) of the Insurance Act, 1943, (Act No. 27 of 1943), as a premium in respect of any kind of policy defined or referred to in that section and under which policy that insurer assumes, in return for such premium, such an obligation as is described in that section in the definition of, or with reference to, the kind of policy in question; (vii) paid to a fund registered or provisionally registered under section 4 of the Pension Funds Act, 1956 (Act No. 24 of 1965), as a contribution contemplated in section 13A of that Act, by or on behalf of a member of that fund; or (viii) paid to a benefit fund, as defined in section 1 of the Income Tax Act, 1962 (Act No. 58 of 1962), as a contribution or a subscription by or on behalf of a member of that fund."

and "the business of a bank",[161] used in the Act are very widely defined and are not entirely satisfactory. They create uncertainty and could well

---

[161] "The business of a bank" means (s. 1(1)) "(a) the acceptance of deposits from the general public (including persons in the employ of the person so accepting deposits) as a regular feature of the business in question; (b) the soliciting of or advertising for deposits; (c) the utilization of money, or of the interest or other income earned on money, accepted by way of deposit as contemplated in paragraph (a) – (i) for the granting by any person, acting as lender in his own name or through the medium of a trust or a nominee, of loans to other persons; (ii) for investment by any person, acting as investor in his own name or through the medium of a trust or a nominee; or (iii) for the financing, wholly or to any material extent, by any person of any other business activity conducted by him in his own name or through the medium of a trust or a nominee; (d) the obtaining, as a regular feature of the business in question, of money through the sale of an asset, to any person other than a bank, subject to an agreement in terms of which the seller undertakes to purchase from the buyer at a future date the asset so sold or any other asset; (e) any other activity which the Registrar has, after consultation with the Governor of the Reserve Bank, by notice in the Gazette declared to be the business of a bank, but does not include – (aa) the acceptance of a deposit by a person who does not hold himself out as accepting deposits on a regular basis and who has not advertised for or solicited such deposit: Provided that – (i) the person accepting deposits as contemplated in this paragraph shall not at any time hold deposits for more than twenty persons or deposits amounting in the aggregate to more than R 500,000; (ii) a person and any person controlled directly or indirectly by him (whether such control is through shareholding or otherwise) or managed by him, and a subsidiary of such last-mentioned person, who accepts deposits as contemplated in this paragraph shall for the purposes of sub-paragraph (i) of this proviso be deemed to be one person; (bb) the borrowing of money from its members by a co-operative, subject to such conditions as may be prescribed; (cc) any activity of a public sector, governmental or other institution, or of any person or category of persons designated by the Registrar, with the approval of the Minister, by notice in the Gazette, provided such activity is performed in accordance with such conditions as the Registrar may with the approval of the Minister determine in the relevant notice; (dd) any activity contemplated in paragraph (a), (b) or (c) – (i) performed by any institution registered or established in terms of, by or under any other Act of Parliament and designated by the Minister by notice in the Gazette; or (ii) performed in terms of any scheme authorized and controlled by, and conducted in accordance with the provisions of, any other Act of Parliament so designated by the Minister, provided such activity is performed in accordance with such conditions as the Minister may determine in the relevant notice; (ee) the acceptance, subject to such conditions as the Registrar may from time to time determine by notice in the Gazette, of money against debentures, bills of exchange or promissory notes or other similar financial instruments, provided the money so accepted is not used, in the case of such acceptance of money by a person other than a bank, for the granting of money loans or credit (other than customary credit in respect of the sale of goods or the provision of services by the issuer of such financial instruments) to the general public; or (ff) the effecting, subject to the provisions of any other Act of Parliament and to such conditions as the Registrar may from time to time determine by notice in the Gazette, of a money lending transaction directly between a lender and a bank as borrower through the intermediation of a third party who does not act as a principal to the transaction (hereinafter in this paragraph referred to as the agent), provided the funds to be lent in terms of the money lending transaction are entrusted by the lender to the agent subject to a written contract of agency in which, in addition to any other terms thereof, at least the following matters shall be recorded: (i) confirmation by the lender that the agent acts as his agent; and (ii) that the lender assumes, except in so far as he may in law have a right of recovery against the agent, all risks connected with the administration by the agent of the funds entrusted to him by the lender, as well as the responsibility to ensure that the agent executes his instructions as recorded in the written contract of agency: Provided that, notwithstanding the preceding provisions of this paragraph, an agent – (i) is a natural or juristic person registered or

lead to expensive and unnecessary litigation. This is an area where the draftsman needs "[a] nice eye, a steady hand, and a sure judgment".[162] Unfortunately, the Act is defective in important respects.

Take one obvious example, the elaborate paragraph (c) in the definition of "the business of a bank" in section 1(1)(xxxvi). This business includes "the utilization of money, or of the interest or other income earned on money, accepted by way of deposit as contemplated in paragraph (a)(i) for the granting by any person, acting as lender in his own name or through the medium of a trust or a nominee, of loans to other persons; (ii) for investment by any person, acting as investor in his own name or through the medium of a trust or a nominee; or (iii) for the financing, wholly or to any material extent, by any person of any other business activity conducted by him in his own name or through the medium of a trust or a nominee". Paragraph (a), which will be referred to again, contains the principal provision concerning the acceptance of deposits from the general public: where a deposit is accepted from the general public, the business of a bank is conducted whether or not the money is utilised in any of the ways set out in so much detail in paragraph (c). Paragraph (c), one is forced to conclude, is entirely unnecessary.

Neither is the definition of "deposit" entirely acceptable. Under the old legislation "deposit" meant a loan for consumption.[163] In the Banks Act the word is defined without reference to a loan but "neutrally", in the sense that the type of transaction giving rise to the deposit is not characterised. A "deposit", if one leaves out the unnecessary elements in the definition,[164] means "money paid … . subject to an agreement in terms of which … . an equal amount or any part thereof will be repaid …" The rest of the definition is descriptive and at best merely indicates that the legislature intended to give a wide meaning to the word.[165]

Since the definition is wide, exceptions had to be provided for; but perhaps it would have been easier, and just as effective, to limit the meaning of "deposit" to loans for consumption and other transactions having substantially the same effect. Be that as it may, the width of the definition makes the exceptions important and shows how difficult it is to

---

Footnote 161 *cont'd*
established in terms of, by or under any other Act of Parliament and the main business activities of whom or of which are regulated or controlled in terms of, by or under such other Act of Parliament; and (ii) has been designated by the Registrar by notice in the Gazette, may, for the purposes of the effecting of the money lending transaction and subject to such conditions as the Registrar may determine in the relevant notice, pool the funds entrusted by the lender to such agent with funds entrusted to such agent by other lenders."

[162] G. Gilmore, "On the Difficulties of Codifying Commercial Law", *Yale Law Journal* 1341 (1948); D. V. Cowen & L. Gering, *The Law of Negotiable Instruments in South Africa* (1985) 141 n. 166.

[163] *Equitable Trust Insurance Co. of SA Ltd v. Registrar of Banks* 1957 2 S.A. 167 (T) and *see* Oelofse, "State Control of Banking Institutions in South Africa", *J.I.B.L.* 34 (1987). *Cf. Langford v. Moore* (1900) 17 S.C. 1, 18–19.

[164] s. 1(1)(x).

[165] *Cf. Equitable Trust Insurance Co. of SA Ltd v. Registrar of Banks* 1957 2 S.A. 167 (T) 168F–H.

comprehend all cases under one formula. Under the first exception (i) deposits and other payments accepted in terms of sales and leases would be excluded, as would payments for the provision of services, such as to an attorney[166] or a broker in terms of a short-term insurance contract. Although paragraph (aa) is formulated in an odd way, it was probably inserted because it is implied in all these contracts that the amount paid would be repaid if the contract is in fact not performed. The examples given in paragraphs (bb) and (cc) would seem to relate to matters such as deposits accepted under the terms of contracts for the sale of immovable property concluded subject to the condition that finance for the balance be obtained.

The second exception (ii) would apply, for example, to margin payments made to a futures broker and which are intended to cover the broker against losses in that very volatile market.[167] Performance deposits also fall within this exception.

The rather curious third exception (iii) probably refers to rental deposits, in the case of both movable and immovable property, to cover the lessor against breakage and other damage to the thing leased.

The fourth and fifth exceptions (iv) and (v) are somewhat misconceived and are discussed below.[168]

The sixth exception (vi) excludes from the definition of "deposit" an amount paid to an insurer registered in terms of the Insurance Act 27 of 1943 as a premium in respect of any policy of insurance defined or referred to in that Act. This exclusion is somewhat surprising since one would not ordinarily include in the term "deposit" premiums paid in respect of an insurance policy: premiums are not paid so that an "equal amount or any part thereof" be repaid; premiums and their policies, generally, serve other purposes. The exception thus gives the impression that premiums are indeed "deposits". The main objection to this provision is that one would have expected the legislature to uphold the validity of transactions under the Insurance Act (and other legislation) and not cast doubt on their legality.

The same objection applies to the seventh exception (vii) dealing with contributions to a fund registered under the Pension Funds Act 24 of 1956.

Paragraph (a) in the definition of "business of a bank" contains the essence of "deposit-taking". In a sense, paragraph (b), by referring to the soliciting and advertising for deposits merely contributes to define the business of "deposit-taking": it could well have provided that a person who solicits or advertises shall be rebuttably *presumed* to be conducting the business of a bank since a person advertising or soliciting for deposits is likely to conduct the business of accepting deposits from the general public.[169]

---

[166] In terms of s. 78 of the Attorneys Act 53 of 1979.

[167] Malan, "Gambling on the Future? Legal Aspects of the Futures Market", *T.S.A.R.* 577 (1990).

[168] Para. 6.

[169] *Cf. S v. Ostilly* 1977 2 S.A. 104 (D) 110E-F and *S v. Rosenthal* 1980 1 S.A. 65 (A) on the repealed Banks Act 23 of 1965.

To determine whether the acceptance of deposits is a "regular feature of the business" requires interpretation and it is clear that the definitions and concepts used to some extent overlap. In a judgment[170] dealing with the previous Banks Act it was said that "the latter business [*i.e.* the business of accepting deposits] can in appropriate circumstances still be carried on even if the deposits do not come from the general public, or their acceptance is not a regular feature of the business. It may, however, be uncertain or difficult to establish in those circumstances that such a business is actually being carried on". All this is relevant and probably also applies to paragraph (a). However, the crucial question is the meaning of "general public". This phrase is not defined. Tucked away in the definitions, one finds statements to the effect that "general public" does not include a bank[171] and that "public" includes a juristic person.[172] Neither of these is particularly helpful and both are somewhat surprising. One would have expected better guidance from the legislature. Of course, there is some help but again this assistance is misconceived. Rather than informing us what "public" and "general public" means, the legislature saw fit to limit the meaning of "deposit" by excluding from it deposits from persons who would not generally have been part of the "general public". A "deposit" is not a "deposit" if it is an amount of money (section 1(1)(x)(iv)) paid by a holding company to its subsidiary, or by a subsidiary to its holding company or by one subsidiary to another subsidiary of the same holding company or (v) paid by a person who, at the time of such payment – (aa) is a close relative of the person to whom such money is paid; (bb) is a director or executive officer of the person to whom such money is paid; or (cc) is a close relative of a director or executive officer of the person to whom such money is paid. One could well argue, subject to what is said below, that deposits made in the circumstances described are not made by the "general public". Central treasury operations, in particular, do not usually entail the acceptance of funds from the "general public". Absent from the exclusions are payments by a person who is a shareholder in, or member of, the person to whom the payment is made. Only directors or executive officers are exempted, not shareholders in companies or members of close corporations. What about the case where the depositor is a juristic person unable to be either director or executive officer? Unless "general public" is interpreted sensibly, joint ventures and similar undertakings where capital is provided by shareholders, members or partners could well run the risk of contravening the Banks Act. Absurd results could follow unless "general public" is given a realistic meaning. Both "general" and "public" must be

---

[170] *S v. Rosenthal* 1980 1 S.A. 65 (A) 80. "Business" is construed widely and includes anything which is an occupation or duty, rather than a leisure activity or hobby; Pennington 33; *Town Investments v. Department of Environment* [1977] 1 All. E.R. 813, 819.

[171] s. 1(1)(xvii).

[172] s. 1(1(xxviii).

interpreted, and it is submitted that not every person, whether a juristic person or not, is part of the general public:[173] the context and facts may exclude him.

The "business of a bank" also includes "the obtaining, as a regular feature of the business in question, of money through the sale of an asset, to any person other than a bank, subject to an agreement in terms of which the seller undertakes to purchase from the buyer at a future date the asset so sold or any other asset".[174] In the regulations issued under the terms of the Act[175] a "repurchase agreement" is defined as "the obtaining of money (which money shall for the purposes of these Regulations be deemed to have been so obtained by way of a loan) through the sale of an asset to any other person subject to an agreement in terms of which the seller undertakes to purchase from the buyer at a future date the asset so sold or any other asset issued by the issuer of, and which have been so issued subject to the same conditions regarding term, interest rate and price as, the asset so sold". These definitions appear to accept the validity of the repurchase agreement as structured by the parties: in other words, the Act is not concerned with simulated transactions but with genuine contracts having the same effect financially as a loan of money. It is clearly envisaged that the object sold consists of securities, but any other *res* can be the object of a repurchase agreement. It should also be noted that it is not necessary, in terms of the definitions, to effect transfer or registration of the article or securities sold. In this event, the so-called "hold in custody repose", the security afforded by the transaction, is greatly diminished. The effect of a repurchase agreement is that the seller obtains from the buyer funds for the period between the sale and the repurchase and that the object sold provide security for payment of the price. The difference between the two prices represents the interest cost.[176]

Certain activities are excluded from the "business of a bank". They are listed as paragraphs (aa) to (ff) under section 1(1)(xxxvi). These "exclusions" give rise to other uncertainties. Should they be interpreted as qualifications of the cases specified as falling under the "business of a bank" or are they inserted by way of instruction and example? It is not clear what was intended and, unfortunately, the wording is such that the meaning of some of the other definitions are obscured.

---

[173] *Cf. S v. Rossouw* 1971 3 S.A. 222 (T) 226 (and 1969 4 S.A. 504 (NC) 509) and the discussion in P. A. Delport, *Die verkryging van kapitaal in die Suid-Afrikaanse maatskappyereg met spesifieke verwysing na die aanbod van aandele aan die publiek* (1986, dissertation) 426 ff; J. T. Pretorius (ed.) *et. al., Hahlo's South African Company Law through the Cases, A Source Book* (1991) 133 ff. See also *R v. Delmayne* [1970] 2 Q.B. 170.

[174] s. 1(1)(xxxvi)(d).

[175] reg. 45: *Government Notice* R2509 (*Government Gazette* 15382) of 28.12.93. Section 78 further declares the following as undesirable practices: (1) "A bank (i) shall not conclude a repurchase agreement in respect of a fictitious asset or an asset created by means of a simulated transaction" and "(j) shall not purport to have concluded a repurchase agreement without – (i) such agreement being substantiated by a written document signed by the other party thereto; and (ii) the details of such agreement being recorded in the accounts of the bank as well as in the accounts, if any, kept by the bank in the name of such other party".

[176] Peat Marwick & McLintock, *KPMG International Handbook of Financial Instruments and Transactions* (1989) 65.

The first paragraph (aa) excludes from the "business of a bank" "*the acceptance of a deposit by a person who does not hold himself out as accepting deposits on a regular basis and who has not advertised for or solicited such deposit*". The distinction between "holding out", "soliciting" and "advertising" and the acceptance of deposits from the general public as "a regular feature of the business" is not self-evident. It seems that there cannot be a "holding-out" without some form of soliciting or advertising; if either soliciting or advertising is present, the acceptance of deposits is likely to be a "general feature of the business". Section 1(3)(a) of the English Act refers to "the person carrying it on does not hold himself out to accept deposits on a day to day basis" and this was interpreted to apply to a person "only if (by way of an express or implicit invitation) he holds himself out as being generally willing on any normal working day to accept such deposits from those persons to whom the invitation is addressed… "[177] This is not particularly helpful, but if one is to accept that "holding out" implies some or other kind of invitation, there would be very little scope for applying the exception in paragraph (aa) to a person whose conduct is already covered by paragraphs (a) and (b) of section 1(1)(xxxvi). However, this exception does not apply where the person accepting deposits as contemplated at any time holds deposits from more than twenty persons or deposits amounting in the aggregate to more than R 500,000.[178] This provision essentially re-enacts the repealed section 1(2A)(iii) which provided that a person shall not be deemed to be carrying on the business of accepting deposits in the circumstances mentioned. It would appear that the present provision was inserted in the Act as a matter of policy: it is necessary since it is quite conceivable that twenty persons or less constitutes the "general public". It is probably also for policy considerations that the amount of R 500, 000 has not been increased.

Paragraph (bb) re-enacts the exception in favour of co-operative societies.[179] Paragraph (cc) allows the Registrar to designate, with the

---

[177] *SCF Finance Co Ltd v. Masri (No. 2)* [1987] 1 All. E.R. 175, 190.

[178] s. 1(1)(xxxvi)(aa)(i). Subpara. (ii) provides that "a person and any person controlled directly or indirectly by him (whether such control is through shareholding or otherwise) or managed by him, and a subsidiary of such last-mentioned person, who accepts deposits as contemplated in this paragraph shall for the purposes of subparagraph (i) of this proviso be deemed to be one person".

[179] s. 1(3) of the Banks Act 23 of 1965. Reg. 46 of the *Regulations relating to Banks Government Notice* R2509 (*Government Gazette* 15382) of 28.12.93 sets out the conditions: "(a) No loan from any individual member shall amount to less than R 1,000, and for the purposes of this paragraph every successive loan from any particular member shall be regarded as a separate loan; (b) a loan shall not be repaid within 12 months after receipt; (c) the co-operative shall in respect of each loan issue an acknowledgment of debt; (d) every loan shall be negotiated on one or other of the following conditions which shall be recorded in the relevant acknowledgment of debt, namely – (i) that the member shall not have the right to demand repayment, but that the co-operative may, after it has held the loan for not less than 12 months, at any time repay such loan upon giving not less than 30 days' prior notice of its intention to repay such loan; or (ii) that the loan shall be repayable at a fixed date to be mentioned in the acknowledgment of debt, but that the board of directors of the co-operative shall have power to defer the repayment if the circumstances of the co-operative as at that date render such deferment necessary, subject to the condition that if the decision of such board is not confirmed at the first succeeding general meeting of the co-operative, the loan shall be repaid within seven days of the date of such meeting."

approval of the Minister, any activity of a public sector, governmental or other institution, or person or category of persons to be exempted, provided such activity is performed in accordance with such conditions as may be determined. The following activities have been exempted:

- The activities by or on behalf of the Teba Savings Fund which is administered by The Employment Bureau of Africa Limited subject to certain conditions.[180]
- Certain activities of mining houses.[181]
- The obtaining of funds by stockbrokers, financial instrument principals and financial instrument traders under the terms of agreements providing for the repurchase of loan stock.[182]
- The issue of commercial paper in accordance with the conditions prescribed.[183] This important exemption regulates comprehensively the issue of commercial paper, which is defined to include any written acknowledgment of debt as well as debentures by companies in terms of the Companies Act 1973.[184] Commercial paper may be issued to obtain operating capital only, and the proceeds may not be used to make loans to the general public.[185] It may be issued in minimum denominations of R 1 m and only by listed companies (*i.e.* companies listed on the Johannesburg Stock Exchange but excluding those listed in the Development or Venture Capital Sectors),[186] by companies having net assets of R 100 m or more, or other approved entities.[187] Instruments listed on a recognised financial exchange, endorsed by a bank, issued for periods of longer than five years or issued or guaranteed by the Central Government are exempted from the requirements set out in the Notice.[188] Commercial paper may be issued only in terms

---

[180] *Government Notice* 2167 (*Government Gazette* 16167) of 14.12.94. The Schedule provides that such activities "(a) are . . . performed solely for the purposes of the achievement of the objective of the said fund, namely the provision of a personal savings service and related services to employees in the mining industry and their beneficiaries; and (b) are authorised by and performed in accordance with the provisions of the Trust Deed of the Teba Savings Fund as approved by the Registrar of Banks and of Building Societies on 30 July 1990".

[181] *Government Notice* 2170 (*Government Gazette* 16167) of 14.12.94.

[182] *Government Notice* 2171 (*Government Gazette* 16167) of 14.12.94.

[183] *Government Notice* 2172 (*Government Gazette* 16167) of 14.12.94. These regulations and earlier ones were issued subsequent to the publication of a position paper by the South African Reserve Bank (Office for Deposit-taking Institutions), *Guidelines Regarding Commercial Paper and Debentures* (October 1991). The regulations give effect to the recommendations made in the position paper. It is believed that the South African market will closely follow developments in the U.K. market (on which *see* Mitchell, *The Sterling Commercial Paper Market* (1988); Peat Marwick & McLintock, *KPMG International Handbook of Financial Instruments and Transactions* (1989) 78 ff; P. Creswell, W. J. L. Blair, G. J. S. Hill & P. R. Wood, 3 *Encyclopedia of Banking Law* (1985) H44.83.

[184] reg. 1.

[185] reg. 4.

[186] reg. 1.

[187] reg. 3(1).

[188] reg. 3(1)A–E.

of a prospectus or placing document complying with certain requirements set in the public interest.[189]

- The activities of a group of persons between whom there exists a
common bond.[190] This exemption is a striking illustration of the rich
but checkered fabric of the South African population. The activities
designated are those that are typically performed by self-help organizations, credit unions, burial societies and the like: the regulation
refers to relief in times of adversity, the granting of annuities, payment
of money in cases of death or illness, the acquisition of land or movable
goods, building, insurance, payment on social occasions or dismissal,
etc.[191] Some of these societies and organisations are referred to as
"stokvels", and a National Stokvels Association of South Africa
(NASASA) to which they belong exists. The designated activities must
be performed by a group belonging either to NASASA or the Savings
and Credit Co-operative League of South Africa (SACCOL) or an approved self-regulatory body.[192] An exempted group must comply with
specific financial and other conditions.[193]

- Securitisation schemes.[194] Asset securitisation is a process whereby
illiquid assets and other receivables of a bank are transferred to a
"special-purpose institution" to sell them off in the form of negotiable
or other instruments. The acceptance by the special-purpose institution
of funds from the public in order to pay for these assets is exempted
from the provisions of the Banks Act subject to the conditions
specified.[195] Despite these enabling regulations, very little use has been
made of securitisation in South Africa to date.

Paragraph (dd) enables the Minister to designate for exemption by notice in
the *Gazette* any activity contemplated in section 1(1)(xxxvi)(a), (b) and (c)
and (i) performed by any institution registered or established in terms of
any scheme authorised or controlled by, and conducted in accordance with
the provisions of any other Act. The following designations have been
made under subparagraph (ii):

- The activities of the Kwazulu Finance and Investment Corporation
Limited.[196]

---

[189] reg. 5.
[190] *Government Notice* 2173 (*Government Gazette* 16167) of 14.12.94.
[191] reg. 2.
[192] reg. 3(c) and (d).
[193] reg. 3.
[194] *Government Notice* 153 (*Government Gazette* 13723) of 3.1.92.
[195] *Government Notice* 153 (*Government Gazette* 13723) of 3.1.92.
[196] *Government Notice* 2169 (*Government Gazette* 16167) of 14.12.94.

- The acceptance of money by a manager in terms of the Participation Bond Act 55 of 1981 subject to certain conditions.[197]
- The acceptance, utilisation or payment of money by a management company or trustee under the Unit Trusts Control Act 54 of 1981.[198]

Paragraph (ee) exempts from the description of the "business of a bank" the acceptance of money against debentures, bills of exchange, promissory notes or other similar financial instruments provided the money is not used, in the case of the acceptance of funds a person other than a bank, for granting money loans or credit (other than customary credit in respect of the sale of goods or provision of services by the issuer of the debentures) to the general public. A provision to this effect is necessary because the obtaining of funds from the public, whether by way of the issue of debentures or otherwise, in order to grant loans or credit to the public is essentially the business of banking. Some form of control appears to be called for.[199] Since it is not always possible to give a precise meaning to the word "debentures",[200] any control measures should also apply to certificates of deposit: there is no doubt that the issue of both involves the accepting of a "deposit" in terms of the Act.[201] The regulations dealing with the issue of commercial paper referred to provide the legal framework for the issue of all these instruments.

Excluded from the "business of a bank" by paragraph (ff) is the effecting of a money lending transaction directly between a bank and a lender through the intermediation of an agent, subject to a specified written agreement and compliance with other conditions.

---

[197] *Government Notice* 195 (*Government Gazett* 13003) of 31.01.91. The conditions are that "(a) the money so accepted is in fact invested for a period of not less than five years in such a participation bond or such participation bonds and remains, after the date of the expiration of the period for which it has been so invested, invested in that participation bond or participation bonds or is reinvested on behalf of the investor concerned in another participation bond or participation bonds included in the scheme, unless it is repaid in accordance with he provisions of the last-mentioned Act to the investor concerned; and (b) in the event of the debt secured by a participation bond in question being repaid in whole or in part by the mortgagor before the expiry of a period of five years from the said period of five years by such manager on behalf of the person first-mentioned in this Schedule upon the security of another participation bond or of other participation bonds included in the scheme in question and acceptable to such person, in accordance with the provisions of section 3(1)(b)(ii) of the last-mentioned Act".

[198] *Government Notice* 196 (*Government Gazett* 13003) of 31.01.91. The Schedule to this notice provides: "The acceptance, payment or utilisation by a – (a) management company registered as such in terms of section 4 of the Unit Trust Control Act, 1981 (Act 54 of 1981); (b) management company in property shares, registered as such a management company in terms of section 30 of the last-mentioned Act; or (c) trustee under a unit trust scheme, registered as such a trustee in terms of section 20 of the last-mentioned Act, of money in the course of and for the purposes of the management of carrying on a unit trust scheme as defined in section 1 of the last-mentioned Act."

[199] Peat Marwick & McLintock 177 ff; T. Prime, *International Bonds and Certificates of Deposit* (1990) 224 ff. *See* s. 79 for limitations of a *bank's* right to issue negotiable certificates of deposit, certain shares, debt instruments and share warrants.

[200] Delport 81 ff.

[201] s. 1(1)(x).

Section 2 of the Banks Act excludes from the application of the Act: the South African Reserve Bank; the Land and Agricultural Bank of South Africa; the Development Bank of Southern Africa; the Corporation for Public Deposits established under section 2 of the Corporation for Public Deposits Act, 1984 (Act No. 46 of 1984); Public Investment Commissioners referred to in section 2 of the Public Investment Commissioners Act, 1984 (Act No. 45 of 1984); a mutual bank; and an institution of body designated by the Minister. The Industrial Development Corporation of South Africa Limited[202] and the Post Office Savings Bank[203] have been so designated.

3.2 Control over banks

The power wielded by banks has always been controversial. Calls for their nationalisation have essentially been motivated by one major consideration only, *viz.* the unease of the political authority with the economic power of the banking industry: banks provide public or quasi-public services and should be both owned and controlled publicly.[204] The control of banking has been a much debated political subject in South Africa: the Freedom Charter of the African National Congress,[205] for example, provides that "[t]he mineral wealth beneath the soil, the banks and monopoly industry shall be transferred to the ownership of the people as a whole". Less specific are other statements,[206] but the debate has lost much of its force with the acceptance of the Constitution of the Republic of South Africa[207] with its entrenched bill of fundamental rights, including the right to property,[208] as well as by the acceptance, often unexpressed, of the principles of a free market economy. This is evidenced by an unexpected embracing of the discarded policies of privatisation of the previous government and has led to a realisation that banks, by remaining in private ownership, could assist in solving the country's social needs: forcing banks to provide banking services at uneconomic prices or in uneconomic locations, as a social service, would be incompatible with the needs of a dynamic and competitive economy.[209] The debate around control of banking institutions

---

[202] *Government Notice* 2169 (*Government Gazette* 16167) of 14.12.94.

[203] *Government Notice* 334 (*Government Gazette* 13744) of 24.01.92.

[204] L. Schuster, *Macht und Moral der Banken* (1977) 133 ff.

[205] As adopted by the ANC in 1955.

[206] § 6.2 *Draft ANC Economic Manifesto for National Conference 11–12 May 1991*: "Development finance institutions and private sector banks will also play an important role in mobilising resources to finance the reconstruction. A democratic government will need to restructure and rationalise the financial sector in order to develop new institutionalised arrangements. Consideration will be given to the establishment of new state and cooperative financial institutions, as well as the transformation of existing ones, to channel domestic and international finance to the critical development needs of the country." For an excellent review of the evolution the ANC policies *see* Lodge, "Context of the Policy Guidelines", 3 *Development and Democracy* 1 (1992) and J. J. Coetzer, *Regsaspekte van beheer oor banke* (LL.M. dissertation, Rand Afrikaans University, 1993) 50 ff.

[207] Act 200 of 1993.

[208] s. 28.

[209] For some aspects of the debate *see The Star* of 13.06.91.

therefore no longer centres on nationalisation or its threat, but rather, on control in a legal and economic sense. This is what the Banks Act addresses; as such its philosophy is:[210]

(1) to prevent the exercising of control, through a majority shareholding, over the affairs of a bank by any one person that is not another bank or a registered controlling company, or by such person and his associates;
(2) to prevent the exercising of control by any one person or by any one person and his associates, through a majority shareholding, over a registered controlling company;
(3) to provide for the registration and cancellation of the registration, of a controlling company; and
(4) to provide for the approval of shareholdings in excess of 10 per cent in banks or controlling companies, and of further increases in such shareholdings, by any one person or by any one person and his associates... .

The aspect underlying these principles "is that a bank should not to be influenced or manipulated for the benefit of a controlling shareholder or his associates, but should be able to fulfil an independent deposit-taking and financial intermediary function in the interest of all shareholders and depositors and an efficiently functioning banking and overall financial system. Given the powerful financial groupings in South Africa, a bank should, in order to retain its independent status, not be controlled by any group, whether through shareholding or otherwise."

Clearly, a banking system along these lines can only function within a free market economy and, in this respect, the Act continues the approach set forth in previous legislation.[211]

Central to the control of ownership in banks is the prohibition[212] against nominee shareholders in banks and bank controlling companies. By requiring shares to be registered in the name of the beneficial shareholder the supervising authority can monitor ownership and control over banks. Any increase in the holdings of a shareholder is subject to approval of the supervising authority: the Act provides for the incremental increase of shareholdings in banks and bank controlling companies in stages exceeding 15 per cent, 24 per cent, 49 per cent and 74 per cent after the shareholder has held the shares in question for a specified time.[213] Although this provision is

---

[210] *Memorandum* published with the Banks Bill 1990 115–117.
[211] *Die Monetêre Stelsel en Monetêre Beleid in Suid-Afrika Finale Verslag van die Kommissie van Ondersoek na die Monetêre Stelsel en Monetêre Beleid in Suid-Afrika* RP 70/1984 §§ 48 ff.
[212] s. 38(1).
[213] s. 37(1) and (2). Section 37 has been amended extensively after several cases involved in the Saambou takeover by an insurance company. *See Nuwe Suid-Afrikaanse Prinsipale Beleggings (Eiendoms) Beperk and others v. Saambou Holdings Limited and others* 1992 4 S.A. 387 (W); *Nuwe Suid-Afrikaanse Prinsipale Beleggings (Eiendoms) Beperk and others v. Saambou Holdings Limited* 1992 4 S.A. 676 (W); *Nuwe Suid-Afrikaanse Prinsipale Beleggings (Edms) Bpk and v. Sloet and others* 1992 4 S.A. 381 (T). The matter is discussed by Itzikowitz, "Financial Institutions and Stock Exchanges", *Annual Survey of South African Law* 319, 342 ff (1992) and by F. R. Malan & M. Larkin, "Control of Banks", *Seminar on the Banks Act 94 of 1990* presented by the Research Unit for Banking Law Rand Afrikaans University Johannesburg on 19 September 1991.

said to ensure that "only fit and proper persons become large shareholders and to prevent the exercising of undue influence on the affairs of a bank or controlling company",[214] Schutz J in *Nuwe Suid-Afrikaanse Beleggings Bpk and another v. Saambou Holdings Ltd and others*,[215] however, found this to be an "unconvincing argument":[216] "How does one judge the performance of a four percenter, or even a twelve percenter? Or ... is there to be an assessment as to whether the applicant has been behaving in an 'unshareholderly way'?" He added:[217]

It seems to me to be very unlikely that Parliament could have intended to link the judgment of applicants to mere shareholdings, sometimes quite small, or even minimal, for a substantial period. What does one say about the person who does not attend meetings, who sends in his proxy in favour of the chairman, and receives his dividends graciously? Surely there are other better ways of judging an aspirant, particularly by inquiring into his other activities, that is other than his being a shareholder in the institution.

One could well quarrel with this: the Second Banking Directive[218] defines a "qualifying holding" as "a direct or indirect holding in an undertaking which represents 10 per cent or more of the capital or of the voting rights or which makes it possible to exercise a significant influence over the management of the undertaking in which a holding subsists." These "qualifying holdings" must be approved by the supervising authorities. It is true that the EU Directive refers not only to a person's shareholding but also to his voting rights or influence over the management of the undertaking. Nevertheless, increases exceeding certain percentages in shareholdings must be notified to the competent authorities so as to enable them to assess "any major shareholder of a credit institution or any inappropriate group structure that could be unsuitable to safe and sound banking management".[219] Surely, the question is not how the performance of a "four percenter" or even a "twelve percenter" should be judged, but whether they have misused their powers or influence as shareholders. One has to concede, of course, that a literal interpretation of the Act can lead to some absurdities, but this does not mean that the provision made for an "incremental increase" in shareholding is meaningless. Amendments subsequent to the these judgments have removed some of the difficulties in interpretation but not all.

---

[214] *Memorandum* 117–119. *Cf.* Aronstam, *Annual Survey of South African Law* 361–2 (1976); Fourie & Butler, "Beperking op die Registrasie van Bankaandele", *Moderne Besigheidsreg* 118 (1984); *Boland Bank Bpk v. Pickfoods Bpk en andere* 1987 4 S.A. 615 (A) *per* Smalberger AJ 635–6.

[215] 1992 4 S.A. 696 (W) 708.

[216] At 36.

[217] At 37.

[218] Article 1 No. 10 Second Council Directive 89/646/EEC of 15.12.89 in Dassesse, Isaacs & Penn 437 ff. *See* Gruson & Feuring, "The New Banking Law of the European Banking Community", 25 *The International Lawyer* 1, 11–13 (1991).

[219] Gruson & Feuring 12; Norton, "The European Community Banking Law Paradigm: A Paradox in Bank Regulation and Supervision – Reflections on the EC Second Banking Directive", in J. J. Norton, C. Cheng & I. Fletcher (eds.), *International Banking Regulation and Supervision: Change and Transformation in the 1990s* (1994) 49, 71–2.

3.3 Directors

The prime responsibility for monitoring the risks inherent in banking lies on management who account to the board of directors who have the main supervisory function over the way in which risks are managed.[220] The directors are indeed, following the Cadbury and King Reports,[221] required to report annually to the Registrar on the effectiveness of the system of internal controls relating to financial and regulatory reporting and compliance with the Banks Act and regulations:[222] they should be aware of the risks inherent in banking and should ensure that they are managed in a prudent manner.[223]

Directors guide and control enterprises. They stand at the very heart of a corporation and the growth of the power and control of directors has steadily diminished the influence of shareholders.[224] The power of directors, if exercised capriciously, threatens all interested parties, employees, shareholders, creditors and the like. The failure by bank directors to observe their customary duties entails dire consequences for the bank and its shareholders and depositors. For these reasons the legislature has anticipated[225] events by introducing in the Banks Act precise measures outlining, albeit in general terms, the duties incumbent on bank directors. Some of these duties merely restate the common law, others perhaps are somewhat wider. It is expressly recognised that every director of a bank and a bank controlling company stands in a fiduciary relationship to the bank or controlling company.[226] This provision, confirming the common law position, is expanded upon: the expression "fiduciary relationship" implies that the director act towards the bank or controlling company "honestly and in good faith" and, in particular, that he manages or represents the bank or controlling company "exclusively in the best interests and for the benefit of the bank and its depositors" or of the controlling company.[227] In addition, every director has to comply with the guidelines and requirements set under the terms of the Banks Act.[228]

No more than 49 per cent of the directors of a bank or a controlling company may be employees of that bank or that controlling company or

---

[220] Pienaar, "The Prudential Requirements of the Deposit-taking Institutions Act 94 of 1990", *T.S.A.R.* 475, 476–7 (1992).

[221] Ch. 13: *The King Report on Corporate Governance* published by the Institute of Directors of Southern Africa (1994) 55.

[222] reg. 37(5).

[223] reg. 37(3).

[224] A. A. Berle and G. C. Means, *The Modern Corporation and Private Property* 3ed (1991) 244.

[225] Notably *The King Report on Corporate Governance* (1994). This report goes further than the Cadbury Report (*Report of the Committee on the Financial Aspects of Corporate Governance* (1992)) in that it seeks to address just about all aspects of corporate governance and not only financial matters. *See* Du Plessis, "Corporate Governance and the Cadbury Report", 6 *S.A. Merc. L.J.* 81 (1994).

[226] s. 60(1).

[227] s. 60(2)(a).

[228] s. 60(2)(b).

their subsidiaries and they may not exercise more than 49 per cent of the vote of all the directors.[229] At least two directors have to be employees.[230]

Although the Registrar is not required to approve the appointment of directors,[231] the prescribed information relating to the proposed directors must be furnished to him before the appointment is made,[232] and the appointment will become effective only when the prescribed information has been furnished.[233] An extensive statement[234] relating to serving or prospective directors as well as executive officers must be given to the supervising authorities, the purpose of which is undoubtedly to determine whether they are fit and proper for the position. Although his consent is not a requirement,[235] the Registrar's view of the suitability of a candidate will obviously be decisive. In determining whether a particular person is fit and proper to hold office as director or executive officer of a bank or a controlling company the Registrar is required to have regard to the general probity of the person, his competence for and soundness of judgment in fulfilling the responsibilities of this office and the diligence with which he is likely to perform his duties.[236] The Registrar may have regard to the previous business and financial conduct and activities of the person and, in particular, to evidence of any offences committed by him or of other specified improper conduct.[237]

The guidelines issued under the Banks Act[238] call upon directors and executive officers to have a basic understanding and knowledge of the business of banking and the laws and customs that govern it. Of course, not every director need be fully conversant with all aspects of banking, but the competence of a director must be commensurate with the nature and scale of the business conducted by that bank or controlling company.[239] A director or an executive officer must perform his functions with diligence and care and with the degree of competence "as can reasonably be expected from a person with his knowledge and experience".[240] They must also ensure that, in view of the public nature of the funds deposited, the risks involved will be managed in a prudent manner.[241] Specific mention is made of the kinds of risk associated with banking; *viz.* the solvency, liquidity, credit, currency, market or position, interest-rate, counterparty, technological and operational risks.[242] The directors are required to report

---

[229] s. 60(3).
[230] reg. 38.
[231] s. 60(6).
[232] s. 60(5)(a).
[233] s. 60(5)(b).
[234] reg. 39.
[235] s. 60(6).
[236] s. 1(1A)(a) (i), (ii) and (iii).
[237] s. 1(1A)(b)(i)–(v).
[238] reg. 37.
[239] reg. 37(1).
[240] reg. 37(2).
[241] reg. 37(3).
[242] reg. 37(4).

annually on the effectiveness of the system of internal controls relating to financial and regulatory reporting and compliance with the Act and regulations.[243]

These guidelines add very little to the common law duties of directors: indeed, for the greater part, they merely confirm them. However, without venturing into this complex field,[244] the question may be put whether the legislature has not indeed created a duty towards creditors, the depositors of a bank, in elaborating the concept of a "fiduciary relationship" in section 60(2)(a)?[245]

4 PRUDENTIAL REQUIREMENTS

The prudential requirements banks must adhere to follow very closely the guidelines set by the Basle Committee on Banking Supervision, and they can be reviewed under the following four headings:[246] capital adequacy, liquid assets, large exposures, the scope of banking activity and market-related risks.

4.1 Capital adequacy

Section 70(2) requires a bank to manage its affairs in such a way that the sum of its issued primary and secondary share capital and its primary and secondary unimpaired reserve funds in the Republic does not amount to less than the greater of either (a) R 50,000,000 (or R 1,000,000 for institutions existing at the time of commencement of the Act) or (b) an amount which represents a prescribed percentage of the sum of amounts calculated by multiplying the average of the amounts of such different categories of assets and other risk exposures in the conduct of its business, as may be prescribed by the risk weights, expressed as percentages, for the different categories of assets and risk exposures.

The "primary share capital" is the capital obtained through the issue of ordinary shares or non-redeemable non-cumulative preference shares.[247] "Secondary share capital" consists of a prescribed percentage of capital obtained through the issue of (a) cumulative preference shares, (b) ordinary or non-cumulative preference shares issued in pursuance of the capital-isation of reserves as a result of a revaluation of assets and (c) certain

---

[243] reg. 37(5).

[244] *e.g.* Sealy, "Directors' 'Wider' Responsibilities – Problems Conceptual, Practical, and Procedural", 13 *Monash University Law Review* 164 (1987); J. T. Pretorius *et. al., Hahlo's Company Law through the Cases* (1991) 376 ff and Botha, "Die plig van direkteure teenoor maatskappyskuldeisers", 4 *S.A. Merc. L.J.* 25 (1992).

[245] Du Plessis, "The Duties of Directors with special reference to Deposit-taking Institutions", *T.S.A.R.* 56 (1993).

[246] Pienaar, "The Prudential Requirements of the Deposit-taking Institutions Act 94 of 1990", *T.S.A.R.* 477 (1992) has made a very useful comparison of the Basle guidelines and the Banks Act.

[247] s. 70(1).

categories of debt instruments.[248] Thus, in accordance with the Basle recommendations, loan capital also ranks as capital.[249] "Primary" and "secondary" "unimpaired reserve funds" are separately defined.[250]

The sum of the primary and secondary share capital and primary and secondary unimpaired reserves is calculated by deducting from the total thereof certain amounts, the most important of which are the depreciation of assets and bad and doubtful debts, operating and accumulated losses, establishment and other costs, assets pledged or encumbered, shares or debt instruments issued by another bank and the amount made available by the bank for the permanent funding of its foreign branches.[251]

To make the calculations for the purposes of paragraph (b) of section 70(2) the regulations promulgated under the terms of the Act must be referred to. The regulations identify a number of asset and risk exposure categories and a certain risk percentage is allocated to each category.[252] A bank must have a share capital and unimpaired reserves which are at least equal to the prescribed percentage of the bank's assets and other risk exposures. The percentage of the amount of a bank's assets and other risk exposures which is to be used to calculate the minimum share capital and unimpaired reserve funds which a bank has to maintain has varied from time to time but was increased from 7 per cent on 21 January 1994 and 8 per cent on 20 January 1995.[253]

4.2 Minimum reserve balance and liquid assets

Whereas the capital requirements of a bank, which act as a cushion to absorb losses should the risks to which banks are exposed materialise,[254] are measured against a bank's assets in the form of its credit granting commitments, the minimum reserve balance and liquid assets requirements do not guard against the solvency risk but against the liquidity risk facing a bank.[255] A bank is required to hold minimum reserve balances with the

---

[248] s. 70(1). In terms of reg. 23(4A) the percentages are respectively 100 for cumulative preference shares, 50 for cumulative shares issued in pursuance of the capitalisation of reserves resulting from a revaluation of assets, 50 for ordinary and non-cumulative preference shares. The debt instruments have to comply with certain requirements, *inter alia* be issued for a period of no less than 5 years; redeemable prior to maturity only with the approval of the Registrar and be subordinated in the event of a liquidation to the claims of other creditors (para. (i), (ii) and (iii) of s. 70(1) "secondary share capital" and reg. 23(5). A subordination agreement is valid and enforceable; *see Ex parte De Villiers & another NNO: in re Carbon Developments (Pty) Ltd (in liquidation)* 1993 1 S.A. 493 (AD) which dispels earlier doubts.

[249] Basle Committee, *International Convergence of Capital Measurement and Capital Standards* (July 1988) paras. 22 and 23.

[250] s. 70(1) and (4) as amended by s. 45 of Act 26 of 1994.

[251] s. 70(5).

[252] reg. 23(p) makes provision for six categories of risk weightings (0, 5, 10, 20, 50, and 100 per cent) which follow very closely the Basle framework (*International Convergence of Capital Measurement and Capital Standards* section 4 and annex 2). The same applies to reporting on off-balance sheet activities (reg. 44(4) and section II(vi) and annex III of the *International Convergence of Capital Measurement and Capital Standards*).

[253] reg. 23(4).

[254] Pienaar 478.

[255] Pienaar 480.

Reserve Bank[256] as well as minimum liquid assets in the Republic in a prescribed percentage.[257]

4.3 Large exposures

The Banks Act, in introducing measures to supervise risk exposures, takes the view that exposures to a customer should not normally exceed 10 per cent[258] of a bank's capital base. If they do, they should be thoroughly examined and provision is made for the approval either by the board of directors or of a committee of which one director who is not an employee of the bank or a subsidiary or the holding company is a member.[259] Exposures in excess of 25 per cent[260] of a bank's capital base should be reported to the supervising authority.[261] The exposures relate to credit risk involving not only one person but also two or more related or interconnected persons.[262]

4.4 Scope of banking activities

Two aspects are of concern here: first, the issue whether banks should be engaged in operations beyond the traditional deposit banking activities and, secondly, whether banks should not be controlled in the sense that the economic power which they wield be restricted or limited.[263] Both questions involve considerations of policy which, at the time of writing, have not quite been resolved.

The holdings of banks in insurance companies are restricted, unless the approval has been obtained, to 49 per cent of the shares in a registered insurer,[264] while bank controlling companies may not invest more than 40 per cent of their capital and reserves in undertakings other than banks or property used mainly to conduct banking business.[265] The amounts a bank may invest in immovable property, whether directly or through subsidiaries, is also limited. These amounts may not exceed the amount of its issued primary and secondary share capital and primary and secondary

---

[256] s. 10A of the South African Reserve Bank Act. 1989 (Act No. 90 of 1989).

[257] s. 72. *See Government Notice* R1537 (*Government Gazette* 15060) of 12.8.93.

[258] reg. 30(1)(a) and *see* the discussion in Dassesse, Isaacs & Penn 199 ff and their discussion of Directive 92/121/EEC of 21.12.92 (Appendix M).

[259] s. 73(1).

[260] reg. 30(1)(b).

[261] s. 73(2).

[262] s. 73(3)(b) refers to two or more persons "the respective exposures to whom are to be regarded as a single exposure because of the fact that they are so interconnected that should one of them experience financial difficulties, another one or all of them would be likely to experience a lack of liquidity". This description probably excludes exposures due to the same geographical or country risk. *Cf.* Pienaar 483–4 and *see* Basle Committee, *Large Exposures* (January 1991) para. IV, 13.

[263] Pienaar 484 and *see* Van Zyl, "Regulering van tradisionele en nie-tradisionele bankaktiwiteite", 1 *S.A. Merc. L.J.* 334 (1989) and 2 *S.A. Merc. L.J.* 17 (1990).

[264] s. 80(3).

[265] s. 50.

unimpaired reserve funds (plus any surplus resulting from a revaluation of assets and which does not qualify as secondary unimpaired reserves).[266]

More important, however, is the evolution of banking activities in the past few years. The Stock Exchanges Control Act 1 of 1985 in the past drew a firm line between banking and broking or investment services. Generally, the business of buying and selling listed securities on behalf of others or on own account was reserved for stockbrokers.[267] The activities of the then merchant banks (and subsequently all the banks) were restricted to buying and selling securities to give effect to a reconstruction, a take-over or on behalf of clients whose funds were administered by the merchant bank.[268] Of course, this could not be tolerated indefinitely, and in 1993[269] the Stock Exchanges Control Act was amended to provide for the admission of derivative broking members to the Johannesburg Stock Exchange. This amendment permitted the admission of natural persons or corporate bodies to restricted membership of the Exchange provided that the person or body corporate is a member of a financial exchange[270] and meets the admission and capital adequacy requirements of the Johannesburg Stock Exchange. The person or body so admitted will be restricted to buying and selling securities specified from time to time in order to manage their risks arising from the creation of financial instruments listed on other exchanges. These "derivative broking members" are allowed to act only as principals. The purpose of the amending Act was to improve liquidity in the equity market and to provide derivative traders, mostly banks, with a cost-effective method of hedging their own trading positions. Derivative members are now able to offset their own positions in the futures and derivatives markets by trading in equities listed on the Johannesburg Stock Exchange. Implementation of this amendment required an amendment of the rules of the Johannesburg Stock Exchange.[271] This was obviously not enough to satisfy the banks and other major financial players and, after publication of the Katz Report in 1994,[272] matters came to a head, and legislation is at present awaited opening the Johannesburg Stock Exchange to banks, as well as foreign broking firms, and allowing dual capacity trading, as well as negotiated commissions.[273] Despite noises to the contrary no fundamental legal principle, but only hard bargaining, seems to have been involved in the change.

---

[266] s. 76(1). Other restrictions on bank activities are contained in ss. 77 and 78.

[267] s. 3 Stock Exchanges Control Act 1 of 1985.

[268] s. 3(2)(c).

[269] Act 104 of 1993.

[270] An exchange licensed in terms of the Financial Markets Control Act 55 of 1989.

[271] *Government Notice* 179 (*Government Gazette* 15529) of 4.3.94.

[272] Johannesburg Stock Exchange, *Report of the Research Sub-Committee on the Future Structure of the Johannesburg Stock Exchange* (April 1994).

[273] *Weekend Star* 8–9 April 1994.

These developments will lead to South African banks becoming more "universal",[274] although perhaps not to the same extent as in Germany.[275] A related development is the introduction of capital adequacy requirements for members of the recognised stock, futures and bond exchanges which could lead to banks being subject to two different regulatory regimes.[276]

5 SOME CONCLUSIONS

The 1990s has been a period of liberalisation and deregulation of the South African banking and financial markets, which has led to the virtual disappearance of some of the traditional institutions and the blurring of boundaries between others. Building societies came to be absorbed by the major banks and the few that remained have been converted into mutual banks. The different classes of banks such as merchant banks, commercial banks and discount houses disappeared with one decisive legislative measure. With the passing of the Banks Act 94 of 1990 all deposit-taking institutions were subjected to the same regulatory regime which did away with artificial institutional boundaries and addressed the function of deposit-taking regardless of the institution involved. Most of the changes were caused by fundamental movements in the financial markets but also coincided with the political emancipation of South Africa and the acceptance of a Constitution which guarantees not only fundamental rights but also the independence of the Central Bank. The amendments of banking laws echo adjustments elsewhere and inspiration for the new legislation often came from Rome or Basle. Initially, however, the Banking Act of 1987, with its accent on deposit-taking, served as the model. In this way, principles reflected in the First Banking Directive were introduced into South African legislation. But the Banks Act of 1990 is also evidence of the profound influence of the Basle guidelines and pronouncements. The transmission[277] or "reception" of the Basle standards for prudential supervision in South African legislation has been practically immediate and often direct and accompanied by explicit references to Basle principles. This trend will no doubt continue and Basle will continue to be the dominating influence in the forging of the South African law of bank regulation. Another tendency, however, is also noticeable: the growing importance of the European

---

[274] Van Zyl, "Regulering van tradisionele en nie-tradisionele bankaktiwiteite", 1 *S.A. Merc. L.J.* 334 (1989) and 2 *S.A. Merc. L.J.* 17 (1990).

[275] Sandrock & Klausing, "Germany. The System of Universal Banking", in R. Cranston (ed.), *European Banking Law, The Banker Customer Relationship* (1993) 61.

[276] The Financial Services Board is at present considering the introduction of capital adequacy requirements based on Council Directives 93/6/EEC of 15.3.1993 (Appendix J to Dassesse, Isaacs & Penn 507) and 93/22/EEC of 10.5.93 on the capital adequacy requirements of investment firms and credit institutions.

[277] Norton, *Standards* 255 ff.

Directives both as a "transmitter' of Basle principles and as an independent source for comparative purposes. The more formal and "legal" nature of the Directives will lead to their increasing importance as a tool for law reform and perhaps as a model for the development of legal institutions beyond the borders of the European Union. Such models prosper best in a comparable social and economic climate.

15. The EEC Directive on Consumer Credit: A Model for Southern Africa?

J. M. Otto[1]

1 INTRODUCTION

Consumer protection will remain a topical issue for as long as complaining consumers, loan sharks in the consumer field and politicians with seemingly well-intended ideals of community protection (often accompanied by motives of self-interest), roam the earth. Consumer protection in various guises is an ongoing saga and consumer credit is no exception. New forms of credit, the ingenuity of the credit industry and the rise of atypical contracts such as the financial lease have all contributed to a dynamic jurisprudence.

There have, of course, always been common law rules protecting consumers of credit. Examples are prohibitions on usurious interest and warranties against defects in goods. Some of the common law forms of protection were effectively annulled or paralysed by a well-known phenomenon called the standard form contract. These contracts invariably excluded or limited common law protection: warranties were excluded,[2] creditors were exempted from liability for misrepresentations and onerous terms were the order of the day.[3] Even provisions authorising self-help by allowing creditors to enter premises and attach goods without a court order were not uncommon.[4] One-sided provisions such as penalty clauses, acceleration clauses, certificate-of-indebtedness clauses and clauses dealing with the jurisdiction of courts favouring creditors were, and still are, common in credit agreements.[5] It is not surprising, therefore, that

---

[1] LL.D., Professor of Mercantile Law, Rand Afrikaans University, Johannesburg.

[2] M. A. Diemont and P. J. Aronstam, *The Law of Credit Agreements and Hire-Purchase in South Africa* (1982) 31; Thornely, "Hire-Purchase Hardships and Hopes", 20 *Cambridge L.J. (C.L.J.)* 43 (1962); Terry, "Consumer Protection Conspicuously Absent", *New Zealand L.J.* 18 (1976); R. A. Hesse, *Consumer Credit 1976; the Anatomy of the Credit Transaction* (1976) 39 ff.

[3] Diemont and Aronstam, *supra*, at 32.

[4] Hicks "A Review of Some Aspects of the Nigerian Law of Consumer Credit", 9 *Nigerian L.J.* 38 (1975). Cf. also Thornely, *supra*, at 43.

[5] *See* J. M. Otto and N. J. Grové, *The Usury Act and Related Matters*, Working Paper 46 of the South African Law Commission (1993) (hereafter *Working Paper 46*) 275; 278; 340; 352.

legislators world-wide took steps to protect their citizens. Initially, credit legislation dealt mainly with money lending transactions and hire-purchase transactions, and usually did so by different legislative means. New forms of credit such as home improvement schemes and the rendering of services on instalments became increasingly popular. The obvious course for legislators to embark upon was to (accept and) pass a single credit Act dealing with the various forms of consumer credit in one instrument. This would prevent fragmentation of legislation,[6] the "regulation of transactions according to their form instead of according to their substance and function"[7] and the situation where credit contracts and the parties thereto were for no logical reason[8] treated differently by different legislative instruments.[9] The modern trend is to replace many Acts with a single credit Act, where possible, dealing with the different forms of consumer credit.[10] Indeed, it was, and still is, a movement in many countries "vom Abzahlungskauf zum Konsumentenkredit".[11]

Statutory protection of consumers reached a pinnacle during the 1960s. The interest in consumer protection and the legal activities in this regard were closely related to the economic prosperity of the time.[12] The next decade did not produce as much activity in all countries and the 1980s can indeed be seen as a period of retrogression.[13] South Africa reached its high water mark in the early 1980s when various Acts were passed in the field of consumer credit.[14] Europe experienced some preparatory work in the 1970s and the 1980s and new legislation was passed in various countries at the beginning of the last decade of this century.[15] This was due to the EEC (as it was called at the time) Directive on consumer credit[16] which is discussed below.

---

[6] Which can lead to malpractices and evasion. N. Reich and H-W. Micklitz, *Consumer Legislation in the Federal Republic of Germany* (1981) 324.

[7] R. M. Goode, *Consumer Credit Law* (1989) 8.

[8] N. J. H. Huls, *Wet op het Consumentenkrediet* (1993) 16.

[9] *Cf.* the *Crowther report* (*Consumer Credit Report of the Committee*, Cmnd. 4596, chairman Lord Crowther (1971) para. 4.2.4.

[10] *See* R. M. Goode, *Consumer Credit Law* 13; the Law Reform Commission of Victoria, *Deregulation of Hire-Purchase* (1986) 1–2.

[11] "From instalment sale to consumer credit". Stauder, "Vom Abzahlungskauf zum Konsumentenkredit", 13 *Zeitschrift für Rechtspolitik* 217 (1980).

[12] Belobaba, "The Development of Consumer Protection Legislation: 1945 to 1984" in I. Bernier and A. Lajoie, *Consumer Protection, Environmental Law and Corporate Power* (1985) 6.

[13] *Cf.* Belobaba, *supra*, 4; G. Borrie, *The Development of Consumer Law and Policy – Bold Spirits and Timorous Souls*, Hamly Lectures, no. 36 (1984) 2.

[14] Notably the Credit Agreements Act 75 of 1980; the amendments to the Usury Act 73 of 1968 by an amendment Act of 1980 that was more voluminous than the main Act itself; the Lay-By Regulations of 1980 and the Alienation of Land Act 68 of 1981 which, amongst other things, protects the purchasers of residential land on instalments in many ways.

[15] *See* F. Graph von Westphalen *et al.*, *Verbraucherkreditgesetz Kommentar* (1991) 13 ff.

[16] Council Directive 87/102/EEC of 22 December 1986 as amended by Council Directive 90/88/EEC of 22 February 1990. An English text of the Directive can be found in A. G. Guest and M. G. Lloyd, *Encyclopedia of Consumer Credit Law* (1975 *et seq.*) 9015 and a German text in P. Seibert, *Handbuch zum Gesetz über Verbraucherkredite* (1991) 92.

2 SIMILAR LEGISLATION IN THE SAME REGION

2.1 The European Union

There are so many obvious reasons for, and advantages of, uniform or comparable legal rules to apply in the same region, continent or sub-continent that they need hardly be stated. The EEC Directive on consumer credit provides a long list of reasons in its preamble for the need for uniformity in consumer credit legislation. Among the reasons are that differences in law can lead to distortions of competition between credit grantors, that these differences may have an influence on the free movement of goods and services and that differences in law and practice result in unequal protection of consumers in the field of consumer credit in different states. The Council of the European Communities added in its Directive that "the establishment of a common market in consumer credit would benefit alike consumers, grantors of credit, manufacturers, wholesalers and retailers of goods and providers of services".[17]

2.2 Southern Africa

The position in Southern Africa is comparable, but hardly identical, to the situation in the European Union. As far as a common legal tradition is concerned, it is well known that most countries in Europe have Roman law as the foundation of their systems and that the roots of their private law codes can be traced back to the magnificent heritage of the Romans. Due to historical reasons this also holds true for most countries in Southern Africa. In fact, it is no exaggeration to say that to a large extent the majority of these countries share a common legal tradition even more uniform than that of many European countries. The common law of countries such as South Africa, Botswana, Lesotho, Zimbabwe, Namibia and Swaziland is a hybrid system: Roman-Dutch law heavily influenced by English law,[18] local customs and new legislation.[19] An interesting feature of this region is that South African judges and advocates have for a long time served, and still do serve, on the benches of some[20] of these countries, applying Roman-Dutch law and local legislation. The most important decisions of the courts in Zimbabwe and Namibia are included in the South African Law Reports. All and all, therefore, there is much common ground.

---

[17] *See* for the text of the Directive, A. G. Guest and M. G. Lloyd, *supra*, 9016.
[18] Amongst others, in the fields of commercial law such as negotiable instruments and company law. The Bills of Exchange Acts of the original provinces of South Africa were all based on the English Bills of Exchange Act, whereas the legislation in Botswana, Lesotho, Swaziland, Namibia, Malawi and Zambia were modelled on the Acts in South Africa or the English legislation. *See* F. R. Malan *et al., Malan on Bills of Exchange, Cheques and Promissory Notes* (1994) 34 ff. *See* as to the history of South African company law and its roots in English law H. S. Cilliers, M. A. Benadé *et al., Entrepreneurial Law* (1993) para. 8.05 ff.
[19] H. R. Hahlo and E. Kahn, *The South African Legal System and its Background* (1973) 578; D. H. Van Zyl, *Beginsels van Regsvergelyking* (1981) 291.
[20] But not all.

There are probably very few legal systems where judges do not refer on a comparative basis to other systems for guidance in their own decisions. This has also been the tradition in Southern Africa and cross-references on a large scale are frequent in the law reports. This does not only occur in common law matters, but also when courts have to interpret legislation that is *in pari materia*. In recent times, this happened particularly in constitutional matters and in the interpretation and application of bills of fundamental human rights.[21] Once countries have similar commercial statutes, the tendency of course is to refer to each other's case law and text-books for guidance. In the field of consumer credit one German writer has indeed predicted that German courts will rely on decisions in France and England in future when difficult questions arise regarding the new German Consumer Credit Act[22] of 1990.[23]

While the legal systems of Africa's subcontinent share substantial common ground, co-operation between South Africa, in particular, and the other countries over the past two decades or so was hardly normal. Granted, trade continued, but there was no uninhibited flow of goods, services, customers or money. After all, some of the countries in the region were engaged in civil war, and their citizens and even the armed forces were often involved in cross-border battles. This apart, close relations with South Africa were frowned upon. Although peace does not reign supreme in the entire region, the political situation has changed dramatically, particularly as far as relations with South Africa are concerned.

It can be expected that more and more large businesses will open branches and establish subsidiaries in neighbouring countries. In the field of consumer credit the advantages of comparable legislation are obvious. Besides the equal protection of debtors and the other considerations mentioned above, life will be far easier for creditors if they are subject to basically the same defences and have to use the same procedures to collect debts. It will save money, time and energy should they be capable of using virtually the same contract documentation for their customers, and training programmes for their staff. Naturally, they will always have to live and cope with differences in the various countries concerned.

---

[21] *See*, for instance, the Zimbabwean Supreme Court referring to the position in Botswana in *In re Munhumeso* 1995 1 S.A. 551 (ZSC) at 556 and the Ciskeian Court in *Ntenteni v. Chairman, Council of State* 1993 4 S.A. 546 (Ck GD) quoting extensively from a decision in Botswana. (Ciskei was an independent homeland under the old South African order but is now once again part of South Africa.) In the South African decision of *Khala v. Minister of Safety and Security* 1994 4 S.A. 218 (W) references to, *inter alia*, decisions of Namibia and Botswana occur. These are only three examples drawn from a large number of recent reported judgments where the courts in Southern Africa referred to decisions in the region as well as to those of other jurisdictions.

[22] *Verbraucherkreditgesetz.*

[23] H.-J. Lwowski *et al., Verbraucherkreditgesetz* (1993) 21.

3 CONSUMER CREDIT LAW IN SOUTHERN AFRICA

3.1 South Africa

Consumer credit in South Africa is regulated by a variety of legislation, as mentioned earlier.[24] Leaving aside the Act dealing with immovable property,[25] the legislative picture is very broadly speaking the following: the *contractual* aspects of credit agreements[26] are mainly provided for by the Credit Agreements Act.[27] The financial aspects[28] are covered by the Usury Act.[29] The Lay-By regulations protect buyers of goods on the lay-by system[30] in various ways, for example by giving them the right to terminate the agreement at any time before it has run its course against forfeiting a small percentage of the amounts already paid.

South Africa's legislation was certainly influenced by the statutes of other countries but many provisions are uniquely South African. For present purposes, one example may be used to illustrate that legislative enactments in

---

[24] Fn. 14 above. *See* for recent sources dealing with consumer credit in South Africa J. M. Otto, *Credit Law Service* (loose-leaf service, 1991 *et seq.*); N. J. Grové and L. Jacobs, *Basic Principles of Consumer Credit Law* (1993); A. D. J. Van Rensburg and S. H. Treisman, *The Practitioner's Guide to the Alienation of Land Act* (1984); J. M. Otto, "Consumer Credit" in W. A. Joubert (ed.), *The Law of South Africa*, First Reissue, Vol. 5, Part 1 (1994).

[25] The Alienation of Land Act.

[26] Such as the contents and form of credit agreements, particular rights of consumers such as the cooling-off right, procedures to be followed in case of breach of contract, etc.

[27] The Act applies to the sale and lease on instalments of durable consumer goods such as motor vehicles, furniture, electrical appliances, sound equipment, jewellery, etc.

[28] The maximum permissible interest rates, the calculation and recalculation of rates, the maximum expenses recoverable, etc.

[29] This Act applies to the sale and lease of all movable goods (and in certain cases even to the sale of land), the rendering of services and money lending transactions.

[30] This system of finance is long established, very popular and widespread in South Africa. There is evidence that lay-bys were also advertised in a newspaper in Zimbabwe as far back as 1957. J. A. Simpson and E. S. C. Weiner, *The Oxford English Dictionary* VIII (1989) 734. A lay-by is a contract of sale in terms of which delivery is not effected until the purchaser has paid a certain part (usually the whole) of the purchase price. The seller remains in possession of the goods in the meantime. It is a useful way of financing transactions with debtors who have no fixed addresses, or little financial resources, or doubtful employment, or who are unable to provide security. It certainly has potential for cross-border transactions. A consumer may want to buy an article on credit but the credit grantor may be reluctant to release the goods to a citizen of another country. It would then be possible to conclude a contract in terms whereof the purchaser pays a deposit and leaves the goods with the seller until his return visit at a future date. The goods will then be delivered against payment of the outstanding amount. This form of contract is also known in New Zealand and Australia. Mackay, "Lay-by Agreements in New Zealand", 6 *Vic. Univ. of Well. L.R.* 11 (1971/73); Lawson, "The Lay-by Sales Act 1971", *N.Z. Univ. L.R.* 181 (1972/73); Lawson, "Protection of the Consumer in New Zealand – Some Recent Developments", *Otago L.R.* 49 (1973/76); J. A. Simpson and E.S.C. Weiner, *supra*, at 734; W. S. Ramson, *The Australian National Dictionary* (1988) 363. In fact Lawson once described the contract as "uniquely Australasian" (1972/73, *N.Z. Univ. L.R.* 181) and "apparently unique to Australia and New Zealand" (1973/76, *Otago L.R.* 61). Its importance as a method of financing has decreased in Australia due to the ready availability of other forms of credit. S. W. Cavanagh and S. Barnes, *Consumer Credit Law in Australia* (1988) para. 113.

far-off Europe may have an influence on domestic attempts to regulate society. South Africa's first comprehensive Act dealing with instalment sales and certain leasing transactions was the Hire-Purchase Act.[31] Some of its sections were clearly based on the Dutch and English legislation at the time.[32] One such provision is a section that gave a purchaser an extra-ordinary right.[33] If the seller recovered possession of the goods as a result of the purchaser's failure to pay his instalments, the purchaser was given the opportunity to pay the arrears within a certain period and to continue with the contract, even though in a technical sense it had been terminated by the seller. Despite differences, this section was clearly based on section 1576v of the Dutch code.[34] When the Hire-Purchase Act was repealed and replaced by the Credit Agreements Act of 1980, this right of redemption was retained (albeit with some amendments)[35] with the result that the Dutch influence is still apparent.

Although South Africa's credit legislation is of reasonably recent origin, the need for drastic reform has been felt for some time. A research committee[36] of the South African Law Commission compiled a report of some 600 pages containing recommendations and draft legislation. The report was published in 1993 as a working paper of the Law Commission.[37] After a number of commentaries on the document were studied a final report was submitted, which in turn was discussed with the Law Commission and amended in various ways. At the time of writing, the future of the entire project is somewhat uncertain.

3.2 Other countries in Southern Africa

It will serve no purpose to describe in detail the credit legislation of the other countries in Southern Africa. General observations will suffice. After having studied various statutes[38] of different countries in the region[39] the following quite interesting conclusions can be drawn:

---

[31] 36 of 1942.

[32] *Cf.* Hamman, "Die Huurkoopwetsontwerp", 5 *T.H.R.H.R. (Journal of Contemporary Roman Dutch Law/Tydskrif vir Hedendaagse Romeins-Hollandse Reg)* 255 (1942).

[33] Sec. 13.

[34] The *Burgerlijk Wetboek.*

[35] *See* for a discussion of the topic J. M. Otto, "Right of Credit Receiver to Reinstatement after Return of Goods to Credit Grantor", 98 *S.A.L.J. (South African Law Journal)* 516 (1981).

[36] Consisting of two law professors, namely J. M. Otto and N. J. Grové, assisted in certain respects by other researchers, and advised by Prof. F. R. Malan.

[37] *See* fn. 5.

[38] The hire-purchase Acts of the countries in particular.

[39] The statutes consulted were the most recent ones available in one of South Africa's leading law libraries which has a very useful collection of foreign materials. It is possible that the legislation of one or more of these countries might have been amended or even repealed or replaced. In some cases the collection in the library bears relatively recent dates, but in other cases, particularly as far as loose-leaf services of statutes are concerned, it unfortunately does not.

(i) Certain statutes are for all practical purposes exactly the same as their South African counterpart. Sadly, however, they are based on outdated and repealed legislation, such as the Hire-Purchase Act of 1942. In one particular country, for historical reasons, the current South African Acts[40] apply.

(ii) Some of the statutes provide an interesting combination of old English legislation[41] and South African legislation. The right of redemption referred to earlier,[42] for instance, is contained in some of these statutes with the result that Dutch law indirectly had an influence on countries with which it never had colonial ties!

(iii) The statutes have provisions that are not based on either English or South African law, *e.g.* provisions protecting purchasers using a negotiable instrument as a means of payment.[43]

Generally speaking, the hire-purchase Acts of these countries belong to a previous generation of consumer credit law. Far be it for me to say that they are valueless[44] or fraught with inadequacies. Every society must decide for itself. What cannot be ignored, however, is the fact that consumer credit is a very dynamic field of law and that it would be shortsighted to turn a blind eye to developments elsewhere. This is of particular relevance where the indications are that greater economic activity and interaction for the region as a whole are at hand.

4 THE EEC (EU) DIRECTIVE

Work on the EEC Directive started in 1974 and took more than a decade before the Directive was finally accepted in 1986.[45] The Directive was preceded by two draft proposals. Member states were, in certain instances,

---

[40] The Credit Agreements Act of 1980 and the Usury Act of 1968.

[41] *e.g.* the Hire-Purchase Act of 1938 which was replaced by the Hire-Purchase Act of 1965. The 1965 Act was in turn buried and succeeded by the Consumer Credit Act of 1974. *See* for a history of English credit law R. M. Goode, *Consumer Credit Law, supra,* at 1 ff.; R. M. Goode, *Hire-Purchase Law and Practice* (1970) 1 ff.

[42] Para. 3.1 *supra.*

[43] Although South Africa's credit Acts always had provisions in this regard, they did not nearly go as far as those of its counterparts in Southern Africa. Provisions to this effect were also introduced into English legislation as late as 1974 by sec. 123–125 of the Consumer Credit Act of 1974. *See* the *Crowther report, supra,* at 285 in this regard. This type of provision has, however, long been fairly common in American consumer legislation. *See* J. M. Otto, "Verhandelbare Dokumente en Reëlmatige Houerskap by Verbruikerstransaksies", 12 *Tydskrif vir die Suid-Afrikaanse Reg/Journal of South African Law (T.S.A.R.)* 26 (1987).

[44] South Africa itself may learn from this legislation, old as they may be. One finds, for instance, useful provisions in them dealing with the appropriation of payments where a debtor has more than one liability towards the same creditor. These provisions are based on English legislation but they are completely absent from South Africa's Acts.

[45] R. M. Goode, *Consumer Credit Law, supra,* at 823; Von Westphalen, *supra,* at 7. *See* for the early history of the proposals P. Latham in R. M. Goode (ed.), *Consumer Credit* (1978) 342.

heavily opposed to some of the original proposals and amendments were sought and obtained by them.[46] The Directive was based on the English Consumer Credit Act[47] but there were French influences as well.[48] The Directive was supplemented by a Directive on the methods to be used in calculating the annual percentage rate of charge.[49]

The Directive is brief and of a general character.[50] It lays down minimum standards of consumer protection to be adopted by member states as part of their national law. Members were supposed to comply with the Directive by 1 January 1990. It is important to note that the Directive did "not preclude Member States from retaining or adopting more stringent provisions to protect consumers".[51] As will be indicated below, this had the effect that the national legislation of different states retained their unique national flavour while conformity was effected at the same time in certain key areas.

There is, of course, another possible route which can achieve the same result. Instead of agreeing to a certain set of principles that are to be embodied in the national legislation of the countries concerned, it is possible for one country to take the lead. It was pointed out above that the Directive was largely based on principles contained in the English Consumer Credit Act of 1974. This Act was once described as "the most comprehensive and sophisticated consumer credit statute ever to have been enacted in any country".[52] This view was to some extent endorsed by a German writer.[53] Were a country in Southern Africa to take the initiative and adopt its own legislation, half of the work will already have been done. This particularly will be the case if such an Act is a comprehensive one covering a wide variety of aspects in the field of consumer credit from which other countries can individually make their selections. It would be even more sensible if the countries, instead of acting individually, agree to certain basic principles deducted from such a comprehensive Act, which serves as a model. It is a sobering thought to note, however, that the infrastructure for co-operation and concerted efforts, to the extent that it does exist, is not as sophisticated as that existing in Europe. It will have to be done on a far more informal basis.

The drafting of consumer legislation is a daunting task, and this is even more so if it is undertaken on a regional basis. It is not only daunting, it is ambitious too. But then it must be remembered that it took Europe almost

---

[46] Emmerich, "Die Verbraucherkreditrichtlinie und die Nationalen Verbraucherkreditgesetze", 38 *Finanzierung Leasing Factoring* 140 (1991).

[47] R. M. Goode, *Consumer Credit Law, supra*, at 823; L. Krämer, *EEC Consumer Law* (1986) 317. The first working paper borrowed freely from United Kingdom Bills. Latham, *supra*, at 342.

[48] Emmerich, *supra*, at 140; Von Westphalen, *supra*, at 7.

[49] *See* A. G. Guest and M. G. Lloyd, *supra*, at 9024/19.

[50] R. M. Goode, *Consumer Credit Law, supra*, at 823.

[51] Art. 15.

[52] R. M. Goode, "The Consumer Credit Act 1974", 34 *C.L.J.* 81 (1975).

[53] "Die umfangreichste und strengste Gesetzgebung zum Schutze der Verbraucher bei Konsumentenkrediten findet sich in England". Von Westphalen, *supra*, at 16.

20 years since the work on its consumer directive started in 1974 until some countries passed their new legislation, as late as the early 1990s.

The European Directive can certainly be used as a model for Southern Africa on which the region can base its legislation. First, some of the principles enacted in the Directive are so sound that they should form part of consumer legislation anywhere. Secondly, the Directive bears proof of the methodology that can be followed in this regard. Thirdly, the experience in Europe shows that it is certainly possible for countries to adopt legislation that conforms to the Directive while at the same time serving their national interests by the inclusion of provisions in their legislation that are absent from similar legislation in neighbouring countries.

5 THE APPLICATION OF THE DIRECTIVE IN SELECTED COUNTRIES

The application of the Directive in Germany, the Netherlands and Belgium will be discussed next. This serves to point out how the legislation of different countries may differ while at the same time meeting minimum standards. Certain aspects only of the Directive will be discussed, as this will suffice to illustrate the principle. Cross-references will be made occasionally to the position in Britain and South Africa. The German Act and the Belgian Act were discussed and analysed[54] at length elsewhere.[55] Naturally some of that discussion will have to be repeated briefly but the emphasis will fall on the Directive as a role model.

5.1 Scope of application of consumer credit legislation

New consumer credit legislation is an emotive issue simply because so many conflicting interests are at stake. It is sometimes difficult for the role players to remain aloof and objective. As Feldman once put it: "These are issues on which it is possible for men of good faith to differ substantially."[56] And nothing is more crucial and more difficult in the field of consumer credit law than the scope of application of consumer credit legislation. The Directive limited its application and with that the application of prospective national legislation. It provided,[57] amongst other things,[58] that the Directive shall not apply to the following:

---

[54] And the Dutch Act compared with them.
[55] *See* J. M. Otto, "Verbruikerskredietwetgewing: Vars Lesse uit Duitsland", Part one, 18 *T.S.A.R.* 395 (1993); Part two, 19 *T.S.A.R.* 119 (1994); Part three, 19 *T.S.A.R.* 278 (1994); Part four, 19 *T.S.A.R.* 485 (1994); J. M. Otto, "Belgiese Verbruikerskrediet: 'n Vergelykende Studie" in three parts to be published in 1995 and 1996 *T.S.A.R.*
[56] L. P. Feldsman, *Consumer Protection. Problems and Prospects* (1976) 47.
[57] Art. 1.
[58] The list in the text above is not an exhaustive replica of art. 1 of the Directive.

(i)   credit transactions relating to land or improvements to buildings;
(ii) leasing agreements where the lessee will not ultimately become the owner;
(iii) credit agreements without any interest or charge;
(iv) current accounts other than credit card accounts;[59]
(v)   small agreements[60] and large agreements;[61] and
(vi) short-term contracts.[62]

The Directive is also limited in its application by virtue of the definitions in article 1. In terms thereof a "consumer" is a *natural* person who does not obtain credit for business purposes. A creditor is a natural or a legal person[63] granting credit in the course of his trade, business or profession. On the other hand, the Directive has a wide application as far as the definition of "credit agreement" is concerned. This is defined as an agreement "whereby a creditor grants or promises to grant to a consumer a credit in the form of a deferred payment, a loan or *other similar financial accommodation*".[64]

The German Consumer Credit Act[65] was drafted in accordance with these principles. There are some differences. The most striking is that, while short-term credit and small loans[66] are excluded, the Act has no ceiling amount. It applies to credit contracts regardless of the amount involved,[67] save for one exception regarding business credit.[68] Ordinary consumer credit is regulated by the Act without any limitation as far as the amount borrowed is concerned. This wide field of application has rightly been criticised as a person can hardly be regarded as a consumer[69] if he concludes contracts for millions of German marks or buys an expensive yacht on credit.[70]

An interesting feature of the German Act is that no mention is made of leasing (hiring) contracts.[71] However, it is generally accepted that the Act

---

[59] Current accounts are covered, however, as far as certain disclosure provisions are concerned.
[60] Of amounts less than 200 ECU.
[61] Amounts exceeding 20,000 ECU.
[62] *i.e.* where the contract period does not exceed three months or where a maximum of four payments are to be made over a period not exceeding 12 months.
[63] Juristic person.
[64] The italics are mine.
[65] The *Verbraucherkreditgesetz* generally referred to in Germany as the *VerbrKrG*.
[66] Beneath 400 D.M.
[67] Wagner-Wieduwilt, "Erfahrungen mit dem Verbraucherkreditgesetz", 32 *Die Bank* 339 (1992).
[68] Namely where the credit is obtained to *start* a business the Act applies up to 100,000 DM. It does not apply to business credit otherwise.
[69] The preamble to the Directive states in this regard: "Whereas credit agreements for very large financial amounts tend to differ from the usual consumer credit agreements . . ."
[70] Schoppmann, "Das Verbraucherkreditgesetz und seine Anwendbarkeit auf Förderdarlehen und Realkredite", 42 *Der Langfristige Kredit (L.K.)* 142 (1991).
[71] Except for para. 3(2) nr. 1 which simply states that *certain* of the Act's provisions do *not* apply to leasing transactions. Indeed, an indirect and tacit way of making the remainder of the Act applicable to them.

will apply to financial leases[72] where full amortisation occurs, but not to operating leases.[73]

The Belgian Act also exempts various forms of short-term credit, business credit, and contracts where small amounts are involved, from its field of operation. Contrary to the German Act, contracts where relatively large amounts[74] of credit are involved are exempted.[75] This will only be the case where the contract is embodied in an authentic act.[76] The effect of this is that wealthy people will also be protected by the Act even if substantial amounts are borrowed by means of an informal instrument of debt and invested in immovable property, shares, gold, works of art, etc.[77]

The Belgian Act did not leave it to the courts, as its German counterpart did, to decide whether leasing contracts fall under the Act. The leasing contract is properly defined[78] and certain provisions apply to leasing contracts only. An important part of the definition is the requirement that, to be a financial lease, an option to purchase must be present – either expressly or tacitly.[79] This is in accordance with article 2(1)(b) of the Directive.

The Dutch Consumer Credit Act[80] also excludes business credit, short-term credit and large amounts from its operation. Contrary to the German and Belgian Acts, and contrary to article 2(1)(f) of the Directive, small loans and other forms of credit are not exempted, despite requests to that effect.[81]

To the layman it may seem strange that the small borrower, of all people, is left unprotected. However, good reasons exist for exempting small loans

---

[72] The words "any other form of financial accommodation" ("einer sonstigen Finanzierungshilfe") in the definition of a credit contract are wide enough to cover leasing contracts.

[73] *See* as to the *VerbrKrG's* influence on leasing contracts H. Bruchner *et al.*, *Verbraucherkreditgesetz* (1992) 59; Graf von Westphalen, *supra*, at 81; Zahn, "Leasingvertrag und Widerrufsbelehrung nach dem Verbraucherkreditgesetz", 44 *Der Betrieb* 687 (1991); Schölermann and Schmid-Burgk, "Das Schriftformerfordernis bei Leasingverträgen nach dem Verbraucherkreditgesetz", 44 *Der Betrieb* 1968 (1991); Seifert, "Aspekten des Verbraucherkreditgesetzes aus Sicht eines Leasingunternehmens", 42 L.K. 144 (1991); Zahn, "Leasingpraxis nach Inkrafttreten des Verbraucherkreditgesetzes", 44 *Der Betrieb* 2171 (1991); Schmid-Burgk and Schölermann, "Probleme bei der Anwendung des neuen Verbraucherkreditgesetzes auf Leasingverträge", 46 *Betriebs Berater* 566 (1991); Peters, "Leasing und Verbraucherkreditgesetz", 46 *Zeitschrift für Wirtschafts- und Bankrecht* 1797 (1992).

[74] 860,000 BF.

[75] Sec. 3(2)(2) of the Belgian Consumer Credit Act *(Wet op het Consumentenkrediet)* of 12 June 1991.

[76] "Authentieke akte". My impression is that this requires a notarially executed document. *See* P. Lettany, *Het Consumentenkrediet de Wet van 12 Juni 1991* (1992) 23.

[77] *Id.*

[78] Sec. 1(10).

[79] *e.g.* where the parties agree to a price that is abnormally low compared with the genuine residual value of the goods. *Memorie van Toelichting* of the Belgian Senate, doc. 916-1, (1989/90) 5.

[80] *Wet op het Consumentenkrediet* of 4 July 1990.

[81] Huls, *supra*, at 25.

from consumer credit legislation. The overhead costs[82] in the case of a small loan are often virtually the same as with large loans, with the effect that the real (proportional) return for the lender is far lower if the same interest rate applies. The effect of this is that large institutions tend to refuse to lend money to small borrowers in legal systems[83] where maximum interest rates are prescribed by the authorities. This in turn drives consumers into the arms of loan sharks in the informal sector who charge exhorbitant rates. This certainly happened in South Africa[84] and small loans, except in the case of overdrawn cheque accounts and credit card transactions, were exempted from the Usury Act.[85] The Directive points to another compelling reason why small loans should fall outside this type of legislation, even in countries with no maximum prescribed rates. As it was put in the preamble to the Directive:

Whereas the application of the provisions of this Directive to agreements for very small amounts could create unnecessary administrative burdens both for consumers and grantors of credit…

The wide definitions of "credit contract" in all three of these Acts ensure that almost any form of credit contract not expressly excluded will be covered by the Act. Consequently, it is generally accepted that the German Act also applies to the rendering of services on credit.[86] The Belgian Act expressly includes the rendering of services in its definition of a sale on instalments.[87] It is indeed the modern trend to regulate services on credit in consumer credit legislation.[88] The Dutch Act is only applicable to the rendering of services to the extent that the authorities declare it applicable to a particular class of service[89] which gives the Act a far more restricted scope of application compared to the Belgian and German Acts.

There are more differences in the three Acts' provisions regarding their scope of application but the discussion above will prove the point that the

---

[82] Such as office rent, salaries, computer expenses, credit investigations and costs in connection with "paper work".

[83] Such as South Africa.

[84] J. M. Otto and N. J. Grové, *Working Paper 46, supra*, at 219.

[85] *See* J. M. Otto, *Credit Law Service, supra*, at para. 11.

[86] Bülow, "Das neue Verbraucherkreditgesetz", 44 *Neue Juristische Wochenschrift* 130 (1991); Seibert, "Das Verbraucherkreditgesetz, insbesodere die erfaßten Geschäfte aus dem Blickwinkel der Gesetzgebung", 45 *Zeitschrift für Wirtschafts- und Bankrecht* 1446 (1991); Mertins, "Das Verbraucherkreditgesetz", 45 *Neue Justiz* 254 (1991).

[87] Sec. 1(9).

[88] The Crowther Committee noted in 1971 that the regulation of services in Britain was "long overdue". *See* p. 295 of the *Crowther report*. The definitions in the British Consumer Credit Act are wide enough to cover these contracts. R. M. Goode, *Consumer Credit Law, supra*, at 87. South Africa's Usury Act regulates the rendering of services and it is explicitly included in the definition of a credit transaction in the Act. The Credit Agreements Act's definition of a credit transaction includes the rendering of services but the Act has never been made applicable to that class of contracts by the responsible Minister.

[89] It has been made applicable to what Huls, *supra*, at 34 calls the travelling agreement ("reisovereenkomst").

Directive was used to accept legislation with basically the same scope, but with differences on a national level as well.

The Directive required member states to protect consumers in various ways. Examples are the disclosure of contractual terms in writing, and other particularly critical areas such as prohibitions or limitations on the use of negotiable instruments, rights regarding advanced payments and the consumer's position *vis-à-vis* third-party assignees. It is unnecessary to deal with all these matters. One was selected and is discussed next to briefly illustrate how the general provisions of the Directive led to highly comparable, but not completely identical, national legislation.

5.2 Payments and security by means of bills of exchange

A debtor under the terms of a consumer credit contract may use bills of exchange and promissory notes as a means of payment or as a means of providing security for future breaches of contract. Sometimes a series of post-dated documents is drawn and delivered to the creditor. It is possible, and does in fact happen, that creditors discount or negotiate these documents to third parties. Should a consumer be unhappy with his contract with the creditor[90] he may find himself in an unenviable position. His normal reaction and remedy would be to withhold payment. However, when confronted by a third party enforcing a negotiable instrument this will be of no avail. He will be held liable against a third party who acted in good faith and who took the document for value. This is well established and is one of the ground rules of the law of negotiable instruments.

Protecting consumers in this situation is a very difficult matter. Choices have to be made: a choice between who should be held responsible, the consumer or the *bona fide* third party;[91] a choice between the free flow of paper and the limitation thereof; a choice between who should be the paramount subject of protection, the individual consumer or the "deep pocket"[92] financier? There are various options available: the use of bills of exchange and promissory notes in consumer transactions may be

---

[90] *e.g.* the creditor commits breach of contract, or committed a misrepresentation during the negotiations preceding the conclusion of the contract, or the goods are defective.

[91] The third party is more often than not a financial institution which has a close relationship with the original creditor. This prompted American and Canadian courts to deny financial institutions with such a connection "the elevated position" of a holder in due course (as Geva, "Reflections on the need to revise the Bills of Exchange Act", 6 *Can. Bus. L.J.* 275 (1981/82) put it) in appropriate circumstances. There are many cases in both jurisdictions dealing with this so-called "close-connectedness doctrine". In the United States this doctrine had its origin in a decision in Arkansas in 1940 (*Commercial Credit Co v. Childs* 199 Ark. 1073, 137 S.W. 2d 260) although there were even earlier signs of the doctrine. Clark, "The Close-Connectedness Doctrine: Preserving Consumer Rights in Credit Transactions", 33 *Ark. L.R.* 491 (1979). *See* as to the history of the doctrine banks, "The FTC Holder in Due Course Rule: A Rule without a Private Remedy", 44 *Montana L.R.* 116 (1983). The *locus classicus* in Canada is *Federal Discount Corporation Ltd v. St Pierre* 1962 O.R. 310 (CA).

[92] As Lawrence and Minan, "The Effect of Abrogating the Holder-in due-Course Doctrine on the Commercialization of Innovative Consumer Products", 64 *Boston Univ. L.R.* 338 (1984) put it.

prohibited entirely,[93] or the creditor may be burdened with the duty to write certain words[94] on the document which will have the effect[95] that no one can become a holder-in-due-course thereof, to name but two possibilities.

The European Directive deals with this problem. The Directive stipulates, without providing any details whatsoever, that consumers must be "suitably protected" when they use bills of exchange (including promissory notes) to make payment or to provide security.[96] The Germans took heed of this Directive, as did the Dutch and the Belgians, each in their own way.

The German Act provides the following in paragraph 10(2):[97] the consumer may not be obliged to enter into a "cambial" agreement relating to the creditor's claims under the terms of the credit agreement. In addition, the creditor may not take a cheque as security for his rights under the terms of the contract. If a bill of exchange or a cheque was issued in contravention of these prohibitions, the consumer may claim its return. Finally, the creditor is liable for any damages suffered by the consumer caused by the delivery of a bill or cheque.

The prohibition on the use of cheques and bills of exchange in the German Act is a somewhat strange provision.[98] It prohibits a "cambial" obligation in the sense that the parties may not agree that the consumer will be *obliged* to issue a bill of exchange. If the consumer, *of his own accord,* uses a bill of exchange as a means of *payment* this will be in order.[99] A cheque may not be taken as security, however. The Act does not define "taking as security" ("zur Sicherung") but this usually means holding the cheque back and only presenting it for payment should the debtor fail to pay the debt in another way.[100]

The German prohibition is a limited one. It does not visit a document with invalidity should the provision be contravened.[101] It does provide some protection, however. Creditors will not be eager to accept negotiable instruments as this will expose them to actions for damages, for instance where the consumer is held liable to a *bona fide* third party.[102]

Section 33 of the Belgian Act, similarly, contains a prohibition on the use of bills and cheques. It forbids a promise or guarantee by a consumer, *or a surety*, by means of a bill of exchange or a promissory note to pay a debt under the terms of a credit contract. It is also forbidden to draw a cheque as security for payment.

---

[93] With the notable exception of cheques payable on demand.

[94] Such as "issued in connection with a consumer credit transaction".

[95] In terms of the relevant credit legislation.

[96] Art. 10.

[97] *See* for a discussion of para. 10(2), in addition to the references in the footnotes below, P. Ulmer and M. Habersack, *Verbraucherkreditgesetz Kommentar* (1992) 194 ff.

[98] Graph von Westphalen, *supra*, at 368.

[99] *Id.*; W. Münstermann and R. Hannes, *Verbraucherkreditgesetz Kommentar* (1991) 370.

[100] *See* Graph von Westphalen, *supra*, at 367. Sec. 123(4) of Britain's Consumer Credit Act specifically defines the taking of a negotiable instrument as security in this way.

[101] Graph von Westphalen, *supra*, at 364; Emmerich, "Das Verbraucherkreditgesetz", 31 *Juristische Schulung* 709 (1991).

[102] Graph von Westphalen, *supra*, at 369.

Contrary to the German Act, a contravention of the section is visited with a criminal sanction.[103] In addition, the creditor is obliged to repay all the "costs"[104] of the agreement to the consumer.[105] This is as far-reaching a sanction as one can imagine.

The Belgian Act also provides that any credit offer must contain a notice in bold letters drawing the consumer's attention to the prohibition on bills of exchange, promissory notes and cheques.[106]

In implementing article 10 of the EEC Directive, the Belgian legislature opted for an absolute prohibition.[107] It considered bills of exchange and promissory notes to be compatible with the relationship between dealers, but was of the opinion that they put consumers in an unequal position.[108]

A contravention of the Belgian Act does not render the document void.[109] Moreover, *bona fide* third parties retain their remedies on the document.[110]

Section 38 of the Dutch Act contains the following prohibitions: The creditor and supplier may not draw a negotiable instrument on the credit receiver or take a promissory note from him for outstanding amounts, nor may he transfer a cheque received as payment to a third party.[111]

6 GENERAL OBSERVATIONS REGARDING THE DIRECTIVE

It was stated above that the Directive is brief and of a general nature.[112] It deals with a relatively small number of consumer credit problems. The question of negotiable instruments was discussed above. Other areas are the form and contents of credit contracts, advertisements, particulars to be supplied in the case of current accounts, repossession of goods, accelerated payments, defences against third-party assignees, actions against credit grantors under certain circumstances where the consumer is unsuccessful in his claim against the supplier of goods or services, to mention the most important aspects of the Directive.

---

[103] Sec. 101(6).

[104] This is defined in sec. 1(5) as all costs of the credit including the interest.

[105] Sec. 96.

[106] Sec. 14(4)(3).

[107] Dambre, "Contractuele Verhoudingen en Driepartijenverhoudingen", 23 *Les Droit des Affairs/Het Ondernemingsrecht (D.A.O.R.)* 60 (1992).

[108] *Report of the Belgian Senate*, doc. 916–2 (1989–1990) 12; Dambre, *supra*, at 60; Meulemans, "Onrechtmatige Bedingen inzake Consumentenkrediet", 28 *Jura Falconis* 4–103 (1991/92).

[109] Lettany, *supra*, at 215; Dambre, *supra*, at 61; Meulemans, *supra*, at 4–104; *Memorie van Toelichting*, *supra*, at 67.

[110] Lettany, *supra*, at 215; Dambre, *supra*, at 61; Meulemans, *supra*, at 4–105.

[111] It is not clear what the consequences of a contravention of the prohibition are. Huls, *supra*, at 101 deals very briefly with the matter and gives an answer in one sentence where he says that what is forbidden is a particular mode of payment. Other forms of payment (he presumably refers to, *inter alia*, cash payments) are legal and may be enforced. From this it can be inferred that the credit contract itself, at least, is not invalid. Sec. 33(e) may have the effect that any agreement regarding bills of exchange, etc. will be invalid as such.

[112] Leaving out the preamble it runs into six pages only in ordinary printed form in Guest and Lloyd's replica (fn. 16, *supra*) thereof.

The Directive provides the skeleton only, the flesh has to be added. Article 8 can serve as an example. It reads:

The customer shall be entitled to discharge his obligations under a credit agreement before the time fixed by the agreement. In this event, in accordance with the rules laid down by the Member States, the consumer shall be entitled to an equitable reduction in the total cost of the credit.

Article 8 thus leaves the member states with a wide discretion. Only two principles apply: the consumer must have a right to accelerate payments and terminate his debt prematurely, and he must obtain a benefit by means of a reduction. How this is effected is left to member states. A state may decide, for instance, to allow the debtor to prepay only after having given notice of his intention to do so and only after the lapse of a certain period,[113] which is not unusual in legislation of this kind.[114] As far as the rebate is concerned, it is also possible to work with different formulae, such as a complete reduction in the outstanding interest or other charges (that would have become payable in future), or a part reduction only, or complete reduction against payment of an administrative fee.

7 CONCLUSION

General principles such as those contained in the Directive are a workable option for countries striving towards similar or uniform legislation. This does not mean that the particular principles in the Directive, or all of them, will be palatable to the countries of Southern Africa, or to lawyers, financiers and dealers engaged in this field. I certainly disagree with some of the principles contained in the Directive, as would others. The issues are too involved to expect general consensus. However, in addition to the methodology behind the Directive, it also provides a set of basic principles of consumer credit law that can be regarded as the latest developments and current thoughts in a region as diverse and as important as that constituted by the member states of the EU.

---

[113] The Belgian Act, for instance, requires a notice of 30 days of the debtor before he may prepay the full outstanding amount in order to be entitled to a reduction. Sec. 23. *See* Lettany, *supra*, at 167 ff.

[114] By comparison sec. 3A of South Africa's Usury Act provides that the parties may agree on the period that must lapse before full payment may occur. A maximum is prescribed, *viz.* 90 days after conclusion of the contract before a notice of accelerated payment may be *given,* and 90 days before *payment* in terms of the notice may occur. The effect is that the creditor may contractually safeguard himself against loss of the debtor's business for 180 days. In terms of sec. 94 of Britain's Consumer Credit Act the debtor may complete his payments at any time by giving notice. No minimum length is laid down for such notice. R. M. Goode, *Consumer Credit Law, supra,* at 539. This is also the position in terms of para. 14 of the German Act and sec. 37(1) of the Dutch Act.

The definition of *consumer* in article 1 of the Directive, for instance, is a striking example of modern thought on consumer protection in the field of granting of credit. The definition, which is very short and simple, encompasses two principles. First, a consumer is defined as a natural person. This means that juristic persons are not regarded as consumers and must look after their own affairs, which is a view not generally reflected in consumer credit legislation of bygone eras.[115] I believe this new trend to be the correct one. Consumer credit legislation must be limited to consumers proper[116] and juristic persons usually operate in a completely different and more professional way. They are accustomed to make use of the services of professional people such as lawyers and accountants and are usually by law required to compile and submit financial statements.[117] Secondly, the definition excludes credit for business or professional purposes. On the face of it this, too, is a sound principle. However, the "purpose of credit test" is a difficult one which may lead to disputes – something that should be kept to a minimum in the field of consumer legislation. Very often, credit is obtained for more than one reason. A businessperson or doctor who buys a motor car often uses it for business or professional purposes, as well as for private, family or personal purposes.[118] If business credit is excluded from this type of legislation, I believe it should be limited to credit granted *solely* for business purposes. It could lead to unnecessary litigation if the test is to be something akin to the "predominant purpose" for which the credit is granted.[119]

---

[115] South Africa's statutes at the moment do not distinguish between natural and juristic persons in their definitions of *credit receiver*. Australia and Britain generally excluded juristic persons from the ambit of their protective legislation. *See, e.g.* the definition of *credit sale contract* and *loan contract* in sec. 5 of New South Wales' Credit Act 94 of 1984 and the definition of *individual* in sec. 189(1) of Britain's Consumer Credit Act which excludes bodies corporate from the definition. *See* further the *Crowther report, supra,* at 246; R. M. Goode, *Consumer Credit Law, supra,* at 93; Guest and Lloyd, *supra,* at 1–004; sec. 4 of the repealed British Hire-Purchase Act of 1965.

[116] Bernitz once put it concisely and correctly: "The use of the *concept* of *consumer protection* should be restricted to protection for private citizens." Bernitz, "Consumer Protection: Aims Methods and Trends in Swedish Consumer Law", 20 *Scandinavian Studies in Law* 25 (1976).

[117] J. M. Otto and N. J. Grové, *Working Paper 46, supra,* at 159. The exclusion of juristic persons from the protection of consumer credit legislation is not altogether without problems and free of criticism. Some people feel that "small" entities should be protected as well. Defining a small entity and working out criteria for what is large and small, however, is a very difficult task. *See* Madsen, "The Impact of Consumer Law on the Law of Contracts in Denmark", 28 *Scandinavian Studies in Law* 91 (1984).

[118] *Crowther report, supra,* at 1; *Molomby report* (*Report on Fair Consumer Credit Laws,* chairman T. Molomby (1972)) 3; *Rogerson report* (*Report on the Law relating to Consumer Credit and Moneylending,* co-ordinator A. Rogerson (1969) 912).

[119] This is the test in applying the Belgian Consumer Credit Act. *Memorie van Toelichting, supra,* at 2; Lettany, *supra,* at 5. The test in Germany, according to the writers, is whether the credit is exclusively or primarily intended for business purposes. Martens, "Anwendungsbereich des Verbraucherkreditgesetzes", 31 *Die Bank* 281 (1991); Bruchner *et al, supra,* at 50. The Dutch Act leaves the matter in the hands of the credit receiver. The Act does not apply where he has signed a declaration that the credit was granted for business or professional purposes. Sec. 4(1)(d) of the *Wet op het Consumentenkrediet.*

The economies and social systems of the countries of Southern Africa differ in many respects from those in Europe.[120] The computer technology and the sophistication of dealers and their staff, to name but two areas, may not always be of the high standard that most European countries are privileged to have. Certain forms of abuse may be more prevalent in Southern Africa than in Europe, and the contrary may also be true. For instance, unconscionable practices relating to debt collection such as simulated legal processes or even physical threats are not unheard of in South Africa, but they are not necessarily a problem in European countries.[121]

It is also true that certain countries simply cannot afford to have sophisticated consumer legislation. They cannot afford the policing associated with this type of legislation and do not always have the manpower to enforce or apply it.[122] Not all countries are capable of implementing a registration system in terms of which credit grantors must be registered. Britain has such a system,[123] as does Belgium.[124] The advantages of a licensing system whereby credit grantors are selected and controlled to some extent are obvious, and it may be the most effective way "of excluding the sharp and dishonest from an area of enterprise while leaving the fair and honest to carry on their activities".[125] It is not the only machinery available, however, and the Directive recognises this. The Directive gives member states three different options: they must ensure that credit grantors obtain official authorisation to do business, or that they are subject to inspections, or that bodies are established with which consumers can lodge complaints. This is another valuable lesson from the Directive, namely that alternatives should, where possible, be available to the countries concerned.

The main issue is not that there are differences among various countries and regions. Everyone knows that. What is of importance is the example set by the Directive and the way in which it was applied by different countries. Therein, I think, lies the value of the Directive. For one, the choice between a comprehensive Act and one that is less so, is better left to the discretion of the countries involved. Belgium, for instance, has a comprehensive Act[126] dealing with a wide variety of subjects; the Netherlands

---

[120] Which, of course, have their own differences.
[121] *Cf.* McQuoid-Mason in A. J. Rycroft (ed.), *Race and the Law in South Africa* (1987) 182. Whether this is a problem in Europe I do not know. The Belgian legislature indeed thought it necessary to deal with debt collecting, including a prohibition on documents simulating legal processes. Sec. 39. *See Memorie van Toelichting, supra*, at 32.
[122] This is of course particularly unfortunate in third world countries where protection is often needed more than in advanced societies simply because developing societies are often more exposed to abuses and malpractices. *See* B. W. Harvey and D. L. Parry, *The Law of Consumer Protection and Fair Trading* (1987) 37; Ross Cranston, *Consumers and the Law* (1984) 9.
[123] *See* Part III of the Consumer Credit Act.
[124] Chap. VII of their Act.
[125] The *Molomby report, supra*, at para. 3.5.1.
[126] The position is the same in Britain. The different states of Australia also accepted comprehensive new credit legislation in the mid-1980s. *See* as to consumer credit in Australia, Cavanagh and Barnes (fn. 30); A. J. Duggan *et al., Regulated Credit. The Credit and Security Aspect* (1989).

has a less comprehensive one, and the German Act is very brief indeed. Each has its advantages. A short Act is usually more simple and on the face of it easy to understand, which is desirable in the case of consumer legislation in particular. That is not the end of the matter, though. A seemingly simple piece of legislation in this field often causes more problems than it provides solutions because so many possibilities for different interpretations are created thereby. It is then left to the courts to provide the answers.[127] This is good news for litigation lawyers, and all very well in wealthy societies. Many societies, on the other hand, are in need of legislation that lay down the rules of the credit game quite comprehensively without necessitating too many court precedents. This, like most of the other problems connected with the drafting of consumer credit legislation, should better be left to individual countries to decide for themselves. But most of the problems will be easier dealt with if a basic set of principles, such as those contained in the Directive, is available.

---

[127] The German Act is such an example. Mertins, *supra*, at 258. *Cf.* also Martens, *supra*, at 282. The Act stimulated an enormous amount of academic jurisprudence. *See* Steiner, "Verbraucherkreditgesetz. Kommentar-Konjunktur", 45 *Zeitschrift für das Gesamte Kreditwesen* 140 (1992).

16. Banking Regulation and Supervision in Egypt: The View from a Developing Country

Ziad A. Baha-Eldin[1]

1 INTRODUCTION

The remarkable growth in literature concerning banking regulation and supervision in recent years has been significant in reflecting the national and international concern over banking systems' safety and soundness. This concern may be attributed to several factors: namely the financial crises which some western industrialised countries have witnessed since the second half of the 1970s led to a growing concern over the safety and soundness of financial institutions and markets, including banks. Such concern has prompted a wide revision of the basis upon which banks had so far been regulated, or unregulated. Moreover, the worldwide trends of economic liberalisation and financial market integration allowed banks, as well as other financial intermediaries, to deal in much wider markets and in a greater scope of activities than had hitherto been possible.

Paradoxically, general economic liberalisation brought with it financial markets reregulation. Further, the late 1970s and 1980s saw a growing trend of international cooperation between bank regulators in an unprecedented manner, as seen by the Basle Committee's guidelines, the most ambitious of which was the 1988 *Report on Capital Adequacy*. With the collapse of communism and the Soviet bloc, an added impetus was given to the need for understanding banking regulation in order to accommodate countries which were trying to embark on a quick transition from centrally regulated, government owned, banking systems to liberal ones where regulation would be kept to a minimum.

One important feature of this growing concern has been the increasing importance of legal writing, which has reflected the significance of legal methods and tools in dealing with the issue of banking regulation. Thus local as well as international efforts to reregulate financial systems in general, including banking sectors, have increasingly relied on legal

---

[1] Postgraduate Researcher in Development Law, London School of Economics, University of London.

expertise not only in the strict area of banking law but also in related topics such as taxation, corporate structures, and bankruptcy, as well as general legal principles.

However, in spite of the growing importance of banking regulation and supervision to countries all over the world, the leading existing legal literature has been largely based on the experiences of banks in the western industrialised markets, and sufficient attention has not been given to the particular circumstances of developing countries.[2] Such circumstances vary according to countries and areas of interest, but broadly speaking include economic conditions, historical experiences, cultural values, and the overall structure of legal systems. These circumstances have an effect on the nature of the banking systems, the regulatory style adopted by the relevant government authorities, as well as the degree of effectiveness of such regulation. Moreover, with the increasing involvement of international organisations – such as the International Monetary Fund, the World Bank and the Bank for International Settlements – in spreading regulatory standards and measures across the world, there is room for concern over the suitability and relevance of such standards and measures to the case of developing countries. However, it is equally important to avoid overemphasising cultural and structural differences between developing and developed countries. A dynamic approach requires that we look not only at differences between the two groups, but also at similarities, as well as potential changes which may narrow, or widen, the gap between them in the future. It is therefore necessary to look at the subject of banking regulation in developing countries as an interplay between several factors and pressures rather than as a mere competition between forces of tradition and forces of modernity.

This chapter will look at the regulation of the banking sector of one particular developing country: Egypt. Its aim is to discuss the interplay of factors and pressures which affect the regulation of banks in Egypt, in a manner which may be helpful in understanding the problems of banking regulation in other developing countries as well.

In 1991, Egypt agreed on an adjustment programme with the International Monetary Fund and the World Bank which included, among other measures, the restructuring of the Egyptian financial system, and wide amendments to the laws governing the regulation of both the securities market and the banking sector. Thus in 1992, the two major laws governing the Egyptian banking system were amended and included, for the first time, comprehensive prudential measures based on the guidelines of the Basle Committee. These amendments, however, came against the backdrop of a complex interplay of several factors and pressures. The first is Egypt's historical experience with colonialism – primarily British – which has been closely linked with the role played by foreign banks in the nineteenth century. Later on, banks figured prominently in the political and

---

[2] The major exception to that is research undertaken or published by the International Monetary Fund and the World Bank.

economic debates and transformations which accompanied the transition from free market to socialist central planning in the early 1960s, and back to liberal market thinking in the mid-1970s. The second is the structure of the banking sector, the type of regulation conducted by the Central Bank of Egypt, and in general the legal tradition which affected the relation of banks with the rest of the financial system. Third, religion and culture have had an effect on banking practices, especially since the rise of the Islamic political movement in the mid-1970s. The religious prohibition on interest and usury has led to a wide debate on the whole legality of "modern" banks not only in Egypt but all over the Arab and Islamic world. Whether the so-called "Islamic banks" have truly presented an alternative to western ones is a matter which remains controversial. Finally, the existence of informal financial activities are an additional factor which has affected banking practices and regulation.

This chapter will summarise the history of banking regulation in Egypt, then describe its current structure and prudential supervision measures. This will be followed by some brief comments on the effect of cultural and religious considerations on the Egyptian banking system.

2 THE HISTORICAL DEVELOPMENT OF THE EGYPTIAN BANKING SECTOR

Egypt's first "modern" bank, The Bank of Egypt, was established in 1856 with financial backing from a number of British institutions and investors.[3] However, this date should not be seen as the beginning of the story, but rather the culmination of events and developments which led to the growth of an Egyptian banking system in the second half of the nineteenth century.

In Egypt, as in other countries, informal financial intermediation in some form or another preceded the rise of financial institutions and markets as we now know them. Moneychangers, wealthy landowners, tax collectors and others, often fulfilled the intermediation function.[4] Research in pre-banking forms of finance is crucial not only for its historical value, but also for the understanding of informal financial arrangements and activities which have persisted until the present time within large sections of Egyptian society.

Since the Arab-Islamic invasion of Egypt in A.D. 641 and until the early twentieth century, the country remained, sometimes in effect and often in name only, part of several Arab-Islamic dynasties and empires, the last of which was the Ottoman Empire (1517–1918).

The appointed governors of the Ottoman rulers relied on Tax Farmers for the collection of taxes. Tax Farmers imposed their own taxes on farmers of

---

[3] R. Wilson, *Banking and Finance in the Arab Middle East* (London: Macmillan Publishers Ltd., 1983), p. 19.
[4] *Id.*

lands under their authority. They were then required to deliver to the Treasury only a fixed portion of the proceeds, in return for keeping the balance as personal profit.[5] Meanwhile, the Egyptian towns were gradually being transformed into commercial and industrial centres, which drew on the surplus production of the agricultural sector. This led to the monetarisation of the villages, and thus to the development of financial intermediation in its simplest forms. Tax Farmers, as owners of the agricultural surplus, became the main source of money and credit. One indirect form of credit was effected by the Tax Farmer paying the taxes himself to the Treasury in the first instance, and collecting them later from the farmers when their crops had grown.[6]

Ottoman control of Egypt, already declining by the end of the eighteenth century, was interrupted in 1798 when a French Army led by Napoleon Bonaparte conquered the country. In 1801, and due to international interference, the French Expedition was forced to abandon Egypt. But in spite of its short duration, the Expedition's influence on Egyptian society was far-reaching. It represented the first direct contact of the Egyptian population with a modern European imperial power, underlined the decline of Ottoman rule, and drew the world's attention to the importance of Egypt in the imperial contest. The end of the Expedition was followed by a restoration of nominal Ottoman rule, but effective power was soon to rest in the hands of an officer from the Ottoman armies, Mohammed Ali, who controlled the country in an independent manner throughout the first half of the nineteenth century.

What Mohammed Ali attempted was no less than a complete transformation and modernisation of the country by taking possession of its resources directly under the control of the state, and imposing a state monopoly on production, distribution, and trade. The introduction in 1820 of a new crop, cotton, proved to be crucial in increasing the public revenue, inflating the price of land, and encouraging the arrival of increasing numbers of foreign merchants, financiers and bankers attracted by speculation on the new crop, and by the forthcoming boom in infrastructure projects.[7]

However, the failure of Mohammed Ali's project, for a variety of domestic and international reasons, forced a shift in economic policy as of the late 1830s. Thus from 1837, a gradual liberalisation was begun, first under Mohammed Ali, then his successors. Gradually, agricultural, manufacturing, and trade monopolies were dismantled. Foreign merchants were permitted to trade freely in agricultural production, including cotton. However, such trade brought with it increasing powers for the foreign merchants under an old Treaty of Capitulations signed between the

---

[5] S. Shaw, *The Financial and Administrative Organization and Development of Ottoman Egypt 1517–1798* (New Jersey: Princeton University Press, 1962), pp. 1–9.

[6] R. Owen, *Cotton and the Egyptian Economy 1820–1914, A Study in Trade and Development* (Oxford: Oxford University Press, 1969), pp. 4–17.

[7] *Id.*, p. 23 (introduction).

Ottoman Empire and European powers in the sixteenth century. The Treaty guaranteed the principle of extra-territoriality whereby the nationals of foreign countries were granted a number of privileges that made them immune from local jurisdiction.[8] By the nineteenth century, those privileges had been extended to a degree that undermined state authority and made foreign nationals practically untouchable.[9]

These were the circumstances in which the Bank of Egypt was established in 1856. However, it was only from 1860, with the beginning of a cotton boom caused by the American Civil War and an accompanying expansion in public infrastructure projects, that banks began to increase in number. Between 1860 and 1880, more than fifteen banks, all foreign, were established in Cairo, Alexandria and the Suez Canal city of Port Said.[10]

The cotton boom did not last for long, and the ultimate fall in cotton prices brought down with it the financial structure, as well as the country's independence. The decline in cotton prices began in 1864, and when the London Stock Exchange crashed in 1866 and no new money was coming from Europe, a large number of Egyptian houses went bankrupt. By 1874, the government's inability to serve the public debt brought direct foreign interference as two officials, an Englishman and a Frenchman, were appointed in the Egyptian treasury to ensure the repayment of the outstanding Government bonds. Further foreign interference led to popular discontent, then to a military movement by Egyptian army officers. In spite of the officers' attempts to reassure foreign bondholders, British forces intervened in 1882, citing the restoration of peace and the safeguard of interests of bondholders as reasons for their interference.[11] Thus began a seventy year long occupation of Egypt by British forces and administration, albeit under the official Ottoman, and later Egyptian, thrones.

The few years that preceded the British occupation saw the beginning of political and legal reforms. An attempt to "modernise" the legal system introduced a dual court structure whereby Mixed Courts had jurisdiction over disputes involving foreigners and used newly drafted Mixed Codes, while Indigenous Courts using equally new Indigenous Codes had jurisdiction over disputes between Egyptians. Both the Mixed and the Indigenous Codes were drafted on the model of European Continental, particularly French, codes. The legal system has remained since that time, even following its unification in 1948, part of the Civil Law tradition in all matters except family law, which has uninterruptedly been based on principles of Islamic Law.

In the early years of British rule, the National Bank of Egypt was established, in 1898, with the intention that it act as the government's bank.

---

[8] M. A. Rifaat, *The Monetary System of Egypt* (London: George Allen and Unwin Ltd., 1935), p. 16.

[9] D. Landes, *Bankers and Pashas* (New York: Harper and Row, 1960), pp. 90–91.

[10] Wilson, *op. cit.*, pp. 21–22 and Rifaat, *op. cit.*, p. 78.

[11] Rifaat, *op. cit.*, p. 26.

Although this privately owned, British-dominated bank did not assume central banking powers, it was the first step towards the regulation of the banking system. Foreign domination of the banking system was not challenged until the twentieth century. Strong nationalist feelings, which followed the end of the First World War and the declaration of Egypt's nominal independence, manifested themselves in the establishment of the first wholly owned Egyptian bank, Banque Misr (Egypt Bank), in 1920.

The following years were characterised by the development and relative sophistication of the liberal economic environment, especially with the increasing involvement of banks in economic life and the growth of securities trading. Political circumstances, however, were deteriorating rapidly. By the early 1950s, popular discontent was rising due to the unfulfilled promises of independence made by the allied forces in the course of the Second World War, the corruption of the Egyptian monarchy, the beginning of a long military confrontation with the newly established state of Israel, and the widening gap between rich and poor. Such feelings led to a military takeover by a group of officers led by Gamal Abdel Nasser in 1952, which overthrew the government, forced the King's abdication, negotiated the evacuation of the British forces, and finally declared Egypt a republic.

Following a period of hesitation, the new republican regime began, as of the mid-1950s, to adopt a gradual transformation of the economy towards socialist central planning. The trend was accelerated following the Suez Crisis in 1956, during which British, French, and Israeli armies were involved in military operations against Egypt. From the point of view of banking activities, a number of legislative developments took place. Law number 22 of 1957 stated that some foreign-owned banks were to be "Egyptianised". In the same year, the Banks and Credit Law number 163 of 1957 was enacted. This was a particularly important step in the development of banking regulation in Egypt, and the law remains, in spite of several amendments, the major and most comprehensive legislation on the subject. One important feature of this Law was the spelling out in clear terms of the role of the National Bank of Egypt as a central bank. The latter remained, however, privately owned until 1960, when it was nationalised.[12] Six months later, in July 1960, the National Bank of Egypt was split into two parts: one renamed the Central Bank of Egypt; the other remained the National Bank of Egypt with a mandate to carry out only ordinary commercial banking activities.[13] Thus an independent, publicly owned, central bank finally came to exist after more than sixty years from its original inception. It remains the basis of banking regulation in Egypt to this day.

In 1961, all banks which had so far remained privately owned were nationalised.[14] This was the final step in the creation of the state's monopoly over the banking sector. What followed during the rest of the 1960s was a

---

[12] Presidential Decree No. 40 of 1960.
[13] Presidential Decree No. 250 of 1960.
[14] Law 117 of 1961.

gradual process of consolidation and specialisation of the public sector banks.

By the mid-1970s, political circumstances had once again changed. President Anwar Al-Sadat, in power since 1970, embarked on a process of liberalisation of the economy, coupled with a redirection of Egypt's foreign affairs towards a peaceful settlement of the conflict with Israel and an increasing reliance on the United States and the western world. From a legislative perspective, the 1974 Foreign Investment Law marked the water-shed.[15] Among other significant measures intended to encourage foreign investment, this Law permitted the establishment of private sector banks, as well as the opening up of branches of foreign banks, although the latter were not permitted to deal in local currency, and thus were prevented from competing with Egyptian banks. But as the prevailing economic thinking was beginning to change, the need arose for a revision of the banking regulatory measures. Whereas the Banks and Credit Law of 1957 remained in place, it was complemented by the 1975 Central Bank and Banking System Law.[16] Both Laws, together with their amendments and imple-menting ministerial decrees, constitute the core of banking regulation in Egypt. The liberalisation policy, however, did not go as planned, nor did it deliver its expected results. Popular discontent, on the rise again by the early 1980s, prevented austerity measures being implemented and finally culminated in President Sadat's assassination in October 1981.

Under Sadat's successor, President Mubarak, the first half of the 1980s was characterised by relatively good economic conditions. But by the second half of the 1980s, the need arose again for the imposition of severe austerity measures. Several rounds of negotiations with international econ-omic organisations were undertaken, but produced little result. However, following the Gulf War, in which Egypt participated alongside the Allied forces to liberate Kuwait, a new programme was finally agreed with the International Monetary Fund and the World Bank, in 1991. The structural adjustment programme agreed with the international economic organ-isations included major provisions concerning the Egyptian banking sector. But it is important to note that the amendments introduced in the banking regulatory system were influenced by other factors, including the collapse of so-called Islamic Investment Companies and the rising international awareness of prudential supervision in line with the Basle Committee prin-ciples, especially following the collapse of Bank of Credit and Commerce International, and its Egyptian subsidiary Bank of Credit and Commerce Misr, as well as the financial troubles which confronted a number of other banks.

The major elements of the new adjustment programme in the area of banking regulation were centred on freeing the interest rates, a gradual implementation of the Basle Committee guidelines on capital adequacy,

---

[15] Law 43 of 1974.
[16] Law 120 of 1975.

minimum capital, lending limits and consolidated supervision. They also included the setting up of a deposit insurance scheme, the opening up of internal competition by permitting branches of foreign banks to deal in local currency, and the gradual privatisation of the banking sector. Thus the two major Laws concerning banking regulation were twice amended in 1992 and 1993.[17] Other relevant legal changes occurred in the Law governing the capital market, and in the investment Law.

The following sections of this chapter will describe in some detail and discuss some aspects of the new banking regulatory system that has resulted from these latest amendments.

3 STRUCTURE OF THE EGYPTIAN BANKING SYSTEM

The current banking regulatory system in Egypt is based on two major Laws, each amended several times and accompanied by a presidential decree which deals with detailed matters not covered by the Law. These are the 1957 Banks and Credit Law,[18] with its implementing decree,[19] and the 1975 Central Bank and Banking System Law,[20] accompanied by the decree promulgating the Statutes of the Central Bank of Egypt.[21] Other directly relevant Laws are the Banking Secrecy Law,[22] and the Capital Market Law,[23] with its implementing decree.[24] Finally, the regulatory system includes regular circulars issued by the Central Bank of Egypt, and dealing with a variety of issues.

The previous Laws, decrees, and circulars deal with banking regulation and supervision in the strict sense, *i.e.* they do not deal with banking operations from a substantive point of view. Substantive provisions are to be found in the principles of the 1948 Civil Code, the 1883 Code of Commerce, other scattered Laws, as well as in banking practices and customs, international agreements and court decisions.

3.1 The Central Bank of Egypt

The Central Bank of Egypt is an autonomous public legal entity domiciled in Cairo.[25] It is managed by a Board of Directors composed of fifteen members, and chaired by the Governor of the Bank. The Governor and his deputy are appointed by presidential decree, in accordance with the Prime Minister's advice, for a renewable period of four years. The Board of Directors is responsible for managing the Bank's affairs and for the

---

[17] Laws 37 of 1992 and 101 of 1993.
[18] Law 163 of 1957.
[19] Currently Presidential Decree No. 187 of 1993.
[20] Law 120 of 1975.
[21] Presidential Decree No. 59 of 1993.
[22] Law 205 of 1990.
[23] Law 95 of 1992.
[24] Ministerial Decree No. 135 of 1993.
[25] Law 120 of 1975, articles 1 and 2.

implementation of monetary, banking and credit policies.[26] Whereas the
Central Bank of Egypt is, by law, an autonomous entity, it is not by any
means independent from Government, and in practice is an integral part of
the executive authority.

Central banks all over the world have, traditionally, performed all or
some of a variety of functions. These include issuing currency, acting as the
Government banker and as a lender of last resort, supervising the implementation of the monetary policy, regulating the banking sector, and generally maintaining the stability of the currency as well as financial and
monetary conditions. Whether or not central banks should combine the
implementation of monetary policy with the supervision over the banking
system is a controversial matter. Whereas the combination of functions may
threaten to create a conflict of interests, particularly in interest rate determination, it may improve the chances of preventing the failure of the
payments system and therefore reducing the potential systemic risk.[27]

The Central Bank of Egypt belongs to the group of regulators which
combine both functions. It issues currency,[28] acts as the Government's
banker,[29] implements the Government's monetary policy,[30] acts as lender
of last resort,[31] and regulates the banking sector.[32] But such an assertion has
to be qualified. The separation of the monetary policy role from banking
supervision only makes sense if the authorities conducting each one are
somewhat independent not only from one another but also from the
Government. But in the Egyptian case, as in other cases where such authorities are under the control of the Government, it would make little difference whether the two functions were combined or separated, as long as
the authority undertaking them is abiding by Government orders. The
whole issue of separation is therefore less relevant in an environment
dominated by the Government's interference.

3.2 Types of banks

In spite of Egypt's relatively long history of banking, no definition exists for
the term "bank" in the different Laws and decrees that have been enacted.
Although commercial, specialised, and investment banks are described,
such descriptions are meant to distinguish between types of banks rather
than to provide a broad definition.

The difficulty, yet necessity, of defining a bank stems from the
continuously expanding range of activities undertaken by banks and other

---

[26] Law 120 of 1975, article 7.
[27] For a recent discussion of the role played by central banks and a comparative study, *see*
    C. Goodhart and D. Schoenmaker, *Institutional Separation Between Supervisory and Monetary
    Agencies* , Special Paper Series Number 52 (London: London School of Economics Financial
    Markets Group, April 1993).
[28] Law 163 of 1957, articles 16 and 17.
[29] Law 163 of 1957, article 18.
[30] Law 163 of 1957, article 1.
[31] Law 163 of 1957, article 50.
[32] Law 163 of 1957, article 1(c).

similar institutions, which is making it increasingly difficult to determine where the boundaries between banks and other financial institutions should lie, if at all. This is why regulators may find it easier to adopt a formal definition of banks rather than a substantive one. In this case, a bank is to be defined as an institution registered as such at the Central Bank, irrespective of the nature and substance of its activities. This is the attitude taken by Egyptian regulators. According to the 1957 Banking and Credit Law, no person, organisation, or establishment not registered according to its provisions may undertake any of the banking operations as a "basic or habitual pursuit".[33] Unfortunately, no definition exists for the term "banking operations".

However, other regulators around the world have chosen to define banks in terms of the substance of their activities. For instance, The European Community, faced with the daunting task of coming up with a definition that would suit all its member countries, stated in its First Directive, that a credit institution is "an undertaking whose business is to receive deposits or other repayable funds from the public and to grant credit for its own account". The Second Directive went further and added a list of activities which banks may be authorised to conduct. In spite of the difficulty of formulating a definition that would encompass all banking activities, and yet be flexible enough to permit for future developments, this second approach is more accurate.

The Egyptian regulatory system recognises different types of banks which can be classified according to one of two criteria: ownership and activity.

According to the ownership classification, banks are either public sector or private sector owned. Following the nationalisations of the 1960s, there only remained a handful of public sector banks. The liberalisation of the economy, begun in the mid-1970s, permitted the establishment of private sector banks either as wholly Egyptian-owned joint-ventures with foreign partners, branches or representative offices of foreign banks.[34]

Fully Egyptian-owned private sector banks, as well as joint-venture banks with international partners incorporated in Egypt and with minimum 51% Egyptian ownership, were permitted to undertake all banking operations. Branches and representative offices of foreign banks, however, were restricted from some operations.

Branches of foreign banks were not permitted to deal in local currency. This situation, thought by the regulators to preserve a protected market for the large public sector banks, was challenged by the foreign banks. The 1991 restructuring programme agreed with the international economic organisations and gave impetus to the lobbying of the foreign banks in this regard. Thus, concerns that foreign banks would dominate the market and drive out local institutions, or that they would engage in "cream skimming" whereby they would capture the more profitable segments of the market,

---

[33] Law 163 of 1957, article 19.
[34] Investment Law 43 of 1974, article 3.

leaving the less profitable to local institutions, were repeatedly voiced. However, in the end, such concerns were overridden by arguments about the need to level the playing field, and to open local currency markets for international competition, which formed part of the restructuring programme. Accordingly, the 1993 amendment to the Banking and Credit Law finally allowed branches of foreign banks to deal in local currency.[35] The fact that such amendment came so late in the liberalisation process indicates the extent to which foreign banks' participation in the domestic banking market was still seen as a potential threat, especially in view of Egypt's historical experience with foreign banks and their association with nineteenth-century colonialism.

Representative offices of foreign banks, on the other hand, were barred from undertaking any banking operations, since their introduction in the early 1980s.[36] Only in 1992 were these offices recognised in the banking legislation,[37] but again on the basis that they would perform neither banking nor any commercial activity. Their role was limited to representing their head offices, undertaking market studies and investment research, as well as providing links between their head offices and Egyptian banks.

The second classification of Egyptian banks is in accordance with the type of activity they are permitted to perform, hence they are either commercial, specialised, or investment/merchant banks. When the first comprehensive banking legislation was enacted in 1957, only two types of banks were envisaged. The first was commercial banks, described as institutions which "habitually" accept deposits payable on demand or after a period not exceeding one year.[38] The second type was non-commercial (later renamed specialised) banks and described as banks whose main business is the financing of real estate, agriculture or industry; while the acceptance of demand deposits is not one of their basic activities.[39]

In 1974, a third type of bank, investment/merchant banks, was recognised, albeit in a gradual and rather curious manner. Following the inauguration of the liberalisation policy in the mid-1970s, the 1974 Investment Law permitted the establishment of private sector banks, as stated above. But, curiously, one of the stated forms of incorporation of such private banks was the so-called Investment and Business Banks, although such type of incorporation did not exist under the banking regulation legislation. The situation, however, was ratified in 1975 with the enactment of the Central Bank and Banking System Law which introduced and described the concept of Investment and Business Banks as banks which would carry out operations related to the pooling and promotion of savings, establish companies, and undertake the financing of Egypt's

---

[35] Law 163 of 1957, article 21–II, as amended.
[36] Company Code No. 159 of 1981, article 173.
[37] Law 163 of 1957, article 21–II, as amended.
[38] Law 163 of 1957, article 38.
[39] Law 163 of 1957, article 43.

foreign debt operations.[40] In effect, the aim of the legislation was the introduction of merchant banking in Egypt.

The same 1975 legislation redefined commercial banks in order to permit them to accept medium- and long-term deposits, so long as they were payable within a fixed period, and to undertake all kinds of financial activities including equity ownership. Finally the Law renamed non-commercial banks as specialised banks, and permitted them a wider scope of activity.[41]

Finally, a word remains to be said about Islamic banks, a number of which now exist in Egypt. In spite of their significance in the market, it would not be appropriate to consider them an independent type of bank, at least not in terms of legal incorporation. The reason is that such banks are incorporated under one of the previously described forms, albeit often under special legislation, and their description as Islamic only relates to the banking operations they choose to undertake. They will therefore be dealt with later in this chapter in the section relating to religious and cultural considerations.

3.3 Supervisory style

It has been said previously that the Central Bank of Egypt is the major regulator of the banking sector. It now remains to be seen how such super-vision is conducted. In spite of the fact that, since 1898, the National Bank of Egypt was established to act as a Government banker, it is difficult to speak of real supervision except in the 1970s, and more so since the early 1990s. The reason for such delayed active supervision is twofold: on the one hand, it is not until the 1957 legislation that the Central Bank's supervision was clearly and sufficiently dealt with in law, and not until 1960 that the Bank became an autonomous, state-owned, entity. On the other hand, by the time such autonomy had been achieved, the country was well into its socialist experience, and in 1961, all banks were nationalised and consolidated in a number of big public sector banks. Accordingly, the Central Bank's super-vision became largely an administrative oversight conducted by one Government agency over another.

The situation was meant to change following the liberalisation of the 1970s, as private sector banks were established. But even then, two restrictions existed: the first was the fact that foreign banks' branches were barred from dealing in local currency, thus they had a limited scope of activity, and the second is that the vast majority of the newly established private sector banks had a majority equity held by one of the big public sector banks. Thus until the late 1980s, the banking sector in Egypt remained largely dominated by the public sector banks, which were largely under the direct control of the Government, leaving little for the Central Bank to regulate independently.

---

[40] Law 120 of 1975, article 17.
[41] Law 120 of 1975, article 16.

The situation began to change dramatically in the early 1990s. On the one hand, the failure of Islamic Investment Companies in the late 1980s and then of the Bank of Credit and Commerce Misr (an Egyptian joint-venture bank) led to the realisation that prudential regulation over financial intermediaries was much needed. On the other hand, with a new impetus given to the liberalisation programme as a result of the agreement with the international economic organisations, branches of foreign banks were permitted to deal in local currency, and a programme of privatising the public sector banks' equity in private sector banks (a policy described as privatising the private sector) was undertaken. This meant that for the first time since its autonomous incorporation, the Central Bank of Egypt began to find itself in a position where it was required to undertake supervision over a banking sector that would eventually become largely outside the direct control of the Government. Following is a description of the Central Bank's supervisory style, in law.

In 1957, the Banks and Credit Law stated that the Central Bank of Egypt should "control banking institutions so as to ensure the soundness of their financial position".[42] The same Law stated that banks had to be registered with the Central Bank and obtain its approval for conducting banking operations.[43] Banks registered with the Central Bank were, and still are, required to submit to it a monthly statement of their financial position, a copy of every report submitted to the shareholders, as well as any other requested information. The Central Bank is also entitled, with the permission of the Ministry of Economy, to review banks' books at their headquarters.[44] Banks are not allowed to merge nor to cease operations without the Central Bank's approval, which also has the authority to delist banks in certain prescribed cases, including situations where a bank "follows a policy which would endanger the public economic interest".[45] Finally, the Board of Directors of the Central Bank is authorised to lay down general rules for the supervision of banks regarding asset valuation, the ratio of loans to loanable value of guarantees, and maturity periods, as well as interest rate determination.[46] The 1975 legislation further strengthened the Central Bank's powers to inspect banks' books[47] and a 1984 amendment made the appointment of board members in any bank conditional upon the Central Bank's approval. In 1992, this provision was extended to branches of foreign banks, and to include as well board members, executive directors, and managers of certain departments.[48]

Following the 1991 agreement with the international economic organisations, the Central Bank's regulatory powers were generally

---

[42] Law 163 of 1957, article 1(c).
[43] Law 163 of 1957, article 19.
[44] Law 163 of 1957, articles 27–29.
[45] Law 163 of 1957, articles 32–34.
[46] Law 163 of 1957, article 37.
[47] Law 120 of 1975, article 9.
[48] Law 163 of 1957, article 24–II, as amended by Law 50 of 1984, article II, and Law 37 of 1992, article II.

increased. It was now in a position to request that any bank facing financial difficulties improve its capitalisation either by increasing its capital or by depositing additional funds with the Central Bank. If the bank facing such difficulty, which in any case was determined by the Central Bank, failed to comply with its requests, the Central Bank would be entitled to either invite public subscription to the proposed capital increase or merge the bank with another, provided that the latter accepted the merger.[49]

These are, in summary, the supervisory powers accorded to the Central Bank of Egypt. They are statute-based, but largely complemented by circulars issued and distributed by the Central Bank. Since the early 1990s, such supervision has been faced with increasing challenges due to the liberalisation of the banking sector. Accordingly, a new structure of prudential measures has been introduced, which is described in the following sections.

4 PRUDENTIAL REGULATION

Prudential regulation is the broad term referring to a wide range of supervisory measures which aim at reducing the risk of bank failure and therefore maintaining the safety, soundness and stability of the banking system. The importance of prudential regulation stems from the notion of "systemic risk", *i.e.*, the belief that one particular bank's failure may affect the public's confidence in other banks, led to a general run on them, and therefore to the collapse of the whole banking system. This unique feature in banks is usually attributed to the fact that they are creators of money, depositories of the society's savings, managers of its payments system, and allocators of credit. Moreover, banks are by their own nature highly leveraged, thus vulnerable to depositor withdrawals.[50] Whether or not one bank's failure would bring down the whole financial system is a controversial assumption, and not universally accepted.

In view of the wide range of measures included in the term "prudential", it is useful to adopt the distinction between preventive and protective prudential regulation.[51] According to this classification, preventive regulation is designed to reduce risk-taking by banks in order to minimise the possibility of crises. These measures include capital adequacy, solvency and liquidity standards, restrictions on permissible activities and on loan concentration, as well as bank examination and auditing practices. Protective regulation, on the other hand, aims at providing support and rescue operations to both banks and depositors once a problem or a crisis has

---

[49] Law 163 of 1957, article 30–II, as amended.

[50] V. Polizatto, "Prudential Regulation and Banking Supervision", in *Financial Regulation: Changing the Rules of the Game*, ed. D. Vittas (Washington, D.C.: The World Bank, 1992), pp. 283–284.

[51] For details of the distinction between preventive and protective regulation, *see* R. Dale, *The Regulation of International Banking* (New Jersey: Prentice Hall Inc., 1986), pp. 55–68.

occurred. This includes depositor insurance schemes, as well as the lender-of-last-resort function of the Central Bank.[52]

Prudential regulation has, traditionally, been a domestic concern which governments and central banks were responsible for conducting. However, since the mid-1970s, the national or domestic nature of such regulation changed dramatically. The unprecedented increase in international banking activity in the past two decades, and the accompanying crises, transformed prudential regulation into a truly global concern.

The relation between the growth of international banking and the rising global concern and cooperation in the area of prudential regulation is due to two reasons. First, international banks, by virtue of their complex structures, represent a challenge to national regulators who may be able to conduct adequate local supervision, but have difficulties in assessing the global position of such banks. Cooperation with other supervisors becomes, therefore, a necessity. Second, the imposition of tight prudential rules may have adverse effects on banks' profitability, at least in the short term, and hence on the competitiveness of the market where such rules are imposed. Accordingly, national banking regulators are reluctant to impose any restrictions unless assured that competing banking centres around the world will follow suit. The so-called flight of banks to soft-regulated systems has become particularly important with the rise in number and importance of developing and emerging markets. This has prompted concerns that the growing international cooperation and convergence in international regulatory standards may be due to the developed countries' attempt to preserve their competitive position as centres of banking and finance, as much as by genuine fears of safety and soundness.[53]

The major manifestation of international cooperation in banking prudential regulation is the set of guidelines issued by the Basle Committee, and in particular the 1975 Basle Concordat, the 1983 Amended Basle Concordat, and the 1988 Report on Capital Requirement.[54] The Basle Committee's 1988 Report is of particular importance as it aimed at setting minimum capital adequacy standards which member countries should gradually introduce, not later than 31 December 1992.[55]

---

[52] *Id.*

[53] *See,* E. Kapstein, *Supervising International Banks: Origins and Implications of the Basle Accord,* Essays in International Finance, No. 185 (New Jersey: Princeton University, Department of Economics, December 1991).

[54] For the background of the formation of the Basle Committee, *see* J. Norton, "Background Note on the Basle Committee", in *Bank Regulation and Supervision in the 1990s,* ed. J. Norton (London: Lloyd's of London Press Ltd., 1991), pp. 82–95. For a detailed analysis of the 1975 Concordat and the 1983 Revised Concordat, *see* R. Dale, *The Regulation of International Banking* (New Jersey: Prentice-Hall, 1986).

[55] P. Hayward, "Prospects for International Co-operation by Bank Supervisors", in *Bank Regulation and Supervision in the 1990s,* ed. J. Norton (London: Lloyd's of London Press Ltd., 1991), pp. 67–81.

The exact provisions of the Basle guidelines are outside the scope of this chapter. However, it is necessary to consider the legal basis upon which different countries, especially developing ones, adhere to such international standards. In other words, since the Basle documents were issued by a limited group of developed countries' supervisors, why do other countries not party to the original discussion nor to the resulting declarations feel obliged to abide by them? The answer to this question lies in the legal nature of the Basle documents.

Formally, the Basle documents have no binding force, not only on third party countries, but even on the countries and institutions represented on the Committee. They are merely reports and recommendations which countries are invited to adopt, and whose implementation depends on the willingness of each country. This is further enhanced by the degree of discretion accorded to supervisors who choose to abide by their content.[56] Nevertheless, the remarkable credibility and seriousness accorded to the Basle documents made them acquire a unique level of universal acceptance. This wide acceptance is due to several reasons. On the one hand, the fact that the original signatories to the Basle reports were the banking supervisors of the G-10 countries, and that they had declared their intention to abide by their requirements, gave the reports a strong initial force. On the other hand, banks and banking systems all over the world could advertise their adherence to the guidelines as a way of acquiring depositor and investor confidence, and gaining a competitive edge, thus forcing other markets to follow suit. The voluntary acceptance of the Basle guidelines suggests that the Basle requirements may be an example of the "soft law" doctrine as applied to international economic matters.[57] However, whereas the "soft law" doctrine would seem to explain the developed countries' acceptance of the Basle guidelines, the situation may be different with developing countries, in particular those with ongoing adjustment programmes with the International Monetary Fund and the World Bank. The reason for this distinction is that international assistance provided through the adjustment programmes is usually made conditional upon a number of measures, which may include the implementation of some of the Basle requirements. In this situation, it becomes possible to consider the adjustment programme itself as the source of obligation. This is true not only of the banking sector reform, but of all aspects of adjustment programmes which acquire a certain degree of enforceability from the conditionality attached to the programmes. Whether this qualifies as a kind of international contractual obligation or not will depend on individual cases.

We now turn to the Egyptian case by discussing briefly some of the prudential measures that have been adopted by the regulatory authorities.

---

[56] C. Thomson, "The Basle Concordat: International Collaboration in Banking Supervision", in *Current Legal Issues Affecting Central Banks*, ed. R. Effros, Volume 1 (Washington D.C.: International Monetary Fund, 1992), pp. 331–332.

[57] J. Norton, footnote to the article by P. Hayward, "Prospects for International Co-operation by Bank Supervisors", in *Bank Regulation and Supervision in the 1990s*, ed. J. Norton (London: Lloyd's of London Press Ltd., 1991), p. 68.

4.1 Preventive regulation

As said previously, a wide range of regulatory measures may be described as prudential. This section will describe two such measures: the restrictions on banking activities, and the capital adequacy requirement.

The scope of activities which banks are permitted to perform is one area of prudential regulation which dates back long before the formation of the Basle Committee. The major issue here is whether financial intermediaries should combine both banking and commerce. In other words, whether the same institution should be permitted to act as a "universal bank", *i.e.*, both as a commercial bank which accepts deposits and offers credit, as well as an investment bank which trades, underwrites and holds securities and other financial instruments.[58]

The debate on universal versus segregated banking has largely centred around the U.S. 1933 Glass-Steagall Act which separated commercial and investment banks. The Act followed the 1929 Stock Market crash which forced a large number of equity holding banks to suspend their operations. The banking crisis, as well as the crash itself, were blamed on banks' heavy involvement in the securities markets, and it seemed obvious at the time that a strict separation should be introduced. The Act has come under strong criticism since then, and, in fact, the original strict separation has been somewhat eroded over the years.[59] German, Swiss, and lately the European Community banking systems, on the other hand, permit universal banks to operate as both commercial and investment banks, as well as to provide a wide range of other financial services.[60]

In Egypt, whereas there is no total separation between commercial and investment banks, some restrictions exist on the activities which commercial banks are permitted to undertake.

The 1957 Banks and Credit Law made a distinction between commercial and investment banks. The same Law prohibited commercial banks from undertaking certain activities, including the ownership of shares of joint-stock companies in excess of 25% of the company's paid-up capital, or in excess of the nominal value of the bank's paid-up capital and reserves.[61]

---

[58] On the issue of universal versus separated banking, *see* R. Dale, *International Banking Deregulation, The Great Banking Experience* (Oxford: Blackwell Publishers, 1992), G. Benston, *The Separation of Commercial and Investment Banking: The Glass-Steagall Act Revisited and Reconsidered* (Oxford: Oxford University Press, 1990), and the whole issue of the *Brooklyn Journal of International Law*, 19, No. 1 (1993).

[59] On the U.S. position, *see* M. Hall, *Banking Regulation and Supervision: A Comparative Study of the U.K., U.S.A. and Japan* (Hants: Edward Elgar Publishing Limited, 1993), L. Goldberg and L. White, ed., *The Deregulation of the Banking and Securities Industries* (Lexington: Lexington Books, 1979), and C. Horn, "The Legal Barrier Between U.S. Investment and Commercial Banking: Its Origins, Application, and Prospects", in *Current Legal Issues Affecting Central Banks*, ed. R. Effros (Washington D.C.: International Monetary Fund, 1992), pp. 279–310.

[60] For Europe, *see* M. Fowle, "1992 – Its Impact on European Banks, Their Structure, Operations and Accounts", in *1992: The Legal Implications for Banking*, ed. R. Cranston (London: Chartered Institute of Bankers and Centre for Commercial Law Studies, Queen Mary and Westfield College, University of London, 1989).

[61] Law 163 of 1957, articles 38–39.

Investment banks, on the other hand, were not restricted in conducting such operations. But, as mentioned previously, following the implementation of a socialist economic system, and the nationalisations of the early 1960s, banks' operations were severely limited, and the Stock Exchange became practically inoperative. The situation remained unchanged, even following the liberalisation efforts of the 1970s and 1980s. Only in 1992, with the restructuring of the financial sector, were the Laws amended significantly.

The 1992 amendment to the Banks and Credit Law retained the distinction and the partial separation of commercial and investment banks, but increased the limit of commercial banks' equity ownership from 25% to 40% of joint-stock companies.[62] The more significant change occurred, however, not in banking legislation, but in the newly enacted Capital Markets Law number 95 of 1992. This Law stated that only broking companies would be allowed to register as members of the Stock Exchange, instead of the previous situation where individual members were accepted.

Such member companies were barred from undertaking any activity other than security trading, broking, underwriting, and clearing, as well as venture capital and portfolio and fund establishment and management.[63] Accordingly, banks, of whatever type, could not become members of the Exchange in their own capacity. However, they could hold equity in member companies which would undertake one of the Exchange activities. Thus commercial banks would be able to own up to 40% of a member company, according to the banking law restriction, while investment banks would be able to wholly own companies registered with the Stock Exchange.

The second area of preventive prudential regulation is the capital adequacy requirement. In the Basle Committee's 1988 agreement on capital adequacy requirements, banking supervisors were advised to impose a minimum risk asset ratio equal to 8% on all internationally active banks under their supervision by 31 December 1992. This ratio is calculated on the basis of expressing the bank's adjusted capital base as a percentage of the total weighted risk assets.[64] The deliberate gradual implementation of the agreement, and the wide discretionary powers accorded to the individual regulators, were aimed at securing the widest international acceptance and adherence. The Central Bank of Egypt, in a circular dated 31 January 1991, informed banks under its supervision that they were to abide by the following capital adequacy timetable: banks which at the end of December 1990 already maintained the 8% ratio were to keep it from then onwards. Banks with a ratio from 7 to 8% were to reach the required 8% ratio by 31 December 1992. Banks with a ratio from 6 to 7% were to reach it by 31 December 1993, and those below 6% to reach it by the end of December

---

[62] Law 163 of 1957, article 39(d), as amended by Law 37 of 1992.
[63] Law 95 of 1992, articles 27 and 29.
[64] Hall, 1993, pp. 188–189.

1995.[65] In April 1991, a new circular stated that banks below the ratio of 6% were now required to reach the 8% target ratio by the end of December 1993 rather than 1995.[66] It is perhaps significant that, since the 1988 Basle agreement, the Central Bank of Egypt did not recommend the adoption of any such ratios until early 1991, which coincided with the agreement with the international economic organisations on a new adjustment programme.

The Central Bank circulars made it clear that, by the end of 1993, all banks operating in Egypt had to reach the 8% capital adequacy benchmark. But whether such a formal declaration has actually been applied remains controversial and an area of debate between Egypt's regulatory authorities and officials of the international economic organisations. This debate has shown that, whereas formal legislation of the guidelines may be the easy step, actual practice and implementation may be difficult to monitor and to judge.

Other preventive measures complement Egypt's network of prudential regulation. These include a reserve requirement, a liquidity requirement, debt valuation and provisioning measures, as well as lending limits, all stated in circulars issued by the Central Bank of Egypt.

4.2 Protective regulation

The Egyptian banking system currently features two protective prudential measures, a deposit insurance fund and the lender-of-last-resort function of the Central Bank.

The deposit insurance fund is a relatively new addition to the Egyptian prudential structure. It was introduced in the 1992 amendment to the Banks and Credit Law. It has an independent legal personality, and is subject to the supervision of the Central Bank.[67] Previous rescue operations by the Central Bank were conducted on an *ad hoc* basis. However, in the end, the regulators were convinced of the need for an institutional method to deal with such potential problems in the future.

The lender-of-last-resort role of the Central Bank is an earlier feature. Since the first comprehensive banking legislation in Egypt, in 1957, the Central Bank was considered responsible for providing emergency funds to banks in trouble.[68] The 1992 amendment, however, gave the Central Bank additional powers when conducting a rescue operation. Thus the new legislation gave the Central Bank of Egypt the authority, in a case where a bank faces difficulties, to request that the bank increases its capitalisation, or deposit additional funds with the Central Bank. If the bank in difficulty fails to comply, the Central Bank is entitled to either invite public subscription in order to achieve the increase in capitalisation, or take the necessary steps to merge the bank with another, provided the latter accepts. One of the advantages of the new provision is that it indicates broad cases where a bank

---

[65] Central Bank of Egypt Circular No. 311 dated 31 January 1991.
[66] The Central Bank of Egypt Circular No. 317 dated 21 April 1991.
[67] Law 163 of 1957, article 31–II, as amended by Law 37 of 1992.
[68] Law 163 of 1957, article 50.

would be considered in trouble, rather than leaving such a decision to the total discretion of the Central Bank.[69]

The setting up of a deposit insurance fund and an elaboration of the-lender-of-last-resort function of the Central Bank have come at a time when serious doubt is being cast on the merits of such measures. According to one school of thinking, this safety net has the adverse effect of encouraging "moral hazard" whereby banks would feel less obliged to pursue a careful business policy, knowing that the monetary authorities would bail them out of any trouble. Moreover, depositors would also be less inclined to make informed choices about which banks to deal with, since their deposits would be safe anyway, thus providing less incentive for the banks to pursue sound policies. The best policy in the long term, according to this theory, is for market discipline to be enforced on banks and depositors alike, even if it is at the cost of an occasional banking collapse. Whereas such a position may make economic sense to those advocating it, it may, on the other hand, prove too costly in practice. This is particularly true in the case of developing countries where the banking system is less sophisticated, disclosure less effective, and choices less available. Until depositors actually have a reasonable degree of access to information, and until the market can provide them with alternatives for depositing their funds, it is difficult to argue that their deposits should remain unprotected, or that market discipline should be the only guarantee for sound banking practices.

5 THE BROADER BACKGROUND: ISLAMIC AND INFORMAL FINANCE

So far, this chapter has been confined to the narrow legal description of the Egyptian banking regulatory system. However, no study of banking regulation would be complete if it did not take into consideration the broader context in which banks operate and are regulated. Banks and banking regulation do not, and cannot, exist in a vacuum. They operate within a social, cultural and political context which is certain to influence such operation. This is true of every country and banking system. But it is particularly relevant to the case of developing countries where such social considerations often go unnoticed or unaccounted for not only by outside observers but also by local ones keen on marketing the image of a modern, western-inspired financial system. Examples of social considerations which may have a significant influence on the way banks operate and are therefore regulated include religious prohibitions and constraints on banking activities as well as the persistence of a large informal financial sector among certain groups of society. Both considerations have had a significant effect on banking in Egypt, and a brief comment about each one follows.

---

[69] Law 163 of 1957, article 30–II, as amended by Law 37 of 1992.

Islamic banks are a relatively new phenomenon. Although early examples can be traced back to the mid-1950s in Egypt, it was only two decades later, in the mid-1970s, that they began to be recognised as a significant and perhaps lasting element of financial systems in a number of Arab and Islamic countries. The simplest description of the whole phenomenon goes as follows: that Islam as a religion forbids usury and interest taking in general, and therefore Islamic banks are those financial institutions which do not deal with interest, neither in lending nor in borrowing. The issue is, however, more complicated: are usury and interest exactly the same thing or does Islam forbid one and not the other? Is the usury prohibition in Islam meant as a moral norm or as a rule of law? Can Islamic banks be a true alternative to conventional, interest-charging, banks or will they remain confined to a "niche" market? Which activities and operations can Islamic banks undertake in order to avoid the usury prohibition, but without sacrificing profitability and competitiveness?

In Egypt, the issue of Islamic banks has been closely related to another broader debate about the application of Islamic Law, *Shari'a*. Until the nineteenth century, the law applied in Egypt was derived from principles of Islamic Law. This situation began to change gradually with the growing influence of the European legal tradition, first through the law of commerce, and then throughout the legal structure. By the late nineteenth century, most of the Egyptian legal system had been drafted on the basis of Continental, especially French, legal principles. Since that time, Egypt has remained part of the Civil Law tradition in all aspects, except in matters of family and succession law, which have been derived from the Islamic legal tradition.

The Egyptian Civil Code, dated 1948, permits the charging of interest, but ties it to the following restrictions:

(1) If a borrower defaults on a debt, then he is charged a rate of interest equal to 4% per annum for civil matters, and 5% in commercial matters.[70]
(2) The borrower and lender may agree in advance on any other interest rate provided it does not exceed 7% per annum.[71]
(3) Interest on interest (compound interest) shall not be charged, nor can the total interest exceed the original capital sum.[72]
(4) If borrower and lender do not agree on an interest rate, then the loan is deemed interest-free.[73]
(5) The court may reduce the interest payment if it decides that the lender has claimed the debt in bad faith.[74]

---

[70] Civil Code No. 131 of 1948, article 226.
[71] Civil Code No. 131 of 1948, article 227.
[72] Civil Law No. 131 of 1948, article 232.
[73] Civil Law No. 131 of 1948, article 542.
[74] Civil Law No 131 of 1948, article 229.

(6) A borrower has total discretion in accelerating repayment, even
without the approval of the creditor, if six months have elapsed from
the day of the loan.[75]

Thus interest charging was restricted by the previous provisions, which
originally applied to banking loans.

However, as such restrictions became incompatible with the economic
circumstances of the 1970s, it became necessary to revise the interest provisions. Thus the 1975 Central Bank and Banking System Law stated that
the Board of Directors of the Central Bank had the authority to determine
the banking interest rates "without being bound by any other legislation".[76]
This was in clear reference to the restrictions of the Civil Code, and since
that time banking interest rates have been unrestricted. The same article
was amended in 1992 to allow banks to determine their own interest rates
independently from the Central Bank.[77] One of the, perhaps, unintended
effects of the banking exemption from Civil Law interest restrictions seems
to be the discouragement of private and informal lending between individuals, because if such lending was ever litigated in court, the interest rate
would be reduced to a maximum of 7% per annum, even at a time when
both inflation and banking interest rates were well into double figures.

These legislative developments coincided, however, with the rise of the
Islamic political movement in the early 1970s in Egypt and elsewhere in the
Islamic world. As this movement gained momentum and popular following, one of its major declarations was the need to "return" to the rule of
Islamic Law. From the banking perspective, this was taken to include forbidding interest charging both by individuals and by banks. The alternative
model was Islamic banks which would use a number of profit and sharing
schemes in order to replace lending with interest. Thus during the first half
of the 1970s, a number of such Islamic banks were established in Egypt, and
attracted a large number of depositors. From the legal point of view, these
banks were incorporated according to the already existing types of banks
provided for in the law, or by special legislation. The only difference
between them and ordinary banks was the fact that their statutes stated
their adherence to the principles of Islamic non-usurious banking.
Currently, a number of Islamic banks are operating in Egypt, although the
large proportion of banking activity remains dominated by conventional
interest-charging banks. Moreover, some of the latter banks have opened
up in-house "Islamic branches".

The issue, however, is not whether banks are called Islamic or not, but
whether in substance they have actually managed to provide a workable
alternative to conventional banks. This remains a contentious issue, as some
of these banks have been seen to conduct ordinary interest-based lending
and deposit-taking under the disguise of Islamic legality and using contracts which are Islamic in name only. This has not been true of all such

---

[75] Civil Code No. 131 of 1948, article 544.
[76] Law 120 of 1975, article 7(d).
[77] Law 120 of 1975, article 7(d), as amended by Law 37 of 1992.

banks, and it is necessary to judge the performance of each of the Islamic banks according to its own practice.

In any case, besides their religious significance, Islamic banks should also be viewed as an example, and an articulation, of the feeling of the ill-ease of large sections of the society with conventional banking. In that sense, Islamic banks are significant in representing one attempt to find alternatives which are derived from particular cultural, political- and historical circumstances.

Islamic banks, however, are not the only manifestation of the need for alternatives to conventional banking. The persistence of informal financial activities is another indicator of the extent to which some members or groups in society may be inclined, for a variety of reasons, to avoid such conventional, and formal banking.

Egypt is no exception to that. It is difficult to estimate the size of informal financial activities in Egypt, by the mere fact of their informality. However, such activities have been the subject of recent research undertaken in rural communities, which has shown the remarkable persistence of wide informal arrangements.[78] Moreover, such research indicates the complex interplay of factors which allow such activities to persist. Religious considerations, social practices, cultural barriers, economic benefits, and lack of accessibility to formal finance are examples of why large sectors of society will avoid formal banking. Whether or not informal finance is a viable, safe, and more suitable alternative for formal banking will depend on individual cases. In any case, the assumption that informal moneylenders are necessarily a negative phenomenon which should be discouraged, and that formal banking and finance is a superior alternative, should at least be challenged. Until formal banking is accessible to everyone, and is sensitive to social and cultural needs, informal finance will remain a flourishing area of activity. Recognising its existence, and attempting to extend some of the formal protections to it may be a better policy than denying the crucial role it still plays.

6 CONCLUDING REMARKS

This chapter has attempted briefly to describe and discuss aspects of the regulation of the Egyptian banking sector. Its aim was to show the interplay of forces and factors which affect the way banks operate, and the way they are regulated in a developing country. The historical experience, the legal tradition, the regulatory style, social and cultural considerations, as well as the influence of international cooperation, are the main such influences. The regulation of developing countries' banking systems has to take account of such factors, in order to respond to real needs, and produce intended results. As long as banking regulation efforts are confined to the narrow provisions of banking legislation, they will be unlikely to improve either the safety, efficiency, or fairness of the Egyptian banking sector.

---

[78] M. Mohieldin, *Informal Finance in Egypt*, paper submitted to the British Society for Middle Eastern Studies Annual Conference, University of Manchester, 12–14 July 1994.

III.   Securities Market Issues

17. Securities Law Models in Emerging Economies

Joseph J. Norton[1]
Hani Sarie-Eldin[2]

1 INTRODUCTION

The notion of economic development connotes a sustainable increase in living standards that encompass welfare, education, health, and environmental protection dimensions.[3] Economic development does not mean only economic growth, but also growth plus change.[4] Economic development has almost always involved a shift in economic policies.[5] This is obvious in relation to Eastern European countries.

The past decade has witnessed, in many developing countries, including Eastern European countries, the implementation of market-oriented reforms. Securities markets are an obvious area of this market-oriented transition. The creation and development of securities markets has received considerable attention from emerging economies as a part of financial liberalisation programmes designed to achieve economic development.[6]

---

[1] Sir John Lubbock Professor of Banking Law, University of London; James L Walsh Distinguished Faculty Fellow and Professor of Law, Southern Methodist University Law School, Dallas, Texas.

[2] Research and Teaching Fellow in Development Law, Centre for Commercial Law Studies, Queen Mary and Westfield College, University of London; Lecturer in Commercial Law, Cairo University.

[3] World Bank, *World Development Report 1991: The Challenge of Development* (1991) p. 31.

[4] G. Meier, *Leading Issues in Economic Development*, 5th edition (1989) p. 4.

[5] Indeed, the development process in these countries is not only about economic reform and transition to market economies, but is also about transition from one-party state-controlled political institutions to Western-styled democratic institutions and governmental processes. *See EC/IS Joint Task Force, Shaping a Market-Economy Legal System* (European Economy No. 2, 1993) ("EC/IS Report"). Further, from the perspective and policies of the European Bank for Reconstruction and Development (EBRD) and the World Bank Group, International Monetary Fund (IMF), and governmental institutions such as the Western countries' export-import banks and governmental aid agencies such as U.S.AID, helping emerging economies, it has become a pre-condition for external assistance to developing countries that economic reform be inextricably linked to political reform. Thus, it was asserted that the transition, in many instances, is not purely an economic process, nor is it solely a political process: it is an intermeshing of the two. *See*, P. Marcer & S. Zechhhini (eds), *The Transition to a Market Economy* (OECD, 1991).

[6] R. Pardy, *Institutional Reform in Emerging Securities Market* (World Bank Working Paper, May 1992) p. 2.

This chapter is concerned mainly with three questions: why; how; and what? Why is there a need for developing countries to create securities markets, and to establish and modernise a specified set of regulations? How can such creation and modernisation be achieved? What are the requirements to build sound and sufficient securities market laws? Part 1 underlines the rationale and objectives of developing securities market laws in emerging economies. Part 2 deals with the legal reform process in the area of securities market law. Part 3 discusses the procedural and substantive aspects of securities markets regulations.

2 RATIONALE AND OBJECTIVES

2.1 The role of the securities markets in the development process

The rationale for creating securities and stock exchange markets laws vary in purposes and in nature.[7]

2.1.1 Alternative funding resource

Capital markets (*i.e.*, securities and stock exchange markets) are thought to provide an alternative funding or capital flows source for emerging economies.[8] It is well known that commercial bank facilities are becoming more and more limited for the purpose of meeting investment and infrastructure development requirements following the debt crisis in the 1980s.[9] As a result, public and intergovernmental sectors, in general, in emerging economies, may lack the external capital funds for necessary development. As such, the development of capital markets may provide a "funding bridge" connecting the developmental needs of an emerging economy with capital sources in the domestic and external private sector.[10] Therefore, capital markets may offer a more suitable alternative funding source or at least a complementary one to private loans.

2.1.2 Privatisation process

With the significant efforts of many emerging economies to privatise their public sectors, a need to create a secondary market for the trading of, and liquidity for, the shareholdings of these privatised entities appears to be

---

[7] For general consideration of capital markets, *see*, F. Fabozzi and F. Modigliani, *Capital Markets* (1992).

[8] For example, annual average net private portfolio equity flows to developing countries increased from 1.3 billion U.S. dollars in 1983–1990 to 39.5 billion U.S. dollars in only 1994. *See* The World Bank, *Global Economic Prospects and Developing Countries* (1995) p. 12.

[9] For example, the annual average net loans made to developing countries has dropped from 42.3 billion U.S. dollars in 1977–1982 to only 3.6 billion U.S. dollars in 1993. *See* The World Bank, *Global Economic Prospects and Developing Countries* (1995) p. 12.

[10] P. Reilly, *Purposes, Issues and Approaches – Capital Market Development* (1988, unpublished report) ("Reilly").

desirable. In the absence of a sound and structured securities market, the privatisation programme may be restricted.[11]

2.1.3 Promotion of small and medium-size business

Most of the economies of developing countries are marked by a significant lack of availability of capital for the development of smaller and medium-sized businesses, businesses which are thought to be the "engines" for future economic reform and development in the these countries.[12] Once again, the securities and stock exchange market is thought to provide a valuable funding source for such businesses. In this respect, the securities market would also provide a vehicle for new issues of stock to support the growth of pre-existing companies or the development of smaller and medium-sized businesses. Further, the creation of a market for long-term business finance through the issuance of debt or equity securities would enhance the economic means of production and the sufficient allocation of capital within that particular society.

2.1.4 National savings

A further objective of developing a securities market is to provide alternative vehicles for national savings (*e.g.*, through collective investment schemes, mutual funds, pension funds, etc.). Moreover, the realities of the modern-day financial world clearly indicate that there are no longer traditional marketplace divisions between money markets and capital markets or between financial institutions dealing within each of these markets.[13] In this light, some form of legal linkage between the money markets and the capital markets would appear desirable.

2.1.5 Attracting foreign investment

The last decade has witnessed a significant change of foreign investment policies in the emerging economies aimed at attracting foreign investors.[14] Establishing a suitable domestic securities and stock exchange regulation structure would provide a highly desirable opportunity to attract direct foreign investment.[15] It should be emphasised that a new issue market will

---

[11] P. Guislain, World Bank Technical Paper No. 186: *Divestiture of State Enterprises: An Overview of the Legal Framework* (1992) pp. 26–27.

[12] *See* R. Strahota, *Report on Developing the Polish Securities Law* (Securities and Exchange Commission, 1993).

[13] *See*, R. Pecchioli, *The Internationalisation of Banking* (OECD, 1983).

[14] *See* generally, United Nations, Centre on Transnational Corporation, *Formation and Implementation of Foreign Investment Policies* (1992).

[15] *Cf.* H. Scott and P. Wellons, *International Finance*, Ch. XVII ("Emerging Markets: Privatisation and Industrial Investors") (1995). For example, Lipper Analytical Services indicates that, at the end of 1991, there were only four emerging market mutual funds in the U.S., but at the end of 1994, there were 47 funds with approximately $8.8 billion in assets. *See* also, weekly "Emerging Market Indicators" in the *Economist*.

invariably require a viable "secondary trading" market for the subsequent trading of these issued shares. Also, to facilitate these securities activities, a network of relevant financial intermediaries (*i.e.*, investment banks, underwriters, broker dealers, stock specialists, analysts, etc.) will be needed.

2.2 Enabling factors

The creation of a viable capital markets scheme in a developing country requires a different set of pre-conditions. As will be discussed, there is a need to develop an overall legal, business and regulatory environment conducive to encouraging private participation in economic development objectives (*i.e.*, a comprehensive legal infrastructure to support the capital market regime). Also, a meaningful educational infrastructure needs to be put in place in both the private and public sectors in order to help, develop, maintain, and monitor the established regime.

Furthermore, the establishment of a macroeconomic environment to increase supply and demand for securities within a particular emerging economy is inevitable. This will often require the creation of an appropriate range of investment vehicle instruments that will evolve to meet these developing supply and demand requirements.

Integrity, transparency, and open and fair access to the market are necessary to create confidence in that market. If the scheme is prone to scandal and insider abuse, if the operational and regulatory "rules of the road" are not made transparent to the various interested parties, and if there is not true open access to these markets, then long-term prospects for the capital market to serve any constructive economic purposes will be sharply curtailed.

In addition, an unequivocal scheme must exist to insure the integrity of these financial markets. There is a need to provide, through the law, a system of adequate investment protection which would include effective disclosure, auditing and enforcement mechanisms. Moreover, a scheme should foster relevant, responsible and accountable financial intermediaries to stimulate and facilitate market operations and transactions. All this will require a considerably developed regulatory (*i.e.*, administrative) structure.

Generally, the regulatory infrastructure would centre on the government body to which is entrusted the power to monitor and to supervise the market. However, such regulatory infrastructure should not be "dense" to the point that it discourages innovation and new investment structures and instruments suitable to the growing needs of an economy. In creating these new opportunities, there needs to be a "base" of flexible regulations that will help identify and avoid untoward market risks. Also, self-regulatory organisations, such as the stock exchange, and professional associations, must be permitted.

Moreover, costs and burdens, on the part of the investors, which are associated with investors' activities should be kept to a minimum for implementing key policy objectives.

Finally, as already indicated, one of the greatest challenges for the development of the operation of a successful capital market is operating an ongoing educational process for the regulators, stock market officials, the various private intermediaries, and for the private investment sector. Such a broad and deep "knowledge base" is necessary to implement the law adequately, and to ensure that the market will operate with vitality, integrity and feasibility.

3 LAW AND TRANSITION: LEGAL REFORM PROCESS

3.1 The instrumental use of law in economic reform

In terms of the legal content of the economic reform dimension of the transition to a market economy, the role of law should be seen, on the one hand, as a means or instrument for implementing effective and efficient policies.[16] On the other hand, law should be seen as a contextual framework within which the implemented economic reforms embrace and maintain a democratic character.[17]

Looking at economic reform and development encompassing our globe today, one quickly observes that the developing countries vary in their economic needs, degree of the sophistication of their markets, availability of legal infrastructure, and macroeconomic status. These differences should be considered, and a general conclusion would be impossible. Launching a universal model for all emerging economies cannot be achieved, and is not desirable.

The constitutional and legal systems of these developing countries are different. Some are based upon reasonably developed, prior legal notions and premisses; others are not. In some developing countries the economic reform, and subsequently the legal reform, start from a "ground-zero" or "near-zero" basis that cries out for new legal models and structures conducive to helping these economies make the transition from a state economy to a free market economy. In this connection, many developing countries looked at the Western models to benefit from in relation to their legal reforms. This issue leads us to discuss the problem of transferability of law, or in other words, can a particular developing country copy an industrialised country's law?

3.2 Comparative law and problems of law's transplantation

As indicated in the previous subsection, the law is used in our modern societies as a principal tool for effecting institutional changes. In this respect, many developing countries sought to copy the law of seemingly successful industrialised countries. This copying or using of "ready-made" laws is explained by two reasons. First, these industrialised countries' models proved to be successful in their economic and legal environment.

---

[16] The instrumental use of law is not limited to economic reforms, but is also used to influence social changes. *See* A. Seidman & R. Seidman, *State and Law in the Development Process* (1994) p. 42; P. Atiyah, *Law and Modern Society* (1983) pp. 72–96.

[17] *See*, the contributions to the Conference on Civil and Commercial Law in Central and Eastern Europe, Leiden, Aug. 4–6, 1993 (hereinafter cited as "Leiden Proceedings").

Second, developing countries need to speed up the economic reforms ; they cannot wait for many years until they develop their own models. However, experience shows that no government can expect to develop by copying some other developed country's successful model. These developing countries should benefit from comparative law methodology, but they should not rely entirely on "ready-made" laws that operate, substantially, in different economic, social, and legal environments.

It is evident that comparative law, particularly of industrialised countries, becomes necessary in helping to facilitate this much needed economic reform.[18] Certainly, one cannot contemplate law reform and use of the comparative methodology in an abstract vacuum of possible "models", as economists and bureaucrats are often prone to do. As already indicated, there is a pre-existing legal and economic environment, which cannot be ignored, even though it is in the process of being disregarded and replaced. This pre-existing environment presents immediate and particularised practical requirements for adaptations and usages within each of the concerned developing countries. There is no model "comparative law garment" that can be superimposed upon each of the developing countries in order to make each progress toward free market economy institutions.

Therefore, the relevance of comparative law methodology is both external and internal. It is external because it should not avoid evaluating available external models and external influences. Obviously, there are lessons to be learned from external models and from other external influences, such as the requirements of international financial institutions in their dealings with these countries and the compelling influence of industrialised models.[19] These external models and influences need, however, to be balanced against and interconnected with the existing internal legal, economic and political environment – with all its present deficiencies, needs and requirements.

As such, there should be a "reconciliation" of the external and internal comparative analyses for purposes of evaluating realistically the internal receptivity and compatibility of any transplantation of external legal models.[20] In certain areas of the law, such as basic contract and commercial law, there may be, to a certain extent, a genuine choice between Civil Law and Common Law models. But, in other more developed and sophisticated areas of law, such as insolvency, banking, and securities law, there may not, to some extent, be any true Civil Law or Common Law models, as significant divergences may exist among the main members of the Civil Law tradition and among the main members of the Common Law tradition. This further complicates the applied comparative analyses.

---

[18] For details of the comparative law approach, *see* R. Schiesnger, H. Badde, M. Damaska & P. Herzog, *Comparative Law: Cases, Text, Materials*, 5th edition (1988); K. Zwlgert & H. Köortz, *Introduction to Comparative Law*, 2 vols, 2nd edition (1987), reprinted in 1992.

[19] Cheryl W. Gray, "The Legal Framework for Private Sector Development in a Transitional Economy: The Case of Poland", 22 *Ga.J. Int'l & Comp. L.* 283 (1992).

[20] Generally on the issue of legal transplants, *see* A. Watson, *Legal Transplants: An Approach to Comparative Law*, 2nd edition (1992).

Furthermore, from a rather mundane but highly relevant viewpoint, there may exist, in various instances, an unhealthy competition between major international law firms pushing one system over another. This is not played out necessarily along the lines of Common Law versus Civil Law, but often more as one major legal centre against another (*e.g.*, London v. New York). This is a valid point because many of these top law firms have been invited by developing countries and international financial institutions to act as consultants to these governments on matters related to legal reforms, and some of these firms were designated to draft model laws to these countries. Obviously, adoption of one model over another could mean long-term business prospects for the law firms from the jurisdictional model that becomes employed in the transitioning economy. This "battlefield approach" can often distort and limit effective comparative law methodology.

Finally, in relation to the economic and legal reform of some emerging economies, such as those of Eastern European countries, one should not dismiss the near "magnetic" influence of the European Community (Union) and its legal environment. Here the EU economic and legal environment no longer serves the Western European democracies as a buffer against the Eastern European socialist bloc. The EU serves as a beckoning "bridge" for luring, in a positive way, the Eastern European countries into viable economic and legal reform. Over the past few years, it has become apparent that virtually all of the Eastern European countries look toward some form of eventual direct or indirect link to the European Union and its member states for the purposes of economic, political, and defence security and stability.[21] Accordingly, the Eastern European countries will most often seek out "EU-compatible" models for their respective reform efforts. Examples of such a model could be the EU banking law and investment services frameworks.[22] However, even though there is this "compelling linkage" between EU models and Eastern European reform efforts, the EU models are often *sui generis*, as they have been designed to foster a common EU internal market through minimal harmonisation of existing national laws in rather special political and economic contexts. Thus, while the "yearning" exists, the eventual compatibility of the EU models with the respective Eastern European countries internal systems remains problematic.

To sum up, in a particular developing country, attempts to copy the "ready-made" law of industrialised countries cannot work. Adaptation to these models, and awareness of social, economic, and legal differences should be taken into account.

---

[21] Furthermore, countries such as the Czech Republic, Slovakia, Hungary and Poland are pressing for membership in the European Union.

[22] Generally, *see* R. Cranston (ed.), *The Single Market and the Law of Banking*, 2nd edition (1995).

3.3 Economic and legal infrastructure

In a particular developing country, the use of law as an instrument for development and reform in a particular area of economic activity requires the founding of a necessary legal and economic infrastructure.

One should not begin grafting a legal or regulatory model on to an emerging economy without first having a sound understanding of that economy's historical and current environment (*i.e.*, its "developmental infrastructure"). This understanding should figure in the political dimensions of economic policy formulation and implementation in the emerging country. This leads one into the nature of a country's political institutions and political processes and also draws one into examining the traditional external political relations and dynamics which, historically, influence the internal policy-making structures.[23]

As to the particular economic policies themselves, one needs to be concerned about both macroeconomic issues and about key microeconomic dimensions (*e.g.*, the specific operations of financial institutions and financial markets).[24]

These political and economic aspects, however, are not sterile in nature, but are often shaped by rather unique social and cultural considerations. As already mentioned, to assume that the developmental infrastructure of all developing countries are the same would be to make a critical mistake. For example, the social and cultural environment of a country such as a Poland is significantly different from that of Uganda, and Argentina is different from Romania, and so on.[25] To apply universal economic and legal models to all developing countries is an obvious mistake. The identification and appreciation of a country's current developmental infrastructure base is not a simple task.

As to the legal component of this developmental infrastructure, a sound understanding of the current state of the particular legal system is important, from a both substantive and a procedural viewpoint. Most developing countries have had constitutional, procedural, and public law legal systems in place for many years. These systems have already shaped many important legal notions, which will influence, inescapably, the carving out of the content, form and implementation of legal reform in those countries.

Further, once the current state of the particular legal system is fully appreciated, then one should begin to evaluate how responsive or non-responsive that system will be to legal reform designed to foster economic development and the transition to a market economy. Here the constitutional fabric within which law has traditionally been held and the nature of the current constitutional alleviation of the role of domestic law in

---

[23] *See* R. Sharlet, "Soviet Legal Reform in Historical Context" in *Legal Reform in USSR* (reprint of symposium, 28 *Colum. J. Trans. L. No. 1* (1990)).

[24] D. McNaughton *et al.*, *Banking Institutions in Developing Markets*, 2 vols. (1992).

[25] *See* generally, *Evolving Legal Framework for Private Sector Development in Central and Eastern Europe* (World Bank Discussion Paper No. 209, 1993).

the lives of the political and bureaucratic institutions within the given state is of utmost importance. Also, pragmatically, the general perception of law by the given populace and that society's receptivity to utilising and accepting law as an instrument of social and political change also become crucial evaluative factors.[26]

One level of understanding to discern how one can link law reform to the current legal environment; another level is to appreciate where significant gaps exist *vis-à-vis* the current legal environment and the desired economic and legal requirements for a given economic and legal reform. In grasping and interrelating these two levels of analyses, the ground of the existing legal environment can be "tilled" and made into a richer and more fertile legal infrastructure to support the moves toward a free market orientated economy and democratic institutions.

Each viable legal infrastructure will probably require modern market economy orientated laws or legal approaches in the following areas (each of which are interconnected into a broader legal matrix):[27] contracts; property and title; secured transactions; company law and sound auditing systems; negotiable instruments; banking and credit laws; judicial process and judicial review; bankruptcy/solvency; public procurement; and taxation. It is only when a system has and can sustain such a developed and transparent legal matrix that serious economic reform can be implemented successfully.

Each of the areas of law above will need to be looked at carefully to determine what is the current state of the law; what are the adequate and non-adequate features of this current law as related to its desired reform goals; and how these gaps can be filled and effective law reform implemented. Only then, when a developing country begins to enhance and to reform these basic areas of private and public law, impacting upon business and commerce and upon financial arrangements, that laws for the actual development of effective and efficient banking and capital markets can be put into place. As such, reform in the area of securities regulation should not be dealt with in isolation of, but in conjunction with, the development of a sound, basic legal infrastructure supportive of and compatible with the development of sophisticated market orientated securities (*i.e.*, capital market) laws.

---

[26] G. Meier, *Politics and Policy Making in Developing Countries, Perspective on the New Political Economy* (1991).

[27] *See* EC/IS Report, Joint Task Force, *Shaping a Market-economy Legal System* (European Economy No. 2, 1993) Ch. 7 ("Legal Foundations of a Market Economy") & Ch. 8 ("Market-oriented Reform Legislation in the Independent States").

4 DEVELOPMENT OF SECURITIES MARKET LAWS: PROCEDURES AND SUBSTANCE

4.1 Regulatory model v. deregulatory approach

The first problem that faces a developing country in relation to the legal reform of the securities market is the issue of market regulation. There is ongoing and overriding tension between law and regulation on the one hand, and effective and efficient economic development on the other. Theoretically, there is the threshold debate as to a "self-regulatory" versus an extensive regulatory model for capital market development.[28] Often, this type of analysis is somewhat contrived. In reality, there probably does not exist in the more industrialised countries any pure examples of either model. For instance, the U.K. is cited as an example of the self-regulatory model; but, this self-regulatory environment is the creature of and operates within an elaborate statutory framework. On the other hand, the United States is cited as an example of an extensive regulatory model. While this is true to some extent, the actual operation of the U.S. stock markets comes under statute, which provides largely for a self-regulatory regime.[29] What this dichotomy between self-regulatory and extensive regulatory models does achieve is to sensitise reformers to the need for, but limitation and burdens of, a regulatory structure.

In many respects, law and regulation may have impedimentary and burdensome dimensions. The following arguments were given in favour of a deregulatory approach. Modern-day market economies seem to suggest a spirit of deregulation and not of comprehensive regulation; although some prudential rules might be desirable.[30] Moreover, it is argued that law and regulations often increase transaction and market costs without any visible proportional increase in market efficiency.[31] Further, many of the legal and regulatory models being grafted on to the emerging economies, particularly those issued by virtue of external conditionality requirements of international financial institutions, are being done without any real scientific knowledge or understanding of their effects.

However, from another perspective, law and regulation can be seen as true enhancers of economic development for the emerging economies, provided the copying of "ready-made" laws of developed countries without any adaptation is avoided. While deregulation, in the abstract, is a desirable goal, deregulation will only make sense when there exists a system that

---

[28] *See*, G. Stigler, "Public Regulation of the Securities Markets", 37 *J. Bus.* 117 (1964); N. Wolfson, *The Modern Corporation v. Regulation* (1984).

[29] *See* generally, M. Steinberg & R. Ferrara, *Securities Practice: Federal and State Enforcement* (1992, as updated).

[30] P. Collier & C. Mayer, "Financial Liberalisation Financial Systems and Economic Growth", 5 *Oxford. Rev. Econ. Pol'y* 1 (1989).

[31] *See* generally, R. Posner & K. Scott (eds), *Economics of Corporation Law and Securities Regulation* (1980).

already has a sound legal, economic, political and social infrastructure. But, in most emerging economies, that basic infrastructure is lacking and needs to be built up and upon. In this sense, well-thought-out legal and regulatory reform can serve as a "foundation stone" for a sound infrastructure. Also, good laws and regulations, by their substantive strength and procedural transparency, can actually be seen as fostering economic efficiency. Further, the realities of the economic development of emerging economies depend upon the external involvement of foreign investors and external governmental and intergovernmental bodies, most of whom look to a sound legal system as a prerequisite for their active involvement in the host economy.[32] In other words, sound and flexible regulations would provide the foreign investor with the transparency that is required to invest in a developing country.

In any event, "regulation" should not become an end in itself and should not be so structured as to create a static, inflexible market environment. In a real sense, the regulatory environment should be used as a means to effect and to promote economic development through the development of viable and sustainable domestic capital markets.

4.2 Drafting, implementation and enforcement concerns

4.2.1 Drafting

The development of a regulatory structure should not be viewed as the creation of a "granite-like" body of law and regulation. This development law reform should be viewed as a "legal process". At an initial stage, this "process" should include open and transparent law formulation and drafting stages and should have broad input, critiques and suggestions from all those affected (or to be affected) constituencies. Further, consultations with, but not over-reliance on, expert consultants from industrialised countries may also be advantageous. The involvement of local lawyers and scholars is highly desirable, if not a pre-condition for a successful law reform.

4.2.2 Implementation

This "process" should entail a series of stages for a sequenced implementation with respect to the creation of a satisfactory securities regulation system. Developing a capital market is a long-term process. Most East Asian countries followed a step-by-step process: liberalise, retrench, deepen. A step-by-step, sequential approach should be anticipated and provided for in the law reform process. Such an approach would then be continually matching the realities and requirements of a particular transition economy and the degree of compatibility and complementariness of the legal system itself.[33]

---

[32] I. Shihata, *Legal Treatment of Foreign Investment: The World Bank Guidelines* (1993).
[33] Reilly, *supra* note 9.

Moreover, identifying and putting in place a suitable administrative and bureaucratic structure, both in terms of the operations of the markets themselves and in terms of the relevant responsible public authorities, should again be viewed as an ongoing process.[34] Implementation of securities law should include training officials who undertake the responsibility to interpret and apply the law.

4.2.3 Enforcement

There will also need to be an effective enforcement process. This will often involve the administrative authorities and the judicial organs of a state. Suitable, transparent, flexible and fair administrative processes and procedures, and the specific and discretionary enforcement authority of the regulator will need to be established. All this will tie into the judicial system, in terms of the use of the court system for civil and criminal enforcement purposes and also in terms of judicial review of administrative decision-making.

Furthermore, it is essential for a successful and effective regulatory system to create workable oversight, monitoring, and revision processes. These processes may be delegated to the primary securities regulator. However, it is desirable to have a body separate from the regulator which is charged with the oversight and monitoring responsibilities and with the authority and duty to recommend suitable revisions to the existing process. What needs to be appreciated in this type of highly sophisticated area of law reform is that there will be a need for periodic revisions, adjustments, and amendments to the processes and to the laws in order to make them more efficient, viable and open. In this connection, there should be, over a period of time, an open evaluation mechanism in respect of the role of the regulator versus the private sector in the enforcement process.

4.3 General issues to be addressed by securities law

4.3.1 Scope of law

The scope of any proposed securities law should not only address specific questions of regulation and supervision but also the related administrative processes along with the monitoring, amendment and enforcement aspects.

Further, the law must define the "security" or "investment" which is covered by its provisions. A determination should be made as to whether the primary focus is on all securities transactions, some transactions, or on those dealing in the securities or investment business or both. The definition could be more open-ended, as in the United States, or more specific, as in the case of the U.K.[35]

---

[34] D. Langevoort, "Theories, Assumptions and Security Regulations: Market Efficiency Revisited", 140 *U. Pa. L.R.* 151 (1992).

[35] *See, e.g.,* W. Butler *et al.,* "Draft Law of the Russian Federation on Securities", 8 *Butterworth's J. Int'l Bank. & Fin. L.* 133 (1993).

4.3.2 Governmental supervision

The securities law should address the role of the regulatory authority, to establish capital adequacy requirements for intermediaries; to organise the relationship between the intermediaries and their clients; to provide for the establishment and operation of different institutions such as the stock exchange and market information system; and to manage the overall shape of the securities market. Another broad determination, as discussed above, is the extent to which the system should be self-regulatory. For example, to what extent should the stock exchanges and the related professional securities bodies be self-regulatory and to what extent should the legislative and regulatory frameworks and the designated government regulatory authorities interrelate with any created self-regulatory scheme or organisations? In this connection, the law should determine the relationship between the governmental regulatory authorities and the self-regulatory organisations.

4.3.3 Information disclosure

A company which intends to raise funds from the public must be required to disclose sufficient and material information. Such disclosure is necessary to allow an investor to assess the company's worth, and to make a good reasoned investment decision. In this respect, it is critical to have an idea as to what exactly is "material" or "sufficient" information for the purposes of disclosure; the time sequence; and procedures for the disclosure, sanctions, and remedies. Related to the nature, type, matter and procedure for disclosure is the issue of how properly to collect and to disseminate the disclosed material information to the public and to the markets.[36] Most information to be disclosed is financial information. Therefore, the proposed securities law must be supported by the adoption of accepted accounting and auditing methods.

4.3.4 Accounting principles and auditing standards

As is evident in the more developed industrialised countries, the process of securities law reform is tied very closely to the development of suitable auditing and corporate law reform. This is not the same level of interconnection as referred to above with respect to the creation of a basic legal developmental infrastructure for securities, but, here the development and reform of auditing principles and corporate laws become an integrated part of the securities law process itself.

While a regulatory structure may come to accept the prevalent "generally acceptable accounting principles and standards" of a particular jurisdiction, it may superimpose more focused and rigorous regulatory securities accounting reporting requirements and principles. In making this determination, reformers might wish to evaluate whether the pre-existing accounting principles and standards are in fact adequate for "material" securities disclosure purposes.

---

[36] *See, e.g.,* H. Kripke, *The Securities and Corporate Disclosure: Regulation in Search of Purpose* (1989).

4.3.5 Other important aspects[37]

In addition to the issues above, the proposed security law should consider the following matters: incentives to increase the supply of and demand for securities; collection and public dissemination of market information; structures of the market, in terms of whether all transactions are required to be conducted on a stock exchange, and relationships between exchanges; requirements as to licensing, qualifications and business conduct of securities brokers and other securities professionals; prevention of fraudulent and manipulative practices in securities transactions, including insider trading and trading on insider information, and market manipulation; clearance and settlement requirements; net liquid capital requirements for brokers and securities professionals; requirements as to margin finance of securities transactions; determination as to whether there should be any special shareholder protection or special rules on tender offers or take-overs; requirements for unit trusts, investment companies and mutual funds; protection of holders of publicly offered bonds and debentures; inspection, subpoena and enforcement powers of government, regulatory authorities and of self-regulatory organisations; penalties and sanctions (civil and/or criminal); civil liability actions available to harmed investors; and judicial proceedings, appeals and judicial review.

5 CONCLUSION

An efficient securities market provides emerging economies with the opportunity to raise funds; to speed privatisation programmes; to facilitate financial liberalisation; and, generally, would contribute to economic growth. The reform of the securities market is a long process. Staged development and staged implementation is often the most desirable implementation strategy.

Experience shows that such reform requires the establishment of a sound macroeconomy that should be conducive to the supply of securities and sufficient demand for them. Further, a coordinated and transparent legal and regulatory infrastructure will be required.

A "ready-made" law used and tested in industrialised countries would not guarantee success if it is copied and employed by a developing country. These models should be used as a guidelines, but nothing more. The initial formulation of the regulation should be realistic and not overly ambitious. Social, economic, and legal differences between industrialised countries and developing countries should be considered carefully.

The reform focus should be on development aims and not regulatory aspects *per se*. Overriding policies and policy options should be understood

---

[37] *See* generally, J. Williams, *Recommended Design For a Securities Law* (1991) (unpublished). For a possible guideline, *see* also American Law Institute, *Proposed Federal Securities Code* (1979).

before specific rules are developed. Moreover, a generally accepted approach to regulation and to the role of administrative discretion should be determined before specific rules are developed.

The law on securities should provide for satisfactory measures to ensure that investors have access to trade facilities and securities instruments. Furthermore, such economic legal reform should be environmental and not piecemeal. Also, as mentioned above, revision of a jurisdiction's company laws and other related business/commercial laws, and public law, should be reviewed for the purpose of removing any impediments to a capital market's development and also for providing the necessary incentives to increase the supply of and demand for securities, and to create the necessary financial instruments to meet such supply and demand. Finally and most importantly, a broad and "deep" educational programme for officials and bureaucrats who undertake the responsibility to apply the regulation is a necessary concomitant.

18.   Blindman's Bluff – A Model for Securities Regulation?

Barry A. K. Rider[1]

1   INTRODUCTION

It would seem that attempts were made, for a variety of reasons, to regulate some of the earliest markets. History records concern about conduct of essentially a manipulative nature in Ancient Egypt and Mesopotamia. The dire effect of practices which undermined the proper operation of the early markets in regard to staple products and other important commodities was well recognised. Of course, this concern was not always to ensure that the market worked efficiently in the interests of all those who depended upon it as a fair and efficient allocator of a scarce resource, whether it be rice or maize or some other product, but, in a number of instances, to ensure the efficacy of price maintenance or the effective collection of taxes. In Britain, whilst it is possible to identify early common law rules, which were later put into statute, relating to cornering, forestalling and regrating,[2] it would seem that even greater attention was focused on practices which deprived those who had the privilege of holding or in some manner servicing the market of their due financial reward. Thus, such records as exist in England indicate concern that the proper dues and levies should be paid by those transporting goods to market and the collection or appropriate charges in the market by those whose privilege it was to hold it, than in activity which was addressed rather more to the price of the commodity in the market. Of course, where staple products were involved or where there was a clear economic or other interest, then attitudes were somewhat different. Nonetheless, it is true that there was, and there remains, a feeling that when goods are placed in a public market the determination of a fair market price should not be dependent upon contrived factors, or at least should not be

---

[1] Director of the Institute of Advanced Legal Studies, University of London, Professor of Law, University of London and Fellow, Tutor and Dean, Jesus College, Cambridge.
[2] *See Russell on Crime* (J. Turner (ed.), 2nd edn, 1964) Ch. 100; B. Rider, C. Abrams and E. Ferran, *CCH Guide to the Financial Services Act* (2nd edn, 1986) 101; and generally E. Swan (ed.), *The Development of the Law of Financial Services* (1993).

the result of actions which are not conventional and to be expected. The integrity of a public market as a "fair" determiner of transactional value is widely recognised and in large measure enshrined in the attitude of the common law.

These considerations were carried forward into the financial markets. Thus, whilst the products traded were essentially different in character, from the very earliest markets there are indications that those responsible for their operation were concerned to discourage conduct which impugned the integrity and independence of the traditional marketplace. Indeed, it was recognised that, to the extent that financial instruments related directly to the viability of trade insofar as they represented the wealth of trade or the means to facilitate it, concern was evident in regard to practices which interfered with public confidence in the assumed fairness of such markets. Indeed, such conduct was seen to be clearly against the interests of trade and therefore against the interests of the nation. For example, in November 1696, Commissioners appointed by the House of Commons "to look after the trade of England" reported to the House that "the pernicious Art of Stock jobbing that, of late, so wholly perverted the End and design of Companies ..." as to undermine public confidence in the then financial markets.[3] The Commissioners illustrated their comments by reference to conduct which would today be clearly recognised as market manipulation, fraud and insider dealing.

2 LEARNING FROM EXPERIENCE

While there is a myth that securities regulation is a creation of this century and outside North America, even the latter half, it is important to realise that concern over regulating the markets is not new. There were laws and regulatory structures in place in London in the Eighteenth Century and even to some degree the Seventeenth Century which in form and substance are not dissimilar to what we have in Britain today. Legislation[4] of the early years of the Eighteenth Century, which was very much influenced by then existing rules in the conduct of business, required those engaged in the conduct of investment business to secure a licence, after showing that they were persons of integrity. There were provisions outlawing transactions which did not involve a licensed trader, which required the recording of bargains and that transactions comported with good practice and honesty. The penalties set out for non-compliance were significantly stricter than those set out in our modern laws. There has, sadly, been a tendency to ignore the experience that not only England but also other countries with a history of trading have, and assume that securities law sprung almost full grown from the brow of the U.S. Congress. Whilst it is true that legislators

---

[3] *House of Commons Journals*, Nov. 25, 1696.
[4] *See* generally B. Rider, G. Abrams and E. Ferran, *supra* note 1, Ch. 1; E. Swan, *supra* note 1 and E. Morgan and W. Thomas, *The Stock Exchange, Its History and Functions* (1962).

both at Federal and state levels created a system of regulation which in terms of sophistication bears little resemblance to the rather parochial and simplistic rules of the older markets, there is a heritage both in terms of experience and, indeed, conceptualisation which should not be ignored. Whilst it has been recognised that the early so called Blue Sky laws in certain U.S. states and Canadian provinces influenced the thinking of U.S. Federal legislators, at least in regard to anti-fraud issues, these provisions in fact have a rather older lineage.

3 MODELS?

There has been considerable discussion over the years, but seemingly more so recently, as to the desirability of certain models of regulation. Indeed, the pressing need to provide many countries in central and eastern Europe with the legal framework to facilitate the creation and trading of capital has provided what might otherwise be primarily an academic debate rather more impetus. Previously, those who were concerned to pursue these discussions with an applied rather than purely academic zeal, were practically confined to work within the limitations of essentially developing third world countries or small, often island, jurisdictions who had a disproportionate appetite for offshore business. The importance of ensuring that countries whose economies are in a state of significant political and economic transition are properly advised, on the most appropriate and efficacious regulatory models to ensure not only the creation of a viable capital market, but their continuity and further development, is now widely appreciated by Western governments – for obvious reasons. Sadly, however, as in the case of developing countries which, in the main, are not as capable of registering such levels of political interest in the minds of Western governments, the flood of advice has not always produced results which are in the interests of anyone other than the advisers. Wholly inappropriate regulatory models have been proposed and in one or two instances put into place, either as a result of profound ignorance, näivety or arrogance on the part of those providing assistance.

Little real debate or for that matter analysis has taken place anywhere as to the justifications of various regulatory devices in the financial markets. In Britain we have assumed that it is appropriate to protect and advance public confidence in the integrity of the markets,[5] but this has been taken as almost an *a priori* assertion and left at that. What amounts to confidence, and to what it is directed have been left unexplained. Indeed, it has not been questioned whether in truth investors or more significantly their advisers and intermediaries actually care about integrity. It is certainly not obvious or easily demonstrable that investors will take active steps to

---

[5] "The primary objective of regulation of the UK equity markets is to enable investors to use these markets with confidence": para 2.1, *The Regulation of the United Kingdom Equity Markets*, report by the Securities and Investments Board, June 1995.

prevent the investment of their funds, which often they will only have indirect control over, in a market where it is thought corporate insiders deal regularly. Professor Homer Kripke[6] has long doubted the relevance in the context of investment decisions of what is essentially integrity-related disclosure. Yet still we create these vast structures of regulation designed to catch, prosecute and thereby discourage insider dealing. Countries that have only recently developed financial markets, such as China, are advised that unless they have laws and enforcement mechanisms to control insiders their markets will be flawed and no one will invest in them. What nonsense! It is nearer the truth that a relatively few number of regulators mainly in the U.S. and in particular in Washington, have discovered that policing insider dealing is a career opportunity, and it is even better to do it from a five star hotel in a foreign country at some other government's expense! Whilst this may seem pure cynicism, if not jealousy, it is the case that in recent years agencies of the U.S. Federal Government, and in particular the Securities and Exchange Commission, are perceived as having launched a "holy war" on insider dealing and more recently money laundering. Whilst taking the profit out of the hands of serious criminals is worthy of a *jihad*, it is hard to see that the same justifications and imperatives apply – with any plausibility – to insider dealing.

Thus, there is a real danger of not just the imposition of inappropriate models on other people, but the dictate of standards. This is all the more unacceptable given the ambiguity which exists in the regulatory structures of many developed countries. In Britain, we have espoused not just the confidence argument, but also free competition or deregulation, albeit in the context of a dramatic increase in law if not order. Transparency in terms of product and operation is also an important element, as is financial soundness and adequacy. The development of standards for admission to the industry and for the conduct of business which demand rather more than honesty and require competence, in general or specific and suitable terms, has been a significant development over the past decade. This reflects the notion that those handling other people's money should be obliged to meet standards of professional competence which might legitimately be expected from persons professing such expertise and skills. The creation of schemes which facilitate the compensation of those who have suffered loss in circumstances where it would not be practical for them to seek redress through the courts, is also becoming a common feature of financial services regulation. To some extent this reflects the idea that the state, or industry, has a responsibility to ensure that certain standards are met and observed within the regulated environment. Thus, in most regulatory systems, the traditional approach of essentially reactive policing is being replaced with a form of control and monitoring which resembles prudential supervision of banks. Regulation and supervision becomes proactive rather than reactive,

---

[6] *See* H. Kripke, "The SEC, The Accountants – Some Myths and Some Realities", 45 *New York University Law Review* 1151 (1970) and H. Kripke, *The Sec and Corporate Disclosure – Regulation in Search of a Purpose* (1979).

and therefore much greater reliance has to be placed on legal devices other than the criminal law, which is often both inappropriate and constitutionally limited. The control of those who are permitted access to the industry in terms of offering a product or a service, remains one of the most effective mechanisms for ensuring that the appropriate standards are observed. The threshold standards in most developed regulatory systems are not limited to issues of integrity and solvency but also address fitness and competence. In some instances, particularly in regard to the financial product, they also address suitability and even quality.

The policies and approaches to regulation in a given jurisdiction are not static, indeed, the dynamic nature of the financial services industry and the ever-increasing tendency to the creation of international markets, ensures the need for constant reappraisal and adaptation. Sadly, significant developments in regulation are invariably a result not of considered research and deliberation, but a scandal which has created a political imperative to impose additional control or refine existing mechanisms.[7] Thus, the process, even in developed jurisdictions, tends to be *ad hoc* and often pragmatic. Given the complexity of the issues requiring attention, it is also the case that no jurisdiction can boast an integrated and therefore efficient structure of control and regulation which consistently and uniformly deals with all sectors and circumstances. Consistency of regulation in the financial sector may well be an ideal that is pursued, but is rarely manifest. To some degree this is inevitable in systems which depend for their efficacy or political acceptability on a large measure of self-regulation, and thus, a number of perhaps not entirely harmonised regulatory initiatives and institutions. Therefore, it is misconceived and dangerous to attempt to select an aspect of regulation in such a jurisdiction and consider it necessarily characteristic of or an efficacious factor in the whole.

Financial services regulation must take account of the economic and political environment within which the markets and industry operate. Thus, even if the form and text of regulation does not necessarily reflect the ascendant political priorities, it is likely that the administration and enforcement of the law and regulatory priorities will. Therefore, a system of securities regulation cannot be reliably looked at in the abstract. It has to be carefully considered against its historical, economic, political and social background. For example, it would have been more or less impossible to understand with any accuracy or feeling how effective the system of self-regulation was in Britain prior to the suspension of exchange control regulation in 1979, without an appreciation of the particular social structure of the City of London at that time. Self-regulation worked effectively because of the high degree of homogeneity and the English class system.

---

[7] Professor Louis Loss has observed in relation to the U.S. Federal laws, "The inevitable result of this episodic kind of legislation, enacted often in response to crises, is a great many inconsistencies, a considerable number of both gaps and overlaps, and in general needless complexity in a field of law that would not make light bedtime reading at best". L. Loss, *Fundamentals of Securities Regulation* (1988) 39.

With greater mobility between classes and internationally, the values and essentially professional and social control mechanisms began to falter. It is equally important to have regard to geographical and demographic considerations. Regulating the financial services industry in Britain was a rather different matter when something like 85 per cent in value of all transactions were executed within a square mile of each other, than it is today, given the profound developments that have taken place in terms of international penetration and technology. In assessing particular characteristics of systems or institutions due regard must also be had to the legal and other environments within which they operate. For example, a great deal of discussion has taken place in Britain and elsewhere as to the efficacy of the traditional criminal justice system in bringing the perpetrators of serious financial frauds to justice. In this debate much attention has been focused on the apparent success of the U.S. Securities and Exchange Commission in policing securities frauds through the use of civil enforcement actions.[8] Therefore, many have called for a similar approach in dealing with insider abuse and fraud in, for example, Britain. The different legal and procedural environment within which the U.S. Securities and Exchange Commission operates and its constitutional inability to prosecute under the criminal law are often ignored, leaving at best a partial picture of the efficacy and ethos of civil enforcement.

The dangers of recommending, without careful consideration and perhaps adaption, the experience of one country to another in the sensitive and critical area of financial regulation should be obvious. Laws and regulatory devices are rather like plants. They exist and are nurtured by their environment. As a New Yorker might not be surprised to discover that palm trees would not be entirely at home on the sidewalks of Broadway, he should not be over-surprised to learn that Rule 10(b)5 of the Securities and Exchange Act 1934 is not a universal remedy for misconduct in the world's financial markets! Laws and systems of financial regulation are rarely if ever exportable. In the same vein, it is unacceptable for academics and others to experiment with the laws of other countries or impose approaches and provisions on other countries, because they cannot convince their own countrymen of their utility. Ironically, the academics that were involved in the American Law Institute's Federal Draft Securities Code programme had rather more success in the third world than they did in persuading Congress of the wisdom of their work. Imperialism can take many forms, but as a general rule it is that which is not entirely appreciated in the home country that is sent overseas!

While there are dangers in prescribing inappropriate regulations for other countries it would be equally unfortunate for states in the process of developing their regulatory structures not to harken to the knowledge and experience of others who have had to deal with similar problems, albeit perhaps at a different time and in a different context. The author would in no way deprecate the need for comparative analysis and discussion and the

---

[8] *See* text at note 90 *et seq.*

provision of expert advice, provided it is offered and taken for what it is. There are no universal models in securities regulation, although there are, of course, more or less agreed model approaches and a few model provisions, for very specific issues. These are matters such as drug money laundering and insider dealing where, as we have seen, there has been a significant political initiative from the U.S. and certain other developed countries. Even model legislation, if a European Community Directive can be considered such, on a matter as specific as insider dealing, has generated considerable controversy and some uncertainty in terms of implementation.[9] There would seem to be little point in attempting to develop in the abstract models for less specific issues of regulation for, for example, the transition economies in Central Europe.

4 A MODEL IN POINT

There are so many issues worthy of discussion that it is inevitable that the selection of any one, will justify criticism from one quarter or another. Nonetheless, the author is of the view that one of the most pressing issues is the challenge, presented to effective policing of the markets, which has arisen through internationalisation. Therefore, this chapter concentrates on this very practical issue and, by looking at the experience of the United Kingdom and Malaysia, seeks to illustrate the points that have already been made in regard to the development of regulatory models. While there is a widespread perception that securities regulation is new in Britain, the author has already indicated that this is in fact not the case. It is true, however, that until comparatively recently the most significant element in regulation was self-regulation. Thus, the new regulatory regime in Britain has apparently been designed for modern conditions, although the debate as to how effectively it has addressed the problems facing the markets today, is far from over. The regulatory structure, since its establishment under the Financial Services Act 1986, has already gone through major changes and there remain areas of regulation which remain unsettled.[10] On the other hand, a number of Central European countries have looked to the British experience in framing their own laws. Indeed, the Financial Services Act 1986 has even been proposed as a model for countries such as Hungary. Such an inappropriate "model" underlines the concern already expressed by the author. The 1986 Act and the regulatory regime that it ordains has been severely criticised in Britain and it would be rash to suppose that it constitutes either a viable or reliable example that should be followed by other and very different jurisdictions. Nonetheless, the British experience is looked at and insofar as it does represent one of the most developed systems of regulation – at least in Europe, it is worthy of analysis. It is also particularly appropriate to look to the situation in Britain when considering

---

[9] *See* generally B. Rider and T. M. Ashe (eds.), *The Fiduciary, Insider and the Conflict* (1995).
[10] *See* B. Rider (ed.), *CCH Financial Services Reporter*, Chs. 1 and 2.

the policing of international markets, given the significance of London as a world financial centre and its particular significance within the European Union. There has also been a great deal of discussion and, indeed, heart searching in Britain in recent years concerning the control of fraud and other abuses.

The selection of Malaysia as a jurisdiction worthy of analysis and comparison may appear to be less obvious. However, the author's choice is not entirely arbitrary, but is justified on the basis of the transition which has occurred in her economy over the last decade and the political and economic imperatives which now drive her economic institutions, which are not wholly unlike those pertaining in several states in Eastern and Central Europe. Furthermore, the regulatory structure in Malaysia has been created from virtually nothing over the past four years or so. In developing what is now a reasonably effective system considerable attention was given to the experience of other jurisdictions, including the U.S. and Australia. The Malaysian Government has also been particularly concerned to ensure that the system is capable of dealing effectively with fraud and related abuses.

5 THE PROBLEM

When questioned as to how far his Writ ran, King Henry II responded as far as his arrows reached! Given the developments that have since taken place in ballistics, such an approach to jurisdiction might have accommodated the extraterritorial zeal of the U.S. Securities and Exchange Commission.[11] However, the law relating to jurisdiction has not kept pace with technology and in England and within those jurisdictions that follow English common law, the criminal law[12] confines itself within the straitjacket of the territorial principle.[13] In other words, the Queen's Writ in criminal matters[14] generally runs to the edge of territorial waters and no

---

[11] *See, e.g., Leasco Data Processing Equipment Corp. v. Maxwell*, 468 F.2d 1326 (2nd Cir. 1972). *See generally* D. Chaikin, "Fraud, Securities Laws and Extraterritoriality in the U.S." in *The Regulation of the British Securities Industry* (B. Rider ed., 1979); A. Neale and M. Stephens, *International Business and National Jurisdiction* (1988). Perhaps one of the most drastic illustrations of the so-called unilateral approach is the U.S. Security and Exchange Commission's proposal for "waiver by conduct" jurisdiction, *see* Sec. Ex. Act Rel. No. 21186 (1984), discussed in W. Hasetine, "International Regulation of Securities Markets", 36 I.C.L.O. 307 (1987).

[12] For example, a murder or manslaughter committed by a British citizen outside the United Kingdom may be tried in England as though it had been committed there. *See* Offences Against the Persons Act 1961, s. 9. Under the same Act, bigamy committed outside the United Kingdom is an offence within English jurisdiction. *Id.* s. 57. For an example of extraterritoriality under Malaysian law, *see* Penal Code, s. 4 (regarding offences against the state).

[13] Law Commission, *The Territorial and Extraterritorial Extent of the Criminal Law* (1979) (Eng.). With regard to economic crimes, *see* L. H. Leigh, "Territorial Jurisdiction and Fraud", *Crim. L.R.* 280 (1988); J. Breslin, *Extraterritorial Control of Securities Frauds* (1989) (unpublished Ph.D. thesis, University of Cambridge).

[14] In fact, the main basis for the common law is territoriality, whether liability be civil or criminal. *See DPP v. Stonehouse* [1978] A.C. 55 per Lord Keith.

further. In a world where transactions can occur on an almost instantaneous basis in or through a number of sovereign jurisdictions, the limits of the criminal justice system become immediately apparent. Today, it is only the most casual or incompetent economic criminal who would venture to confine his illicit activities to within a single jurisdiction.[15]

6 THE GLOBAL IMPERATIVE

It is not only for criminal and antisocial reasons that so much in the world of finance and commerce today stretches beyond national frontiers.[16] Development in communications, technology, and the general mobility of capital and persons, have all contributed irresistibly to a highly interdependent world economy, with truly international markets.[17] For a host of sound commercial reasons, a significant proportion of any nation's business transactions will involve a multiplicity of jurisdictions.

This is perhaps nowhere more apparent than in the corporate securities industry.[18] The international "character" of securities markets is nothing new. Some of the earliest English joint stock companies were concerned with foreign trade. For example, in February 1553, Sebastian Cabot formed a company with 240 shareholders to trade with Russia. A year earlier a company had been chartered with the rather more romantic object of "discovery of regions, dominions, islands and places unknown". Indeed, some of the earliest recorded trading in script and bonds within the City of London was in regard to such companies.[19] In fact some of the most ancient "markets" appear to have been concerned primarily with "foreign goods".[20] The securities markets of today often constitute markets for paper issued by foreign issuers and may be operated by members who have direct or indirect foreign interests, trading for or on behalf of persons outside the jurisdiction. While the degree of internationalisation obviously varies from one market to another, virtually every market is subject, to some extent, to the essentially international imperative of money.[21] Surprisingly, little

---

[15] *See* generally B. Rider, *The Promotion and Development of International Cooperation to Combat Commercial and Economic Crime* (Commonwealth Secretariat, 1980).

[16] *See* generally *Internationalisation of the Securities Markets* (U.S. Securities and Exchange Commission Report, 1987).

[17] D. Ayling, *The Internationalisation of Stock Markets* (1986).

[18] P. Stonhm, *Global Stock Market Reforms* (1987).

[19] *See* A. Jenkins, *The Stock Exchange Story* (1973); H. Berman, *The Stock Exchange* (1962); E. Morgan and W. Thomas, *The Stock Exchange* (1962).

[20] *See* R. Hodges, *Primitive and Peasant Markets* (1988); M. Silver, *Economic Structure of the Ancient Near East* (1985).

[21] *See* generally *The Market for International Issues* (OECD Committee on Financial Markets, 1972); B. Brown, *The Flight of International Capital – A Contemporary History* (1987); G. Pivato (ed.), *The Stock Exchange – Aims and Efficiency of the Exchange in the Modern Economic and Social Contexts* (1972). Even relatively undeveloped markets are unable to ignore the impact of internationalism. *See* K. Doodha, *Stock Exchanges in A Developing Economy* (University of Bombay, 1962); B. Rider and S. Fung, *Regulating the Chinese Stock Market* (1989).

attention has been given to the implications of internationalisation of the securities markets on what are essentially domestic structures of securities regulation.[22] While economists and even politicians have long recognised the significance of internationalisation, few lawyers have, and those that have, have perceived relevant issues solely in terms of national jurisdiction.[23] This somewhat parochial approach is not confined to Britain. In fact, other than North America, where jurisdictional disputes are endemic, very few jurisdictions have given any real consideration to the problem. It is almost entirely futile to search for learned writings on the impact of transnational transactions in securities on traditional models of regulation in the Commonwealth or Europe. To some extent this reflects the undeveloped stage of learning and research in corporate securities regulation in these jurisdictions.

7 THE TRADITIONAL RESPONSE

Traditionally, the approach of the Common Law to the control and regulation of foreign financial transactions has been to simply assert domestic jurisdiction through whatever normative system was applicable. Thus, in England, a foreign issuer desirous of seeing its securities quoted on the Stock Exchange was required to comply with English law as scrupulously as was possible. This naturally varied a great deal in practice, given the general requirements available for domestic issuers. Indeed, in some instances, because specific statutory exemptions might not be available for a foreign company, the more demanding "self-regulatory" requirements of the market would be applied. Until recently, members of the various organised markets[24] were required to be domestic and the strict

---

[22] *See* generally S. Heberton and B. Gibson, "International Aspects of Securities Legislation" in 3 *Proposals for a Securities Market Law for Canada* (Government of Canada, 1979); B. Rider, *Final Report to the Government of Barbados on the Securities Exchange of Barbados and a Regional Capital Market* (1979).

[23] *See* B. Rider, "Combating International Commercial Crime", 2 *L.M.C.L.Q.* 217 (1985); D. Chaikin, *Combating International Fraud* (unpublished Ph.D. dissertation, University of Cambridge, 1983) (on file with author). Indeed, even Professor L. C. B. Gower, in his review of investor protection in Britain, barely mentioned the impact of internationalisation, devoting only a few paragraphs to the "offshore problem" in his initial Discussion Document and Final Report. *See* L. C. B. Gower, *Department of Trade, Review of Investor Protection – A Discussion Document* (1982) (Eng.); L. C. B. Gower, *Department of Trade, Review of Investor Protection – Final Report*, Cmnd. 9125 1.19 (1985) (Eng.) (hereinafter *Final Report*).

[24] In Britain, the securities industry has been more or less confined within the "square mile" of the City of London. *See* generally W. Clarke, *Inside the City* (1979); A. Hilton, *City Within a State* (1987); H. McRae and F. Cairncross, *Capital City* (1985); B. Rider and E. Hew, "The Regulation of Corporation and Securities Law in Britain – The Beginning of The Real Debate", 19 *Malay. L. Rev.* 144 (1977).

requirements of exchange control regulation[25] effectively separated the domestic and international financial worlds.[26] In large measure, this is also the experience of Malaysia.

In Britain, the criminal law was, and still is, equally simplistic and parochial. In the context of the securities markets, the most relevant area of the criminal law is that relating to fraud and cheating.[27] A special working party of the English Law Commission has recently described the primary feature of the present common law rules on jurisdiction in fraud matter as that of "insularity".[28] These rules generally provide that a triable crime will be committed where and only where its last element takes place within territorial jurisdiction.[29]

The Common Law distinguishes between so called result crimes and conduct crimes. In the case of the first category, there will be jurisdiction if the proscribed result occurred within territorial jurisdiction. In the case of conduct crimes, it does not generally matter that the consequences occurred beyond the shores, if the proscribed result occurred within the territorial jurisdiction. This seemingly clear application results in ludicrous decisions. The development of electronic and other modern methods of transferring money and dealing in securities across national boundaries has naturally produced further problems. The implications of the restrictive attitude of the English courts were manifest in *R. v. Tomsett*,[30] where a telex operator employed by a Swiss bank in London wrongfully diverted a large sum of money in an account in New York to another account in Geneva. English Common Law rules exclude from jurisdiction conspiracies to commit frauds outside the country. Consequently, when the operator successfully argued that the theft did not take place in England, he was successful in avoiding the jurisdiction of the English courts.

The English Law Commission's working party recognised that the approach of the English courts "may well be perceived by other countries as an insular, indeed chauvinistic indifference to their interests, a perception that may be damaging to the interests of the United Kingdom".[31]

---

[25] *See* J. Plender and P. Wallace, *The Square Mile* (1985); T. M. Ashe, "Securities Transactions and Exchange Control" in *The Regulation of the British Securities Industry* (B. Rider ed., 1979).

[26] *See* B. Rider, C. Abrams and E. Ferran, *CCH Guide to the Financial Services Act* (2nd edn, 1986) (Eng.) (hereinafter *CCH Guide*).

[27] B. Rider, "Policing the International Financial Markets", 16 *Brook. J. Int'l L.* 199 (1990). *See* generally M. Clarke, *Regulating the City* (1986); L. Leigh, *The Control of Commercial Fraud* (1982); L. Leigh, "Securities Regulation: Problems in Relation to Sanctions" in 3 *Proposals for a Securities Market Law for Canada* (Government of Canada, 1979); M. Levi, *Regulating Fraud* (1987).

[28] *Jurisdiction over Fraud Offences with a Foreign Element – A Consultation Paper* (The Criminal Law Team of The Law Commission, 1987) (hereinafter *Jurisdiction over Fraud Offences*).

[29] *See* generally A. Arlidge and J. Parry, *Fraud* (1985). Of course, the Malaysian law in relation to fraud and cheating offences is not necessarily so restricted. *See* generally P. R. Glazebrook, *Fraud Offences in Singapore and Malaysia*, Address at First Regional Symposium on Economic Crime, Awana, Malaysia (1991).

[30] [1985] Crim. L.R. 369.

[31] *Jurisdiction over Fraud Offences*, *supra* note 28, at 24, para. 1.4.

Thus, the Law Commission's working party made sensible recommendations in regard to jurisdiction. Specifically, it recommended that if any "act or omission forming part of the offence, or any event necessary to the completion of any offence" occurs within England, English courts have jurisdiction to hear such matters.[32] The Commission excluded from its proposals offences relating to investments, as such offences often involve other considerations. The Law Commission's proposals have now been enacted in the Criminal Justice Act of 1993[33] in regard to the more general offences in English law, and those crimes relating specifically to the financial investments are now governed by their own special rules relating to jurisdiction.

In regard to British securities regulation, the Securities and Exchange Commission's Division of Corporate Finance, in its report on internationalisation to the U.S. Congress in July 1987, observed that "the extent of extra-territorial jurisdiction claimed by the U.K. regulatory agencies has never been subject to much discussion".[34] The same could be said for most countries, especially Malaysia. However, Britain's Financial Services Act of 1986 created an entirely new regime of regulation and supervision of the securities industry in Britain. As has already been pointed out, prior to this Act, the structure of control was essentially self-regulatory. Within this system of self-control there were many forms of regulation and numerous bodies, including some that exercised formal control, and on occasions even an official mandate, and others that functioned as little more than clubs.[35] While this worked well when the City of London was essentially a close knit, homogenous "village", with post-World War II changes in the London population and business dealings – in particular with the suspension of exchange control regulation in 1979 – the traditional forms of restraint provided no protection against the "incompetent, let alone the fraudulent".[36]

The various authorities that sought to "police" the City before 1986 were able to exercise their powers without excessive regard to the normal constraints of legal jurisdiction. For example, the City Panel on Take-overs and Mergers was prepared to "apply" the strict letter of the Take-over Code to

---

[32] This would be essentially the same as § 1.03(1)(a) of the American Law Institute's Model Penal Code. *See* Model Penal Code, § 1.03(1)(a).

[33] *See* generally Criminal Justice Act 1993, s. 62 (concerning insider dealing); Financial Service Act 1986, s. 47 (concerning market frauds). In relation to the position in Malaysia, *see* Securities Industry Act 1983, ss. 84–91 (regarding market frauds).

[34] U.S. Securities and Exchange Commission, *Report to U.S. Congress on Internationalization of Securities Regulation* (U.S. Securities and Exchange Commission, Division of Corporate Finance, 1987).

[35] *See* generally E. Hew, "The Anatomy of Regulation in the Securities Industry" in *The Regulation of the British Securities Industry* (B. Rider ed., 1979); B. Rider and E. Hew, "The Regulation of Corporation and Securities Laws in Britain – the Beginning of the Real Debate", 19 *Malay. L. Rev.* 144 (1977) (hereinafter *The Regulation of Corporation and Securities Laws in Britain*).

[36] *See* Blond Briggs and B. Rider, *Insider Trading* (1983); Clarke, *supra* note 14, at 23; R. Spiegelberg, *The City: Power Without Accountability* (1973); T. Haddon, "Fraud in the City: The Role of the Criminal Law", Crim. L.R. 500 (1985).

Malaysian companies and individuals who attempted to take control over a British public company. Indeed, one of the alleged advantages of self-regulation was its ability to reach beyond the strict limits of legal jurisdiction. In contrast, a senior civil servant in the Department of Trade and Industry observed that "the fundamental purpose of the Financial Services Act is to create a safe environment in which those who consume investment services within the United Kingdom can do so with confidence".[37] Thus, the philosophy of the Financial Services Act 1986, insofar as there is a cogent one,[38] is simply to control the financial services industry within the traditional territorial jurisdiction. Where the relevant activity occurs outside the United Kingdom, the controls "go no further than is justifiable in accordance with established rules of international law and the principles of international good manners".[39] Of course, the weakness with this somewhat gentlemanly approach is that crooks do not invariably observe "good manners"! There is a convincing argument in favour of responsible states not permitting their jurisdictions to be abused by crooks as "safe havens". This is surely a principle of "good neighbourliness" let alone good manners.[40]

The Financial Services Act and the regime that it creates has been described as little more than a "compromise package". It makes a determined, and albeit not entirely successful effort, to satisfy everyone's vested interests and preconceptions. It is no less a compromise in its attempt to accommodate the foreign aspects of securities regulation. To some extent the hands of the Government were tied by the Treaty of Rome,[41] and in other cases, such as in regard to the U.S. and Japan, economic and political considerations dictated a spirit of compromise. Under the new regime, an investment business that is based in, and regulated by, the laws and regulations of another member country of the European Communities (EC) is allowed to operate freely in Britain. "Harmonisation" of financial services regulation within the Union was the goal of the Communities but today this has been watered down to the attainment of mere "equivalence".[42] The primary structure of regulation for financial and banking institutions within the Communities is "home state" authorisation with mutual recognition of each other's authorisation procedures on the basis that they are broadly equivalent. In practice, this might well mean that some European countries operate systems of regulation that are far less demanding than

---

[37] J. Rickford, *Development in the U.K. – Securities Regulation, an International Perspective* (paper presented at a conference organised by the Centre for Commercial Law Studies, Queen Mary College, 1986).

[38] *See CCH Guide, supra* note 26.

[39] Rickford, *supra* note 37.

[40] *See* generally B. Rider, "Policing the City – Combating Fraud and Other Abuses in the Corporate Securities Industry", 41 *Current Legal Probs.* 47 (1988) (hereinafter *Policing the City*).

[41] Treaty of Rome Establishing the European Economic Community, Mar. 25, 1957, 298 U.N.T.S. 167.

[42] *See* B. Rider and T. M. Ashe, *European Securities Regulation* (1993).

others. It is certain that some systems of regulation will be far less exacting both in terms of application and administration than those set down under the Financial Services Act in Britain. The temptation for British and overseas firms to relocate in a more "hospitable" and probably warmer jurisdiction is obvious. Consequently, it may well be that in time, European integration of financial services will, instead of enhancing the effectiveness of regulation, militate in favour of a lowering of standards, at least in Britain. Countries should be also be aware of these dangers in the context of regional initiatives.

While the general approach to securities regulation in Britain is essentially what it has always been, there are one or two exceptions where British regulations do in effect extend beyond national boundaries. High pressure selling of securities, either through cold calling or from "bucket shops", has become an increasing problem in Europe and for that matter elsewhere in recent years.[43] Malaysia has been used by such operators as both a base for launching attacks on investors throughout the Asia-Pacific region and as a target itself. The "boiler room merchants" who learned their trade in Canada and the United States moved their operations to Europe, and in particular Amsterdam, during the late 1970s. They then plied their despicable trade with seemingly virtual impunity.[44] The practice of "share hawking" is not new in Britain, the British Government set up a committee under Sir Archibald Bodkin in 1936 to inquire into such undesirable practices, and the recommendations of this committee[45] led to the enactment of the Prevention of Fraud (Investments) Act of 1939.[46] Indeed, the Commissioners appointed by Parliament in 1696 reported that fraudulent promoters of worthless shares were selling such "with Advantage, to ignorant Men, drawn in by the Reputation, falsely raised, and artfully spread, concerning the thriving state of their Stock".[47] It would seem that the profession of the "loader" is not a new one.

---

[43] *See* M. Bose and C. Gunn, *Fraud* (1989); R. Bosworth-Davies, *Fraud in The City* (1988); D. Francis, *Contrepreneurs* (1988); D. Henry, "Funny Money Stocks", *Forbes*, Sept. 23, 1985, at 38.

[44] *See*, D. Francis, *supra* note 43, at 45. For example, Irving Kott and Thomas Quinn established their organisations and then disseminated a plethora of worthless stocks on an unsuspecting, but often greedy public, invariably employing inexperienced and dishonest salesmen to even engage in cold calling and high-pressure telephone selling. *See id.* Thomas Quinn and his network was one subject of a special meeting organised by the General Secretariat of ICPO-Interpol on Feb. 14, 1980. See "Boiler Plate at Full Steam", 128 *N.L.J.* 618 (1988). A number of these operations have organised crime connections and those operating in Malaysia certainly did. *See*, H. L. Ooi, *Cold Calling and High Pressure Selling of Securities* (1992); M. Rowe, *Fraud in Trade Finance 43* (1989); A. Shipman and B. Rider, *International Organized Crime* (International Chamber of Commerce, 1987); A. Gibson, *The Global Corporate Intelligence Function* (Fourth I.M.B. Lecture at Queen Mary College, Nov. 15., 1988).

[45] *See* generally R. Pennington, *The Investor and the Law* (1968); C. H. Welch, "The Department of Trade and Supervision of The Securities Markets" in *The Regulation of the British Securities Industry* (B. Rider ed., 1979).

[46] The Prevention of Fraud (Investment) Act of 1939 was re-enacted with minor amendments as the Prevention of Fraud (Investment) Act of 1958. Before the Financial Services Act 1986, this represented the principal piece of securities regulation in Britain.

[47] *House of Commons J.*, Nov. 25, 1696.

Section 56(1) of the British Financial Services Act prohibits any person from doing any investment business in consequence of an unsolicited call made on a person in the United Kingdom or from the United Kingdom on a person elsewhere.[48] This prohibition creates a "civil offence" insofar as any resulting contract will not be enforceable against the investor approached, and thus, the investor will be able to recover money or property transferred under the contract or compensation. It is important to note that this provision extends to "cold calling" by individuals in the United Kingdom on persons overseas. One of the reasons that criminal liability was not imposed is that it was thought unjustifiable to extend the reach of the criminal law in this way. It is of interest to note that in the recent judgment of the European Court in *Alpine Investments BV* v. *Minister van Financiën*[49] the Court held that similar "cold calling" regulations in the Netherlands, whilst inhibiting freedom of services within the Communities, were nonetheless justified on the basis of a Member State's right to protect investors. Where the unsolicited call is made from outside the United Kingdom, it is questionable whether a foreign court would apply English law in assisting an investor in recovering his money or property. Should the call be made from a European country it is, at least arguable, that an English court could take jurisdiction under section 4 of the EC Brussels Convention of 1968[50] on the basis that it is a "consumer contract". An order of the English High Court would therefore be enforceable throughout the Community under the Civil Jurisdiction and Judgments Act of 1982.[51]

In assessing the credibility of any new regime of regulation, however, it is necessary to measure what has so far been achieved against its guiding philosophy and objectives. Sadly, as has already been pointed out, little thought has been given to the philosophical issues of securities regulation, and such debate as there has been has tended to concentrate on such matters as insider dealing.[52] While it is true that some of the earliest laws seeking to regulate markets were based upon the importance of promoting and maintaining public confidence in their integrity and thus, efficiency,[53] concentration on this aspect tends to obscure the essentially facilitative nature of securities regulation.[54] While it is also possible to discern a number of philosophical threads in, for example, the Financial Services Act,

---

[48] *See* generally *CCH Guide*, *supra* note 26.

[49] Case C–384/93, May 10, 1995.

[50] 1968/09/27 [1968] *O.J.* 189.

[51] Civil Jurisdiction and Judgments Act 1982.

[52] *See* B. Rider and H. L. Ffrench, *The Regulation Of Insider Trading* (1979); B. Rider, *Insider Trading* (1983); B. Rider, "Insider Trading? A Crime of Our Times", 42 *Current Legal Probs.* 47 (1989).

[53] *See* note 2 *supra*. As we have seen, in England there were laws as early as the reign of Edward I that sought to ensure the integrity of public markets and the ancient offences of forestalling, engrossing, and regrating still survive today within conspiracy to defraud, *see Russell on Crime* (J. Turner ed., 12th edn, 1964).

[54] *See* generally C. Goodhart *et al.*, *The Operation and Regulation of Financial Markets* (1987); L. S. Sealy, *Company Law and Commercial Reality* (1984); L. S. Sealy, "Tomorrow's Company Law", 2 *Company Law* 195 (1981).

not the least being the need to promote and protect public confidence, it is difficult to characterise one as dominant. For example, the British Government's White Paper,[55] which sought to set out the legislative aims of the new law, advocates increased competition as a means of improving both integrity and competence within the industry. Many would consider this highly debatable.

The Malaysian laws are, with respect, no more profound in their logic or application. The Securities Industry Act of 1983,[56] as amended, borrows significantly from outdated and indeed superseded legislation in Australia. The philosophy of the relevant New South Wales and Victoria provisions, while perhaps more discernible than in the British legislation, is questionable as an appropriate approach for Malaysia. The Malaysian markets and financial services industry are very different from those in Australia. The economic and political policies that have circumscribed the development of market capitalism in Malaysia are hardly mirrored in an economy such as that in New South Wales.

In any case, the philosophical foundations of the Australian law have themselves been questioned if not undermined by subsequent events. Sadly, more recent Malaysian legislation, such as The Securities Commission Act of 1992,[57] indicates that few if any lessons have been learnt in this context. It, too, is a mish-mash of philosophies that rest ill at ease with each other. To place in one agency responsibility for promoting the markets and at the same time regulating and policing them, is considered by many commentators to be a recipe for, if not disaster, at least schizophrenia![58]

8   THE REGULATOR'S POWER

Prior to the Financial Services Act of 1986, there were certain statutory provisions regulating the British investment industry and the purchase and sale of securities. Under the Companies Acts and the Prevention of Fraud

---

[55] *Financial Services in the United Kingdom: A New Framework for Investor Protection* (1985) Cmnd. 9432 (HMSO) and *see* also *Final Report, supra* note 23; B. Rider, "Analysis and Appraisal of The City Revolution" in *The Practical Implications of the Financial Services Act* (CCH, 1986); L. C. B. Gower, "Big Bang and City Regulation", M.L.R.1 (1988); B. Rider, "Protecting the Prudent Investor", 6 *Company Law* 54 (1985).

[56] *See* generally B. Rider, *Report Commissioned by the F.P.L.C., A Malaysian S.E.C.* (1991) (hereinafter *Malaysian S.E.C.*).

[57] *See* The Securities Commission Act 1992. *See* also B. Rider, *Policing the Malaysian Markets*, paper submitted to Malaysian F.P.L.C. (1992).

[58] For example, s. 15(1)(k) of the Securities Commission Act provides that the Securities Commission shall be responsible for encouraging development of the securities and future markets in Malaysia. At the same time, s. 15(1)(i) provides that the Commission should "suppress illegal, dishonourable and improper practices . . ." *Id.* Indeed, profound doubts have arisen as to the viability of protecting private investors and creating competitive markets for professional investors within a single law in Britain. But *see* A. Large, *Making the Two Tier System Work* (1993) and *SIB Regulation of the UK Equity Markets* (SIB, 1995).

(Investments) Act of 1958,[59] the structure of regulation was essentially self-regulatory. Although there was considerable discussion as to the effectiveness of this system it became increasingly apparent that it could not deal with fraud and therefore could not adequately protect investors.[60]

In 1986, a committee under Roskill L. J., appointed to consider the form and conduct of fraud trials, reported that "the public no longer believes that the system ... is capable of bringing the perpetrators of serious fraud expeditiously and effectively to book. The overwhelming weight of evidence laid before us suggests that the public is right."[61] Although a certain amount of "tinkering" with the system of supervision and regulation took place prior to the Financial Services Act of 1986,[62] it was generally the view that a system of self-regulation was inadequate, given the developments that had taken place in the market and the way in which business was transacted. The Government appointed Professor L. C. B. Gower in 1981 to review and report on the adequacy of the regulatory scheme and both during his inquiries and subsequently, he made it clear that he favoured the establishment of a new authority along the lines of the U.S. Securities and Exchange Commission – a view shared by many, albeit mostly outside the City of London.[63]

While it is unjust and unhelpful to judge the Financial Services Act too harshly until the "dust settles", it has taken rather longer than most thought it would for the new regime to settle.[64] The system established under the Act is a curious mixture of both official regulation and supervision on the basis of direct statutory authority and various permutations of delegated

---

[59] Companies Act 1985; Prevention of Frauds (Investments)Act 1958 (Eng.). *See* generally R. Pennington, *supra* note 45, at 49, C. M. Schmitthoff, *Commercial Law in a Changing Economic Climate* (1974) 27; C. M. Schmitthoff, *Remarks* (conference organised by the International Faculty of Securities Regulation in London, 1976) "[A]s regards investor protection, it would only be a slight exaggeration to maintain that we have no law at all".

[60] *See* M. Clarke, *Regulating the City* (1985); T. Hadden, *The Control of Company Fraud* (1968); T. Hadden, "Fraud in the City; Enforcing the Rules", 1 *Company Law* 9 (1980). *See* generally *The Third Report of the Trade and Industry Select Committee*, House of Commons, U.K. Parliament, Company Investigations (1990).

[61] *Report of the Fraud Trial Committee* (1986). A report prepared by a special working party convened by the Director of Public Prosecutions had come to a similar conclusion in 1979.

[62] *See* generally *The Regulation of Corporation and Securities Laws in Britain*, *supra* note 24, at 30; B. Rider, "The British Council for the Securities Industry", 42 *Revue de la Banque* 303 (1978); B. Rider and E. Hew, "The Structure of Regulation and Supervision in the Field of Corporation and Securities Laws and Britain", 41 *Revue de la Banque* 83 (1977).

[63] *See Final Report*, *supra* note 23, at 3.12. *See* also "Big Bang and City Regulation", *supra* note 55, at 1. Many have expressed the view that it is inevitable that sooner or later Britain will have to establish a securities and exchange commission, *see* B. Rider, *Policing the City in the 21st Century* (King's College, London University, 1994). The Securities and Investments Board, which is incorporated as a private company with limited liability, is perceived by many as taking unto itself more and more responsibility in the area of enforcement. *See* Large, *supra* note 58, at 42. It is also interesting that the Securities and Investments Board, with the support of the U.S. Securities and Exchange Commission, has successfully contended before the U.S. courts that it is performing a "governmental function" and is therefore entitled to immunity (under FSIA 28 USC 1602-11) *see European American Corp Inc. v. SIB* No 89–2333 (JGP) D.C./DC 4/5/90, 22 *Sec. Reps. & Law Reps.* 595 (1990).

[64] *See* B. Rider (ed.), *CCH Financial Services Reporter*, Chs. 1 and 2.

and essentially contractual authority.[65] Regardless of what jurists might argue about the normative and educative effect of rules that remain in practical terms unenforced, common sense would incline towards the view that rules that cannot be enforced are a delusion that brings the legal system into disrepute. The Act does provide the Securities and Investment Board and the Department of the Trade and Industry with a number of significant powers. Such powers include the ability to require cooperation in conducting inquiries, and, in certain circumstances, the ability to actually intervene and control conduct of business. It is not necessary to detail all these powers here.[66] What is of more relevance is to note that scant attention was paid to the institutional aspects of effective supervision and surveillance.

When the Act first came into operation, enforcement took a relatively low priority.[67] Few authorities sought to give any real attention to the needs of this important function. In a system that requires confidence in its efficiency and integrity for its credibility, there was and still is a risk of disaster.[68] Fortunately, over the past two or three years, the Securities and Investment Board (SIB) had addressed these issues with a good deal more determination and foresight, and there is now a germ of credibility in the system.[69] Unfortunately, the British Government exhibited no greater willingness to take the institutional aspects of enforcement more seriously. The Department of Trade and Industry and the Treasury,[70] aside from losing several key officials to the new authorities, have experienced considerable difficulty in recruiting competent lawyers and experienced enforcement personnel. For example, the section that deals with insider dealing cases relies, by its own admission, almost exclusively on the Insider Dealing Unit of the London Stock Exchange for detection and preliminary

---

[65] *See* B. Rider, "Self-regulation: The British Approach to Policing Conduct in the Securities Business, with Particular Reference to the Role of the City Panel on Take-Overs and Mergers in the Regulation of Insider Trading", 1 *J. Comp. Corp. L. & Sec. Reg.* 319 (1978). *See supra* text accompanying note 62. The Government, which by no means was wholly receptive to Professor Gower's proposals, did accept the need to ensure that the new scheme of regulation was properly policed, however.

[66] *See* generally *CCH Guide*, at 55.

[67] *See* generally *Policing the City, supra* note 40, at 61 (citing the statement of the first chairman of the Securities and Investments Board, namely that "I [the chairman] am a regulator, a watchdog and a policeman – in that order".). The chairman of the Malaysian Securities Commission, Dato' Dr. Munir has taken the same stance, although he had more recently emphasised the significance of enforcement. *Cf.* Dato' Dr. Munir, Chairman, Malaysian Securities Commission, *Address* (Second Regional Symposium on Economic Crime in Kuala Lumpur, 1993); Dato' Dr. Munir, Chairman, Malaysia Securities Commission, *Address* (Third Regional Symposium in Kuala Lumpur, 1994).

[68] This has been most dramatically illustrated with the collapse of Baring Investment Bank, *see Report of the Board of Banking Supervision Inquiry into the Collapse of Barings* (HMSO, 1995) and the so-called Robert Maxwell affair.

[69] *See* generally A. Large, *supra* note 58 and the *SIB Review Implementation* (SIB, 1993).

[70] The powers that were afforded to the Department of Trade and Industry under the Financial Services Act have now been transferred in the main to the Treasury.

investigation.[71] The London Stock Exchange's Insider Dealing Unit is responsible for monitoring and investigating instances of possible insider abuse on the stock market. While it operates within a self-regulatory jurisdiction, it is impossible for either the Department of Trade and Industry or the SIB to eventually appoint members of this Unit to conduct investigations and prosecutions and thereby to have access to the statutory powers of investigation in the Financial Services Act of 1986. Given the virtual absence of effective policing in the corporate securities industry prior to 1986, it is perhaps not surprising that there is not only a dearth of suitable "regulators", but also little relevant expertise.

The experience in Malaysia has not been appreciably different. Regulatory experience in Malaysia is at a premium and the Malaysian Securities Commission must be congratulated on its ability to have attracted to its ranks a number of well-qualified young professionals from other government departments and the private sector. It remains to be seen, however, whether they contemplate a long-term career with the Commission. Similar problems occur in the embryo compliance "industry", both in Britain and Malaysia. The Malaysian Securities Commission is well aware of the importance of creating a compliance culture, serviced by a compliance "industry", but at present it is doubtful whether the resources in terms of manpower and expertise exist to fashion an effective compliance regime in most businesses. In Britain, an effective compliance structure in financial intermediaries has been dictated rather more by the onerous anti-money laundering provisions in the Criminal Justice Act 1993 and Drug Trafficking Act 1994 than the obligations, such as they are, under the Financial Services Act 1986.

It is not necessary for us to chart the historical development of securities regulation in Malaysia, although it should be appreciated that the Malaysian stock market, in Kuala Lumpur, is not new and has a history that dates back to the end of the last century. Securities regulation in Malaysia has developed pragmatically and has often been used to further specific economic and political objectives, in addition to simply creating an efficient capital market and financial services industry. The pragmatic development of regulation is reflected in the number and diversity of organisations involved in administering the markets. Indeed, one of the reasons for creating the Malaysian Securities Commission in 1993 was to provide a "one-stop agency".[72] As a result, however, while a good deal of centralisation of authority has been achieved, there are still a number of other bodies with responsibility for matters pertaining to the nation's

---

[71] Controversy has centred on the "economics" of the Department of Trade and Industry and Treasury appointing very expensive barristers and accountants to conduct its inspections under the provisions of The Companies Act 1985. Indeed, every effort is made to persuade the Stock Exchange to continue the investigation, given the cost implications. *See* generally *Third Report of the Trade and Industry Select Committee*, House of Commons, U.K. Parliament, Company Investigations (1990).

[72] *See* generally *A Malaysian S.E.C.*, *supra* note 56.

capital markets.[73] Nevertheless, the Securities Commission is given regulatory and enforcement oversight over all of these entities and inevitably, it is in this oversight that the success of this new regulatory system will be judged.

9 THE ACID TEST

Much of the discussion that took place as to the adequacy of the various structures of British regulation has focused on the ability of those charged with policing the financial services industry to secure convictions before the ordinary criminal courts for fraud and abuses, such as insider dealing.[74] The same is equally true in Malaysia, where it has been said that "perhaps one of the most serious ills of the securities industry is the perilous yet elusive abuse called insider trading ... insider trading is one of the most serious threats to the Malaysian securities markets".[75]

In 1878, a Royal Commission on the London Stock Exchange, appointed under Lord Penzance, expressed concern about the lack of enforceability of various rules and regulations, and called for responsibility for policing these laws, to be placed in a "public functionary".[76] Attempts were made during the 1970s and early 1980s to improve the prosecution of cases of fraud in England, for example, by the strengthening the staff of the Director of Public Prosecutions and the creation of Fraud Investigation Groups.[77] However, prosecution is only one factor in combating fraud. As the committee sitting under Roskill L.J. observed,[78] deficiencies in the procedures for investigation and in the trial process itself are equally important stumbling blocks.

As a result of the recommendations of the Roskill Committee, the Criminal Justice Act of 1987 provided for the establishment of the Serious Fraud Office (SFO). The Act entrusts far-ranging inquisitorial powers to the Director of this office – powers analogous to those afforded to the Department of Trade and Industry under the Companies Act of 1985 and the Financial Services Act of 1986. However, the power afforded the Director is predicated on the basis that the matter involves a "serious or complex fraud". It must also be emphasised that the SFO's powers are for the purpose of investigating crime with a view to prosecution, whereas the

---

[73] In Britain the Financial Services Act 1986 has not reduced the number of agencies concerned at one level or another with "policing" the securities industry. There are over 15 such agencies, although the Securities and Investments Board is actively concerned to ensure adequate coordination and, indeed, rationalisation. *See* B. Rider (ed), *CCH Financial Services Reporter*, Ch. 2 and A. Large, *supra* note 58.

[74] *See* "Blowing the Whistle on Foul Play in the City", *Financial Decisions*, Apr. 1989, at 35.

[75] Puan Zainun Ali, Registrar of Companies, *Address* (Fifth Annual Conference of the Securities Industry in Malaysia, Sept. 5, 1989).

[76] Government Printer (1878).

[77] D. Lanham, *et al.*, *Criminal Fraud* (Law Book Company, 1987); S. Froomkin, "Problems of Investigating and Prosecuting Commercial Crime Offences", II *C.L.B.* No. 2 (1985); B. Rider, *Report to the Attorney General of Hong Kong on Combating Commercial Crime* (1979).

[78] *See supra* notes 61–63 and accompanying text.

inquisitorial powers of the Department of Trade and Industry and its inspectors are more in the nature of a public inquiry.[79]

The Malaysian Registrar of Companies, under the Companies Act of 1965 and Securities Industry Act of 1983,[80] has similar powers of inquiry. However, section 38 of the Securities Commission Act of 1992 gives investigating officers appointed by the Commission the power to demand evidence, which can then be used against an alleged fraudster.[81] As such, the Malaysian legislation is broader than the investigatory provisions in any of the British legislation. In Britain, evidence demanded from an alleged perpetrator cannot be used other than in cross-examination. That is, it cannot be used in the prosecution's case-in-chief.

While there is little doubt that the establishment of the SFO in Britain and the resources that it has been able to attract are significant advances in the fight against fraud, its impact on the policing of securities laws remain doubtful. Although the Office has not shown a reluctance to concern itself with frauds in the investment world, it interprets its statutory mandate restrictively. Consequently, it has been stated by an Assistant Director of the SFO: "Insider dealing on its own is essentially a regulatory offence, and as such is unlikely to qualify ..."[82]

The SFO, whilst achieving a conviction rate of over 60 per cent, has been undermined by a series of spectacular failures involving extremely expensive trials. There have also been cases where even a conviction has resulted in nothing but derisory penalties. Indeed, the present Director has gone as far as expressing the view that many instances of abuse in the financial world would be better dealt with under the essentially contractual disciplinary jurisdiction of the various self-regulatory authorities.[83]

In Malaysia, all prosecutions require the consent of the Public Prosecutor, although under the Securities Commission Act of 1992, the Securities Commission can, subject to the requirement of consent from the Public Prosecutor, conduct prosecutions itself.[84] Whether there would be advantage in Malaysia having a Serious Frauds Office is a much wider

---

[79] The Director's powers of investigation under s. 2 of the Criminal Justice Act 1987, are almost a unique example of such powers being vested in a prosecutor in England. It has been remarked that in this regard the process is similar to the inquisitorial powers of an examining magistrate in Civil Law systems, and although not a particularly accurate comparison, this does emphasise their unusual character.

[80] Companies Act 1965; Securities Commission Act 1992, s. 38.

[81] The Securities Commission Act 1992, s. 38.

[82] Letter from Assistant Director of the Serious Fraud Office (Dec. 7, 1988); *see* also Criminal Justice Act 1987, s. 1(3) (the determination of what constitutes a "serious or complex" fraud is left for the Director to determine "on reasonable grounds"); C. Wolman, "UK Treads Carefully Over Insider Dealing", *Financial Times*, Feb. 7, 1989. For a discussion of insider dealing enforcement *see* B. Rider and T. M. Ashe, *Insider Crime* (1993); B. Rider, *Insider Trading* (1983); B. Rider, "The Policing of Insider Trading in Britain" in *European Insider Dealing Regulation* (1991). In regard to Malaysia, *see* B. Rider and H. L. Ffrench, *The Regulation of Insider Trading* (1979).

[83] *See* generally B. Rider, "Civilising the Law – The Use of Civil and Administrative Proceedings to Enforce Financial Services Law", 3 *Journal of Financial Crime* 11 (1995).

[84] Securities Commission Act 1992.

question. Malaysia has not had a particularly good record in securing convictions for serious cases of economic crime, in common with many other
countries some of which, such as its new neighbour, Singapore, already
possess a specialised prosecutorial agency that deals with investment fraud.

It is, in the view of the author, unfortunate that the discussion of the
effectiveness of securities law and corporate regulation in Britain and elsewhere has focused so much on the ability of the traditional criminal justice
system to bring fraudsters to book. It has long been recognised that effective control and regulation of financial markets involves devices other and
in addition to the ordinary criminal law.[85] For example, as we have already
seen, the Statute of 1697, "To Restrain the number of ill Practice of Brokers
and Stockjobbers", contained provisions that sought to regulate the
embryonic securities industry in a manner not too different from that under
the Financial Services Act of 1986. Brokers had to be licensed and be of
"proven value". Not only were they required to eschew fraud, but also to
"adhere to good and fair principles". The Act required the posting of bonds
for good behaviour and indemnity. There were also provisions for the
recording of bargains.[86] In this early law, one can discern such concepts as
"authorisation", "fit and proper" and even the notion that the "spirit" is
more important than the "letter" of the rules.[87] In practical terms, adequate
control, and vetting of those seeking admission to the securities industry or
the markets and the prudential regulation of such is likely to be far more
cost-effective than resort to the criminal law on an *ex post facto* basis.

The criminal law has not proven to be an efficient device in combating
economic crime for a host of technical, practical, procedural, and institutional reasons.[88] It requires a high standard of proof, is generally slow
and exacting in its procedures, and is restrictive and cautious in the evidence it will allow to be adduced. Few jurisdictions have achieved a
significant level of success in policing financial misconduct by relying
primarily, let alone exclusively, on this blunt and very expensive tool. Even
the Royal Commission sitting under Lord Penzance in 1878, to which
reference has already been made, recognised that the criminal law was too
inflexible and slow.[89] When one considers the developments that have
taken place in the financial markets since the time of Lord Penzance's
deliberations, the problems facing the criminal justice system must be so
much greater. Internationalisation of the markets is a major difficulty
serving to confound detection, fragment and diversify investigations, place

---

[85] For a somewhat "exotic" example, *see* the rules relating to stabilisation of the commodity
markets in China: G. Boulais, 55 *Manuel du Code Chinois*, 754b (Variations Sinologiques,
Shanghai, 1924) (prohibiting persons from rural areas from purchasing more than a *shih* of
rice in Peking). *See also The Market in History* (B. Anderson and A. Latham (eds), 1986).

[86] *See An Act to Prevent the Infamous Practice of Stock-Jobbing 1734* (The International Stock
Exchange, 1986).

[87] *See e.g.*, General Principle 1, *U.K. City Code on Take-Overs and Mergers and The Principles, Care
Conduct of Business Rules* (SIB, 1992).

[88] *See* generally B. Rider, "Combating International Commercial Crime", 2 *L.M.C.L.Q.* 217
(1985).

[89] *See supra* note 76.

witnesses and evidence out of evidential and often financial reach and render conventional criminal processes ineffectual or disproportionately expensive.

10 ALTERNATIVE ENFORCEMENT MODELS

In the author's view the civil law is far more likely to provide an effective enforcement tool than the criminal law. In certain jurisdictions, most noticeably that of the United States, the civil law had long been used to assist in the enforcement of what are essentially penal or regulatory laws.[90] Under section 21(d) of the U.S. Securities and Exchange Act of 1934, the Securities and Exchange Commission is empowered to bring suit to enjoin violations not only of the Federal laws, but various rules and regulations made under the authority of such.[91] It is by this authority that the Securities and Exchange Commission has achieved comparative success in policing both the general anti-fraud provisions in the Federal laws and, in particular, insider abuse. By bringing injunctive suits against those suspected of violating the Federal law, the Securities and Exchanges Commission has been relatively successful in securing court orders enjoining future violations, disgorgement of profits and exacting certain other undertakings, such as entering into an approved in-house compliance procedure. Given the tremendous costs involved in litigation and the robust stance of the Commission, in a high proportion of these proceedings court orders have been made on the basis of consent, as defendants are willingly to accept the injunction and other orders, rather than risking incurring the costs, inconvenience, and embarrassing publicity associated with a long trial. The practical importance of such an order is that a further violation of the relevant law or a rule made under it, amounts to contempt of court for which traditional criminal law sanctions are, of course, available.

Regulatory authorities in other jurisdictions have shown far less courage and ingenuity than the U.S. Securities and Exchange Commission in seeking the assistance of civil courts in policing the securities markets. Of course, much depends upon the receptiveness and boldness of the judiciary. For example, until comparatively recently, English courts have not always exhibited great eagerness to become involved in this area.[92] Nonetheless, section 61 of the Financial Services Act 1986,[93] now provides both the Department of Trade and Industry, as well as the Securities and

---

[90] *See* generally L. Loss, *Fundamentals of Securities Regulation* (2nd edn) (hereinafter *Fundamentals of Securities Regulation*).

[91] 15 U.S.C. §§ 77a-80c-3 (1988).

[92] For example, in *Prudential Assurance Ltd* v. *Newman Industries Ltd (No. 2)* [1981] Ch. 257, Lord Justice Templeman stated that "in our view the voluntary regulation is a matter for the City. The compulsory regulation of companies is a matter for Parliament".

[93] *See* also s. 6 of the Financial Services Act pertaining to unauthorised investment business. This provision has been used already on a number of occasions.

Investments Board, with a statutory power to apply to the courts for injunctions and restitution orders in cases of violations of certain provisions in the Act and rules made under its statutory authority.[94] It remains to be seen whether this power will be used with the same degree of enthusiasm that the U.S. agencies have exhibited in bringing civil enforcement suits. While the Securities and Investments Board has on several occasions indicated that it attaches practical significance to this power, it remains uncertain whether sufficient resources will be made available for it to be fashioned into the sort of weapon that plays in important role in the United States.[95]

In the context of Malaysia, it is doubted whether the Malaysian Securities Commission has the legal authority and standing to bring similar civil actions. Section 16 of the Securities Commission Act of 1922 states that "[t]he Commission shall have all such powers as may be necessary to carry out its functions under this Act".[96] It has been contended that this broad provision gives the Commission the power to bring civil enforcement suits. However, the flaw with this argument is that the section does not address the issue of *locus standi*. The Commission would not have *locus standi* to proceed in a civil action against someone who had breached, for example, a provision of the Securities Industry Act or one of the Commission's own rules. Obviously, this is a serious weakness in the Malaysian legislation and one that requires urgent attention.[97]

Not only is civil enforcement often quicker, cheaper and more effective than the laborious and expensive processes of the criminal law, it does have a greater potential for reaching overseas.[98] It is an accepted principle of international law that one state will not enforce another state's laws.[99] No such rule exists in regard to the civil law. Given the incidence of serious international fraud, some judges have been prepared to seize this possibility and allow the pursuit of fraudsters and their ill-gotten gains. Although it may not be acceptable for the Hong Kong courts to directly enforce U.S. anti-insider dealing laws, they can order a bank in Hong Kong to freeze money in an account, that is the proceeds of insider dealing in the U.S., on the basis that the bank had knowledge that the money was

---

[94] *See* generally *CCH Guide*, at 192.

[95] Note also the creation of a statutory tort action for "private investors" under s. 62 of the Financial Services Act of 1986 and *see* B. Rider, *supra* note 83.

[96] Securities Commission Act 1992, s. 16.

[97] Under s. 100 of the Securities Industry Act of 1983, the Registrar of Companies does have authority to apply to the High Court for orders in relation to breaches of the Securities Industry Act 1983, as does the Kuala Lumpur Stock Exchange in regard to its own rules. Securities Act 1983, s. 100.

[98] *See* generally B. Rider, "A safe haven for fraud?", 10 *Company Law* 46 (1989); B. Rider and D. Chaikin, *Mutual Assistance in Criminal Matters: A Commonwealth Perspective* (Commonwealth Secretariat, 1983), and B. Rider, *supra* note 83.

[99] *Dicey and Morris on the Conflict of Laws* (Stevens ed., 11th edn). *See* also *AG of New Zealand* v. *Ortiz* [1984] A.C. 1; *Re State of Norway's Applications* [1989] 1 All E.R. 745; *AG for The UK* v. *Heinemann* [1988] 78 A.L.R. 449.

allegedly obtained in breach of trust.[100] On ordinary trust law principles the bank becomes a constructive trustee.[101] Moreover, even in cases where a person does not actually hold the proceeds of a breach of trust, provided they know or suspect the truth, they may well be held liable as if they were in fact a constructive trustee to make restitution, if they assist in laundering the money in question.[102]

English courts have also been prepared to order that assets should not be removed from its jurisdiction in circumstances where litigation has commenced or is about to be commenced and it is likely that property within the jurisdiction will not fully satisfy a judgment.[103] Indeed, in exceptional circumstances, English courts have been prepared to order defendants to disclose not only their assets within its jurisdiction, but outside the jurisdiction and to freeze the transfer of such.[104] The courts have also been prepared in the context of civil actions to prevent defendants and potential defendants from leaving the jurisdiction.[105] Furthermore, the arrangements for recognising and enforcing foreign orders and judgments in civil proceedings are far more developed than in regard to criminal matters.[106]

As one might expect, U.S. courts have been no less imaginative than their English cousins. The Singapore courts have also shown themselves willing and able to use the civil law effectively against international fraudsters,

---

[100] *Nanus Asia Co.* v. *Standard Chartered Bank* [1990] 1 H.K.L.R. 396 (H.K. High Ct.). *See* also *AG for Hong Kong* v. *Reid* [1994] 1 All E.R. 1. Note also the approach in *AG for the U.K.* v. *Wellington Newspaper Ltd* [1988] 1 N.Z.L.R. 129 (New Zealand). *See* generally B. Rider, "Fei Chien Laundries and The Pursuit of Flying Money", 1 *J. of Int'l Planning* 77 (1992) (hereinafter *Pursuit of Flying Money*).

[101] *See* for example, *Lipkin Gorman* v. *Kurponale Ltd* [1991] 2 A.C. 548.

[102] *Agip (Africa) Ltd* v. *Jackson* [1990] Ch. 265 and [1991] Ch. 547 and *Royal Brunei Airlines Sdn Bhd* v. *Tan* [1995] P.C., *The Times*, May 29, 1995.

[103] *See* generally Supreme Court Act 1987, s. 37; *Mareva Compania Naviera* v. *International Bulk Carriers*, 2 Lloyd's Rep. 509 (1975); *Felixstowe Dock & Railway Co.* v. *U.S. Lines, Inc.* [1989] 2 W.L.R. 109. Similar proceedings to freeze money in bank accounts or other property have been brought by law enforcement agencies in relation to the proceeds of fraud, *see* in particular *SIB* v. *Pantell (No. 2)* [1991] 4 All E.R. 88. *See West Mercia Constabulary* v. *Wagner* [1981] 3 All E.R. 378; *Chief Constable of Kent* v. *V.* [1983] Q.B. 34. But note the limitations of the common law in regard to derivative property in *Chief Constable of Leicestershire* v. *M.* [1989] 1 W.L.R. 20. Additionally, note the provisions in regard to "profitable" crimes in Part VI of the Criminal Justice Act 1988 relating to restraint of property and confiscature. *See* Criminal Justice Act, 1988, Pt. V (Eng.); *see* also D. Feldman, *Criminal Confiscation Orders – The New Law* (Butterworths, 1988). In regard to disclosure of assets, *see* Bankers Book Evidence Act 1879, s. 7; *A.v. C.*, [1980] 2 All E.R. 347; *Bankers Trust* v. *Shapira* [1980] 2 W.L.R. 174.

[104] *Babanaft International* v. *Bassatne* [1989] 2 W.L.R. 232; *Derby & Co.* v. *Weldon (No. 2)* [1989] W.L.R. 276; *Republic of Haiti* v. *Duvalier* [1989] 2 W.L.R. 261.

[105] Note also the flexibility of the English courts in regard to service of process on defendants who are out of their jurisdiction. *See Barclays Bank of Switzerland* v. *Hahn* [1989] 1 W.L.R. 261 (1989).

[106] *See, e.g.,* J. McClean and W. Patchett, *The Recognition and Enforcement of Judgement and Orders and the Service of Process within the Commonwealth* (Commonwealth Secretariat, 1979).

such as in the Pertimina bribes litigation.[107] It remains to be seen whether the Malaysian Courts will be as bold.[108]

It is the view of the author that more reliance should be placed on the civil law, in policing the securities markets, particularly in regard to abuses such as insider dealing and market frauds.[109] Some jurisdictions have already gone a little down this road.[110] Others are actively considering creating specific civil actions for breaches of regulatory provisions. While it would not be appropriate for the civil law to altogether replace the prospect of criminal liability, the civil law should be allowed to operate as a more flexible and probably efficacious weapon. In the case of insider dealing regulation, there is considerable advantage in an express right of action being given, by statute, to the issuer of securities in which the insider dealing takes place. While it may be difficult to justify such an action on traditional principles of loss, causation and reliance, this liability should not be viewed as compensatory or for that matter restitutionary – as it is under the Malaysian legislation.[111] It would exist simply to deprive the wrongdoer of his ill-gotten gains, and operate through the intermediation of the issuer – which has at least some interest in achieving a fair market in its shares.

There are of course other devices that can be utilised to improve not only the mechanisms of enforcement, but the detection of abuse in the first place.[112] Increasing attention, especially by the Kuala Lumpur Stock Exchange, is being given to various forms of stock market surveillance. However, little attention has been given to other forms of monitoring except in regard to the prudential regulation of financial intermediaries' solvency. The area of loss prevention and minimisation is probably one of the most important in the regulation and control of all forms of economic abuse. Despite the development of these various mechanisms, there is little evidence of the development or refinement of effective systems.

For example, in Britain, the various self-regulatory agencies have the primary responsibility for "authorising" those activities in the investment business. They are required to satisfy themselves that before such a person is permitted to operate an investment business he is a "fit and proper person" to do so.

---

[107] *Sumitomo Bank Ltd* v. *Kartika Ratna Thahir* [1993] I S.L.R. 735.

[108] Mr. Justice George (President of The Commonwealth Court, Malaysia) speaking at the Second Regional Symposium on Economic Crime, Kuala Lumpur 1993, expressed his personal support for the developments that have taken place in other Commonwealth jurisdictions and said that he would be well disposed to such authorities if cited in an appropriate case before his court. Justice George, *Address* (Second Regional Symposium on Economic Crime in Kuala Lumpur, 1993).

[109] B. Rider, *The Unacceptable Insider* (Legal Research Foundation, University of Auckland, 1987); *Pursuit of Flying Money, supra* note 100, at 77.

[110] *See* Securities Law Reform Act 1989 (N.Z.).

[111] *See* Malaysia Companies Act 1965, s. 132A and Securities Industry Act 1983, ss. 89–91.

[112] In regard to the use of "timely disclosure" obligations *see* B. Rider, "Insider Trading – A Question of Confidence", 77 *L.S. Gaz.* 113 (1980); B. Rider, *Proposals for a Securities Exchange Law of Barbados* (1981) 85. *See* also Securities Exchange Act 1982, ss. 58, 59 (Barbados).

Another aspect of loss prevention that receives scant attention in most jurisdictions is the adequate policing of disclosure and reporting obligations. In most regulatory systems there are various reporting obligations imposed on enterprises and those involved in the financial services industry. Usually one of the first indications that something is amiss is that the reporting obligations will be ignored or that false information will be provided. However, enforcement of these provisions is invariably given a very low priority.

11 FACILITATOR LIABILITY

There are, of course, many other ways in which securities regulation can be rendered more effective. One particularly fruitful approach is to focus regulation and thus potential liability much more on the "facilitators" of abusive or illegal conduct. To some extent this has long been done in the United States[113] and to a lesser extent in Britain.[114] By using aider and abettor concepts and even the law of conspiracy,[115] it is possible to cast a significantly wider net over those who knowingly facilitate or connive in the frauds of others. Expanding notions of "control liability"[116] and placing specific obligations on those in a supervisory role to ensure the effectiveness of compliance,[117] are all steps in the right direction. The professional adviser or intermediary who knowingly or recklessly and perhaps even negligently, facilitates the commission of a securities fraud, betrays the trust and respect that society places in him as a professional.[118] Furthermore, from a purely pragmatic standpoint, given their standing, advisers and intermediaries constitute relatively easy targets within the jurisdiction. They are also, by virtue of the professional constraints within which they operate, far more susceptible to other regulatory procedures and to discipline. For example, they will be bound to comply with more onerous recording and reporting provisions, violations of which are themselves grounds for enforcement action against them.

---

[113] The Draft Federal Securities Code, which is essentially a restatement of the present law, provides the following:

> [An] agent or other person who knowingly causes or gives substantial assistance to conduct by another person giving rise to liability under the Code . . . with knowledge that the conduct is unlawful or a breach of duty, or involves a fraudulent or manipulative act, a misrepresentation, or nondisclosure of a material fact by an insider . . . is liable as a principal. A person may cause or give substantial assistance to conduct by inaction or silence when he has a duty to act or speak.

See Fundamentals of Securities Regulation, supra note 89, at 1016.

[114] *See AGIP* v. *Jackson* [1992] 4 All E.R. 385, 451 and *SIB* v. *Pantell (No. 2)* 4 All E.R. 88.

[115] *See* also the Racketeer Influenced and Corrupt Organization Act 1964, U.S.C. §§ 1962(a) (1988).

[116] *See Fundamentals of Securities Regulation, supra* note 90, at 101.

[117] *See* Insider Trading and Securities Fraud Act 1988, 15 U.S.C. §§ 78e(e) (50), 78o(f), 78t-1. 78u-1, 78kk(c), 806-4a (1988 and Supp. 1993).

[118] YB Dato' Hamid Syed Jaafar Albar, Malaysian Minister of Law, *Address* (Third Regional Symposium on Economic Crime in Kuala Lumpur, Mar. 28, 1994).

What is certain, however, is that there are no panaceas in policing the financial markets domestically, let alone internationally. Regulation in this complex area of economic activity is a multifaceted problem calling for a diversified and flexible response from law enforcement and those charged with regulatory oversight. To attempt to administer what are essentially property-related crimes and procedures, often fashioned by criminal courts a hundred years ago, is like trying to fight a modern war with King Henry II's bow and arrows!

12 CRIMES OF THE POWERFUL!

A factor that is not always recognised in policing the securities markets and which affects regulation at all levels, is the increasing amount of organised crime involvement. Organised crime regards securities frauds as a low risk/high reward activity.[119] Although it is dangerous to sensationalise both the extent and menace of organised crime, it is even more irresponsible to ignore what is a very real threat.[120] Although police agencies have different perceptions of organised crime, it is clear that in recent years both traditional and other forms of organised crime have increasingly moved into "white collar crime" and in particular securities frauds,[121] and other related activity. Their activities have ranged from simple theft of script, to sophisticated schemes to market worthless shares or manipulate markets.[122]

---

[119] *Communique to Commonwealth Law Ministers Meeting, Harare, Zimbabwe* (1986) para. 59: "Ministers recognised an increasing trend of organised crime to become involved in economic offences, as these offer high rewards with relatively little risk of apprehension". This development was also acknowledged by Commonwealth Law Ministers at their meetings in Canada in 1977, in Barbados in 1980, in Sri Lanka in 1983, and by the Commonwealth Heads of Government at their meeting in the Bahamas in November 1987. The United Nations has on a number of occasions specifically recognised the move by organised crime into the sphere of economic crime, *see* for example, *Report of the UNCTAD Secretariat on Maritime Fraud*, Items 3 and 4 of Provisional Agenda, U.N. Doc. TD/B/C.4/AC4/8 (1985), and the resolution of the Seventh Congress of the United Nations on Crime Prevention and Criminal Justice, on organised crime. Other organisations such as ICPO-Interpol and the Customs Cooperation Council have not been slow to acknowledge this development either. *See* also D. Carter, "International Organised Crime Emerging Trends in Entrepreneurial Crime", 10 *Journal of Contemporary Criminal Justice* 236 (1994).

[120] *See* Shipman and B. Rider, *supra* note 44: B. Rider, *Organised Crime Report to the Home Affairs Committee*, House of Commons, U.K. Parliament (1994); *Minutes of Evidence and Memoranda* (HMSO, 1994) and also *Organised Crime, Report of The Home Affairs Committee* (HMSO, 1995). *See* also *Organised Economic Crime* (Commonwealth Secretariat 1986); B. Rider, "The Financial World at Risk: The Dangers of Organised Crime, Money Laundering and Corruption", 8 *Managerial Auditing J.* 3 (1993).

[121] *See* generally *Organised Crime*, 53rd ANZAAS Cong. (May 20, 1983) 23 (Australian Government printer, D. Meagher ed., 1983); U.S. President's Commission on Organized Crime, Report to the President, *The Impact: Organized Crime Today* (1986); *Papers* (conference organised by the General Secretariat of ICPO-Interpol, Feb. 14–15, 1989).

[122] *See* M. G. Yeager, "The Gangster as White Collar Criminal: Organised Crime and Stolen Securities" in *The Crime Society* (1976) 47.

Some groups have used the traditional tools of violence, corruption, and extortion to facilitate their frauds and manipulations. There have been instances where corporate executives have been blackmailed or bribed into betraying corporate confidences so that information can be sold and utilised for dealing.

Not only is organised crime concerned with engaging in various forms of fraud to make money, which can then be used for investing in other criminal enterprises or penetrating legitimate businesses,[123] but also to launder the proceeds of other crimes ranging from simple robberies to illicit trafficking in drugs. Many of these methods involve the securities markets and financial intermediaries. The U.S. Presidential Commission on Organized Crime, in its Interim Report to the President, stated that "every financial institution ... should assume it is a potential target for use by organized crime in money laundering schemes".[124] The London Stock Exchange[125] has also recognised this in the context of laundering profits from drug trafficking and has warned its members accordingly. Of course, the risk to the financial intermediary is not simply that of a criminal prosecution, but is also the risk of corruption and loss of confidence. If effective action is to be taken to discourage the commission of serious crimes that give rise to such profits in the first place, it is important that this money should not become legitimised.[126] The criminal pipeline of illicit funds has to be fractured.

The problems facing those charged with combating securities offences and abuses are bad enough, without the balance being even more tilted against them by the involvement of organised crime groups with access to vast resources.

---

[123] *See* M. Bers, U.S. Justice Dep't, *The Penetration of Legitimate Business By Organized Crime* (1970).

[124] "The Cash Connection: Organised Crime", *Financial Institutions and Money Laundering* 1 (1984). *See* also E. Nadelman, "Unlaundering Dirty Money", 18 *InterAmerican Law Rev.* 33 (1986).

[125] Letter to Member Firms from M. E. Fidler, Secretary to the Council (Oct. 14, 1986). The Institute of Chartered Accountants for England and Wales issued a similar statement on Dec. 14, 1987. The Chairman of The Hong Kong Securities and Futures Commission also drew attention to the dangers facing those engaged in business in the financial sector in Apr. 1993.

[126] In Britain, it is considered preferable to seek the assistance of financial institutions on an informal basis in reporting suspicious transactions to the authorities than imposing a formal reporting requirement in regard to certain categories of transaction as is done under the Bank Secrecy Act, 12 U.S.C. §§ 1951–1959 (1988). Nevertheless, persons who knowingly assist in laundering the proceeds of a serious crime are guilty of an offence in Britain and this has, in practice, encouraged a significant amount of cooperation. Additionally, the Prevention of Terrorism (Temporary Provisions) Act of 1989 makes it a crime to be concerned in an arrangement whereby money is made available to a person "knowing or having reasonable cause to suspect that it may be used by that person for purposes of terrorism". Prevention of Terrorism (Temporary Provisions) Act 1989. *See* D. Wheatley, [1989] *N.L.J.* 499. *See* generally Drug Trafficking Act 1994 and the Criminal Justice Act 1993.

13 INTERNATIONAL COOPERATION

Faced with all these problems, it is not surprising that those charged with protecting and advancing the capital markets are giving more and more attention to international and regional cooperation.[127] It is now generally accepted, even in the United States, that cooperation is far more profitable in the long term than simply a unilateral assertion of jurisdiction extra-territorially.[128] On the other hand, it is possible to have some sympathy with Judge Owen, who, sitting in the Southern District Court of New York, in an enforcement action brought by the U.S. Securities and Exchange Commission to freeze the profit that the defendant had made from insider dealing in the U.S. expressed the view that "in Hong Kong they practically give you a medal for doing this sort of thing [insider trading]" and thus, refused to defer jurisdiction to the Hong Kong courts where the money had been sent.[129] As a result, Judge Cruden, in Hong Kong, took the view that "this Court will always take whatever effective steps are legally available to it under Hong Kong law, to deal with illegal or morally reprehensible com-mercial conduct ... " By way of rebuke to his New York colleague he asked "where a conflict of law does arise ... the dispute should be approached in a spirit of judicial comity rather than judicial competitiveness. Whatever the approach of other courts, this is the sympathetic approach followed by this Court".[130]

While most legal systems do not deliberately attempt to frustrate the law enforcement efforts of other nations, concern for sovereignty and the inevitable lack of political and cultural interface in certain areas, can render meaningful cooperation unpredictable. Even in Commonwealth countries, which share a common legal heritage and where specific legal inhibitions on the exchange of information are rare, cooperation cannot always be assured. In cases where mandatory procedures are required before information can be secured, let alone furnished to a foreign agency or tri-bunal, it is almost always necessary to establish "double criminality" in the sense that the matter that is the basis of the inquiry or request for assistance would also be a criminal offence had the relevant conduct occurred within

---

[127] *See* "Enforcement of the Securities Laws" in *An International Market in Internationalization of the Securities Markets*, Report of the Staff of the Securities and Exchange Commission to the U.S. Congress (1987); S. Heberton and B. Gibson, "3 International Aspects of Securities Legislation" in *Proposals for a Securities Market Law for Canada* (Government of Canada, 1979); W. Hasetine, *supra* note 11.

[128] *See Regulation of International Securities Markets*, Policy Statement of the U.S. Securities and Exchange Commission (1988) 11; J. Grundfest, *International Cooperation in Securities Enforcement – A New U.S. Initiative* (1988).

[129] *See Nanus Asia Co.* v. *Standard Chartered Bank* [1990] 1 H.K.L.R. 396 (H.K. High Ct.).

[130] Insider dealing has long been a matter of interest to the authorities in Hong Kong: *see* B. Rider, "Insider Trading: Hong Kong Style", 128 *N.L.J.* 897 (1978). *See* also B. Rider, "The Regulation of Insider Trading in Hong Kong", 17 *Malay. L. Rev.* 310 (1979).

the jurisdiction of the country whose assistance is sought.[131] Even where mandatory procedures are not necessary the matter will often only be considered sufficiently serious and worthy of expending precious law enforcement resources if the relevant conduct is readily recognisable as criminal.

This problem has manifested itself on countless occasions when the authorities of a developing country have sought assistance from the British police in regard to an exchange control matter, which no matter how seriously it may be regarded overseas, is not regarded in Britain as a crime or even worthy of official interest. As the English Law Commission's Working Group[132] recognised, a failure on the part of both countries to appreciate the perspective of the other is highly damaging to international cooperation in general terms.[133]

In a number of jurisdictions, for a host of reasons – some more acceptable than others – legislation has been enacted that provides for the secrecy of certain categories of information, or actually forbids disclosing information to foreign authorities.[134] These secrecy and blocking laws are usually more

---

[131] There are, of course, a variety of procedures available for taking evidence out of jurisdiction. In Britain, the main provision is contained in s. 29 of the Criminal Justice Act 1988, which now governs the procedure for letters of request. *See* Criminal Justice Act 1988, s. 29; C. Emmins and G. Scanlan, *Blackstone's Guide to Criminal Justice Act 1988* (1988). Where evidence is obtained pursuant to mandatory procedures at common law, it cannot be passed to external authorities. *See AG for Hong Kong* v. *Ocean Timber Transportation Ltd* [1979] H.K.L.R. 298 (H.K.). Evidence can be obtained for foreign courts, where a criminal matter is pending before that court, under both s. 5 of the Extraction Act of 1873 as amended, and under the Bankers Books Evidence Act of 1879.
　　The procedures for assisting foreign tribunals in civil matters are far less restrictive, under the Evidence (Proceedings in Other Jurisdictions) Act of 1875. This Act has been generously interpreted by the English courts. In *Re State of Norway's Application* [1989] 1 All E.R. 745, the House of Lords held that a letter of request issued by the Norwegian court did not amount to the attempted enforcement of Norwegian revenue laws in England, but was merely seeking the assistance of the English courts to obtain evidence to enable Norwegian revenue laws to be enforced.
　　The U.S. courts have shown themselves willing to assist foreign agencies. *See, e.g. Re Letter of Request from the Crown Prosecution Service of the United Kingdom*, 870 F. 2d 686 (D.C. Cir. 1989).

[132] *Jurisdiction Over Fraud Offences, supra* note 28.

[133] Certain developing countries seriously question why they should willingly assist countries like Britain and the United States in drug inquiries when the more developed jurisdictions ignore them for assistance when seeking to protect their economies. *See* B. Rider, *U.S. Dep't State, International Cooperation – Fact or Fiction*, Paper presented to White House Conference for a Drug Free America (1988). The then-head of C.I.D. in Malaysia, Datuk Khan, criticised the attitude of U.S. law enforcement agencies in this context. According to Datuk Z. Khan, cooperation was in practice a "one-way street" leading to Washington. Datuk Z. Khan, Head of C.I.D., *Address* (Second Symposium on Economic and Narcotic Crimes in Taipei, 1993).

[134] *See* generally U.S. Senate, *Staff Study: Crime and Secrecy: The Use of Offshore Banks and Companies: Permanent Sub-Committee on Investigations* (U.S. Gov't Printer, 1983); I. Walter, *Secret Money* (1985); *Offshore Haven Banks, Trusts and Companies, The Business of Crime in the Euromarkets* (1984); Prager and B. Rider, "Money Laundering – The Risk to Small States" in *Memoranda for Meeting of Senior Law Officers of Small Commonwealth States* (1983).

related to banking and financial activities,[135] however, in some countries, they extend to professional and business information.[136] While most legal systems, even those containing such provisions, permit the taking and disclosure of information in limited circumstances, in practical terms the institutional and cost factors tend to militate against the effectiveness of such procedures. Furthermore, most systems require a criminal investigation to be existent and are extremely careful to screen out "fishing expeditions". Indeed, in the case of an offshore bank in Labuan, the new Malaysian offshore centre, disclosure of information relating to accounts can be obtained by the Royal Malaysia Police or Bank Negara (*i.e.* the Central Bank) upon application to the High Court only in regard to the current investigation of a specific serious crime committed in Malaysia.[137] This is a major problem in securities regulation, as many matters would not be susceptible to being characterised as "criminal". For example, in Malaysia, the laundering of the proceeds of insider dealing is not *per se* a crime, although it is now in Britain and the United States. Hence, there will be a problem of finding double criminality.[138] There is no doubt that some countries have deliberately created almost impenetrable secrecy barriers, simply to attract business and in particular "flight money". A few have been willing to promote their facilities without any proper regard as to who might wish to avail themselves of the advantage of anonymity. In addition to secrecy and blocking statutes, an ever-increasing number of countries have been prepared to permit a variety of banks and other financial institutions to establish themselves within their territory, primarily to engage in business overseas. These offshore banks and other institutions, operating behind walls of secrecy, often with little prudential or other regulatory oversight, provide an excellent facility for the international fraudster and money launderer.[139] Sadly, in some jurisdictions, it is not only the banks and other financial institutions that are prepared to prostitute themselves, as there would

---

[135] The British Protection of Trading Interests Act of 1980 requires persons doing business in Britain to report to the Secretary of State foreign compulsory orders and allow the Secretary of State to dictate the response, under threat of a criminal sanction: British Protection of Trading Interests Act 1980. Under s. 181 of the Financial Services Act 1986, the Department of Trade and Industry may block the disclosure of information by regulatory authorities in Britain to an overseas agency even where the request is voluntary, Financial Services Act 1986, s. 181. *See* also The Canadian Foreign Extraterritorial Measure Act 1984–85, c. 49; The French Law No. 80-538, July 15, 1980.

[136] *See, e.g.,* Swiss Civil Code, art. 28 (Switz.); Banking Secrecy Financial Privacy and Related Restrictions (1979).

[137] *See* B. Rider, *Offshore Banking in Labuan* (paper submitted to Royal Malaysian Police Force at the Symposium on The Misuse and Abuse of Offshore Banks, 1992).

[138] This was the problem that the U.S. authorities encountered in seeking assistance from the Swiss, under their 1976 Treaty on insider dealing cases. *See infra* note 141. *See* generally J. Siegel, "U.S. Insider Prohibition in Conflict with Swiss Bank Secrecy", 4 *J. of Comp. Corp. L. & Sec. Reg.* 353 (1982); D. A. Szak, "International Cooperation in Insider Trading Cases", 40 *Wash. & Lee L. Rev.* 1149 (1980).

[139] Barrons, *See Where Hot Money Hides* (July 11, 1983); P. Willoughby, *The Law and Practice of Tax Havens; Uses and Abuses* (address at the Eighth Commonwealth Law Conference in Jamaica, 1986).

appear to be a ready supply of lawyers and accountants to also service this type of business.[140]

In practical terms, the insertion of a so-called "haven" jurisdiction in the commission of a securities fraud, will cause tremendous problems for investigators. In many such cases it will be sufficient to effectively frustrate any meaningful legal process. Consequently, even where there are procedures for cooperation between responsible states, much will depend upon the degree of involvement of a "haven" jurisdiction. There are, of course, "havens" or "international finance centres" that provide *bona fide* services which are properly administered and supervised, such as Labuan, but unfortunately these are the exception rather than the rule.

14 MEMORANDA OF UNDERSTANDING

To regularise procedures for obtaining mutual assistance in legal proceedings there is a tendency for countries to negotiate treaties, or at least memoranda of understanding (MOUs). Most countries have at least some bilateral arrangements for extradition, but, in the context of the securities markets, few cases ever reach the stage of an extradition request. As has already been pointed out, a serious problem in securing cooperation in this area, is that many "securities offences" are not "ordinary criminal offences", or fail to meet the usual requirements of double criminality. For example, until comparatively recently, insider dealing was not an extradition crime in English law, and consequently it was not possible for the British Government to "surrender" a person to, for example, the U.S. authorities, even though there are comprehensive extradition arrangements between Britain and the U.S. This problem manifested itself under the U.S.–Swiss Treaty on Mutual Assistance in Criminal Matters.[141]

Comprehensive Mutual Assistance Treaties (MLATs) for cooperation in criminal matters are now the goal of many countries and already some progress has been made. In 1986, Commonwealth governments, encouraged by Malaysia, endorsed a new scheme for mutual assistance in criminal matters within the Commonwealth. The so-called "Harare Scheme"[142] provides an agreed vehicle for Commonwealth jurisdictions to furnish comprehensive mutual assistance, subject, of course, to specific enactment within their own domestic law. To some extent, the Commonwealth

---

[140] *See,* for example, *Report of the Commission of Inquiry Appointed to Inquire into the Illegal use of the Bahamas for the Trans-shipment of Dangerous Drugs* (1984) (Bah.).

[141] Treaty on Manual Assistance in Criminal Matters (May 25, 1973) U.S.–Switz., 27 U.S.T. 2019, 1052 U.N.T.S. 61.

[142] The Commonwealth Scheme for Mutual Assistance in Criminal Matters (1986). *See* also The Commonwealth Scheme for The Rendition of Fugitive Offenders (1966) (amended 1986); The Commonwealth Scheme for The Transfer of Convicted Prisoners (1986). *See* generally T. Huckle, *Mutual Judicial Assistance and Economic Crime* (Commonwealth Secretariat, 1985).

Scheme mirrors the European Convention on Mutual Assistance in Criminal Matters. While both the European Convention and Harare Scheme are significant steps in fostering effective mutual cooperation, from the standpoint of the securities regulator, they are of little practical relevance. The European Convention is primarily concerned with criminal proceedings – under the Civil Law, and thus, does not always fit well into common law systems. Indeed, the view of the British Home Office, until comparatively recently, was that the two systems were wholly incompatible. It was upon this basis that the British Government refused the proposal that there should be a mutual assistance treaty between Britain and Switzerland.

Of particular interest is the Convention on Insider Trading of the Council of Europe.[143] This Convention provides for cooperation between signatory states, not only in investigating cases of insider dealing, but also in the monitoring of markets to ensure "equal access to information for all users of the stock market". Similar arrangements are required for member countries of the European Union, in the Council Directive for coordination regulations on insider dealing.[144] Article 8 of this instrument provides that the relevant enforcement agencies in each Member State are bound to assist the authorities in other member countries in enforcing their laws against insider abuse. There are, of course, other instruments of the European Community that also require cooperation between authorities concerned with policing the financial markets and banking institutions.[145] To date, while enhancement of cooperation has been discussed by law enforcement and regulatory authorities in other regions, most noticeably Latin America, the Asia Pacific region, and Caribbean, nothing of substance has emerged to compare with developments within Europe.[146]

It is in the area of MOUs that most progress has, however, been made and is likely to be made in the foreseeable future.[147] The U.S. Securities and Exchange Commission has adopted a consensual approach to cooperation and has signed MOUs with over thirty-five countries. Of course, to what extent agreements that have been signed can be described as "consensual", particularly with some of the smaller Caribbean countries, may be

---

[143] *See* B. Rider and T. M. Ashe, *The European Insider Dealing Directive* (Univ. of Siena, 1993).

[144] Council Directive 89/07/29, 1989 *O.J.* 192.

[145] *See, e.g.*, Council Directive 82/121/EEC (regarding investment services and information published by listed issuers).

[146] *See* generally B. Rider and C. Nakajima, *International Initiatives in Securities Regulation* (Cambridge, 1993).

[147] *See International Securities Enforcement Cooperation Act of 1988*, Report of the Committee on Banking, U.S. Senate (U.S. Govt. Printer, 1988). MOUs play an important role in other areas of law enforcement, such as narcotics and in particular the exchange of financial information in regard to assets derived from illicit trafficking in drugs. *See* generally E. Nadelmann, "Unlaundering Dirty Money Abroad: U.S. Foreign Policy and Financial Secrecy Jurisdictions", 18 *InterAmerican Law Rev.* 33 (1986). The Double Taxation Agreements should also be noted: *see, e.g.*, Convention Between the Government of the U.K. On Behalf of the Government of Bermuda; The Government of the U.S.A. Relating to the Taxation of Insurance Enterprises and Mutual Assistance in Tax Matters.

questioned.[148] Nonetheless, it is perfectly acceptable for the U.S. authorities, given their expertise, resources and obvious self-interest in promoting effective cooperation in policing the world's capital markets to take the lead in this regard. While the U.S. Securities and Exchange Commission has attempted to "standardise" the various arrangements that it has already negotiated and is presently negotiating; it has not always proved feasible. Most MOUs that the U.S. Government has negotiated provide for "co-operation" in the exchange of information not only for investigatory and traditional law enforcement purposes, but also for surveillance and monitoring. The Securities and Exchange Commission is eager to convert as many of these "agreements" into binding treaties and to add the significant obligation to use, where possible, available mandatory procedures to obtain information and evidence in furtherance of a request for assistance.

The Insider Trading and Securities Enforcement Act of 1988[149] expands dramatically the powers of the U.S. Securities and Exchange Commission to respond to a request for assistance from a foreign securities authority. The Commission "in its discretion" may use its mandatory and subpoena procedures for obtaining information on behalf of a foreign authority, provided that the authority confirms that the matter under inquiry relates to a violation of its own securities law, whether or not the same conduct would amount to a violation of U.S. laws had it occurred within its jurisdiction. There must also be an undertaking of reciprocity. This provision gives the Commission a wide-ranging and practical means of assisting foreign agencies, and although it has been indicated that there is no question of assistance being conditional on an existing MOU, the Commission will be far more inclined to exercise its discretion in circumstances where there is such an arrangement, if for no other reason than that reciprocity is assured.

Given the prerequisite of reciprocity, a number of other jurisdictions have been "encouraged" to amend their laws to facilitate the execution of foreign assistance requests. Under the English Common Law, it is more or less certain that statutory powers of investigation, such as those for obtaining and executing a search warrant, may only be used in regard to a matter for which there is proper jurisdiction, and even then the results of such an inquiry cannot normally be handed over to a foreign authority.

The British Companies Act of 1989 seeks to bring the English law in line with that in the United States, so far as securities regulation is concerned, and the Criminal Justice (International Cooperation) Act 1990 and Criminal

---

[37] The Treaty between the United Kingdom and the United States Concerning the Cayman Islands relating to Mutual Legal Assistance in Criminal Matters was not universally welcomed in the Caymans, where it remains a controversial matter: *see* R. Nash, "US and Caymans Sign Crime Pact", *N.Y. Times*, July 4, 1986. Even in Bermuda, criticism is still made of the Government and in particular, the former Attorney General for being too cooperative with Washington. Indeed, it would seem that even the Swiss required a little "inducement" before they agreed to the 1974 Treaty. *See* B. Rider and M. L. Ffrench, *The Regulation of Insider Trading* (1979).

[149] *See* 15 U.S.C. §§ 78a–80 (1988).

Justice Act 1993 address the problem generally. The 1989 Act empowers the Department of Trade and Industry to conduct an inquiry, using mandatory procedures to compel production of documents and witnesses, at the request of an "overseas regulatory authority" that exercises a function corresponding to that of the Department of Trade and Industry, or the Securities and Investment Board, under the Financial Services Act of 1986. In considering whether to exercise its wide investigatory powers, the Department may take account of reciprocity and whether the relevant violation would be objectionable under a parallel provision of English law. It is important to note, however, that unlike the U.S. statute, cooperation is not ruled out by lack of reciprocity.

Other provisions in the Companies Act 1989 and Financial Services Act 1986 significantly strengthen the role of MOUs in policing the securities markets. Where satisfactory arrangements have been negotiated with another regulatory authority, whether domestic or foreign, it will be open to the Securities and Investment Board, or one of the other self-regulatory authorities, to rely on the information that other foreign authorities provide in the discharge of its regulatory and enforcement functions. While there is a widespread feeling among the various regulatory authorities that information can be as easily obtained through informal contacts other than MOUs, it is only information that is communicated pursuant to a "satisfactory arrangement" that may be directly relied upon in this manner.

At present, the British Government, through the Department of Trade and Industry, has eight signed MOUs. There are a number of other special agreements for financial information, but these are not primarily directed at enforcement. The Securities and Investment Board has itself negotiated a number of MOUs with a great variety of overseas authorities, concerned primarily with the exchange of information for authorisation purposes and the capital adequacy rules. The Securities and Futures Association has also placed on a formal basis many of the informal arrangements that it operated before the Financial Services Act of 1986 in regard to the Stock Exchange. Perhaps one of the most significant is the MOU that it has signed with the North American Securities Administrators Association (NASAA) on exchange of enforcement information. Various self-regulatory authorities in Britain have also ensured that their own rules permit a substantial degree of interface with these various arrangements.

The Government of Malaysia has also recognised the importance of developing a network of formal and informal agreements designed to promote the exchange of information and international cooperation. To date, the Securities Commission has signed five MOUs. Other arrangements are being negotiated with a number of other countries. Of course, the Malaysian Central Bank also has a number of similar arrangements in relation to its role as supervisor of financial institutions. The law does not, however, currently permit Malaysian authorities, such as the Securities Commission or the Registrar of Companies, to use their statutory powers of investigation on behalf of a foreign agency inquiring into matters that do not involve an infraction of the laws of Malaysia.

15 DISCLOSURE IN CONJUNCTION WITH INVESTIGATORY POWERS

Reference has already been made to the almost "inquisitional" powers entrusted to the Director of the Serious Fraud Office, in Britain, under section 2 of the Criminal Justice Act of 1987.

In determining whether it is appropriate for the SFO to pursue a matter that has been referred to it, inquiries may well have to be initiated and, consequently, the Office might well come into possession of information which is highly relevant to the responsibilities of some other authority. Section 3 of the Criminal Justice Act of 1987 empowers the SFO to disclose information that is obtained pursuant to its statutory powers, to various prosecutorial and regulatory authorities, including "anybody having supervisory, regulatory or disciplinary functions in relation to any profession or any area of commercial activity". Therefore, it is in order for the Director to disclose relevant information to the various bodies operating under the Financial Services Act of 1986, and in practice this is done regularly.

This provision further states that the Office may disclose such information to "any person or body having, under the law of any country or territory outside the United Kingdom" corresponding powers and responsibilities. Thus, in appropriate cases, the Director could disclose information that the SFO has already obtained, pursuant to its statutory powers, to a securities regulatory authority in another jurisdiction.

The Director is also authorised to enter into "agreements" to "supply information" or to "receive information" from other relevant authorities, and these can be of a general or restrictive nature. So far, the Director has only sought to utilise this particular power to agree with foreign authorities that information disclosed by his office, or received by him, will be used for specific purposes. Obviously, occasions arise where other agencies are prepared to disclose information to the Office, but are concerned that it shall only be used for specific purposes. By the same token, the Director may himself wish to impose such restrictions on further disclosure or use. This can be achieved through the expedient of an "agreement" under section 3 of the Criminal Justice Act of 1987. It should be noted, however, that under the Director's general power to disclose information to other agencies, or under his power to negotiate "agreements" for such cooperation, he is not empowered to actually utilise his investigatory powers in response to a request for assistance from either a domestic or foreign authority. Rather, he is only authorised to pass on information that he has already obtained. Of course, the dividing line is not a clear one, and it may well be necessary for the Director to use his powers to obtain information upon which he can properly resolve whether a serious fraud has been committed within his jurisdiction.

While it is probable that most systems of law do not actually impose the constraints on sharing information that they are often thought to do,[150] it is

---

[150] *See Gartside v. Outram*, (1856) 26 L.J. 113. "The true doctrine is that there is no confidence as to the disclosure of iniquity. You cannot make me the confidant of a crime of a Fraud . . ."

understandable that those who might well have to face civil and other actions for alleged improper disclosure act with a degree of circumspection. Section 179 of the Financial Services Act of 1986 provides that it is a criminal offence for certain "primary recipients" of "restricted information" to disclose it, without the authority of the person to whom it relates, or for a person who receives such information from a "primary recipient" to do so.[151] Restricted information is defined to include information that is obtained by a primary recipient in the discharge of, or for the discharge of its functions under the Act, or rules and regulations made thereunder. The category of "primary recipient" is limited to those agencies which have legal responsibilities and powers to obtain information under the Act. Thus, the Department of Trade and Industry and the Securities and Investments Board are included, but the other self-regulatory authorities are not, as their powers to obtain information arise by virtue of the contractual arrangements that they are required to have in place for their members. The position in regard to information that they might obtain under their own rules is governed by those rules and the general law. Of course, if a self-regulatory authority receives "restricted information" from the Securities and Investment Board, it will be subject to the restrictions in section 179.

Section 180 of the Financial Services Act contains a number of exceptions to the general prohibition contained within section 179. These exceptions include the disclosure of information for a criminal, civil or disciplinary proceeding, or for the proper performance of some regulatory or legal function, or where the identity of the person concerned remains confidential. In *Melton Medes Ltd* v. *The Securities and Investments Board*,[152] Lightman J. held that the Securities and Investments Board had acted properly in disclosing information to beneficiaries of a pension fund who had initiated an action against Melton Medes Ltd. The Court considered that it was appropriate for the Securities and Investments Board to disclose even "restricted information" in such circumstances as it was within its mandate to assist in the protection of investors. Section 180(3) further provides that section 179 will not restrict the disclosure of information "for the purpose of enabling or assisting any public or other authority for the time being designated for the purposes of section 180" by the Department of Trade and Industry. The Department has been willing to designate a wide class of agencies and authorities under this provision, and has made clear that the restriction in section 179 does not preclude the disclosure of "restricted information" to an authority outside the United Kingdom that performs functions corresponding to those of the Department of Trade and Industry under the Financial Services Act of 1986 or under the anti-insider dealing law. Of course, under section 181, the Department may direct that information shall not be disclosed to any person or authority outside the United Kingdom

---

[151] Financial Services Act 1986, s. 179.
[152] [1995] 2 W.L.R. 247.

where the Secretary of State considers such to be against the public interest.[153]

There are no such similar provisions under Malaysian law in regard to the Securities Commission and it is to be regretted that the Malaysian authorities do not have the ability to share information that they have, under their investigatory powers. Information received by regulatory authorities in the exercise of their functions will generally be restricted in the sense that it should not be disclosed other than for the purpose for which it was obtained, or for another which is legally justifiable, such as the prosecution of crime. Section 43 of the Securities Commission Act of 1992 is a good example of such a provision. In many cases, there will be specific legal obligations on the recipients of such information preventing free or even controlled disclosure and even in the case of those authorities not operating under direct statutory power, the general law and their own rules may well produce a similar result.

It should be clear from the discussion so far that there are inevitable limitations to the effectiveness of international cooperation through bilateral devices. Consequently, thought has been given to various multi-national initiatives. Comparatively early in the life of the European Community, suggestions were made for a Euro-Securities and Exchange Commission,[154] and although this is still many years off, increased co-operation will lead to a *de facto* integration in many areas. The Organisation for Economic Cooperation and Development (OECD) provides a forum for specialised discussion of international fiscal matters and has shown some interest in securities regulation. However, it has never been seriously suggested that the OECD should perform a regulatory or policing function, or for that matter even coordinate such. The same is true, at even a lower level, of organisations such as the International Federation of Stock Exchanges (*Fédération Internationales des Bourses de Valeurs*).

Considerable ignorance exists as to both the constitutional limitations and capabilities of the International Criminal Police Organisation (ICPO-Interpol). It is often assumed, quite erroneously, that ICPO-Interpol provides a facility for investigating international securities frauds and pursuing the offenders. In fact, the ICPO-Interpol network is primarily directed at the facilitation of communications between ordinary police forces, which are its exclusive members. Securities regulatory authorities are not members of this network and in most jurisdictions are not permitted access to it. Furthermore, article 3 of the Constitution of ICPO-Interpol confines the organisation's mandate to "ordinary criminal law offences". Many of the matters that are of concern to those charged with regulating the securities markets would not fall within this definition. Of course, this is not to

---

[153] *See CCH Guide, supra* note 26.
[154] *European Community*, Report of the Committee of Experts on the Development of a European Capital Market (1966) 235. *See* generally, Rider and Ffrench, *supra* note 148, at 275.

say that on occasions the ICPO-Interpol network cannot be used to communicate police information concerning securities fraudsters both effectively and with security. It is clear, however, that the role of ICPO-Interpol in policing the securities markets is minimal and is most unlikely to increase. To some extent, this reflects the fact that in many countries the investigation of matters such as insider dealing and stock market fraud has been substantially taken out of the hands of the ordinary police and given to specialised agencies.

Commonwealth governments, recognising the limits of "police force to police force" cooperation, launched an initiative in 1977. This led to the establishment of a special office within the Commonwealth Secretariat in 1980. Unlike the General Secretariat of ICPO-Interpol, the Commonwealth secretariat is an intergovernmental organisation with full diplomatic privileges. This office was mandated to conduct investigations and to develop and deploy intelligence, on a proactive and preventive basis, in regard to economic crime and related matters.

From 1981 to 1989, the Unit responded to over 3,400 requests for assistance and handled in excess of 2,000 cases. About 35 per cent of these involved securities-related offences, and an additional 20 per cent would have been relevant to authorities charged with policing the financial markets.

Since 1990, however, the Commonwealth Unit has been rendered in practical terms "unoperational" and is now only a shallow reflection of what it was and what governments intended it should be.

The International Organisation of Securities Commission and Similar Organisations (IOSCO) had discussed international cooperation in policing the markets on a number of occasions but, in practice, little has been achieved. The Constitution of IOSCO does provide for mutual assistance between its members, and there is no doubt that the facility, through its regular meetings, provided for regulators to meet with each other and discuss common problems is beneficial. Consideration has been given within IOSCO to setting up a limited database, but given the absence of a viable Secretariat or the necessary resources, little headway has been made.

Mention has already been made of various regional initiatives to facilitate cooperation between law enforcement agencies. This approach has been encouraged by the U.S. Government and bodies such as the OECD, particularly in regard to combating money laundering, and Regional Financial Action Task Forces, have been constituted within the overall framework of the programme ordained by the G-7 countries, with U.N. support.

Some of the Caribbean states have also explored establishing a Carricom group of securities regulators, but outside the area of "harmonisation of company law", little has been achieved given the embryonic state of the many of the capital markets in the region. Discussions have also taken place in Africa and the Middle East along the same lines as in the Caribbean, but to even less effect. Since 1965, various proposals have been circulating within the Asia Pacific region for the establishment of a contact group between regulators.

At this point in time, it is difficult to predict how successful these various international initiatives will be. What is perhaps more significant, is the increasing interest in proper policing of the international financial markets taken by central banks. The American Bar Association has suggested that the Bank for International Settlements should assume a far greater role in coordinating enforcement in this area. Several influential central bankers have lent their weight to this proposal, but there is no sign of this being taken up, other than in the context of anti-money laundering initiatives.

16 A LINE IN THE SAND

As should be clear from the discussion above, the author is particularly concerned that countries, at a critical stage in their national development, should be assisted in achieving a structure of regulation in the financial sector which facilitates the sort of development that the relevant society aspires to. Of course, in an interdependent world, it is not practical or sensible to view such issues in an entirely domestic and thus, parochial manner. For example, whilst few would contend that it is not within the sovereign right of a state to charter and permit the operation of banks and other financial institutions within its territory, it is being recognised increasingly that the world community has a legitimate interest in ensuring they are not utilised to facilitate heinous activities in other countries. It has long been recognised that a state has the right, if not the duty, to ensure that it does not become a haven for criminals to perpetrate frauds on others. For example, in *SEC* v. *Kasser*[155] the Court of Appeals for the Third Circuit emphasised that Congress must have intended the Securities and Exchange Commission to have the necessary authority to act against those who were using the U.S. as a base to go out and defraud foreign investors. The Court emphasised "We are reluctant to conclude that Congress intended to allow the U.S. to become a 'Barbary Coast' as it were, harboring international securities 'pirates'". By the same token some states have been prepared to contemplate extreme action on an extraterritorial basis to protect their national interest. Indeed, the U.S. Supreme Court has accepted that, in cases of complicity in the murder of U.S. law enforcement personnel involved in undercover action against illicit drug trafficking, it is legally permissible for Federal agents to go as far as to "kidnap" suspects in foreign jurisdictions so that they can stand trial in the U.S. The U.S. Justice Department has been prepared to countenance conduct no less dramatic against those who have threatened the integrity of its national securities markets through fraud. In Operation De Niro, U.S. Federal agents, with the consent of the British Government established an offshore bank in Anguilla and operated for several months until December 1994 so as to "entrap" money launderers and fraudsters. The determination of, at least, U.S. agencies to protect their perceived national interest should not be underestimated. Thus, it is at the international level that regulatory structures are perhaps most tested. Already in central and eastern Europe we are seeing operations develop,

---

[155] 548n F. 2d 109 (3rd Cir. 1977) and also *IIT* v. *Cornfeld* 619 F. 2d 909 (2nd Cir. 1980).

which may in time present a serious challenge to Western economies. The OECD, Council of Europe and General Secretariat of ICPO-Interpol have already drawn attention to the activities of banking and other financial institutions in central and eastern Europe in regard to money laundering operations. Indeed, it would seem that there has already been a significant degree of penetration by what might be considered organised crime factions of the banking sector in certain countries. Concern has already been voiced that those states which are developing capital markets, invariably to facilitate the crucial and sensitive privatisation of their economies, face significant risks of seeing their financial intermediaries come under the direct or indirect influence of antisocial and criminal groups. It would be rash and perverse to dismiss these concerns as mere sensationalism.

Therefore, in discussing whether regulatory models are of practical utility, the author has fastened upon the issue of policing the markets in the context of cross-border threats to their integrity and stability. The author's scepticism as to the value of pervading, let alone universal, models has already been underlined. Such models, often peddled by the so-called international expert, are products rather more of the word processor than anything else. The models advanced as state of the art solutions, often funded by well-meaning "know-how funds" and international organisations, are about as well trimmed and enduring as the U.S.$ 40 suit that you can purchase whilst in transit in Bangkok. Experience is of value, but it is particular to the circumstances in which it is gained, and this must not be lost sight of. Whilst there is an international interest in preventing fraud and abuse, it must be remembered that the definition of fraud is not universal in every respect and that there are different national and even regional imperatives. To simply assert the imperative of investor confidence is about as worthy and as cost-effective as the crusaders asserting their aspirations over Jerusalem. In the final analysis we must be concerned with a careful analysis of risk and then the strategic determination of resources to achieve what are credible and worthy objectives. Of course if you can get the ERBD to pay for it and have the services of a nice professor, so much the better!

19. The Experience of Japan in Adoption and Adaptation

Chizu Nakajima[1]

1 INTRODUCTION

The history of legal development in Japan is marked by three stages of reception of foreign laws and their subsequent adaptation. Though at each stage a very different legal system was adopted, such adoption had a common purpose – to resolve either political or economic problems within Japan at the time. The first reception of foreign law took place at the beginning of the eighth century[2] when the Chinese legal system was adopted. This changed drastically the indigenous customary law that had previously existed in Japan and brought about the centralisation of authority by nationalising ownership of land.[3] Though there is no trace of the direct heritage of the Chinese legal system in modern Japanese law, its influence can nevertheless be found in Japan. The Confucian ideals of harmony, closely linked to the once-imported Chinese legal system, have been ingrained in Japanese society and have influenced all aspects of society including modern-day business.[4]

The second stage of development was the adoption of the European civil law system at the beginning of the Meiji era, when Japan officially opened itself to the outside world, in 1868.[5] The purpose of such adoption was for Japan to be accepted in the international community as a civilised nation. In order to remain autonomous and to amend the unequal treaties concluded

---

[1] Senior Lecturer in Law, City University, London.
[2] Two statutes based on the Chinese legal system were enacted in 701 and 718 respectively and they came into force in 702 and 757 respectively. *See* S. Dando, *Hogaku Nyumon (Guide to Jurisprudence)* (1978), at 51–52.
[3] *See* P. Lansing & M. Wechselblatt, "Doing Business in Japan: the Importance of the Unwritten Law", 17 Int'l Law. 647 (1983), at 647.
[4] *See* Dando, *supra*, at 51–52.
[5] Japan had a 400 year period of self-imposed isolation until then.

with the Western nations,[6] Japan had to introduce a Western legal system so as to be recognised as a modern nation.[7] A French lawyer, Boissonade,[8] was invited to Japan to draft the Civil Code, Criminal Code and Criminal Procedural Code. Whilst the latter two were enacted after some alterations, the Civil Code was abandoned as it was deemed to be too alien to the Japanese customs. German lawyers were invited to draft the Commercial Code and Civil Procedural Code. The Civil Code was subsequently drafted by Japanese scholars who based themselves on the German Civil Code. The Japanese Constitution was drafted based on the German constitutional monarchy, as opposed to the British, whereby the authority of the democratically elected parliament was restricted so that the Government, which at the time meant the Emperor, retained most of the power. The German system of civil law was chosen whilst the English system of common law was rejected as it was thought to attach too much importance to individual rights with developed adversarial relationships which were difficult for the Japanese to accept. Another reason for choosing the German system was perhaps due to the fact that it was far easier to copy as the law was codified whilst the common law system was not, as it was based on precedents.

Realising the need to catch up with the West, the Meiji government encouraged commercial activities by recognising the merchant class and giving assistance to those engaged in commerce. Under this policy of commercial expansion, *zaibatsu*, large family-owned holding companies, eventually emerged and came to control the majority of Japanese economy. The Meiji Government also recognised the need for developing stock markets and, in order to regulate them, the rules of the London Stock Exchange were adopted on the advice given by Boissonade,[9] and the Stock Transaction Ordinance of 1874 (STO) was enacted. The STO was an attempt to reform the highly speculative nature of dealing methods that originated from the traditional rice market.[10] The STO failed to function as the rules were designed for stock transactions carried out on permanent stock exchanges whilst there was no permanent exchange and very few stocks were being traded in Japan at the time. The rules designed to curb speculative practices met with strong opposition from the market participants, who wished to preserve the speculative nature of their dealing practices.[11] No stock exchange was established under the STO.

---

[6] These treaties, signed in the 1850s by the previous government of the Tokugawa Shogunate, had recognised extraterritoriality for foreign nationals in Japan whereby no foreigners would be made defendants in civil or criminal cases in Japanese courts. *See* H. Tanaka, "The Role of Law in Japanese Society: Comparison with the West", 19:2 U.B.C. Law Review 375 (1985), at 378.

[7] *See* Dando, *supra*, at 52.

[8] His full name was Gustave Emile Boissonade de Fontarabie.

[9] *See* K. Kanzaki, *Shokentorihikiho* (Securities and Exchange Law) (1987), at 56.

[10] M. J. Happe, "Inside the Japanese Stock Market: An Assessment", 5:73 Am.U.J.Int'l. & Pol'y 87 (1989) at 100.

[11] *See* Kanzaki, *supra*, at 57.

The Meiji government, nevertheless, needed urgently to establish stock exchanges in order to distribute a large number of bonds that it had issued. The STO was replaced by the Stock Exchange Ordinance of 1878 (SEO), which established the Tokyo and Osaka Stock Exchanges. The rules of the SEO were modelled on the Rice Exchange Ordinance of 1877, which was based on the speculative dealing practices on the rice exchanges developed during the Tokugawa period.[12] The speculative dealing practices on the two exchanges were further encouraged by the fact that the exchanges were formed as stock corporations whose shares were traded on the exchanges which were run as business enterprises deriving their revenues from commissions.[13] No proper regulation of the exchanges was feasible under such a system.

Several unsuccessful attempts for reform were made before the enactment of the Exchange Law of 1893, which remained the main body of securities regulation until the end of the Second World War. One such attempt was the "Bourse Ordinance" of 1887 which aimed to bring about fundamental changes in the structure of the stock exchange by abolishing the formation of exchanges as stock corporations and replacing them with memberships.[14] It also introduced the separation of functions by allowing the members to operate only in a single capacity, either for their own account (like jobbers) or for their clients (like brokers). Spot transactions were introduced and restrictions were put on "time transactions"[15] in an attempt to discourage speculative transactions. The move to alter the traditional dealing practices met with much opposition from the market participants and the statute was never implemented.

The enactment of the Exchange Law of 1893 reversed the course of development in securities regulation by incorporating key provisions of the SEO of 1878. The Exchange Law reintroduced the formation of exchanges as stock corporations and endorsed "time transactions" as well as spot transactions. Though the Meiji Government hoped that this statute would help Japan's industrialisation by facilitating provision of long-term capital through the stock exchanges, the aim was not to be served. The majority of stock-holdings in major corporations came to be held by *zaibatsu*, which provided their capital. Even the shares distributed amongst the general public, which represented a very small proportion of shares in issue, were mostly traded off the exchanges.[16] Individuals played an insignificant part in the securities markets and the speculative nature of share dealings continued to prevail in Japan.[17]

---

[12] *Id.*

[13] *See* M. Tatsuta, *Securities Regulation in Japan* (1970), at 8–9 and Happe, *supra*, at 101.

[14] *See* Kanzaki, *supra*, at 58.

[15] Time transactions could be settled either by counter-sale and set-off or delivery of stock certificates. Investors hoped to make a profit in a balance between selling and purchase prices, rather like in futures transactions commonly found on commodity exchanges, *see* Tatsuta, *supra*, at 9.

[16] *See* Tatsuta, *supra*, at 9.

[17] The contemporary Japanese securities markets have changed very little in this respect – some 65% of corporate equities in issue are said to be locked in financial groups' cross-holdings. Due to the low liquidity, the price movements tend to be more volatile than other major markets.

During the Second World War, when the entire Japanese economy was controlled by the wartime Government, the Japan Securities Exchange Law was enacted in 1943 to consolidate all stock exchanges into a single securities exchange, which had the character of a quasi-public corporation.[18] The Government appointed officers, who were deemed to be public servants, and made a financial distribution. Though its enactment was part of the Government's emergency measures in order to have a further control over the warring nation's economy, it, nevertheless, made a significant step towards the establishment of modern securities markets. It abolished the formation of stock exchanges as stock companies and prohibited time transactions exempt on the exchange and helped to reduce speculative transactions and provided investor protection. However, the wartime economy had no strength to develop real investment markets and the system collapsed when the War ended.[19]

2 THE SUPERIMPOSITION OF THE COMMON LAW SYSTEM

After the Second World War, the Occupation authority (SCAP)[20] set about bringing reforms to Japan to democratise it in every respect, including its economy.[21] Based on the "New Deal" conviction that political reforms are inadequate and only fundamental economic changes could be effective,[22] the SCAP believed that creating American-style democracy was a necessary process to transform Japan into "a peaceful, stable and thoroughly democratic nation".[23] Such economic reform was to be achieved by democratising corporate ownership,[24] which had been dominated by *zaibatsu*, through securities investment by the masses; and to facilitate this, the SCAP decided to establish a new legal framework based on the anti-monopoly philosophy in the U.S. This became the third stage of the reception of foreign legal system in Japan. An essentially feudal society, with emphasis on the Confucian values of harmony and a legal framework borrowed from the European (mostly German) civil law system, was to adopt a common law system inspired by the democratic ideals of the U.S. It is not surprising that even the Japanese scholars admit that there might well have been some "indigestion" in the process.[25]

---

[18] Kanzaki, *supra*, at 61–62 and Tatsuta, *supra*, at 9–10.

[19] Kanzaki, *supra*, at 60–62.

[20] The SCAP, Supreme Commander of the Allied Powers, referred to General McArthur himself or the American bureaucracy in Occupied Japan as a whole. In this text, it is used to refer to the latter. *See* generally W. M. Tsutsui, *Banking Policy in Japan* (1988).

[21] Joseph Dodge, the financial adviser to General McArthur from early 1949 to the end of the Occupation in 1952, aimed to lay the foundation of an American-style "democratic" economy – that is, a competitive, free-enterprise, decentralised, capitalist economy – as the basis of Japan's economic resurgence. *See* Tsutsui, *supra*, at 97 and accompanying note 17.

[22] *See* Tsutsui, *supra*, at 39, quoting the remarks by a member of the SCAP, Ted Cohen.

[23] *Id.*

[24] *See* Kanzaki, *supra*, at 35–37.

[25] *See* Dando, *supra*, at 55–56.

With the aim of democratisation of Japan's economy in mind, the Securities and Exchange Law (SEL)[26] was enacted in 1948 to regulate issuance and distribution of securities comprehensively under one statute, for the purpose of the adequate running of the national economy and protection of investors.[27] The SEL of 1948, modelled on the U.S.'s Securities Act of 1933 and Securities Exchange Act of 1934, was, in effect, forced upon Japan by the SCAP as its enactment was part of the conditions for reopening the stock exchange that had been closed down after the War.[28] The emphasis on the democratisation of corporate ownership reflects the fact that the SCAP identified the *zaibatsu* as hindrance to achieving their goal.[29] The *zaibatsu* were family-owned groups of closely held companies with holding companies governing over them. This meant that the majority of shares in large corporations were owned by *zaibatsu* holding companies and the banks within their groups and that individuals played an insignificant role in securities markets as investors.[30] The SCAP implemented the dissolution of the *zaibatsu* and the enactment of the SEL and other statutes, including one that prohibits holding companies,[31] in order to decentralise the economy and to encourage the development of the securities markets.[32]

Despite the SCAP's plan to widen share ownership by encouraging the development of securities markets, the *zaibatsu* banks that had dominated the Japanese Government and corporate finance did not become part of the dissolution plan. The *zaibatsu* banks' direct control over the companies within their own groups was severed by forcing them to dispose of their shares and prohibiting the directors of *zaibatsu* banks from holding directorships in other companies. Though the reason for the SCAP's somewhat lenient stance in regard to the *zaibatsu* banks is not well documented,[33] it seems that Japan's economic recovery was given priority over the anti-monopoly ideals that the SCAP intended to introduce in Japan as the outbreak of the Korean War made Japan a strategic base for the American

---

[26] *Shokentorihikiho*, Law No. 25 of 1948.

[27] Article 1 of the SEL.

[28] It is, therefore, thought to have been enacted without much deliberation. *See* Tatsuta, *supra*, at 10.

[29] *See* Tsutsui, *supra*, at 39–40. The Americans maintained that the *zaibatsu* were largely responsible for the rise of militarism in Japan leading up to the Second World War.

[30] *See* Happe, *supra*, at 101–102.

[31] *Shitekidokusen No Kinshi Oyobi Torihiki No Kakuno Ni Kansuru Horitsu* (Law concerning the Prohibition of Private Monopolies and the Maintenance of Fair Trading), Law No. 54 of 1947, commonly known as the Antimonopoly Law. This statute, which prohibits the establishment of holding companies under its Article 9, was "pushed through the Japanese Diet", *see* generally, Note, "Trustbusting in Japan: Cartels and Government – Business Cooperation", 94 *Harv. L. Rev.* (1981) at 1064.

[32] *See* Kanzaki, *supra*, at 63–68.

[33] *See* Tsutsui, *supra*, at 46, noting that the documentary evidence is "elusive" and that the explanation has to be based on "conjecture".

forces, while the threat of communism in China required a stronger independent Japan.[34] The banks were left untouched[35] to ensure the continuation of the flow of capital to the industries that desperately needed it for reconstruction after the Second World War and the anti-monopolistic economic plan was only pursued half-heartedly.[36] Indeed, ever since that time, there has been a constant tug of war between the pursuit of free competition that the U.S. tried to transplant to Japan by superimposing its legal framework, and the Japanese tradition of a cooperative business environment, which is often perceived by the foreign observers as collusion.[37]

3 THE ADAPTATION OF THE SEL

Japan's aversion to confrontation and the forced nature of reforms during the Occupation meant that the legal framework that Japan adopted for its newly democratised economy was, in effect, a direct copy of the relevant statutes in the U.S. and it, to a large extent, has remained so to this day. Since its enactment in 1948, the SEL has been amended more than twenty times, but many of the amendments closely followed the changes made to the statutes in the U.S. For example, the amendment made to the SEL in 1971, requiring the issuers of the securities listed on the exchange or quoted over the counter to file semi-annual and current reports, was based on the amendments made to the U.S. Securities Exchange Act in 1964.[38]

3.1 The abolition of the JSEC

Some subsequent amendments of the SEL have had the effect of nullifying the regulatory mechanism that the SCAP had established under the SEL to ensure the democratic development of securities markets in Japan. One such change was the abolition of the Japanese Securities Exchange Commission (JSEC) in 1952, as soon as the Occupation ended. The JSEC, modelled on the American SEC, was established as an independent agency to regulate the securities industry in 1948. Though the official explanation for the abolition was that it was to simplify the administrative structure,[39]

---

[34] *See* Note in 94 *Harv. L. Rev.*(1981), *supra*, at 1067.
[35] The exemption of *zaibatsu* banks from the SCAP's dissolution plan contributed significantly to regrouping of companies in the form of *keiretsu, see* Happe, *supra*, at 103. Despite the prohibition on banks to own more than 5% of equity holding in any other company, under the Banking Law of 1081, through cross-holdings there are six major *keiretsu*, four of which are former *zaibatsu*. The difference between *keiretsu* and *zaibatsu* is that the former is no longer controlled by one family like the latter was. On *keiretsu, see* generally, Y. Fujigane, "Financial Keiretsu Strengthen Solidarity", Tokyo Business Today (Feb. 1991), at 26–30.
[36] *See* Note, *supra*, at 1067.
[37] *See* Note, *supra*, at 1064, commenting that the American business community complain that "Japanese industry and government are so intertwined as to give Japanese companies competitive edge".
[38] Prior to the amendment, the continuous disclosure of company information was only required by means of submitting annual reports: *see* Kanzaki, *supra*, at 87.
[39] *See* Misao Tatsuta, "Enforcement of Japanese Securities Legislation", 1 *J. Comp. Corp. L. & Sec. Reg.* 95 (1978) at 122.

the real reason behind this was that the autonomous nature of the JSEC could not easily be accepted by government officials and it seems that it was abolished as soon as the Japanese Government was in full control of its affairs.[40] The function of the JSEC was absorbed into the Ministry of Finance and it eventually became the Securities Bureau. This absorption enabled the Government "to coordinate securities regulation with the perceived needs of economic growth (and occasionally to subordinate it, when economic development or long-standing business clashed with investor protection)".[41]

What the internationalisation of Japanese economy brought about to Japanese society was an urgent need to make adjustments to the system to maintain the harmony that society had been enjoying. Thus, in order to maintain harmony within Japan and to avert confrontations with other countries, Japan chose to use extra-legal means to realise Japan's post-war national interest – the recovery of its economy. By having an essentially American legal framework, Japan sought acceptance by other leading nations in the international marketplace, but at the same time ensured the running of its domestic economy through informal means of administrative guidance.[42] It is informal in the sense that adherence to the administrative guidance is at the discretion of the individual business to which the relevant ministry or government agency specifically addresses it. Albeit informal, its implementation is ensured through sanctions in the form of "a use of government power, often in a totally unrelated field, to punish non-compliance with regulatory requests",[43] thus, it has "the interesting quality of being officially voluntary but unofficially binding"[44] and is unique to Japan.[45]

3.2 The adaptation of the Glass-Steagall Act[46]

Japanese banks are prohibited from conducting securities business except in certain limited circumstances, under Article 65 of the Securities and Exchange Law. This provision was modelled on the U.S. Glass-Steagall Act, a collective name for sections 16, 20, 21 and 32 of the U.S. Banking Act 1933. However, the reason for its introduction in Japan and the circumstances in which it was introduced differed considerably from those of its American counterpart.

---

[40] *See* Tatsuta, *supra*, at 96–97.
[41] *See* B. A. Banoff, "The Regulation of Insider Trading in the United States, United Kingdom, and Japan", 9 *Mich. Y.B. of Int'l Legal Stud.* 145 (1988) at 163.
[42] Known as *gyoseishido* in Japanese, it can be defined as "all the different means whereby the ministries and agencies of the Japanese government exert formal and informal regulating authority over business in Japan", see Charles R. Stevens, "Japanese Law and the Japanese Legal System, Perspectives for the American Business Lawyer", 27 *Bus. Law.* 1259 (1972) at 1264.
[43] *See* Stevens, *supra* , at 1264.
[44] *See* Lansing & Wechselblatt, *supra*, at 657.
[45] *See, Happe, supra*, at 117.
[46] *See* generally, C. Nakajima, "Conflicts of Interest in Japan", in Rider & Ashe, *The Fiduciary, the Insider and the Conflict* (1995), Ch. 11, at 165.

In the United States, the Glass-Steagall Act was enacted because Congress sought to control abuses in the financial sector by separating commercial and investment banking after a series of bank failures between 1929 and 1933, caused, apparently, by the operation of the banks' securities affiliates. Before the Second World War, there were no restrictions on securities operations by banks in Japan. In the 1920s, there were widespread bank failures in Japan, but they were due to over-lending to closely related clients, including companies owned by the same families as the banks – rather than the banks' involvement in securities operations. After the banking collapses in Japan, the majority of deposits were absorbed by what became known as the "Big Five" banks which formed the basis of the creation of *zaibatsu*.

The primary aim of the Japanese Government's policy to separate banking and securities business was to develop the securities markets by breaking the traditional dominance of the *zaibatsu* banks in underwriting. This differed greatly from the reason for such segregation in the United States, which was primarily to protect depositors' money. By barring the banks from underwriting securities other than government securities, Japan attempted to give a boost to the new independent securities companies. The divergence of the types of securities operation that banks of the respective countries are permitted to engage in, albeit the similarity in the statutory framework, reflect the difference in their policies.

First, Article 65 of the SEL explicitly authorises banks to purchase for their own account stocks and shares of any corporations,[47] whilst the U.S. banks are prohibited from purchasing investment securities other than marketable debt instruments.[48] Though Article 11 of the Anti-Monopoly Law of 1947 prohibits financial institutions from acquiring more than 5% of equity in another company, banks have managed to re-create, through cross-holdings, *keiretsu*, the post-war version of *zaibatsu*. Also, through cross-holdings in related companies, banks can acquire controlling interests in securities affiliates within their *keiretsu*.

Secondly, whilst banks in the U.S. are prohibited from purchasing shares in any company, they are allowed to act as agency brokers, acting upon the order and for the account of their customers. The SEL permits Japanese banks to "purchase and sell securities upon the written order of clients" as one of the exceptions under Article 65. In practice, banks cannot take advantage of this exception as the existing rules of the stock exchanges prevent securities houses from dealing directly with banks. Despite the fact that this operation is merely a service to the banks' customers and therefore bears no risk to the depositors' money other than that of the customer on whose behalf the bank is acting, this area is preserved for securities companies.

The Japanese Government's attempt to allow securities companies to strengthen their operation and to develop the equity market, by keeping

---

[47] SEL Art. 65, para. 1.
[48] Section 16, U.S. Banking Act 1933.

banks out of underwriting and broking operations in corporate shares, did not meet with much success. Due to the high demand for capital from industry during the rapid growth of the Japanese economy from the mid-1950s to mid-1960s, bank lending soared. By the early 1970s, 80% of corporate finance was dominated by bank lending.

The Japanese Government promulgated in 1992 the Financial System Reform Law (the Reform Law), the main feature of which was to ease the strict separation imposed on banks and securities companies under Article 65 of the SEL. Since the mid-1980s two advisory committees (one on the banking industry and the other on the securities industry) appointed by the Ministry of Finance (MOF) had been discussing various methods by which to ease the segregation of the two businesses. Other leading financial centres were studied and different options were explored. For example, the German "universal banking system" was considered to be somewhat "alien" to the Japanese financial sector, in which financial institutions are divided according to their functions. A compromise came in the form of the "segmented approach" whereby banks, trust banks and securities companies are able to enter into each other's business by setting up separate subsidiaries. Reflecting the securities industry's fierce opposition to the banks' entering the securities business, the resulting legislation incorporates a large number of restrictions on the operations of banks as parent companies, and on those of their securities subsidiaries.

4 THE REGULATION OF INSIDER DEALING

4.1 Introduction of the insider dealing provisions in Japan

Japan now has a set of detailed provisions prohibiting insider dealing. Substantive provisions to regulate insider dealing[49] and impose criminal sanctions for their violation came into effect on 25 May 1988 when a bill was passed to amend the SEL. This move to regulate insider dealing was prompted by pressures from other leading financial centres[50] in Japan – whose stock market in Tokyo[51] had become the largest in the world[52] – to

---

[49] The Securities and Exchange Law had contained, since its enactment in 1948, three provisions which could have been applied to the regulation of insider dealing: Art. 58, general anti-fraud provision, based on Rule 10b-5 promulgated by the SEC of the United States in 1942; Art. 189, issuer's recovery of short-swing profits from its insiders, based on Section 16(b) of the U.S.'s 1934 Act; and Art. 50, prohibition of the management and employees of the securities companies from engaging in activities which either prejudice the protection of investors, or which are detrimental to the fairness of transactions, or undermine the credibility of the securities industry.

[50] For example, Rudnistsky, Sloan and Fuhrman, "The Land of the Rising Stock", Forbes, 18 May 1987, at 140, describing the Japanese stock markets as more like the U.S. market of 60 years ago.

[51] There are five other stock exchanges in Japan and Tokyo is the largest amongst them.

[52] In terms of the total market capitalisation, the Tokyo stock market was the largest in the world until it collapsed at the end of 1990, followed by New York, then London. It still retains the second place.

bring the standards of fairness[53] in the market up to their level. Also, at that time, a major scandal[54] concerning insider dealing erupted in Japan[55] which drew the Japanese people's attention to the lack of regulation to tackle this embarrassment. Indeed, an eminent Japanese corporate lawyer had predicted that there would not be "proper regulation" of insider dealing "unless a shocking event of scandalous insider trading [came] out".[56]

Under the newly enacted Article 190–2, insider dealing in securities of listed corporations[57] was rendered criminal by prohibiting "corporate-related persons", who have obtained "material facts" through their relationships with the corporations concerned, from buying or selling the securities of the said corporation until the "material facts" are disclosed. In other words, "corporate-related persons" either disclose the material facts or abstain from dealing. Article 190–2 concerns the issuer whilst Article 190–3 deals with persons related to the offeror in a tender offer and information generated from the offeree. The definitions of "material facts" and "related persons" are further detailed by the relevant Ministerial Ordinances and Cabinet Orders.[58]

By the enactment of Articles 190–2 and 190–3, insider dealing became a specific criminal offence as stipulated under Article 200.[59] For the state to

---

[53] "Fairness" was the prime issue on the agenda when insider dealing regulation was discussed by the Japanese Government. *See* Securities and Exchange Council (Shoken Torihiki Shingikai) Report, *Naibusha Torihiki no Kisei no Arikata ni Tsuite* (How Insider Dealing should be Regulated), 24 Feb. 1988.

[54] For the scandals to prompt major changes does not seem to be a phenomenon peculiar to Japan, *see* an observation made by B. A. K. Rider, *Insider Trading* (1983), at 6.

[55] Tateho Chemical Industries had accumulated massive losses from the Government Bond Futures Market, and one of the leading banks that had come to its rescue sold the shares it held in the company the day before the losses were publicly announced. This was investigated by the Osaka Stock Exchange through which the transaction in question was carried out but not enough evidence was found for the transaction to be a violation of securities regulation. It, nevertheless, sparked off criticism of the government with regard to this matter.

[56] *See* M. Tatsuta, *Corporate Disclosure under Japanese Law*, Convegno Internazionale di Studi Sull'Informazione Societaria (1981), at 14.

[57] This provision excluded corporate securities traded over the counter. The reason for the exclusion was given to be the lack of volume of shares traded over the counter, which stood at less than a thousandth of that traded on the stock exchanges; and it was felt that it would be sufficient to regulate only the companies listed on the exchanges. However, it was also felt that as the trade volume grew, the same regulatory regime would be eventually extended to cover the OTC market. *See* Y. Yokobatake, *Insaida Torihiki Kisei To Bassoku* (Insider Dealing Regulation and the Penalties) (1989), at 34–35. Also, companies within the scope of insider dealing regulation do not include their subsidiary, parent or associated companies unless the inside information of such company is received from a primary insider of such company, whereas the Insider Dealing Act in the U.K. includes the company's subsidiary, company's holding company, holding company's subsidiary and foreign companies.

[58] The two insider dealing provisions, Articles 190–2 and 190–3 have delegated the more technical issues and matters closely related to economic activities to relevant Ministerial Ordinances and Cabinet Orders, to accommodate flexibility for change if necessary in the future. *See* Yokobatake, *supra* at 17.

[59] It provides for a penalty of maximum six months' imprisonment or a fine of a maximum 500,000 yen (approx. £2,000).

decide to intervene in the activities of stock market investors, the nature of these acts must have sufficiently grave consequences for the free market economy.[60] Indeed, Article 1 of the SEL states that "[t]he objective of the present Law [is] to attain a fair issuance, buying and selling or other transactions with respect to securities and the smooth circulation thereof for the purpose of contributing to the proper operation of national economy and the protection of investors". In order to analyse the justification for regulation of insider dealing by criminal sanction, the background to the law must be considered.

4.2 Securities Exchange Council Report[61]

The Securities and Exchange Council is vested with the task of discussing the issues relating to stock issuance and transactions under the auspices of the Ministry of Finance, as prescribed by Article 165 of the SEL. The preparation to amend the SEL had already been in progress in the Securities and Exchange Council in the context of improving the corporate disclosure system and creating futures markets. In October 1987, when an urgent need for tougher regulation of insider dealing arose in response to the pressures, the Securities and Exchange Council established the Special Sub-committee on Unfair Trading in order to improve the "soundness and transparency of the securities market".[62] The Sub-committee convened seven times, including several sessions involving practitioners from the banking and securities industries, in several sessions, principally to discuss issues related to insider dealing. Their findings were submitted as a report to the Finance Minister by the Securities and Exchange Council and recommended amendments to the existing Securities and Exchange Law to regulate insider dealing.[63] Rather than proposing a separate bill for insider dealing regulation, the Government chose to incorporate the changes into the proposed amendments in regard to disclosure and the futures market in order to reduce any chance of objection.[64] All this took place in a space of four months.

The reason for imposing sanctions on the acts described under Articles 190–2 and 190–3 seem to hinge on the "unfairness" of such acts. The Securities and Exchange Council Report states in the introductory section that the reason for the proposed amendment of the SEL is that a person who is in a special position through personal involvement in generating non-public information, or who has ready access to such information that could influence the investment decisions of the public, is at a marked advantage over other investors who cannot obtain such information until it is

---

[60] Article 1 of the SEL states the objective of this law to be "to manage the smooth running of the national economy and to protect (its) investors".

[61] The Securities and Exchange Council Report, *supra*.

[62] Morimoto, *"Fukoseitorihiki no kisei"* (The Regulation of Unfair Trading), 1294 Shojihoumu, 5 August 1992, at 10.

[63] *See* generally, Securities and Exchange Council Report, *supra*.

[64] T. Akashi, "Regulation of Insider Trading in Japan", 6 Columbia Law Rev. (1989) 1296, at 1303.

publicly disclosed. "If such privileged trading is left unregulated, it will undermine the fairness and soundness of the securities markets, causing the loss of investors' confidence."[65] The Report also explains that the aim of the proposed amendment is to address typical cases of insider dealing[66] involving the issuer of corporate securities, or offeror/offeree in a tender offer situation.

The reasoning above suggests that the purpose of the amendment was to ensure the "fairness" and "soundness" of the market in order, in turn, to maintain investors' confidence in the market. However, the amendment was not to ensure that all the investors would have an equal access to corporate information, as this would be impossible to achieve and would not result in loss of investors' confidence in the market if the information was not obtained through the special position with the company outlined above.[67] For this reason, fortuitous receipt of information would not give rise to prohibition of dealing in the securities of the company concerned.

Because the reason for regulating insider dealing under the SEL is to prohibit dealings by those in privileged positions in order to maintain investor confidence, whether the duty of care or duty of loyalty owed to the issuer is breached by dealing in the securities of the issuer is thought to have no relevance. Some commentators even assert that it is wrong to base the regulation of insider dealing on the breach of either duty of care or duty of loyalty.[68] Equally, breach of duties owed to the conduit of information is thought to have no basis for the regulation of insider dealing. This is because it is generally believed that, although such misappropriation of information by someone who is neither an insider or tippee should be prohibited, it should not come within the scope of insider dealing regulation, which is directed at the protection of investors.[69]

Unfortunately, this was the extent of discussions held with regard to the criminality of insider dealing prior to the 1988 amendment. The legislators' comments suggest that they avoided further deliberation altogether[70] and focused only on providing for typical cases of insider dealing that they collected from abroad,[71] namely the U.S.,[72] though they admitted that there was room for further discussion.[73]

---

[65] Securities and Exchange Council Report, *supra*, introductory remarks.

[66] As there had been no case of insider dealing tried by Japanese courts , the Council had to draw on experiences of other countries, mainly the U.S. and U.K.

[67] Kanzaki, "Naibusha torihiki no kinshi – Sono kihonteki kozo (Prohibition of Insider Dealing – its basic structure)", 806 *Kinyu Shoji Hanrei* (Cases in Financial and Commercial Laws) (1989), at 123.

[68] Kanzaki, *supra*, at 124 note 10, stating that the U.S. Federal Court decisions had been evolved around the fiduciary duties owed to the issuing company of which the securities had been dealt, but recently "such reasoning is showing flaws".

[69] *Id.*, at 125 note 13.

[70] *See* Yokobatake, *supra*, at 9–11 on the criminality of insider dealing, and the House of Councillors Finance Committee Report (14) at 19.

[71] *See supra*, note 73.

[72] Article 200 of the Civil Procedural Code of Japan recognises the validity of the decisions by foreign law courts provided they fulfil certain conditions including that they must not violate the public order or general good of the people in Japan.

[73] *See* the Securities Council Report, *supra*, Section 3.4.(3) Civil Liability. Also, Yokobatake, *supra*, at 9–11 and 19.

4.3 Further amendments

The Special Sub-committee continued making recommendations to the Ministry of Finance to amend the SEL, including a report on regulation of the over-the-counter (OTC) market. On the Sub-committee's recommendation, a new Sixth Chapter entitled "Regulation of Securities Trading"[74] was created in order to bring together all the provisions within the existing SEL related to the regulation of unfair trading, including insider dealing, and the application of these provisions was extended to cover the OTC market. However, these amendments have not made any substantial changes to the regulation of unfair trading practices such as insider dealing.

4.4 Insider

Article 166, as amended,[75] prohibits a "corporate related person"(primary insider)[76] from trading in the securities (including options) of a listed company with which he has a connection as an insider, whilst in possession of material non-public information relating to the said company. Paragraph 1, items 1 to 5 describe in detail the categories of persons who would be deemed insiders. They include company executives and employees,[77] and shareholders who own more than 10% of a company's shares.[78] A person who has a contractual relationship with the issuer is also an insider.[79] Former insiders are also subject to the same prohibition as insiders within one year[80] of termination of their relationship with the company concerned.

Article 167, which has very similar wording to that of Article 166, regulates insider dealing in a tender offer situation. Those related to a company which is making a takeover bid for another company cannot deal in the securities of either company.

---

[74] Articles 157 to 171.

[75] The amendment in 1992 moved the insider dealing provisions created in the 1988 Amendment, Articles 190–2 and 190–3, to the newly created Chapter Six and renumbered them Articles 166 and 167 respectively. It also expanded the scope of the provisions to include the companies whose shares are traded on the OTC market.

[76] This is a literal translation of the term used in the relevant provisions. Many commentators have translated this term as "corporate insider" but in order not to confuse this with bodies corporate which can also be liable for violation of the insider dealing regulation in Japan, the author chooses to use either the literal translation or the term used commonly in the U.K., "primary insider".

[77] Item 1.

[78] Item 2. Under Article 293-6, para. 1, such shareholders have a right to look over the books of the company.

[79] Item 4.

[80] Acknowledging the fact that it is within six months of termination of employment under the U.K. regulation, as all listed companies publish annual reports it was to be assumed that they would have disclosed any material fact by the end of one year. *See* statement made by Fujita, the House of Councillors Finance Committee Report (15) (19 May 1988), at 24.

Insiders under these provisions include companies as well as individuals. Thus, penalties would be imposed on both an insider company and an officer, agent or employee of such company who actually carried out insider dealing on behalf of the company. This is because Japanese culture attaches importance to "group" and "society" rather than the "individual", and because the insider dealing regulations do not place emphasis upon the dishonest state of the mind of the trader.

As the act of insider dealing is prohibited when it is intentional, an insider has to be aware of the following facts:

(1) that he is an insider;
(2) that he has obtained material facts in connection with his duties;
(3) that the material facts have not been disclosed.

Also as an attempt[81] does not constitute an offence in the regulation of insider dealing, the transaction in question must have been completed.[82] However, the offender does not have to gain profit from the actual transaction, so, "no profit" does not constitute a defence. What matters is whether he has dealt after he has obtained the information, but the prosecution does not have to prove that the accused dealt on the inside information.[83] Knowledge of the material facts does not have to be so specific for the offence to be committed, as it is deemed that even partial knowledge of material facts cannot be obtained by the general investors unless disclosure takes place.[84] For example, it is thought that there is sufficient knowledge of the material facts in circumstances where an employee knows that the turnover forecast for his company has been revised up enough to affect the share price, but there is no precise awareness that the revision exceeds the limits, set to be either more than plus or minus 10% of the most recent publicly available forecast, as stipulated in the Ministerial Ordinance.[85]

The above-mentioned insiders are all prohibited from dealing on the "material facts" they have obtained during the course of their duties. The unitary prohibition on dealing on the information obtained during the course of their duties seems to suggest that the legislators had good reason to believe that these duties imposed responsibility on those that were conducting them to keep the information confidential. However, the picture

---

[81] This is an exception to the general provision on attempts under Article 43 of the Criminal Code.
[82] The definition seems to be that a transaction is deemed completed only when the actual bargain is completed on the stock exchange by a securities company, only through whom the orders can be placed and dealt on the exchange, though delivery of money or share certificates is not required.
[83] Yokobatake, *supra*, at 17.
[84] *Id.*, at 35.
[85] Article 4, para. 1, Ministerial Ordinance concerning Regulation on Trading of Share Certificates or similar Instruments by Corporate Insiders (Ministry of Finance Ordinance No. 10 of 1989).

looks quite different when the information is divulged by a "corporate-related person" to a third party. This situation is considered next.

4.5 Tipper and tippee

As the act of insider dealing has to be intentional in order to contravene Article 166, paragraph 2, a tippee must be aware of the following factors:[86]

(1) The tipper is a "corporate related person" who has obtained "material facts" in connection with his duties.
(2) The information divulged to the tippee is considered to be "material facts".
(3) These "material facts" have not been disclosed.

Even if the tippee was unaware of some or all of the factors above on receipt of the information, as long as he has the relevant knowledge on completion[87] of the relevant transaction, he has committed an offence.[88] Partial knowledge[89] of the material facts is sufficient for the offence, as in the case of primary insiders. However, because the tippee has to be aware of the three factors above, fortuitous receipt of information does not prohibit the recipient of the information from dealing.

Violation of the insider dealing regulations under Articles 166 and 167 would only occur when a primary insider or his tippee traded whilst in possession of inside information. The present insider dealing regulation under the SEL prohibits the act of dealing while in possession of inside information, but imposes no liability on the act of divulging inside information to non-insiders. In other words, the act of tipping inside information itself is not a criminal offence. The legislators clearly stated that the tippers are not within the scope of criminal sanctions under the SEL (unless they themselves have dealt), although they thought that in some cases the tipper might be criminally liable as an abettor or aider to the tippee under the general provisions of the Criminal Code.[90]

Only those who receive inside information directly from primary insiders are within the scope of the regulation. The legislators saw difficulties in delimiting the scope of tippees if the prohibition went beyond first stage tippees.[91] For the purpose of defining the offence, it was felt necessary to distinguish between information and rumour. Accordingly, one could deal

---

[86] *See* the statement made by Fujita, Director of the Securities Bureau, Ministry of Finance, House of Councillors Finance Committee Report (15) (19 May 1988), at 13.
[87] *See supra*, note 88.
[88] Yokobatake, *supra*, at 207.
[89] *See supra*, p. 402.
[90] *See* the statement by Fujita, Director of the Securities Bureau, Ministry of Finance, House of Councillors Finance Committee Report (15) (19 May 1988), at 20, explaining that, as sanctions imposed by the SEL (Art. 200 para. 4) are criminal sanctions, he thinks that other general principles under the Criminal Code could be applied to some cases of non-dealing tippers under Article 61 para. 1 for abetting or Article 62 para. 1 for soliciting.
[91] Fujita, *supra*, at 19–20.

on the basis of inside information acquired from a spouse or relative of an executive officer of the company since they would not be primary insiders. Also, investment experts with easy access to "leaked" information would be able to deal freely without committing any offence. However, if a tipper was using someone merely as an instrument for communicating the information, the person who received the information and traded after obtaining such information could be deemed a primary insider.[92] Similarly, secondary tippees could be prosecuted for conspiracy along with a primary tippee, provided there was sufficient evidence of a conspiracy or understanding with the informants.[93]

As discussed above,[94] the justification for regulation of insider dealing hinges on the "unfairness" of dealings conducted by those in a privileged position with the company[95] in relation to the securities traded. If this is left unregulated, undermining of the fairness and soundness of the securities markets results, which in turn would causes loss of investor confidence in the markets.[96]

In other words, there is no test of whether the person is in breach of his duty to the company. Indeed, the legislators, having acknowledged the issues related to various duties of corporate related persons, decided not to address them in the 1988 amendment.[97] It was argued that it would be too far-fetched to apply breach of confidence as proscribed under the Criminal Code[98] or the special provision proscribing the breach of trust by corporate insiders under the Commercial Code[99] to sanction misappropriation of information or breach of trust where there is no property loss to the company concerned, however unfair the act in question might be. Furthermore, it was thought that the internal order of a corporation or protection of interests of a corporation would not be within the proper scope of the SEL.[100]

One commentator clearly states that it is wrong to base the reasoning for the prohibition of insider dealing on any breach of duty owed to the

---

[92] *Id.*

[93] The Criminal Code of Japan, Articles 60 and 61. Article 60 provides, "Two or more persons who jointly commit a criminal act shall all be dealt with as principals". Article 61, para. 1 provides, "A person who instigates and causes another to commit a crime shall be quasi-considered a principal".

[94] *See supra*, section on Securities Council Report.

[95] It is assumed that the tippee (only first stage tippees are within the scope of the regulation) also enjoys the privilege. *See* Yokobatake, *id.*, at 122.

[96] This view seems to be shared by the British, *see* Rider, *Insider Trading, supra*, at 5.

[97] Yokobatake, *supra*, at 10–11.

[98] Article 247 of the Criminal Code imposes imprisonment of up to five years or a maximum fine of two hundred thousand yen (£1,000) on a person in a position to administer the affairs of another person if he causes such other person property loss by committing an act in violation of duty with intention of promoting his own interest or of a third person.

[99] Article 486 of the Commercial Code imposes tougher sanctions on the corporate directors in breach of trust proscribed under Article 247 of the Criminal Code, *supra*, note 40. The sanctions prescribed under Article 486 is imprisonment of up to seven years or a maximum fine of three million yen (£15,000).

[100] Yokobatake, *supra*, at 10–11.

company of the securities traded in violation of the insider dealing provisions, even though under the Japanese Commercial Code[101] company directors owe duty of loyalty to their company.[102] This, he explains, is because the aim of prohibiting insider dealing is to maintain investor confidence and the breach of duty referred to in this context has no relevance.[103]

There is a provision[104] in the SEL which imposes the duty of confidence – but only on those who are or have been officers or employees of a stock exchange – by prohibiting the divulgence or misuse of information by the members of the exchange, such as their financial situations, obtained during the course of their duties. This provision is applied *mutatis mutandis* to the officers and employees of a securities finance company.[105] Anyone in breach of these provisions is criminally liable under Article 204 of the SEL, which imposes a maximum penalty of one year's imprisonment or a fine of one hundred thousand yen. Such person may also be liable under the general tort provision of the Civil Code.[106]

4.6 What constitutes inside information?

4.6.1 Materiality

Inside information is referred to as "material facts" in The SEL. Article 166, paragraph 2 gives an extensive list of facts that are considered to be "material" within the meaning of the provision under three main categories: (1) facts decided by the company; (2) facts occurred to the company; (3) amount of net sales and profit.

The test for materiality is what impact the piece of information in question would have on the decisions of other investors in general if it became known to them – in other words how price-sensitive it is. The statutory provisions give detailed definitions of material facts, which are further elaborated by relevant Ministerial Ordinances in order to avoid the previous problem of ambiguity.[107]

The definition of "company" under the insider dealing provisions does not include a subsidiary, parent, or other associated company of the company in which shares may be traded. Therefore, executive officers,

---

[101] Article 254–3 of the Commercial Code.

[102] Kanzaki, *supra*, at 124 note 10 thereof.

[103] *See supra*, section on tipper and tippee.

[104] Article 106.

[105] Securities finance companies were set up, between 1949 and 1950, as financial institutions specialising in making loans of cash or securities to the securities companies which in turn provide their clients with cash or securities in order to offer them credit for margin trading. Three such companies still operate in Japan.

[106] Article 709 of the Civil Code. Tanaka & Horiguchi state the possibility of the civil liability under the provision, *see* Tanaka & Horiguchi, *Shokentorihikiho* (The Securities and Exchange Law) (1990), at 663.

[107] For example, the reason for the ineffectiveness of the anti-fraud provision, Article 58, was that it was too broad and therefore the meaning was too ambiguous.

agents or employees of a company will be free to deal in the securities of a subsidiary, parent or associated company unless they receive inside information on the subsidiary, parent or associated company from a primary insider of one of these. Also, major shareholders of a company can deal in the securities of its associated company on the basis of information about their company which may also be price-sensitive information in relation to shares of the associated company.

(a) *Facts decided by the company*[108]   The first category of material facts are important decisions taken by the company where its relevant managers have taken decisions relating to the conduct of business where there may be a direct impact on the value of securities. In this category, since a decision made by the corporate business decision-making organ (or decision-maker) is a material fact, there is the question as to when such a decision has been made. In a company which follows a bottom-up decision-making process, a proposal is outside the meaning of "decision", even if there is certainty that the matter would finally be decided as proposed.

Furthermore, even if a "decision" is not formal, tacit understanding among even the representative directors would not satisfy the requirement and some express agreement among them would be required. Factual and legal questions would arise in individual cases as to when such a "decision" has been made. The effectiveness of this provision would be extremely narrow if it only applied to formal decisions by the board of directors.

A total of sixteen corporate decisions are regarded as material unless they are of such minor nature that the authorities may deem them to be unimportant. Under Ministerial Ordinance No. 10,[109] certain matters which are immaterial to the investment decisions of investors are excluded from these regulations.

The SEL lists eight corporate decisions considered to be "material information". It includes, for example, decisions in relation to mergers; liquidation of the company; developments and commercialisation of new products and technology; proposed issues of shares or convertible bonds; and reduction of capital or stock split.

An additional eight corporate decisions are listed in Article 28 of Cabinet Order No. 23.[110] These include establishment of a new business tie, discontinuance or abolition of a line of business, or a petition for bankruptcy.

(b) *Facts occurred to the company*   The second group of material facts are incidents such as physical or transactional damage to the corporation and change in its control. This item is concerned with material action which

---

[108] SEL, Article 166, para. 2 (1).

[109] Ministerial Ordinance Concerning Regulation on Trading of Share Certificates or Similar Instruments by Corporate Insiders, Ministry of Finance Ordinance No. 10 of 1989 (3 February 1989), Article 1.

[110] Cabinet Order Concerning the Amendment to the Enforcement Order of the Securities and Exchange Law, Cabinet Order No. 23 of 1989 (3 February 1989).

may affect the company and does not involve any decision made by the company. A company may be affected by actions taken by others. Where these actions are known, they may affect the value of the company's securities and give an unfair advantage to any related officers dealing in the securities.

The SEL sets out three major events which are regarded as material and one catch-all provision. Article 29 of Cabinet Order No. 23 lists eleven further incidents considered to be material facts. These include the fact that the company is about to be sued, the fact that a government agency has issued a discontinuance of business order against the company, and any exemptions which may have been granted to the company in relation to any of its liabilities. Once again, a transaction may be excused if the event involved is of such minor nature as not to be considered material.[111]

(c) Amount of net sales and profit[112]   The third category is concerned with material information relating to projected sales and earnings. Generally, this item sets up a detailed comparison with the latest publicly announced prediction figures. More specifically, the authorities will consider as material: any variation over 10% in projected amount of sales; any variation over 30% in relation to recurring profits of the company; and variation of over 5% in the value of the net assets used in estimating recurring profit, or any variation over 2.5% in the valuation of net assets in returning net profit.

(d) General   In addition to the three above, SEL Article 166, paragraph 2, item (4), acting as a catch-all provision, describes important facts concerning the management, business or property of the company which are considered to have significant influence on the investment decisions of investors and, therefore, constitute material facts. Decisions and incidents, which may be material but have been left out of the list of material facts, may be covered by this provision. The materiality of information under item (4) will be judged in the light of other information provided for under paragraph 2 of Article 166. Article 167, paragraph 2 deals with material facts in tender offer and similar schemes.

4.6.2 Undisclosed

"Material facts" are considered "disclosed" to the public only when such information is made available by the issuer through a specified person, such as a corporate representative or a person authorised by him, and distributed to more than two news media[113] as prescribed by a Cabinet Ordinance.[114] Twelve hours must elapse after such disclosure before those

---

[111] Ministerial Ordinance No. 10, Article 2.
[112] SEL, Article 166, para. 2(3).
[113] Twelve hours must elapse after the disclosure to the media.
[114] Cabinet Ordinance No. 321 of 1965, Article 30 (as amended by Cabinet Ordinance No. 23 of 1989). They have to be major news agencies covering current and economic and industrial events.

related to the company will be allowed to deal in the securities. Alternatively, when documents, such as registration statements or tender offers, contain material facts, they have to be made available for public inspection by the Minister of Finance before those affected by the insider dealing provisions can trade.

In addition to the direct regulation of insider dealing, the SEL attempts to address the issue through enhanced disclosure obligations on publicly traded companies. Beyond the requirement of semi-annual reports, companies are now also required to report publicly and promptly any business forecast predicting a change in sales of over 10% to be derived from the introduction of a new product.[115]

4.7 Exemptions

Article 166, paragraph 5 lists, in detail, eight transactions by primary insiders that are exempted from prohibition of insider dealing. Generally, if an insider is obliged to sell or buy stocks unavoidably, he will be exempted from the provisions on insider dealing. For example, a director or high-ranking official is allowed to buy his company's shares as a "defence" when his company becomes a target of a tender offer bid, provided he obtains a board resolution to do so.[116] This is because the Japanese Commercial Code prohibits any company from buying or preserving its own shares.[117]

Another exemption is the "employees' stockholding group".[118] Although Japan has no legal concept of "stock-option", it has become customary for employees to purchase company shares and employers usually encourage them to do so. As a result, almost all of the listed companies have such "groups". Subject to each employee's consent, the company deducts a set amount from the employee's salary and conveys it to the group, which is an independent legal entity, similar to an association. Normally, the corporate secretary in charge of general affairs is appointed as caretaker or supervisor of the group. He collects all the deducted cash from the employees' salaries and purchases the company's shares at the stock exchange on a set day each month. Such a scheme is seen as a preventative measure against green-mailers and arbitrageurs. Even though a group supervisor is in a position to know the company's material facts, the monthly purchase does not constitute insider dealing.

Another exemption is transactions between primary insiders or tippees off the market.[119] A primary insider is permitted to deal with another primary insider or his tippee face to face, provided that the buyer does not then sell the shares he has just bought on the market. The reason for this exemption is that as the transaction is not carried out on the market, it does not affect it and will not damage the investors' confidence in the fairness

---

[115] SEL, Article 166, para. 4.
[116] SEL, Article 167, para. 6, item 5.
[117] The Commercial Code of Japan, Article 210. This provision is currently under review.
[118] SEL, Article 166, para. 5, item 8 and Ministerial Ordinance, Article 6, para 3.
[119] Article 190-2, para. 5, item 7 of the SEL.

and soundness of the market. This underlines the policy behind the regulation of insider dealing, which is to maintain the integrity of the market in Japan.

4.8 Article 50 of the SEL: Corporate information and market information

The insider dealing regulations only cover non-public information concerning the issuers of securities that are traded on the securities exchanges or OTC market. The Securities and Exchange Council, though recognising that market information – information concerning the supply and demand of securities in the market – can be price-sensitive, decided not to bring it into the scope of the regulation.[120] It was explained that whilst market information such as large orders from institutional investors,[121] stock accumulation by "speculator groups",[122] recommendations by the top securities houses and information concerning trading of securities by these securities houses could influence investment decisions, there are other types of market information such as the identity of securities individual investors are trading in. It seems that the exclusion of market information was decided on the basis that it is difficult to have an objective standard for what constitutes "price-sensitive" information and, therefore, it is not appropriate to impose a uniform restriction through criminal sanctions.[123]

Nevertheless, such information could have a significant impact on the market, particularly in Japan, where there is an extensive system of cross-holding of shares amongst the companies to perpetuate business relationships and as a result over 65% of issued shares are kept out of the market.[124] This makes it easy for the institutional investors and brokerage houses, which together control a large portion of the shares traded on the market, to influence the prices. This fact was recognised by the legislators who have sought to regulate the use of such market information by the securities companies, though such action is rare. The Soundness Ordinance, Article 1, paragraph 5, is based on the SEL, Article 50, paragraphs 1–5, which prohibits amongst other unsound conducts, "the directors and employees of securities houses to buy or sell securities on the basis of the information regarding the clients' orders and any other information that

---

[120] *See* House of Representatives Committee of Finance Report (15) (11 May 1988), at 39 (statement made by Mr. Fujita , Director of the Securities Bureau, Ministry of Finance).

[121] *See* Happe, *supra*, at 107 n. 136, quoting from Perlmutter, that "the large investors and brokerage firms control a large percentage of the limited floating shares available and therefore unilaterally influence share price".

[122] They are known as *shite shudan*. They are often backed by Japanese criminal organisations, known as *Yakuza*, and engage in accumulating stocks for the purpose of raiding corporations, price manipulation, or green mailing. A boss of one such organisation has recently been prosecuted for the violation of Article 125 of the SEL which proscribes market manipulation.

[123] Yokobatake, *supra*, at 12.

[124] Happe, *supra*, at 106–107.

they have obtained by virtue of their position or through their duties". On violation of the above provision, an administrative sanction, such as revocation or suspension of the licence of the employee or of the securities house, could be imposed by the Ministry of Finance, though such action is rare.[125] Furthermore, the directors and officers of the securities house in question could also be held liable for damages "if their conduct reflects bad faith or a gross breach of their duties" under Article 266–3 of the Commercial Code.[126] However, despite the existence of these enforcement measures provided by law, regulators seem to prefer issuing warnings and the securities houses have instituted in-house guidelines.[127]

Other types of market information, such as the Government's economic policy, are outside the scope of regulation as it is thought that the impact on the price of individual stock is too indirect for the criminal sanctions to be imposed on transactions executed on such information.[128] However, if the regulation of insider dealing is to ensure the fairness of the market, should the market participants with access to such information be allowed to use it? Public officials, including Members of Parliament, are, like other insiders, prohibited from dealing on confidential corporate information. However, they are free to trade on information such as the Government's economic policy as it is outside the scope of the regulation. This issue will be looked at more closely when administrative sanctions are discussed.

4.9 Article 164[129]

Article 189 before the 1988 amendment, this provision, modelled on Section 16(b) of the U.S. Securities Exchange Act 1934, requires directors or major shareholders (shareholders with over 10% holding in a company) to return to the company profits derived from any sale and purchase, or purchase and sale, of the issuer's shares within a six-month period. Other shareholders may bring an action against such major shareholders, if the issuer, after demand, fails to bring its own action. However, in 1953, the Government repealed Article 188 of the SEL, which required insiders to report their trades to the Government. This provision had been easy to evade as it did not require the reporting of beneficial ownership and the Government did not publicise the reports.

The Government chose to repeal Article 188 rather than to make its enforcement more effective. As a result, Article 189 was emasculated and only two actions were ever brought under the system. The SEL amendment of 1988, reinstated under Article 188 (Article 163 as amended in 1992) the reporting requirement imposed on directors and major shareholders.

---

[125] There have only been eight cases of administrative sanctions all of which led to a suspension of part of the violators' business for one to three days.

[126] Happe, *supra*, at 114.

[127] *See* Banoff, *supra*, at 166.

[128] Yokobatake, *supra*, at 13.

[129] Article 189 was renumbered Article 164 in the 1992 amendment to be included in the newly created Chapter Six, which brought together all the existing provisions within the SEL, concerning unfair trading practices.

4.10 Article 157[130]

Article 157,[131] as amended, of the SEL, is a general anti-fraud provision, closely modelled on Section 10(b) of the U.S. Securities Exchange Act of 1934. It provides that :

No person shall effect such acts as are mentioned in any of the following items:
(1) To employ any fraudulent device, scheme or artifice with respect to the purchase and sale of any securities or similar tradings. . .

The Securities and Exchange Council, in its report published in 1976, expressed its doubts over the possibility of applying this anti-fraud provision to the regulation of insider dealing by saying "As for the application of Article 58 (Article 157 as amended), from a standpoint of the intention of the legislators [of the said Article] which was to generally prohibit fraudulent and unfair transactions, an immediate extension of its application to insider dealing is limited."[132]

Indeed, Article 157 has only been applied once[133] in a case[134] that did not concern insider dealing, but is significant as it defined "fraudulent device" under Article 157, item 1 to be an act of deceit by serving the defendant's or another's interest by intentionally inducing the plaintiff's justifiable reliance on his misrepresentation. It also ruled that the "fraudulent device" is not necessarily so vague as to render the provision null and void under Article 31[135] of the Japanese Constitution.[136]

Despite the doubts expressed in the past over the application of Article 157 to insider dealing, given the fact that the provision was left intact in the SEL, both Articles 166 or 167 and Article 157 could be invoked if fraudulent intent was involved,[137] at least in theory. Also, because Article 157 goes on to determine whether the transaction in question is substantially unfair or not, if convicted the penalties will be heavier than those under 166 or 167.[138]

---

[130] Previously Article 58 of the SEL. *See supra*, note 91.

[131] It was slightly amended in 1988, when the specific provisions on regulation of insider dealing were incorporated in the SEL, to provide for dealing in futures and options.

[132] The Securities and Exchange Council, *Kabunushikousei no Henka to Shihonshijou no Arikata nitsuite* (On Changes in Shareholding Structure and Capital Markets) (1976), at 38. *See* also Kanzaki, *supra*, at 612. This view was expressed again in the Council's report which formed the base for the amendment of the SEL in 1988, *see* the Report, Section 3.1.(1).

[133] *See* Akashi, *supra*, at 1298, whereas Banoff claims that there have been a small number of disciplinary cases against brokerage houses under Article 58, *see* Banoff, *supra*, at 164.

[134] *Nasu Kogyo* case, Tokyo Kosai (Tokyo High Court), judgment of 10 July 1963, affirmed judgment on 25 May 1965, Saikosai (Supreme Court of Japan).

[135] It guarantees due process of law in criminal prosecutions.

[136] Akashi, *supra*, at 1298.

[137] Fujita, *supra*, at 11. Also Yokobatake, *supra*, at 14–15.

[138] Yokobatake, *supra*, at 18. Under Article 157, the penalties are imprisonment of up to 3 years and a maximum fine of 3 million yen as provided under Article 197, item 2, whereas under Articles 166 or 167, the penalties are imprisonment of up to six months and a maximum fine of 50 thousand yen.

Similarly, both Articles 157 and 50 could be invoked against unfair acts by securities companies, their directors or other employees in connection with their duties. These provisions would not be mutually exclusive as there is no criminal sanction provided under Article 50 whereas there is under Article 157.[139] However, the situations above are still theoretical as none has been tested by the Japanese courts.

5 ADMINISTRATIVE SANCTIONS

There are other forms of regulation imposed on the securities companies in Japan by various administrative means[140] with regard to prohibition of insider dealing. The Ministry of Finance issued a circular notice[141] in 1971,[142] instructing securities companies when accepting orders from the issuer's directors, officers, principal shareholders, etc. to take necessary steps, such as the following:

(1) Check the background and purpose of their orders if necessary.
(2) Draw the client's attention to the fact that the transaction might be deemed to be insider dealing.
(3) Refuse to take orders if necessary.
(4) Report to the relevant stock exchange on refusal of such order.

The stock exchanges also issued several notices, including several to listed companies, warning that purchase or sale of securities of the companies by their insiders might violate Article 58 (Article 157 as amended). The notices urged them to be fully aware of this fact[143] and asked the securities companies to take necessary measures, such as warning and refusal of orders, if such are received from insiders there is possible violation of Article 157. In fact one of the stock exchanges disclosed in its notice that it had censured a member of the exchange which transacted an order from an insider.[144]

5.1 The Sound Management Rules

The Ministerial Ordinance on Sound Management,[145] promulgated in 1965, was amended in order to add items (8) to (10),[146] providing for prohibition

---

[139] *See* Kanzaki, *Shoken Torihikiho* (Securities Regulation) (1987), at 597–599.
[140] Administrative guidance, as they are collectively referred to, is regarded as an important method of regulation by the authorities and this view is confirmed in the Council Report.
[141] This is known as *tsutatsu* which is not publicly disclosed as it is regarded as communication between the MOF and the institutions to which it has been issued.
[142] Despite the nature of *tsutatsu*, explained in the previous note, this is cited by Kanzaki, *supra*, at 592 and Akashi, *supra*, at 1301. This particular notice was sent to the Directors of the Regional Finance Bureaux and the President of the Japanese Securities Dealers Association.
[143] Kanzaki, *supra*, at 592–593.
[144] *Id.*
[145] Ministry of Finance Ordinance No. 60 of 1965, as amended on 10 August 1988.
[146] The text is of the author's own translation of the summary of the three items.

on securities companies of such acts, directly reflecting insider dealing regulation under the SEL. These cover:

(8) Acceptance of a client's instructions for the purchase or sale of securities with knowledge that such client's purchase or sale is or could be a violation of Articles 190–2[147] or 190–3[148] of the SEL.

(9) Solicitation of the purchase or sale of securities by providing the client with inside information.

(10) Trading securities on his or its account (as it is addressed to both the body corporate and individuals working for them) based on the inside information.

The most significant of the three above is item (9), which prohibits specifically the act of divulging inside information regardless of whether or not anyone has dealt as a result. It cannot, however, be concluded from this that the Japanese system imposes a duty of confidentiality imposed on securities companies, or any individuals with capacity to give investment advice, not to disclose the information.

6 BASIC PRINCIPLES APPLIED TO INSIDER DEALING REGULATION IN JAPAN

The following can be identified as the underlying principles of the present regime of insider dealing regulation in Japan.

First, the reason for regulating insider dealing is to maintain the soundness and fairness of the securities markets which in turn secures investor confidence.

Second, an offence is committed if a corporate insider deals on undisclosed price-sensitive information, or a tippee does on the information received from the insider. This prohibition on dealing on inside information must mean that the system recognises that there is some sort of duty attached to a person in a special position (corporate insider) with the issuer (a company). The exact nature of this duty is unclear, as there has been no discussion.

Third, an offence is committed only when the purchase or sale of the securities in question is complete. In other words, an act of tipping itself does not constitute an offence. Therefore, when a tipper divulges inside information and a tippee does not deal, no offence is committed. This must mean that, whilst a duty of some kind is recognised between the issuing company and its insider, no criminal liability is attached to breach of confidentiality between the issuer and its insiders.

---

[147] Article 166 as amended in 1992.
[148] Article 167 as amended in 1992.

7 CASES AFTER THE AMENDMENT TO THE SEL IN 1988

7.1 Nisshin Kisen

The first case of insider dealing after the insider dealing provisions were enacted in 1988 was decided in September 1990 when the president of a finance company that had participated in a third party placement of shares in a shipping company called Nisshin Kisen was convicted of violation of Article 190–2,[149] prohibiting insider dealing, and was fined 200,000 yen (approx. £1,000). Mito had agreed to underwrite 350 thousand shares in a third party placing of new shares issued by Nisshin Kisen in order to finance the purchase of a hotel in Australia. Believing that the share price of Nisshin Kisen would go up on the back of the news of this acquisition, Mito bought 7,000 shares worth about £75,000, the day before the announcement, in the name of a friend. He did not manage to sell the shares when the share price went up, against the market trend, which prompted the rumour that there had been insider dealing.

The prosecution was brought forward through "abbreviated procedures" for the following three reasons. First, the number of shares involved was relatively low. Second, the accused did not sell the shares concerned, therefore he did not make any profit. Third, the accused had already taken the social responsibility by resigning as the president of the finance company.

This decision was criticised as too lenient and the imposition of much larger fines was recommended by some commentators to make insider dealing economically unattractive.[150]

7.2 Macross

The most recent case was decided in September 1992. Kamijo, a former executive director of an electrical goods retailer, Macross, was convicted of insider dealing and was fined 500,000 yen (approx. £2,500). Kamijo heard during the board meeting of the company, Macross, that one of the other directors at the time had "window-dressed" the company accounts with some four billion yen's worth (approx. £20 million) of phantom sales and, as a result, the company's expected profit was to be reduced substantially. Thinking that Macross's share price would plunge if the information above was made public, Kamijo sold 12,000 shares held in his wife's name and 10,000 shares held in his own and avoided a loss of approximately £90,000.

The prosecution had asked for four months' imprisonment The judge, though recognising the importance of punishing insider dealing in order to maintain the fairness of securities transactions, decided to impose a fine as the accused had given away a portion of the loss he had avoided as a donation and the proceedings had been prolonged for nearly a year.[151]

---

[149] Article 166 as amended in 1992.
[150] For example, *see* comments made by Kanzaki quoted in *Asahi Shinbun*, 27 September 1990, morning edition, at 31.
[151] *See* the judge's comments quoted in *Nihonkeizai Shinbun*, 26 September 1992, morning edition, at 31.

7.3 The establishment of the SESC

In July 1992, an amendment to the SEL[152] established the Securities and Exchange Surveillance Commission (SESC) in an attempt to step up the enforcement of the Securities and Exchange Law. Since its establishment the SESC has yet to make its mark in the Japanese business community, that has still to recover from the burst of its "bubble economy". On 10 February 1995, the SESC filed a complaint against a Japanese bank and a machinery company with the Tokyo district prosecutors for alleged insider dealing. The alleged insider dealing involved share dealings in Shin Nihon Kokudo Kogyo, a small construction company, by Shimizu Bank, a regional bank, and Marubeni Construction Machinery Sales, an affliate company of Marubeni, a leading trading company. It is alleged that, in March 1994, just before Shin Nihon announced its default on a 150 million yen (approximately £1 million) promissory note, executives of Shimizu Bank sold 40,000 shares and officials of Marubeni sold 5,000 shares on the respective companies' account. Shin Nihon shares were suspended only a day after the alleged share dealings by the two companies and Shin Nihon subsequently went into bankruptcy.

The SESC, since its creation, has been fraught with difficulty in proving allegations of such stock market abuses as insider dealing and market manipulation which are within its remit of its responsibility. Insider dealing became a crime punishable by imprisonment of up to six months and/or a maximum fine of 500,000 yen (approximately £3,000) in 1988. So far, the SESC has had very few successful prosecutions, including the most recent case concerning share dealings in Nihon Shoji, a pharmaceutical company, last year. The SESC filed a complaint against 32 people in October last year with the Osaka District Prosecutors' Office for alleged insider dealing.

8 CIVIL LIABILITY

The amendment to the SEL in 1988 which created specific criminal offences for insider dealing did not include provisions for civil liability. The reason for exclusion seems to be that the drafters of the amendment thought it premature to include such liability, "since issues such as the standing to sue, the adjudicative procedure, etc. needed to be discussed", though, apparently, "it is agreed that a system of compensation should be introduced into the Law".[153]

The commentators seem to agree[154] that those "victims" that have suffered loss as a result of insider dealing can use Article 157, 166 or 167 as a basis of a civil damage action for tort under Article 709 of the Civil Code

---

[152] *Shokentorihiki touno kosei wo kakuhosurutameno shokentorihikiho touno ichibuwo kaiseisuru houritsu* (Law to Amend the SEL etc. in Order to Ensure the Fairness in Securities Trading), Law No. 73 of 1992.

[153] *See* H. Oda, *Regulation of Insider Trading in Japan, Japanese Banking, Securities and Anti-monopoly Law*, Oda & Grice ed. (1988), at 92.

[154] *Id. See* also Tatsuta, *Corporate Disclosure under Japanese Law, supra*, at 14.

or breach of contract.[155] However, the provision imposes a heavy burden of proof such as the existence of fault, a causal relationship, and quantity of damages,[156] which are all hard to prove. No court case has yet awarded damages based on a violation of the insider dealing regulations.[157] The most recent case,[158] and the only civil action brought so far on the basis of Article 166 (formerly 190-2), was dismissed in October 1991 on the grounds that the court did not find a direct causal relationship between the insider's failure to disclose inside information and the loss suffered by other investors who dealt in the securities to which such information was related. The plaintiff bought 494,000 shares in Japan Line worth 302,982,000 yen (approx. £2 million) through the Tokyo Stock Exchange on 19 December 1988. But on 23 December, when a drastic reduction in capital as a result of a merger between Japan Line and Yamashita Shin-nihonkisen was announced, the share price of Japan Line plummeted from 623 yen per share to 180 yen per share. The plaintiff claimed that the defendant, a principal shareholder of Japan Line, had obtained the information about the merger and resultant capital decrease and had sold his Japan Line shares four days prior to the announcement of such information. Those shares had been acquired by the plaintiff through the Tokyo Stock Exchange. The plaintiff claimed 214,062,000 yen – the difference between what the plaintiff paid and what the shares were worth after the fall – from the defendant as damages sustained as a result of the defendant's insider dealing. The defendant denied that he had known about the merger before the announcement, and claimed that as the plaintiff bought the shares through a stock exchange. Where it was impossible to determine which buyer bought from which seller or vice versa there was no causal link between his sale of Japan Line shares and the plaintiff's loss. The court, though confirming that damages claims for insider dealing can be made in tort if the causal link is established, dismissed the plaintiff's claim on the grounds that the trading in question was executed on an exchange where it is impossible to determine who is on the other side of the trade and that, as there is no clause requiring causal links under the present insider dealing regulation, no causal link could be established.

Article 164[159] of the SEL provides for an issuer's right to claim from an officer or principal shareholder[160] any profit derived from purchase within

---

[155] Kojima, Chapter 22 in *Insider Trading*, ed. Gaillard (1992), at 339.
[156] Oda, *supra*. See also Securities and Exchange Council Report, *Naibusha Torihiki no Kisei no Arikatani tsuite* (1988), Section 3.4.(3), though recognising the need for an effective means of providing civil remedies, the Council felt that more discussion was required and that they were to tackle this as a medium- to long-term issue.
[157] Kojima cites a judgment given by Tokyo District Court on 31 March 1987, in which a client brought a damages claim against a securities distributor alleging that the distributor's solicitation violated Article 58 of the SEL, and therefore constituted a tort as well as a breach of contract. Though the court dismissed the client's claim, it confirmed as a general theory that violation of Article 58 can be used as a basis for a civil damage claim. This decision was upheld by Tokyo High Court on 20 October 1988.
[158] Tokyo District Court Decision, 29 October 1991, reported in *Kinyuu Shoji Hanrei* No. 898, 29–33 and No. 902, 45–51.
[159] Article 164 (formerly Article 189), para. 2.
[160] This refers to any shareholder who owns more than 10% of the issued shares.

six months after sale, or sale within six months after purchase. If the issuer does not make this claim within sixty days of a request made by its shareholder, the provision gives such shareholder the right to bring a class action against the officer or principal shareholder who gained such profit.[161] However, this does not work in reality as the legal costs have to be borne by the shareholder bringing the action even if he wins the case and the profits are to be paid back directly to the relevant company. In other words, what is in it for the shareholders?

9 OUT OF COURT SETTLEMENT

Due to the inaccessibility of civil actions and the general dislike of litigation in Japanese society, disputes are often settled out of court. Unfair securities transactions are no exception to this preferred solution.

In May 1993, a newspaper[162] reported that Nikko Securities had paid three clients a total of 1 billion yen as a settlement. A salesman had been using his client's money to buy and sell shares without their authorisation, and had run up a huge loss due to the fall in the market. Though the salesman responsible for the loss has been dismissed by Nikko, the MOF is investigating this incident as his conduct contravenes the rules of the JSDA.[163]

10 SELF-REGULATION

The Securities and Exchange Council Report submitted prior to the 1988 amendment of the SEL emphasised the importance of the prevention of insider dealing,[164] as well as the imposition of adequate sanctions.[165] For this reason, it strongly recommended that securities companies should tighten self-regulation with regard to the flow of inside information, and take positive actions such as putting into place a barrier to stop the flow of such information, in the form of a "Chinese Wall".

Since June 1973, securities companies have operated self-imposed rules[166] with regard to their employees engaged in corporate related duties.[167] These rules have focused on the separation of underwriting and broking businesses within the securities companies and stated that:

---

[161] Article 164 (formerly Article 189), para. 2.

[162] *Asahi Shimbun*, 22 May 1993.

[163] The Japanese Securities Dealers Association.

[164] The emphasis was repeated in the subsequent resolution of the Diet, *see* Yokobatake, *supra*, at 21.

[165] In fact, the order in which the Report recommended changed to prevention and then sanctions halfway through the drafting of the Report, *see* Kawamoto, *Insaida torihiki no mizenboushitaisei* (Prevention of Insider Dealing), Shojihoumu No. 1166, 5 December 1988, at 11.

[166] A set of in-house rules entitled *Houjinkankeishain fukumukitei* (The conduct rules for employees engaged in corporate related duties), were put into effect by all the securities houses with a capital of over 3 billion yen (£20 million).

[167] Henshubu (Editorial Section), *Shoji Houmu* No. 1151, 5 July 1988, at 3.

(1) Employees engaged in corporate related duties (those dealing with corporate clients in underwriting sections, etc.), should take due control over undisclosed information concerning their corporate clients obtained during the course of their duties in order to ensure that such information is not used by the broking department.

(2) Such employees as described above should not accept any orders from the issuers' officers, principal shareholders or related companies if such orders are clearly based on corporate related information (inside information).[168]

(3) Such employees as described above should not, in principle, accept any sale orders from the officers, of securities of their companies, if they have sold such securities within the previous six months or accept purchase orders of such securities, if they have been sold within the same period.

There was a response to the recommendations made in the Securities Council Report by the Japanese Securities Dealers Association (JSDA), the self-regulatory organisation vested with the responsibility of promoting fair practices by member firms in securities transactions, ensuring investor protection through its conduct rules, for adequate sanctions against breach.[169] The JSDA amended their Rules of Fair Practice[170] to provide that members should implement a set of in-house rules for the prevention of insider dealing.

The model in-house rules, "Insider Dealing Control Rules",[171] drawn up under the amended Rules of Fair Practice were brought into effect by all the member firms. The most notable characteristic of these rules is that all information related to corporate clients is to be collected in a "Trading Control Room"[172] whose members are prohibited from dealing in any securities.

10.1 Control of corporate related information

The "Insider Dealing Control Rules" refer to price-sensitive information as "corporate related information", definitions of which, under Article 2, are in line with the definitions of "material facts", given under Article 166 paragraph 2, except that the scope of the Rules is somewhat wider as it includes such items as window dressing of accounts by the issuer or the danger of bankruptcy.[173] Any such information has to be reported to the head of the Trading Control Room via the chief of the section.

---

[168] A definition of "corporate related information" was later given in detail in *Naibusha torihiki kanri kisoku* (Insider Dealing Control Rules), *see supra* note 17.

[169] Articles 71, items 1, 2 and 5 of the SEL.

[170] Rule No. 9, *Kyoukaiin no toushikanyu kokyakukanri ni kansuru kitei* (Rules concerning inducement of investment and treatment of customers).

[171] *Naibusha torihiki kanri kisoku* consisting of six chapters and twenty-one clauses, replaced the earlier rules, *Houjinkankeishain fukumukitei* (The conduct rules for employees engaged in corporate related duties), *see supra*, note 146.

[172] Its functions are similar to those of a compliance department of a U.K. financial institution.

[173] *See* Otake, *Kakukai kara no kosatsu – shokenkai* (Securities Industry's Perspective [of Insider Dealing]), 806 *Kinyu Shouji Hanrei*, August 1988, at 36.

Any document containing such information as described above has to be kept within the relevant department and away from the rest of the firm. When preparing investment information material for circulation within the firm, the material has to be checked in consultation with the Trading Control Room so that it does not contain any inside information.

10.2 Prohibited conduct

A securities company is prohibited from dealing in securities on its own account using inside information. Any officer and employee of a securities company is also prohibited from dealing in the securities of his corporate client regardless of whether or not he is in possession of inside information.

Any officer or employee of a securities company is prohibited from communicating inside information to anyone else unless such act, as in underwriting, is deemed necessary by the Trading Control Room.

Any officer or employee is also prohibited from soliciting customers on the information concerning such securities as cautioned by the Trading Control Room.

10.3 Control of customers

When a customer orders a sale or purchase of securities, the employee of a securities company that receives the order has to complete a "customer registration card" by writing his name, contact address, position held in his company, financial record, experience of securities investment, nature of trade, etc. This card is then sent via the branch manager or section chief to the head of the Trading Control Room where the details are stored in the computer database.[174] The cards are used by the Trading Control Room to monitor dealings in the securities by the officers and principal shareholders of the companies so that it can inform the relevant companies if the disgorgement provision is enforceable.[175]

10.4 Prohibited orders

No officer or employee of a securities company should accept any orders from the issuers' officers, principal shareholders or related companies if such orders are clearly based on inside information.

No officer or employee should, in principle, accept any sale orders from the officers for securities of their companies if they have sold such securities within the previous six months, or accept purchase orders of such securities if they have been sold within the same period.

---

[174] One major securities company is said to have held some five hundred entries, 90% of which were those of financial institutions, on their database by the end of June 1990, *see Shoji Houmu* No. 1225, 25 August 1990, at 17.

[175] Article 164 of the SEL gives a company the right to ask for the return of short-swing profit gained by its officers and principal shareholders within the six-month period.

10.5 Control of trades

The Trading Control Room can prohibit the company from dealing on its own account in the securities which relate to inside information, and order that such securities are not recommended by the company and that its employees ask their customers the reason for placing orders for such securities to be sold or bought.

11 THE PROBLEMS OF ADOPTING FOREIGN LAWS

It seems to be a common practice for the learned scholars of American–Japanese comparative law to cite the cases brought to the American courts in order to predict or dictate the direction of the Japanese regulation of insider dealing.[176] However, most seem to overlook one major difference between the systems of regulating insider dealing in the two countries. Whilst the new Japanese regime of regulation of insider dealing imposes criminal sanctions on violation of the relevant provisions in the Securities and Exchange Law, the American approach under the Federal Securities Act is to consider criminal liability "as a last resort", though it constitutes a criminal offence "to wilfully violate any of the [SEC] Acts' provisions or rules made thereunder, or indeed any order or subpoena of the Commission".[177] Contrary to the general perception and the image that the SEC may promote, the SEC cannot itself prosecute for the violation above.[178] It is up to the Attorney General, to whom the SEC gives the evidence, to decide whether proceedings should be brought.[179] Indeed, in dealing with insider dealing cases, the Americans seem reluctant to bring criminal prosecutions unless "there is both a degree of specificity and moral turpitude".[180] Though the number of criminal cases are on the increase,[181] much more emphasis is placed on the SEC's ability to bring civil actions against the violators in federal courts for injunctive relief, disgorgement, and civil penalties of up to three times the defendant's profits.[182] The SEC seem to be succeeding with this approach.[183]

Whilst the Americans strengthened[184] the civil enforcement actions against wrongdoers[185] by the SEC, the Japanese took the option of enforcement

---

[176] There have been many articles published on the subject since the amendment of the Securities and Exchange Law of Japan in 1988, including, probably, many that the author is not even aware of, published both in English and Japanese, and, indeed, on drafting the amendment many of the concepts were drawn from the American experience of dealing with the problem.

[177] *See* Rider & Ffrench, *The Regulation of Insider Trading* (1979), at 47.

[178] The staff of the SEC are known to utter words such as "we prosecute" whilst they can only sue the suspected violators for civil liabilities.

[179] *See* Rider, *supra*, at 47.

[180] *Id.*, at 48, citing Professor Loss' view.

[181] *See* Banoff, *supra*, at 152.

[182] *Id.*

[183] *Id.*, at 153. *See also* Rider, *Insider Trading – A Crime of Our Times*, at 79.

[184] *See* Insider Trading Sanctions Act of 1984 and that of 1988.

[185] Rider, *supra*, at 79.

through criminal sanctions. This choice is understandable given the well-known reluctance of the Japanese to litigate[186] and the need to be seen to take tough measures to regulate.[187] Furthermore, Japan abolished the SEC, which was established under American direction during the Occupation, as soon as the Occupation ended, and therefore there is no autonomous regulatory authority[188] to take civil actions. Prior to the amendment of the SEL to introduce insider dealing provisions, there were certain provisions within the SEL which could have been applied to prohibit insider dealing but they were never enforced. However, as they look so similar to the American Federal Laws, given that the SEL was modelled on them,[189] they gave the false impression to American-trained lawyers that they were enforced in similar ways, while to Japanese lawyers that they could not go wrong if they followed the American examples.

Even after the amendment in 1988, the same tradition continues. This can have quite dangerous implications for enforcement of the insider dealing provisions. Japanese academics have followed closely the development of insider dealing cases in the U.S. and the reasoning for or against the prosecution. Eminent corporate lawyers in Japan have published a number of articles in which they analyse insider dealing cases in the U.S.[190] Criminal prosecutions have reached the Federal Supreme Court, but it can be misleading to base one's view on the theories that have come out of these American cases in order to draw any meaningful conclusions as to the direction of regulation that Japan should follow. It should not be forgotten that these cases have involved civil proceedings somewhere on the way and that criminal prosecutions are, after all, the last resort, whereas in Japan, whilst civil actions are, as discussed above, theoretically possible, they are not likely.

12 CONCLUSION

The reception of the American common law system, with developed concepts in regard to individuals' rights, resulted in a clash with the unique Japanese legal consciousness, which could be characterised as non-litigious[191] with a great emphasis on group harmony.[192] The pursuit of

---

[186] *See* Happe, *supra*, at 124–128.
[187] One of the prime reasons for the introduction of insider dealing provisions was to respond to international criticism, therefore it required a high profile.
[188] The Ministry of Finance is responsible for regulating the entire financial sector in Japan.
[189] The SEL, enacted in 1948 to regulate issuance and distribution of securities comprehensively, was modelled on the Securities Act of 1933 and Securities Exchange Act of 1934, both of the U.S.
[190] For example, Namiki, *Naibusha torihiki no tekiyou kakudai nitsuite* (Towards the Extension of Application of Insider Dealing Regulation), *Hogakukenkyu* Vol. 65 No. 8 (Aug. 1992), at 1–22.
[191] According to a survey conducted around 1975, the per capita number of civil lawsuits in the U.K. was approximately ten times that of Japan: *see* Tanaka, *supra*, at 377.
[192] *See* Lansing & Wechselblatt, *supra*, at 650.

individual enterprise and economic freedom based on the "New Deal" policy directed by Roosevelt[193] contradicted the cooperative business environment in Japan,[194] where the economy had been dominated by a handful of *zaibatsu*, which in turn had been "closely tied" with the Government,[195] sharing the same economic goals.[196] The Japanese Government's reluctance to enforce the regulations has been widening the gap between what is written in law and what is being done in practice. It seems that the Japanese Government is generally not apprehensive about the gap between law and practice.[197] Nevertheless, from time to time, attempts to narrow this gap are prompted by criticisms, mostly from outside Japan, and are made by adopting new statutes and rules, often taken from another country, rather than by tightening the enforcement.

While individuals' rights are regarded as secondary to the national economic interest in Japan, it is not feasible to see that the U.S. model of regulation could be superimposed on Japan and expect it to sit comfortably. At the same time, the U.K. model could not work as the Japanese financial sector has never had self-regulation in the form upon which the City of London has based its regulation. The Japanese financial sector's main concern will continue to be the mitigation of commercial interests between the participants. It is arguable that investor protection in respect of fairness is least pertinent to global harmonisation.[198] After all, whilst the stock market continued to rise, no one in Japan questioned or criticised the regulatory system.

13 REFERENCES

Shokentorihikiho (The Securities and Exchange Law), Law No. 25 of 1948.

T. Akashi, "Regulation of Insider Trading in Japan", 6 Columbia Law Rev. (1989) 1296.

B. A. Banoff, "The Regulation of Insider Trading in the United States, United Kingdom and Japan", 9 Michigan Yearbook of Int'l Legal Studies 145, at 163.

M. J. Happe, "Inside the Japanese Stock Market: An Assessment", 5 Am. U.J. Int'l L. & Pol'y (1989).

K. Kanzaki, *Shokentorihikiho* (The Securities and Exchange Law) (1987), at 56.

---

[193] *See* Tsutsui, *supra*, at 38–39.
[194] *See* Note, *supra*, at 1064.
[195] *See* Happe, *supra*, at 102.
[196] *See* Happe, *supra*, at 105–106.
[197] *See* Banoff, *supra*, at 167.
[198] A number of economists have been arguing this for some time: *see* for example, B. Steil, "Regulatory Foundation for Global Capital Markets", (The AMEX Bank Review Second Prize Essay) in 6 *Finance and the International Economy* 62 (1992).

K. Kanzaki, "*Naibusha torihiki no kinshi – Sono kihonteki kozo* (Prohibition of Insider Dealing – its basic structure)", 806 Kinyu Shoji Hanrei (Cases in Financial and Commercial Laws) (1989).

C. Nakajima, "Conflicts of Interest in Japan", in Rider & Ashe, *The Fiduciary, the Insider and the Conflict* (1995), Ch. 11 at 165.

B. A. K. Rider, *Insider Trading* (1983).

Rider & Ffrench, *The Regulation of Insider Trading* (1979).

Tanaka & Horiguchi, *Shokentorihikiho* (The Securities and Exchange Law) (1990).

M. Tatsuta, *Securities Regulation in Japan* (1970).

W. M. Tsutsui, *Banking Policy in Japan* (1988).

Y. Yokobatake, *Insaida Torihiki Kisei To Bassoku* (Insider Dealing Regulation and the Penalties) (1989).

20. Emerging Securities Markets – A View of Internationalization from the U.S.

Marc I. Steinberg[1]

1 INTRODUCTION

For emerging capital securities markets,[2] is the United States approach useful when determining the structure and components of such markets? Does the U.S. system serve as a panacea for these developing markets or as an inflexible bureaucratic maze to be sidestepped with impunity? Stated succinctly, the answer is that the U.S. model may be useful in certain contexts but that each emerging capital market should adhere to an approach compatible with its culture and reflective of the costs and efficiencies implicated.

Today, with the continual need for the infusion of funds and the increased competition of obtaining such funds from traditional sources, countries with emerging economies look with ardor to establishing attractive capital markets in order to procure sought-after capital from private sources, frequently from abroad. Countries spanning the globe from continent to continent seek access to a healthful cut of this elusive pie. Even countries within geographic regions join together for this common purpose.[3]

Countries with emerging securities markets are not alone in their quest for inducing the inflow of capital. They compete not only with the supposedly sophisticated securities markets in, for example, New York,

---

[1] Rupert and Lillian Radford Professor of Law, School of Law, Southern Methodist University. Visiting Professorial Fellow, Banking and Finance Law Unit, Centre for Commercial Law Studies, University of London. Of Counsel, Winstead, Sechrest & Minick, Dallas, Texas.
  I thank Professor George Martinez for his helpful comments. I also thank Professor Joseph Norton for his support, professionalism, and friendship.
[2] *See*, H. Scott & P. Wellons, "Emerging Markets: Privatization and Institutional Investors" in *International Finance: Transactions, Policy and Regulation* 965–1004 (1995).
[3] *See, e.g.*, Angola-Botswana-Lesotho-Malawi Mozambique-Namibia-Swaziland-Tanzania-Zambia-Zimbabwe: Treaty of the Southern African Development Community, 32 *I.L.M.* 116 (1993) (Introductory Note by Rosalind H. Thomas). *See* generally, Winn, "How to Make Poor Countries Rich and How to Enrich our Poor", 77 *Iowa L. Rev.* 899 (1992).

London and Tokyo but also with a host of markets that have strong regional or at least local impact in procuring capital (including, for example, the Singapore, Johannesburg, and Stockholm Exchanges).

Therefore, the challenge facing emerging capital markets is daunting. They compete for a finite amount of private investment in an increasingly competitive world. They must persuade astute investors to impart capital in their respective countries rather than in seemingly countless other venues that provide greater comfort. With the availability of readily accessible capital markets having relatively long-standing stability, what benefits can an emerging market offer to attract investors? Key inducements, for example, are: the realistic lure of impressive profit; a relatively stable political climate; liquidity and negotiability of investment; control over one's investment; and regulation that promotes market integrity and ethical business practices (without unduly infringing upon privacy concerns and entrepreneurial creativity).[4] Of course, the reality may be such that the preceding inducements serve merely as platitudes, incapable of effective implementation. Political instability, inexperience with capital markets, and the absence of funding to establish (and maintain) regulatory oversight may prevail. In such an event, successfully inducing the inflow of capital may well depend on the ability of such emerging capital markets to persuade investors that substantial profits are likely to be made. Certainly, this task of persuasion is easier in a country such as China as compared to Uganda.[5]

Needless to say, there is no fixed agenda to which emerging securities markets must adhere. *A la carte* serves as the menu of preference. Given different cultures, political climates, and degrees of access to internal and/or traditional sources of capital, each country's realities call for distinct choices. Hence, rather than designating a "set menu" for emerging capital markets, the more prudent course is to identify those components worthy of consideration. In this endeavor, due to its impact and supposed respect in the world capital markets, the U.S. system is a key source that should be explored.

Irrespective of the contours of the framework ultimately adopted, it must receive approbation by participants in the affected securities market. The system adhered to will be difficult enough to effectuate; skepticism at the outset will reduce such likelihood to virtually nil. Therefore, input, dialogue and consensus are essential; affected constituencies must "buy into" the framework's sensibility and prospect for success. Also, skilled draftsmanship in formulating statutes and regulations in this complex area should be a top priority. A clearly written statute (accompanied by coherent legislative history) will serve as a valuable resource when the meaning and scope of the statute are later questioned.[6]

---

[4] *See,* Pardy, "Institutional Reform in Emerging Securities Markets", Policy Research Working Papers, Country Economics Department, The World Bank WPS 907 (1992).

[5] But *see,* "Foreigners Shun New Issues in China", *USA Today,* Int'l ed., July 24, 1995, at 6B.

[6] *See, e.g., Ernst & Ernst v. Hochfelder,* 425 U.S. 185 (1976).

This chapter thus analyzes those ingredients that an emerging capital securities market may embrace. In this task, to some extent, the U.S. framework serves as a model for possible adaptation as well as those from other countries, such as England. Utilizing this approach, the chapter will address several key issues that emerging capital securities markets may wish to consider, namely:

(1) the choice between government and self-regulation;
(2) personnel and funding needs to enforce the laws and other norms deemed worthy of protection;
(3) government civil versus criminal enforcement;
(4) the merits of a private attorney general approach;
(5) opting for a disclosure rather than a merit-based system;
(6) facilitating access to and growth of their respective securities markets; and
(7) the delicate task of overseeing the activities of financial intermediaries.

Undoubtedly, a number of the foregoing issues are related and should be considered in a unified manner. This is not surprising. Given the complexity and wide spectrum of choices facing each respective securities market, there exists the ever-present challenge to respond in a cohesive, consistent fashion that adequately addresses the underlying problem cost-effectively while not being perceived as either too zealous or too lax by interested parties. To do so effectively remains an awesome if not impossible choice for any capital securities market, let alone an "emerging" market.

2 GOVERNMENT REGULATOR OR "SRO"?

Irrespective of the sophistication of a particular capital securities market, it is clear that some form of oversight or regulation is appropriate. The options include, for example:

(1) a central government regulator having extensive authority;
(2) government regulation by means of regional bodies;
(3) self-regulation conducted by stock exchanges and/or other self-regulatory organizations (SROs) established to oversee issuers and financial intermediaries (such as brokers, dealers, investment advisers, and clearing agents); and
(4) some combination of the foregoing.[7]

---

[7] In the United States, federal, state, and SRO regulations are all employed. Of course, the underlying circumstances often will dictate the scope of activity of the applicable regulator(s). *See*, L. Loss & J. Seligman, *Securities Regulation* (3d ed. 1989).

Government regulation along the lines of a United States model Securities and Exchange Commission (SEC) evokes fear of stringent government regulation that impedes capital formation and entrepreneurial creativity. According to such critics, the resulting bureaucratic maze with its accompanying high transaction costs is a burden that emerging and even more developed securities markets can ill afford.[8]

On the other hand, to induce investors to enter these markets, there ordinarily must be in place an oversight authority to help engender much needed confidence in market integrity. Where sharp practices prevail (or are so perceived), mechanisms should be implemented to enforce applicable law and to deter fraud. In such circumstances, much can be said for speaking loudly and carrying a big stick. In those countries where an SRO, by custom or law, cannot command such presence, a government regulator is the preferable route.

Regardless of whether a U.S.-type SEC is established or self-regulation or some hybrid, adequate powers should be provided. Such powers include, for example:

(1) investigatory authority (such as the ability to issue subpoenas demanding the production of relevant documents and the appearance of individuals to testify under oath);

(2) enforcement authority enabling the regulator to seek either directly or efficiently through a different regulatory source remedial relief (such as injunctions, disgorgement, and the appointment of a receiver) as well as punitive measures (including civil fines, forfeitures, and criminal prosecution); and

(3) the wherewithal to secure judicial relief (such as criminal contempt) in the event of a subject person's non-compliance with an order previously imposed.[9]

Whether a particular capital securities market opts for a government regulator or SRO oversight may depend on such factors as the applicable country's culture, resources, and level of sophistication in this area. There are difficult choices to be made. It may soundly be argued that a country with little expertise that seeks to develop a securities market would be imprudent from both a cost and efficiency perspective to establish a U.S.-type SEC. This putting the cart before the horse approach elevates theory over reality, reflecting waste with little tangible benefit. On the contrary, it may be asserted with some justification that, unless the prospects for economic gain are strikingly encouraging, investors outside of the host country will not enter a market that lacks basic regulatory oversight. Hence, in

---

[8] *See*, Helner, "Stock Exchange Law: The Need for Legislation and Research" in *Stock Exchange and Corporation Law* 61, 62 (C. Roos ed. 1984) (stating that "the very detailed regulation in the American Securities Act is not attractive to [Sweden]").

[9] *See*, M. Steinberg & R. Ferrara, *Securities Practice: Federal and State Enforcement* (1985 & 1995 supp.).

order to induce the inflow of foreign capital, it may be necessary for a country with an emerging capital securities market to establish a governmental regulatory body.

3 MONEY AND RESOURCES – SEEMINGLY ALWAYS A KEY DILEMMA

Irrespective of a market's level of sophistication, funding and resources for adequate oversight pose a continuing dilemma. When demands are high for such crucial matters as education, health care, defense, and infrastructure, the zeal for pursuing inside traders and stock manipulators more effectively by appropriating generous funds is not surprisingly chilled. This dilemma is exacerbated for emerging securities markets frequently situated in countries with pressing human and societal demands.

Yet, sufficient funding and resources are key to the success of a securities oversight framework. For example, the most rigorous statutes have little impact if there exists a lack of funds to hire, retain, and school the requisite number and variety of personnel to administer competently the regulatory regimen. Hence, without the necessary human and financial resources, even egregious violations go undetected and the most elaborate regulatory framework proves futile.[10]

Therefore, a review of key characteristics in this context is to the point. Clearly, the personnel employed by the subject SRO or governmental body must be competent and qualified. They must have the requisite education and training to administer the pertinent framework. Sending employees abroad to acquire the necessary acumen should be a matter of priority as should inviting experts from abroad to lend their insights. Also, there should be a "critical mass" of employees in both numbers and specialties. In addition to adequate support staff, attorneys, accountants, financial analysts, and investigators should comprise the scene. Personnel alone is not sufficient. Given the ingenuity of those bent on fraud, the requisite technology must be available to the enforcers. Of course, the degree of the technology demanded will depend on the complexity of the particular securities market.

With vigorous investigatory and enforcement powers, competent oversight personnel in both number and specialty and the use of appropriate technology, much can be accomplished. Nonetheless, there remains the task of attracting and retaining personnel of high caliber. Some suggestions are offered. Certainly, employment with the applicable SRO or government regulator should be perceived as a position having respect and status. Salaries (and other compensation benefits) should be set as near as economically feasible to that earned by comparable persons in the private sector.

---

[10] For example, although South Africa has a fairly detailed insider trading prohibition as well as regulatory personnel to pursue alleged violators, thus far not one prosecution has been initiated. *See* generally, van Zyl, "South Africa: Insider Trading Regulation and Enforcement", 15 *The Company Lawyer* No. 3, at 92 (1994).

The same holds true for office accommodations. They should be of similar quality as those used by respected professional firms in the host country. To reward those who perform admirably, periodic salary increases and promotion opportunities for more demanding positions should be made available. And last, the objective of achieving excellent performance should be part of the culture and ethos of the applicable regulator as viewed from both within and outside.[11]

The foregoing ideals can be actualized only with strong financial support. Put simply, it will "take plenty of money".[12] With more pressing personal and societal demands facing countries with emerging securities markets, how can these funds feasibly be raised? A number of sources come to mind. First, a registration fee may be collected when an issuer opts to have an offering of its securities. Second, financial intermediaries, such as broker-dealers and investment advisers, may be required to pay an annual or other periodic registration fee to the applicable body as a condition of "doing business". Third, companies and other types of business enterprises may be subject to an annual franchise tax. Fourth, the relevant stock exchange may collect a fee from companies listed on the exchange as a privilege of having their securities traded on such exchange. Fifth, the relevant stock exchange likewise may impose a "user fee" upon broker-dealers to reflect their engaging in business through exchange facilities. Sixth, the SRO or the government regulator may levy (or seek the levying through court order of) money penalties against securities law violators.[13]

Collection of sufficient revenues without posing a disincentive for companies and financial intermediaries to enter the applicable securities market is a delicate task. If the charges levied are viewed as excessive, they will induce the relevant "players" to divert at least a significant amount of their activity to other less intrusive markets. This point becomes accentuated with respect to the imposition of money penalties which not only may be costly but also carry a stigma to one's reputation.

In light of the personal and societal needs of countries with emerging securities markets, there also exists the distinct possibility that the particular government will make use of the fees generated to serve other more pressing needs. Leaving the applicable SRO or government regulator with meager funding disserves the long-term economic interest of procuring the inflow of foreign capital. By providing an adequate level of funding for the SRO or government regulator to oversee the applicable securities market, there will exist a greater likelihood of instilling investor confidence.

---

[11] *See*, Mann, "What Constitutes a Successful Securities Regulatory Regime?", 3 *Australian J. Corp. L.* 178 (1993); Miller, "S.E.C.: Watchdog 1929 Lacked", *New York Times*, Oct. 31, 1979, at D.1; J. Seligman, *The Transformation of Wall Street – A History of the Securities and Exchange Commission and Modern Corporate Finance* (1982).

[12] G. Harrison, *Got My Mind Set On You* (1987).

[13] The SEC and the states tap a number of these sources. *See*, M. Steinberg, *Securities Regulation* (2d ed. 1993); Cary, "Federalism and Corporate Law: Reflections Upon Delaware", 83 *Yale L.J.* 663 (1974).

On the other hand, allowing the applicable regulator to be entirely self-funding from the fees and penalties collected, creates the risk that a bloated bureaucracy will emerge and that corruption will serve as the order of the day. Tying personnel salaries and perquisites to the revenues generated is fraught with risk. For example, if the levying of money fines against alleged violators directly redounds to the financial benefit of the enforcers, non-meritorious cases may be pursued and excessive fines may be assessed. Such an occurrence would be catastrophic to the success of any emerging securities market (except in those markets where the market players, including investors, expect handsome returns).

4 GOVERNMENT ENFORCEMENT – CIVIL VERSUS CRIMINAL

When an alleged violation of the securities laws occurs, should civil and/or criminal enforcement be pursued? For illustration purposes, the SEC may bring civil enforcement action seeking a wide range of relief, such as the entry of a cease and desist order, ordering of an injunction, appointment of a receiver, levying of money penalties, imposition of an officer and director bar, and ordering of disgorgement of ill-gotten profits.[14] Moreover, the SEC may institute criminal contempt actions against those who have not obeyed injunctions previously issued.[15]

In addition, the U.S. Department of Justice may criminally prosecute accused violators of the federal securities laws. Hefty criminal sentences of up to ten years' imprisonment may be imposed for many violations as well as severe money fines (*e.g.*, for illegal insider trading, stock manipulation, filing with the SEC materially false statements).[16] Added to the prosecutors' criminal arsenal under U.S. law are statutes that may be invoked in addition to or in lieu of the federal securities laws. These statutes include the federal mail and wire fraud provisions as well as the Racketeer Influenced Corrupt Organizations Act (RICO).[17]

The state securities laws (or "blue sky" laws) enacted by each of the fifty states likewise provide for both government civil and criminal enforcement. Indeed, some of the state securities laws are more onerous than the federal

---

[14] *See, e.g., Aaron v. SEC*, 446 U.S. 680 (1980); M. Steinberg & R. Ferrara, *Securities Practice: Federal and State Enforcement* (1985 & 1995 supp.); Dent, "Ancillary Relief in Federal Securities Law: A Study in Federal Remedies", 67 *Minn. L. Rev.* 865 (1983).

[15] *See, e.g., United States v. Custer Channel Wing Corp.*, 376 F. 2d 675 (4th Cir. 1967).

[16] *See*, Section 32(a) of the Securities Exchange Act, 15 U.S.C. § 78ff(a); Mathews, "Criminal Prosecutions Under the Federal Securities Laws and Related Statutes", 39 *Geo. Wash. L. Rev.* 901 (1971).

[17] *See, Carpenter v. United States*, 485 U.S. 19 (1987) (federal mail and wire fraud statutes); *United States v. Turkette*, 452 U.S. 576 (1981) (criminal RICO statute). Nonetheless, violations often go undetected. *See*, Emshwiller, "How Career Swindlers Run Rings Around SEC and Prosecutors", *Wall Street Journal*, May 12, 1995, at A1; Stecklow, "Owing $500 Million, New Era Charity Seeks Refuge from Creditors", *Wall Street Journal*, May 16, 1995, at A1.

statutes. For example, a number of states authorize criminal liability premised on principles of strict liability.[18]

The SROs in the United States also have significant civil enforcement powers. For example, the stock exchanges may assess censures, bars, and money fines upon broker-dealers and their associated persons who violate the federal securities laws or the respective exchange's rules. An exchange can also delist a security. Moreover, the National Association of Securities Dealers (NASD) has broad authority to discipline those subject to its regulation.[19]

In contrast to the United States, many countries today, both in emerging and more developed securities markets, rely chiefly (if not solely) on criminal enforcement. It may be questioned whether this is the most effective approach. Today, in a number of these countries such practices as insider trading are made criminal where less than a decade ago they were viewed as standard fare or at worst a slap against one's reputation.[20] From current experience, it appears at this time that judges and juries are reluctant to criminally convict supposedly "reputable" business persons for practices that were part of the societal mainstream a short while ago. Indeed, in a number of countries, there have been few if any convictions for illegal insider trading (although the practice continues to occur with some frequency).[21]

Although the climate in the United States points toward increased criminalization of the securities laws,[22] this situation should be viewed from a historical perspective. Insider trading serves as a useful example. Although the major U.S. securities Acts were enacted in the 1930s,[23] it was not until the early 1960s that the SEC instituted a key civil enforcement proceeding based on illegal insider trading.[24] A significant appellate court

---

[18] *See, Buffo v. State*, 415 So. 2d 1158 (Ala. 1982); J. Long, *Blue Sky Law* § 8.02[2][b] (1995); Sargent, "A Blue Sky State of Mind: The Meaning of 'Willfully' in Blue Sky Criminal Cases", 20 *Sec. Reg. L.J.* 96 (1992).

[19] *See*, A. Bromberg & L. Lowenfels, *Securities Fraud and Commodities Fraud* § 13.4(1520) (1995); Pickard & Djinis, "NASD Disciplinary Proceedings: Practice and Procedure", 37 *Bus. Law.* 1213 (1982).

[20] *See*, Tunc, "A French Lawyer Looks at American Corporation Laws and Securities Regulation", 130 *U. Pa. L. Rev.* 757, 762 (1982) (observing that in France tipping of inside information viewed as "a social duty . . . expected of relatives and friends"). *See also*, "Escaping Through the Net", *The Economist*, at 95 (Nov. 7, 1992); von Dryander, "The German Securities Trading Act: Insider Trading and Other Secondary Market Regulation", 9 *Insights* No. 1, at 26 (Jan. 1995). Prior to the insider trading legislation in Germany, insider trading was proscribed pursuant to self-regulatory rules that became binding upon parties on a contractual basis. *See*, Eising & Glasser, "Stock Exchange Rules in Germany and the Treatment of Insider Trading", 14 *Int'l Bus. L.* 191 (1986).

[21] *See*, note 10 *supra* (South Africa). Australia's experience thus far has been similar. *See*, Tomasic, "Insider Trading Law Reform in Australia", 9 *Comp. & Sec. L.J.* 121 (1991).

[22] *See*, Janvey, "Criminal Prosecution of Insider Trading", 15 *Sec. Reg. L.J.* 136 (1987).

[23] The Securities Act of 1933 and The Securities Exchange Act of 1934 are the major U.S. Securities Acts.

[24] *In re Cady, Roberts & Co.*, 40 S.E.C. 907 (1961).

decision based on an SEC civil action was not handed down until the late 1960s.[25] Some ten years later, the U.S. Department of Justice brought the initial criminal prosecutions for insider trading violations.[26] Hence, criminal prosecution was initiated only after successful civil enforcement made clear that the practice at issue was illegitimate from a consensual point of view. Although it seems doubtful that such an enforcement policy was part of a grand strategic plan, the government's current success in the criminal arena[27] underscores the merits of this approach.

To buttress this proposition, the heavier burden of proof in a criminal as compared to a civil proceeding perhaps has prompted judges and juries to refrain from criminally convicting based on circumstantial evidence.[28] From a prosecutor's viewpoint, financial frauds like insider trading or stock manipulation are not necessarily subject to direct evidence; if a conviction is to be had, circumstantial evidence frequently remains essential. With some exceptions, prosecutors in the United States have been more successful in this respect.[29]

Stated succinctly, it is not suggested that regulators in emerging capital markets abandon criminal enforcement efforts. Rather, the point is that civil regulatory remedies should be made available and should be invoked on a frequent basis. Successful enforcement actions in civil suits will encourage compliance, stimulate securities enforcement efforts in other contexts, and facilitate a consensual understanding of behavior subject to sanction. Criminal enforcement under this scenario would become the "heavy club" to be swung against those deemed sufficiently blameworthy to deserve the slammer (*i.e.,* imprisonment).

5 PRIVATE ATTORNEY GENERAL – PUBLIC BENEFIT OR SOCIETAL WASTE?

Today, in the vast majority of countries having securities markets, complex private securities litigation is a rarity. With prohibitions against attorney contingency fees, the presence of a "loser pays" structure, and significant barriers to hurdle for initiating class action or derivative suits, this trend (in the absence of modification) will continue.[30]

---

[25] *SEC v. Texas Gulf Sulphur Co.,* 401 F. 2d 833 (2d Cir. 1968).

[26] *See, e.g., Chiarella v. United States,* 445 U.S. 222 (1980).

[27] *See, e.g., United States v. Bilzerian,* 926 F. 2d 1285 (2d Cir. 1991). Nonetheless, even today, the government frequently fails to prevail. *See, e.g., United States v. Mulheren,* 938 F. 2d 364 (2d Cir. 1991).

[28] *See,* Bostock, "Australia's New Insider Trading Laws", 10 *Comp. & Sec. L.J.* 165 (1992).

[29] *See* Testimony of Michael D. Mann, Director of SEC's Office of International Affairs Concerning the International Antitrust Enforcement Assistance Act Before the U.S. Senate Subcommittee on Antitrust, Monopolies, and Business Rights, Committee of the Judiciary (Aug. 4, 1994) ("As a general matter, the Commission's investigations involve extensive document review and are often predicated on circumstantial evidence gleaned from the documents and from testimony".). *See also, SEC v. Switzer,* 590 F. Supp. 756 (W. D. Okla. 1989).

[30] *See,* Redmond, "The Reform of Directors' Duties", 15 *U. New So. Wales L.J.* 86 (1991).

On the other hand, the private attorney general approach has gained acceptance in the United States. Over thirty years ago, the U.S. Supreme Court emphasized that private suits based on securities law violations were a "necessary supplement" to SEC enforcement action.[31] With allowance for contingency fees, award of generous attorneys' fees, recognition of the class action and derivative suit as useful mechanisms to redress investor injury, and application of the general rule that each party (win or lose) bears its own costs, private securities lawsuits seeking damages (as well as other relief at times) proliferate the U.S. legal landscape.[32]

To opponents, many of these suits constitute vexatious litigation or, to use a pejorative term, "strike suits".[33] The only clear winners, according to these critics, are the attorneys. Annoyed by the time expenditures involved and bad publicity, defendants opt to settle many of these actions. Shareholders receive relatively modest financial recompense.[34] In reaction to those alleged consequences, the U.S. Congress is in the process of considering amendments to the Federal Securities Acts to make such actions more difficult to bring. The contours of any such legislation, if enacted, remain somewhat uncertain at this time.[35]

In light of the foregoing, should an emerging securities market authorize aggrieved investors to initiate private actions for damages against such persons as directors, officers, broker-dealers, investment bankers, accountants and attorneys for allegedly engaging in fraudulent practices? The costs of doing so appear unacceptably high. Having such a system in place would present a strong incentive for issuers and financial intermediaries to take their business to more hospitable surroundings. Although investors supposedly would benefit, it is unlikely that the existence of such a regimen would be influential in their decisions where to provide capital. After all, investors in emerging markets understand that risk is an integral part of the process; generally, so long as the prospect for profit is reasonable and minimally acceptable regulatory standards are implemented effectively, the venture is given serious consideration. In short, investors in these markets ordinarily do not anticipate bringing a lawsuit based on securities fraud in the host country. Rather, if they seek to protect themselves in this context, they do so through contractual warranties or through the conducting of negotiations or other aspects of the transaction that cause U.S. subject matter jurisdiction to apply.[36]

---

[31] *See, J.I. Case v. Borak,* 377 U.S. 426 (1964).

[32] *See,* Kritzer, "Searching for Winners in a Loser Pays System", 78 *Am. Bar Assoc. J.* 55 (Nov. 1992).

[33] *See, Blue Chip Stamps v. Manor Drug Stores,* 421 U.S. 723 (1975) (referring to "the danger of vexatious litigation").

[34] *See,* Alexander, "Do the Merits Matter? A Study of Settlements in Securities Class Actions", 43 *Stan. L. Rev.* 497 (1991).

[35] *See,* 27 Sec. Reg. & L. Rep. (BNA) 975 (describing Senate-passed bill); 27 Sec. Reg. & L. Rep. (BNA) 392 (1995) (describing House-passed bill). *See* generally, *Contract with America* (E. Gillespie & B. Schelhas, eds. 1994).

[36] *See, Richards v. Lloyd's of London* [1995 Transfer Binder] Fed. Sec. L. Rep. (CCH) para. 98,801 (S.D. Cal. 1995).

Moreover, most emerging capital markets are ill suited for the type of complex litigation prevalent in the United States. The particular country's goals of efficiency and satisfying more important needs render such a framework imprudent. When judges and lawyers are not numerous, where their level of expertise on such complex matters is not impressive, and where the citizenry and the government must have expeditious access to the courts in order to resolve vital matters relating to the human condition, the prospect of opening up the floodgates of litigation to redress sophisticated investor woes sounds like utter nonsense.

Nonetheless, there are two key countervailing interests: investor compensation and deterrence of fraudulent practices. Provided that the costs of providing monetary relief to aggrieved investors are acceptable, these interests ought to be pursued. The proper forum for doing so is in the SRO or civil government enforcement setting. In bringing such a proceeding, the applicable regulator (where appropriate) should seek an order of disgorgement of the alleged violator's ill-gotten gains. If so granted, the amount disgorged should be held for the benefit of parties defrauded by the violator's conduct. In this fashion, aggrieved investors will be afforded some meaningful measure of relief without undue intrusion upon the judiciary.

To accomplish this objective in hopefully a more effective manner, consideration should be given to establishing an administrative tribunal within the particular securities authority. Hearing examiners with expertise in securities law and having no relationship with the securities authority would be appointed to decide the cases brought. Depending on the norms of the particular country, appeal to a court from an adverse determination by the hearing examiner may be available. Such appeal may be provided as a matter of right or only if the sanctions levied surpass certain levels of severity. Again, the degree of process accorded, of course, is best left to the customs and norms of the applicable country. Even so, the foregoing may well represent a model for adaptation.[37]

6 REGULATION OF OFFERINGS – DISCLOSURE VERSUS MERIT REGULATION

In securities offerings conducted in their markets, should such emerging markets opt for a disclosure and/or merit-based approach? In a disclosure framework, all material information[38] normally should be disclosed in the form of written offering materials. This information should include, for example:

---

[37] *See,* generally Committee on Federal Regulation of Securities, "Report of Task Force on the SEC Administrative Law Judge Process", 47 *Bus. Law.* 1731 (1992).

[38] "Material" information may be defined as (1) such information that a reasonable investor would consider important in the making of a decision to buy or sell; or (2) such information that is deemed "price sensitive". *See, Basic, Inc. v. Levinson,* 485 U.S. 224 (1988); Australian Corp. L. § 1002G, discussed in Bostock, *supra* note 28, at 172.

(1) material historical information relating to such elements as assets, earnings, nature of operations, and managerial self-dealing;
(2) the purposes for which the proceeds derived from the offering will be used;
(3) reasonably accurate financial statements prepared in compliance with recognized accounting practices and auditing standards; and
(4) forward-looking developments, events, and contingencies that are reasonably likely to occur and to have a material financial effect on the enterprise.[39]

By contrast, merit regulation enables the securities authority, even if there is accurate and full disclosure, to prevent the offering from being conducted if it is determined that such offering is "unfair, unjust or inequitable". Such a determination may be reached, for example, if the insiders purchased their stock at extremely low prices, seek to retain inequitable stock options or warrants, or where the planned underwriter "spread" is deemed excessive.[40]

In the United States, the federal securities laws focus on disclosure. Merit regulation is adhered to by a number of states, perhaps most notably California and Texas.[41] By calling for disclosure, however, the SEC nonetheless impacts upon substantive fairness. In other words, if self-dealing transactions must be disclosed, the insiders are less likely to engage in such practices. Moreover, if such disclosure of insider dealings reveals unacceptably abusive practices, the investment community will be far less likely to support the contemplated offering.[42]

For emerging securities markets, it is suggested that a disclosure approach should be adopted to the exclusion of a merit-based system. In a number of such markets, there exists the risk that adherence to merit regulation will serve as a subterfuge for government assessments of character, integrity, and goodness – a quasi-return, under the guise of capitalism, to the way business used to be conducted in such countries. Such risk should not be undertaken, for merit regulation's costs exceed the speculative benefits that might otherwise be received. Clearly, implementation of a market efficient merit system calls for sophisticated and time-consuming judgments to be made. With efficient allocation of sparse resources a necessity for emerging securities markets, such markets should refrain from indulging in the luxury of a merit-based system.

Nonetheless, adoption of a disclosure approach alone leaves a gap that needs to be filled. Although a disclosure-based system calls for revelation of material insider dealings, such a system fails to address the propriety of even blatantly unfair insider rip-offs. Nonetheless, if attractive profits are

---

[39] *See*, SEC Forms of Registrations S-1, S-2, S-3; SEC Financial Reporting Release No. 36 (1989). *Cf. Gower Report (U.K.)* on "Review of Investor Protection" (Part I – 1984, Part II – 1985), with SEC, "Report of the SEC's Advisory Committee on Corporate Disclosure" (1977).
[40] *See*, Tyler, "More About Blue Sky", 39 *Wash. & Lee L. Rev.* 899 (1982).
[41] *See*, ABA Task Force, "Report on State Regulation of Securities Offerings", 41 *Bus. Law.* 785 (1986).
[42] *See*, Weiss, "Disclosure and Corporate Accountability", 34 *Bus. Law.* 575 (1979).

anticipated, many astute investors will purchase the subject securities irrespective of unfair insider dealings.[43]

Irrespective of such investor nonchalance, a regulatory system should not stand dormant. Moreover, the problem is exacerbated after the offering is completed, especially when the insiders sell substantial amounts of stock in the offering while retaining a sufficient percentage to retain control over the enterprise. In such a scenario, such insiders would have even greater incentive to unduly benefit themselves at the expense of the enterprise and unaffiliated security holders.

To rectify this abusive situation in a cost-effective fashion, consideration should be given to directing the SRO or government securities regulator to promulgate rules of fair practice to redress egregious misconduct. Such rules, for example, could provide, after a proceeding before a hearing officer as described above, that the offending transactions be rescinded and that restitution be made. Although such rules of fair practice should be adopted and invoked cautiously, they may serve as a relatively efficient mechanism to discipline insider abuse.[44]

7 FACILITATING ACCESS TO CAPITAL MARKETS

Facilitating access to initial and secondary capital markets is key to the success of emerging securities markets. Mechanisms should be implemented to allow for the development of attractive markets where issuers, investors, and financial intermediaries are accommodated in a manner that finds acceptance. The balance struck depends on such factors as the type of investor participation (*i.e.*, institutional or individual), the applicable market's realistic attainment of some meaningful degree of sophistication, and the deployment of sufficient resources (in terms of funding, personnel, and technology).

With respect to *initial* capital markets, three types of offering scenarios are addressed:

(1) limited offerings made to a finite number of investors with some investors having financial acumen;
(2) offerings made in markets comprised solely of institutional (and other presumably sophisticated) investors; and
(3) offerings directed at the general public, thereby encompassing the uninitiated.

Depending on the context, the affected market that develops may be either private or public in character. For example, an initial offering made

---

[43] *See, generally*, Siegel, "The Long March to a Market Economy: The PRC's Corporate and Securities Law Reform", *infra, see* Ch 23.

[44] *Cf.* Raisler & Geldermann, "The CFTC's New Reparation Rules: In Search of a Fair, Responsive, and Practical Forum for Resolving Commodity-Related Disputes", 40 *Bus. Law.* 537 (1985).

by an issuer to twenty persons normally is private. However, if those persons thereupon sell their interests to 500 different investors, a public market will emerge. Accordingly, that an initial offering is made to few investors does not foreclose the possibility that a public market will eventuate. This prospect affects issues relating to disclosure, market abuse, and regulatory oversight.[45]

7.1 "Limited" offerings

Where issuers seek to offer securities to a limited number of investors, questions arise relating to the proper degree of government or SRO oversight. For example, should there be mandated disclosure in this context? Should the issuer's offering statement be subject to review by the regulatory authority? Should there be restrictions on purchasers reselling their securities to avoid the emergence of a public market where a lack of adequate information exists concerning the subject issuer and the securities?

Generally, in a limited offering, unlike one that is public, there is less government or SRO regulation. No disclosure document may be required to be filed with the regulatory authority and, if all purchasers are sophisticated, there may be no mandated delivery of information. Prohibitions against fraud nonetheless apply in this context.[46] For oversight and fee generating purposes, a form notifying the regulatory authority of the offering may be demanded of issuers and financial intermediaries.[47]

Generally, a limited offering may be viewed as having certain characteristics depending on the construction given by the affected emerging securities market. In this regard, such offerings are made to a finite number of investors. That number may be ten, thirty-five, one hundred or some other number that the regulatory overseer concludes meets capital raising needs without adversely impacting on market integrity. Nonetheless, at some point, the offering of securities on a widespread basis should signify that the offering is public (rather than limited).

Whether a monetary ceiling should exist for an offering to qualify as "limited" is another issue. For example, an offering is limited under U.S. law in certain contexts if the amount raised does not exceed $5 million during any twelve-month period. Otherwise, registration of the offering with the SEC is mandated.[48] For emerging capital markets, a distinction on a monetary basis between limited and public offerings should not be implemented. Rather, more relevant criteria focus on the manner of solicitation

---

[45] *See, SEC v. Ralston Purina Co.*, 346 U.S. 119 (1953); SEC Securities Act Release No. 6389 (1982).

[46] *See,* Warren, "Review of Regulation D: The Present Exemption Regimen for Limited Offerings Under the Securities Act of 1933", 33 *Am. U.L. Rev.* 355 (1984).

[47] *Cf.* Form D that (although not fee generating) must be filed with the SEC when a Regulation D limited offering is made. *See,* SEC Securities Act Release No. 6825 (1989); Sargent, "The New Regulation D: Deregulation, Federalism and the Dynamics of Regulatory Reform", 68 *Wash. U.L.Q.* 225 (1990).

[48] *See,* M. Steinberg, *Understanding Securities Law* 38-48 (1989); sources cited notes 45–47 *supra*.

(*e.g.*, advertisements in newspapers versus by means of preexisting relationships), number of offerees, and restrictions on resale. Also, irrespective of the monetary amount sought to be raised in the offering, needed revenues can be raised by the regulatory authority assessing fees upon the issuer and financial intermediaries for the privilege of conducting the offering.

If the issuer and financial intermediaries engage in advertising or general solicitation,[49] there is good reason to require that an offering document adequately describing the issuer, the terms of the offering, and the securities offered be transmitted promptly to all offerees. Otherwise, promoters will have free rein to "hype" the offering, creating a "hot issue", and thereby condition members of the public to purchase the securities without their being privy to sufficient information. Because the prospect for fraud is greater in this setting, it may be prudent to require that the offering statement be filed with and reviewed by the securities regulator.[50]

No doubt, promoters also can "hype" an offering where investors are few in number. Sophisticated investors, however, are more likely to distinguish "hype" from "reality" and to demand the delivery of adequate disclosure. Where investors are unsophisticated, on the contrary, there is the need for such investors to receive a basic information package. Nonetheless, due to the monetary costs incurred by issuers to generate a formal disclosure document, application of effectively implemented provisions directed against fraudulent practices may be deemed sufficient where the offering amount is relatively small.

An additional concern is that a supposed limited offering may be in reality a public one where purchasers of large holdings "dump" their securities on the market. If adequate information is not in the public domain, a distribution of securities would have occurred in contravention of investor protection and market integrity objectives. To ameliorate this situation, restrictions on resales may be considered, such as those relating to holding periods (*e.g.*, security must be held for a two-year period) and percentage of stock sold during a specified period (*e.g.*, up to one per cent of the issuer's outstanding stock during a three-month period).[51]

A sound balance must be struck. Imposing overly stringent requirements on issuers and financial intermediaries in the limited offering setting will dissuade these participants from resorting to this capital raising device. Nonetheless, there is legitimate concern that many investors in these types of offerings in emerging capital markets will be individual citizens who

---

[49] Certain SEC rules exempting limited or private offerings from registration prohibit advertising or general solicitation. *See*, SEC Rules 505, 506, 17 C.F.R. § 230.505, 230.506; sources cited notes 45–48 *supra*.

[50] *See* generally, R. Janvey, *Regulation of the Securities and Commodities Markets* paras. 4.01–4.02 (1992); Goldstein, Ramshaw & Ackerson, "An Investment Masquerade: A Descriptive Overview of Penny Stock Fraud and the Federal Securities Laws", 47 *Bus. Law.* 773 (1992).

[51] *Cf.* SEC Rule 144, 17 C.F.R. § 230.144 which sets forth certain criteria that a shareholder must satisfy in order to come within the rule's protection. *See*, Steinberg & Kempler, "The Application and Effectiveness of SEC Rule 144", 49 *Ohio St. L.J.* 473 (1988).

have relatively modest savings and limited financial sophistication. Loss of individual investors' savings in speculative investments will have repercussions throughout the affected economy and therefore is a matter of serious concern.[52]

7.2 Institutional investors markets

Generally, institutional investors are financially sophisticated. They have the acumen, experience, personnel and financial wherewithal to make astute investment decisions. They also have the leverage, particularly when acting in concert with other like investors, to induce the issuer to disclose sufficient information. Because there exists a "level playing field" in this context, there is good reason to allow the various participants to fend for themselves. Hence, arguably only rules relating to fraud need to be applied here.

Under this framework, an emerging securities market may seek to develop a stock exchange where solely institutional (or other sophisticated) investors having a specific net worth (such as $5 million) may participate. For each issuer that seeks to list its securities on the exchange, negotiations would ensue among the participants (the subject issuer, financial intermediaries, and prospective investors) concerning the degree of disclosure that the issuer would provide to the market on a periodic basis, with respect to which the issuer would be contractually bound to comply. Alternatively, the exchange (or governmental regulator) may promulgate minimum disclosure guidelines that all listed companies must meet, while still enabling the parties to negotiate more rigorous requirements.

The prohibitions against fraud should apply in this setting. SRO or government overseers, therefore, would monitor occurrence of fraudulent practices and, depending on the framework adopted, help ensure compliance with applicable disclosure mandates. Procurement of the necessary fees from market participants to fund this mechanism should be attainable.

This framework should be attractive to market participants. Costs of raising capital for issuers are minimized. Qualified institutions can fend for themselves, negotiating the requisite degree of disclosure in both the initial and secondary markets as a condition for investing in the subject issuer. Mandated disclosure, if any, imposed by regulators is not overly burdensome. Surveillance directed against fraud remains within the purview of the SRO and government authorities.[53]

---

[52] *See*, Jennings, "The Role of the State in Corporate Regulation and Investor Protection", 23 *Law & Contemp. Prob.* 193 (1958). *See* also, F. Fabozzi & F. Modigiliani, *Capital Markets* (1992); Gray, "The Legal Framework for Private Sector Development in a Transitional Economy: The Case of Poland", 22 *Ga. J. Int'l & Comp. L.* 283 (1982).

[53] *See*, Steinberg & Lansdale, "Regulation S and Rule 144A: Creating a Workable Fiction in an Expanding Global Securities Market", 29 *Int'l Law.* 43 (1995).

7.3 Public offerings

When issuers elect to tap unsophisticated investors for funds on a wide-spread basis, the need for disclosure and surveillance should prevail. Investors in these types of offerings normally are citizens of the country where the emerging securities market is situated. Being uninitiated investors, they are more easily induced to part with their funds on the basis of false hopes and outright lies. Although sound regulation cannot prevent the overly gullible from being manipulated, it can minimize the degree of investor intoxication enveloping such offerings.[54]

Requiring sufficient disclosure and implementing adequate surveillance against fraud should deter sharp practices. If a regulatory authority has been established, the filing with such authority of the applicable disclosure documents transmitted to investors should be mandated. Application of a cost-benefit analysis in this context calls for these measures. Although capital raising may be impeded, this downside is outweighed by the realistic prospect that, in the absence of use of these measures, a significant number of the country's citizenry will suffer financial harm (some of catastrophic magnitude). Such loss would redound to the applicable country's economic detriment in terms of both consumer spending power and savings. Indeed, for those individuals who were to incur severe financial loss, basic needs such as food and housing may no longer be afforded. Hence, unlike offerings made to sophisticated or foreign investors, a far greater likelihood of adverse economic consequences impacting on domestic affairs persists in this setting. Therefore, greater prudence should be demanded.[55]

7.4 Secondary markets

In order for an emerging securities market to prove successful, a sound secondary trading market must develop. Without the presence of a liquid secondary market that is efficient in pricing and maintains basic standards of fair practice, sophisticated investors will be reluctant to participate.

To develop a sound secondary trading market, certain conditions must be met. First, there must be a sufficient number of buyers and sellers so that liquidity of investment is enhanced. Second, adequacy of disclosure is key to enable market participants to make informed investment decisions. Where the applicable market consists of solely sophisticated investors (normally institutions) having an impressive net worth, then the extent of disclosure called for may be subject to negotiation as a matter of contract between the issuer, financial intermediaries, and affected investors. The understanding reached should be enforceable as well by the subject

---

[54] *See*, Seligman, "The Historical Need for a Mandatory Corporate Disclosure System", 9 *J. Corp. L.* 1 (1979).

[55] Hence, securities regulation is focused at problems "as old as the cupidity of sellers and the gullibility of buyers". 1 L. Loss, *Securities Regulation* 3 (2d ed. 1961); sources cited note 52 *supra*.

exchange, with delisting of the issuer an alternative sanction for non-compliance.[56] Third, financial intermediaries, such as broker-dealers, market-makers, and specialists, should exist in sufficient numbers with each having adequate capital to facilitate market liquidity. And, fourth, given the continual threat of abusive activity (*e.g.,* stock manipulation, insider trading, and undisclosed excessive brokerage commissions) as well as the lack of financial security (*e.g.,* failure by broker-dealers to have sufficient net capital or provide for accurate recording of trades), there should be adequate surveillance and enforcement measures implemented.[57]

Fulfillment of the foregoing conditions, of course, will not ensure the presence of an attractive secondary trading market. To induce foreign investment, the value of the securities purchased and the prospect for bountiful profit are key and, depending on the applicable market, may override other considerations. Moreover, cost considerations may prevent an emerging securities market from expending the resources necessary for an optimal secondary trading market to exist. Nonetheless, satisfaction of the conditions above should normally provide great impetus for facilitating the development of an effective secondary trading market.

8 OVERSEEING FINANCIAL INTERMEDIARY CONDUCT – INDEED A DELICATE TASK

Financial intermediaries are essential players in capital markets. They provide needed liquidity, structuring of transactions, and, at times, capital to emerging securities markets. Their roles may range from an investment banker orchestrating a distribution of securities on behalf of an issuer, to that of a broker acting as agent for its clientele, to that of a dealer engaging in transactions for its own account. Because of their function in the structuring and consummation of securities offerings, mergers, and acquisitions (euphemistically called "deals"), financial intermediaries (particularly investment bankers) frequently hold the "passkey". Phrased differently, financial intermediaries often control the red or green light to the successful completion and marketing of securities deals.[58]

With this power comes the risk of abuse. As alluded to previously,[59] financial intermediaries may engage in improper conduct such as stock manipulation, insider trading, charging undisclosed excessive commissions, and a broad range of other unfair practices in contravention of what is known as the "shingle" theory.[60] They also may run foul of

---

[56] *See* generally, Doherty, Okun, Korostoff & Nofi, "The Enforcement Role of the New York Stock Exchange", 85 *Nw. U.L. Rev.* 637 (1991).

[57] *See,* sources cited notes 9, 19, 50, 56 *supra*.

[58] *See, Chris-Craft Industries, Inc. v. Piper Aircraft Corp.*, 480 F. 2d 341, 380 (2d Cir. 1973); M. Steinberg, *Securities Regulation: Liabilities and Remedies*, § 5.04[4] (1995).

[59] *See, supra* notes 56–57 and accompanying text.

[60] The "shingle" theory posits that a broker-dealer, by hanging out its "shingle", impliedly represents that its behavior and the conduct of its employees will be equitable and will comply with professional norms. *See, Hanly v. SEC*, 415 F. 2d 589, 596–597 (2d Cir. 1969).

standards relating to financial integrity. Failure to retain adequate capital, accurately record trades, and provide effective settlement and clearing mechanisms will wreak havoc not only on the delinquent financial intermediary, but, if severe, upon the affected capital markets.[61]

Emerging securities markets, therefore, must oversee financial intermediary practices from both fraud and financial integrity perspectives. Definitive rules administered by the applicable regulator having sufficient enforcement powers should be effectuated. In this context, three key concepts are registration, oversight, and enforcement.

Registration by such financial intermediaries as investment advisers, brokers, and dealers with the applicable government regulator or SRO should be mandated. Compulsory registration enables the regulator to qualify those meeting defined standards, acts as a tracking procedure for identifying subject intermediaries under its oversight authority, and serves as a fee-generating vehicle for costs incurred. These fees (as well as a tax levied on brokerage commissions) also may be used to establish a system of investor insurance to provide protection against catastrophe should a broker-dealer become insolvent or abscond from the jurisdiction with its customers' assets.[62]

To help ensure market integrity, oversight by the applicable regulator over financial intermediaries is crucial. Such broker-dealer, investment adviser, or other intermediary should be required to subscribe to enumerated rules of fair practice and financial integrity, file reports with the regulator detailing its compliance with capital adequacy standards, and be subject to inspections by SRO or government personnel for ascertaining its adherence to specified financial and operational directives. Because of the adverse fallout that all too realistically may occur due to a broker-dealer's insolvency or grossly abusive practices, the applicable regulator should assume an active oversight function in this setting.[63]

To induce financial intermediaries to follow specified requirements and to redress instances of misconduct, the applicable regulator must have sufficient enforcement powers. The powers provided should cover the broad range of prospective non-compliance. For technical violations causing relatively little harm, entry of a cease and desist order should be appropriate for a first-time violator. For repeat violators and for more serious offenders, such as where fraud is perpetrated on certain clients or where a broker-dealer fails to carry sufficient net capital, heftier penalties are warranted. Examples include levying a significant monetary fine and suspending for a certain period of time the subject violator from engaging in certain (or all) of its business activities. For egregious violators or where there is a systematic breakdown throughout the organization, extreme

---

[61] *See*, R. Janvey, note 50 *supra*.

[62] *See* generally, Crespi, "The Reach of the Federal Registration Requirements for Broker-Dealers and Investment Advisors", 17 *Sec. Reg. L.J.* 339 (1990); Lipton, "A Primer on Broker-Dealer Registration", 36 *Cath. U.L. Rev.* 899 (1987).

[63] *See*, A. Bromberg & L. Lowenfels, *supra* note 19, at § 5.7; R. Janvey, *supra* note 50, at paras. 4.01–4.02; M. Steinberg & R. Ferrara, *supra* note 9, at §§ 2:17, 13:01–13:11.

measures may be necessary. In such circumstances, the regulator may seek to bar the violator from conducting business, have a receiver appointed to preserve assets, and pursue criminal prosecution.[64]

Thus, the applicable regulator should have within its enforcement arsenal a wide array of weaponry, deploying the appropriate mechanisms to disarm its intended targets. Although granting such enforcement powers may lead to overzealousness on occasion, the risks posed justify this risk. An efficiently run regulatory structure, containing levels of internal review by relatively detached personnel, along with independent scrutiny by a judge or hearing examiner, should rein in much of the overreaching that otherwise might ensue. Moreover, in view of the tenuous situation that most emerging capital markets experience, there is widespread recognition that enforcement powers should be finely tuned and used only where clearly necessary. Otherwise, legitimate and well-heeled financial intermediaries will take their activities elsewhere, leaving the affected country without an essential player in its capital market structure.[65]

Irrespective of an emerging capital market's adoption of relatively comprehensive procedures with respect to financial intermediaries situated within its borders, vigilance also needs to be directed at rogue "cross-border" broker-dealer practices. In today's awesomely paced technological world, there exists the continual threat of fraud by financial intermediaries and other market participants from locations abroad, having adverse ramifications in the affected emerging securities market. To help guard against such cross-border abuses, understandings of cooperation should be entered into with securities authorities from other nations. Pursuant to such understandings, each regulator agrees to provide law enforcement assistance and technological support to the other when there is a violation of its laws perpetrated from the other's jurisdiction. This mutuality of obligation approach, based on the concept of reciprocity, should ameliorate to some extent cross-border market abuses.[66]

9 CONCLUSION

The foregoing discussion illustrates the difficult challenge facing emerging securities markets. To attract a continual flow of outside capital, such markets must ordinarily offer the realistic lure of attractive profit, implement a sufficiently credible regulatory framework to provide foreign institutional investors with some degree of comfort, and induce the

---

[64] *See, e.g., SEC v. Prudential Securities* [1993 Transfer Binder] Fed. Sec. L. Rep. (CCH) para. 97,780 (D.D.C. 1992); *SEC v. Milken* [1989–1990 Transfer Binder] Fed. Sec. L. Rep. (CCH) para. 95,200 (S.D.N.Y. 1990); *In re Rooney Pace, Inc.* [1987–1988 Transfer Binder] Fed. Sec. L. Rep. (CCH) para. 84,206 (SEC 1987).

[65] *See,* H. Scott & P. Wellons, *supra* note 2, at 1000–1004. *See* also, Butler *et al.,* "Draft Law of the Russian Federation on Securities", 8 *Butterworth's J. Int'l Bank. & Fin. L.* 133 (1993).

[66] *See,* Pitt & Hardison, "Games Without Frontiers: Trends in the International Response to Insider Trading", 55 *Law & Cont. Prob.* 199 (1992).

participation of sophisticated financial intermediaries while engaging in delicate yet effective oversight. Certainly, this task is difficult at best.

Even for those emerging markets that seek to attract principally domestic sources of capital, tough issues must be addressed. While seeking to facilitate the development of an active securities exchange, perceptions will exist that the market should function without impediment and that regulation should play the role of nominal bystander. In this context, however, proliferation of abusive practices impacts directly on the affected country's citizenry. Severe losses suffered by its investor-citizens may spell economic disaster in terms of diminished consumer spending power and even inability to purchase essential goods on the same level as before the débâcle. Hence, sensitive benefit/loss assessments must be made. The balance struck should involve considerations that focus on promoting capital formation, facilitating the presence of a viable securities market, and providing some meaningful protection for its citizen-investors against the specter of rampant securities market fraud.

Determinations should also be made by emerging capital markets with respect to specific market abuses and corporate control transactions. For example, statutes and rules may be prescribed relating to insider trading practices[67] as well as mergers and acquisitions.[68] The specificity and detail of the approach adopted with respect to such practices and events will reflect policy considerations as well as perceptions of acceptable business conduct.

To help ensure periodic review of the framework then in place, institution of "sunset" provisions may be incorporated in statutes and regulations.[69] Such an approach may be useful for emerging capital markets that foresee incremental change. While not foreclosing in any way revision of applicable statutes and regulations at an earlier point, "sunset" provisions seek to compel reconsideration of the existing framework by a specified date in the future. However, the huge drawback attendant upon such a timed review is the risk that the governing authorities will be concerned with more pressing priorities or a different climate will prevail in the legislature, thereby causing insufficient attention to be focused on the issue. Indeed, if preoccupied with more urgent matters, the legislature may allow the applicable statutes to lapse, leaving no governing law in existence. This prospect should give one pause before endorsing the use of "sunset" provisions.

Irrespective of the contours of the system in place for an emerging securities market, a frequently important criterion impacting on ultimate success or failure is whether the various participants lend their support. Without receiving such approbation from affected constituencies, the road to success

---

[67] *See* generally, M. Steinberg & W. Wang, *Insider Trading* (1996).

[68] *See* generally, H. French, *International Law of Take-Overs and Mergers* (1987); N. Poser, *International Securities Regulation* (1991); *Tender Offers: Developments and Commentaries* (M. Steinberg ed. 1985).

[69] *See*, 27 Sec. Reg. & L. Rep. (BNA) 853 (June 2, 1995) (concept of U.S. federal agency funded through user fee).

may be far too arduous. Enabling key players to provide input, engage in dialogue, and reach consensus will facilitate their "buying into" the system. By having a perceived stake in this framework, hopefully they will be more receptive to work toward its success. Thus, emerging securities markets embark on a difficult journey. Persuading affected constituencies to embrace the framework adopted represents for many emerging securities markets a critical determinant.

10 REFERENCES

A. Bromberg & L. Lowenfels, *Securities Fraud and Commodities Fraud* (1995).

F. Fabozzi & F. Modigliani, *Capital Markets* (1992).

H. Ffrench, *International Law of Take-Overs and Mergers* (1987).

Gower Report (U.K.), on "Review of Investor Protection" (Part I – 1984, Part II – 1985).

R. Janvey, *Regulation of the Securities and Commodities Markets* (1992).

L. Loss & J. Seligman, *Securities Regulation* (3d ed. 1989).

N. Poser, *International Securities Regulation* (1991).

H. Scott & P. Wellons, "Emerging Markets: Privatization and Institutional Investors" in *International Finance: Transactions, Policy and Regulation* 965–1004 (1995).

I. Shihata, *Legal Treatment of Foreign Investment* (1993).

M. Steinberg, *Securities Regulation: Liabilities and Remedies* (1995).

M. Steinberg, *Understanding Securities Law* (2d ed. 1996).

M. Steinberg & R. Ferrara, *Securities Practice: Federal and State Enforcement* (1985 & 1995 supp.).

M. Steinberg & W. Wang, *Insider Trading* (1996).

Trubek, "Toward a Social Theory of Law: An Essay on the Study of Law and Development", 82 *Yale L.J.* 1 (1972).

U.S. SEC, *Report on the Internationalization of Securities Markets* (1987).

21. The U.K. Model of Securities Regulation

Eva Lomnicka[1]
Jane Welch[2]

1 INTRODUCTION

This chapter seeks to describe the essential features of the U.K. securities regulation system and, perhaps more importantly, how it has fared in the relatively few years that it has been operating. In characterising it as a "model", of course no claim is made that it is appropriate for wholesale transplant elsewhere. It is presented as a model in the sense of a viable system from which lessons may be learnt – just as in devising the U.K. regime, lessons were learned from securities regulation systems already existing elsewhere.[3]

A word about the background to the present U.K. system is necessary both to explain how the current system came about and to make the obvious point that no regulatory system is imposed in a vacuum but is necessarily a product of the environment – political, legal, economic and social – into which it is established.

The present U.K. system was largely introduced by the Financial Services Act 1986[4] and came into force, for most purposes, in April 1988.[5] By the

---

[1] M.A. (Cantab); LL.B. (Cantab), Professor of Law, King's College, University of London, Barrister.
[2] B.A. (Mod) (Dublin); LL.M. (London), Head of Legal Advice Department, The Securities and Investments Board, London. Written in a personal capacity and therefore the views expressed are not those of the SIB.
[3] In drawing up his proposals, Professor Gower (*see* below) looked at "models" elsewhere and the U.K. "model" that eventually emerged was especially influenced by experience in the U.S., Canada and Australia. Professor Gower had studied the U.S. securities regulation system in his youth and he made clear that this (coupled with some fact-finding visits to other jurisdictions during his inquiry) informed his approach.
[4] *See infra* as to other relevant measures, especially the Public Offers of Securities Regulations 1995, S.I. 1995 No. 1537 (concerning public offers of securities not listed on the Official List of the London Stock Exchange), the Criminal Justice Act 1993, Part V (insider dealing) and the Takeover Code.
[5] *See* the "commencement order": S.I. 1988 No. 740 (C. 22).

beginning of the 1980s London was already a major financial centre with sophisticated trading facilities for securities which, as far as regulation was concerned, relied primarily on so-called "self regulation" by the markets themselves, backed up by some rather outdated, piecemeal statutory legislation.[6] A number of factors combined to render reform desirable. Domestically, there were clear deficiencies in the existing system, especially from the investor protection point of view.[7] Internationally, there was a need to ensure that London maintained its competitive standing as an international financial centre.[8] The existence of a largely successful securities industry meant that evolution and reform of what was already there, not root and branch upheaval, was the obvious way forward. Consistent with the prevailing political philosophy, regulation was not seen as having any role in steering the financial services industry in any particular direction: that was for market forces to determine.[9] Moreover, it was clearly desirable to involve practitioners in the reforming process so that the new system was workable and not destructive of the many sound aspects of it. Such involvement also increased the likelihood that the new system would have the support of those affected by it.

The process by which the new regime was introduced was, of course, reflective of how such matters are achieved in the U.K. generally. It had a number of stages which sought to arrive at the optimum result whilst involving and so preparing those who were going to be most affected. Thus not only the final "model" itself, but also the means whereby it was arrived at, may be of interest.

The government department responsible, then the Department of Trade,[10] commissioned their resident company law consultant, Professor Jim Gower, to propose reforms and his final report[11] became the basis of the Financial Services Act 1986. As is often the case in a complex law reforming project, a two-stage process was adopted: first a very tentative Discussion Document was issued[12] which described the existing system, pin-pointing

---

[6] Mainly the Prevention of Frauds (Investment) Act 1958, largely re-enacting the 1938 Act of the same name which sought to control (i) the then (in 1938) emerging unit trust (mutual funds) industry and (ii) share-pushing. The system pre-FSA 1986 is documented in Gower, *Review of Investor Protection: A Discussion Document* (HMSO, Jan. 1982), Chap. 3 (hereafter: "Gower, Green Paper").

[7] There had been financial scandals in the investment management sphere. Moreover, the Stock Exchange's Rulebook was challenged in the Restrictive Practices Court as being anti-competitive and this made a re-examination of that aspect of securities regulation desirable. *See* further, Gower, "'Big Bang' and City Regulation" (1988) 51 M.L.R. 1.

[8] "In all developed countries proper regulation to protect the interests of investors is seen as a necessary element in the healthy development of financial services": *Financial Services in the United Kingdom: A new framework for investor protection* (Jan. 1985), Cmnd. 9432, para. 1.2 (hereafter "the White Paper").

[9] *See* further, the *White Paper*, esp. Chap. 3.

[10] Since June 1992, the Treasury has had overall responsibility for most aspects of financial services regulation: The Transfer of Functions (Financial Services) Order 1992, S.I. 1992 No. 1315.

[11] Gower, *Review of Investor Protection, Part I* (Jan. 1984), Cmnd. 9125 (hereafter "Gower Report").

[12] Gower, *Review of Investor Protection: A Discussion Document* (HMSO, Jan. 1982), (hereafter: "Gower, Green Paper").

its deficiencies and signposting possible routes to reform. In the light of responses received, Professor Gower produced a final report[13] which set out with some precision his recommendations for a revised regulatory system. The impetus for reform having gathered momentum, the government accepted the need to legislate and set out its proposals in a White Paper[14] which largely (but by no means entirely) reflected Professor Gower's ideas.[15] Despite this comparatively lengthy consultative process, with plenty of opportunity for interested parties to submit their views, the Financial Services Act 1986 had a rather difficult passage through the legislative process. Thus many last-minute amendments[16] were made which ultimately detracted from its coherence.

However, the process did all it could to involve those affected by it and to prepare them for the inevitable changes it introduced. There was then a time-lag between the enactment of the legislation[17] and its implementation[18] – giving the industry (and regulators) time to establish the requisite systems.

The framers of the new Financial Services Act 1986 regime deliberately built into the system a degree of flexibility[19] but even so, significant amendments to the Act itself were made in 1989[20] and part of it[21] was repealed before ever being brought into force. The degrees to which and ease with which a regime may be altered of course depends on the constitutional proprieties of the country in question. In the U.K. there are a number of conventions which require Parliament itself to approve certain types of lawmaking, for example, the creation (or extension) of criminal offences, the imposition of taxation, and thus the extent to which the regime may be speedily altered is necessarily limited by this factor.

2 THE REGIME IN GENERAL

The regulatory approach adopted in the U.K. is to regulate the activity of "investment business" by means of a system of licensing (or authorisation) which both vets who can operate and then seeks to regulate how they operate. The issue of definitions is considered in greater detail below and is obviously crucial in deciding the reach of the regulatory regime. In essence,

---

[13] *See* n. 11, *supra.*

[14] *See* the *White Paper, supra.*

[15] Professor Gower produced a critique of the *White Paper*, noting how it departed from his proposals: Gower, *Review of Investor Protection, Part II* (July 1985).

[16] Especially to the definition provision: Sched. 1 (*see* below). In particular, the important Sched. 1 para. 23 was an afterthought.

[17] In November 1986.

[18] *See* n. 5, *supra.*

[19] In particular, the scope of the Act can be altered by secondary legislation: *see infra.*

[20] By the Companies Act 1989: *see infra.*

[21] Part V. It was repealed and replaced by Public Offers of Securities Regulations 1995, S.I. 1995 No. 1537: *see infra.*

the Financial Services Act 1986 defines "investment" and then uses this term to define the activity which is regulated: the carrying on of "investment business" in the United Kingdom.

One immediate problem is determining the territorial reach of the regime. This is particularly problematic because, of all businesses, investment business transcends national boundaries. In conformity with notions of international comity (and recognising the consequent territorial limitations of law enforcement), States normally seek only to regulate activities within their borders and the scope of the U.K. regime reflects this. Thus the Financial Services Act 1986 only seeks to regulate persons carrying on investment business and investment advertising "in the United Kingdom".[22] "Carrying on business in the United Kingdom" is then defined[23] in terms of maintaining a permanent place of investment business in the U.K.[24] or engaging in the U.K. in investment business.[25] Thus, in so far as persons operate either from the U.K. (even if they target markets elsewhere) or into the U.K., the U.K. regime, in principle, catches them. There is a distinction between the business for which authorisation is required by the Act (investment business in the U.K., as defined) and, once a person is authorised, the investment business which is consequently regulated. Thus, once a person is carrying on investment business in the U.K., then the regulatory regime applies to them and this regulatory regime is not co-extensive with investment business in the U.K. Further, due to the global nature of securities activities, the U.K. regulators play their part in liaising and co-operating with their counterparts elsewhere. Moreover, they are statutorily empowered[26] to take enforcement action in the U.K. in support of overseas regulators.[27]

A second consideration which any regulatory regime faces is that it necessarily restricts competition and thus needs to be accommodated within the domestic (and for members of the EU, the EC) competition regime. As far as domestic competition law is concerned, the Financial Services Act 1986 establishes a special competition regime which provides for the special scrutiny of the securities regulation regime so that it does not distort competition more than is necessary for the protection of consumers.[28] As far as EC competition law is concerned, in theory there are no specific concessions for domestic[29] investor protection regimes.[30] Thus the

---

[22] *See* FSA, s. 3 (investment business); s. 57 (advertising). *See* also s. 56 (unsolicited calls to or from the U.K.).

[23] In FSA, s. 1(3).

[24] FSA, s. 1(3)(a).

[25] FSA, s. 1(3)(b): here the definition of "investment business" is subject to certain exclusions in Sched. 1, Part IV and the operator is termed an "overseas person".

[26] *See* FSA, Part I, Chap. XV, added by the Companies Act 1989.

[27] *See* especially, FSA, s. 128C.

[28] *See* FSA, Part I, Chap. XIV and *see* n. 7, *supra*.

[29] The London Stock Exchange, when acting as competent authority under FSA, Part IV (*i.e.* provisions enacted in consequence of EC law) is a special case.

[30] Indeed, DG IV made clear its view that the Minimum Commissions Agreement previously operated by the life assurance industry was anti-competitive and this delayed the recognition of the relevant SRO: LAUTRO.

relevant notifications have, in general, been made to the Commission and no action is expected to be taken by it.

3 SCOPE OF THE REGULATORY SYSTEM

The initial issue in establishing any regulatory system is to decide on its reach. This will depend on the existing domestic markets and anticipated further developments. Two aspects of the U.K.'s approach merit mention: the inherent flexibility of its scope and the breadth of its reach.

Securities markets evolve rapidly and any regulatory system must be responsive to these changes. Indeed, one of the lessons Professor Gower drew from the old U.K. system was that it had "ossified".[31] There are at least two ways of dealing with the ossification problem. One is to define the scope of the regime in such a general way that it can accommodate new developments.[32] This creates uncertainty until the point is settled by litigation. Another approach is to adopt a precise definition but allow it to be altered easily and rapidly. In the interests of clarity and certainty, the U.K. has chosen the latter route. The definitions of "investment" and "investment business" – which determine the reach of the U.K. Financial Services Act 1986 – are very prolix.[33] They are not without difficulty[34] but they may be altered swiftly by secondary legislation,[35] although in conformity with our constitutional conventions,[36] any extension of the definition (which entails extending the scope of a criminal offence[37]) requires the affirmative resolution procedure to be adopted. As a matter of history, the U.K. definitions have been altered a number of times, largely to rectify initial deficiencies in drafting,[38] illustrating the desirability of getting the regime right to start with as far as possible. One practical problem encountered in the U.K. resulting from the ease with which the definition may be altered, which is a consequence of deficiencies in the publication of legislation that has subsequently been amended, is discovering the exact terms of the most recent version. The problem has been ameliorated by the SIB periodically publishing the definition, as amended.[39]

---

[31] *Gower, Green Paper*, Chap. 5, esp. paras. 5.02, 5.06. Thus it was unclear what constituted a "security" within the Prevention of Fraud Investments Act 1958 and the definition failed to catch novel forms of investment.

[32] *See* the "catch-all" definition of "security" in the U.S. Securities Act 1933, s. 2(1) and the voluminous case-law it has spawned.

[33] *See* FSA, Sched. I, Part I ("investment") and Parts II–III ("investment business").

[34] Provisions which have caused particular difficulty are Sched. 1, para. 2 (meaning of "debenture"), s. 75 (meaning of collective investment scheme)) and Sched. 1, para. 13 (arranging deals in investments).

[35] Under FSA, s. 2.

[36] *See supra.*

[37] FSA, s. 4 renders carrying on investment business in the U.K. without authorisation (or exemption) a criminal offence, *see* further *infra.*

[38] For example, certain Government index-linked investments were later excluded by the Financial Services Act 1986 (Restriction of Scope of Act and Meaning of Collective Investment Scheme) Order 1990, S.I. 1990 No. 349, Art. 2 (amending Sched. 1, paras. 3 and 9).

[39] As "Guidance Releases".

The U.K. definitions of "investment" and "investment business", as well as being very specific, are also very wide. The decision was taken to include "all types of property except physical objects over which the purchaser has exclusive control after their acquisition".[40] Thus, the definition of investment covers all investment media from traditional securities,[41] including interests in collective investment schemes,[42] through to financial and commodities derivatives[43] and (a peculiarity of the U.K. market where a favourable tax regime for investing in this way exists) to certain life assurance policies.[44] In other contexts, for example in the EC[45] and the U.S., the scope of securities regulation is narrower, in particular in not extending to commodities derivatives.[46] Having one regulator responsible for all forms of investment obviously avoids demarcation disputes. However, U.K. securities regulation, in common with other such regimes, does stop short of regulating bank deposits[47] although certificates of deposit are expressly included.

4 INSTITUTIONAL QUESTIONS

Much debate in the U.K. centred (and still centres) on the institutional nature of the regulatory bodies. This may appear puzzling to persons from other legal systems where a government agency – whether or not aided by self-regulating associations – is the obvious form of regulator. The debate is explicable in terms of the previous U.K. system which was largely self-regulatory in the sense of having evolved without direct legislative intervention,[48] by market players deciding that it was in their interests that they regulate their operations themselves. Many aspects of self-regulation were regarded as desirable: it was close to and therefore sensitive to the nature of the market, it operated quickly and flexibly, it had the support of the market operators themselves and it was self-funding.[49] Thus, the received wisdom was that "self-regulation" was to be preserved as much as possible.

---

[40] *Gower Report*, para. 4.02.

[41] *i.e.,* shares and loan stock: FSA, Sched. 1 paras. 1–3, 4 (warrants), 5 (ADRs and EDRs).

[42] FSA, Sched. 1, para. 6.

[43] FSA, Sched. 1, paras. 7 (*certain* options), 8 (futures), 9 (contracts for differences).

[44] FSA, Sched. 1, para. 10 – if the policy is used as an investment vehicle and is not merely term assurance.

[45] *See* the Investment Services Directive (Directive 93/22, (1993) O.J. L141/27), Annex, which defines the scope of that measure.

[46] In the EU there are no concrete plans to extend harmonisation to commodities futures firms. In the U.S., commodities markets are regulated not by the SEC but by the CFTC (Commodities Futures Trading Commission).

[47] For the avoidance of doubt they are excluded from the definition of "investment" by FSA. Sched. 1, para. 2, Note (c). Banking is regulated by the Bank of England under the Banking Act 1987.

[48] However, self-regulation was sometimes set up in order to forestall statutory regulation, as was the case in the setting up of the Takeover Panel noted below.

[49] In so far as a government agency is not responsible, it enables government to distance itself from any regulatory failings – unless they become so great that the government is criticised for not taking responsibility.

There was also a fear, verging on paranoia, that the markets would be stifled by an insensitive, bureaucratic and lawyer-dominated governmental agency along the U.S. SEC model.[50] Thus, much energy was spent in devising a regime which retained a degree of "self-regulation", albeit within a statutory framework. The statutory framework was necessary in order to address the obvious drawbacks of "pure" self-regulation: agency-capture, limited enforcement and investigative powers and lack of political accountability. In addition, the European Convention on Human Rights[51] requires the intervention of a "tribunal established by law" if a person's livelihood is at risk. In consequence, the Financial Services Act 1986 requires regulators to have public interest representation[52] and to act in the public interest[53] and there is a degree of political accountability.[54]

The end result is a notoriously complex institutional system which requires some explaining. Regulatory powers are given to a minister answerable to Parliament but those powers may be (and have been) transferred[55] to a "body ready and willing" to undertake them which satisfies various statutory criteria (a "designated agency"): the SIB. The SIB is a private corporation (technically a company limited by guarantee) and as a matter of history, was incorporated in June 1986 whilst the Financial Services Act 1986 was going through its legislative stages, in anticipation of becoming the designated agency. Indeed, the SIB lobbied in favour of certain provisions in the Financial Services Act 1986 which were going to affect it.[56] Thus the central, umbrella regulatory body in the financial services area is a private corporation exercising statutory powers delegated to it by government. These powers may be revoked and in this way the activities of the SIB are, to a limited extent, subject to political control.[57] Again, the degree of political control and thus accountability in relation to securities regulation is a delicate matter that reflects what is regarded as constitutionally appropriate. Some argue that the public interest is not

---

[50] *See Gower Report*, Chap. 3 which pointed out that these caricatures of the SEC were exaggerated.

[51] Art. 6.

[52] *See* FSA, Sched. 7, para. 1 (constitution of SIB); Sched. 2, para. 5 (governing body of SROs).

[53] *See* the requirement that they promote and maintain high standards of integrity and fair dealing: FSA, Sched. 7, para. 5 (SIB); Sched. 2, para. 7 (SROs).

[54] Considered *infra*. The issue of limited enforcement and investigative powers is dealt with by giving the SIB certain statutory powers see especially ss. 6, 61 (considered *infra*), 105 (investigation powers). As for the need for a tribunal established by law, *see infra* as to direct authorisation by the SIB (n. 58) and the possibility of appeals against its authorisation and disciplinary decisions to the Financial Services Tribunal.

[55] FSA, s. 114.

[56] For example, it argued strongly that it and its officers should be immune from liability in damages whilst exercising regulatory functions. *See* now, s. 187 noted *infra*.

[57] The SIB must produce an annual report (FSA, s. 117) which is laid before Parliament and its Chairman appears before and is questioned by the Treasury Select Committee. Its governing body is appointed jointly by the Treasury and the Bank of England (FSA, Sched. 7, para. 1).

served by having the regulators so far removed from parliamentary accountability[58] whilst others view this distance between government and financial services regulation as entirely proper.

The SIB in turn recognises "self-regulating organisations", or SROs (and, for professionals such as lawyers and accountants peripherally engaged in investment business, existing professional bodies) which have to satisfy it as to various statutory criteria.[59] The recognised SROs are in fact the front-line regulators since it is mainly[60] they who confer authorisation on persons carrying on investment business by admitting them to membership[61] and then regulating how they operate. (The recognised professional bodies perform a similar function in authorising their professional members by a process of "certification"[62].) By the process of admission to membership, SROs vet their members by deciding if they are "fit and proper" to undertake the relevant types of investment businesses regulated by the SRO.[63] Again, the SROs are private bodies but the criteria they have to satisfy for recognition[64] seek to ensure that they are credible regulatory agencies operating in the public interest.

Ensuring that appropriate SROs emerged and obtained recognition was not an easy exercise. Originally, five functionally based SROs obtained recognition.[65] Most arose from a regrouping of existing associations of market operators. For various reasons, including limited resources, a redrawing of the demarcation lines occurred and now[66] there are three SROs: SFA,[67] IMRO[68] and PIA.[69]

The evolution of the U.K. regime from the institutional point of view is instructive for a number of reasons. In so far as there existed an old regime with strengths – for example, the positive aspects of self-regulation – these

---

[58] As noted *infra*, the front-line regulators of authorised firms are the SROs which are even further removed from political accountability.

[59] FSA, s. 10 (SROs) and s. 18 (RPBs). The criteria are set out in those sections and in Sched. 2 and 3 respectively.

[60] Authorisation is also obtainable from the SIB (FSA, s. 25), but it strongly encourages firms to seek authorisation from the relevant SRO.

[61] FSA, s. 7.

[62] FSA, s. 15. Some firms are authorised "automatically" by virtue of provisions in the FSA, *viz.* ss. 22, 23, 24. Moreover, banks based and authorised in other EEA States may take advantage of the Second Banking Directive "passport" and operate in the U.K. without further authorisation: *see* the Banking Coordination (Second Council Directive) Regulations 1992, S.I. 1992 No. 3218.

[63] *See* FSA, Sched. 2, para. 1.

[64] *See* n. 59, *supra*.

[65] TSA (The Securities Association), FIMBRA (Financial Intermediaries, Mangers and Brokers Regulatory Association), LAUTRO (Life Assurance and Unit Trust Regulatory Organisation), IMRO (Investment Management Regulatory Organisation) and AFBD (Association of Futures Brokers and Dealers).

[66] In April 1991, TSA and AFBD merged to form the SFA. PIA was recognised as an SRO in the summer of 1994.

[67] The Securities and Futures Authority.

[68] *See* n. 65, *supra*.

[69] Personal Investment Authority, comprising ex-members of FIMBRA, LAUTRO and (to some extent) IMRO, and covering the retail sector. However, FIMBRA and LAUTRO presently remain authorised for transitional purposes.

aspects were carefully retained whilst their weaknesses were tackled. The price paid was institutional and operational[70] complexity. Moreover, it was realised that regulatory resources, both in terms of financial cost and expertise, were limited and thus a concentration of them in a few regulators was positively encouraged.[71] This had the added advantage of reducing demarcation disputes between regulators which are not only wasteful of resources but risk problems falling through the cracks. Despite there being a tradition of regulation, the financial services industry needed some persuading that the new regime was necessary. In particular, the relevance of the public interest was not always appreciated by some of the SRO members who were more used to regarding their "regulator" as a trade association acting in their interests. This was particularly so as the costs of regulation (including the costs of prosecuting the unregulated) are paid for by membership fees from the regulated. Again, this is consistent with the political philosophy of the time in the U.K. – that government funding should be kept to the minimum – but when the regulated fund their own regulation they naturally expect considerable say in how this regulation affects them. This is, of course, part of the wider problem of striking the right balance between the needs of the market operators on the one hand and the market users and wider public interest on the other.

5 JUDICIAL CONTROL OF REGULATORS

The role of litigation, in particular in challenging how regulators operate,[72] has caused debate in the U.K. both from the private and public law point of view. By way of background, received wisdom is that, in the financial markets context, litigation is to be avoided as being disruptive of the smooth operation of markets in general and regulation in particular.[73] The law reflects this approach.

As far as public law is concerned, the activities of persons undertaking public functions are susceptible to judicial review.[74] This is not an appeals procedure whereby the merits of a decision are examined[75] but a means of ensuring that the decision-making process was proper. One of the problems raised by having self-regulatory, private bodies involved in financial services regulation was the question whether they were susceptible to judicial

---

[70] *See* the discussion of the rulebooks and sanctions *infra*.

[71] The SIB orchestrated the establishment of the PIA when it became clear that the existing SRO network (in particular FIMBRA) could be improved.

[72] *See* also *infra* as to s. 62 litigation.

[73] For example, *see* the comments of the Court of Appeal in the *Datafin* case, noted *infra*.

[74] Supreme Court Act 1981, s. 31. For the procedure, *see The Supreme Court Practice* (The White Book), RSC, Ord. 53.

[75] Except in so far as the decision way be judged irrational or *"Wednesbury* unreasonable" (after the decision of that name establishing this ground of challenge: *Associated Provincial Picture Houses Ltd. v. Wednesbury Corp.* [1948] 1 K.B. 223).

review at all. In a landmark case[76] the courts decided that, as the Takeover Panel[77] clearly operated in the public domain, its decision were judicially reviewable, although the judgment went on to stress the need of the courts to be sensitive to the disruptive nature of litigation in exercising their judicial review functions. This established the important principle that decisions of private bodies, if exercising public functions, were judicially reviewable and subsequent case-law confirmed that the decisions of both the SIB[78] and SROs[79] may be challenged in this way.[80] However, the emerging case-law in the context of the judicial review of financial markets regulation generally[81] indicates that the courts are cautious in upholding challenges too readily. Two main reasons are given for this. First, as noted above, there is the view that the litigation disturbs the smooth operation of the financial markets and is often one of many tactical devices used by market operators. Thus, courts will use their discretion to refuse leave to consider the issue at all if it is an unmeritorious, tactical challenge, will not exercise their discretion to stop the decision taking effect pending resolution of the dispute and, in giving relief, will be likely not to overrule any decision but declare prospectively how it should have been taken. Secondly, the courts appear to be displaying deference to the expertise of regulators which they are not ready to criticise.[82]

As far as private law is concerned, the Financial Services Act 1986,[83] confers immunity from liability in damages on the regulators unless they act "in bad faith".[84] The rationale behind this immunity is that regulators should not be inhibited from regulating effectively, by fears of liability to huge damages claims should their activities cause loss. To borrow a term from the medical negligence field, the policy is to discourage "defensive regulation". In fact, as far as negligence claims are concerned, this immunity probably reflects the common law where regulators have generally escaped liability.[85] However, in other contexts this immunity has been invoked.[86]

---

[76] *R v. Panel on Takeovers and Mergers ex parte Datafin* [1987] Q.B. 815 (CA).

[77] Considered briefly *infra*.

[78] *R v. SIB ex parte IFAA, The Times*, 18 May 1995 – although there was never any real doubt that the SIB was subject to judicial review as it exercises delegated statutory powers.

[79] *See*, most recently, *R v. LAUTRO ex parte Ross* [1993] Q.B. 17; *R. v. SFA ex parte Panton, Lexis*, 20 June 1994.

[80] The decisions of the Investors' Compensation Scheme have also been challenged: *SIB v. FIMBRA* [1992] Ch. 268 and, most recently, *R v. ICS ex parte Bowden*, (HL), 18 July 1995.

[81] The Court of Appeal decision in *R v. ICS ex parte Bowden* [1995] 1 All E.R. 214, which was reversed by the House of Lords (*see* previous note) was against this trend.

[82] *See* Bingham J's comments in *R v. SFA ex parte Panton*, n. 77, *supra*.

[83] s. 187. This immunity applies only to the SIB, SROs and Stock Exchange (in its capacity as "competent authority in relation to listing) but not (in conformity with constitutional convention) the Treasury.

[84] Other regulators, such as the Bank of England (Banking Act 1987, s. 1(4)), the Council of Lloyd's Insurance Market (Lloyd's Act 1982, s. 14) and auditors' regulators (Companies Act 1989, s. 48) also have similar immunities.

[85] *See Yuen Kun Yeu v. AG of Hong Kong* [1988] A.C. 175 (PC); *Minories Finance Ltd v. Arthur Young* [1989] 2 All E.R. 105; *Davis v. Radcliffe* [1990] 1 W.L.R. 821.

[86] *Melton Medes v. SIB, The Times*, 27 July 1994 and *see SIB v. Lloyd-Wright* [1994] 1 B.C.L.C. 147.

6 REGULATORY METHODS

The U.K. regime uses two traditional methods of regulation: pre-vetting of operators and then subjecting them to a regulatory regime.[87] Both aspects have an effect on competition and, as noted above, the U.K. has addressed the problem of accommodating its regulatory regime within its domestic competition law. As the front-line regulators – the SROs – are technically private bodies, their regulatory powers derive from contract. This results in some limitations; in particular, they have no power over non-members. This is a significant drawback of so-called "pure" self-regulation and, therefore, the Financial Services Act 1986 contains provisions which seeks to remedy this.[88]

6.1 "Fit and proper"

The U.K.'s system of pre-vetting seeks both to be fair to the applicants themselves and to ensure that only "fit and proper" persons are able to operate. As to the former aspect, SIB and SRO rules as to admission, discipline and expulsion "must be fair and reasonable and include adequate provision for appeals".[89] The decisions of the SIB (only[90]) are subject to an appeal to a Financial Services Tribunal.[91] Incidentally, the Tribunal is one of the few aspects of the regime which is publicly funded, in order to ensure the Tribunal's independence.[92] Moreover, there is the possibility, noted above, of challenging regulatory decisions by judicial review. There is no definition of "fit and proper" but from the beginning, the SIB[93] made clear that this connoted: honesty, solvency and competence. Recently, a fourth consideration – the need for adequate internal compliance systems – has been added. One of the beneficial consequences of the new regime has been to extend the focus of vetting from the relatively uncontroversial (and easily objectively verifiable) aspects of honesty and solvency to competence. Thus in proactive mode, the SIB has encouraged the SROs to raise competency standards by providing training and examinations for their members.[94] To ensure that they remain "fit and proper", once admitted to membership, members are subject to monitoring by their SRO.[95]

---

[87] However, in contrast to regulation of, for example, banking and insurance, securities regulation in the U.K. makes extensive use of conduct of business regulation.

[88] Thus the SIB is given statutory power to pursue unauthorised persons. Note also that the SIB has rule-making powers over all authorised persons in areas where the (contractual) SRO rules could not achieve the required result: ss. 51 (cancellation), 54 (compensation fund), 55 (client money). Sometimes the SIB is given rule-making powers where uniformity is particularly required (*e.g.* s. 76(3)).

[89] FSA, Sched. 2, para. 2 – a condition of recognition by the SIB: *see supra*.

[90] A disappointed SRO applicant has to apply to the SIB, be rejected and then challenge that rejection.

[91] FSA, Part I, Chap. IX.

[92] FSA, s. 210.

[93] In its explanatory literature.

[94] It commissioned a report on the issue (Consultative Paper No. 40) and subsequently set up a Training and Competence Panel at the SIB. Again (*see* n. 87, *supra*), this is a special feature of securities regulation, in contrast to banking and insurance regulation.

[95] *See* further, *infra*.

6.2 Rules of conduct

Each SRO has an elaborate rulebook which seeks to regulate how their members operate. Again, the history of the evolution of the SRO rulebooks is instructive in illustrating the unique institutional nature of U.K. securities regulation and, incidentally, in showing how important it is to get the detail of the regulation right.

Before the Financial Services Act 1986, certain "licensed dealers" did have some conduct of business rules imposed upon them[96] and so the concept of regulating at least some types of investment business in this way was not new. However, it was decided to extend conduct of business regulation to all authorised[97] investment businesses and thus a central aspect of the new regime is that each SRO have conduct of business rules applicable to its members. To ensure that the rulebooks were drafted to an appropriate standard – bearing in mind that the SROs, as private bodies, were themselves to be responsible for this – the technique was adopted of requiring[98] the SIB to draft a rulebook[99] and then requiring each SRO, as a condition of recognition,[100] to produce a rulebook which provided "equivalent investor protection". Thus the SIB drafted a lengthy rulebook, complying with certain criteria articulated in the Financial Services Act 1986 (including the important principle that regulation differentiate between different classes of investor – professional and private[101]) and this became the blueprint for the SRO rulebooks. As each SRO applied for recognition, the SIB assessed its proposed rules against its own prototype and, after requiring amendments, recognised each SRO in turn. The result was a proliferation of six differently worded rulebooks (not counting the conduct of investment business rules of the recognised professional bodies) and much dissatisfaction and confusion.

In retrospect – and here the U.K. experience enables clear lessons to be learnt – this SIB blueprint approach was probably not the ideal way of ensuring that the SROs drafted rules of the requisite standard. Again it was a price being paid for "self-regulation" – giving the SROs freedom to devise their own rulebooks, subject only to satisfying the SIB that their investor protection standards were appropriate. However, again in retrospect, perhaps it was salutary to require each SRO to take the initiative and consider how best to deliver investor protection to its members' customers. In any event, a new approach (the "new settlement") was adopted[102] which in essence entailed the SIB drafting a series of relatively simply drafted "core

---

[96] The Licensed Dealers (Conduct of Business) Rules made under the Prevention of Fraud (Investments) Act 1958.

[97] "Exempted persons" (*see* FSA, Part I, Chap. IV) are not subject to conduct of business regulation.

[98] As a condition of designation and transfer of statutory powers (see FSA, s. 114).

[99] *See* esp., FSA, ss. 48, 49, 51, 52, 55, 56, 107.

[100] FSA, s. 10 and Sched. 2, para. 3.

[101] FSA, s. 114 and Sched. 8.

[102] This required primary legislation and the FSA was accordingly amended by the Companies Act 1989.

rules" which were intended to be applied to all SRO members, with the SROs being able to qualify and modify these in relation to their members.[103] To meet complaints that the spirit behind the new regime was obscured by the mass of detailed rules, the SIB also issued (ten) very generally worded "Statements of Principle"[104] which sought to encapsulate the ethos of the regime. This approach undermined the self-regulatory nature of the regime in limiting the rule-making power of the SROs, but it did result in the achievement of some level of consistency between the SRO rulebooks and was therefore judged worthwhile. The "equivalence" test was changed to one of "adequacy"[105] so that the SRO rulebooks (*i.e.*, the SIB's core rules as amplified by the SRO's rules) now had to provide an "adequate level of protection for investors". Moreover, in response to criticism about the financial burdens of the regime, a new provision[106] required the SIB and SROs to have arrangements for taking account of the compliance costs of any rules they framed. It is a measure of the dissatisfaction of the old blue-print approach that it was thought worthwhile, so soon after it had been adopted, both to use parliamentary time to amend the Financial Services Act 1986 and to redraft the rulebooks in order to achieve a workable set of rules.

As a final twist, once the SROs had (as they had to)[107] incorporated the SIB's core rules into their rulebooks, the SIB decided[108] that it would no longer impose its core rules on SRO members – although it retains the power to do so should the SRO rulebooks cease to provide "adequate" investor protection. Thus the face of "self-regulation" – in that the SROs are again theoretically responsible for the content of their rulebooks – has been saved.

It should be noted that, in some areas, in particular where the contractual nature of SRO rules are unable to deliver the required result (for example, affecting the rights of third parties), the Financial Services Act 1986 confers regulation-making power on the SIB in relation to *all* authorised persons.[109] Moreover, the SIB authorises and makes regulations concerning collective investment schemes.[110]

6.3 Rulebooks: content

Although a consideration of the detail of the SRO rulebooks is clearly out of place here, it is useful to note the areas they cover. Conduct of business is

---

[103] *See* FSA, ss. 63A–63B added by Companies Act 1989, s. 194. The modifications (in practice, derogations) had to be agreed with the SIB.
[104] Under FSA, s. 47A, added by Companies Act 1989, s. 192.
[105] FSA, Sched. 2, para. 3 was amended by Companies Act 1989, s. 203.
[106] FSA, Sched. 2, para. 3A (SROs) and Sched. 7, para. 2A (SIB), added by Companies Act 1989, s. 204.
[107] In fact only IMRO and SFA did so.
[108] The Financial Services (Dedesignation) Rules and Regulations 1994.
[109] *See* FSA, ss. 51 (cancellation, n. 115 *infra*), 54 (compensation scheme), 55 (clients' money).
[110] FSA, Part I, Chap. VIII. Ensuring uniformity is the rationale behind reserving to the SIB the power to make regulations under s. 76(3).

regulated with some precision,[111] in particular, obligations are imposed as to "know your customer"[112] and as to extensive disclosure[113] and an attempt is made to deal with conflicts of interest.[114] As noted above, an important aspect of these rules is the distinction made between professional and private investors – the obligations to the latter being considerably more onerous. Provision is also made (by SIB regulations) for a "cooling-off" period in relation to certain retail sales[115] and agreements made in consequence of unsolicited calls in certain circumstances (again, in the retail context) are rendered unenforceable.[116] Investment businesses must also comply with the relevant financial resources rules[117] which seek to minimise the risk of insolvency and reflect the risks inherent in the nature of the business undertaken. The regime seeks to encourage a culture of openness and co-operation with regulators[118] and this is underpinned by a requirement to report periodically, and more frequently in the case of various occurrences, to the relevant regulator.[119]

7 MONITORING, SANCTIONS AND ENFORCEMENT

Of course, the real test of the effectiveness of any regulatory regime is whether, at a practical level, compliance with it is properly monitored and, if necessary, enforced. However, the role of the law is to ensure that the relevant powers are available to the regulators – it is then a matter of how these are resourced and operated – and the framers of the U.K. regime have been astute to ensure that a wide variety of powers are at least theoretically present. At a general level, each SRO is obliged to have "adequate" arrangements and resources for the effective monitoring and enforcement of its rulebook.[120] As regards monitoring, the SROs have reserved powers in their rulebooks to seek information from their members and to make spot checks.

As regards enforcement, the U.K. regime is underpinned by a wide variety of enforcement mechanisms: disciplinary, criminal and civil action.

---

[111] The SIB's statutory conduct of business rule-making power is in FSA, s. 48.
[112] Reflecting Statement of Principle 4.
[113] Reflecting Statement of Principle 5.
[114] Note Statement of Principle 6. "Chinese Walls", for the purposes of the rules, are sanctioned (*see* FSA, s. 48(2)(h)).
[115] *See* the SIB's cancellation rules made under FSA, s. 51. Because they alter the general law (which, of course, cannot be done by SRO rules as they are merely contractual in nature), they apply to all authorised persons.
[116] The SIB's statutory rule-making power is in FSA, s. 56. On unenforceability, *see* further below.
[117] The SIB's statutory rule-making power is in FSA, s. 49.
[118] *See* Statement of Principle 10.
[119] The SIB's statutory rule-making power is in FSA, s. 52.
[120] FSA, Sched. 2, para. 4 – a condition of recognition by the SIB, *see supra*.

7.1 Disciplinary actions by regulators

Perhaps the most significant inducement for investment businesses to comply with their regulators' rulebook is the disciplinary power available. Again, as far as SROs are concerned, these powers derive from the contract of membership.[121] These powers, which are subject to appeals procedures,[122] range from a power to publicly censure,[123] through to powers of intervention in the conduct of business,[124] and culminating in powers of suspension and expulsion from membership.[125] The SROs have all reserved the power to fine their members and relatively large fines and the attendant publicity surrounding their imposition has proved a useful disciplinary tool. Anomalously, the SIB, which derives its disciplinary powers over the few firms it directly regulates from the Financial Services Act 1986, has no statutory power to levy fines.

Reflective of the principle of "self-regulation", the SIB is generally[126] not given disciplinary powers over SRO members. In practice, this has proved a frustration to the SIB when swift action is needed but not forthcoming from the SRO. Thus, just as in the area of the lines of demarcation between the rulebooks, so in the area of discipline some would view this price paid for self-regulation as too high.

7.2 Criminal sanctions

The criminal sanction is reserved for a limited number of contraventions. This is in line with the general U.K. approach to the role of the criminal law. Thus, as a matter of theoretical justification, the view is taken that only certain types of particularly antisocial conduct should be criminalised and as a matter of practicalities the criminal process is generally regarded as too cumbersome a means to enforce financial services regulation. In consequence,[127] operating without requisite authorisation is a criminal offence,[128] as is investment advertising by unauthorised persons without the requisite approval.[129] Otherwise, once a person is authorised, breach of the rulebook is not a criminal offence.[130] However, authorised persons of

---

[121] But reflect the statutory enforcement powers of the SIB, in so far as this is possible by way of contractual provision.

[122] As is required by FSA, Sched. 2, para. 2, noted *supra*.

[123] For the SIB's analogous statutory power in relation to persons authorised by it, *see* FSA, s. 60.

[124] For the SIB's analogous statutory power in relation to persons authorised by it, *see* FSA, Part I, Chap. VI.

[125] For the SIB's analogous statutory power in relation to persons authorised by it, *see* FSA, ss. 28–29.

[126] But *see* s. 61, considered *infra*, and s. 64(4) (limited power of intervention).

[127] But *see* FSA, s. 200 (making false or misleading statements to the SIB (but not SROs) is a criminal offence).

[128] FSA, s. 4 – an offence of strict liability, although there is a due diligence defence.

[129] FSA, s. 57(3). Cold-calling as such, if not permitted, is *not* rendered criminal by FSA, s. 56.

[130] Confirmed by FSA, s. 62(4). The furnishing of false information in purported compliance with the SIB's rules and regulations (but not those of SRO rules) is a criminal offence: FSA, s. 200(1)(b).

course remain subject to the general law, for example on insider dealing,[131] and money laundering.[132] Moreover, the Financial Services Act 1986 does create[133] two specific offences in relation to market conduct which apply to everyone: making misleading statements[134] and market manipulation.[135]

7.3 Civil sanctions

The general civil law, especially that concerning contracts, delictual liability and breach of confidence, of course applies to underpin the regulatory regime. Indeed, as emphasised above, the source of the power that SROs have over their members is the general law of contract (with all its limitations). The U.S. experience with express and implied rights of action for securities regulation violations[136] prompted the U.K. to introduce an express statutory right of action for, *inter alia*, breaches of the SRO rule-books.[137] Many argued that this added little to the general law in that breaches of the rulebooks almost always also give rise to breaches of contract or tort liability.[138] However, being able to point to a specific rule and showing that it had been broken probably did increase the likelihood of claims being made. Again, looking to the U.S. experience, the financial services sector feared that such an express right of action would encourage a litigious climate – hitherto noticeably absent in the U.K. markets – to the detriment of the smooth operation of the markets.[139] These anxieties[140] induced the government, as a corollary to the introduction of the "new settlement" in 1989,[141] to amend the Financial Services Act 1986 by generally limiting the right of action to private investors (as defined by regulation).[142] Thus, in addition to their usual common law rights, private

---

[131] *See* Criminal Justice Act 1993, Part V.

[132] *See* Criminal Justice Act 1993, ss. 29–35. (inserting new ss. 93A–93F into Criminal Justice Act 1988).

[133] One offence (that in s. 47(1)) is a re-enactment of the Prevention of Fraud (Investments) Act 1958, s. 13.

[134] FSA, s. 47(1).

[135] FSA, s. 47(2). Acting in conformity with the SIB's rules in relation to Chinese Walls and certain stabilisation of market activities is not a breach of this provision: FSA, s. 48(6)–(9).

[136] For example, for breach of the catch-all, anti-fraud provision in Securities and Exchange Act 1943, s. 10(b) and SEC Rule 10(b)–5 made thereunder. *See Kardon v. National Gypsum Co.*, 69 F. Supp 512 (E.D. Pa 1946).

[137] FSA, s. 62. Rights of action are also conferred by FSA, s. 131(7) (promotion of life assurance), s. 156B(5) (offer of listed securities without a prospectus) and s. 185(6) (breach of partial restriction notice).

[138] The relationship between the regulatory rules and common law fiduciary duties was considered by the Law Commission in its Consultation Paper No. 124: *Fiduciary Duties and Regulatory Rules: A Consultation Paper* (1992) (HMSO).

[139] *See supra*.

[140] Section 62 was also partly blamed for the prolix and legalistic nature of the original rulebook (*see supra*). As there were, in effect, potentially creating legal liability for their breach, it was regarded as desirable to define that liability precisely.

[141] *See supra*.

[142] FSA, s. 62A, added by Companies Act 1989, s. 193. The relevant regulations are: the Financial Services (Restriction of Right of Action) Regulations 1992, S.I. 1991 No. 493.

investors have an added statutory cause of action if they can establish a breach of the rulebook. In practice, this has proved a useful "extra" claim in usually being easier to establish – all that needs be proved is that the rule was breached[143] and that loss was suffered – than general common law claims. It has also enabled the Investors' Compensation Scheme[144] to process claims relatively quickly on the basis of claims for relatively easy-to-establish breaches of the rules.

A second novel (from the U.K. point of view) aspect of the enforcement of the U.K. regime is the statutory power given to the SIB[145] to bring civil enforcement proceedings for certain breaches of the regulatory regime. Again this is modelled on the U.S. SEC's power to obtain injunctions and disgorgement orders against recalcitrant firms. Individual investors often do not do have the stamina or resources to sue for their losses – which are often individually relatively small although collectively may be very large – and thus there is clearly a role for the regulator to take the initiative on their behalf.[146] The Act[147] provides for three types of court order which the SIB may obtain: injunctions, restitution and disgorgement orders. Moreover, as a matter of general law, the courts have held that, despite the novel nature of the proceedings, the SIB has *locus standi* to apply for an order freezing assets pending the determination of the action.[148]

Turning to the orders available, the restitution order requires the undoing of any transactions and remedying of the contravention.[149] It is available not only against the contravener but also against a "person knowingly concerned in the contravention". Although the case-law on this is as yet sparse,[150] in particular it is unclear how strictly "knowingly" will be interpreted and how actively a person needs to be "concerned"; the provision is a clear incentive to persons who are not themselves subject to the regulatory regime but who may facilitate its breach, to ensure that it is adhered to. The "disgorgement"[151] order enables the SIB to obtain disgorgement of profits and (in theory) compensation for losses suffered as a result of the breach of the regime.[152] The court may order the recovery of "such sum as appears to the court just", having regard to profits made and losses caused and thus, although there is no reported case-law as yet, it would seem that triple damages or some such exemplary damages are not obtainable. In the U.K. there is no tradition, as there is in the U.S., for

---

[143] Often, especially after the "new settlement", the duty imposed by the rule is qualified and thus breach may not be easy to establish.

[144] Established under FSA, s. 54.

[145] And the Department of Trade and Industry.

[146] Individuals are not helped by the UK's legal system, which does not (as such) permit class actions or contingency fees (legal aid being very limited).

[147] FSA, ss. 6, 61.

[148] A so-called "Mareva" injunction: *SIB v. Pantell* [1990] Ch. 426.

[149] FSA, s. 6(2) and s. 61(1).

[150] The only reported decision is *SIB v. Pantell (No. 2)* [1993] Ch. 256 where it was held that solicitors acting for a contravener might be persons "knowingly concerned".

[151] This term is not used in the Act.

[152] FSA, s. 6(4) and s. 61(4).

awarding triple damages and the jurisdiction to order exemplary damages
is very limited. Thus, there have as yet been few calls for the U.K. to expand
the remedial powers of the courts in this way.

Finally, an effective method of encouraging compliance with a regulatory
regime is rendering certain transactions in breach of it unenforceable. As a
matter of general law, the status of contracts made in breach of regulatory
regimes is by no means clear[153] and the Financial Services Act 1986 not only
clarifies this issue but deliberately (and very selectively) uses unenforce-
ablity to underpin selected aspects of its regime. Thus, subject to the discretion of the court, transactions in breach of certain aspects of the regulatory
regime are unenforceable against and may be avoided by the investor. The
relevant breaches which have this consequence are: breach of the general
obligation to be authorised in order to carry on investment business in the
U.K.,[154] breach by unauthorised persons of the advertising provisions[155] and
breach of the unsolicited calls provisions.[156] However, given the drastic
effect unenforceability has on commercial transactions, this device is used
sparingly and so other breaches of the regime – in particular, breaches by
authorised persons of their rulebook – do not have this invalidating
effect.[157]

8 INVESTMENT MARKETS

The regulation of investment markets or exchanges in the U.K. is achieved
in the following way. Operation of an investment market in the U.K. constitutes the carrying on of investment business within the meaning of the
Financial Services Act 1986.[158] Thus, *prima facie*, such activity is subject to
the requirements of authorisation and regulation under that Act.[159] Indeed
the over-the-counter market, in so far as it exists, is regulated in this way by
the operators' SROs. However, an "investment exchange" may become
exempted from the usual SRO regimes by obtaining "recognition" from
the SIB.[160] For overseas investment exchanges[161] – which may, of course,

---

[153] For case-law seeking to resolve the issue in the related insurance context, *see Bedford
     Insurance v. Inst. de Resseguros do Brazil* [1985] 1 Q.B. 966 (insured could not enforce
     insurance contract written by unauthorised insurer), not followed in *Stewart v. Oriental Fire
     and Marine Insurance Co. Ltd* [1985] 1 Q.B. 989. The matter is clarified by FSA, s. 132. *See also
     Hughes v. Asset Managers plc* [1995] 2 All E.R. 669 (CA) (contracts in breach of Prevention of
     Fraud (Investments) Act 1958 not impeachable.
[154] FSA, s. 5.
[155] FSA, s. 57(5)–(10).
[156] FSA, s. 56(2)–(6).
[157] FSA, s. 62(4) makes this clear in relation to rule breaches (and see s. 47A(3) – breach of
     Statements of Principle).
[158] FSA, s. 1 and Sched. 1, Parts II–III – in particular dealing and arranging deals in
     investments.
[159] FSA, s. 3.
[160] FSA, s. 36 – not to be confused with recognition of SROs (or RPBs) which enable these
     bodies to confer authorisation of their members.
[161] Those with head offices outside the U.K.

undertake investment business in the U.K. – recognition is obtainable from the Treasury.[162] The status of "recognised investment exchange" and thus exemption is, however, only accorded to exchanges which satisfy certain criteria as to, *inter alia*, investor protection and liquidity of investments.[163] Moreover, the exchange has to subject itself to a degree of regulation by the SIB. Thus the end result is that the established exchanges such as The London Stock Exchange are in effect regulated by the SIB. However, other more informal dealing arrangements, if falling within the territorial reach of the Financial Services Act 1986, are regulated by virtue of those effecting them having to be authorised and regulated by an SRO in the usual way.

The U.K. regime does avoid the difficulty of defining what an "exchange" is. Apart from the need to be one for recognition purposes, nothing turns on whether an "exchange" exists. The question is whether the activities constitute investment business in the U.K.

As far as the regulation of the U.K. securities markets and the related issue of public offers of securities is concerned, the U.K. system has no particularly special or unique features. These matters have been the subject of significant harmonisation by the EC[164] (as it then was) and the U.K. regime reflects this. Thus, the listing of securities on the Official List of the London Stock Exchange and offers of such securities are governed by Part IV of the Financial Services Act 1986 and secondary legislation made thereunder, which implements the relevant Directives. Securities not qualifying for official listing were eligible for the so-called Unlisted Securities Market (the USM) but this is now being replaced by the Alternative Investment Market (the AIM). As far as public offers of "unlisted" securities[165] are concerned, the original intention was to regulate these under Part V of the Financial Services Act 1986, which was drafted in anticipation of EC harmonisation activity. However, eventually[166] it was decided that the Part V regime was far from ideal and therefore it has been repealed and replaced by the Public Offers of Securities Regulations 1995.[167]

---

[162] FSA, s. 40 – a function not delegable to the SIB (s. 114(6)).

[163] FSA, s. 37 and Sched. 4. Again, a special competition regime is provided for by FSA, Part I, Chap. XIV.

[164] In particular, the Listing Particulars Directive (Directive 80/390/EEC, (1980) O.J. L100/1), as amended by the two mutual recognition directives, Directives 87/345 and 90/211), the Admissions Directive (Directive 79/279, (1979) O.J. 166/21) and the Public Offers (Prospectus) Directive (Directive 89/298/EEC, (1989) O.J. L 124/8).

[165] *i.e.*, securities not listed (or subject to an application for listing) on the Official List of the London Stock Exchange. Thus, this would include securities listed or quoted on other markets, whether in the U.K. (*e.g.* on AIM) or elsewhere.

[166] After two consultation documents, one from the DTI in July 1990 (*Listing Particulars and Public Offer Prospectuses: Implementation of Part V of the FSA 1986 and Related EC Directives*) and one from the Treasury in July 1994 (*Revised Implementation of the EC Prospectus Directive*).

[167] S.I. 1995 No. 1537.

9 TAKEOVERS

Because of its unique nature and history, brief mention should be make of takeover regulation in the U.K. In the late 1950s, disquiet was voiced about the unregulated nature of takeover activity and inevitably there were calls for some form of statutory control. To pre-empt this, a City working group[168] devised what was to become the "Code" of principles and rules to govern the conduct of takeovers:[169] the City Code on Takeovers and Mergers. The Code only concerns itself with ensuring that all target share-holders are treated alike, that there is extensive disclosure and that devices aimed at frustrating the bid are not used. It does not address either the merits of the bid (a matter left to the target shareholders to decide) or the competition effects (which may be referred to the relevant government agency to consider). Initially, it was hoped that the Code would be adhered to without more – an illustration of how effective "self-regulation" in its purest form was at that time perceived to be – but this proved too opti-mistic. Thus in 1968, a body was established to administer the Code: the Panel on Takeovers and Mergers. This is presided over by an independent Chairman[170] and comprises representatives of City institutions. The Panel has been vividly and accurately described[171] as performing its important regulatory function "without visible means of legal support". This is because it has no formal enforcement powers – it is not even in contractual relationship with those it seeks to regulate – and has been largely untouched by legislation.[172] However, in practice, the Panel's rulings are almost invariably obeyed, the real sanction being "cold-shouldering" (*i.e.*, exclusion from the U.K. financial markets) and disciplinary action by another regulator.[173] Moreover, the courts have shown deference to the importance of operating in accordance with the Code when making judgments about market behaviour.[174]

The Panel is regarded as so effective a regulator that there are no serious moves to alter how it operates or to bring it within any statutory structure. Indeed, it was held up as an example of how successful "self-regulation" could be during the debates on the Financial Services Act 1986.[175] Moreover,

---

[168] Orchestrated by the Bank of England.

[169] Preceeded by "Notes on Amagamation of British Businesses".

[170] Often an eminent QC.

[171] In the *Datafin* case, see n. 76 above.

[172] There are oblique references in statutes, for example, FSA, s. 47A(2) enables the SIB to require compliance with any "code … issued by another person" and, as anticipated, the SIB has endorsed the Takeover Code for this purpose.

[173] Thus the London Stock Exchange can suspend the listing of shares affected by breaches of the Code and the FSA regulators also require compliance with the Code by their members.

[174] For example, *Re St Piran Ltd* [1981] 1 W.L.R. 1300; *Re Chez Nico (Resturants)* [1991] B.C.C. 736.

[175] Despite the *Gower Report* assuming it would be brought under the umbrella of its proposed regulatory regime, the *White Paper* decided to leave it alone: para. 13.0.

there was grave disquiet[176] that the EC harmonisation activity in this area[177] would require the U.K. to move away from this unique way of regulating takeovers.

10 CONCLUSION

This discussion has examined some aspects of the U.K.'s domestic securities regulation system. It has been seen that the regime is characterised by a complex institutional structure, usually described as: practitioner-based, statutorily backed regulation. This is a product of the history of such regulation in the U.K., which relied heavily on so-called "self-regulation", and is responsible for the institutional complexities and consequent operational problems noted above. The new U.K. regime still attaches importance to maintaining self-regulation as a central feature of the regime and illustrates how legislative intervention can be used to address the inherent weaknesses of such regulation and make it more responsive to the public interest. Institutional questions apart, other notable features of the U.K. regime are its wide reach and its capacity to respond to changes in the markets. Otherwise, it uses traditional regulatory methods: pre-vetting and imposition of rules as to conduct and financial resources. Moreover, it is underpinned by a wide variety of sanctions, disciplinary, civil and criminal. In devising it, aspects of securities regulation "models" elsewhere[178] were influential and the U.K. regime in turn has influenced subsequent developments in securities regulation.[179] With the inevitable increase in co-operation and interaction between regulators world-wide[180] and harmonisation initiatives,[181] this learning process can only continue.

11 REFERENCES

Blair, *Financial Services: The New Core Rules* (1991) (Blackstone Press).

Fiduciary Duties and Regulatory Rules: A Consultation Paper, Law Commission Consultation Paper No. 124 (1992) (HMSO).

---

[176] Now largely laid to rest.
[177] *See* the EC Commission's Amended Proposal for its 13th Company Law Directive, (1990) O.J. C240/7.
[178] For example, the U.S. "model" is reflected in FSA, s. 62 (express right of action) and ss. 6, 61 (disgorgement orders).
[179] For example, the idea of "Statements of Principle" has been adopted elsewhere and endorsed by IOSCO.
[180] An inevitable response to the global nature of the markets.
[181] *See* the EC's Investment Services Directive, (Directive 93/22, (1993) O.J. L141/27). The U.K. regime largely meets the minimum standards required by this Directive and the modifications needed for its implementation are expected to be in force by the requisite deadline (1 January 1996).

Financial Services in the United Kingdom: A new framework for investor protection (Jan. 1985), Cmnd. 9432.

Gower, *Review of Investor Protection: A Discussion Document* (HMSO, Jan. 1982).

Gower, *Review of Investor Protection, Part I* (Jan. 1984), Cmnd 9125.

Gower, *Review of Investor Protection, Part II* (July 1985).

Lomnicka and Powell, *Encyclopedia of Financial Services Law* (1987) (Sweet and Maxwell).

Page and Ferguson, *Investor Protection* (1992) (Weidenfeld and Nicolson).

Rider *et. al., Guide to the Financial Services Act 1986* (2nd ed. 1989) (CCH Editions Ltd).

Whittaker *et. al., Financial Services: Law and Practice* (1987) (Butterworths).

22.   Starting from Ground Zero: The New Bulgarian Securities Act

Georgi Spasov[1]

1 BACKGROUND ISSUES

1.1 Abstracts on regulation

1.1.1 Regulation

Any regulation is limitation. Therefore, it is usually unwelcome for one reason or another. Sometimes it is believed to be inevitable for one reason, although still unwelcome for another reason.

Securities regulation is yet a manifestation of this dichotomy. It is meant to ensure a fair environment for business, wherein everyone involved wants to appropriate the money of (some of) the others involved. Thus securities regulation should state the rules of the game so that any eventual appropriation may be readily classified as legal or illegal.

Diminishing the barriers to eventual classification as illegal in effect increases investor protection. Investor protection is important for two main reasons :

- legally, the investor is the weaker party, as he is to perform first, letting his money go, and waiting for the performance, promised in consideration;
- politically, investors are numerous and in democratic regimes are a serious social factor.

For all these reasons, all the countries in the world, where securities trading is a relevant business, tend to introduce certain regulation in favour of the

---

[1] Senior Assistant Professor of Commercial Law, Kliment Ohridski University in Sofia, Bulgaria and Partner with Bratoev, Konov, Krastevich & Spasov Lawyers' Partnership. He has been of Counsel to the Economic Commission of the Bulgarian Parliament in drafting the Securities, Stock Exchange and Investment Companies Act.

investors: "... legislation was designed to protect investors from market abuses rather than to alter the structure of the markets".[2] From the economic point of view, such regulation is not necessarily in favour of the investors, as limitations might affect their own return, and finally the costs of regulation are borne by the investors directly, or indirectly – as tax-payers. But from a legal point of view, regulation acts as a kind of insurance policy – it improves the chances of the investors, at least in the two crucial points: investment decision-making; and, return performance to the investors. Thus, the state itself becomes engaged into securities exchange (which otherwise is a private business), legislative authorities being involved obligatorily, and, depending on the particular regulatory model, executive authorities might come to be involved as well. Usually, the judiciary authorities also back-up the effectiveness of the national regulatory scheme.

1.1.2 Market and regulation

Securities regulation is a national business. Philosophers say that the market is one of the factors forming the nation. It seems to have extended to securities markets as well. Thus, every interested country regulates its own securities market, even if it just translates some other country's legislation. It is a matter of sovereignty.

The problems of fixing a model for a securities market are many, because it is a very sophisticated phenomenon, even if as yet undeveloped. Most of its facets might be objects of studies of models by themselves. Usually, a market is compared to the general notion of other such markets, and the defining of the model of a market is therefore done mainly through comparative law studies.

In this aspect, a model of a securities market is inseparable from the model of its regulation. What is more, as economically all securities markets are much the same, it is their regulation that actually brings in the specifics of the model. Thus, a securities market seems to be greatly defined by the applicable regulation, which is in fact the legal framework.

Probably, a securities market is sketched by the three fundamental determinants:

(1) what is on the market;
(2) who is at the market;
(3) how does the market operate.

Speaking of regulatory models, the points will be:

(1) how are the above three basic determinants regulated;
(2) what is compliance and what is its cost;
(3) what risks face non-compliance.

---

[2] Poser, "Restructuring the Stock Markets: A Critical Look at the SEC's National Market System", 56 *N.Y.U.L. Rev.* 883 (1981).

In order to be evaluated properly, a market has to be well-functioning one. It may be a paradox, but it is easier to define as a whole an operating market than an emerging one.[3] The greater problem with defining an "Emerging Market" is that it is more imperfect than a "regular" one, at least for two reasons:

(1) there is no "critical mass" of securities to initiate incessant trade;
(2) there is no "investor confidence", but mere curiosity or, even *mala fide* planning.

Thus there is no integrity of the market.

2 A MARKET IN *STATUS NASCENDI*

2.1 General status

The problem of regulating the securities market in Bulgaria is, of course, of major social importance. With the development of a market-oriented economy and private enterprise over the past few years this problem had to be resolved quickly because of the two traditional considerations: one positive – promotion and facilitation of the investment capital market to the overall benefit of the economic system; and one negative – avoidance of instances of elaborate deception of the investors. However, in the meantime, the securities market in Bulgaria started to develop in the actual absence of any specific regulation, which resulted in several "bubbles" and "pyramids" affairs, bringing social frustration and lack of confidence in the market. Yet, from the viewpoint of the public (certainly not from that of the affected persons) it might be considered to be a kind of useful experience.

The existing securities market in Bulgaria is expected to be enhanced by its regulation. But it is, and will be for some period of time, classified as an "Emerging Financial Market" under any relevant criterion.

2.2 Specific features

One of the points is that there is no "critical mass of securities" yet in order to launch a proper market. At the moment most of the trading is done in governmental securities which are themselves quite safe though not very attractive for dividends. Another issue is privatisation, including mass privatisation through possibly transferable vouchers, but these are so far unlikely to be regulated as securities and their circulation as securities exchange. There are actually no institutional investors such as pension or other funds, and even if such exist, they are piloted by some bank.

---

[3] *e.g.*, U.S. House of Representatives, Report No. 101 – 524 (1990): "In addition to the linkage of the securities and futures markets, the overall marketplace has become increasingly institutional, with significant numbers of institutional portfolio managers utilising indexing strategies to trade the market 'as a whole' through purchases of portfolio of securities, rather than by making judgements regarding the investment value of individual stocks."

In fact, most of the raising of corporate finance is done at the money market, expensively and for short terms, which is modelling the national economy (especially private enterprises) towards commercial intermediation and trade, but not investments and production. Credit substitutes such as leasing, forfeiting, and other forms of commercial credit are flourishing, and even some of the occasional typical investment market operations are completed by the universal banks, all of them being under the tight control of the regulating National Bank. The few attempts to raise finance for private enterprises at the investment market (except for the equity of some banks and tourism companies) have actually been unsuccessful. Some of the trading at the stock (and also commodities and stock) exchanges all over the country is rumoured to be manipulative, and exercised by the issuers for the purpose of elaborate advertising only. Yet there are one or two stock exchanges that try to cope with the classical tasks of the institution.

2.3 The ground

It is at this amateur stage that the legal regulation is expected to come forth, and introduce the whole pattern of the securities market and its environment immediately and most effectively. In such circumstances the approach obviously has to be a more administrative than market one – Regulation v. Free Market. It looks very anti-democratic (which is a sensitive field now in Bulgaria), but it seems also to be true that securities markets always require a strict regulatory regime within a market economy.

3 GENESIS OF THE BULGARIAN SECURITIES ACT

3.1 The zero level

The activities over preparation and adoption of the laws on the regulation of securities and securities exchange have been launched in Bulgaria since 1992, within some two years of the shift towards a market economy. Then the Government and Harvard University concluded the so-called "Harvard Contract", under which there should be prepared drafts by eminent European experts in the area of securities, which drafts were to be further discussed by Bulgarian experts. This programme was sponsored by the World Bank through the Technical Aid Loan.

Thus, certain drafts and opinions were rendered by Prof. E. Weemersh from the University of Ghent in Belgium, Prof. K. Hoptt from the University of Munich in Germany, and Mr. H. Shwartze from the German Society for Development of the Stock Exchanges and the Financial Markets in Central and Eastern Europe, seated in Frankfurt. On the basis of these drafts there were held several meetings and discussions, where different Bulgarian experts in the theory and practice also opined on the problems. In 1994 a special committee of experts was formed, under the auspices of the Ministry of Justice, which was to summarise the results of all the work done so far and to prepare and introduce the drafts (Green Papers) – one on Securities and one on Securities Exchange – to the Cabinet. This was completed by the autumn of 1994 and on September 21st, the then Cabinet approved the drafts and sent the White Papers to the Parliament.

Unfortunately, nothing more was done then, as the Cabinet resigned, which finally resulted in dissolution of the Parliament (The 36th Regular People's Assembly) itself.

3.2 Speeding up the draft

Immediately after the formation of the new regular Cabinet in January 1995, the work on the draft was resumed, and bringing a draft into the Parliament (The 37th Regular People's Assembly) was considered to be a priority task. A new committee was formed, headed by the Minister of Justice personally, which amended the drafts and introduced the notion of moulding the existing two separate drafts into one consolidated draft. The reasons for this amendment were found in the interdependence between the matters covered by the drafts and the aspiration to avoid eventual disturbances because of legal techniques. Perhaps another factor was the tendency of codifying laws attributable to all continental legal systems, the Bulgarian one being one of them. The draft was then approved promptly by the Cabinet, which brought it to the Parliament on March 20th, 1995.

Some two weeks later, exercising the right of legislative initiative, a member of the Parliament introduced an alternative draft of his own, prepared with the assistance of an adviser of his – an American national. Respectively, the second draft was more or less a direct translation of parts of the 1933 Securities Act and the 1934 Securities Exchange Act, as well as of some of the Regulations, issued by the Securities Exchange Commission. It was an important disadvantage of this draft, that it was definitely not concurrent with the existing legislation, especially in the matters of civil and criminal procedure.

The two drafts were brought to the attention of the Economic Committee of the Parliament as a leading Committee, and to the Budget Committee and the Civil Service Committee as supporting ones. It should be noted here that all these committees are subdivisions of the Parliament and consist only of members of the Parliament.

The Economic Committee held several sessions in order to discuss the two drafts. It was agreed that the White Paper of the Cabinet was much more operative and adherent to the current Bulgarian legislation and general legal doctrine, and that the other draft should be used partially so as to adopt some particular solutions on disclosure and liability of the persons involved in issuing, promoting and trading in securities. The curious point was that there were quite similar approaches in the two drafts, regarding the status of the Regulatory Body and the impact of the new Act on the provisions within the existing Bulgarian legislation.

Upon the initiative of the Economic Committee, certain assistance was requested from the experts of the World Bank, which reacted quite promptly, suggesting answers to several questions put up by the Committee.[4]

---

[4] Especially productive was Mr. Terry M. Chuppe, Executive Director, Emerging Markets Institute; who produced a Report on the Bulgarian Securities Law.

The sessions of the Economic Committee invited large public attention and a lot of governmental (the Bulgarian National Bank, the Competition Protection Commission, the Mass Privatisation Centre) and non-governmental agencies or bodies (the Association of the Financial Brokerage Houses, the Association of the Authorised Representatives of Securities Dealers, some existing stock exchanges and brokers) sent their representatives to the open discussions, and/or sent some considerations in written form.

After some hard work over particular texts of the draft, the Economic Committee prepared its final revision for the plenary session of the Parliament. Because of the complex and voluminous text of the draft, it had to be adopted in several parts, each in extensive debates of the members of the Parliament. Finally, on June 29th, 1995 the draft was adopted by the Parliament in the whole. The President would not find reasons to exercise his right of veto, and the procedures were completed by its official publication on July 14th. Three days later, after the general, for Bulgaria, *vocatio legis* period, it was automatically enacted.

3.3 Legal environment

3.3.1 Reception

The Act is quite specific – Securities, Stock Exchanges and Investment Companies Act (SSEICA) – that it takes into consideration the basic requirements of the European Union for the relevant fields, such as:

(1) Council Directive, co-ordinating the requirements for the drawing-up, scrutiny and distribution of the prospectus to be published when transferable securities are offered to the public;[5]
(2) Council Directive on information to be published on a regular basis by companies the shares of which have been admitted to official stock-exchange listing;[6]
(3) Council Directive on the approximation of the laws, regulations and administrative provisions, relating to undertakings for collective investment in transferable securities;[7]
(4) Council Directive on the information to be published when a major holding in a listed company is acquired or disposed of;[8]
(5) Council Directive on investment services in the securities field;[9]
(6) Council Directive on insider dealing.[10]

---

[5] (EEC) 89/298.
[6] (EEC) 82/121.
[7] (EEC) 85/611.
[8] (EEC) 88/627.
[9] (EEC) 93/22.
[10] (EEC) 89/592.

These specifics have been noted particularly in the introductory report of the Minister of Justice to the Cabinet, and such a reference is by itself a precedent in Bulgarian lawmaking procedures. Of course, the named directives, as said above, were "taken in consideration", and not always and in the whole directly implemented.[11]

3.3.2 Succession

The Act in question fits the general concepts of the Bulgarian legal system, as well as the existing Acts, such as the 1991 Commercial Act, the 1992 Banking and Credit Activities Act, the 1950 Obligations and Contracts Act, the 1992 Competition Protection Act, the 1992 Foreign Economic Activities and Protection of Foreign Investments Act, as well as the 1952 Civil Procedure Code. In fact, the enactment of SSEICA brought amendments only to the Commercial Act and the Banking and Credit Activities Act, which was actually otherwise required by the jurisprudence as certain provisions within them had proved inoperative.

4 MARKET MODEL POINTS WITHIN THE ACT

4.1 What is traded at the market?

4.1.1 Definition of security

(a) *Traded securities*　There was much dissension over the definition of a security within the SSEICA, especially over making it inclusive of derivatives. Most of these problems in fact originated from the lack of understanding as to where the money market ends and where the investment market begins. It was finally agreed by the experts, certainly not unanimously, that the regime of securities should apply to (s. 2):

(1) equity;
(2) bonds;
(3) other documents or rights, related to equity and bonds.

The infiniteness of the last catch-all point is of crucial importance. In former variants the explicit mention of options, futures and derivatives of such was discussed, but there would be more problems than usual, as the terms are not legally defined, which is disastrous for a continental type of legal system. In fact, all these instruments are based on transfer of rights in the general civil law theory, but it is always difficult to explain such a transfer in relation to immaterial "choses in action".

---

[11] The Treaty for Association of the Republic of Bulgaria to the European Communities was enforced on 1.2.1995 and provides for a 10-year transitional period for harmonisation of laws and regulations.

Any privatisation equity and vouchers were initially excluded from the list, considering their specific and temporary role at the market. The legislators preferred not to use these even to boost the securities markets to the critical mass of securities in turnover, because it could distort the securities market at the very beginning. Perhaps privatisation vouchers could relate in a way to the general investment market, but it would be a matter of regulation within another piece of legislation.

(b) Dematerialised securities   Of much importance is, that despite severe obstructions on the part of "classically oriented" lawyers, a major problem received treatment within the SSEICA, for the first time in Bulgarian law – the problem of legalising the trade in dematerialised securities. The Act provides for acknowledging the electronic transfers of equity and bonds that were never issued on paper, though at the current stage the Bulgarian securities market is mostly "the Belgian dentist" oriented, and in practice certain "dematerialisation" comes from non-issuance of actual certificates, but only of acknowledgement receipts for equity or bond participation. The only properly dematerialised market is that of the governmental bonds, which is run, at present, jointly by the National Bank and the Ministry of Finance, and is subject to specific regulation by Ordinances of those two institutions.

(c) Investment contracts   There was much discussion about the placing of trading in options, futures and derivatives in commodities into the scope of regulation of the Act. This was dropped for reasons of purity of the matters regulated, which is disappointing, because these latter instruments are not now regulated at all, and are, in fact, purely financial tools, or, at least, are being mainly used as financial tools. Much discussion followed one suggestion in the White Paper, addressing a specific Bulgarian problem: the intent to regulate through the SSEICA the various ways of investment in building enterprises.[12] These and similar considerations were brought to the attachment of "investment contracts" to the securities, regulated by the Act. An investment contract will be any contract in written form, under which an investor would transfer money or other property rights to another person, for the purpose of investing in economic activity, and in consideration of a promise for income – s. 3, para. 2.

An interesting point of distinction between the securities under s. 2 and the investment contracts (s. 3) is that the former are regulated by the Act "if these could be publicly offered", and the latter – "if these are being publicly offered".

(d) Public offers   Any type of security, either under s. 2 or under s. 3, falls under regulation in a case where it is connected to a public offering. An

---

[12] Most Bulgarian families aspire to own their flats or houses, and there is no legal possibility for a long-term lease. It is also difficult to arrange for a *hypotheque* (mortgage) and a lot of people took various instruments, offered by *bona* or *mala fide* building entrepreneurs. Quite a few of these instruments are actually to be covered by the SSEICA. There are no "building societies" (as in the U.K.) or equivalent regulation yet.

offering will be irrebuttably deemed to be public, if either one of the following has occurred:

(1) the offer is made to 50 persons or more;
(2) the offer is made to an unlimited number of people, including through the mass-media; or
(3) a person takes part in the offering who is neither a licensed investment intermediary, nor the legal owner of the offered securities.

(e) Unregulated investments   Any other security-like object of trade will be exempted from the regime of SSEICA. Actually, the traditional notion of securities as "negotiable instruments" is cut short by the definitions above, as bills of exchange, cheques, etc. will not be subject to this regulation at all, although still being named also as "securities".

Another specific point is the position of foreign "hard" currency. Bulgarian currency[13] is not convertible in the sense of Article VIII of the International Monetary Fund, and because of inflation processes in an emerging economy, it is highly volatile. Therefore, foreign convertible currency is an investment from an economic point of view, and a lot of people would keep their savings in such. From a legal point of view foreign currency is not legal tender,[14] and therefore it is rather a "chose in action" than money. Yet its regulation is left to the money market and the National Bank, instead of leaving it to public trade at the stock exchanges, for example. Thus it is easier to maintain the existing strict exchange control, and to exercise the strongly monetary politics of the National Bank.

4.2 Dealing in corporate control

4.2.1 Basic points

It is one of the specific features of a securities regulatory system, whether or not it dares to introduce provisions on dealings in corporate control. The choice of the Bulgarian system is to try to do it, and at several stages. Through being regulated, corporate control in a way becomes an object of securities trading itself, though not being security in itself, but being a certain position, related to other securities and their value.

The basic point is that corporate control becomes relevant only in connection with companies, whose shares are offered publicly under the provisions of SSEICA. All the others are exempt from the regulations.

Control is then monitored on the basis of votes, attributed to shares. Under Bulgarian law, even non-voting equity might acquire votes in certain circumstances, and then these should be counted as well.

---

[13] Bulgarian lev (pl. – leva), quoted as BGL; recently floating around 66 BGL per 1 U.S.$; or 105 BGL per 1 U.K. pound sterling.
[14] Obligations and Contracts Act 1950, s. 10.

4.2.2 Transfer issues

Thus any acquisition or disposal of 10% or more and of every 10% of the votes in the general meeting of a publicly offered company by one person or more, acting in concert, brings a duty to inform the company itself, the Commission, and, if the shares are traded at a stock exchange, the latter as well. Those informed are to publish the information accordingly.

4.2.3 Proxy issues

Corporate control manipulations are also to be monitored as regards representation by proxies. Anyone, who would offer to a single shareholder or a group of shareholders, owning 5% or more of the votes, to act as his or their proxy, ought to inform the company at least 10 days in advance of the meeting. The company should in turn inform the Commission and the rest of the shareholders.

4.2.4 Tender offers

Corporate control has also been treated by the SSEICA in terms of regulating tender offers for acquisition of publicly offered shares. Anyone, who would on his own, or through others, acting in concert, try to acquire 25% or more of the votes in the general meeting, is obliged to do it by producing a public offer bid to all shareholders of voting stock. The offer may be made public only after the Commission has added its confirmation to the draft. In terms of investor protection, there are specific requirements on the minimum price, the term for eventual acceptance and depositing the money for paying of the price, or the shares, offered in exchange through the bid. The controlling shareholders and the members of the board of the bidder (if it be another company) have to declare their existing votes in the general meeting of the target company.

5 WHO IS WHO AT THE MARKET

5.1 The Commission

5.1.1 Position

The Bulgarian securities market is to be headed by the Commission on Securities and Stock Exchanges (the Commission), which is to be responsible for all the regulation and also for development of the market.

It was long argued whether the Commission should be accountable to the Parliament, or to the Cabinet (or even the Ministry of Finance). Strong arguments were shown for attaching it to the Cabinet, by comparisons with Japan, Poland (the Cabinet jointly with the National Bank), Hungary, Turkey, Thailand, China and, in a way, Korea. It is believed that for an emerging securities market it is quite helpful to engage the governmental and executive administration instruments in this regulation, and even the *ex officio* appointment of members of the Commission is recommended so that promotion and development of the market be guaranteed. This also seems to be the constant advisory practice of the World Bank.

The Commission consists of seven members, appointed by the Cabinet; it has a legal personality of its own; and is financed jointly by income from its own activities and the state budget. It collects certain fees, but, considering the undeveloped state of the securities market in the country, the legislators did not believe in the ability of full self-funding of the Commission. Also, the legislators would not like to create an institution that would depend only on the penalties imposed by itself, and thus indirectly induce it to distortions. Therefore, despite its own problems, the state budget is to be the supporting resource in this case. On the other hand, funding is one of the most important aspects of independence. Personal independence is guaranteed to the members of the Commission institutionally, as once elected, they cannot be removed (without a very serious reason) from the position before the end of a five-year term of service.

The independence of the institution itself might not be the best thing for the Commission of an emerging market, considering the importance of its strategic role in the development of the market and enlightening its environment. It seems proper that, at the beginning, some interaction between governmental ministries, agencies and other regulators within the financial area will probably promote the goals of securities regulation.

5.1.2 Functions

The Commission is entrusted to monitor, control and promote the securities market, and, in fact, is responsible for its integrity and effectiveness. It controls the primary access to the market by licensing all the professionals acting there, and then continues to monitor them. It is notable that the Commission might extend its jurisdiction and control over persons who are in breach of the SSEICA, although these have not been licensed by itself, thus preventing much flagrant disobedience.

Because of its specific situation within the system of the institutions of the civil service, the Commission will issue its own normative Acts not directly, but through Acts of the Cabinet, the latter being drafted by the Commission. This peculiar mechanism engages the Cabinet directly with the securities market, and, also, opens a door for judicial control over such Acts, which might end in their cancellation for reasons of contradiction with the law.

The Commission (heading the investment market) will keep close contact with the Bulgarian National Bank, the regulator of the money market, but it will not be entitled to access to banking secrets, though it could be granted such permission by the courts under the procedure for the public prosecutor in criminal cases. The Commission is itself bound to keep any secrets its members and staff come to know in the line of their duties, but, in principle, all the activities of the Commission are public and transparent. It corresponds to the policies of disclosure as the basic instrument of investor protection in SSEICA.

5.2 Stock exchanges

5.2.1 Position

There were debates over the number and status of the stock exchanges. International experience shows a variety of solutions. In Poland, it is provided that stock exchanges are shareholding companies without any requirement for minimum endowment capital, and the Warsaw exchange is wholly owned by the state. In Hungary, an exchange might be a shareholding company with a minimum endowment capital of 150,000,000 Hungarian forints. In Japan, the Tokyo stock exchange is an incorporated organisation under a membership system, restricted to securities companies. In Germany, the exchange is not a shareholding company, and so on.

At one time it was planned that in Bulgaria there would be only one stock exchange, controlled by the government through majority shareholding (51%). This was argued by some members of the Parliament and contested by the Competition Protection Commission regarding the White Paper, and it was finally considered that such a monopoly might not be proper, and the position should be open on competitive basis.

Now, any company that answers to the requirements in the SSEICA must be licensed by the Commission. It was agreed that if a candidate meets all the requirements, the Commission could not refuse admission without stating a good reason, and if so, its decision can be appealed in court.

5.2.2 Structure

The stock exchanges are to be commercial (shareholding) companies rather than non-profit organisations, although it is hardly likely to produce much profit at the existing market. Yet a strange text was passed in order to create a mixture of these, forbidding the exchanges to form and distribute dividends at all. The quasi-public character of the exchanges, perhaps in deference to the opinions that a stock exchange should be an organ of the state, is underlined by another peculiar provision, stating that in case there is a demand for subscription of 20% or more of the registered capital, the general meeting of the stock exchange is obliged to vote for increasing the registered capital and adopting the new shareholders.

The endowment capital requirement for establishing a stock exchange was gradually lifted to 100 million Bulgarian leva, and, for purpose of comparison, the required endowment capital for a bank, for example, is 450 million Bulgarian leva. Thus it is believed that the existing dozens of stock exchanges will merge, into only one stock exchange. Out of these considerations arose also the problems of the interrelation between participation in the capital of the stock exchange and the membership of such. After discussion, it was agreed that there will be no conditioning of membership on the subscription of capital, as it is, for example, in Japan. But one investment intermediary may be a member of only one stock exchange, and within one year a stock exchange has to list at least 20 members, otherwise it will lose its licence within the expiration of six more months.

5.2.3 Functions

Otherwise, recognised stock exchanges are to be remarkably free in exercising discretion in their function. The regulator is to monitor only the structure as there are provided specific limitations such as prohibitions on controlling more than 5% of the voting stock by a single person or by persons acting in concert; and the requirement that a minimum of two-thirds the capital is to be subscribed by banks and/or licensed financial intermediaries; and that all the capital may consist only of voting equity.

The SSEICA actually neglects self-regulation, except for the stock exchanges, which may extend their own further requirements to the members for listing of shares, and to the investment intermediaries in order to choose whom to work for. Actually the stock exchanges are to be, in comparative terms, a type of self-regulating organisation of their own, supervised by the Securities Commission.

Further, stock exchanges have to provide for the organisation of a clearing system for the transactions, carried out by them, and for exchange arbitration courts at each one. A strange point is that the latter would hear the appeals of refusals for admission to membership to the exchange, while the arbitrators in the list are appointed by the same exchange.

5.3 Investment intermediaries

5.3.1 Position

The SSEICA does not differentiate between "brokers" and "dealers" in the classic meaning of these terms. Instead, the Act introduces a general institution of "investment intermediary", which is to answer to a number of requirements in order to fit the image of a creditworthy institution.

Initially, it was provided that the investment intermediaries would not engage in any activities other than those of trading in securities. Then it was agreed that, considering the particular problems of the emerging, undeveloped market (that there might not be enough transactions on the market for the intermediaries to live on); as well as the recent, but already established practice in the country, the intermediaries would be allowed to carry out also activities at the money market, and be separately licensed by the National Bank under the 1992 Banking and Credit Activities Act, *i.e.* to act also as financial intermediaries. In no other circumstances may a licensed intermediary conduct any other commercial activities.

5.3.2 Structure

There was also much discussion over the forms of company that could be eligible as investment intermediaries. The majority of the experts agreed on admission only of limited liability companies (so-called "capital" – as opposed to "personal", companies), but there was much pressure for the admission of sole traders and natural persons into the market. On this issue the Act is based on the principle that persons may act only under the licence of a company,[15] thus preserving the availability of the general claim in tort against the principal jointly with the agent, under section 49 of the Law of Obligations and Contracts.

---

[15] *Cf.* Financial Services Act (U.K.), s. 44.

Investment intermediaries may now qualify for a licence if they are formed as banks (already licensed by the National Bank), as joint-stock shareholding companies, or as limited liability companies.[16] A specific point is, that the choice between the forms is not based on the minimum required capital for the registration, which is the general principle in the Commercial Act, as regardless of the form, the investment intermediary has to have 1,000,000 leva paid in endowment capital. If the intermediary be a shareholding company, it may not issue bearer shares, or shares with more than one vote. Any other forms of companies, which are personal, or where control is not based on participation in the capital, are out of the market.

5.3.3 Functional regulation

After being admitted to the market, the intermediaries are subject to standing obligations to maintain certain levels of capital adequacy and liquidity of their funds, following roughly the EC Directive.[17] It is believed that, thus, the confidence in the emerging market will be much strengthened. An interesting point is that the Commission is free to release some of the smaller-scale intermediaries from certain capital requirements. Those who are thus relaxed, correspondingly, will not be entitled to become underwriters, market-makers, or otherwise undertake greater risks in deals.

A very radical tool of consumer protection, which is unknown in the other branches of Bulgarian law, is the prohibition on "cold-calling" in investment services. It is a twofold prohibition, with the intention to be a catch-all: an investment adviser may not offer advice to people who did not ask for such and consult on questions which are not asked by his client.

5.3.4 Fiduciary issues

Any Securities Act nowadays follows some case-law legal system. Such reception by a continental law system inevitably brings some interaction between the legislative models. Thus, the SSEICA for the first time introduces into the Bulgarian legislation (which is purely continental) the notion of trust. Any investment intermediary has to act as trustee for the investments of his clients, as there is a general duty to keep the portfolio of its clients' securities apart from the portfolio of the intermediary's own securities. Thus, the securities, entrusted by clients, cannot be used for speculative manipulations, and are easily identifiable in case of insolvency, or such, of the intermediary. The latter provides excellent opportunities for tracing claims for the clients as a class of insolvency creditors, which is quite beneficial to them, in comparison with the general provisions of Bulgarian law of contract, as influenced by "false wealth" fears. There is also a continuing obligation to report monthly on the procedures for keeping the portfolios apart, to the Commission.

---

[16] In the matter of company forms Bulgarian legislation is closer to the German one, and liability of members may be limited either by proportional fraction participation in the stock (*GmbH*, or "limited company" in the text), or by shareholding (*AG*, or "joint-stock"/"shareholding" company in the text).

[17] 93/22/ECD.

There is another fiduciary point about investment intermediaries – client relationship. The professional intermediary is obliged to provide for "privileged performance" of a client's order in regard of an identical transaction for his own account, which actually means that an intermediary is obliged to let his client have the better of two identical transactions. The wording "privileged" is broad enough to cover, for example, such situations, where if the price falls, the intermediary is obliged to order for himself first, and then, at the lower price, order for his client who has given identical order.

5.4 Banks

5.4.1 Banks as investment intermediaries

The interrelation between money market and investment market and the role of banks in the investment market, also raised many interesting problems for discussion among the experts. Especially serious was the discussion whether the banks should participate in the investment market directly – on the basis of their banking licences, or should be specially licensed and supervised by the Securities Commission for their investment business. The experts could not reach agreement on this problem, but the idea of the single licence prevailed within the Parliament, as there were fears of confrontation between the National Bank and the Securities Commission as parallel supervisors.

All Bulgarian banks, unlike for example the U.S. banks,[18] are universal, as there is no prohibition upon them participating directly in the securities markets, following only the general formulae of solvency, liquidity, etc. and prudential standards. This universality brings certain difficulties in the realisation of their role in the investment market, and some misunderstanding of the specific risks and the corresponding regulation, thus bringing, perhaps, an overall misunderstanding of the position and the role of the regulatory body.

The World Bank stood on the point that universal banks should be licensed by the specific regulator (the Commission in this case) for any single facet of their activities (which is the English way of regulation) with a view to the integrity of the market and the equality of access for professional structures, but the Bulgarian legislator was more inclined to rely on the public notion of the unfeasibility of banks, and the ability of the National Bank to control them by itself alone.

5.4.2 Classic banking

Banks appear in the SSEICA not only as investment intermediaries, but in their classic functions as well. Thus there are provisions of a quite fiduciary

---

[18] Note, "A Conduct-Oriented Approach to the Glass-Steagall Act", 91 *Yale L.J.* 102 (1981): "The Glass-Steagall Act requires that commercial banking be separated from investment banking . . ."; *Cf.* Norton, J. & Whitley, S.C., *Banking Law Manual*, (1982), par. 16.02: "The Glass-Steagall Act does not, however, create an absolute barrier between commercial and investment banking."

character in regard to the banking services rendered to investment companies, some privileges to become shareholders in stock exchanges, etc.

5.5 Investment companies

5.5.1 Structure

One of the most unclear questions within the White Paper was the delicate problem about the structures designed to accumulate capital from the original investors and be professional investors themselves. These were named investment companies and actually depart from the traditional notions of collective investment schemes and the related institutions.

Investment companies could be only shareholding companies with only voting shares, which could only invest in others' securities. Originally, there was an idea to bring also into the regulation companies which would invest only in immovable property, which was in fact an attempt to "borrow" some regulation and attach it in order to stop certain manipulations of the housing market. For reasons of inconsistency, this idea was dropped, and the permissible portfolio of an investment company is now in accordance with the general definition of "security" within the SSEICA.

There was also much debate over management and representation of the investment companies, especially as to whether these should be managed only by an outside body – licensed intermediary; or by their own boards. Finally, it was left to the shareholders' meeting to opt for either of these possibilities. If they chose the former, there is an upper limit (5% of the weighted assets for the year) on the annual remuneration of the intermediary, as protection for the investors of the company. The initial idea, in the White Paper, of joint representation by at least two executive directors (following the pattern established for banks) was overturned.

The investment companies may be of two types – "open" and "closed", which expresses roughly the idea of "public" and "private" companies. The difference arises from the method of providing liquidity of the investments in the shares of these companies – an "open" company is that whose shares are listed and traded at a stock exchange, and a "closed" one is that which has undertaken to buy back its own shares at the investors' demand. If an "open" investment company is delisted, it will be regulated under the rules for a "closed" one.

As the international practice has shown that the monitoring of capital adequacy, liquidity and similar features is a reliable guarantee for stability, these requirements for investment companies are very strict (especially for the "open" ones) and to some extent the EC rules have been adapted. An investment company has to be licensed by the Commission.

5.5.2 Fiduciary issues

In regard of the investment companies, there are also certain provisions of a fiduciary character and related to trust, which notion, as already mentioned, is quite a novelty in Bulgarian law. Thus, an investment company may keep its assets only with a depository bank, and the latter is to keep these assets in trust for the company. The investment company may not be controlled by a single person, or persons, acting in concert or itself control someone else by investing more than 5% (30% for the "closed" company) of its capital (especially in other investment companies) or otherwise control an issuer of securities. There are express prohibitions on capital participation, borrowing or using guarantees, or interlocking directorates with the depository bank and/or the investment intermediary employed.

5.6 Insiders

Of course, the White Paper made much use of the experience and the advanced securities regulation in other states, and provided for some prevention of misuse of inside information, though it is not yet an actual problem in Bulgaria. Inside information is broadly defined in a catch-all frame, pointing to a few well-known specifics, such as materiality, non-public, related to an issuer or to securities, etc.

Insiders, as defined in the SSEICA, are all the directors of an issuer; all of the directors of a company controlling, or controlled by an issuer; any person or group of persons owning 10% or more of the votes of an issuer and in possession of inside information; and any person who for reasons of his profession, activities or relations to an issuer or a person from the categories listed above, has access to inside information. Thus tippees are also treated as primary insiders.

6 HOW IS THE TRADING ORGANISED?

A great part of the matters that could be discussed under this title were already discussed above, and yet there are some points to be highlighted.

6.1 Prospectus

Any public offering of securities, regardless of whether it is an issue for the underwriting or direct distribution at the primary market or a public offer at the secondary market, has to be started by a prospectus. It is believed that this is the best way to guarantee equal access to the material information. There is a point of merit regulation here, as the Commission has to approve or disapprove the prospectus, and without such approval it is illegal to make public offers of securities. The SSEICA provides that the Commission refuses granting of an approval if the applicant-issuer has defaulted payments, liquidity problems, liabilities to connected persons, or (which is the catch-all merit point) did not provide enough for the investors' protection. Besides its grant of approval, the Commission is not expected to investigate the information into the prospectuses and could not be liable for any losses because of misstatement, omission or fraud. Such eventual liability is to be shared by the signatories to the prospectus.

There are a few exemptions from the requirement for a prospectus, for securities that have traditionally been recognised as riskless, such as gilts, securities of recognised international institutions, bonds convertible into shares and non-cash dividends.

The obligation to disclose information is continuous for the issuer; which is to submit quarterly, semi-annual and annual reports to the Commission, as well as to its stock exchange, if the securities be listed; and to inform these institutions *ad hoc* if a material change in the reported facts occurs.

An important procedural guarantee for the position of the *bona fide* investor, is his right to claim the rescission of any transaction with securities within three months of the performance, if there was a breach of the rules about the prospectus. As Bulgarian law does not comprise any class actions, in such a case each investor will have to file his own claim.

6.2 Listing of securities

The listing standards provided within the SSEICA are also essential for the classification of the model of the securities market. These standards certainly avoid merit regulation and tend to disclosure-based regulation, but, for example, only securities for which a prospectus has been issued and approved by the Commission, are eligible for listing. Also the Commission is to establish the general frame of requirements for the listing standards and each stock exchange, in compliance with those, may specify its own requirements. In no circumstances may a stock exchange refuse listing of "gilt-edged" (governmental) securities. Certain merit regulation elements may be also found in the powers of the Commission to waive a few of the formal requirements in regard of newly incorporated companies. Perhaps, however, this should be avoided, and the responsibility laid in full upon the issuer and the underwriter or promoter, as is originally planned within the draft Act. On the other hand, an emerging market should not rely only on fair disclosure, so the concept of joint liability seems adequate.

6.3 Over-the-counter trading

Perhaps, the position of over-the-counter trading should also be clarified. The underlying concept in the SSEICA is that the public over-the-counter market be also regulated and deals be performed only by licensed persons. But the criterion for the separation of the markets comes not from the securities being traded at a stock exchange, or not, as such; it comes from the securities being offered to the public regardless of the marketing method. Exempt from regulation would be, for example, an offer to less than 50 addressees, in private mail (circulars also qualify for the exemption); or an offer from the legal owner of securities for their direct sale.

6.4 Short sales

Short sales are not forbidden but are to be specially regulated by Cabinet Order, which is to be drafted by the Commission. So, until the adoption of such order, these sales shall be treated as unlawful. Unfortunately, within the SSEICA there is no time limit for the introduction of such order. The "open" investment companies shall not be able to enter into short sales especially provided for them in the SSEICA.

6.5 Other general rules of stock exchange transactions

6.5.1 Discretion

Stock exchanges are quite free to introduce trading rules of their own, but still have to abide by some general requirements. For example, any payments for transactions at the exchange have to be made only through the banking system. The exchanges have to organise a clearing system of their own for the clearance of the transactions there, but cash settlements are made finally into bank accounts.

6.5.2 Suspension of trade

Also, for purposes of investor protection and/or market integrity, a stock exchange may suspend the trading of listed securities for up to three days upon simple notice to the Commission. If the proposed term is to be more than three days, it needs the special permission of the Commission.

6.5.3 Derivatives trading

Forward trading and trading in options are conditional on the written consent of the issuer and the permission of the stock exchange. The issuer is free to cancel such trade at any time and the stock exchange is obliged to suspend the trading within one year of the notification.

6.5.4 Central Depository

All transactions in securities are to be registered at the Central Depository. This is a shareholding company to be formed by the National Bank and the Ministry of Finance and all the participants at the securities market may take a share in its capital if they wish to do so. In case the capital as designed by the Bank and the Ministry is not subscribed in full by June 30th 1996, the two institutions above are to pay in the rest as underwriters with a firm commitment. Besides keeping the public register, the Central Depository will also offer safe custody of paper-based securities and act as clearing house for dematerialised securities.

7 RISKS OF NON-COMPLIANCE

7.1 Judicial control

The controlling position of the courts is another important aspect of regulation, especially as the Commission has itself to comply with the requirements, fixed by the SSEICA, although no civil action for damages may be brought against it. It is provided that the acts and the decisions of the Commission may be appealed at court. It is highly unlikely that the court will engage in deciding on the merits of a case, and probably will keep to controlling the formal response of these acts to law and superior normative acts. It is also very important to provide for the enforcement of investor securities contracts, in order to promote the integrity and confidence in such a volatile market, and the systemic risk is much higher in an emerging market. Thus it is provided that each stock exchange is to organise an arbitration court of its own, whose decisions are final, binding and directly enforceable.

7.2 Civil liabilities

The most important issues of civil liabilities as provided in the SSEICA have already been discussed above. The general point is that the SSEICA provides special claims for damages thus relieving investors (and their lawyers) from the burden of qualifying under the general claims in contract or in tort. The other specific point is that the SSEICA provides a few instances of the voidability of contracts breaching its rules, and which is perhaps unique in Bulgarian law – that sometimes the undue performance of the contract will make it voidable.

7.3 Administrative offences and disciplining

The Commission operates a variety of measures to impose compliance with the rules of the SSEICA, starting from proscription of particular acts (compliance orders) and calling meetings of the boards of directors of the suspects; through making the offences public knowledge by any media; to suspension of the trade in particular securities and revocation of licence. For any offences by banks the Commission has to inform the National Bank, and it may not revoke the licence of a bank itself, but may only ask this from the National Bank and the latter is to take the decision.

7.4 Penalties and pending criminal liability

In cases of breach of certain provisions of the SSEICA as listed at the end of the Act, the Commission may impose penalties upon the guilty persons within the range from 200,000 to 1,000,000 Bulgarian leva. In a case where any activity, subject to prior licensing, has been carried out at the investment market, the penalty varies from 500,000 to 2,000,000 leva. In addition to the personal fines, the legal entities may be also penalised by fines from 1,000,000 to 5,000,000 leva. Also, any illegal income is to be confiscated. These penalties are subject to the clause "provided it is not a criminal offence" in anticipation of further reformation of the Criminal Code. *De lege ferenda*, certain offences will be incorporated there as crimes, but it is not within the Bulgarian legislative technique to introduce criminal sanctions through Acts other than the Criminal Code itself. Anyhow, the SSEICA does not provide for any settlement between the Commission and offenders in consideration of waiving claims or such.

8 SECURITIES MARKET MODEL ISSUES

8.1 Complex phenomenon

The problem of defining the model of a certain type of such a complex phenomenon as a securities market, is of course, multi-facial. It is far more difficult if this market has just come to exist and there is not actually a market in the economic sense but it has to be created by way of the regulation of the legal framework itself. Therefore, it is particularly difficult to speak of the model of a market, which at its best has only a legal framework and some practice before the framework was introduced. It means, in fact, to define the targets and the goals of a contemplated regulatory system more than defining the actual situation.

The comparative history of securities regulation is quite amazing. In 1934, the U.S. became the first country in the world to establish a national regulatory body, which was manifestly independent, whose rule-making was remarkably transparent, and whose investigation powers are frightening.[19] In the U.K. formal regulation – in the form of deregulation – was introduced only in 1986 through the Financial Services Act (FSA), which designated the Securities and Investments Board (SIB), whose extensive powers are channelled through a network of second-tier organisations, and regulation is at the cost of the regulated bodies and persons only.[20] In Germany, it appears that a regulatory body was introduced only at the beginning of 1995 – the Federal Securities Supervisory Office, which is to monitor and discipline the market, providing uniformity and abiding by the EC rules. And, in Bulgaria, the institution was created that should create the market through regulating it at the very beginning. "Regulation was first" comes quite like "Chaos was first".

8.2 Regulatory concept

Perhaps the basis for the classification should be the regulatory concept. Such a concept involves different policy options, varying from extensive administrative management to free market self-regulation. Historically, the securities market has sprung up as an epitome of private ingenuity to meet economic demands for accumulation of capital and spreading of the risks, through their multiplication to different persons. It was only after the shortcomings of this system of raising capital showed up that public authorities started to try to mix up and regulate some of the risks to some extent by legal means.

It seems nowadays that there is a world-wide tendency of shifting from the tradition of self-regulation by the expert practitioners themselves to the fashion of strong governmental regulation of the market. Perhaps the changes in this direction are most notably seen in the U.K. model, comparing the concept before and after the adoption and implementation of the

---

[19] Steinberg, M. & Ferrara, R., *Securities Practice: Federal and State Enforcement*, para. 4.01. (1985 & 1992 Supp.): "the federal securities laws authorise the Securities and Exchange Commission . . . to adjudicate a myriad of administrative proceedings."

[20] Pennington, R., *The Law of Investment Markets* (1990), para. 3.01. ". . . the most effective, practical and economical way to regulate the investment markets and investment activities would be to combine regulation by the representative organisations whose members are engaged in the various branches of investment business, with a supervisory and residual degree of regulation by a Government appointed body acting as an agent of the state".

Financial Services Act 1986. The mode of stricter administrative control[21] is often considered to be of U.S. origin, which might mean that the 1929 Wall Street crisis had more effect on policy considerations in the U.S. than all that happened since the 17th century South Sea Bubble collapse in the U.K. Speaking of the same problem in terms of an emerging investment market, there is still the same dilemma: whether to start from where everyone has started and let history work its way out; or to take notice and consideration of the experience of the other countries in the world and try to put up legal barriers even before the market has been started. It is rather a question of "to be or not to be", but any position is only a starting one. It is a fashion among the emerging financial markets to follow the most advanced regime, which is believed to be the U.S. model of disclosure standards regulation,[22] as juxtaposed with a system of merit regulation,[23] closely connected to governmental control. It is very tempting to learn from the experience and the mistakes of the others, and to adopt directly the most advanced system of regulation. But it also seems true, in a way, that the securities market has to be brought up gradually, as if it were a child. Therefore, one cannot expect a most advanced regulatory system to fit an emerging financial market. Every new market has to gain some experience of its own, before being able to accept the rationalisation of the operations there.

After the mode of regulation has been chosen, then the next problem arises – what bodies should exercise powers of regulation? If it be one body only, then even a pattern of total control has to rest with that only regulator. If not, the legal framework has to provide for the division of powers and responsibilities between the different bodies. Then becomes relevant the question as to whether these bodies should be independent institutions, different governmental agencies, or whether some of the functions and responsibilities should be transferred to private bodies, themselves participants in the same regulated market.

Reviewing the current Bulgarian practice, the model of the money market shows that all the powers concentrate into a sovereign body, independent from the Government, and in theory accountable to the Parliament – the National Bank. What is more, the Government is under the obligation to be "lender of last resort" to the National Bank, upon request. The state-owned stock in banks is concentrated under the directions of the International Monetary Fund and the World Bank, into a shareholding company,

---

[21] *The Work of the SEC* (Published by the SEC) (1982): "The Securities and Exchange Commission (SEC) was created on July 2, 1934 by an act of Congress entitled the Securities Exchange Act of 1934. It is an independent, bipartisan, quasi-judicial agency of the United States Government."

[22] Sargent & Greenberg, "Research in Securities Regulation: Access to the Sources of the Law", 75 *Law Libr. J.* 98, 108 (1982): "A disclosure approach, in short, presumes that the investor need merely be informed – that is, be given the facts required to make an informed investment decision."

[23] *Id.* "The 'merit' jurisdictions also embrace the concept of full disclosure but go further. They presume that the state has an obligation to protect its citizens from making bad investments."

co-owned by the Government and the National Bank (and with some minor participation of some other state bodies). There is an Association of the Commercial Banks, which is a non-profit company, designed to promote the agreed policies of the banks, but it has not been granted any powers.

As for the position and tasks of the investment market regulatory body, it is usually considered that, for an emerging market, the Securities Commission is to be responsible both for the regulation and for the development of the market. Perhaps the strongest point of criticism of the Bulgarian White Paper by the World Bank (the help of the latter was requested by the Parliament, asking for the answers to some questions) is that the Securities Commission was first structured as a regulatory, but not as a development agency. The World Bank also found the Bulgarian Securities Commission a relatively weak, though independent body. The strategic problem with the regulatory body is that, whoever assumes the mandate of management, a system has to assume the responsibility of failures as well, both political and social, as well as purely financial. It seems that this aspect of liability for eventual failures, which could occur in an emerging market, are underestimated by the Government, which opted for direct control over the Commission and the market, thus engaging itself with the corresponding responsibility and increased budget expenditures.

9 CONCLUSION

Thus, the Bulgarian legal framework of the model, drafted by Belgian and German professors first, and much adjusted afterwards, is said to be generally oriented towards reproducing the U.S. regulatory model of a strong and (to some extent) independent Commission, ruling over a market subject to broad requirements for disclosure. The primary responsibility for regulation and the modelling of the market is left with the Securities Commission, which so far is to be accountable to the Cabinet. From the standpoint of legal technique, the Bulgarian model looks closer to the U.K. one, as the SSEICA seems to be the only piece of legislation intended to regulate the market, together with some future Cabinet orders, provided for in the same Act.[24]

However, the specifics of the regulation provided for in Bulgaria tend to show that it is not actually a matter of functional regulation only, and is not of merit regulation only. It is a matter of something that could be provisionally named "total regulation", in case no allusion is made to former political regimes. In fact, the Bulgarian model regulates the regulatory body itself; the objects of trade at the market; all the subjects (participants) in the market; access to that market (through licensing only), the latter being con-

---

[24] Pennington, R. *op. cit.*, para. 3.01: "The scheme of the Financial Services Act 1986 for the regulation of the investment markets in the United Kingdom differs from the American system in that a complete system of regulation is being introduced in the United Kingdom by a single piece of legislation, whereas the American system has grown up gradually over 50 years . . ."

ditional on some specific requirements; and the market activities; as well as the resolution of any disputes related to that market and the sanctions for offences. Any single aspect of these reveals some specific features; for this reason the sum is also specific.

Thus, it seems that in general the model is one of total control, centralised with the Commission, with some relaxation in the stock exchanges only. This model is in fact very much a copy of that of the regulation of the money market by the National Bank, and thus, besides the obvious subordination of the investment market regulation to the money market regulation, some parity seems to be introduced between the two hopefully competing markets, which could be very effective from a macroeconomic point of view.

23. The Long Walk to a Market Economy: An Examination of the New Company and Securities Laws of the People's Republic of China

Stanley Siegel[1]

1 INTRODUCTION

With a speed and sophistication that has amazed many observers, the People's Republic of China has adopted many of the components of a market economy. This economic development has been so rapid that its institutions – companies, share trading and stock exchanges – often have come into existence and operation before the laws were enacted to validate and regulate them. Borrowing from the laws and practices of many nations, China has enacted laws and regulations of considerable sophistication to govern its unique "socialist market economy". This chapter examines the development of the capital markets, and the related company and securities laws, in the People's Republic of China (PRC).

2 THE DEVELOPMENT OF COMPANIES AND COMPANY LAW IN THE PRC

2.1 The origins of contemporary company laws

The contemporary history of private limited liability companies in China comprises a period of fewer than ten years. The first companies limited by shares were organized under regional regulations adopted in Guangdong and Shanghai in 1986 and 1987. Indeed, until 1992, such companies were governed only by local regulations, most importantly those promulgated in

---

[1] Professor of Law, New York University School of Law, New York.

Shenzhen,[2] Shanghai,[3] and Guangdong.[4] Among the more remarkable developments in contemporary China – further discussed below – were the organization of stock exchanges and the commencement of public trading of shares pursuant to these tentative municipal regulations, before the enactment of a national company law governing the issuance of shares or, indeed, the organization and regulation of the issuing companies.

National legislation concerning companies commenced with the issuance in 1972 of the Share System Procedures[5] and the Standards Opinion.[6] The PRC Company Law (the "Company Law") was formally adopted on December 29, 1993 (effective July 1, 1994) at the Fifth Session of the Standing Committee of the Eighth National People's Congress.[7] Although it is on its face the governing law of limited liability companies, the Company Law does not address a number of important areas. Therefore, the Share Procedures and the Standards Opinion (as well as some of the municipal provisions) continue to govern certain aspects of corporate organization and governance. Committees of the National People's Congress are presently at various stages in the drafting and submission of other laws relative to companies.[8]

2.2 The "socialist market economy"

From the outset, the regulations and laws governing companies have contemplated the continuation of a substantial role for the government in the overall supervision and governance of the economy. The "share system" of enterprise ownership – *i.e.*, ownership of enterprises in the form of

---

[2] Shenzhen Municipal People's Government, Companies Limited by Shares Tentative Provisions (March 17, 1992), 2 *China's New Companies* 30–67 (*Asia Law & Practice*, 1993). *See* also, Shenzhen Special Economic Zone, Companies Limited by Shares Regulations (April 26, 1993, effective October 1, 1993) (amending and replacing in part, and with respect to certain companies, the Companies Limited by Shares Tentative Provisions), 2 *China's New Companies* 68–100 (*Asia Law & Practice*, 1993). [Unless otherwise noted, citations to laws, regulations and other official pronouncements of the PRC or municipalities thereof are to unofficial English translations.]

[3] Shanghai Municipal People's Government, Companies Limited by Shares Tentative Provisions (May 18, 1992), 2 *China's New Companies* 2–27 (*Asia Law & Practice*, 1993).

[4] Standing Committee of the Eighth People's Conference of Guangdong Province, Guangdong Province Company Regulations (May 14, 1993), 2 *China's New Companies* 145–180 (*Asia Law & Practice*, 1993).

[5] PRC Share System Experimental Enterprise Procedures (the "Share System Procedures"), promulgated by the State Commission for Restructuring the Economy, the State Planning Commission, the Ministry of Finance, the People's Bank of China and the State Council Production Office (May 15, 1992), 1 *China's New Companies* 6–10 (*Asia Law & Practice*, 1993).

[6] PRC Standards for Companies Limited by Shares Opinion (the "Standards Opinion") promulgated by the State Commission for Restructuring the Economy (May 15, 1992), 1 *China's New Companies* 11–38 (*Asia Law & Practice*, 1993).

[7] The official text of the Company Law, with a parallel unofficial English translation, is available in *China Law & Practice* (March 9, 1994) at pages 7–55.

[8] The author met recently with a drafting committee of the National People's Congress that is in the initial stages of preparing a statute to govern the organization and operation of single-shareholder corporations and proprietorships. As of this writing, no draft of that statute has been publicly circulated.

companies limited by shares or limited liability companies[9] – is viewed as one of the routes toward a more effective socialist economy. It is intended that the creation and operation of companies limited by shares and limited liability companies will:

... change the enterprise management system, promote the separation of political and enterprise responsibility, allow enterprise management autonomy, responsibility for profit and loss, self-development and self-regulation ... open up new channels for finance and capital ... promote the rational flow of production factors ...[10]

However, the principles that govern these enterprises also include the following:

Maintain the leading position of the public ownership system and protect public assets ... Carry out the national industrial policy ...[11]

The role of companies in the overall economic scheme of the PRC is stated in the first article of the Company Law:

This Law is formulated in accordance with the Constitution in order to suit the requirements of establishing a modern enterprise system, to standardize the organization and activities of companies, to protect the lawful rights and interests of companies, shareholders and creditors, *to safeguard the social and economic order, and to promote the development of the socialist market economy.*[12]

Similarly, the interim regulations on trading of shares and the draft securities law state their purpose of "developing the socialist market economy",[13] and "promoting the sound development of the socialist market economy".[14]

---

[9] The Chinese procedures, opinions and laws divide share enterprises into "companies limited by shares" and "limited liability companies". *See, e.g.,* Share System Procedures, art. 3. In the United States, these two forms are roughly analogous, respectively, to the corporation (public company limited by shares in England, AG in Germany, SA in France) and the close corporation (private company limited by shares in England, GmbH in Germany, SaRL in France). The two forms are collectively referred to herein as "companies".

[10] Share System Procedures, art. 1.

[11] *Id.*, art. 2.

[12] People's Republic of China, Company Law, art. 1 (emphasis added).

[13] Interim Regulations on the Administration of the Issue and Trading of Shares, promulgated by the State Council, April 22, 1993 (the "Interim Regulations"), art. 1. The Interim Regulations – but not the Seventh Draft – contain a further strong statement of principles:

Article 4. Shares may be issued and traded, provided the overriding socialist principle of public ownership is maintained and the national assets are protected against encroachment.

[14] Securities Law of the People's Republic of China (the "Seventh Draft") , art. 1 (7th Draft, August 18, 1993). The Interim Regulations and the Seventh Draft are discussed in further detail later in this chapter.

Moreover, the Company Law contemplates a degree of intervention and control of corporate operations by the State:

Under the macroscopic adjustment and control of the state, companies shall independently organize production and operation in accordance with market demand, and shall aim to raise economic benefits and labor productivity and to maintain and increase the value of assets.[15]

These objectives are evidenced in the substantive provisions of the laws that they preface. The developing corporate structure and capital markets in China have many – but not all – of the salient features of financial markets in nations with developed market economies. And while there is considerable evidence that these characteristics of a market economy will increase as the Chinese capital markets develop and expand, it would at the moment be clearly erroneous to suggest that the PRC is moving toward implementation of a full capitalist economy. A preliminary examination of the regulations and laws reveals the key differences.

2.3 Provisions of the company laws

In its general structure and provisions, the PRC Company Law (as well as several of the other regulations and procedures that preceded or coexist with it) resembles the company laws of Western Europe, upon which it was evidently based in significant part. The distribution of authority and powers among the shareholders, the board of directors, and the corporate officers is similar[16] – though clearly not identical[17] – to the structures set forth in the European company laws. Provisions on issuance of shares are generally similar to the European provisions,[18] but again with a few

---

[15] *Id.*, art. 5.

[16] With respect to limited liability companies, *see* Company Law, arts. 38 (shareholders' meeting), 46 (board of directors), 50 (manager), 59–63 (duties of directors, supervisors and manager). With respect to companies limited by shares, *see* Company Law, arts. 103 (shareholders' meeting), 112 (board of directors), 119 (manager), 124, 126 (supervisory board).

[17] *See, e.g.*, the list of functions and powers of the shareholders' general meeting in Company Law, art. 103, which includes the following:

    (1) To decide on the business policies and investment plans of the company . . .
    (3) To elect and replace supervisors from among the shareholders' representatives and to decide on matters concerning the remuneration of supervisors . . .
    (6) To consider and approve the company's proposed annual budgets and final accounts . . .

[18] *See* Company Law, arts. 131 (issuance not below par value); 134 (maintenance of share register); 143–146 (assignability of shares), 149 (limitations on share repurchase).

significant variations.[19] The provisions on financial disclosure set a high standard,[20] and the Law imposes unique provisions designed to assure the retention of reserves out of income.[21]

Several features, however, render the developing company laws of the PRC more restrictive than the company laws of other market economy nations. Most important among these are substantive government review of establishment, and limitations on the raising of capital and the carrying on of business activities.

2.3.1 Organizational approval

The Share System Procedures require approval of the State Commission for Restructuring the Economy (or of subsidiary provincial, regional or municipal departments) for establishment of companies. The Procedures further require that companies must obtain the approval of the People's Bank of China for the public issuance of shares.[22] These approval procedures are detailed in the Standards Opinion, which requires the submission of multiple documents (including an establishment agreement, an application form, a feasibility study report, an asset verification report, a share prospectus and an industry management department examination and approval opinion) to the appropriate government authorizing department, under the State Commission for Restructuring the Economy.[23] Similar approval requirements are included in the Company Law, though phrased in more general terms. Moreover, the requirements appear to depend on the form of the company. Thus, the establishment of a company limited by shares is subject to approval of an authorized department of the State Council or of a provincial People's Government.[24] Approval of the establishment of a

---

[19] *See, e.g.,* Company Law, art. 137, which sets forth conditions for the issuance by a company of new shares, including among the conditions the following:

> (2) The company has been continuously profitable for the last three years and is able to pay dividends to its shareholders . . .
> (4) The company's anticipated profit rate can reach the interest rate of bank deposits for the same period . . .

[20] *See* Company Law, art. 175, requiring that the accounting report of the company include not only a balance sheet and income statement, but also a statement of changes in financial position, and an "explanatory statement on financial condition". Financial accounting systems are subject to regulations of the State Council's department in charge of finance. Company Law, art. 174. Development and implementation of accounting principles for business organizations in the PRC are at an early stage. Evaluation of the effectiveness of accounting disclosure in practice is beyond the scope of this discussion.

[21] *See* Company Law, art. 177, requiring allocation of 10% of after-tax profits to a "statutory common reserve" and between 5% and 10% of after-tax profits to a "statutory provident fund".

[22] Share System Procedures, art. 8. The approval requirement is also contained in Standards Opinion, art. 18.

[23] Standards Opinion, art. 13(4). Following approval of these documents, the promoters must apply to the Administration for Industry and Commerce to commence procedures for the establishment of the company. *Id.,* art. 13(6).

[24] Company Law, art. 77.

limited liability company appears to be less elaborate, although the Company Law provides – somewhat obscurely – that "if laws and administrative regulations provide that relevant authorities must carry out examination and approval", the approval document must be submitted as part of the registration of the company.[25] The language and context of these governing procedures and laws indicate clearly that these approvals are not restricted to mere assurance of technical or administrative compliance with the organizational requirements. Rather, their intent is to retain power over establishment of new companies as part of overall governmental economic planning.

2.3.2 Limitations on the raising of capital

The Standards Opinion requires that both initial public offerings and additional stock issuances be approved by the People's Bank.[26] This approval is neither pro forma nor merely administrative; although the Standards Opinion is silent on the matter, it appears that the People's Bank exercises substantive authority to limit the raising of capital in accordance with fiscal and other governmental policies. Similarly, companies authorized to raise capital from foreign investors must obtain People's Bank approval for the issuance of "B" shares.[27] The Company Law is silent on the subject of People's Bank approval of issuance of shares to foreign investors, but as suggested below, the Share System Procedures and the Standards Opinion appear still to govern these issuances. The Company Law requires at least two approvals for the issuance of new shares. The first, by the State Council's department for the administration of securities, appears to be in the nature of administrative, reporting and disclosure review, pursuant to the now substantially developed securities regulatory structure of the PRC.[28] The second, approval by "a department authorized by the State Council or ... the People's Government at the provincial level",[29] is the same substantive review of the raising of capital originally implemented by the Standards Opinion.

These substantive limitations on the raising of capital are mirrored in the Interim Regulations on the Administration and Trading of Shares and in the Draft Securities Law, discussed below.

2.3.3 Governmental management authority

The Share System Procedures retain a degree of governmental administrative authority over companies. Although the responsible government department "should create autonomous business conditions for the enterprise", the guiding principle is that the government administrative departments will "manage ... enterprises according to the principles of 'planning,

---

[25] Company Law, art. 27.
[26] Standards Opinion, arts. 28, 34.
[27] Standards Opinion, art. 29.
[28] *See* text following note 39, below.
[29] Company Law, art. 139.

coordination, service, supervision' and work according to responsibility".[30] The Company Law makes no mention of governmental administration, but the combined effects of direct and indirect government stock ownership (discussed below) and the expansive role of the shareholders' meeting suggest the likelihood of a continued government voice in company operations.

3 THE EMERGENCE OF A CAPITAL MARKET IN CHINA

3.1 Exchange and over-the-counter trading of securities

Securities trading commenced in China in 1987, and until 1992 was primarily in debt securities. Since then, secondary trading has been overwhelmingly in equities. Exchange trading on two organized exchanges (Shanghai and Shenzhen) began in December 1990, expanding nearly geometrically in each succeeding year. From 1987 to 1990, total securities trading volume increased from 100 million RMB to 13.5 billion RMB, of which 19% was in equities in 1990. Following the establishment of exchange trading, the statistics were as follows (billion RMB):

Table 1

Year	Total	% Equity
1991	55.5	8%
1992	172.9	80%
1993	377.3	97%

As of the end of 1993, the Shanghai exchange had 481 members (of whom 388 were floor traders), and the Shenzhen exchange had 426 members (of whom 280 were floor traders). A handful of foreign traders have seats on each of the exchanges.

Organized over-the-counter trading, on the model of the American NASDAQ system, commenced in the second half of 1993 with the establishment of the STAQ and NET systems. STAQ, with 55 terminal cities and nearly 400 members (both dial-in and directly linked) trades primarily debt instruments and legal-person shares. NET trades similar securities, with 14 terminal cities and nearly 200 members.

In short, China has in place and in full operation most of the physical systems and commercial structures of a contemporary debt and equity trading market, including exchanges, dispersed trading markets and the associated infrastructure (members, brokers, dealers, reporting systems, computer and communications networks). The legal structure, both

---

[30] Share System Procedures, art. 9.

organizational (company law) and regulatory (securities law) necessary for the maintenance of this system is rapidly being developed.

That these structures could be developed and implemented in well under a decade is cause for admiration, if not amazement. The rapidity of these developments is, however, not without its problems and its limits. These may be understood by examining in greater detail the nature of the traded securities and the administrative and legal limitations of the market system.

3.2 Forms of stock; stock ownership

Shares of stock in Chinese corporations admitted to exchange trading are divided into at least two, and often three or more, categories. These categories are not based on the relative rights, preferences and privileges of the shares (which are identical), but rather on their ownership, trading base, and currency denomination.

The classification of company shares on the basis of their ownership originated with the Share System Procedures,[31] and was further elaborated in the Standards Opinion.[32] Shares are divided into four categories:

(i)   State shares: shares received by departments and organizations of the State with the right to represent the State in the investment of State assets.

(ii) Legal person shares: shares received by "enterprise legal persons" or by business work units and collectives, investing their legally disposable assets in a company.

(iii) Individual shares ("A" Shares): shares received by individual Chinese investors.[33]

(iv) Foreign investment shares ("B" Shares): shares received by foreign investors.[34]

The Company Law is silent on the subject of classification of shares on the basis of ownership,[35] but at least four factors evidence the continuation of the classification system under the new law. First, the Company Law recognizes companies organized prior to the implementation of the Company

---

[31] Share System Procedures, art. 4.

[32] Standards Opinion, art. 24.

[33] "A" shares may not be purchased by foreign, Hong Kong, Taiwan and Macau investors: Standards Opinion, art. 29.

[34] "B" shares, also known as "special renminbi shares", may be issued by a company that is authorized to have foreign investors upon the approval of the People's Bank of China. Although they are denominated in renminbi, they may be subscribed and traded in foreign currencies. They may be bought and sold only by foreign, Hong Kong, Taiwan and Macau investors.

[35] *See* Company Law, part four, arts. 129–158. *Cf.* Company Law, art. 85:

> Upon approval by the State Council's department for the administration of securities, a company limited by shares may offer shares to the public outside the PRC. *The specific measures shall be provided by the State Council in special regulations.* (emphasis added)

Law;[36] second, the Company Law contains numerous delegations of authority to the State Council, which through its various organs participated in the implementation of the Share System Procedures and the Standards Opinion; third, previously classified shares continue to trade actively (and within their legal limitations) on the exchanges; and finally, it appears that listings following the enactment of the Company Law continue to follow these share classifications.

Both "A" and "B" Shares are listed on the Shenzhen or Shanghai exchange, and both are denominated in RMB. However, the "B" shares are subscribed for and traded in non-Chinese currency (Hong Kong dollars on the Shenzhen exchange, and United States dollars on the Shanghai exchange), and are owned by non-PRC citizens. Though their rights are nominally identical to the equivalent "A" Shares, their trading patterns and prices are widely different. Legal Person Shares do not presently trade on the exchanges, but a small number of issues are traded in an over-the-counter market analogous to NASDAQ.

There are additional classifications which, though not specified in the Standards Opinion, are within its parameters. "H" Shares are primarily listed on the Hong Kong exchange, and though denominated in RMB, are subscribed for and traded in Hong Kong dollars by non-PRC citizens. In addition, a number of companies have issued American Depositary Receipts, which are traded on exchanges or over-the-counter.

Because the share categories carry restrictions on ownership and trading, they affect the distribution of corporate ownership and control. For many companies, State Shares combined with Legal Person Shares represent an absolute majority of outstanding shares or the single largest voting share block, with the result that the government (whether directly or indirectly) retains effective voting control. Statistics on direct and indirect government ownership are not available, nor have studies been published on the degree to which the government has used its direct and indirect stock ownership to affect company policies. There is no reason to assume, however, that directors elected by holders of State Shares and Legal Person Shares do not play an active role in company management. There is, furthermore, no indication that government ownership will be systematically reduced (whether through formal privatization or simply through exchange trading of State Shares and Legal Person Shares). Direct, internal government participation appears to be a permanent fixture of the corporate system of the PRC.

The distinction between "A" Shares and the other categories of traded shares also has considerable structural significance. Issuance of "B" and "H" shares, as well as ADRs, shifts at least a portion of corporate ownership and control to non-PRC citizens. Correspondingly, retention of separate "A" Shares assures retention within the PRC of a determinable fraction of the ownership and control structure of each corporation. And, since authorization to issue shares of every category remains within the

---

[36] *See* Company Law, art. 229. Those companies are required to comply with the Company Law pursuant to implementing measures to be formulated by the State Council.

State's power of allotment, the overall national effect of the public-trading capital market remains subject to government control.

The nature of these limitations on the capital markets can only be roughly estimated, given the limited data available. Some sense of these limitations can be gained from statistics on the two categories of publicly traded shares. As of December 31, 1994, 169 companies had securities listed on the Shanghai exchange and 120 companies had securities listed on the Shenzhen exchange. The nature of those securities is summarized in the following statistics:[37]

Table 2

	"A" Shares	"B" Shares
Listed Securities:		
Shanghai	169	34
Shenzhen	118	24
Total Par Value of Listed Securities (billion RMB):		
Shanghai	38.7	3.1
Shenzhen	20.5	1.6
Total Market Value of Listed Securities (billion RMB):		
Shanghai	248.1	11.7
Shenzhen	103.2	5.8
Trading Volume (January 1–December 31: millions of shares)		
Shanghai	63,432	2,243
Shenzhen	35,369	289

These statistics suggest an equity trading market that, while clearly open to outside investment, is nevertheless heavily weighted in favor of investment and trading by PRC citizens. Whatever may be the relative domestic merits of this approach from a political, social or economic perspective, the PRC capital market is on its face lacking *at the international level* one of the two distinguishing elements of an open capital market: free access of investors to investment opportunities. And, as noted earlier (and for different reasons), the Chinese structure lacks at both domestic and international levels the second element of an open capital market: free access of enterprises to sources of capital.

Thus, despite the existence of two vital and important securities exchanges, despite the facts that a significant number of debt and equity securities are owned and traded by a substantial number of investors and that fully or partially privately owned enterprises are thriving in the PRC, it would be an overstatement to suggest that China now has an open capital market in the sense that such markets exist in the traditional free-market nations.

---

[37] The statistics were accumulated by the China Securities Regulatory Commission and supplied to the author. The statistical compilation is available on request.

4 SECURITIES REGULATION

Just as the creation and operation of companies in the PRC preceded the drafting and adoption of a company law, the creation of exchanges and the commencement of public trading of securities has preceded the drafting and adoption of a securities law. A similar process of experimentation with preliminary regulations, and of the preparation of multiple draft laws, has characterized the company law and the securities law development. And while the company law is now in effect, the securities law presently remains in draft form, despite several years of consideration of various versions thereof.

4.1 The interim regulations; role of the CSRC

All trading and issuance of shares within the PRC is now governed by the Interim Regulations on the Administration of the Issue and Trading of Shares (the "Interim Regulations"), promulgated by the State Council on April 22, 1993.[38] The Interim Regulations designate the State Council Securities Policies Committee as the national authority in charge of administering the stock market, and the China Securities Regulatory Commission (the CSRC) as the regulatory agency.[39] The Interim Regulations, though preliminary and brief, encompass most of the components of a general securities regulatory scheme. Many of the provisions are not far removed in substance from the securities laws and exchange regulations of the established market countries. Among these are the prospectus requirements,[40] listing requirements,[41] and continuing disclosure provisions.[42] Some provisions, however, impose detailed regulation of procedures or practices that in other nations, such as the United States, are largely regulated by industry practice or individual negotiation, such as the details of underwriting.[43]

The principal distinguishing characteristic of the Interim Regulations is retention of State substantive approval authority over the raising of capital. This approval authority, not to be confused with administrative approval of disclosure documents or even with "merit regulation" of public offerings, is a central feature of governmental control over access to the financial markets. The Interim Regulations provide that after the application to issue shares has been examined for financial position, expert opinions, asset appraisals and other legal matters:

---

[38] Citations to the "Interim Regulations", are to an unofficial and unpublished English translation, available from the author.

[39] Interim Regulations, art. 5.

[40] Interim Regulations, arts. 15 (contents), 17 (signatures), 18 (expert opinions), 19 (no disclosures prior to permission from CSRC).

[41] Interim Regulations, arts. 31–38.

[42] Interim Regulations, arts. 57–64.

[43] *See* Interim Regulations, arts. 20–28.

... the enterprise can apply for its shares to be issued to the public in accordance with the jurisdiction of its local government ... or the department in charge of the enterprise which is under the administration of the central government ... [44]

In approving the issuance of shares, the designated approving authorities, in turn, are subject to nationally assigned capital quotas:

The local government shall examine and approve the application of the local enterprise within the quota assigned by the state; the department in charge of a centrally-administered enterprise shall examine and approve the application of the enterprise after consulting with the local government in whose jurisdiction the enterprise is located ...[45]

Following substantive approval by the local government or the national department in charge of the enterprise, the application for issuance of shares is submitted for approval to the CSRC, and then to the listing committee of the exchange on which the shares are to be traded.[46] However, the CSRC does not have responsibility for the substantive quota review on share issuance. The quota review procedures and criteria are, to the best of the author's knowledge, not published and not necessarily uniformly applied throughout the PRC.

The CSRC, as the regulatory agency, has developed considerable experience and expertise in the administration of the Interim Regulations. The forms, filing procedures, and approval criteria of the CSRC are well developed, and the CSRC maintains real-time monitoring of the trading on both exchanges, by means of satellite and other communications media. Members of its senior staff have consulted widely with securities regulators, underwriters and stock exchange officials in other nations, in connection with the implementation of the Interim Regulations and as part of the process of commenting on the drafts of the Securities Law.

4.2 Drafting of the proposed law: the single authority in charge

The Securities Law of the People's Republic of China, drawing on statutes and model laws of many nations and numerous commentators, is the product of an extensive drafting process. The Seventh Draft (of August 18, 1993)[47] was made available for review in connection with an International Colloquium on China's Securities Legal System and the Standardization of Securities Markets (the "Colloquium").[48] The End Draft of the law, which is

---

[44] Interim Regulations, art. 12(1).

[45] Interim Regulations, art. 12(2).

[46] Interim Regulations, art. 12(3).

[47] The Securities Law of the People's Republic of China (7th Draft, August 18, 1993), unofficially translated into English for the use of the International Colloquium on China's Securities Legal System and the Standardization of Securities Markets) [hereinafter cited as "Seventh Draft"].

[48] The author and William J. Williams, Jr., of Sullivan & Cromwell, were the two American participants in this Colloquium, held in Beijing on November 16–19, 1993. Many of the comments herein concerning provisions of the Seventh Draft draw upon the insights of Mr. Williams, though he bears no responsibility for any omissions or misstatements in this chapter.

believed to be based substantially on the Seventh Draft and to reflect at least some of the comments made at the Colloquium, is presently under joint consideration by the Commission of Legislative Affairs of the Standing Committee of the National People's Congress and the Financial and Economic Committee of the National People's Congress. That draft has not, however, been released for comment outside the PRC.

The Seventh Draft designates the State Securities Commission as the "authority in charge" of the securities markets in the PRC.[49] The language of the draft implies, but does not clearly state, the intent that the Commission will be the single authority exclusively responsible for administering and enforcing the Securities Law. Some participants in the Colloquium urged divided administrative control, and there have been suggestions in the financial press that delay in the enactment of the new Law may be attributable in part to desires on the part of the Ministry of Finance and the People's Bank to exercise control. Thus, while the Seventh Draft appears (for example) to grant power to the State Securities Commission to provide rules for the issuance of "B" Shares,[50] it seems reasonable to speculate that the Law as finally enacted may retain that authority in the People's Bank. The Seventh Draft contains no provisions directly analogous to those in the Interim Regulations recognizing governmental authority with respect to quotas on the issuance of shares, but since its coverage is limited to securities *regulation* (as contrasted with *authorization for issuance*), there is no reason to believe that it is intended to abolish the quota requirements.[51] Finally, regulation of accounting principles throughout the PRC is presently within the jurisdiction of the Ministry of Finance, and the Seventh Draft does not shift the authority to the State Securities Commission.[52] In short, whether or not the Seventh Draft's single authority is retained, the fact of divided governmental authority over securities issuance and regulation, as well as corporate disclosure, is likely to be a fixture of the PRC financial markets.

4.3 Basic elements of the Seventh Draft

Although the overall structure of securities issuance in the PRC contains important elements of substantive government review and approval, and the possibility of merit regulation of securities issuance is present in the Seventh Draft (as noted and criticized by several commentators at the

---

[49] Seventh Draft, art. 5.

[50] Seventh Draft, arts. 3, 4.

[51] This conclusion is buttressed by a general clause at the end of the list of conditions to be satisfied for establishment of a corporation and issuance of stock: "Other conditions as may be described by the authority in charge": Seventh Draft, art. 9(5).

[52] *See* Seventh Draft, art. 140(6), which grants authority only "to supervise securities issuers to disclose information". Compare Interim Regulations, art. 59(13), which contains a requirement of submitting audited financial statements, but similarly grants no authority to the CSRC to prescribe accounting principles or auditing standards.

Colloquium)[53] the Seventh Draft on its face establishes a disclosure regulation scheme.[54] Disclosure obligations are in a form familiar to Western commentators, including a prospectus requirement,[55] review by the authority in charge,[56] and prohibitions on sale prior to approval of the application and in the absence of a prospectus.[57] Some worrisome omissions and provisions include the absence of permission to use a preliminary prospectus; the absolute requirements that issuance of stock and bonds be underwritten[58] and that trading take place only on exchanges or recognized over-the-counter markets;[59] the exclusion from the coverage of the Law of governmental bonds;[60] and the inclusion of substantive conditions for the issuance of stock[61] and bonds.[62] These features were all the subject of comment at the Colloquium, and it is not clear which will be carried forward to the enacted version of the End Draft.

The continuing disclosure requirements of the Seventh Draft include an annual report,[63] a semi-annual report[64] and periodic reporting of significant

---

[53] *See* Seventh Draft, art. 8: "The issuance of securities must be approved by the authority in charge." This approval requirement may be interpreted to encompass merit review, *e.g.*, of the quality of the issuer and its securities, as suggested by other provisions of the Seventh Draft. *See, e.g.*, Seventh Draft, art. 7, requiring as part of the application for issuance of stock the submission of "a feasibility study on the use of the proceeds". However, the Seventh Draft sets forth no criteria for merit review.

[54] Securities regulatory legislation may generally be categorized under the two headings of disclosure regulation and merit regulation. The first, exemplified by the Federal securities laws in the United States, aims to protect investors by requiring disclosure for certain events (such as securities offerings and shareholder votes) and by requiring continuing periodic (annual and interim) disclosure by the company. Coupled with the disclosure requirements are civil and criminal penalties and administrative procedures, as well as the possibility of private actions, in the event of non-disclosure, misdisclosure and fraudulent or deceptive schemes. Merit regulation, typified by many of the state securities laws in the United States, grants to the regulator the authority to limit or preclude issuance of certain securities based on their investment quality, or to limit the potential investors therein, based on their knowledge, financial resources or other criteria. The two approaches are not mutually exclusive, and some regulatory statutes contain components of both.

[55] Seventh Draft, arts. 13 (stock), 17 (bonds).

[56] Seventh Draft, art. 19.

[57] Seventh Draft, art. 21.

[58] Seventh Draft, art. 22.

[59] Seventh Draft, art. 32.

[60] Seventh Draft, art. 7.

[61] For example, upon initial issuance of stock, promoters must subscribe for no less than 35% of the shares, the public must subscribe for no less than 25%: Seventh Draft, art. 9.

[62] A proposed issuer of bonds must satisfy the following standards:

(1) The trustworthiness of the bond to be issued has, according to the rating of a rating institution, met the standard stipulated by the authority in charge;
(2) The ratio between the total bonds issued by the issuer . . . and the value of the net assets owned by the issuer has not gone beyond the level stipulated by the authority in charge; and
(3) Other conditions as may be stipulated by the authority in charge.

Seventh Draft, art. 15.

[63] Seventh Draft, art. 24.

[64] Seventh Draft, art. 25.

events.[65] The required signers of these reports – promoters, directors and the lead underwriter in the case of a prospectus; directors and major managerial staff in the case of other reports – are held jointly and severally liable for "false or serious misleading statements or material omissions" therein.[66] Professionals are held to "the common practice and ethical standards" of their professions, and are similarly jointly and severally liable for the work for which they are responsible.[67] These provisions, however, do not set forth a standard of materiality nor do they deal with such issues as the applicability of a reliance or a purchase or sale requirement and the measurement of damages. Also strikingly missing from the Seventh Draft is any regulation of the required disclosures to shareholders associated with proxy solicitation, whether for election of the board of directors or for approval of significant corporate changes, such as amendment of the articles of incorporation or merger.

At least one cautionary note should be sounded concerning the disclosure regime of the Seventh Draft, which has as a principal subject mandating financial disclosure in the form of financial statements, notes, commentaries and audit reports. The limited information available to Western commentators suggests that while Chinese financial disclosure may in form be similar to the disclosures made in the established market economies, the accounting principles and audit practices of the PRC have not yet been standardized in rules or in practices sufficiently to allow unqualified reliance thereon.

The Seventh Draft contains anti-fraud provisions and prohibitions on insider trading[68] and short-swing trading,[69] supported by civil and criminal penalties.[70] In general, the penalties include confiscation of any illegal gains,[71] and fines of a multiple of the illegal gains[72] or of stated ranges and amounts.[73] A general provision establishes liability for civil damages and criminal liability.[74] It is too early to predict the form that these provisions

---

[65] Seventh Draft, art. 26.

[66] Seventh Draft, art. 30.

[67] Seventh Draft, art. 31.

[68] Seventh Draft, art. 50. Extensive provisions prohibiting market manipulation and "any kind of scheme to cheat customers" are contained in Seventh Draft, arts. 51, 52.

[69] *See* Seventh Draft, art. 46, inspired by and substantively similar to Securities Exchange Act of 1934, § 16(b).

[70] Seventh Draft, arts. 151–162.

[71] *See, e.g.,* Seventh Draft, arts. 152 (insider trading), 153 (market manipulation), 154 (cheating on customers by securities dealing institutions, *et al.*). Though these provisions do not clearly so state, they imply that the profits will be confiscated by the State. It is unclear whether confiscation and private recovery of damages, *e.g.,* pursuant to Seventh Draft, art. 158, are mutually exclusive. The context of these provisions, including punitive recoveries, suggests that multiple recoveries (*e.g.,* by confiscation and through private civil recovery) are contemplated.

[72] Seventh Draft, arts. 152, 153 (fine of three to 30 times the amount of the illegal gains).

[73] The fines are set at between RMB 10,000 and RMB 500,000 yuan. *E.g.,* Seventh Draft, arts. 151 (failure to file reports); 155 (issuance of security not in conformity with procedures); 156 (establishment of securities dealing and similar associations not in accordance with procedures).

[74] Seventh Draft, art. 158.

will ultimately take in actual practice, since the legal system of the PRC has very little experience with private civil actions for damages, which now play an important role in developed securities regulation structures elsewhere, particularly the United States.

Also within the Seventh Draft are provisions regulating take-overs,[75] registration of exchanges and non-exchange trading,[76] and investment funds,[77] as well as a structure for establishment of one or more self-regulatory organizations.[78] Even a cursory reading of the proposed law leads to the conclusion that, despite its occasional problems and peculiarities, it establishes a comprehensive securities regulatory system of considerable sophistication. The rapid development of a securities trading market in the PRC has been reflected in the drafting of a law (and its implementation at least in part, even prior to enactment) suited to the crucial task of regulating that market. It is reasonable to expect that the End Draft, as finally adopted, will therefore formally establish an informed and advanced market regulatory scheme.

5 CONCLUSION

A study of the corporate and securities laws of The People's Republic of China reveals at least three formidable problems. The first is the difficulty of rapidly creating and regulating a network of financial markets where none has previously existed. The second is assuring the competitive effectiveness and compatibility of those markets in the world economy. The third, and possibly most daunting, challenge is to reconcile these components of the market economy with China's political, social and economic framework in the form of the "socialist market economy". Although the first decade of these developments in the PRC has not been without setbacks, the progress in achieving these goals is impressive. China, it now appears, will adopt and absorb those elements of market law and practice that fit its political and social structure, and fashion alternative laws and practices where needed to implement its unique economic vision.

---

[75] Seventh Draft, arts. 57–63.
[76] Seventh Draft, arts. 109–132.
[77] Seventh Draft, arts. 92–108.
[78] Seventh Draft, arts. 83–91. The Seventh Draft does not, on its face, require the creation of a *single* self-regulatory association. Experience in the United States with coordination of rules and regulations among multiple self-regulatory associations, including the National Association of Securities Dealers (NASD) and the various exchanges, suggests that there would be advantages to a single organization.

24. International Financial Organisations, Financial Markets and the Transition Process in Eastern Europe

Mads Andenas[1]

1 INTRODUCTION

This volume has brought together chapters on financial market reform in developing and transition economies. Some of them deal directly with financial market reform, others with models for such reform. Several concern the role of international financial institutions (IFIs).[2] This chapter poses some questions about the role of IFIs and financial markets in the transition process of the former communist countries of eastern Europe.

It is argued in this chapter that IFIs were badly prepared for their role in this transition process. Their approaches give priority to solving problems of deregulation of the private sector and reduction of the public sector. Their advice and instruments of policy are based on the situation in the developing or the market economies. Most important for the ideological basis is of course the current economic policy formulation in the dominating member states, the Group of Seven or the wider circle of OECD countries, with the United States in the lead. Their relevance to the transition economies of the new IFI members could be expected to be limited. However, policies and instruments were modified only to a very limited extent, and the entire conceptual framework, including economic targets, that had been applied to the old IFI members was retained.

---

[1] Director, Centre of European Law, King's College, University of London. Honorary Director of Studies, Institute of Advanced Legal Studies, University of London and Former Legal Adviser, European Bank for Reconstruction and Development, London.
[2] The IFIs discussed in this chapter include the development banks, mainly the World Bank Group, including the World Bank (state-guaranteed lending) and the International Finance Corporation (private sector lending and investment), and the European Bank for Reconstruction and Development (both state-guaranteed and private sector operations). They also include the International Monetary Fund, which provides member states with credits as part of an international monetary system but is increasingly becoming a vehicle for economic aid from its dominating members (the Group of Seven and the OECD countries) to other member states with not only monetary problems but more structural economic problems.

An important consequence of this is the limited concern with institutional reform. Although institutional reform was placed high on the reform agenda as formulated by the IFIs early on, this had few practical consequences. The International Monetary Fund (IMF) was concerned with familiar macroeconomic targets. The development banks, the World Bank Group and the European Bank of Reconstruction and Development expended their resources on financing a wide range of individual projects having only limited impact.

There was sporadic and not very successful involvement in the financial market institutions of the transition economies of the new members. The IMF was occupied mainly with monetary policy, and its concern with credit was to restrict it. The development banks were themselves direct providers of credit, and their engagement in payment systems and capitalisation of banks coincided with the need, long into the transition period, for a local banking system to administrate a large volume of credit from the IFIs to small and medium-sized businesses.

In retrospect, it seems surprising that the fundamental role of the financial sector in the transition from "plan" to "market" could be overlooked to such an extent. The replacement of the plan by the financial market would bring the transition close to completion, but few of the early activities of the IFIs aimed at financial markets or institutions.

When the projects appeared, they dealt with the capitalisation of the new private banks or newly privatised banks and with payment systems between them: the regulatory side was not given any priority. The state bank system was mainly considered as part of a privatisation process.

Investor protection, in a market with unparalleled functions in the redistribution of ownership of assets of highly industrialised transition economies, has not been a concern. The limited involvement of the IFIs dealt with other issues, and it has been left to the European Commission to provide assistance, as part of the implementation of European Union standards. Admittedly, investor protection issues may be politically controversial and there may have been a risk of them drawing attention away from the privatisation process.

The effectiveness of the way in which IFIs organise their work in the area of institutional reform is limited in different ways. IFIs are highly project- or deal-driven and activities that are not part of a project will be supported only if they provide support, very directly and swiftly, for projects. Project finance techniques and the goal of a high ratio of private sector projects constrain involvement in public sector projects without any immediate prospect of privatisation or easily identifiable income streams, or, rather, both. Institutional reform projects can rarely be linked to a specific project so as to provide the necessary justification. Even the funds that are made especially available for non-core activities, for instance those coming directly from member states for the purpose of institutional reform, sectoral surveys and project preparation, are used mostly for activities relating to the lending and investment operations.

There are even stronger limitations in the way in which development banks operate when they are involved with institutional reform issues. To a large extent, this has been dealt with by hiring consultants, based on competitive tendering, with little, if any, relevant experience in areas such as drafting of legislation, the political process generally or the country itself (and its language in particular) with which the project is concerned.

The main question is whether the IFI approach to institutional reform had any effects on the way in which the transition economies developed. A second question is what lessons have been learnt, and whether is it possible to improve the performance in this area.

2 IFIs IN EASTERN EUROPE

The IFIs approached the problems of deregulation of the private sector and reduction of the public sector of the transition economies in the way they do in other member states. They have a strong doctrine and highly developed practice based on their experience of dealing with these issues in the developing or the market economies. Their policies reflect the currently accepted economic policy in the relevant ministries in the dominating member states, the Group of Seven or the wider circle of OECD countries. United States economic theory and policy is very influential.

There are several reasons why the relevance to the transition economies of the new IFI members could be expected to be limited. There was no established economic doctrine dealing with the transition from a centrally planned to a market economy: the approaches had to be speculative. The intuitive response was to apply the established doctrine with as few modifications as possible.

Policies and instruments were in fact modified only to a very limited extent. The entire conceptual framework that had been applied to the old IFI members was retained. That would, for instance, mean that the IMF in many ways treated the strongest transition economies very similarly to the OECD countries, even when it came to economic targets, which clearly made very little sense. The World Bank would offer the same projects as it would to Third World countries, and the EBRD would adopt the World Bank approach.

What about the institutional interplay which is so important to the understanding of the role of the IFIs? They have as their clients the governments of the member states. No project will be initiated by a development bank without the support of the concerned member, even if it is a private sector project not dependent upon state guarantee. IMF conditionality is more often than not formulated to give maximum support to the member state's ministry of finance in its fight to gain control over public spending and inflation against spending departments of state and parliament. Most of what the IMF publishes about the economic affairs of members will be with their consent. The OECD, which publishes much more statistical materials and reports, will also consult intensely with the member states concerned, and both timing of publication and content of reports will aim at providing maximum support to members who attempt largely to place themselves within the generally accepted targets for economic policy. With member states at the margin of what is acceptable, the negotiations may become more antagonistic.

The problem with the new member states, obviously a long way from being able to meet established targets, was that they did not have the experience of these kinds of negotiations. IFIs could influence them more strongly than they could older members. They would quickly establish client relationships in the new members' governments, and these would be more dominated by the IFIs than in the case of established members. What could be seen as useful prodding of OECD governments in the right direction could be turned into the imposition of strict and doctrinaire policies.

3   IFI INVOLVEMENT IN LEGAL AND INSTITUTIONAL REFORM

The limited concern, at least in the initial phase, with institutional reform might seem surprising. It was in fact placed high on the reform agenda as formulated by the IFIs and other international bodies early on: however, this had few practical consequences.

The IMF provided advice on institutional reform to developing countries. It offered a basic kit for getting a central bank up and running, and provided even more basic advice on banking supervision and on taxation. For industrialised countries, its concern with exchange controls had become less relevant. The IMF teams, travelling to the capitals of prospective members, would prepare them by offering an institutional model with a strong and independent central bank, responsible for banking supervision, and otherwise focus on the familiar macroeconomic targets: the latter would remain the focus of the dealings with a new member.

The development banks, the World Bank Group and the European Bank of Reconstruction and Development expended their resources, which seem extremely limited compared to the task, on financing a wide range of individual projects with only limited impact.

Development banks have limited experience in the field of institutional reform. They are organised in a way which solidly places the emphasis on projects they can finance, either by providing credit or direct investment, often with other financial institutions or investors, private or public. It is difficult to justify involvement in institutional reform on the basis of their direct and immediate contribution to individual projects.

Other international organisations could be better placed to contribute to institutional reform. OECD provided important contributions from an early stage of the transition process, but again on a very limited scale. The European Commission has by far the most extensive programmes, and they have clear and relevant targets in the harmonisation of European Union standards.

Complementary parts could be carved out for the different international organisations: this was not done. In fact, the institutional reform projects of the IFIs had even less impact, as they overlapped considerably with those of the OECD and the European Commission. At the same time, the latter projects did not meet the need for such projects in a way which made IFI involvement entirely superfluous.

4 IFI INVOLVEMENT IN FINANCIAL MARKET REFORM

There was sporadic and not very successful IFI involvement in the financial market institutions of the transition economies of the new members. As mentioned above, the IMF was occupied mainly with monetary policy, and its concern with credit was to restrict it, adopting the methods of a member state's ministry of finance but avoiding the many restraints of domestic policy.

The development banks were themselves providers of direct credit (not particularly coordinated with the macroeconomic policies propagated by the IMF, perhaps because this credit was too limited to have any effect on the demand in most countries). Their engagement in payment systems and capitalisation of banks came at a later stage. It coincided with the need, long into the transition period, for a local banking system to administrate all credit from the IFIs to small and medium-sized businesses.

The fundamental role of the financial sector in the transition from plan to market did not have much impact on the involvement of the IFIs at the early stage of transition. It seems as if it was involvement in other sectors or policies that brought home the importance of financial markets. It seems surprising that this could be overlooked to such an extent for so long: anyone should be able to figure out that the replacement of the plan by the financial market would bring the transition close to completion.

Few of the early activities of the IFIs were aimed at financial markets or institutions. When the projects appeared, they dealt with the capitalisation of the new private banks or newly privatised banks and with payment systems between them. The regulatory side was not given any priority by the development banks and the IMF's involvement remained very limited. The state bank system, with the potential for providing mechanisms of transition, was only considered as part of a privatisation process.

The approach to investor protection seems to replicate the most traditional textbook version, which was not updated in the light of the past decade and a half's privatisation experiences in the United Kingdom and elsewhere. If anything, these recent experiences should be very relevant indeed.

The role of investor protection takes on a completely new dimension in a market with unparalleled functions in the redistribution of ownership of assets of the highly industrialised transition economies. This seems not to have been a concern: the limited involvement of the institutions dealt with other issues. It is the European Commission that has provided assistance in this area, not as part of a particular agenda for transition economies but as consequence of the implementation of European Union standards generally in countries with varying degrees of association with the European Union.

The oversight must to some extent reflect that investor protection issues may be politically controversial. There may have been a risk of them drawing attention away from the privatisation process itself and, in effect, slowing it down. It still seems difficult to defend this as a position. Without certain minimum guarantees for an equitable distribution process, a transition process will meet considerable opposition. A financial market with a minimum investor protection programe could have provided an important contribution to such guarantees.

Index

International Economic Development Law

1. J.J. Norton, T.L. Bloodworth and T.K. Pennington (eds.), *NAFTA and Beyond. A New Framework for Doing Business in the Americas.* 1995
   ISBN 0–7923–3239–3

2. N. Kofele-Kale: *International Law of Responsibility for Economic Crimes.* Holding Heads of State and Other High Ranking State Officials Individually Liable for Acts of Fraudulent Enrichment. 1995
   ISBN 0–7923–3358–6

3. Hani Sarie-Eldin: *Consortia Agreements in the International Construction Industry.* With Special Reference to Egypt. 1996   ISBN 90–411–0912–9

4. J.J. Norton and Mads Andenas: *Emerging Financial Markets and the Role of International Financial Organisations.* 1996   ISBN 90–411–0909–9

KLUWER LAW INTERNATIONAL – LONDON, THE HAGUE, BOSTON

M-44